Franklin D. Roosevelt

ALSO BY ROGER DANIELS

The Politics of Prejudice (1961)
American Racism (with Harry H. J. Kitano, 1970)
The Bonus March (1971)
Concentration Camps, USA (1971)
The Decision to Relocate the Japanese Americans (1975)
Concentration Camps, North America (1981)
Asian Americans, Emerging Minorities (with Harry H. J. Kitano, 1987)
Asian America: Chinese and Japanese in the United States since 1850 (1988)
History of Indian Immigration to the United States (1989)
Coming to America (1990)
Prisoners without Trial (1993)
Not Like Us (1997)
American Immigration: A Student Companion (2001)
Debating American Immigration (with Otis L. Graham, 2001)
Guarding the Golden Door (2004)
The Japanese American Cases (2013)
Franklin D. Roosevelt: Road to the New Deal, 1882–1939 (2015)

FRANKLIN D. ROOSEVELT

The War Years, 1939–1945

Roger Daniels

UNIVERSITY OF ILLINOIS PRESS

URBANA, CHICAGO, AND SPRINGFIELD

Library of Congress Cataloging-in-Publication Data
Daniels, Roger, author.
Franklin D. Roosevelt / Roger Daniels.
2 volumes cm
Includes bibliographical references and index.
Contents: v. 1. Road to the New Deal, 1882–1939 —
v. 2. The War Years, 1939–1945.
ISBN 978-0-252-03951-5 (v. 1 : hardcover : alk. paper) —
ISBN 978-0-252-09762-1 (v. 1 : e-book) —
ISBN 978-0-252-03952-2 (v. 2 : hardcover : alk. paper) —
ISBN 978-0-252-09764-5 (v. 2 : e-book)
1. Roosevelt, Franklin D. (Franklin Delano), 1882–1945. 2. Presidents—United
States—Biography. 3. United States—Politics and government—1933–1945. I. Title.
E807.D336   2015
973.917092—dc23   2015005243
[B]

Contents

Preface

THIS VOLUME, LIKE ITS PREDECESSOR, focuses on the words that Franklin Roosevelt directed at the American people. Thus, its chief source remains the public record of those words in speeches, press conferences, other public papers, and the press, particularly the *New York Times,* then much more a paper of record than today's feature- and opinion-heavy journal. Even more than in the previous volume, it also depends on witnesses who recorded their impressions of what the president said in contemporary documents and later articles, books, and memoirs. After Pearl Harbor, extreme secrecy about the whereabouts of the president was invoked. This meant that meaningful daily reportorial contact with him was greatly reduced, and the White House press corps often spent weeks without seeing him. Even when correspondents knew that the president was not in Washington, they could not report it, and for long periods of time they had only vague notions of where he was. However, during the foreshortened periods of preelection activity in 1942 and 1944, reporters did have access to the president on a daily basis. Thus, this volume depends more heavily on witnesses from his official and political associates. Happily, two of them have left us accounts, based on their own writing created contemporaneously, which provide some day-to-day details.

Of course, the focus in this volume shifts to foreign affairs and Roosevelt's growing mastery of them. Continuing the trend begun with the 1937 quarantine speech in Chicago, he shepherded public opinion so that it increasingly supported his verbal encouragement of Hitler's opponents and, after the fall of France, seemed briefly to be even more eager for military aid to Britain than the president himself. Unlike Abraham Lincoln, the only other American president deeply engaged in military direction in wartime, Roosevelt had an effective command of military and diplomatic information, and his informed direction of strategic military and diplomatic affairs was unprecedented.

Unlike Lincoln, who spent much of the Civil War trying to find winning generals, Roosevelt, by the time of Pearl Harbor, already had in place a team of top military commanders that he had selected. It would continue largely unchanged until the final victory, which he did not live to see. What is even more remarkable, it seems to me, is that even in the darkest days of the war in the weeks after Pearl Harbor, Roosevelt kept part of his attention fixed on the problem of a viable postwar peace. On January 1, 1942, at a time when each new day seemed to produce further disasters in the Pacific—and knowing that worse was yet to come—he orchestrated a joint declaration of twenty-five "united nations" pledging support for a postwar international organization, a concept he first raised in the initial conference with Churchill in August 1941. We know from his own words and the testimony of others that the specter of Wilson's failures at Versailles and after were often before him as he consciously strove to secure a better result. For military matters, I rely almost exclusively on volumes published by the government in the series the United States Army in World War Two, the well-known "Green Books" still being published by the army.

Although a small library of books has been devoted to describing "the wartime mess in Washington," Roosevelt's management of what he named "the Arsenal of Democracy" was, in the final analysis, an undoubted success. Not only did it produce what Stalin described as the machines necessary for victory, but it did so with remarkably little inflation. Roosevelt's management led to a higher level of a more general relative prosperity than America had ever known in the industrial era. His farsighted insertion of language inserted into the 1939 Reorganization Act, described in *Franklin D. Roosevelt: Road to the New Deal, 1882–1939,* enabled him to govern in large part by executive orders that were all but immune from congressional interferences, even though Congress, as a body, was increasingly alienated by his continued domination. Congress, although it all but surrendered its authority over military spending, did frustrate some of Roosevelt's attempts to stem the growing enrichment of the managerial class by refusing to enact, among other things, the annual cap of twenty-five thousand dollars on individual salaries he proposed. Even more significantly, it largely ignored administration requests to make the revenue code more effective. It also canceled, over his protests, previously enacted increases in Social Security taxes.

Finally, Roosevelt biographers have to deal with the vexing question of his health, especially during the closing months of his presidency. I have made a consistent attempt throughout to examine Roosevelt's health and what he and others said about it even before the onset of the polio that made him a "cripple." Roosevelt, as governor and president, often used that word, but never, as far as I can tell, explicitly applied it to himself. I have, whenever possible, used the testimony of reliable witnesses, professional and lay. I also utilize, as best I can, the evidence of a most unreliable witness, the official White House physician. White House physicians, as a class, are, as we say today, not only doctors of medicine, but doctors of spin as well. Roosevelt's official White House physician violated not only his Hippocratic oath, but federal statutes as well in a long-successful cover-up of his mis- and malfeasances.

Acknowledgments

ALTHOUGH THE ACTUAL WRITING OF THIS BOOK took place in the past dozen years, my entire formal education, all but two years of it in public institutions, and those who taught me must be acknowledged. My teachers in the Miami public schools pushed me to read beyond textbooks and to question what I read. When I finally got to college in the 1950s, faculty members in the History Department at the University of Houston gave me what I now realize was an inordinate amount of personal attention. I shall always be grateful to them, particularly Louis Kestenberg and Charles Bacarisse. During my graduate work at the University of California at Los Angeles (UCLA), apart from my mentor, Theodore Saloutos, I was most influenced by Eugene N. Anderson.

In a long professional career at five American universities with visiting stints at two Canadian and four European universities and guest lectures at dozens of others as well as professional encounters of various kinds, I came into contact with a considerable number of the historians of my time. I can mention only a few. Al Larson at Wyoming, Ed Saveth at Fredonia, and Bill Aeschbacher at Cincinnati were instrumental in bringing me to those places. I learned much from the men—and eventually women—who became my departmental colleagues, but here I will mention only two: Zane Miller, who was the rock upon whom the modern Cincinnati department was built, and Henry Winkler, who joined us there as a president who actually taught classes regularly while president. Of colleagues in the larger profession, none were more important for me than Rudolph Vecoli, the acknowledged leader of the immigration historians of our generation, and Robert Skotheim, a historiographer who became a college president and then re-created the Huntington Library.

As I note elsewhere, teaching about the Democratic Roosevelt helped me to envisage the kind of narrative I wanted to present. I am particularly grateful to those students who wanted more information and those who didn't quite get it. Questions from both groups helped me to understand some of the inadequacies of what I had originally presented. In the same way that newspapers can claim to be the first drafts of history, my classroom lectures provided the foundation on which I built my narrative. I continue to maintain contact not only with former colleagues and graduate colleagues from all of my permanent appointments, but also with a few former undergraduate students such as James E. Wright from Platteville and Sue Fawn Chung from UCLA.

Among the platoons of historians and others who enabled my efforts in these Roosevelt volumes, Judith M. Daniels, a historian and editor in her own right, must take precedence. Everything I have accomplished since 1960 owes much to her probing intelligence. Beginning with conversations about whether even to attempt a Roosevelt biography, she has participated in every phase of the process, listening to me read daily work product and commenting upon it, editing chapter drafts and redrafts in more versions than I am now able to count. Above all, her faith that I would endure after my original publisher could no longer continue sustained my resolve at times when scrapping the project seemed the better part of valor.

The writing process itself, begun in Cincinnati, was largely completed in Bellevue, Washington, from late 2005, much of it based on materials acquired in visits to the FDR Library, the Truman Library, and various branches of the National Archives. I can no longer retrieve the names of most of the skilled librarians and archivists who helped to continue my education, as I am twenty-three hundred miles away from my stored papers, so I can here mention only the senior reference librarian at UCLA in the 1950s, a Ms. Grey, and Sally Moffitt, the history bibliographer at Cincinnati's Langsam Library who still gently guides students and faculty through bibliographic labyrinths.

Of those persons directly connected with the forging of these volumes, the three most vital, apart from Judith, are two persons in the book trade and one historian. Ivan R. Dee, who had published an earlier book of mine, contracted to publish the biography and provided good advice and a valuable full first editing of the entire text. To our mutual regret, economic considerations made it impossible for him to continue. He facilitated my affiliation with agent Georges Borchardt, who negotiated the contract with the University of Illinois Press. Its editor in chief, Laurie Matheson, led me through a complete reediting, whose aim was to prune a hundred thousand words from the text, and did so with intelligence, precision, and grace. Early in the writing, I asked Max Paul Friedman to look over what I had to say about international relations. He generously took on reading the draft chapters as they were written, giving good advice and encouragement on every aspect of the work. Most of this was via e-mail, but I remember particularly a long dinner conversation in Washington, D.C., in which we talked out some of the thrust of the volumes.

To many of my doctoral students, particularly those who wrote on Roosevelt-era subjects, I owe a double debt: not only did I learn much by preparing to help them pursue their specific topics, but their findings invariably expanded my knowledge. In addition, some of them answered my queries and made suggestions as I worked on the text. I thus thank Mike Anderson, Allan Austin, Mark Cowett, Kirsten Gardner, Barbara Hahn, Andy Kersten, Kris Lindenmeyer, Bob Miller, Nina Mjackij, Rick Reiman, and Matthais Reiss.

Of my senior colleagues in the larger profession, Frank Freidel, whose five biographical volumes about Franklin Roosevelt remain unrivaled, gave encouragement and advice and commented on a first brief outline for what became these volumes. Most of the assistance I received is acknowledged in the footnotes and in the list of works consulted, but I must mention two government historians, Jan Kenneth Hermann of the U.S. Navy and Larry DeWitt of Social Security, for materials gleaned from their own researches.

Of the large squad of specialists who put the materials together, I worked personally with senior project editor Tad Ringo, copy editor Annette Wenda, and indexer June Sawyers, each a skilled professional who imposed their high standards cheerfully while improving the final result. Behind the scenes, art director Dustin Hubbart transformed my vague suggestions into two stunning covers and Lisa Connery composed the pages producing a clean, effective look. Many others, unknown to me, toiled to produce a most attractive volume.

Abbreviations

AAA	Agricultural Adjustment Administration
ANB	*American National Biography*
AVG	American Volunteer Group (Flying Tigers)
BEW	Board of Economic Warfare
CCC	Civilian Conservation Corps
CIO	Committee/Congress of Industrial Organizations
DALLEK	Robert Dallek, *Franklin D. Roosevelt and American Foreign Policy, 1932–1945*
DNC	Democratic National Committee
EO	Executive Order
EOP	Executive Office of the President
ER	Eleanor Roosevelt
FBI	Federal Bureau of Investigation
FCC	Federal Communications Commission
FDR	Franklin Delano Roosevelt
FDRL	Franklin Delano Roosevelt Library, Hyde Park, N.Y.
FDR Letters	Elliott Roosevelt, ed., *F.D.R.: His Personal Letters,* 3 vols.
FERA	Federal Emergency Relief Administration
FLA	Federal Loan Agency
FRB	Federal Reserve Board
FSA	Farm Security Administration (1937–46); Federal Security Administration (1939–53)
FTC	Federal Trade Commission
FWA	Federal Works Agency
HASSETT	William D. Hassett, *Off the Record with FDR, 1942–1945*
HIST STATS	U.S. Department of Commerce, *Historical Statistics of the United States: Colonial Times to 1957*
MOWM	March on Washington Movement
NDAC	National Defense Advisory Committee
NDMB	National Defense Mediation Board
NRA	National Recovery Administration
NWLB	National War Labor Board

NYT	*New York Times*
OCD	Office of Civilian Defense
OEM	Office of Emergency Management
OGR	Office of Government Reports
OPA	Office of Price Administration
OPM	Office of Production Management
OWM/OWMR	Office of War Mobilization and Reconversion
PPA	Samuel I. Rosenman, ed., *Public Papers and Addresses of Franklin D. Roosevelt,* 13 vols.
PRA	President's Reemployment Agreement
Press Conf	FDR, *The Complete Presidential Press Conferences of Franklin D. Roosevelt,* 25 vols.
RFC	Reconstruction Finance Corporation
SPAB	Supply Priorities and Allocations Board
UMW	United Mine Workers
UNRRA	United Nations Relief and Rehabilitation Administraion
USDA	United States Department of Agriculture
USHA	United States Housing Authority
USPHS	United States Public Health Service
VA	Veterans Administration
WRA	War Relocation Authority
WRB	War Refugee Board

Franklin D. Roosevelt
The War Years, 1939–1945

1 Reform, Neutrality, and War
1939

ROOSEVELT'S ANNUAL MESSAGE IN EARLY 1939, and the congressional response to it, prefigured his relations with Congress for the remainder of his presidency. As long as his chief concern was national defense and eventually the prosecution of the war, he could usually count on majority support drawn from both sides of the aisle for most of his proposals. But when he endeavored to expand the New Deal, he would often encounter serious difficulties.

The president began by speaking of the endangered peace, asserting that although war had been "averted . . . storms from abroad" threatened America. He went on to warn that "the world has grown so small and weapons of attack so swift that no nation can be safe in its will to peace . . . weapons of defense give the only safety." He promised to send a special message on defense in a few days. As long as he spoke of danger and defense, it was clear from the response in the Capitol chamber and the remarks that followed that he had the support of the overwhelming majority. Isolationists, however, were troubled by his use of the phrase "methods short of war" and his observation, made as the final victory of Franco's revolt in Spain became increasingly certain, that "our neutrality laws . . . may actually give aid to an aggressor and deny it to the victim." They feared, correctly, that this presaged an attempt to alter the Neutrality Act.

Roosevelt went on to redefine national defense, dividing it into three elements. The first two—"armed forces . . . strong enough to ward off sudden attack [and achieve] ultimate victory" and "key facilities [that can be] rapidly expanded to meet all needs"—were generally agreed upon. But his insistence that the nation's program of social and economic reform was "a part of defense, as basic as armaments themselves," did not receive similar acceptance.

Much of the rest of the address was a defense of New Deal liberalism, comparable in many ways to his recent speech at the University of North Carolina. But, thinking of his national audience, Roosevelt avoided using either the words *New Deal* or any form of the word *liberal*. Instead, he spoke of "what we have accomplished since 1933" and of "reform," while arguing that all of it contributed to "national preparedness." The president itemized his achievements: "conserving and developing national resources"; "trying to provide necessary food, shelter and medical care"; "putting agriculture on a sounder basis"; "strengthening the weakest spot in our system of industrial supply—its long smouldering labor disputes"; "cleaned up our credit system"; and "giving . . . youth new opportunities and education."

While admitting that some things remained to be done—"better provision for our older people" and better care "for the medically needy"—there was no trumpet call for a vast program of reform. The major immediate goal he set for the Congress was his revised reorganization bill, and he allowed that since 1933 Congress had met all or part of the nation's "pressing needs." "We have now passed the period of internal conflict in the launching of our program of social reform. Our full energies may now be released to reinvigorate the processes of recovery in order to preserve our reforms, and to give every man and woman who wants to work a real job at a living wage."

Since, as he spoke, unemployment, always a lagging indicator, was still about 18 percent—in round numbers some ten million persons—providing jobs for everyone was a herculean goal for which he made no concrete proposals. The Works Progress Administration rolls had peaked in November at 3.35 million, serving at best a third of the unemployed, and were already being cut by his administration. One of the fights with Congress in 1939 would be over how much to cut the WPA. At no time during the 1930s did the administration attempt to provide directly for even half of the unemployed. Roosevelt did not talk about unemployment in any detail, but there would soon be a special message on the WPA, which he did not mention in the annual message. The president admitted that "dictatorships," using methods "we abhor," had at least temporarily solved their unemployment problems. He asked: "Can we compete with them by boldly seeking methods of putting idle men and idle capital together and, at the same time, remain within our American way of life, within the Bill of Rights, and within the bounds of what is, from our point of view, civilization itself?" He spoke of the "great unemployment of capital" and argued, correctly, with his newfound economic sophistication, that the widespread notion that "we are overburdened with debt" was false: "Despite our Federal Government expenditures the entire debt of our national economic system, public and private together, is no larger today than it was in 1929, and the interest thereon is far less than it was in 1929."

This kind of macroeconomic thinking was too counterintuitive to be effective and, in fact, would have been rejected by the Roosevelt of 1936–37. Most Americans, including most members of Congress, believed that the economic maxims of Ben Franklin's Poor Richard or Dickens's Mr. Micawber applied equally to personal and governmental budgets. Roosevelt never got traction with this argument and stopped using it.

He did, however, directly challenge those in Congress who sought to cut spending. He again used the concept of national income. In the June 1938 Fireside Chat, with the outcome of his stimulus package in doubt, he could only offer the hope that national income would not "fall below sixty billion dollars." Eighteen months later, with that level seemingly sustained, he could raise the possibility of increased spending—he called it "investing"—to create an $80 billion economy, but he warned that some thought the United States was "only a sixty billion dollar country."

He insisted that it did not seem logical, "at the moment we seek to increase production and consumption, for the Federal Government to consider a drastic curtailment of its own investments." He acknowledged the point of view that advocated eliminating "enough activities of government to bring the expenses of government immediately into balance with the income of government." But to accomplish this, Congress "will have to reduce the present . . . activities of government by one third," drastically curtailing a number of big-ticket items ranging from "aid to agriculture" to "national defense." "The Congress," he continued, "has the power to do this."

Rejecting that point of view, he argued that maintaining the current level of government was necessary and that the United States could not become "an eighty billion dollar nation in the near future if government cuts its operations by one-third. . . . [I]f we were to try it, we would invite disaster." Referring to his mistakes of 1937 without specifically admitting them, he added that "we have learned that it is unsafe to make abrupt reductions at any time in our net expenditure program."[1]

Although his argument was not particularly effective, Roosevelt had assimilated enough of what some of his tutors had been telling him to put forth an essentially Keynesian position—though he never let the dreaded word pass his lips in public. Sam Rosenman, who helped write this speech and devotes four pages to it in his memoir, never discusses the argument and probably did not understand that it was a Keynesian premise. His only mention of the economist is to recount what "Lord Keynes" said to him about Lend-Lease in London in 1945.[2]

The budget message the next day proposed spending $9 billion for the fiscal year ending June 30, 1940. It estimated that the national debt—the accumulated deficit—which had been some $37 billion on June 30, 1938, would be $44.5 billion by mid-1940. Aware of the growing hostility toward deficit spending—what he termed "recovery spending"—Roosevelt put a colloquial passage into the otherwise ponderous budget message. "We have not been throwing the taxpayers' money out of the window or into the sea. We have been buying real values with it. Let me repeat: The greater part of the budgetary deficits that have been incurred have gone for permanent, tangible additions to our national wealth. The balance has been an investment in the conservation of our human resources, and I do not regard a penny of it as wasted."[3]

It probably did little to change popular preconceptions. A Gallup poll published a day after the budget message but taken sometime in the previous fall reported that 61 percent of respondents (46 percent of Democrats and 89 percent of Republicans) thought that the government was spending "too much" and that the numbers had not changed significantly since 1935. A similar poll in 1934 had found that only about 40 percent thought that the government was spending too much. Other poll numbers published two days later showed the president's popularity at 58 percent, up from 54.4 percent just before the 1938 elections.[4]

Two other messages supplemented the budget message: a deficiency request for $875 million to keep the WPA going went to Congress at the same time as the budget message, while the promised additional request for national defense expenditures went up a week later.[5] Predictably, the WPA request drew initial negative reactions. Roosevelt's message reviewed the results of the stimulus package that Congress had approved and observed that the money then appropriated would run out at the end of the month. His request, he thought, would fund 3 million WPA jobs in February and March, with the number gradually diminishing until it reached 2.7 million in June.

The House cut the appropriation to $725 million, and early in February the Senate agreed; Roosevelt signed it and immediately sent a request for the missing $150 million. When that was not forthcoming, he repeated his request on March 14, which resulted in the appropriation of $100 million on April 11. Thus, Roosevelt had gotten all but $50 million of the requested appropriation, 95 percent of what he asked for.[6]

Two more major appointments followed: Frank Murphy to be attorney general and Felix Frankfurter to fill the vacancy on the Supreme Court created by the death of the liberal Benjamin Cardozo the previous July. Both, plus recess appointee Hopkins, had to be confirmed. Murphy replaced Homer Cummings, who resigned at age sixty-nine after serving almost five years. His undistinguished tenure's most important event was the terrible advice he gave Roosevelt in the Court fight. If Murphy had been reelected governor of Michigan, the post would have probably gone to Roosevelt's confidant Robert H. Jackson, who was solicitor general.

It was thought that Murphy would have a difficult confirmation hearing in view of his refusal to use the power of the state to break the sit-down strikes in Detroit in 1937, but that was not to be the case. To the surprise of many, Vice President Garner made efforts on his behalf after Murphy's production of a letter he had written to John L. Lewis, informing Lewis that if a settlement were not reached quickly he would enforce the court order that the strikers leave or be removed from the General Motors plants. Murphy was confirmed 87–7, with a majority of GOP senators positive. Frankfurter, known as the mentor of many New Dealers, won Senate approval without a dissenting vote. Harry Hopkins's appointment drew a heavy attack, though confirmation was never in doubt; the vote was 58–27.

During the entire session, Roosevelt filled 631 positions requiring Senate confirmation, of which 12 were turned down, only 2 of them major positions. Both were federal circuit court judgeships—one in Virginia, the other in Nevada—which ran afoul of the extraconstitutional tradition of "senatorial courtesy," whereby the Senate refuses to "advise and consent" to the appointment of federal judges and prosecutors opposed by a senator from the state in which they would serve. Roosevelt made an issue of one and ignored the other. He had originally made a recess appointment of state judge Floyd H. Roberts to a new judgeship in the Western District of Virginia on July 6, 1938, despite the fact that the state's senators, Carter Glass and Harry Byrd, had recommended two other candidates. Roberts sat until the full Senate defeated his nomination by a vote of 72–9 without debate. Roosevelt, who had corresponded with Glass about his appointment philosophy as early as March 1938, was putting down a marker by deliberately challenging the extraconstitutional tradition begun during George Washington's administration. The Senate has almost always rejected appointments to positions in the home state of senators who have declared that the appointment is "personally obnoxious" to them. After the rejection, Roosevelt wrote a public letter to Judge Roberts, praising his service and attesting that there had been no criticism of him as a judge. The president insisted that the Constitution intended the "advice" to come from the Senate as a whole.[7]

The Jackson Day Dinner that wound up the first week of the year gave Roosevelt a chance to rally Democrats and speak for the first time about the 1938 election. He began by acting out an imaginary conversation with the seventh president that had Jackson saying to him:

> Young fellow, do you realize that if you live out the term you now have, you'll be the only president of any party who had two full terms with a majority of his own party in both the House and the Senate all the time, the only President since—who do you suppose?—why, son, since James Monroe . . . Tell your fellows to learn to count. Some of you Democrats today get scared and let the other fellows tell you you've lost an election just because you don't have majorities so big that you can go to sleep without sentries.

Switching back to his own voice, Roosevelt offered a formula for victory in 1940, noting that "millions who had never been Democrats" put the party in power in 1932 and kept it there in 1936 to get "certain things done." The way for the party to stay in power was to continue to "get those things done which non-Democrats, as well as Democrats, put it in power to do." He continued to insist that to win again, the Democrats must continue to be a liberal party and "act as a party in power" by continuing to pursue liberal policies. He invited "nominal Democrats . . . convinced that our party should be a conservative party" to join the Republicans. As Roosevelt surely expected, no such defections occurred among congressional Democrats.[8]

The national defense proposal was ready late in the second week: the basic decisions had been made at a White House meeting in September 1938. At that meeting, Roosevelt, against the wishes of many of the military brass, initiated a policy of giving top priority to aircraft production and pilot training, which General Henry Harley "Hap" Arnold (1886–1950), who led the U.S. Army Air Forces from 1938 to 1946, called the Air Corps' "Magna Carta." Initial goals of seventy-five hundred military planes, total aircraft production of twenty thousand planes, and training twenty thousand pilots had been established later in the fall. These and similar decisions were very much presidential decisions, and for the rest of his presidency the problems of military preparedness would absorb more and more of Roosevelt's time and energy. All American presidents have been, by virtue of the Constitution, "commanders in chief," but no previous peacetime president had exercised those powers so fully, and only Abraham Lincoln had actually functioned in that role. From his earliest days in the White House, Roosevelt did not merely decide on options presented to him by civilian and military officials but actively participated in shaping those decisions, often revamping and rejecting his official advice.[9]

The national defense message began with Roosevelt reemphasizing that it was "imperative that we take immediate steps for the protection of our liberties" but warning that "it would be unwise to yield to any form of hysteria." Seeking to appear to be moderate on the subject, he warned against both extremes: those who claimed that it was necessary to spend "billions of additional money" as well as those who felt that "no further additions" were needed. Citing his experience—"those of us who took part in the conduct of the World War"—he explained that after the declaration of war in April 1917, no American units took part in engagements until May 1918, and that relatively speaking "we are not much more ready" to conduct large-scale land or air operations today. He also assured the public that neither "the Congress or the President have any thought of taking part in any war on European soil."

Roosevelt asked for $525 million in military expenditures beyond the amount in the budget message for "a well-rounded program, considered by me as Commander-in-Chief . . . for the necessities of defense." He noted, accurately, that the existing air defenses were "utterly inadequate." Of the total, $450 million was for the army and $321 million was for building planes for both services, plus $10 million a year for training civilian pilots. The unannounced September goal of seventy-five hundred planes had been pushed up to eighty-two hundred. An amount of $27 million was devoted to "implementing the military defenses of the Panama Canal," reflecting the ongoing delusion that the canal was a major enemy target.[10] Although there were even some complaints about defense spending, Congress agreed to this and additional requests. In this instance, Roosevelt got what he asked for in a bill he signed in early April, and by the end of that month he was asking for, and got, an additional $185 million for the army.[11]

Ever the opportunist, Roosevelt had been quietly encouraging the British and French governments to place orders for advanced military aircraft. He was willing to allow them in some instances to take delivery of aircraft for which the U.S. Army was waiting. He had initial discussions with a French representative as early as January 1938, and in October he had an unreported meeting at Hyde Park with Jean Monnet (1888–1979), the remarkable Frenchman who would become one of the key architects of postwar Europe. Monnet was in the United States to purchase planes for France. Roosevelt smoothed the purchase and suggested to Monnet that if war came, the French could get around the Neutrality Act by setting up plants in Canada—adjacent to aircraft manufacturing centers in Detroit and Buffalo—to assemble American-made parts into aircraft. That product of the president's fertile brain never materialized, but Monnet's mission did result in a firm order for six hundred planes, most of which were delivered before France fell in June 1940. Roosevelt and Monnet discussed an additional order for fifteen hundred more for 1940.[12]

The propriety of Roosevelt's conspiring with a foreign agent to evade an act of Congress can be raised, but had he been challenged he would have answered that he was acting in the national interest. His motives were twofold. He hoped that additional aircraft in the hands of Hitler's potential enemies might have some deterrent value and perhaps strengthen the resolve of the Western powers. More important, in the long run, additional orders would aid the rapid expansion of the American aircraft industry and, incidentally, lessen American unemployment. Less far-sighted American military officers, including General Arnold, resented these orders because they somewhat delayed the American buildup. They were also opposed by Secretary of War Harry Woodring, the Kansas Democrat who had been promoted from assistant secretary after seven months in an acting capacity following George Dern's death in August 1936. A competent administrator, Woodring was an isolationist who for the next seventeen months opposed not only selling advanced military aircraft abroad but also much of Roosevelt's foreign policy.

The covert but legal policy of giving friendly foreign governments access to experimental military aircraft was first made public—it had been revealed to some key legislators—following the crash in the parking lot of the Los Angeles Municipal Airport of a prototype of what became the Douglas A-20 Havoc, the most widely produced two-engine American bomber during World War II. The test pilot bailed out and was killed when his parachute failed to open, but his passenger survived the crash. After first being identified as a Douglas company mechanic, he was revealed to be Captain Paul Chemidlin, a Frenchman attached to Monnet's purchasing mission. Congressional isolationists were aroused, and Roosevelt invited the Senate Military Affairs Committee, which was thick with isolationists, to the White House for a briefing. It satisfied most but not all of them.[13]

By mid-January, Roosevelt was ready to push additions to old domestic reforms as well as new ones. He began by sending Congress a report he had requested from the Social Security Board (SSB), pointing out that more than 2.5 million "needy old people, . . . blind persons, and dependent children" were receiving $500 million in annual benefits, that 3.5 million unemployed persons had received $400 million in benefits in the past year, and that the program itself now contained 42.5 million accounts, though retirement benefits were not yet being paid. Roosevelt suggested a number of improvements, which, after a series of hearings, were approved overwhelmingly by Congress, 361–2 in the House and 57–8 in the Senate.

These 1939 amendments added about 1.1 million persons to the Social Security system, including bank employees and seamen; advanced the first retirement payments from 1942 to 1940; changed the basis for computing the retirement benefit from "accumulated" to "average" wages, which made for a significant increase in retirement benefits for persons who joined the system close to the time for their retirement; provided for wives aged over sixty-five of insured husbands to receive a benefit equal to half of their husbands'; enabled widows of retirees to receive three quarters of what their husbands had received; and provided benefits for children under eighteen years of insured workers who died before reaching retirement age. None of these changes affected the major gaps in coverage—farm workers and domestic servants—but they did establish a tradition, envisaged in the original act, of steady improvement of the system. In signing the bill in mid-August, Roosevelt argued that the amendments "represent another tremendous step forward [converting] the federal old age insurance system into [an] old age and survivors' insurance system."[14]

A historian of Social Security writes: "The original Act provided only retirement benefits, and only to the worker. The 1939 Amendments made a fundamental change in the Social Security program. The Amendments added two new categories of benefits: payments to the spouse and minor children of a retired worker (so-called dependents benefits) and survivors benefits paid to the family in the event of the premature death of a covered worker. This change transformed Social Security from a retirement program for workers into a *family-based* economic security program."[15] Despite this the 1939 amendments to the Social Security Act did not bring it up to the standard that Roosevelt had called for in 1938, as they did not "include all those who need its protection." This was still the case toward the end of Barack Obama's second term in 2015.

Continuing his commitment to reform, Roosevelt followed the Social Security message with one on health care a week later, sending Congress the recommendations of Josephine Roche's interdepartmental Committee on Health and Welfare. After observing that "the health of the people is a public concern" and that "ill health" was a "major cause" of both economic loss and dependency, the president reviewed the evolution of the committee's proposals since 1935 without referring to his decision not to include health insurance in the 1935 Social Security Act. The committee recognized the existence of both "serious unmet needs for medical service" and "our failure to make full application of the growing powers of medical science to prevent or control disease and disability." Roosevelt endorsed the committee's proposals, which sought to improve health through the device of matching federal grants to the states. These had been used extensively since the Progressive Era and in such New Deal programs as aid to dependent children, and in most such programs they were supplemented by state funds. The 1939 amendments to the Social Security Act, noted above, included provisions for an $11 million annual appropriation to aid state health programs.[16]

Roosevelt's failure to recommend any form of health insurance at this time reflected not only the caution of what Frank Freidel described as a "New Dealer with brakes on"—"driving at reduced speed" would be more appropriate—but also the history of attempts to get health insurance in modern America.

The first such push had come in emulation of pre–World War I European health plans when the American Association for Labor Legislation, on the assumption that a national bill would be unconstitutional, crafted a model bill to be introduced in state legislatures. It called for compulsory enrollment of most manual laborers earning $100 a month or less and provided for their income protection and medical care. According to the historian of the movement, this plan initially had the support of many physicians, but during and after World War I opinion turned against it: the formal opposition of the American Medical Association (AMA) in 1920 provided the coup de grâce.

Just before the Great Depression set in, Baylor University Hospital in Dallas began offering hospitalization insurance to the city's teachers for 50 cents a month. Soon similar plans were created, and by the mid-1930s Blue Cross and similar hospitalization schemes came into being. Initially, they too were opposed by the AMA, which urged Americans "to save for sickness" instead. In 1932 Hoover's interior secretary, Ray Lyman Wilbur, a physician, released a report by the nonpartisan Committee on the Costs of Medical Care, funded by some of the nation's most prestigious foundations, whose majority report included recommendations that "all basic public health services should be extended to the entire population" and that "medical costs should be placed on a group payment basis through insurance, taxation, or both." A minority report opposing both insurance and taxation was endorsed by the AMA. In 1937, with discussion of government health insurance on the rise, the physicians' trade union relented and approved participation in such plans as long as they in no way limited the compensation of its members.[17]

In late February 1939, Senator Robert F. Wagner, who had long favored doing something about health care, introduced a bill embracing the Roche committee's recommendations. He insisted, "We must take action now to conquer this last remaining frontier of social security in America." Wagner's bill did not establish any form of health insurance, but it would have made it possible for a state that did so to receive federal funds to help support it. The bill authorized spending $80 million the first year and at least $275 million in the third. As was the case with existing health programs in the developed nations that had them, Wagner's plan was to be financed from general funds rather than payroll taxes. The money would go in matching grants to states in five areas: child and maternal health, state public health services, state systems of temporary disability insurance, construction of hospitals and health centers, and "general programs of medical care." To be eligible for federal money, a state had to conform to established federal medical standards.

Opposition quickly developed among congressional conservatives, while Frank Gannett's National Committee to Uphold Constitutional Government—performing the propaganda functions once funded by the Liberty League—and the AMA led the opposition to any kind of government-sponsored health care. The physicians' organization raised funds to fight the bill by having its various chapters levy assessments and marshaled pharmaceutical houses and drugstore chains to pay for and distribute literature opposing the bill. In May the 174 delegates to the AMA's national convention voted to a man to condemn the Wagner bill. At Senate hearings, the chair of the AMA's board of trustees testified that the bill should not be passed, but he had to admit that he had not read it.

The loudest voice of the medical profession in those years was Morris Fishbein, M.D. (1889–1976), who had never practiced medicine. After a peculiar residency during which he spent much time doing autopsies at Chicago's Cook County Hospital and gained little experience with live patients, he went to work on the American Medical Association's journal and in 1924 became its editor. He led the fight against what the AMA had long called "socialized medicine" and insisted that the Wagner bill, if passed, would become its opening wedge. When it became apparent in May 1939 that Wagner's bill would not get out of committee, Fishbein celebrated by philosophizing: "A little sickness is not too great a price to pay for maintaining democracy in times like these."[18]

Wagner was prepared to renew the fight in the next Congress, but Roosevelt had decided by the end of the year not to push to get the bill out of committee. Instead, he placed immediate emphasis on a more limited program to build hospitals in the poorest parts of the nation where local governments did not have enough funds to be able to qualify for Public Works Administration (PWA) matching grants. As he told an end-of-year press conference, the problem with the Wagner bill was that the matching-grant requirement meant that most of the aid went to the richest states. Roosevelt was thinking about a program that would be fully funded by the federal government and would build hospitals in places where there were none, at one point speaking about "the fifty areas in the United States that most need hospital facilities."[19]

At about that time, there were changes in the medical program closest to his heart. In the run-up to the annual Birthday Ball, it became clear that there was public confusion about the distribution of its revenues as well as some resentment by local organizers about the fact that in 1938, as Roosevelt had announced, all of the funds collected had gone to the new national foundation. In New York, General Hugh Johnson, who despite his break with the New Deal continued to head the New York drive, made it clear that money from the national drive no longer went to the Warm Springs Foundation and that half the funds raised in New York would stay there and half would go to the national foundation. The fifty-fifty split was a return to earlier practice. Some days later, the president used the device of a public letter to the national foundation's Keith Morgan to reemphasize the fifty-fifty split without acknowledging that giving the entire net proceeds of the 1938 Birthday Ball to the national foundation had ignored what Roosevelt called the "American principle of local self-determination" in his radio address on the night of his birthday. A new feature of the 1939 celebration was a White House luncheon for a dozen stars of screen and stage, hosted by the first lady, which drew inaugural-size crowds hoping for a glimpse of celebrities and further associated the White House with them.[20]

February, as was often the case, was filled with congressional hearings and committee work. The biggest political event was the retirement of eighty-two-year-old Louis D. Brandeis, frail and ill, who sent the president a one-sentence letter on February 13: "Pursuant to the act of March 1, 1937, I retire this day from regular active service on the bench." Roosevelt, despite his disappointment about some of the decisions of the man he referred to as "Isaiah," responded graciously, telling the justice—whose 1916 appointment had been opposed by every living president of the American Bar Association (ABA)—that "I hope you will realize, as all your old friends do, how unanimous the nation has been in its gratitude to you." The buzz in the press was that the appointment of a westerner was called for, and the immediate favorite was Washington's senator Lewis B. Schwellenbach (1894–1948), who had been a last-ditch supporter of the president in the Court fight. But the next day, the word went out that another Washingtonian, William O. Douglas (1898–1980), the former Yale professor who had succeeded Joe Kennedy as chair of the Securities and Exchange Commission (SEC), was the likely choice. Douglas was nominated in mid-March; unanimously recommended by the Senate Judiciary Committee, which had asked him no questions; and easily confirmed early in April by a vote of 62–4. At forty he was the youngest justice in more than a century.[21] The two 1939 appointments meant that Roosevelt had put four justices on the Court in less than twenty months, each of them, despite many differences, a New Dealer.

Some months later, Roosevelt issued a tendentious signing statement, claiming that a minor administrative reform marked the final triumph of "the comprehensive proposal for judicial reorganization which I made to Congress" in 1937, a.k.a. the Court-packing plan. First, he ticked off a list of seven recent statutes that accomplished "six of the actual recommendations" he had made in 1937 and claimed that "the seventh" (which he failed to describe) "has been accomplished through the opinions of the Supreme Court itself." Some press commentary suggested that the president was responding to the recent comments by the current ABA president who had complained that the Court's recent decisions had brought most national activities "within the ambit of federal control" and that "the American people must look to the Legislature rather than the judiciary for the preservation of liberty."[22]

Not until March did Congress again take up executive reorganization, which it had failed to pass in 1937 and rejected in 1938. From the very beginning of the New Deal, Roosevelt had sought, and often achieved, greater control of the entire federal establishment. His major administrative device was the executive order (EO). With it he could create, without resort to Congress, the so-called alphabet soup of temporary agencies and coordinating bodies such as the CCC (Civilian Conservation Corps) and the NEC (National Emergency Council). Most of these would need congressional funding, but some could be supported for a time from funds available to the president. As noted, he had shown his ambition to control the independent regulatory agencies in August 1933 when he summarily removed a truculent probusiness conservative Republican member of the Federal Trade Commission (FTC) on the grounds that he was not in sympathy with the presidential program. William E. Humphrey, who had been reappointed by Hoover in 1931 to a second six-year term, had refused to resign and sued the government for his salary. Humphrey died in 1934 with the case still pending, but his executor continued the suit, which in May 1935 was decided by the Supreme Court against the government. The 9–0 decision reversed a previous ruling and held that persons appointed to positions for which Congress had stipulated specific terms could not be removed without appropriate cause.[23]

The 1939 version of the reorganization bill had been significantly toned down by Roosevelt and his congressional advisers. The major features of the 1939 version were:

1. The 1939 version required the president to submit specific plans to which Congress could apply what has come to be called a legislative veto, instead of giving the president virtually carte blanche to make changes once the bill was passed.
2. An act of Congress continued to be required to create a new department, instead of allowing the president to create new government departments—that is, cabinet-level bodies—by executive order.
3. The president was expressly forbidden to abolish any of the ten cabinet-level departments or any of a list of twenty-one subcabinet bodies or to appoint anyone to head a subcabinet body with the title of secretary or give such a person a cabinet-level salary.[24]
4. The president and his advisers had dropped provisions giving the president greater authority over the civil service and the General Accounting Office.

5. A proposal authorizing the president to appoint six administrative assistants at salaries of ten thousand dollars continued in all versions of the bill.

The changes were surely a curb on Roosevelt's administrative ambitions, but the bill still gave him wide powers.

In both the House and the Senate, the major bone of contention was the terms of the legislative veto. The administration's proposal required majority "no" votes in both houses within sixty days to negate a presidential proposal. A "no" vote in one house, or the failure of one or both houses to vote, would permit the president's proposal to become law. Congress was not required to pass it and could not amend it.

As had been the case in the Court fight two years earlier, the congressional opposition was spearheaded by Democrats, this time led by Hatton W. Sumners (1875–1962) of Texas, chair of the Judiciary Committee in the House, and Burton K. Wheeler in the Senate. They wanted either house to be able to veto the plans. The president's floor leaders, Lindsay C. Warren (1889–1976) of North Carolina in the House who had come to Congress in 1925 and whom Roosevelt would appoint comptroller general in 1940, and Jimmy Byrnes of South Carolina in the Senate, preserved the two-house requirement with some difficulty. In the House, Sumners's one-house veto amendment originally prevailed by a teller vote of 176–156 in the Committee of the Whole, but after Graham and other administration leaders marshaled their forces the amendment was defeated on a roll-call vote, 209–193. The Senate votes were even closer. Wheeler's amendment originally passed, 45–44, but was reconsidered the next day and lost, 46–44. The votes on the bill's final passage were overwhelming: the House approved, 246–123, and the Senate by 63–23, and Roosevelt signed it into law on April 4. The law, as we say now, sunset in January 1941, but in December 1941 the first War Powers Act gave Roosevelt very broad authority to move subcabinet units around, and reorganization was an ongoing process throughout the rest of Roosevelt's presidency.[25]

While most scholars treat the reduced scope of his powers as a major setback for Roosevelt, the chief architect of reorganization, the pragmatic Louis Brownlow, saw it differently. Writing in 1957, he argued that Roosevelt got essentially what he wanted. Congress prevented him from creating the two departments that he had in mind: a Department of Welfare, which surely would have gone to Harry Hopkins, and a Department of Public Works. But he was able to create the Federal Security Agency (FSA) and the Federal Works Agency (FWA) and to appoint persons with the title of administrator to run them. While Brownlow could shrug off the differences as unimportant, the American underclasses would have been much better served by a cabinet Department of Welfare headed by a dynamic reformer like Hopkins than by a mere agency headed by Paul V. McNutt, an ambitious Indiana politician with no discernible moral compass.[26]

The appointment of Hopkins to the not particularly comfortable cabinet seat in the Department of Commerce at the end of 1938 had indicated that Roosevelt understood what was possible.

Before he sent a reorganization plan to Congress, the president needed someone to manage the process. Since a key part of the Reorganization Plan would include moving the Bureau of the Budget from the Treasury to the planned Executive Office of the President (EOP), Roosevelt finally decided to appoint a successor to budget director Lew Douglas, who had resigned in 1934. Morgenthau's man Daniel Bell had served as an acting director for nearly five years. Roosevelt chose Harold D. Smith (1897–1947), a professional administrator with ties to the University of Michigan who had been Frank Murphy's budget director and came with strong recommendations from the new attorney general and from Brownlow. When Roosevelt summoned him to Washington and offered him the job, Smith hesitated, saying that he still had bridges to burn in Michigan. Roosevelt handed him a book of matches and said, "Start burning."

Smith was quickly sworn in on April 16 and put to work drafting Reorganization Plan No. 1, which was submitted to Congress on April 25; Plan No. 2 went up on May 9. Under his direction, the Bureau of the Budget not only performed its basic duty of compiling the budget for the president's approval but became his administrative staff. It analyzed every bill passed by Congress for the president's action, had to approve proposals to Congress from any part of the executive branch, drafted most executive orders, and generally managed the operation of the executive branch.[27]

Smith, essentially nonpolitical, described himself as "an independent Republican with Socialist leanings who frequently votes Democratic." He quickly gained Roosevelt's confidence and made the budget director's office more powerful than it might have been in other hands. Included in his job description, however, was the injunction to "keep the President informed of the progress of activities by agencies of the government with respect to work proposed, work actually initiated, and work completed."

Robert Sherwood reported that he knew "of no one whose judgment and integrity and downright common sense the President trusted more completely" than Smith. After the budget director and his staff moved into the White House and the adjoining old War, Navy, State Building, Smith became the most important single civilian administrator in Washington. And while Smith's diary is filled with familiar complaints about the president's notoriously bad administrative habits, shortly before he died he told Robert Sherwood that, upon reflection, he no longer thought that Roosevelt was "a very erratic administrator."

But now, when I look back, I can really begin to see the size of his programs. They were by far the largest and most complex programs that any president ever put through. People like me who had the responsibility of watching the pennies could only see the five or six or seven percent of the programs that went wrong, through inefficient organization or direction. But now I can see in perspective the ninety-three or—four or -five percent that went right—including the winning of the biggest war in history—because of unbelievably skillful organization and direction. . . . Roosevelt must have been one of the greatest geniuses as an administrator that ever lived. What we couldn't appreciate at the time was that he was a real *artist* in government.[28]

In submitting Plan No. 1 to Congress, Roosevelt explained that his "whole purpose" was "to improve the administrative management of the Republic" by reducing the numbers of agencies reporting to him and giving him assistance in dealing with the executive branch. The plan created, in addition to the EOP, three other major entities: the Federal Security Agency, the Federal Works Agency, and the Federal Loan Agency (FLA).

The Bureau of the Budget was the major element in the EOP; the budget director became responsible for the whole unit. Its personnel grew tenfold, from fifty to five hundred persons, during Roosevelt's presidency. Two independent bodies, the Central Statistical Bureau and the National Resources Planning Board, were also attached to the EOP, and the two committees directing them abolished, as was the Federal Employment Stabilization Office in the Department of Commerce. The employees and assets of the attached and abolished agencies were also transferred to the EOP to be utilized or transferred at the discretion of the budget director.

Roosevelt assured Congress that the task of the six administrative assistants provided for in the bill, the ones with "a passion for anonymity," would be "to help me get information and condense and summarize it—they are not to become in any sense Assistant Presidents nor are they to have any authority over anybody in any department or agency." That proved to be the case and remained so in the Roosevelt era and beyond, but many of their later successors, particularly Sherman Adams in the Eisenhower administration and H. R. Haldeman and John Ehrlichman in the Nixon administration, became notorious for exercising precisely those functions that Roosevelt proscribed.

The Federal Security Agency got the United States Employment Service from the Labor Department; the Office of Education, including its commissioner, from Interior; the Public Health Service, including the surgeon general, from Treasury; the National Youth Administration (NYA), which had been part of the WPA; and two independent bodies, the Social Security Board and the Civilian Conservation Corps.

The Federal Works Agency got both the independent WPA and Interior's PWA, plus the Bureau of Public Roads from Agriculture, the Public Buildings Branch from the Treasury, and from Interior the National Park Service's Branch of Building Management and the United States Housing Authority.

The Federal Loan Agency grouped mostly independent agencies: the Reconstruction Finance Corporation (RFC), the Electric Home and Farm Authority, the Federal Home Loan Bank Board, the Federal Housing Administration, and the Export-Import Bank. Three lending agencies primarily devoted to financing farms and crops were transferred to Agriculture.[29]

Many of the transfers in and out of established departments were hotly contested by such acquisitive administrators as Henry Wallace and Harold Ickes. In addition to Ickes's never satisfied desire for Agriculture's Forest Service, his ambition to expand his scope was notorious. As Brownlow tells the story, Roosevelt during a small meeting about Plan No. 1, at a time when most of the proposed transfers were still a very closely held secret, turned to the newcomer, Harold Smith, and explained:

> If I may address Dishonest Harold, Honest Harold has a peculiar trait. He is as honest as he is reputed to be, but he is like an honest cop patrolling a city market. He won't let anybody steal a peanut, but every once in a while he will reward himself with an apple here or a banana there as a tribute to his own honesty. Thus it is with Harold Ickes. He won't let anyone else take a bureau away from him, but he will be glad to pick up one or two if convenient in order to maintain his strict honesty.

Then, turning to Charles Merriam—Ickes had managed his unsuccessful 1919 campaign to be mayor of Chicago—Roosevelt continued, demonstrating his reluctance to deliver bad news: "I think you had better talk to Honest Harold and tell him we are actually taking the Office of Education away from him and putting it in a new agency."

Brownlow explains that he and Merriam invited Ickes for lunch, but Merriam was "loathe to act" and Ickes, who suspected that the pair had bad news for him, grew increasingly nervous. The lunch over and Ickes preparing to leave, Brownlow finally spoke up:

> Mr. Secretary, the plans are going up and one bureau is being taken away from the Department of the Interior.
>
> Ickes, as expected—"Oh how he bristled" Brownlow comments—asks: "What's that? What's that?"
>
> Brownlow responds: "The Office of Education."
>
> Ickes, relieved: "Thank God. I never wanted the so-and-so anyhow."[30]

Sending Plan No. 2 to Congress two weeks later, the president explained that while the first plan had to do with "overall management," the second concerned primarily "a more logical grouping of existing units" within the various departments and the further elimination of some independent agencies. Appended to the report was the following one-page chart.[31]

The President's Reorganization Plans 1 and 2
Effective July 1, 1939

EXECUTIVE OFFICE OF THE PRESIDENT

Bureau of the Budget (Treasury)
    Central Statistical Board (independent)
    Central Statistical Committee* (independent)
    National Resources Planning Board[1] (independent)
    Federal Employment Stabilization Office*
      (Commerce)
National Emergency Council*[2] (independent)

STATE DEPARTMENT

Foreign Commerce Service (Commerce)
Foreign Agriculture Service (Agriculture)
Foreign Service Buildings Commission
    (independent)

AGRICULTURE DEPARTMENT

Farm Credit Administration (independent)
    Federal Farm Mortgage Corporation
      (independent)
Commodity Credit Corporation (independent)
Rural Electrification Administration (independent)

INTERIOR DEPARTMENT

Bureau of Fisheries (Commerce)
Bureau of Insular Affairs (War)
Bureau of Biological Survey (Agriculture)
National Bituminous Coal Commission*[3]
    (independent)
Consumers' Counsel of NBCC* (independent)
Mt. Rushmore National Memorial Commission
    (independent)

JUSTICE DEPARTMENT

Federal Prison Industries, Inc. (independent)
National Training School for Boys (independent)

NATIONAL ARCHIVES

Codification Board* (independent)

COMMERCE DEPARTMENT

Inland Waterways Corporation (War)

FEDERAL WORKS AGENCY

Public Roads Administration[4] (Agriculture)
Public Works Administration (independent)
Work Projects Administration[5] (independent)
United States Housing Authority (Interior)
Public Buildings Administration[6]

FEDERAL SECURITY AGENCY

Office of Education (Interior)
    U.S. Film Service (National Emergency Council)
    Radio Division (National Emergency Council)
Public Health Service (Treasury)
Social Security Board (independent)
    U.S. Employment Service (Labor)
National Youth Administration (independent)
Civilian Conservation Corps (independent)
American Printing House for Blind (Treasury)

FEDERAL LOAN AGENCY

Reconstruction Finance Corporation (independent)
RFC Mortgage Company (independent)
Disaster Loan Corporation (independent)
Electric Home and Farm Authority (independent)
Federal National Mortgage Association
    (independent)
Export-Import Bank of Washington (independent)
Federal Housing Administration (independent)
Federal Home Loan Bank Board (independent)
    Home Owners' Loan Corporation (FHLBB)
    Federal Savings & Loan Insurance Corp.
    (FSLIC)

TREASURY DEPARTMENT

Bureau of Lighthouses (Commerce)
War Finance Corporation* (independent)
Director General of Railroads* (independent)

Notes

Note: Parentheses indicate former status of agencies
*Functions transferred as shown, office abolished.
[1] Formerly called the National Resources Committee.
[2] Now called the Office of Government Reports.
[3] Now called the Bituminous Coal Division.
[4] Formerly called the Bureau of Public Roads.
[5] Formerly called the Works Progress Administration.
[6] Composed of Public Buildings Branch (Treasury) and Buildings Management Branch (Interior).
Source: Samuel I. Rosenman, comp., *The Public Papers and Addresses of Franklin D. Roosevelt,* 1939 volume, *War—and Neutrality,* 334.

The president had told his press conference in Warm Springs in April, where he signed the bill, that he had given no "thought of what to do about any" reorganization details. He waited until July to name his first three assistants and took two more months to make the dimensions of the EOP clear. On September 9, in the midst of a number of actions triggered by Hitler's invasion of Poland and the beginning of what became World War II, the president issued an executive order "reorganizing" the EOP into six divisions: a "White House Office," the "Bureau of the Budget," the "National Resources Planning Board," the "Liaison Office for Personnel Management," the "Office of Government Reports," and, "in the event of a national emergency," an office to manage that emergency, "as the President shall determine."[32]

The functions of each were laid out. A three-part White House Office would now consist of, first, the "Secretaries to the President," which was still the three authorized positions inherited from Herbert Hoover. Steve Early and Marvin McIntyre were still in place but had been promoted from assistant secretaries after Louis Howe's death. Jimmy Roosevelt's appointment to fill Howe's slot but not his shoes was short lived; in early 1939, after his son's resignation, Roosevelt, in an unprecedented move, named his longtime military aide Colonel Edwin M. (Pa) Watson to fill the third secretary's position and ordered his promotion to brigadier general.[33] The other two parts were, second, the "Executive Clerk," still Rudolph Forster, with his traditional duties plus a considerable staff that could be temporarily expanded for such events as inaugurations by borrowing personnel from other parts of the executive branch, and, third, the new element, the six "Administrative Assistants to the President," who were to "get information and summarize it for his use" and to have no executive authority whatsoever. Consistent with Roosevelt's previous statements about them, more space is devoted in his order to what they may *not* do than is spent describing their duties.

Of the first three assistants, appointed shortly after the Reorganization Act went into effect on July 1, two, economist Lauchlin Currie (1902–93) and William H. McReynolds (1880–1951), a permanent civil servant, were keepers and still on the president's staff when he died. The third, James H. Rowe Jr. (1909–84), was one of many who passed through. He had come to Washington in 1933, fresh from Harvard Law School and a protégé of both Frankfurter and Tom Corcoran, and was a kind of legal utility infielder. He began doing legal chores for the National Emergency Council, had a stint as one of Justice Holmes's law clerks, and then more lawyering for the RFC, the PWA, and the SEC, the Democratic National Committee (DNC), and as an assistant to Pa Watson, before he took on similar tasks for the president for some two years. In late 1941, the president named him an assistant attorney general. He left Washington in 1943 to become a naval officer. Rowe's original White House appointment was taken by Washington insiders to mean that Corcoran, who with his alter ego, Ben Cohen, had been the gossips' favorite for one of "the selfless six," would not be appointed.[34]

Although McReynolds and Currie had similar tenures, the nature of their assignments could not have been more different. The civil servant McReynolds, who had begun his federal career in Theodore Roosevelt's administration and was known among senior bureaucrats as "Mr. Mac," was essentially a liaison officer between the White House and the Civil Service Commission. The original Brownlow plan had proposed abolition of the Civil Service Commission, placing more direct control of career employees in the president's hands. Specifically forbidden to do that by Congress, the flexible Roosevelt exercised his control through McReynolds, who met once or twice a week with the commissioners to inform them of Roosevelt's suggestions. The Eisenhower administration later modified the process by bringing the chair of the Civil Service Commission into the EOP.[35]

Currie's appointment had both symbolic and real importance. As the first trained economist on the White House staff, his appointment represented an obvious triumph for what the *New York Times* called advocates "of the 'spending for recovery' theory." Marriner Eccles reports that when Roosevelt phoned to tell him that he was "going to steal Lauch Currie" for his staff, he "baited the hook" by adding, "You, of course, see the advantages . . . of having a friend in court who can represent you and speak for *your* point of view." Currie's successful performance led to the creation of the Council of Economic Advisers, which he helped to set up in the EOP early in the Truman administration.[36]

Currie's advanced economic views were certainly important. One scholar of planning has called him the 'the fairest-haired economic planner in the New Deal . . . who possessed that rare combination of intellectual charm and economic persuasiveness . . . capable of restraining Roosevelt from relapsing toward the balanced budget." Currie, describing the advocacy of a number of broadly Keynesian economists in "winning converts," wrote, "We did not sleep much, but when we did the *General Theory* kept working. With the work on the Works Financing Act of 1939 and our long discussions on a major revision of the Social Security System, Roosevelt finally gathered a firm grasp of the theory."

But many of Currie's tasks were not those most bosses would have assigned to an economist, including two essentially diplomatic missions to China during which he met in Chungking with both Chiang Kai-shek and Chou En-lai. None of the more than a dozen other administrative assistants appointed by Roosevelt had such varied chores.[37]

Despite the glamour of the select six, the most important innovation in the reorganization plan was the transformation of the Bureau of the Budget that took place along with its physical move. As described in the executive order, it had eight interlocking missions. The first two were traditional: to assist the president in preparing the budget and to administer it. The other six transformed it into a supervisory agency intended to help the president manage the rest of the executive branch while serving as a watchdog over it. The bureau was now responsible for developing improved plans of administrative management and informing executive departments and agencies about them; helping the president bring about a more efficient and economical government; assisting the president by clearing and coordinating departmental advice on proposed legislation and, as had been the case previously, making recommendations on proposed legislation; assisting in the consideration, clearance, and, where necessary, preparation of executive orders; planning and promoting the improvement and coordination of federal and other statistical services; and keeping the president informed of the progress "of activities by agencies of the Government with respect to work proposed, work actually initiated, and work completed, together with the relative timing of work among the several agencies of the Government."[38] Unlike the provisions about the president's administrative assistants, the order placed no limit on the activities of the Budget Bureau.[39]

One reason that we do not read much about the Budget Bureau or the other parts of the Executive Office of the President is because while Roosevelt arranged to have almost every aspect of the war written about, no one was ever assigned to write a history of the expanded White House. My notion is that this was not an oversight and that Franklin Roosevelt intended to write or at least supervise that project himself when he retired to his Hyde Park library. Another reason for neglect is that most historians and others who have written about the war years have had little interest in administrative details.

On March 30, as Roosevelt was preparing to leave for a Warm Springs vacation, Harold Ickes came to the White House and secured his approval for the black contralto Marian Anderson to give what became an epochal recital at the Lincoln Memorial on Easter Sunday. The Daughters of the American Revolution had refused to make an exception to its white-only policy for its auditorium, Constitution Hall, then the only first-class cultural venue in the nation's capital. This was consistent with general segregation practices throughout the District of Columbia. A controversy had been sparked by Eleanor Roosevelt's discussing her resignation from the organization in her newspaper column, *My Day*. The event, at the Lincoln Memorial, attended by seventy-five thousand persons black and white, became the first major public protest against Jim Crow in the nation's capital.[40]

Ironically, Roosevelt's first stop on the way to Warm Springs was at Tuskegee, Alabama, to visit the institution founded by Booker T. Washington and partially funded by the state of Alabama at which segregation was not publicly challenged. Introduced by Tuskegee's emeritus president Robert Russa Moton (1867–1940) as "the best friend of the Negro race or any race high or low anywhere in the world," Roosevelt made polite, mildly inspirational remarks, and in closing addressed the students as "my boy and girl friends." (In another address that day at Auburn, Alabama's agricultural school for whites, he addressed "you young men and women.") While at Tuskegee, he visited the hospital, spoke with the renowned black scientist Dr. George Washington Carver, and shook hands with patients in wheelchairs, as he often did.

The seeming inconsistency between Roosevelt's enabling an important symbolic attack on segregation in the nation's capital and his acceptance of it on Alabama campuses was in fact typical of Roosevelt's strategic behavior as the leader of a party whose traditional strength lay in the solid South. In a little-noticed 1935 public statement, he praised "the white people of the South" for providing a new agricultural building at Tuskegee "as an endorsement of the splendid work being done there in the teaching of scientific agriculture. . . . As an adopted citizen of the South I have great faith in Tuskegee."[41]

It is not certain that Roosevelt's end-of-March visit to Tuskegee had anything to do with Basil O'Connor's announcement two months later at the end of May that the national foundation had approved a $161,000 grant, the largest it had yet made, to build the Tuskegee Polio Center and maintain it for one year. The center would not only provide care but also train black doctors, nurses, and physiotherapists. Naomi Rogers, in a splendid study, has demonstrated that there had been growing pressure from the African American community, expressed by its medical professionals and the black press, about the almost total lack of polio treatment facilities for their people and about the lily-white health care provided at the Warm Springs facility. There were also complaints about black contributions to the March of Dimes being used to support facilities that would not treat them. Although O'Connor claimed in private communications to the trustees that only "professional colored promoters" and other troublemakers were complaining, he nevertheless saw the way the wind was blowing, and the Tuskegee grant was one result. Two of those "troublemakers" were Franklin and Eleanor Roosevelt, each of whom had raised the question of a separate cottage for black patients.[42]

Roosevelt's ten days at Warm Springs were quite informal and quiet, as the transcripts of his four al fresco press conferences indicate. One complex headline said it all: "Roosevelt Happy in Georgia: His Spirits Rise in Warm Springs to Song and Jest as He Revels in a Free Life." The president recycled old jokes, claiming that he would make his chief guest, Harry Hopkins, who was sitting next to him in the little car he drove himself, "take a bath. . . . He has not had one for two months." But over this calm hung the growing expectations of a major war. In mid-March, Hitler, violating the Munich Agreement, dismembered the remains of the Czech Republic, leading Neville Chamberlain to withdraw the British ambassador from Berlin and declare the end of appeasement. Later that month, Madrid fell, ending the Spanish Civil War, and on April 3 the United States formally recognized the Franco regime. On March 23, Lithuania had surrendered the Baltic port of Memel to Germany; eight days later, England and France announced that they would go to war if Poland were attacked. On April 1, Mussolini invaded Albania.

Roosevelt in Warm Springs gave a frank off-the-record assessment of the economic aspects of German and Italian aggression to be attributed to White House sources. Five days later, as his special train was about to leave the Warm Springs station, the president, as was his custom, appeared on its rear platform and, smiling, spoke briefly to the small waiting crowd: "My friends of Warm Springs: I have had a fine holiday here with you all. I'll be back in the fall if we don't have a war." While the suddenly silent crowd waited for an elaboration, Roosevelt waved, and on the arm of Pa Watson he turned and reentered his car, leaving the crowd and the nation to wonder just what he meant.

In a story datelined from the president's northbound train on Easter Sunday, the *Times'* White House correspondent wrote that "well-informed sources close to the president revealed" that in recent transatlantic telephone conversations, diplomats had "told the President that the probability of war in a few weeks was very high." With the leisure of an evening deadline, the *Times*man described the wire-service reporters throwing "a few hastily scribbled lines" about the president's statement to "waiting telegraph company attendants" as the train pulled out of the Warm Springs station.[43]

Roosevelt returned to an anxious Washington. Before he left the train, he had a short meeting with Cordell Hull, who came to Union Station to brief him on what had happened while he was en route. Later the president found time, as he put it, to throw out the first Easter egg for a crowd of some fifty thousand children and adults as he and Eleanor watched the festivities from the South Portico of the White House.[44]

At Roosevelt's regular Tuesday press conference, for which he had "no news," reporters pressed him for an interpretation of his parting remark at Warm Springs. He eventually referred them to an editorial in the *Washington Post*, a paper that rarely supported his policies.

THE PRESIDENT: . . . It is very good.

Q: Did you inspire it, sir?

THE PRESIDENT: No . . . I almost fell out of bed when I read it, but it is very good, very clear, and very honest. (Turning to the stenographer) Henry Kannee, will you [put] the . . . editorial into the [press conference] minutes so that posterity will know what I am talking about.

The editorial, which began by quoting Roosevelt's warning sentence at the Warm Springs station, argued that by using the collective pronoun *we*, he was alerting Americans as well as Europeans that any general European war would affect not only the combatants but all of Western civilization, including the United States, whether or not it actually entered the conflict.[45]

Later that week, speaking to the Pan American Union, Roosevelt called upon Europe for peace while affirming his resolve to defend the Western Hemisphere.

"We, too, have a stake in world affairs," he insisted, and he made it clear that he was prepared to defend the hemisphere, including Canada, from both military and economic attack. Later that day, speaking at Mount Vernon, where George Washington had learned of his election as president on April 14, 1789, Roosevelt kicked off the 150th anniversary celebration of Washington's assumption of the presidency. In the course of his speech, he speculated about Washington's feelings that day and was sure that the first president would have refused the summons had the times been normal. But it was "clear" to Roosevelt that Washington believed that the permanence of the new republic was at stake. Therefore, against his inclination, he accepted the call and set out two days later for the then arduous journey to New York City and inauguration on the last day of the month. Naturally, many of the readers of political tea leaves saw this as an indication of Roosevelt's intention to accept a third term in 1940 if war came.[46]

That Saturday morning, a hastily called press conference garnered only about 25 of some 150 accredited correspondents to hear the president's gloss on the essentially identical messages he had sent to Hitler and Mussolini at 9:00 p.m. the night before. Hull, Assistant Secretary Sumner Welles, and Senate Foreign Relations chair Key Pittman were silent spectators. Explaining that he sent the one to Hitler because he was a head of state and Hull sent the one to the Italian premier, Roosevelt told reporters that last night, "the Secretary of State and I . . . both slept with a clearer conscience than we had before." The messages asked the two dictators to "give assurance that your armed forces will not attack or invade" thirty-one enumerated nations in Europe and the Middle East "for at least ten years." It is impossible to believe that Roosevelt thought that his reasonable proposal sent to unreasonable men would cause them to change their behavior. Apart from his conscience, he could hope that his appeal might bolster the morale of the British and French, but surely his effort was largely intended for domestic consumption.[47]

Neither dictator even deigned to reply, and the controlled press in each nation immediately sneered at the proposal, while London and Paris papers largely praised it. The *Sunday Express* went so far as to headline an editorial on Roosevelt's messages "The Greatest Man in the World." The American reaction was more varied. A cynical senatorial isolationist, like Hiram Johnson, scoffed privately that Roosevelt "wanted to knock down two dictators in Europe, so that one may be firmly implanted in America," while an idealist like Gerald P. Nye felt that it was "a grand way to approach this immediate situation." Reporters covering Capitol Hill generalized that "most Democrats and some Republicans" had varying degrees of praise for the president. It was, after all, difficult to oppose an appeal for peace. In terms of practical politics, it was one more element in the struggle to amend the Neutrality Act, which would continue for most of the year.[48]

After a series of conferences with congressional leaders, Roosevelt decided that the Neutrality Act revision should go first to the House, where isolationist strength was weaker and whose Committee on Foreign Affairs now had a new chair, a New York Democrat, Sol Bloom (1870–1949). Bloom, a rags-to-riches son of immigrants whose earliest encounter with "foreign affairs" involved importing the belly dancer known as Little Egypt to the 1893 Chicago World's Fair, was an enthusiastic supporter of Roosevelt's foreign policy. On May 1, 1939, the cash-and-carry provisions of the 1937 Neutrality Act expired, so the existing law again forbade the export to belligerents of arms, ammunition, and implements of war. Roosevelt and Hull wanted a law that gave them legal ways to continue to send military supplies to Britain and France in the event of war. Aid to China remained unaffected, as the United States had not officially recognized the war in progress in Asia. Bloom and his committee drafted a bill giving the president wider latitude than he had ever had, and the committee approved it on a straight party vote, 12–8. But at the end of June, the House accepted an amendment by a Republican member of the committee, barring the export of "arms and ammunition" to belligerents but saying nothing about "implements of war." This would have enabled the continued export of aircraft to belligerents. It was adopted by a vote of 159–157 and reaffirmed by a vote of 180–176. About 100 Democrats ducked the first vote and some 60 the second.[49]

Roosevelt was thus forced to rely upon the Senate Committee on Foreign Relations, on which prominent isolationists were overrepresented. After the Fourth of July recess, the parliamentary situation in the Senate was that 34 senators were pledged to filibuster any neutrality bill, and adjournment was near. Under those circumstances, the Senate committee voted 12–11 to postpone any action on a neutrality bill until the second session of Congress in January. Five Democrats had joined all 7 Republicans on the committee in blocking the administration measure; even had the proposal prevailed in committee, though, passage by the full Senate seems to have been unlikely. Roosevelt, Hull, and administration leaders in Congress struggled in vain to find a way to bring neutrality legislation to the floor. On July 14, Roosevelt released a terse three-paragraph statement to the Congress, to which was appended a prolix twenty-six-hundred-word policy statement from Hull that the president said had his "full approval." His own position was stated in two sentences. "It has been abundantly clear to me for some time that for the cause of peace and in the interest of American neutrality and security, it is highly advisable that the Congress at this session should take certain much needed action. I see no reason to change that opinion." It seems clear that the president knew he was licked and was just going through the motions and making a record.

On the night of July 18, Roosevelt and Hull had a three-hour conference with the vice president; Senators Alben Barkley and Charles McNary, the Senate majority and minority leaders; Foreign Affairs chair Pittman; plus William Borah and Vermont's Warren R. Austin (1877–1962), ranking Republican members of the Foreign Affairs Committee. At its conclusion, the White House reported Barkley and McNary agreed that "no action on neutrality legislation can be obtained" now, that the Senate "would consider neutrality legislation at the beginning of the next session," and that the president and Hull held that failure of the Senate to take action now "would weaken the leadership of the United States" in responding to events during the remainder of the year. Clearly, the failure of congressional Democrats to follow Roosevelt's lead reflected all the differences between them since the Court fight as well as differences about foreign policy.[50]

At his next press conference, Roosevelt gave his account of the meeting:

THE PRESIDENT: There weren't any clashes. . . . There was only one disagreement between two people [Borah and Hull]. Senator Borah did intimate rather clearly and definitely that his information [was better than that of the State Department]. It was all in very parliamentary language.

The politics of it, according to Roosevelt, was that "the members of the Senate who have decided to defer action until January have been gambling that the possibility [of war] won't eventuate. Therefore there is nothing further to discuss. The country understands it."[51]

With neutrality no longer an issue, the business of the session was concluded in the first week of August. While the disaffection of many Democratic legislators was obvious, the session's accomplishments were impressive: most important were the Reorganization Act, the Social Security revision, and the greatly increased military spending discussed earlier. Total authorized expenditures were more than $13 billion, higher than any previous New Deal session, nearly $2 billion of it for military expansion. In addition to the supplemental relief funds voted early in the year, a new relief bill appropriated more than $1.7 billion for relief in the coming year, the bulk of it for the WPA at roughly the levels requested by the president. Congress abolished the controversial Federal Theater Project while leaving other WPA cultural projects alone, and for the first time it applied certain restrictive rules about how work relief was to be administered.

Congress only tinkered with the tax code, wiping out what was left of an undistributed profits tax and substituting a flat 18 percent levy. The House Ways and Means Committee did agree to make a recess study of the revenue code. Other important matters left for the second session included pending amendments to the Wagner Act and the wages and hours legislation, railroad reorganization measures, and aspects of the president's health program. An end-of-session revolt in the House resulted in unexpected defeats for two further stimulus measures, a $1.85 billion lending measure for public works and an $800 million housing bill. The former, after passing the Senate 52–28, lost in a 193–166 House vote made possible by 47 Democrats joining the negative majority. The housing bill lost in the House by a similar vote.[52]

Roosevelt made no special report to the people about the 1939 session, but he did comment on its results in press conferences and issued specific statements about several new measures. He had understood that defeats were coming. As compared to his reactions to the Court fight, his public demeanor was quite restrained. Being rebuffed on this or that matter was something he had experienced regularly in New York, where he had never enjoyed a legislative majority. Responding to the defeat of the public works lending bill, he simply pointed out that though it was justified as an economy move, it would actually cost the taxpayers in two ways: the money not appropriated would have stimulated the economy and put more people to work, taking some off the relief rolls, and its defeat would surely increase those rolls further. He made and remade the point that this was the responsibility of Congress, and he fully expected those or similar appropriations to be approved in future sessions. In signing the Hatch Act, touted as an anti–New Deal measure, which limited the right of most federal employees to participate actively in politics or coerce the participation of others, Roosevelt took the unusual step of sending a message to Congress about an approved bill. Noting that he had called for such a measure in his January 5 message on the WPA, he warned of its possible conflict with the civil rights of federal employees and suggested that it be extended to a much more numerous group, employees of state and local governments. The bill's author, New Mexico's senator Carl Hatch, generally an administration supporter, told reporters that he was "deeply gratified" by Roosevelt's approval. He promised to follow up on the president's proposal to extend it to nonfederal employees, which was accomplished in part by a statute in 1940.[53]

At his next news conference, with adjournment approaching, Roosevelt continued his seemingly passive response to setbacks. When asked to comment on the House's defeat of the housing bill, he replied with a stock Latin quotation, "Res ipsa loquitur" (The thing speaks for itself), and enjoyed answering a question about Ohio's Robert A. Taft's presidential aspirations with a question of his own.

Q: Do you agree or disagree with the statement of Senator Taft to the effect that no sensible person will want to be president after 1941? (Laughter)

THE PRESIDENT: Did he say that about his own candidacy?

Q: He said it about his own candidacy.

Q: Won't you answer?

THE PRESIDENT: Don't you think that is an awfully good answer that I have already given? (Laughter)

Asked about the apparent duplication of effort in dam building, with some projects supervised by the Army Corps of Engineers (for example, Fort Peck) and others by Interior's Bureau of Reclamation (for example, Boulder and Grand Coulee), he gave a long, serious answer, explaining at some length the rough rule of thumb used to divide the work. The Corps did work on the Mississippi, plus harbors and flood control, while Reclamation did the rest of the work. When a report was called for on the work of either group, it was done by its rival.[54]

Just before Roosevelt left for Hyde Park, where he would spend a week working through some 350 bills that came to him with departmental and agency recommendations attached, the White House issued two statements designed to show the president in charge and not besieged, as the press had been depicting him. One was the president's statement claiming victory in the Court fight, discussed above, and the other harked back to the days of the 1933 Economy Act and instructed government departments to make the cuts in administrative costs envisaged by the Reorganization Act.[55]

Questioned at Hyde Park about his differences with Congress, Roosevelt, with Eleanor at his elbow chiming in and occasionally prompting him, again made the point that Congress—all the Republicans and a small minority of Democrats—were making two "bets" with the nation: on neutrality that there would be no crisis before January and on reducing spending that "industry and business will take up the whole slack." He hoped they would win both bets, but if they lost, "the Nation must and will hold them solely responsible."

Roosevelt argued in a message sent to a Young Democrats meeting in Pittsburgh that "Republican and Democratic reactionaries want to undo what we have accomplished in these last few years and return to the unrestricted individualism of the previous century." Harking back to his Jackson Day Dinner speech, he warned that if in 1940 "we nominate conservative candidates . . . I personally, for my own self respect and because of my long service in and belief in liberal democracy, will find it impossible to have any active part in such an unfortunate suicide of the old Democratic Party." White House sources told reporters that in the coming session, the president would revert to his former practice of listing certain bills as "must" legislation.[56]

In a formal signing statement for the Social Security Act amendments, he praised the changes and called for continuing improvement, noting that despite the expansion of coverage many workers were still excluded and that "in my opinion, it is imperative that these insurance benefits be extended to workers in all occupations." But he did not then or ever formally suggest extending Social Security to the two largest excluded groups: domestic servants and agricultural workers.[57]

Unlike 1937 and 1938 when popular attention was focused on the dramatic struggles between the president and Congress, the focus of national concern was elsewhere that summer, on the danger of a European war. But for large numbers of Americans, the summer of 1939, with economic conditions again approaching the 1937 levels of what seemed a kind of prosperity, was a time of relaxation. Millions attended one of the two World's Fairs, in New York and San Francisco, and more than a few went to both. Roosevelt had sent a sunny radio message to San Francisco's February opening, calling it "an instrument of international good will"; he planned to visit it in the fall. He personally opened New York's "World of Tomorrow" at the end of April, claiming that "our wagon is still hitched to a star . . . a star of friendship . . . of progress of mankind . . . of greater happiness and less hardship . . . of international good will, and, above all, a star of peace."[58]

The great presidential event of the summer was the June 7–12 royal visit of Britain's forty-four-year-old king, George VI—the great-great-great grandson of George III—and his queen, part of the first visit to the New World by a reigning British monarch. The royal couple were in the United States on just four of their forty-four days in North America. The rest of their tour was, understandably, spent in Canada and Newfoundland, as they traveled by train to the Pacific Coast and back. The two days in the American capital went according to protocol: an afternoon garden reception at the British Embassy, which housed the royal couple; a formal dinner and musical entertainment at the White House the first day, followed by a reception with members of Congress in the Rotunda of the Capitol; lunch aboard the presidential yacht the second day with both Roosevelts and a very short cruise across the Potomac to visit Mount Vernon; the inspection of a CCC camp, their one encounter with the New Deal; and then the laying of a wreath at the Tomb of the Unknown Soldier in Arlington, closing with an informal tea in the White House and a formal dinner for the Roosevelts at the British Embassy.

After an overnight train trip to Red Bank, New Jersey, and a drive to Sandy Hook, the royal party boarded the destroyer USS *Warrington,* which landed them at the tip of Manhattan, where they were briefly greeted by Governor Herbert Lehman and Mayor Fiorello La Guardia. A waiting motorcade escorted them to the World's Fair. After a luncheon there and a brief tour of the fair, the party was driven back to Columbia University—an institution chartered in 1754 as "King's College" by George II—and briefly inspected its library. Then their motorcade went up to Hyde Park, arriving before dinner.[59]

The two days at Hyde Park, scripted by Roosevelt, were great American theater. The press was not permitted to enter the house or go to the scene of the famous picnic and got all its information from White House and State Department staff. Although the area was awash with troops—a battalion of army regulars from West Point guarded the house and grounds, while a thousand New York National Guardsmen guarded the approaches to the village of Hyde Park itself—within the cordon informality reigned. The royal pair were hosted by Eleanor and Franklin in Sara's house, and the three greeted the royal party on their porch. Eleanor had explained to reporters that they wanted it to be as simple as a dinner for royalty and twenty-three other guests, including three Roosevelt sons and their wives, could be. The queen, at least, was convinced that this was the case, writing her mother-in-law, "They are such a charming and united family and living so like English people when they come to their country house."

But the real public relations coup came on the final afternoon, when the Roosevelts took the royal couple on what was described as a "picnic" and, to the reported horror of the eighty-five-year-old Sara, fed them "hot dogs." The royal "picnic" was on the porch of the hilltop cottage Roosevelt had built largely for Eleanor and her friends. (A real picnic—blankets on the grass—would have involved serious public relations problems for a closet paraplegic.) Before the picnic, both couples attended Sunday services at St. James; Roosevelt drove the royal couple and his daughter-in-law Betsy Cushing Roosevelt to the picnic in his small car, and the two heads of state—and no one else—had a swim in the cottage's spring-fed pool. After another formal dinner in the Roosevelt home, the visitors and their entourage, which included Canadian premier Mackenzie King, left to return to Canada for the remainder of their tour. Franklin, Eleanor, and Sara went down to the Hyde Park station to see their royal guests off.[60]

Although Roosevelt had told the press beforehand that his talks with the king would "not amount to very much," we now know, thanks to the dutiful monarch's handwritten notes for his ministers, the king's version of what was said.

"I had two good conversations with the President," the king's notes began, and he "seemed genuinely glad that I had been able to pay him this visit." At the first, with "Mr. Mackenzie King present," they talked of the "firm & trusted" Canadian-American friendship, and "FDR mentioned that he thought it was a waste of money to build a Canadian fleet as he had already laid his plans for the defense of the Pacific Coast of Canada." A parenthetical remark indicates that the president also brought up the scheme we know he had already discussed with Jean Monnet of assembling American aircraft parts in Canada.

The king's report of the second conversation, when they were alone, shows that Roosevelt was incredibly indiscreet, probably because he knew that the king would report his remarks. He showed him on charts just where his naval patrols would go if war came. "If he saw a U-boat he would sink her at once & wait for the consequences." With less accuracy, Roosevelt assured the king that "if London was bombed USA would come in. Offensive air warfare was better than defensive & he hoped we should do the same on Berlin."

Other remarks reported by the king show that Roosevelt already knew some of what he would want from Britain in case of war, including bases in Trinidad and Bermuda and nickel from Canada. He warned that the war-debt question should not be reopened.[61] These notions, expressed in June 1939, need to be kept in mind when Roosevelt's actions and statements after war broke out are considered. Some two months later, as he was disposing of the last bills from the congressional session, Roosevelt's staff informally told reporters that should there be a crisis in which war in Europe or the Far East seemed imminent, he would convoke a special session of Congress to repeal the mandatory arms embargo provisions of the Neutrality Act and return to the traditional provisions of international law.

Later that day, the president was driven to New York, where he boarded the USS *Tuscaloosa* for a ten-day North Atlantic cruise with one planned landfall at Campobello, accompanied only by members of his personal staff. A small press contingent would follow on the destroyer USS *Ward*. After Roosevelt held a brief conference with Mayor La Guardia and George Meany (1894–1980) of the state American Federation of Labor (AFL) about WPA wages, the ship sailed without ceremony on August 12. There was a brief stop off Portsmouth, New Hampshire, for the commander in chief to view the ongoing salvage operations to recover the submarine USS *Squalus,* which had sunk on its test cruise that May. Roosevelt arrived at Campobello, where his son Franklin and his family awaited him at his mother's cottage. Sara was in Europe.[62]

When correspondents caught up with him on the island and showed him a newspaper story describing Chicago mayor Edward J. Kelly's call for a draft of Roosevelt for a third term at the Young Democrats convention, the president made no comment beyond referring to his letter to the same meeting. Some New Dealers had talked publicly about a third term immediately after the 1936 election, but Kelly's call, and the enthusiastic reaction it provoked at the convention, was the first such demonstration.

Much more controversy was set off by the president's announcement that he would move Thanksgiving—the only nationally celebrated holiday not fixed by federal law—from the last Thursday in November, which that year was November 30, to November 23. He noted that he had been receiving complaints from "retail people" that Thanksgiving came too close to Christmas "for the past six years." It had been a "movable feast" until after the Civil War, so there was "nothing sacred" about it.

Although merchants were gratified by the extension of the Christmas shopping season, traditionalists howled. With good reason, football coaches who had scheduled Turkey Day games complained. The chair of the selectmen of Plymouth, Massachusetts, the Pilgrims' hometown, insisted that "we . . . consider the day sacred." The result was almost a civil war of proclamations. More than two months later, in wartime, Roosevelt's solemn proclamation ignored commercial motives, referenced the Pilgrims and George Washington, gave thanks to the "Ruler of the Universe" for "the strength . . . to carry on our daily labors," and closed with the hope that "the activities of peace shall reign on every continent." The edict was binding only in the District of Columbia and on federal employees everywhere. Elsewhere, gubernatorial proclamations were in effect. Twenty-three of them followed the president and set the holiday on the fourth Thursday, while twenty-three others stayed with the fifth. The generous governors of Colorado and Texas declared both dates to be public holidays. After two more years of divided celebrations and continued controversies, the president gave in—too late to change the 1941 dates—and announced that he would return to the traditional Thursday in 1942. Pending congressional legislation then was passed and signed, setting the fourth Thursday as a statutory holiday beginning in 1942.[63]

From Campobello the president's cruiser, beset by evening fog, put in at Halifax one night and at tiny Sydney on Cape Breton Island the next, anchoring off Newfoundland on the next three nights. An unofficial and unrecorded press conference aboard the *Tuscaloosa* produced the "news" that the only fish caught so far were a large salmon landed by Pa Watson and a skate by Dr. Ross McIntire. At each of the stops, an expected rendezvous with a plane bringing up a mail pouch from Washington was prevented by fog. The next day, as the fog continued, Roosevelt ordered the cruise shortened so he could attend to business—largely signing papers that would permit various WPA projects to begin. On August 21, back in Halifax, Roosevelt finally got the mail pouch that had been sent up by train. He stayed aboard the cruiser but told officials who visited him that he would head for Washington via Annapolis, arriving there four days later, but if news from Europe required it he would land at New York and take a train back to the capital.[64] Although Eleanor flew repeatedly, Roosevelt had not been in a plane since his 1932 flight to the Chicago convention.

Although the August 23 announcement of a nonaggression pact between the former and future enemies, Hitler's Germany and Stalin's USSR, stunned many world leaders, Roosevelt had been aware that the Soviets were negotiating with both the Western allies and the Germans and had sent them word in early August that a treaty with Hitler would merely delay his attack on Russia until after he had beaten France. The memory of this accurate analysis probably contributed to the high regard in which Roosevelt was later publicly held by Stalin. News of the pact set off the last desperate crisis before the outbreak of what became World War II. Hitler made further public demands on Poland, seeking to gain the city of Danzig (today's Gdansk) and direct land connection with Germany's East Prussian province through the so-called Polish corridor, and privately set his war plans in motion. Britain and France gave verbal support to Poland and began mobilization. Roosevelt, still at sea, ordered a change in plans that transferred his party to the escorting destroyer *Lang,* which put him ashore at Sandy Hook for a drive to Red Bank, New Jersey, and a train trip to the capital. Before boarding the train, he spoke to the State Department by phone and authorized the dispatch of the first of three peace messages. It went to Italian king Victor Emmanuel, urging him "to formulate proposals for a pacific solution of the present crisis."

The other two, sent around midnight after his arrival in Washington, went to Hitler and the president of Poland, asking each to enter into direct discussions or submit to arbitration or conciliation. When the beleaguered Pole made an all but instant positive response, Roosevelt sent a second appeal to Hitler. As Roosevelt must have expected, none had the slightest effect on events. He may have acted, as he had claimed about his April peace message, to ease his conscience, but it is more likely that his chief motive was to boost his reputation as a man of peace. In a brief press conference on August 26, he refused to say that he would call a special session of Congress, explaining that when he said "imminent" he meant "certain," claiming that he still had hopes for peace.[65]

All that was left for Roosevelt to do was what Woodrow Wilson had called "watchful waiting" during the early crises of what soon became known as World War I. That waiting came to an end at 2:50 a.m. on September 1 when the president was awakened in the White House to a telephone call from Ambassador William Bullitt in Paris. Bullitt told him that German troops had invaded Poland.[66]

2 Beginning an Undeclared War
1939–40

IN A BRIEF MIDMORNING SEPTEMBER 1 press conference, Roosevelt called for calm and answered the inevitable question "Can we stay out?" on the record:

> THE PRESIDENT: Only this, that I not only sincerely hope so, but I believe we can and that every effort will be made by the Administration to do so.

Asked whether he would call Congress into special session to amend the Neutrality Act, he teasingly answered that Congress would meet sometime between "September 1 and January 2." That afternoon the White House announced that the president would address the nation on Sunday evening, September 3, between 10:00 and 10:15, a favorite time for Fireside Chats. By the time the stock market closed in New York, many stocks and most commodities had risen significantly. War would bring further stimulus to the economy.[1]

By the time Roosevelt spoke, Britain and France had redeemed their promises to Poland by declaring war on Germany. But they made no efforts, then or later, to send the Poles important aid and did not attack Germany, while in Poland German troops advanced and the Luftwaffe bombed Warsaw.

In his Fireside Chat, the president played off Wilson's words, in the parallel situation just twenty-five years before. The twenty-eighth president had written in August 1914: "The United States must be neutral in fact as well as in name during these days that are to try men's souls. We must be impartial in thought as well as in action, must put a curb upon our sentiments as well as upon every transaction that might be construed as a preference of one party to the struggle before another."[2] Roosevelt very carefully took a more realistic position:

> This nation will remain a neutral nation, but I cannot ask that every American remain neutral in thought as well. Even a neutral has a right to take account of facts. Even a neutral cannot be asked to close his mind or his conscience.
>
> I have said not once, but many times, that I have seen war and that I hate war. I say that again and again.
>
> I hope the United States will keep out of this war. I believe that it will. And I give you assurance and reassurance that every effort of your Government will be directed toward that end.

As long as it remains within my power to prevent, there will be no black-out of peace in the United States.

In his brief chat, a mere twelve hundred words, the president acknowledged that it was "impossible to predict the future" and insisted that "every ship that sails the sea, every battle that is fought, does affect the American future." He nevertheless admonished: "Let no man or woman thoughtlessly or falsely talk of America sending its armies to European fields." He held that "national safety" was paramount, and that included "the safety of the Western Hemisphere" and the seas around it. It followed therefore that "we seek to keep war from our own firesides by keeping war from coming to the Americas."[3]

Knowing what we now know, to what degree do these words reflect Roosevelt's actual beliefs at the time? If he had been frank with the American people, he would have indicated that his administration was determined to continue helping those governments that were defending themselves from aggression. To do that, he would ask Congress to amend the Neutrality Act. Instead, after a one-sentence "simple plea that partisanship and selfishness be adjourned," he closed with the passage already quoted.

What were Roosevelt's chief concerns in September 1939? Although anyone parsing his chat could easily conclude that he was concerned only with the Western Hemisphere and Europe, this was definitely not the case. Japan was never far from his thoughts. The Pacific rival had been the "most probable enemy" in American naval doctrine since early in the century, and his evolving views on the Japanese threat are well documented, as are his hopes for China.[4] Since the settlement of the Panay incident of December 1937, relations with Japan had continued to deteriorate, though there had been no flash point. The emergence of the Berlin-Rome-Tokyo Axis and Japanese exultation in German successes were worrying factors, but it was Japan's continuing undeclared war in China and Roosevelt's support for Chiang Kai-shek's government that were the basic issues between Tokyo and Washington. At the end of July 1939, a note from Hull to the Japanese ambassador, sent after consultation with the president, had given the required six months' notice that the United States would terminate the commercial treaty with Japan that had been in effect since 1911. This was, as reporters were advised, a necessary precondition if an arms embargo against Japan were desired once the Neutrality Act was appropriately amended. Asked about it in his press conference, Roosevelt refused to comment and referred reporters to the State Department.[5]

It is clear that in the Western Hemisphere, the president wanted to maintain and strengthen the unity of purpose seemingly achieved by the Lima declaration of December 1938. He and some Latin American leaders were concerned about possible dangers to some nations in the hemisphere from external military threats and from internal subversion by German colonists and local fascist groups. Whether he believed in these dangers, which he would continue to tout, is not at all clear.[6] Roosevelt is celebrated for helping Americans conquer fear in the depths of the Depression; it is not often noted that he used fear in wartime to spur adherence to his prescribed goals. In any event, rearming to repel a threat to the Western Hemisphere was difficult for isolationist politicians to oppose.

Roosevelt's 1939 vision of how the war might go stressed a policy of meeting German threats first. This meant building up American military forces, particularly naval and air forces, and continuing to furnish aircraft, armaments, and other sinews of war on a cash-and-carry basis to Britain and France. As American power grew, Roosevelt would extend Atlantic patrols against German submarines as he had conveyed to the British king. Within days of war's outbreak, he had the State Department negotiate limited and unpublicized use of British bases in Bermuda, St. Lucia, and Trinidad.[7] Much to the annoyance of army planners, he refused to expand the size of ground forces in any meaningful way until well into 1940.

Roosevelt had been preparing to exercise his authority and become a functional commander in chief. Lincoln, the only previous president to do that, had only to walk over to War Secretary Stanton's office to do so. Roosevelt brought the military leaders to him, first administratively and later by establishing a secure communications center, the White House Map Room, in his official home. As we have seen, he overrode his advisers and pushed through his plans for increased aircraft production. He also made institutional changes before war broke out in Europe. The earliest of these was his choice of Brigadier General George C. Marshall (1880–1959) as army chief of staff after a Sunday-afternoon interview at the White House on April 23, 1939. This came despite the fact that, early in his tenure as deputy chief, Marshall had disagreed with Roosevelt publicly in the November 1938 meeting at which Roosevelt mandated a concentration on airpower.

As Marshall later told the story, Roosevelt had asked him toward the end of the White House conference, "Don't you think so, George?" Marshall replied, "Mr. President, I'm sorry but I don't agree with that at all." He remembered that the president gave him a surprised look—"very startled"—and that ended the conference. Some of Marshall's colleagues told him that he had ruined his chances to become chief of staff, a job that he had long coveted. Much of the press reaction to his appointment emphasized that in selecting Marshall, Roosevelt had passed over "twenty major generals and fourteen brigadiers" who were senior to him. In fact, he was very much the inside candidate, even though he was not a West Pointer but a graduate of the Virginia Military Institute. He had the support of both War Secretary Harry Woodring and Assistant Secretary Louis Johnson and, perhaps more important, the strong support of the greatest World War I American commander, General John J. Pershing (1860–1948). In addition, as deputy he had developed a relationship with Harry Hopkins that Marshall thought had been a major factor in Roosevelt's decision. Whatever the reasons for his appointment, Marshall's contribution to American victory was second only to Roosevelt's.[8]

On July 5, 1939, Roosevelt had issued two unpublicized—and therefore secret—orders transferring the Joint Army-Navy Board, the Joint Army-Navy Munitions Board, and a number of military bureaucracies into the Executive Office of the Presidency, even though the executive order establishing the EOP would not be issued until September 8.[9]

In the days after the Fireside Chat on the war, Roosevelt issued a number of policy announcements and got his enlarged White House ready for the tasks before it. The first of the required proclamations of neutrality was not issued until September 5, which allowed some vessels to sail with war materials before the automatic embargo went into effect. Two separate neutrality proclamations were issued: the first covered the requirements under existing international law, while the second laid out the requirements of the existing American neutrality statute originally adopted in May 1937, making it unlawful "to export . . . arms, ammunition, or implements of war to any belligerent . . . or to any neutral state for transshipment" to a belligerent.[10]

At his press conference, after explaining the neutrality proclamations, Roosevelt announced that American vessels would not be convoyed but would proceed "with all lights burning and the American flag painted all over them." Asked about the Cunard passenger liner *Athenia*, which had been torpedoed and sunk off Ireland on September 3, Roosevelt, who did not yet have all the details, called it a violation of international law. He reminded reporters that the Neutrality Act gave Americans abroad ninety days to sail home on belligerent ships, but obviously they would be safer on American-flag vessels. The State Department estimated that some one hundred thousand Americans were in Europe.[11]

In a separate presidential announcement, Roosevelt "requested" that the attorney general instruct the Federal Bureau of Investigation to "take charge of investigative work in matters relating to sabotage, espionage, and violations of neutrality regulations," the first of a number of pronouncements enhancing the power of the FBI and its director, J. Edgar Hoover. The threat of war had already caused an increase in the then tiny and not secret intelligence budget. Asked at his January budget press conference:

Q: Anything in here for counter-espionage?

THE PRESIDENT: Yes, there were some increased items for F.B.I., Naval Intelligence and Military Intelligence . . . [aggregating] $125,000.

Acting budget director Daniel Bell broke the figures down, showing that the bulk of the money, $75,000, went to the FBI.[12]

In his September 8 press conference, Roosevelt proclaimed "a limited national emergency . . . for the proper observance, safeguarding and enforcing of the neutrality of the United States." He insisted that he was not putting the nation "on a war basis. . . . We are going to keep the Nation on a peace basis." One immediate consequence was the triggering of a clause the State Department had put in its 1940 appropriation statute allowing the president to expend as much as $500,000 for the protection of American citizens abroad in case of an officially declared emergency. He stopped being coy about a special session of Congress, conceding that one would be called soon to amend the Neutrality Act. He also announced executive orders increasing the authorized size of the armed forces, which remained relatively small. The navy would grow to 145,000 from a current 120,000, still well below its statutory limit of 191,000. The army would increase to 227,000 men from 120,000, also below its 280,000 authorized limit. Roosevelt indicated that much of the army increase was to garrison outlying defenses, specifying Puerto Rico and the Panama Canal and saying nothing about the Pacific garrisons; he also authorized 150 additional FBI agents.[13]

The executive order that brought the new EOP into being did not mention the secret military additions to it, but the order did describe the absorption of one previously unmentioned entity into the enlarged White House: the Office of Government Reports (OGR). This was merely the first of a number of competing propaganda agencies promoting "information" and occasionally "disinformation" during World War II.[14]

The White House issued an optimistic statement describing the confusion existing in previous wartime agencies, which the new arrangement was intended to prevent. Set up in a time of stress, these special facilities sometimes have worked at cross-purposes both internally and between themselves and the established agencies. But the statement describes very well the confusion that would often occur in Roosevelt's wartime capital.[15]

A final executive order addressed the first of many actions aimed at dampening the inflation inevitable in a wartime situation. Explaining that "the increased world demand for sugar" as a result of the war had caused a rise in prices, speculation, and hoarding, the president used his new emergency powers to suspend the quotas that since 1934 had limited the production of American sugar. In a later note, he explained that the wholesale price of raw sugar had gone up a third in the first six days of September and that his action had so reduced the price that he was able to revoke the proclamation and restore the quota by year's end.[16] The ability to do this kind of fine-tuning quickly from the White House was just one of the benefits of having an economist on hand.

His flurry of postconflict business over, Roosevelt left Washington for a short Hyde Park weekend to show that all was normal. Beforehand, the Secret Service asked that the schedule and route of the president's trip not be published, a practice that continued through the rest of his presidency, except for the two presidential election campaigns. In Hyde Park, reporters were told that the president had gotten his first full night's sleep since war broke out, as there had been no very early-morning calls from Europe. Seeking to demonstrate his desire to "adjourn" politics, Roosevelt sent out feelers to Alfred Landon and Frank Knox about taking cabinet posts; Knox was interested, but Landon made a public statement that the way for Roosevelt to get his support would be for him to renounce publicly any aspirations for a third term. The president also, through Norman Davis, head of the American Red Cross, asked Herbert Hoover to come and see him about organizing overseas relief efforts, but Hoover turned him down. After Pearl Harbor, Hoover volunteered his services, but Roosevelt never responded.[17]

A presidential proclamation on September 13 declared that "public interests require" the convening of an extra session of Congress at noon on September 21. The repeal of the arms embargo required the construction of a bipartisan coalition. The White House let it be known that a meeting of congressional leaders with the president would include Republicans. This was not only another example of Roosevelt's efforts to adjourn politics but a tactical necessity. The president could count on majorities in each chamber, but the possibility of a filibuster in the Senate, which could not be broken unless sixty-four of the ninety-six senators voted for cloture, a distinct if outside possibility. Right on cue, Senator Frederick Van Nuys (D-IN), who had been part of the twelve-to-eleven majority on the Senate Foreign Affairs Committee in blocking consideration of an arms-embargo repeal in July, announced that he would vote to bring the measure to the floor in the special session.[18]

There were, of course, isolationists in both parties, largely from the Midwest and beyond. In addition, the Nazi-Soviet pact had transformed American Communists as well as most of the much more numerous groups on the Left. Almost overnight they switched from supporting interventionist politics to become some of the most vehement opponents of Roosevelt's international and defense policies. Most of these were only temporary adherents to what is usually called isolationism; most quickly reverted when Hitler invaded the USSR in June 1941.

The White House conference of September 20 in which fourteen political leaders, including six Republicans—Landon, Knox, Senate minority leader Charles McNary (OR), House minority leader Joe Martin (MA), Senator Warren Austin (VT), and the ranking minority member of the House Rules Committee, Carl E. Mapes (MI), none of them isolationists—recommended that rather than a full repeal of the Neutrality Act, a cash-and-carry provision be substituted for the prohibition of exporting arms and implements of war to belligerents. Thanks to a rare transcript of the meeting, we can observe Roosevelt in action. He began by reminding the conferees of his plea to forget partisanship "for a while anyway." He went on to review the war developments, underlined the benefits to the economy that would result from the resumption of the now forbidden arms shipments, and gave a brief account of previous American policy. He argued that, save for an aberration in the Jeffersonian era and the period since the adoption of the 1935 Neutrality Act, the United States had followed the policy he now wished to pursue. The president made an unusual admission of error. Speaking of the 1935 Neutrality Act, he said, "I regret that the Congress passed that Act. I regret equally that I signed that act."

He noted that the Nazi press publicized on its front pages "every remark" that Missouri Democrat "Bennett Clark makes, that Borah makes, that Hiram Johnson makes, that Hamilton Fish makes." Roosevelt had made—and continued to make—similar observations, both publicly and privately.

Some of his own private comments were outrageous. For example, when it was clear that the Senate would not allow a vote on revising the Neutrality Act at the end of June 1939, he ranted in a late-night phone call to Henry Morgenthau: "I think we ought to introduce a bill for statues of Austin, Vandenberg, Lodge, and Taft—the four of them—to be erected in Berlin and put the swastika on them." Morgenthau dutifully wrote down this and a lot of other similar nonsense or dictated it to a secretary to be preserved in his "diary" where it would embarrass historians friendly to Roosevelt and delight hostile ones. Wiser members of his circle simply ignored them.

As the conference was closing, Roosevelt insisted on a formal statement for reporters: "They will write their own story if you don't write it for them." The five-sentence statement stressed "with unanimous accord" that all desired to keep the nation "neutral and at peace," that "in a wholly nonpartisan spirit" the conference agreed that the chief goal was "the repeal of the embargo and a return to the processes of international law," and that the "consensus" was for the Senate Foreign Relations Committee to begin the process. Landon, seeking to make space for himself though he was publicly committed to repeal of the arms embargo, told reporters that he would have preferred that Congress remain in session as long as the emergency lasted. Key Pittman announced that his Foreign Relations Committee would immediately take up the Bloom bill, already passed by the House and still on the congressional agenda until the formal end of the session on December 31.

According to Senate post office employees, a flood of telegrams and mail against repeal soon poured in, much of it obviously sparked by Father Charles Coughlin. The same security concerns that blacked out news of Roosevelt's itinerary caused a change of rules at the Capitol: entry to the public galleries now required a card from a member of Congress, and no packages could be brought in by any visitor.[19]

Roosevelt's address in Congress, broadcast nationally and transmitted worldwide in Spanish, French, and German, in keeping with his nonpartisan public approach to the question of neutrality attacked no one. He assumed that "every member of the Senate and of the House of Representatives, and every member of the Executive Branch," wanted "to keep us out of war." He threw down a gauntlet before his opponents, making a proposition that he knew they could not accept.

Because I am wholly willing to ascribe an honorable desire for peace to those who hold different views from my own as to what those measures should be, I trust that these gentlemen will be sufficiently generous to ascribe equally lofty purposes to those with whom they disagree. Let no man or group in any walk of life assume exclusive protectorate over the future well-being of America, because I conceive that regardless of party or section the mantle of peace and of patriotism is wide enough to cover us all. Let no group assume the exclusive label of the "peace bloc." We all belong to it.

He then justified his own and his predecessors' actions, noting that "since 1931" (Japan's seizure of Manchuria), unnamed nations everywhere except in the Americas had ignored the council table and prepared for war. "For many years the primary purpose of our foreign policy has been that this nation and this Government should strive to the utmost to aid in avoiding war among nations. But [since war has come] this Government must lose no time or effort to keep our nation from being drawn into the war. In my candid judgment we shall succeed in those efforts."

After reviewing and quoting some of his own recent statements, the president argued that since 1789, the nation's policy "with one notable exception has been based on international law." Referring to what was then the least successful war in American history, he cited the "Embargo and Non-Intercourse Acts . . . the major cause of bringing us into active participation in European wars in our own War of 1812. It is merely reciting history to recall to you that one of the results of the policy of embargo and non-intercourse was the burning in 1814 of part of this Capitol in which we are assembled today." The "next deviation by statute," he continued, was "the Neutrality Act of 1935." Mirroring his mea culpa of the preceding day's conference, he regretted that "the Congress passed that Act. I regret equally that I signed that Act."

After reminding his listeners that he had wanted a change in the Neutrality Act in July, he asked Congress to do just one thing in the special session: to "remove the embargo provisions" of the act. He pointed out the inconsistencies of the act—it barred exporting "completed implements of war" but permitted sending "uncompleted implements of war" and other goods and products. In addition, those cargoes could be sent in "American flag ships to belligerent nations." This, he argued, was a "definite danger to our neutrality and our peace." He spoke briefly about the material gains in employment and profits that would flow from the change and stressed the inconsistency of embargoing only arms: "Let those who seek to retain the present embargo position be wholly consistent.

Let them seek new legislation to cut off cotton and cloth and copper and meat and wheat and a thousand other articles from all of the nations at war."

"The crux of the issue," he insisted, was repealing the embargo and returning to international law. Several other generally agreed-upon actions should then follow, put into effect either by executive action or by statute: American ships should be kept from war zones, American citizens barred from traveling on belligerent ships, foreign buyers required to take title of goods for belligerents in the United States, and belligerents to pay cash for everything.

Taking care of these matters, which were unresolved in the run-up to war in 1917, along with the return to international law, Roosevelt insisted, were "better calculated than any other means to keep us out of war."

He reminded his listeners of recent increases in the defense budget and of the emergency measures he had ordered since the outbreak of war. He announced that congressional leaders in both parties had agreed to stay in Washington for consultation until the new Congress met in January and that if new developments warranted, he would recall Congress again. "Darker periods might lie ahead," he warned, concluding:

> Destiny first made us, with our sister nations on this Hemisphere, joint heirs of European culture. Fate seems now to compel us to assume the task of helping to maintain in the Western world a citadel wherein that civilization may be kept alive. The peace, the integrity, and the safety of the Americas—these must be kept firm and serene.
>
> In a period when it is sometimes said that free discussion is no longer compatible with national safety, may you by your deeds show the world that we of the United States are one people, of one mind, one spirit, one clear resolution, walking before God in the light of the living.[20]

The immediate reaction, from both Congress and the press, was largely favorable. An overnight nationwide sampling of newspaper editorials showed widespread approval of the president's message: even the normally hostile *Los Angeles Times* praised the president's "fair and logical spirit and . . . clear grasp," while Frank Knox, speaking for the Republican leadership, praised "one of the greatest speeches Roosevelt ever made." A Gallup poll taken shortly before the speech found Roosevelt approved by 61 percent of major party voters—near the level of his 1936 landslide and up from 56.6 percent in August; in a poll taken shortly after the speech, 57 percent favored changing the law to allow Britain and France to buy war materials, up from 50 percent shortly before war was declared. Soon after that, Gallup reported that 43 percent of likely voters were ready to vote for Roosevelt in a third term if the war continued, up from 33 percent in May and 40 percent in August.[21]

Surely, Roosevelt's hand was also strengthened when in October, the Pan-American conference he had convoked issued the Declaration of Panama. In it the republics of the hemisphere, in response to Roosevelt's call for a "neutrality zone," proclaimed an area, described in degrees of latitude and longitude, extending from the Canadian border to the southern tip of South America and from three hundred to a thousand miles east of the coasts that was "to be free from the commission of any hostile act by any non-American belligerent." They pledged to monitor this vast zone. Although Roosevelt had glibly told the British king about the way he planned to patrol in case of war, as matters stood in the fall of 1939—and for some time to come—the American navy did not have the forces to oversee any significant part of that area. Roosevelt, who admitted this off the record, told reporters that they should concentrate on the text of the declaration and that things "will work out alright." Nevertheless, the unanimous agreement in Panama, another fruit of the Good Neighbor policy, was a useful talking point for his supporters in the congressional debates on neutrality.[22]

Most of the bipartisan Senate isolationist bloc was not persuaded by Roosevelt's speech or impressed by any of the administration's actions after September 1. California's Hiram Johnson met with twenty-three other senators in his office shortly after the president left the Capitol, the same office from which he had led the successful fight against ratifying the Versailles Treaty in 1919. They knew that they faced a difficult battle; just how difficult became clear when the Senate Foreign Relations Committee, which had kept the Neutrality Act repeal off the floor by a 12–11 vote in June, reported it favorably with a 16–7 vote on September 28. A long and bitter senatorial debate took up most of October in which the ultimate weapon, the filibuster, was threatened but not used. The final Senate vote went Roosevelt's way on October 27, 63–30. The House spent three days of debate before passing it on November 2, 243–181; the approval of the necessary conference report, after some members had gone home, passed both houses by similar but numerically smaller majorities. The president affixed his signature on November 4 and immediately issued the two required proclamations.[23]

Whatever his private fulminations, Roosevelt kept his public cool during the final struggle over amending the Neutrality Act. In a radio address to the annual *New York Herald Tribune* Forum as the Senate debate was reaching its climax, he threw "bouquets" to the majority of the press and radio for its international coverage and asked "to be pardoned" for wishing for a similar treatment of domestic news. Again describing himself as "just a little bit left of center," he did complain, without naming any individuals, about those who were "beating their breasts and proclaiming against sending the boys of American mothers to fight on the battlefields of Europe." This was, he said, "a shameless and dishonest fake." He insisted that "no person in any responsible place in the national administration in Washington . . . has ever suggested in any manner or form the remotest possibility of sending the boys of American mothers to fight on the battlefields of Europe."[24] While it can be argued that his statement was technically true, a franker statement would have been that the president's policies were to assist Britain and France in defeating Hitler's forces so that it would not be necessary to send American troops to Europe.

Many of the isolationists, who, as their historian Wayne Cole points out, "from 1939 onward . . . were never able to defeat any presidential aid-short-of-war proposal actually put to vote in Congress," made extreme statements and were, on many matters, divided. A number of them came to favor keeping the embargo on arms while adopting cash and carry.[25] Charles A. Lindbergh, who became the most important isolationist orator in 1940, during the 1939 battle proposed distinguishing between offensive and defensive weapons: he would permit the export of pursuit planes and antiaircraft guns and ban the export of bombers and field artillery. After his well-publicized 1938 trip to the Third Reich during which he inspected the Luftwaffe and German aircraft production and accepted a medal from Hitler, Lindbergh had briefed American air force officers thoroughly on what he had learned and in April 1938 had a friendly meeting with Roosevelt. Before he made his first speech as an isolationist spokesman in mid-September 1939, he recorded in his journal that an army colonel brought him a verbal message from Secretary Woodring, who had isolationist connections, offering him, presumably with Roosevelt's approval, "a secretaryship of air [that] would be created in the cabinet and given to me" if he did not make the speech. No documents connect Roosevelt with the supposed offer, and its details are dubious. Congress, in passing the Reorganization Act, specifically barred the president from creating new departments, and the military establishment would have resisted a separate air force. Any legitimate offer would have been at a subcabinet level, as an under- or assistant secretary in the War Department. In that speech, Lindbergh's first since 1931, carried on all three radio networks, he warned that "if we enter fighting for democracy abroad, we may end by losing it at home." He also argued, curiously for an advanced student of airpower, that the Atlantic and Pacific still protected the United States from attack.[26]

While Congress debated the Neutrality Act, a Russian-born, American-educated economist and banker, Alexander Sachs (1893–1973), who had entrée to the White House because he had been chief economist of the National Recovery Administration (NRA), brought to Roosevelt and read him on October 11 the now famous eight-paragraph letter dated signed by Albert Einstein on August 2 but written by a then little-known Hungarian refugee physicist, Leo Szilard (1898–1964). It explained that recent well-known experiments made it "almost certain" that "nuclear chain reactions in a large mass of uranium" would produce "vast amounts of power" and that "it is conceivable—but much less certain—that extremely powerful bombs of a new type" would be possible that "if exploded in a port might destroy the whole port together with the surrounding territory." The letter went on to point out that the United States had little uranium, that Canada and Czechoslovakia had more, and that the largest known supply was in the Belgian Congo. The letter closed by noting that the Germans had stopped the export of the Czech uranium it now controlled and warning that the Germans were "repeating some of the American experiments" at Berlin's Kaiser Wilhelm Institute, "where the son of the German Under Secretary of State was attached."

The combination of Einstein's prestige and Sachs's advocacy captured Roosevelt's attention. He created the Advisory Committee on Uranium headed by Lyman J. Briggs (1874–1963), an American physicist who headed the federal National Bureau of Standards, which held its first meeting on October 21—just ten days after the Sachs visit. On November 1, using NBS funds, Briggs's committee awarded the first federal atomic research grant of six thousand dollars to Columbia University, where Szilard and other refugee physicists, including Italian Enrico Fermi (1901–54), were working. Briggs would function as administrator for what came to be called the Manhattan Project. Roosevelt's insistence that qualified scientists, and not the military, make scientific decisions was crucial to the successful prosecution of the war. Later, his own personal military adviser Admiral William D. Leahy (1875–1959) would assure him, "as an expert in explosives," that an atomic bomb would never work. What was crucial, here, was that work got under way; it would be twenty-five months before the major commitment to try to make a bomb was taken.[27]

Meanwhile, the war in Europe went on. Hitler's army overran western Poland in a matter of weeks in what the Germans called a "blitzkrieg"—literally "lightning war"—and, by prearrangement, Stalin's army seized the eastern portion of Poland on September 17. Soon thereafter, the Soviets annexed the three Baltic republics of Estonia, Latvia, and Lithuania and incorporated them into the USSR. It had been negotiating with its neighbor and onetime imperial province Finland since 1938 over territorial adjustments Stalin considered vital for the defense of Leningrad, today's St. Petersburg, and offering territorial concessions to the Finns elsewhere. On November 9 these negotiations were broken off, and on November 30 the USSR invaded Finland, beginning the so-called Winter War.

On October 11, when apparently both sides were optimistic about a peaceful resolution, Roosevelt had sent a brief "personal" message to President Mikhail Kalinin of the Soviet Union, urging that his country make "no demands on Finland inconsistent with its independence." Roosevelt was assured that "despite the tendentious versions" of the negotiations being circulated, Moscow would respect Finland's sovereignty. After the Winter War began, the president made no secret of his sympathy for the Finns and condemned the Soviet attack and bombings, a position all but universally held by Americans except for Communists and some fellow travelers.[28]

The relative lack of military activity in the West—British bombers flew over German territory and dropped leaflets—caused British critics of Prime Minister Neville Chamberlain's war policy to coin the fake German term *sitzkrieg* to describe what others called the "phony war." Allied troops massed in the elaborate, largely underground French fortifications in the Maginot line faced German troops just kilometers away in less elaborate but quite formidable defenses called the Siegfried line.

Only at sea was there serious conflict between Germany and the Allies, the other two Axis powers temporarily remaining neutral. The one major surface engagement was in the Western Hemisphere in mid-December, as three British cruisers damaged the German pocket battleship *Graf Spee* in the Battle of the River Plate, forcing it to seek temporary refuge in Montevideo on December 13. Facing internment, the *Graf Spee* left port on December 17 and while still in Uruguay's territorial waters was scuttled by its commander. In its short wartime career—it had sailed from Wilhelmshaven on August 21—it sank nine merchant ships. That the battle happened well within the hemisphere, with destruction of the battleship in full view of spectators onshore, made Roosevelt's continuing warnings about dangers to the various American republics more believable.

Much more significant was the damage done by German submarines, sixteen of which were sent into the Atlantic before hostilities commenced. Apart from sinking the *Athenia,* the major blow struck by German naval action during the phony-war period was the penetration of the British home-fleet anchorage at Scapa Flow, in the Orkney Islands, by a submarine that torpedoed and sank the battleship HMS *Royal Oak.* Roosevelt, naval buff that he was, followed these developments closely, but he refrained from public comment.

When Winston Churchill, who had become first lord of the admiralty as Britain declared war, sent Roosevelt details of the River Plate engagement, the president thanked him and commented on the "extraordinarily well fought action of your three cruisers."[29] The message from Churchill was part of a correspondence begun in the first days of the war when Roosevelt sent the Briton one of his chatty notes:

My dear Churchill—

It is because you and I occupied similar positions in the World War that I want you to know how glad I am that you are back again in the Admiralty. . . . What I want you and the Prime Minister to know is that I shall at all times welcome it if you will keep me in touch personally with anything you want me to know about. You can always send sealed letters through your [diplomatic] pouch or ours.

Although Roosevelt and Churchill eventually developed a real friendship, it had not been love at first sight. In an unpublished memoir, Joe Kennedy says that when he asked Roosevelt during a White House bedroom conversation in December why he had inaugurated secret conversations with Churchill, bypassing his embassy, the president told him, "I have always disliked him since the time I went to England in 1918. He acted like a stinker at a dinner I attended lording it all over us. . . . I'm giving him attention now because there is a strong possibility that he will become the prime minister and I want to get my hand in now."[30]

Even though war had come, the president was able to free himself to spend Thanksgiving at Warm Springs; work on the budget due in January would pursue him there. At the traditional dinner, with Eleanor seated at his right and a six-year-old polio patient at his left, he carved a very large turkey and after dinner spoke about war, peace, and segregation. Referring to his remarks on leaving Georgia that spring, he noted that despite the war he had managed to get back and that he hoped that "next spring there won't be any war." The segregation he referred to in speaking to the assembled white patients and visitors, and the black waiters and cooks who served them, was not the racial segregation still sanctioned by the courts and in effect at Warm Springs, but the isolation of the "crippled" person who "was segregated . . . put up in the attic. It was one of the things you didn't talk about." He went on to celebrate the changes in such attitudes that Warm Springs was helping to bring about.[31]

Budget director Harold Smith had been flown down to discuss the budget for the fiscal year July 1, 1940–June 30, 1941, the day before a Warm Springs press conference, so reporters asked Roosevelt what the two had accomplished. When Roosevelt gave one of his no-news-today answers, a reporter responded:

> Q: We had him down at the cottage and he talks more than [Smith's predecessor] Danny Bell did but there is less news in it.
> THE PRESIDENT: I will tell you what we did yesterday: We did Justice and Treasury.

His tongue loosened, Roosevelt went on to give an interesting disquisition on the mysterious budget-making process that had been going on for about six weeks.

> THE PRESIDENT: We did the usual thing. . . . Here is the process . . . somebody has to trim the payroll in any [unit] that is doing normal work with nothing new. . . . I would take the total of this fiscal year and [by] a rule of thumb . . . for instance, on a bureau that costs three hundred thousand dollars a year to run I would take out three thousand dollars. Well, that means . . . two $1500 positions. . . . [I]n dollars and cents it doesn't amount to an awful lot but it is a good thing for the government to prune the tree.

For those burgeoning parts of the government especially concerned with problems caused by the war and American neutrality, he explained that there would be an "A" and a "B" budget, "A" representing what would have been spent had there been no war and "B" representing estimated extra expenses. For the navy, he was estimating $500 million for the "B" budget. Roosevelt had floated dual budget notions before in not very successful attempts to minimize deficit spending, arguing that emergency relief expenditures be considered separately in an otherwise balanced budget.[32]

Although preparing for war, Roosevelt continued to speak of peace. Just before Christmas, he announced the appointment of Myron C. Taylor as his "personal representative" to the Vatican, led since May by Pius XII, who as papal nuncio had met with Roosevelt at Hyde Park in 1936. This restored a formal relationship between the United See and the Holy See, which had been broken just after the Civil War. The resumption was widely praised, but Southern Baptists, Lutherans, and Seventh-Day Adventists criticized what they viewed as a violation of the traditional divide between state and church. In a letter to the pope, Roosevelt wrote, "When the time shall come for the reestablishment of world peace on a surer foundation, it is of the utmost importance to humanity and to religion that common ideals shall have united expression."[33] Informed observers were given to understand that the president intended to make a major peace move or moves early in the coming year.

Roosevelt used the airwaves for a Christmas greeting, which mixed anxiety, hope, and a plug for the New Deal. Speaking from the Ellipse south of the White House to a crowd of several thousand and a nationwide radio audience, and with four generations of his family around him, he noted that the year "began with a dread of evil things to come" and was ending "with the horror of another war." Thanking "God for the interlude of Christmas," he wished "all of my countrymen the old greeting—'Merry Christmas—Happy Christmas.'" Noting his own penchant for rereading Dickens's *A Christmas Carol,* he remarked that he always thought of "Bob Crachit's humble home as a counterpart of millions of our own American homes" and that even "Scrooge found that Christmas wasn't a humbug . . . and took to himself the spirit of neighborliness." Claiming that "today neighborliness . . . has gradually spread . . . to the whole nation," he went on to identify that neighborliness with his own programs: "Who a generation ago would have thought that a week from tomorrow . . . tens of thousands of elderly men and women in every State . . . county . . . city would begin to receive checks every month for old age retirement insurance."

He also spoke about "unemployment insurance" and aid to "the needy, the blind, and the crippled children . . . which will reach down to the millions of Bob Crachits, the Marthas and the Tiny Tims of our own four-room homes." And while Roosevelt said nothing in this message about his opponents, he certainly must have expected many of his listeners to connect them with an unrepentant Scrooge. He ended by reading the Beatitudes from the Sermon on the Mount; the year before he had read the passage from Isaiah about disarmament.[34]

The formal appointment of Charles Edison (1890–1969), son of inventor Thomas Edison, as secretary of the navy at year's end formalized his more than three-year de facto leadership of the Navy Department as assistant secretary. Claude Swanson had died in July 1939. Before that, in one of his chatty letters, Roosevelt told Josephus Daniels, "Swanson is too sick a man to do much, but I haven't the heart to let him go. . . . [Y]ou know I am my own secretary of the navy." At the time of Edison's formal appointment, Roosevelt told him that he wanted him to run for governor of New Jersey in the fall so as to clip the wings of Jersey City's Frank Hague, the most noisome of the nation's Democratic bosses. Elected, Edison later claimed success in a job of political "slum clearance."[35]

Roosevelt opened his 1940 annual message insisting that no one should imagine that "our Government is abandoning . . . its domestic policies" just because his address was largely devoted to foreign affairs. But there was no indication of what, if anything, would be proposed in the way of new programs. Nor, for that matter, were there any new insights given into American foreign policy. Senator Borah, who had announced that he would not attend because "it's dangerous to listen to Roosevelt because he could recite an example in algebra and make it interesting," could have attended safely. Neither of the two most pressing questions—whether Roosevelt would run for a third term and how his policy of aid to the Allies would be implemented—was even alluded to, much less answered. He did say that more would be spent on national defense and less on most other items and that taxes would have to be raised to pay for defense, and he asked that the reciprocal trade program, which would expire in June, be reauthorized.[36]

The more prosaic budget message, after a one-paragraph summary, began with a spirited defense of prewar New Deal fiscal policy of more than a thousand words that provides a convenient point to assess the oft-repeated charge that Roosevelt's New Deal was a failure. Of course, the ultimate judgment should be of the Roosevelt era that extends beyond his life span, but the more limited evaluation is so often made that it cannot be ignored.

Roosevelt's January 1940 assessment began with a denigration of the old order: "The relatively low and constant level of [federal] expenditures throughout the nineteen-twenties reflected the relatively minor role played by the Government in those years. . . . In the early thirties—prior to 1933—fiscal policy was exceedingly simple in theory and extraordinarily disastrous in practice. It consisted in trying to keep expenditures as low as possible in the face of shrinking national income. Persistence in the attempt came near to bankrupting both our people and our government." In contrast, he argued, his fiscal policy was more realistic. "All about were idle men, idle factories, and idle funds, and yet the people were in desperate need of more goods than they had the purchasing power to acquire. . . . The deliberate use of Government funds and Government credit . . . had a profound effect both on Government and private incomes." National income rose from $42 billion in 1933 to $72 billion in 1937, an increase of 69 percent. Tax revenues grew from $1 billion in fiscal 1933 to more than $5 billion in fiscal 1937. People, as opposed to corporations, paid $3 billion "more in taxes, but they had nearly ten times more than that . . . to spend on other things."

Claiming that by 1937, "rapid progress was made toward a balanced budget"—it would have been more appropriate to speak of a shrinking annual increase in the deficit—the president admitted that then

> maladjustments in the economic system began to appear and caused a recession in economic activity. The recession was due to a variety of causes stemming in the main from over-optimism which led the Government to curtail its net expenditures too abruptly and business to expand production and raise prices too sharply for consumers to keep pace. A large volume of unsold goods piled up.
>
> If the recession were not to feed on itself and become another depression the buying power of the people . . . had to be maintained. To this end, in the spring of 1938, I recommended a further use of Government credit and the Congress acted on my recommendation.

Roosevelt argued that the "soundness" of his remedy was "strikingly demonstrated." He compared the $42 billion decline in national income and the "four-year period of liquidation and inflation" in 1929–32 with a 1937–38 decline that "scarcely exceeded" $8 billion. He noted that "productive activity turned up within nine months" in 1937–38 and insisted that the 1938–39 experience should "remove any doubt as to the effectiveness of a fiscal policy related to economic need."

He did recognize that "employment still lags considerably below the levels of 1929" and that many "younger workers have not found employment, and many others have been displaced by machines." He called for guarding "the gains we have made" and "pressing on to attain full employment."

"We must, therefore," he concluded, "avoid the danger of too drastic or too sudden a curtailment of Government support." In what was, for a sitting politician, a reasonably fair assessment, he argued that his "aims [had been] substantially but not fully attained." An even fairer historical assessment would be aims partially but not fully attained. The two chief macroeconomic effects of almost seven years of Roosevelt's evolving economic policies were that the decline was stopped in 1933 and that erratic but meaningful recovery had taken place. Accompanying these changes was a transformation of the structure of the federal government, making it much more capable of guiding—and misguiding—the economy. Those were no mean achievements. The New Deal was not a failure, even though it did not restore full prosperity.

Roosevelt's modest January projections for fiscal 1941 would be made irrelevant by events even before fiscal 1940 ended, but they should be briefly noted. He foresaw total spending of $8.4 billion, grouped under seven headings:

Category	Cost in Billions
National defense	$1.8
Work relief programs	$1.3
Pensions, retirements, and assistance	$1.2
Public works and investments	$1.1
Interest on the public debt	$1.1
Regular operating	$1.0
Agricultural programs	$0.9

He forecast a reduced deficit increase of $1.7 billion and assumed a projected $460 million increase in income taxes that some congressional leaders predicted would not be adopted in an election year. Underlining the year's low-key start, the White House announced the cancellation of one of the biweekly press conferences because Roosevelt "had no news." It was the first such cancellation during Roosevelt's presidency.[37]

The political year began, as usual, with a Jackson Day Dinner. In December Roosevelt, in what he said was a move toward unity, had invited Senate minority leader McNary and two other leading Republican legislators to attend, offering them a free dinner and a nonpartisan speech. Not surprisingly, they turned him down. It was grist for Roosevelt's mill, just as their attendance would have been. After a salutation that included an ad-libbed "Candidates Here and Candidates There," he began what he called "a plate-side chat" with a fairy tale:

Once upon a time—and in a campaign year every speech ought to start that way—once upon a time there was a school teacher, who, after describing Heaven in alluring and golden terms, asked her class of small boys how many of them wanted to go to Heaven. With eyes that sparkled at the thought every small boy in the class held up his hand—except one. Teacher said, "Why Charlie, Charlie McNary—Charlie, you don't want to go to Heaven? Why Not?" "Teacher," he said, "sure I want to go to Heaven, but" pointing to the rest of the boys in the room—"not with that bunch."

Roosevelt then briefly explained about the refused invitation, speculated about why the Republicans didn't come, and then guessed that the real reason was that, "like the little boy, they didn't want to go to heaven with this bunch." Roosevelt eventually got serious, but he ignored the question everyone there wanted answered and didn't even give a hint about whether he would run. He did assure his audience that the path for victory in November was to continue to attract independent voters, as he had done in 1936. At his press conference the next day, when asked to comment on Jackson Day speeches by Secretary Wallace and Attorney General designate Robert Jackson calling for him to run again, Roosevelt said he hadn't read them. But when Steve Early was asked if the pair would be rebuked, as was the case in the fall when the agriculture secretary had said the same thing, his boss responded, "Of course not."[38]

With a war on, foreign affairs were not a matter for jokes. Working within the terms of the Neutrality Act, Roosevelt made some symbolic gestures of cautious support for the beleaguered Finns. In December the Export-Import Bank made a $10 million loan to the Finnish purchasing agent in the United States. After being turned down by congressional leaders whom he asked to initiate economic aid—they said the initiative should come from him or the secretary of state—Roosevelt requested an additional $20 million loan a month and a half after war began. Congress approved it a month and a half later, which was ten days before the war ended on March 12.[39] Like almost all of what has come to be called "foreign aid," the money was not transferred to the Finns, but was spent in the United States to purchase American goods and services, thus boosting the American economy.

During the beginning of what the press called the "phony war"—the period between conquest of Poland and the elimination of the Baltic states—Roosevelt began to take cautious public notice of what Gunnar Myrdal would call "an American dilemma"—the unequal treatment of black Americans in what was supposed to be a democratic society.

For what Steve Early called "sentimental reasons," Roosevelt chose his fifty-eighth birthday to send a message to Congress calling for the construction of fifty small hospitals "in needy areas of the country," which he had mentioned in his press conference a month earlier, and noting that they "should not be constructed in communities where public or private or private institutions" already existed. He also proposed that projects be approved by the surgeon general of the Public Health Service. He specifically stated that he continued to support the broader proposal from his interdepartmental committee and, presumably, Senator Wagner's health care bill. He added that "special provisions should be made for the care of the tuberculous in many areas of the South; the present acute needs for the care of Negro patients should also be met." Almost seven full years into his presidency, this is the first time that Roosevelt used the word *Negro* in a message to Congress. He asked Congress to appropriate between $7.5 and $10 million for the Public Health Service to inaugurate the program. Despite the modest price tag and AMA support, this limited, low-budget program could not win majority support in Congress. A further indication of his serious intentions about expanding federal health programs was his persuading Josephine Roche to withdraw her resignation as head of the Interdepartmental Committee to Coordinate Health and Welfare Activities and in removing its activities from the control of FSA administrator Paul McNutt.[40]

Yet eleven days before, in a radio address given before the final session of the 1939–40 White House Conference on Children in a Democracy, he made no reference to race. The president embraced its report, which bore significant legislative results only in 1943. He reminded the delegates that when he had opened the conference back in April 1939, he had asked them to consider "how a democracy can best serve its children" and "how children can best be helped" to become preservers and protectors of democracy as adults. "A succession of world events has shown us that our democracy must be strengthened," he said, and "national defense, in the broadest term, calls for adequate munitions and implements of war and at the same time, it calls for educated, healthy and happy citizens. Neither requisite taken alone without the other, will give us national security." He endorsed the findings of the conference, which had reported great progress since the prior meeting, and agreed that "we still have a long way to go." "The Conference tells me that more than half the children of America are in families that do not have enough money to provide adequate shelter, food, clothing, medical care and educational opportunities."

Reminding his audience that he had been criticized for highlighting "one-third of America—the ill-clothed, ill-housed, ill-fed," he was glad that the conference report sustained him. Agreeing that public assistance of many kinds was necessary, he added a traditional caution that "the Federal treasury has a bottom." He set out two general policies, without specific proposals to achieve them: "first, to increase the average of incomes in the poorer communities, in the poorer groups, and in the poorer areas of the nation; and, second, to insist that every community should pay taxes in accordance with ability to pay."

Then, departing from his text, he spoke of John Steinbeck's *The Grapes of Wrath*.

> There are 500,000 Americans that live in the covers of that book. I would like to see the Columbia Basin devoted to the care of the 500,000 people represented in "Grapes of Wrath."
>
> Migratory families, children who have no homes, families who can put down no roots, cannot live in a community. That calls for special consideration. But I am being practical. I am trying to find a place for them to go.
>
> This means, in its simplest terms, a program for the permanent resettlement of at least one million people in the Columbia Basin and a lot of other places.[41]

No such resettlement program ever took place, although California and the Pacific Northwest would gain more than a million persons from interstate migration during the war years and beyond. That gain came largely in the coastal urban areas rather than in the interior.

That evening he made a brief thank-you addressed to the participants in "more than twenty-five thousand parties" celebrating his birthday and to the nation. Talking, as usual, about Warm Springs, he did not mention, then or ever, that although its food service was by black cooks and waiters, the patients and visitors they served were all white.[42]

An ongoing consequence of the Nazi-Soviet pact, in addition to the previously noted temporary addition of many on the Left to the isolationist forces, was the alienation of sizable elements of the American Left from support for the New Deal. These were largely members of a whole variety of trade unions and social organizations, many of which were led by Communist Party (CP) members, mostly covert. One such, the Workers Alliance, an organization of WPA workers, mocked the president with a song that went "The New Deal came and stayed for a while, / But all that's left is Roosevelt's smile."[43]

The Left organizations that both Franklin and Eleanor were most concerned about was the American Youth Congress (AYC, 1934–41), which claimed 4.5 million members, mostly of college and college-age youth. When some of its leaders and other left-wing youth were summoned to appear before the House Committee on Un-American Activities (HUAC) in late November 1939, Eleanor counseled them on their testimony and created a sensation by coming to the hearing and sitting with those summoned. Two months later, a "Youth Citizenship Institute" brought some 5,000 delegates to Washington to lobby for a never-enacted American Youth Act that would have provided funds to expand existing federal work-study programs and whose goal was to ensure that no one would have to drop out of college for lack of funds. Eleanor arranged accommodations in federal facilities, including Fort Myer, for several hundred. Just as Governor Roosevelt had invited left-wing hunger marchers into his office, he asked the youth delegates to listen to him on the White House lawn.

Despite a driving rain, a White House count of 4,466 persons inside the gates assembled to hear the president, speaking from the shelter of the portico, address them as "Fellow Citizens" instead of his trademark "My Friends." In his long broadcast speech of more than three thousand words, there were few of the ingratiating touches—humor, anecdotes, and flattery—that Roosevelt normally used to create sympathy with his audience. Instead, it was what Joe Lash, an approving witness, calls "a spanking." Rather than creating a bond, the president made a separation: "Some of us realize that if we had a different form of government this kind of meeting on the White House lawn could not take place."

After long passages replete with statistics in which he outlined the accomplishments of the New Deal, he ended his speech by focusing on a recent AYC resolution opposing American loans to Finland, based "not on the ground that we ought to spend the money here among our own needy unemployed, but on the ground that such action was, 'an attempt to force America into the imperialistic war.'"

Roosevelt dismissed this as "unadulterated twaddle" and insisted that no one with "common sense believes that Finland had any ulterior designs on the integrity or the safety of the Soviet Union." He claimed that after the revolution, "I recognized that many leaders in Russia" were improving the lives of the common people. But he "disliked the regimentation," "abhorred the indiscriminate killings of thousands of innocent victims," and "heartily deprecated the banishment of religion—though I knew that some day Russia would return to religion." He insisted:

> The Soviet Union . . . is run by a dictatorship as absolute as any other dictatorship in the world. It has allied itself with another dictatorship and it has invaded a neighbor. . . . It has been said that some of you are Communists. . . . As Americans you have a legal and constitutional right to call yourselves Communists. . . . You have a right peacefully and openly to advocate certain ideals of theoretical Communism; but as Americans you have not only a right but a sacred duty to confine your advocacy . . . to the methods prescribed by the Constitution . . . and you have no American right, by act or deed of any kind, to subvert the Government and Constitution of the United States.

After this verbal trouncing, the president, ignoring what the *Times* correspondent called "the almost entirely silent" reaction to this part of the speech "with a few faint boos" from the back of the crowd, closed with almost a benediction. "The things you and I represent are essentially the same, and it will be your task, when I'm gone from the scene, to carry on the fight for a liberal Government. . . . Above all, we must help those who have proved that they will try to make things a little better for the people of our nation. . . . So I say to you, keep your ideals high, keep both feet on the ground and keep everlastingly at it."[44]

That afternoon some of the same crowd cheered and laughed as labor's John L. Lewis responded to Roosevelt with an even longer speech in the Labor Department's auditorium, chastising the president for criticizing the Youth Congress's positions and chiding him for failing to solve the problem of unemployment and for not using the Department of Justice to challenge the poll taxes of eight southern states. He warned that the nation's "common people" were afraid of being dragged into war and that any statesman who did so would be held "strictly accountable."[45]

Most who have treated this episode write as if the Roosevelts immediately wrote off the American Youth Congress, but that was not the case. Eleanor continued to defend it publicly, and almost four months later the president, abetted by his wife and Harry Hopkins, and with his son Elliott in attendance, held what is called a press conference for a racially integrated group of "Representatives of the American Youth Congress in the State Dining Room of the White House." It went on for some three hours, during which the participants were served beer.[46]

While ignoring the third-term speculation that increasingly dominated the political agenda as winter turned to spring, the president continued to urge preparedness and defend his New Deal legacy. Using the latest data, he noted that national income had grown from $40 billion in 1932 to $68 billion in 1939, a rise of 71 percent, with a nearly comparable rise in wages and salaries for the same period. The growth of cash farm income for the two years was even more impressive, up 82 percent: from $4.7 billion for 1932 to $7.7 billion in 1939, plus $0.8 billion in federal payments.[47]

After urging Congress to "make immediately available" $15 million already authorized to purchase various strategic materials, Roosevelt told reporters that he would be leaving for his winter cruise the next day, February 14. His train would take him to meet the cruiser USS *Tuscaloosa* at an undisclosed port for unknown destinations for a cruise of about ten days. Only the three wire-service correspondents would sail with him on one of two accompanying destroyers. The press tended to make a meal of the obvious security precautions with headlines about a "mystery cruise." The cruise took Roosevelt and his small party—his doctor, Ross McIntire; Pa Watson; and his naval colleague Captain Daniel J. Callaghan (1890–1934)—from Pensacola, Florida, across the Gulf of Mexico, through the Panama Canal to Cocos Island, some 350 miles out in the Pacific and back to Pensacola fifteen days later. In an onboard press conference after his return, he stressed the importance of perfecting the defense of the Panama Canal and spoke of his meetings with the presidents of Panama and adjoining Costa Rica and Colombia, who had agreed to cooperate in the defense of the canal in their own self-interest. It is clear that the president and his military planners, following traditional American defense doctrine, were expending large sums on the defense of the canal. Yet none of America's enemies had the means of attacking it, and the money could have been put to better use elsewhere.[48]

Roosevelt returned just in time for the seventh anniversary of his presidency. With cabinet and other officials and members of his family, he attended services in the church adjacent to the White House, which were given a special significance by the thought that it might be the last. The Reverend Endicott Peabody, one of four celebrants, set the tone, calling for "peace [and ending] all bitterness and misunderstanding in both church and state." On Capitol Hill, dueling senators gave opposing views of the New Deal. Senate majority leader Barkley claimed that the "Roosevelt Administration has now convinced the American people that their grievances" are the proper concern of government, while Senate minority leader Austin called for a "new administration" with "an attitude of friendliness toward all activities that are lawful [and] tend to produce wealth." Pundit Arthur Krock reduced domestic politics to two questions: "Will the President run again?" and, if not, "Whom will he choose as his loyal successor?"[49]

Roosevelt steadfastly refused to discuss or even comment on either of those questions. Meanwhile, little legislation was completed other than deficiency appropriations. The major domestic accomplishment in March and early April was sending up Plan No. 3 under the Reorganization Act, which dealt with consolidating duplicate bureaus and offices in the Treasury, Interior, and Agriculture Departments; in Labor's Immigration and Naturalization Service; and in the Civil Aviation Authority. It also abolished Interior's General Land Office, which had distributed much of the national domain that was granted to individuals under such legislation as the Homestead Act of 1862. The agency had once done "a land office business" but was now redundant.[50]

Difficult as it is to credit today, many supposedly well-informed observers, encouraged by the continuing phony war in the West, believed that a window of opportunity existed for some kind of negotiated peace between Hitler and his Anglo-French opponents before the better weather for fighting returned in the spring. Roosevelt, despite having no real hope for peace, sparked the international boomlet in peace talk by sending Sumner Welles on a month-long mission to Europe just before the president left on the *Tuscaloosa*. Welles met first with Mussolini, still a neutral, and then with Hitler, before going on to consult with officials in Paris and London. Roosevelt, who noted privately that the chances for any progress toward peace were "one in a thousand" and would require the attributes of both the "Holy Ghost and Jack Dempsey," was not as negative in his formal statements. Officially, he said at the beginning that Welles's "visit is solely for the purpose of advising [him and Hull] as to present conditions in Europe" and that the envoy was not authorized to make "proposals or commitments." After Welles returned and reported, Roosevelt announced, "He has not received nor has he brought back to me, any peace proposal from any source [but Welles's information] will undoubtedly be of the greatest value when the time comes for the establishment of peace."

Although nothing of substance had occurred diplomatically, the political benefits of Roosevelt's gambit were not inconsiderable. It did not hurt the perceptions of a president who was being labeled a "warmonger" to have his name associated with a peace mission on front pages for more than a month. A Gallup poll published before Welles returned in late March showed 58 percent of those with opinions favored his mission's purposes.[51]

But three weeks after Welles's return, the phony war came to an end as Hitler launched land, sea, and airborne invasions of neutral Norway and Denmark, and hopes for peace quickly turned to fears about Allied defeat.

3 Breaking Precedents in War and Politics
1940

THE NEWS OF THE GERMAN INCURSIONS into Scandinavia reached the State Department about one in the morning on April 9. Roosevelt was at Hyde Park, and Secretary Hull was vacationing in Atlantic City; each hurried to Washington by train and conferred at the White House with Sumner Welles and Assistant Secretary of War Louis A. Johnson. At immediate issue were the details of a neutrality proclamation and an executive order to reflect the spread of the war and beyond that to decide what actions were called for to prevent Greenland and Iceland from falling into German hands. Greenland, a huge, barren offshore island of North America with a population of 17,000, was a Danish colony; Iceland, a medium-size Atlantic island (forty thousand square miles) with a population of some 150,000, including a handful of refugees from Nazism, was independent, with ties to the Danish crown. Some of Roosevelt's worst fears were realized: the real war in the West had begun, and he knew that the British and French were not ready.

The paperwork was a fairly simple matter: a proclamation redefining the combat area and an executive order freezing all Danish and Norwegian funds in the United States were signed the next day. As the war spread in 1940–41, similar executive orders froze the funds of other nations overrun by Germany or associated with it, amounting by early October 1940 to four billion dollars. Similar exchange controls had been put in place during World War I and during the banking crisis of 1933. Roosevelt also issued a statement condemning the aggression and warned that "if civilization is to survive, the rights of smaller nations must be protected."[1]

Roosevelt was willing to leave Iceland, for a time, largely to the British, who executed a military occupation early in May. It was welcomed by the Icelandic government, which had declared its full independence after the German occupation of Denmark. Greenland, clearly a part of the Western Hemisphere, was another matter. Roosevelt privately warned off the British and Canadians from intervening, as it would be a violation of the "no transfer" aspect of the Monroe Doctrine, and publicly expressed concern about the fate of Greenland. He had the State Department send consular officers on a Coast Guard cutter rather than a naval vessel to establish a "provisional consulate" in Greenland. Later, the United States assumed responsibility for getting food and other necessary supplies to Greenland and provided limited armaments for its defense. Months later, American naval forces thwarted German attempts to set up weather stations there.[2] While it is now understood that one of the fundamental long-term results of World War II was a fatal blow to European colonial systems, few have realized that the process began in the frozen lands of the North Atlantic.

No major changes were made in the American defense program as a result of the wider war. Roosevelt issued his Reorganization Plan No. 4, whose most controversial provision was to merge two independent bodies regulating aviation into the Civil Aviation Board and place it in the Department of Commerce; it was unsuccessfully opposed by Senator Pat McCarran (D-NV) (1876–1954). But the president's request for reauthorization of the Reorganization Act, which was due to expire on January 20, 1941, and to eliminate the ban exempting twenty-one administrative agencies from reorganization, failed to pass. His authority to approve reciprocal trade agreements without further recourse to Congress was extended for three years.[3]

In broadcast speeches to the Pan-American Union and the Young Democrats, the president struck very different notes, but in neither did he talk about the expanding war he most feared. In the former, speaking of the Western Hemisphere, four successive paragraphs began with the words *peace reigns,* even as Allied forces were being driven out of Norway.

He assured the Young Democrats that, although "not speaking tonight of world affairs," your "government is keeping a cool head and a steady hand" and "keeping out of wars that are going on in Europe and in Asia."[4]

Roosevelt spoke to the Young Democrats from Warm Springs. On leaving Washington, he had told reporters that he was ready to return immediately "if another country is invaded." With him at Warm Springs were his naval aide Captain Dan Callaghan; William D. Hassett (1880–1965); filing in for his boss, the ill McIntyre, Basil O'Connor; and, for the first time, Lauchlin Currie. Asked whether Currie had come to assist with the budget, Roosevelt said that they would talk about "that old science of economics. It means everything and nothing." Roosevelt got a rest and a suntan from driving his open roadster on short country rides.[5]

The early days of May were quiet but uneasy for the president. Returning early from a weekend at Hyde Park and asked why he left early, he answered, "Nothing; nothing in particular, just the general feeling that I have sometimes in these days—if I stay away too long, I begin to feel nervous about the general situation. There isn't anything to justify it but after I have been away from Washington a few days I say to myself, 'My God, what is going to break this afternoon on the European front?'"[6]

On the night of May 9–10, Ambassador John Cudahy phoned from Brussels, giving the government its first news of the German invasion of the Low

Countries. Roosevelt, up most of the night, signed an executive order freezing the assets of the Netherlands, Belgium, and Luxembourg; it was in operation before the New York markets opened. At his press conference a little before noon, the president declared himself "in full sympathy" with the Netherlands' Queen Wilhelmina, who had described the unprovoked attack by the Germans and vowed that "I and my government will now do our duty."[7]

Within days she and her government ministers were in London as a government in exile. French and British armies moved north into Belgium to meet the German forces, but most were soon driven back into France in a retreat that became a rout for the French. In Britain Chamberlain's government fell, and on the day that the Germans attacked, Winston Churchill became prime minister and minister of defense and brought into his cabinet Labour Party leaders who had refused to enter a Chamberlain cabinet. Roosevelt shifted the defense program into high gear with an accelerated program that surprised not only most politicians but also his own military advisers. And, many historians now believe, whatever reservations he may have had about running for a third term were swept away by the dangers that a German-controlled Europe presented. Aid to Britain would become an important concern, and new fears about Germany gaining control of the French and British fleets in case of victory or even a negotiated peace with Britain made aid to Britain an even more vital factor in the defense of the United States.

During the six days after the Germans unleashed their blitzkrieg, the pace and scope of American military preparations were totally transformed. Roosevelt had almost nonstop meetings in the White House with civilian and military officials and congressional leaders, with the results presented to Congress and the American people. On the evening of the first day, Roosevelt inserted a passage into a previously prepared broadcast speech to a Pan-American scientific Congress in Washington, asserting that "we Americans of the three Americas are shocked and angered" by the day's "tragic news." He reminded the audience before him that at the hemispheric conferences in Buenos Aires and Lima, "we discussed a dim and unpleasant possibility . . . that the Americans might have to become the guardian of Western culture, the protector of Christian civilization. [Then] it was merely a fear. Today the fear has become a fact." He closed with an incredible claim and a firm resolve: "I am a pacifist. You, my fellow citizens of the twenty-one American Republics, are pacifists too. But . . . if it be necessary [we] will act together to protect and defend by every means at our command our science, our culture, our American freedom and our civilization."[8]

Three days later, White House sources told the press that a request for an additional $500 million for defense was being prepared. But in a press conference the next afternoon, the president compared the situation with a fire in a big city, which obviously would have a financial impact on later city budgets, but "the newspaper men and women covering the fire do not make the following year's budgets the lead of their stories." He was not concerned at the moment with how the bill would be paid. It could, he said, "come out of taxes or it can come out of borrowings, or it can come out of a combination of the two, but the important thing is the national defense rather than the next years' method of paying for it." Two days later, the press could cite "reports" saying that the president would ask for an additional $750 million for military spending in the coming fiscal year.[9]

On May 16, Roosevelt broadcast an early-afternoon message to Congress. An Associated Press map on the front pages of many newspapers that morning showed that the German forces—what we now know were massive armored units supported by tactical airpower—had broken through thinly held French lines, taken Sedan, and crossed the Meuse River. They would reach the English Channel four days later, trapping, so it seemed, most of the British army deployed on the Continent.

As the president entered the House chamber and while he was helped up the long ramp created so he could reach the rostrum, the lawmakers, "ignoring party affiliation," rose and applauded "wildly" in what a reporter interpreted as "a demonstration of national unity in a time of international crisis."

"These are ominous days," Roosevelt began. The "brutal force of modern offensive warfare has been loosed in all its horror." He proceeded to lay out the immediate dangers to the United States and its sister republics, making potential threats to the United States seem more immediate than they actually were. He would continue this tactic until after the United States began offensive operations late in 1942. He outlined the relative ease of air attacks on New England from bases in Greenland and, stretching plausibility, made "St. Louis, Kansas City, and Omaha" seem likely targets of "modern bombers," although, in fact, there was no existing aircraft that could execute the raids he warned of. The first inaugural sought to banish fear; this speech knowingly conjured up false ones.

Most of the speech merely spelled out in greater detail what White House and other sources had been saying for several days. Roosevelt's calculation of total new spending was almost $1.2 billion, which ran the total for the coming year to $3 billion, including two separate $100 million items for money to be spent at the discretion of the president. Much of this was spent for hemisphere defense projects, including an arrangement with Pan American Airways to expand its existing airports in Latin America for military use.[10] The speech contained one bombshell and an important caveat. The bombshell was Roosevelt's call for the nation's aircraft production facilities to be "geared up . . . to turn out at least 50,000 planes a year [and] plan at this time a program that would provide us with 50,000 military and naval planes." The caveat, which preceded it, was: "I ask the Congress not to take any action which would in any way hamper or delay the delivery of American-made planes to foreign nations which have ordered them, or seek to order new planes. That, from the point of view of our own national defense, would be extremely short-sighted."

The reason for the caveat was that both the immediate goal of fifty thousand planes and the ongoing policy of sending many of the most modern planes to Britain and France were opposed by the president's military advisers, and they were joined in opposition to the overseas shipments by Secretary of War Woodring. Roosevelt wished to counter, in advance, any testimony that might oppose his plan. Army and navy chiefs opposed the goal of fifty thousand planes, as they had the goal of ten thousand planes in November 1938, because they thought these plans premature and likely to delay the development of more traditional land and naval weapons. They also opposed giving priority to British and French orders as depriving American forces of assets they would need should France and Britain fall.

The president closed his speech with a rhetorical flourish largely absent from what had gone before: "Our security is not a matter of weapons alone. The arm that wields them must be strong, the eye that guides them clear, the will that directs them indomitable. These are the characteristics of a free people, a people devoted to the institutions they themselves have built, a people willing to defend a way of life that is precious to them all, a people who put their faith in God."[11]

The speech was a great success. The congressional ovation that greeted the president continued throughout the speech with the greatest burst of applause coming after the call for fifty thousand planes. Only one member of the Senate, Kansas Republican Clyde Reed, was negative, remarking, "Patriotism, what crimes are committed in thy name." A few criticisms came from House members, but the support there was also overwhelming. Minority Leader Martin said bluntly, "We are for the program. It might as well be enacted speedily and get it over with." His Massachusetts colleague George Tinkham, who had been in Congress since 1915, took a position adopted by many isolationists: "[Defending] the American Continent is thoroughly justified, but preparation to carry on an aggressive war in Europe, which has been implicit in Mr. Roosevelt's policy for three years, is indefensible." Some Republicans complained about the president's two $100 million "blank checks," but the bulk of House Republicans followed their leader: the asked-for appropriations, and more, were quickly enacted.

The most strident congressional criticism came from Fiorello La Guardia's left-wing protégé Vito Marcantonio (American Labor Party) (1902–54), who found the speech "tragically reminiscent of 1917 . . . a blitzkrieg on American peace."[12]

Most national Republican leaders had good things to say about the president's speech. Herbert Hoover declared that the "president was right that our defense armament should be revised" and that "there can be no partisanship in national defense." Alf Landon praised Roosevelt's "splendid address" and his call for national unity, but complained that the latter came "tragically late." Two presidential aspirants, Tom Dewey and Michigan's senator Arthur Vandenberg, favored the call for defense but insisted that Republicans could do a better job than New Dealers, with the latter calling for an "insulated America." The only national Republican leader to be totally negative was the extreme right-wing New York publisher Frank Gannett, who spoke of Roosevelt's "self-proclaimed failure to provide adequate defense" after spending billions and insisted that there was "no immediate danger."[13]

More important, from Roosevelt's point of view, was the evidence that the people overwhelmingly approved his approach. A Gallup poll question, which asked if respondents favored Roosevelt's defense spending plan, was approved by a whopping 86 percent to 14 percent of those with opinions, and only one respondent in twenty was undecided or had no opinion. A very large majority, 76 percent, was willing to pay additional taxes for defense. Party and region made little difference: 93 percent of Democrats and 83 percent of Republicans approved, and even in the isolationist Midwest 76 percent of respondents were favorable.[14]

In a Saturday press conference the morning after the speech, the president offered no clear plans for reaching the goal of fifty thousand planes. He insisted that there would be "no Government operated plants" and, in response to reporters' speculations, conceded that the government might finance the plants but not run them. He noted that for strategic reasons, new plants would not be built on the Western and Eastern Seaboards, where the bulk of the industry was then located. He also spoke of plans to recommission thirty-five decommissioned World War I destroyers. Later in the day, the White House announced that there would be a Monday-morning planning meeting of aviation industry executives and military officials in Secretary Morgenthau's office, and the president would meet with Jesse Jones about possible RFC financing of new plants. Informally, War and Navy Department officials let it be known that the production of thirty thousand planes for the coming year was an interim goal.[15]

The drafting and submission of Reorganization Plan No. 5, Roosevelt said in a May 22 message to Congress, was triggered by the "startling sequence of international events" since mid-April that had "revealed a pressing need" to move the control of immigration from the Labor Department to the Justice Department. In a 1941 note in his *Public Papers,* Roosevelt claimed that because of "a dangerous threat from abroad in the form of the fifth column and other activities," he had felt it "expedient" to make the transfer "in order to cope with this danger, as a matter of national defense." The action was another example of his use of fear to gain support for war measures.[16]

Congress soon passed, and Roosevelt signed, the Alien Registration Act. This was a complex forty-one-section statute organized into three separate titles. Title I authorized a sentence of ten years in jail and a fine of ten thousand dollars for anyone "undermining the morale of the armed forces" or who "advocates, abets, advises, or teaches" the violent overthrow of the government. It was, in fact, a peacetime sedition act. Title II invented new grounds for deportation, most of which involved "subversive activities." Title III was the Alien Registration Act, requiring all aliens to register, be fingerprinted, and keep the government informed of any change of address, but it did not require them to carry their registration cards. Versions of Titles I and II had been introduced in 1939 by Representative Howard W. Smith (1883–1976) without result, but when the Justice Department sent over a draft of the Alien Registration Act in late May 1941, he bundled it with his two measures into what was called the Smith Act. In his signing statement, Roosevelt mentioned only the third title, and, as he later noted, that process was made as little threatening as possible. At his insistence, aliens registered at post offices, not police stations.[17]

But the Roosevelt administration did eventually institute sedition prosecutions under the act, most significantly in the July 1941 indictment and later conviction of members of the Socialist Workers Party in Minneapolis, some of whom had won control of a dissident and militant local of the Teamsters Union (AFL), whose national president, Daniel J. Tobin, was a pillar of national Democratic Party politics. The jury refused to convict anyone on the sedition charges, but did convict eighteen persons of conspiracy to create insubordination in the armed forces and recommended leniency. The judge gave twelve of those convicted sixteen months and the others a year and a day.[18] The Roosevelt administration made no further use of the Smith Act, but it was used by the Truman and Eisenhower administrations to convict most of the leaders of the American Communist Party. The act's approval is one of three major actions by Roosevelt that contributed significantly to what can be called the American national security state. (The other two, incarcerating Japanese Americans and condemning German saboteurs to trial by military commission, are discussed in subsequent chapters.)

As war news from the Low Countries and France worsened, the secret communications from Churchill became increasingly urgent. During the first eight months of the correspondence, there were a total of eleven messages, eight from Churchill, three from Roosevelt, dealing almost exclusively with naval matters. Five days after he became prime minister, an eloquent and frank letter from Churchill gave Roosevelt an insider's view to supplement the telephoned and written reports from his ambassadors.

"Although I have changed my office," the Briton began, "I am sure you would not want me to discontinue our intimate, private correspondence. . . ."

The scene has darkened swiftly. The enemy have a marked preponderance in the air. . . . I think myself the battle on land has only just begun. . . . Hitler is working with specialized units in tanks and air. The small countries are simply smashed up, one by one, like matchwood. We must expect . . . that Mussolini will hurry in to share the loot of civilization. We expect to be attacked here ourselves, both from the air and by parachute and air borne troops in the near future. . . . If necessary, we shall continue the war alone and we are not afraid of that. But I trust you realize, Mr. President, that the voice and force of the United States may count for nothing if they are withheld too long. You may have a completely subjugated, Nazified Europe established with astonishing swiftness, and the weight may be more than we can bear. All I ask now is that you should proclaim nonbelligerency, which would mean that you would help us with everything short of actually engaging armed forces.

Then came the shopping and wish list under six headings:

1. "the loan of forty or fifty of your older destroyers."
2. "several hundred of your latest types of aircraft."
3. "anti-aircraft equipment and ammunition."
4. [Since] "our ore supply" from Sweden and elsewhere "is being compromised . . . it [is] necessary to purchase steel . . . and other materials" from the United States. "We shall go on paying dollars as long as we can, but I should like to feel reasonably sure that when we can pay no more, you will give us the stuff all the same."
5. Noting "reports of possible German parachute or air borne descents in Ireland . . . the visit of a United States squadron to Irish ports . . . would be invaluable."
6. "I am looking to you to keep that Japanese dog quiet in the Pacific, using Singapore in any way convenient."[19]

Roosevelt answered the next day, saying that he was "most happy" to continue the correspondence and was "giving every possible consideration to the suggestions made in your message." Most of Roosevelt's letter dealt with the destroyers. Sending them would have to be authorized by "Congress and I am not certain that it would be wise" to "ask Congress at this moment." He added two separate "furthermores"—we need them ourselves, and, even if we could do it, it would take "six or seven weeks." The other points were dealt with briskly. The president said that "we are now doing everything in our power" to make the "latest types of aircraft" available. The request for antiaircraft equipment should be taken up with the "proper authorities here in Washington" who had already approved steel purchases. He would give further consideration to the Irish port visit and said that the "American fleet is now concentrated in Hawaii" and would stay there. He did not directly mention the question of what to do when the dollars ran out, but he promised "to communicate again soon" when he had made a final decision about "other matters."[20]

The prime minister responded briefly on May 18: "We are determined to persevere to the very end whatever the result of the great battle now raging in France. . . . We must expect to be attacked here on the Dutch model before very long and we hope to give a good account of ourselves. But if American assistance is to play any part it must be available [soon]." After Churchill had heard from his Washington ambassador, Lord Lothian, about his meetings with Roosevelt, he responded more fully on May 20. "Lothian has reported his conversations with you. I understand your difficulties, but I am very sorry about the destroyers. . . . The battle of France is full of danger to both sides. . . . Our most vital need is . . . the delivery at the earliest possible date of the largest possible number of Curtis P-40 fighters now in course of delivery to your army." Then, answering concerns raised by Roosevelt with Lothian, Churchill made some grim observations:

> Our intention is whatever happens to fight on to the end in this Island and, provided we can get the help for which we ask, we hope to run them very close in the air battles in view of [our] individual superiority. Members of the present administration would likely go down during this process should it result adversely, but in no conceivable circumstances will we consent to surrender. If members of the present administration were finished and others came in to parlay amid the ruins, you must not be blind to the fact that the sole remaining bargaining counter would be the fleet, and if this country was left by the United States to its fate no one would have the right to blame those responsible if they made the best terms they could for the surviving inhabitants. Excuse me, Mr. President, putting this nightmare bluntly. I could not answer for my successors who in utter despair and hopelessness might well have to accommodate themselves to the German will. However there is no need at present to dwell upon such ideas. Once more thanking you for your good will.[21]

What must be remembered is that these were secret messages. Churchill's name did not pass Roosevelt's lips publicly, even in a press conference, until September 1940, and that was "off the record." But dealing with these and further Churchill requests had never been far from Roosevelt's mind. During that period, twenty-one additional messages had been exchanged, fifteen from Churchill and six from Roosevelt. Roosevelt had to be convinced that Churchill would take hold, and he wanted formal assurances that the British fleet would not be surrendered even if Britain were conquered. Then he had to find ways to make helping Britain politically acceptable. This would have been the case even if Roosevelt had not been engaged in an unprecedented election campaign to win a third presidential term.

Roosevelt was most immediately concerned with strengthening support for his arms buildup by drawing in elements that had rarely supported the New Deal. On the eve of a Fireside Chat on national defense, the White House announced that leading industrialists were to be called to help plan and coordinate the defense program.[22]

That chat on May 26, the first since he spoke at the onset of war in Europe, came eleven days after Churchill's first message. It contained not a word about military aid to the Allies and must have been a great disappointment to them. The morning papers had maps showing the Low Countries almost completely overrun, and the accompanying texts warned of Allied troops being cut off by German armored forces that had streamed into France through the Ardennes gap and were headed toward the English Channel.

The president, focusing on "subjects that directly affect the future of the United States," began his Sunday-evening talk by expressing shock "at the almost incredible eyewitness stories" about the sufferings of millions of "women and children and old men" fleeing "on the once peaceful roads of Belgium and France," trying "to escape bombs and shells and fire and machine gunning." "Each one of you," he told his audience, "has a way of helping them." After describing the efforts of the American Red Cross, he ended his appeal: "Please—I beg of you—please give generously . . . to your nearest Red Cross chapter. . . . I ask this in the name of our common humanity."

Then, at his most casual, he shifted from Europe to America. "Let us sit down together, you and I, to consider our own pressing problems." He began with what would be a theme of his reelection campaign: blaming, but not yet naming, the isolationists, as the "many among us who [had] closed their eyes" to what was happening in Europe, "honestly and sincerely thinking that the many hundreds of miles of salt water" were protection enough. Then his attack narrowed to "some of us who were persuaded" that we could safely retire "within our continental boundaries." The final trope shifted to "a few among us who have deliberately and consciously closed their eyes because they were determined to be opposed to their government, its foreign policy and every other policy, to be partisan, and to believe that anything that the government did was wholly wrong."

Then, responding to critics he did not name, there followed a long and detailed accounting of American defense expenditures since 1933, which showed a considerable buildup, resulting in the strongest peacetime forces the country had ever had. He pledged to continue the buildup of the nation's armed forces but insisted that "while our Navy and our airplanes and our guns and our ships may be our first lines of defense, it is still clear that way down at the bottom, underlying them all, giving them their strength, sustenance and power, are the spirit and morale of a free people."

The president went on to guarantee that the reforms of the New Deal would not be overturned by the need to concentrate on defense. "We must make sure," he insisted, "that there be no breakdown or cancellation of any of the great social gains we have made in these past years." After specifically mentioning the gains achieved by labor and the Social Security system as reforms to be protected and expanded "to other groups who do not now enjoy them," he added: "There is nothing in our present emergency to justify a retreat from any of our social objectives—from conservation of natural resources, assistance to agriculture, housing, and help to the under-privileged." In the same vein, he made an implied promise that he would be unable to keep: "Our present emergency and a common sense of decency make it imperative that no new group of war millionaires shall come into being in this nation as a result of the struggles abroad. The American people will not relish the idea of any American citizen growing rich and fat in an emergency of blood and slaughter and human suffering." He coupled this with a pledge to protect consumers from "the rising spiral of costs of all kinds" that had characterized the 1914–18 experience, a pledge more successfully redeemed than similar pledges given in connection with the National Recovery Act.

Having dealt with hopes, Roosevelt again turned to fears, fears that he may have believed to be real but that were largely chimerical and were nicely calculated to discredit domestic opponents of his internationalist policies. "Today's threat to our national security is not a matter of military weapons alone. We know of new methods of attack. The Trojan Horse. The Fifth Column that betrays a nation unprepared for treachery. Spies, saboteurs and traitors are the actors in this new strategy. With all of these we must and will deal vigorously." Roosevelt went on to use language that could be interpreted to mean that any deviation from national unity in a time of crisis was tantamount to subversion and treachery. It could be parsed to argue that in the final analysis, Roosevelt would endorse an Americanized version of Hitler's slogan, "Ein Volk, ein Reich, ein Führer" (One people, one empire, one leader). Such an extreme view is unjustified, but there was a tendency in Roosevelt's makeup, as in the makeup of many strong leaders, to view any opposition as disloyalty and even subversion. And even when, as in this chat, he employed the politics of fear, he soon returned to what Lincoln would have styled his "better Angel," the politics of hope.

The peroration echoed his second inaugural. "This . . . is the task of our generation, yours and mine. But we build and defend not for our generation alone. We defend the foundations laid down by our fathers. We build a life for generations yet unborn. We defend and we build a way of life, not for America alone, but for all mankind. Ours is a high duty, a noble task. . . . In common affection for all mankind, your prayers join with mine—that God will heal the wounds and the hearts of humanity."[23]

Public opinion had, in some respects, gone further than the president was willing to recommend publicly. Gallup reported that only 7 percent favored going to war after the invasion of the Low Countries, up from 3.5 percent in December. More important, "a large majority said they would prefer to vote for a candidate who promised the Allies all the help they need short of going to war than to vote for a candidate who promised no more help than is now being given." The same poll found that a small majority approved "sending war planes to the Allies on credit if they cannot pay cash." More specifically, a scholar at Princeton reported that in April, only a third of those polled favored extending credit to the Allies, but by the end of May half were willing to do so. In addition, a whole spectrum of pressure groups arose to mobilize public opinion in what one contemporary scholar called "the battle against isolation." The most influential of these groups was William Allen White's Committee to Defend America by Aiding the Allies.[24]

As Roosevelt was speaking, the crucial evacuation of the British army and some French soldiers from Dunkirk across the English Channel to safety in England by an armada consisting largely of small, privately owned boats had begun. Between May 25 and June 4, some 338,000 men were retrieved, but almost all their weapons were left behind. In Parliament, on June 4, Churchill made his great speech to the British people—"We shall fight them on the beaches. . . . [W]e shall never surrender"—which ended with a public appeal to Roosevelt: "And even if, which I do not for a moment believe, this island or a large part of it were subjugated and starving, then our Empire beyond the seas, armed and guarded by the British fleet would carry on the struggle. Until, in God's good time, the New World, with all its power and might, steps forth to the rescue and liberation of the old."

Roosevelt sent no significant private message to Churchill during the crucial rescue operation, but sent him in effect a public one six days after it ended. He had long planned to make a brief appearance at the University of Virginia's commencement, at which his son Franklin would receive a law degree, but after he returned from a weekend cruise, he had Steve Early phone reporters that his speech would be broadcast at 6:30 p.m. and contain "an important pronouncement." The speech's most remembered phrase, describing Mussolini's attack on the reeling French as "the hand that held the dagger has plunged it into the back of its neighbor"—but the important passage followed it: "We send forth our prayers and our hopes to those beyond the seas who are maintaining with magnificent valor their battle for freedom. In our American unity, we will pursue two obvious and simultaneous courses: we will extend to the opponents of force the material resources of this nation; and, at the same time, we will harness and speed up the use of those resources in order that we ourselves in the Americas may have equipment and training equal to the task of any emergency and every defense."[25]

That verbal commitment, which was followed by action, was another important instance in which Roosevelt rejected the official advice he received from General Marshall and his planners who had little faith in the ability of Britain to resist successfully after the defeat of France. They disputed, in vain, Roosevelt's determination to send materials needed for the expanding American forces to

Britain to replace equipment destroyed or abandoned in France when its soldiers were evacuated. They believed, among other things, that the Germans would be able to dictate peace terms. Roosevelt's basic assumption in June 1940, that by the fall and winter of that year "Britain and the British Empire [would be] still intact," turned out to be more accurate than the planners' view. By the fall and after Britain's continuing resistance to German air attacks, and the failure of the Germans even to attempt an invasion of Britain, the military planners changed their estimate.

Churchill, of course, got the message in Roosevelt's speech. "We all listened to you last night," he wrote the next morning, "and were fortified by the grand scope of your declaration." But he reiterated his appeal for more aid, especially "the thirty or forty old destroyers you have already had reconditioned. . . . If while we have to guard the East Coast against invasion a new heavy German-Italian submarine attack is launched against our commerce the strain may be beyond our resources; *and the ocean traffic by which we live may be strangled. Not a day should be lost.*" Churchill continued to press for the destroyers, other and quicker aid, and even an American declaration of war until, in mid-August, Roosevelt wrote him that "it may be possible" to send the destroyers.[26]

American reactions to Roosevelt's speech were largely positive. A compilation of editorial opinions by the *New York Times* and the Associated Press showed general approval: the most common theme was that the president, in offering aid, was in tune with popular opinion. Congressional comment was also generally favorable, with isolationists expressing concern about the dangers of aid leading to direct involvement in the fighting. The leading Republican candidates for the presidency were divided about Roosevelt's foreign policy. Front-runner Tom Dewey found Roosevelt too emotional when what was called for was a "cool head," and he heard in the speech "the voice of a belligerent." Dewey observed that "if the President intends to involve us in this war he should say so openly." The dark horse Wendell Willkie, judged to be the runner-up, put himself on record: "I think that the President is too secretive and too emotional about the details of his foreign policy, but generally I am in full accord with his program."

Two less favored midwestern candidates were also divided. The former isolationist Senator Arthur Vandenberg supported "all out help to the Allies short of war or impairing [American] defenses," while Ohio's freshman senator, Robert A. Taft, speaking in Alabama, urged "five steps to keep us safe from attack," one of which was Roosevelt's abandonment of the third term.[27]

At his press conference the day after the speech, the president read a letter he was sending to Congress asking that fifty million dollars be added to the pending relief bill and given to the Red Cross for the relief of refugees in Europe. Among a series of questions, most about foreign affairs, which he deflected one way or another, one question made news:

Q: Do you care to comment on the page ad today, put out by the Committee—

THE PRESIDENT: (interposing) Bill White's?

Q: Yes, sir.

THE PRESIDENT: Well, I had not read it and I read this morning that Bob Sherwood wrote it so I read it then. It is a great piece of work, extremely educational for the people of this country and, without going into a specific endorsement of every phase, it is a mighty good thing that Bill White and his committee are getting things like that out for the education of this country.

Since the committee's ad, headed "STOP HITLER NOW," was effective and shrewd support for the president's program, its conclusion is worth quoting:

There is nothing shameful in our desire to stay out of war, to save our youth from the dive bombers and the flame throwing tanks in the unutterable hell of modern warfare. But is there not evidence of suicidal insanity in our failure to help those who now stand between us and the creators of this hell?

We can help—if we act now—before it is too late. We can help by sending planes, guns, munitions, food. We can help to end the fear that American boys will fight and die in another Flanders, closer to home.[28]

The transformation of American public opinion was quickened by the shock of the total collapse of the French army, and especially by the fall of Paris, for which millions of Americans who had never been to Europe had formed a sentimental attachment created by books and especially motion pictures. German propaganda was particularly inept, giving film coverage of a triumphant Hitler viewing Paris from the Eiffel Tower, which was soon shown in American theaters. Even before that time, Congress was passing legislation giving Roosevelt everything he asked for in terms of defense legislation. One correspondent had argued, on the eve of Italy's entering the war, that Congress was "thirty days behind the trend" of public opinion and that "even the President for once, is being outdistanced." In the days that followed, against all the norms of politics, Congress was willing to impose new taxes in an election year, needing little urging from Secretary Morgenthau. The House passed a sizable tax bill and raised the debt limit with unprecedented near unanimity, 396 to 6. And though Roosevelt told his press conference more than once that "there was no special reason" for Congress to prolong its session, Congress continued to sit until the new Congress, elected in November, took over on January 3, 1941, and that Congress sat without recess until December 16, 1942.[29]

The management of the war effort, essentially an attempt to transform the supposedly free market–driven American economy into one closer to what economists called a "command economy," was a major point of contention between Roosevelt and critics both friendly and unfriendly during the war and in innumerable postmortems afterward.[30] The major political focal point of the argument was the insistent demand for some kind of single authority—most often called a czar—to manage production and all its problems for the president. As we have seen, Republican politicians were quick to make this an issue, as were such friends of the president as Bernard Baruch, who would regularly post himself on a bench in Lafayette Park across the street from the White House to pontificate about how the war and everything else should be run, using his own experience in running the War Industries Board for Woodrow Wilson as a template.

The last thing that Roosevelt was prepared to countenance was the appointment of any kind of a czar or czar-like committee or bureau to run the domestic side of defense and later the war. He was determined to keep control in his own hands and to use the Bureau of the Budget and other means within the Executive Office of the President as his agents. Even before war came, he was creating new instruments to ensure his personal control. Back in early August 1939, the assistant secretaries of war and of the navy, in their statutory authority as joint chairs of the long-standing Army and Navy Munitions Board, announced the formation of the War Resources Board, a civilian advisory committee to their joint board. Both bodies would report only to the president and not to their putative bosses, the service secretaries. The War Resources Board was headed by Edward R. Stettinius Jr. (1900–1949), chairman of the board of U.S. Steel. In late November 1939, Roosevelt wrote to thank Stettinius and his colleagues for their report and dissolved the War Resources Board. Stettinius's sign-off letter said that the board had "rendered the principal service for which it was appointed." The demise of the War Resources Board left the Army and Navy Munitions Board intact but now under the direct control of the president instead of the cabinet secretaries.[31]

The so-called Stettinius report, which recommended something like the War Industries Board of World War I, had been described even before it was delivered to the president in a planted story in late September 1939 obviously inspired by Tom Corcoran, claiming that the impending report of the War Resources Board represented a triumph for New Dealers, as it meant that control in any future emergency would be vested in the political bureaucracy rather than placed in the hands of industrial leaders on loan to the government. At the end of May 1940, a second planted story inspired by Steve Early revealed that a board "directly responsible to the President to supervise industrial mobilization for defense and not a coordinating agency in which industrial experts would be responsible to departmental officials was recommended in the still secret report of the advisory board headed by Edward R. Stettinius, Jr., which was disbanded after war started last Fall."[32]

Early knew that the next day, the president intended to unveil a new body, the National Defense Advisory Committee (NDAC), composed of both business leaders such as Stettinius and New Dealers, to help him manage the defense program. He did so at an afternoon press conference during which he may have been sleep deprived: he had been roused at 4:30 a.m. to take a call from Ambassador Bullitt in Paris to tell him that the king of the Belgians had just surrendered. Roosevelt explained that as a 1916 law that had been passed for Woodrow Wilson was still on the books, no new legislation for the NDAC was needed. In the course of discussing it, he showed uncharacteristic confusion, conflating the Council on National Defense, which was by statute composed of cabinet members, and the NDAC, which the cabinet group was supposed to suggest to the president. When asked about the cabinet committee's role, Roosevelt responded, "You need not bother about that," and indicated that the legal requirement that the committee members report to appropriate department heads would be ignored. And shortly after announcing that William McReynolds, his assistant who specialized in the federal bureaucracy, would be the committee's secretary, he forgot for a moment that he had done so. To the final question, which asked where the committee would be housed, Roosevelt blurted out: "Going to be housed? Oh, my God, I do not know."[33]

The seven appointees, who got no pay and could keep their day jobs, appealed to different constituencies: three business executives, one relatively conservative Democrat with ties to agriculture, and three New Deal liberals. Four of them—Stettinius; William S. Knudsen (1879–1948), president of General Motors; Sidney Hillman (1887–1946), president of the Amalgamated Clothing Workers (CIO); and Leon Henderson, an economist who was then a member of the SEC—were to play key roles in the war economy, but not as members of the NDAC, which did not long endure. But that was a case not of failure but of evolutionary redundancy, as many of the various functions of the committee were transferred to entities created later.[34]

What the president did not mention was that, in an unpublicized administrative order issued on May 25, he had activated the Office of Emergency Management in the Executive Office of the President, which had been authorized in the 1939 Reorganization Plan but had lain dormant until that moment. The OEM became the "home" for various defense and war-planning agencies. As budget director Smith realized later, Roosevelt was improvising, within the law, "a new government within a government" to run the war.[35]

Roosevelt attended the first meeting of the NDAC on May 30. We have a transcript of the meeting, which was attended by all committee members, except Hillman, who had the flu, plus McReynolds, seven cabinet members, budget director Smith, Senate majority leader Barkley and House majority leader Sam Rayburn, General Marshall and chief of naval operations Admiral Harold R. Stark (1888–1972), Steve Early, and military aides Watson and Callaghan.

Roosevelt, who did almost all of the talking in the hourlong meeting, spoke frankly about some of his present fears: "I will tell you all that I know in the international situation in a very few words: It is extremely serious for England and France. . . . It would hurt their morale terribly if we mention it out loud, but it looks very serious." After noting that he expected Italy to join in, he said:

> That will mean the complete domination of Europe by the Nazi forces, with the Fascists acting as their lieutenants. It will mean the complete domination of Africa . . . and a very definite desire on the part of the people who run Germany to destroy the power of the British Empire and England especially.
>
> It does not mean of necessity that they will be coming over here but it means possibly that they would set up an economic union, a tariff union, which they would control entirely and then say to the people outside, "Yes you can join . . . on our terms" [and saying] to nations where they have a large infiltration . . . for example to the Argentine, "If you will join our economic European union, we will take all of your meat, your wheat and your corn . . . the export of which you live on. We will take them on our terms."

Roosevelt then described the limited choices that would be offered with payment in barter on Germany's terms:

> That will be a peaceful process in the sense that the Germans and the Italians send no armed forces over to our hemisphere . . . make no effort to take over Canada or the British West Indies or the French West Indies. . . .
>
> But on the other hand a victor of that kind may think at the beginning that he is not going to conquer the whole world but, when the time comes and he has conquered Europe and Africa and got Asia all settled up with Japan and has some kind of practical agreement with Russia, it may be human nature for victors of that kind to say, "I have taken two-thirds of the world and I am all armed and ready to go, why shouldn't I go whole hog and control, in a military way, the last third of the world, the Americas?"

The two congressional leaders then asked about future military appropriations and were told that requests for another one billion dollars were being prepared. That would make four billion dollars for the session so far. The president also explained, in response to a question from Senator Barkley about legal authority, that it was contained in the unrepealed 1916 statute.

At this point, the Danish-born Knudsen, who had literally worked his way up from a common laborer's job in a shipyard, asked, "Where do we head up at the moment?"

THE PRESIDENT: At the moment you head up in the Federal Reserve Building and Mr. McReynolds will start there—
MR. KNUDSEN: (Interposing) I beg your pardon; I meant, who is our boss?
THE PRESIDENT: Who is your boss? Well, I guess I am.

There was a good deal of laughter, but it was a good question and a good answer. The whole purpose of the exercise, going back to the 1939 version of the Reorganization Act, was to make Roosevelt literally the boss, without intermediaries, in the management of what became the deadliest war in history.

That would have been a good place for the meeting to have ended, like a first-act curtain line, but it went on for perhaps another quarter hour. Roosevelt said there would be an initial appropriation of one million dollars to get their offices staffed and then switched to what in his public speeches he had been calling "fifth column" activity.

> Well, I will give you an illustration on fifth column. The Secretary of Labor the other day had recommended to her very, very highly, a technical man who was pretty thoroughly familiar with the whole subject of employment and she was going to appoint him. Luckily, she called up somebody in the [AFL] and she was warned against him. We followed the thing down and found [that he] was absolutely 100 per cent affiliated and associated with the Communist movement in the country. You have to be careful on that. Also be careful not to get pro-Germans. There are a good many Americans who love efficiency and are pro-Germans for that reason. We even have them in the ranks of the officers of the Army and Navy and we have to be pretty darned careful . . . about the heart of the fellow we are getting, as well as his head.[36]

At the end of June 1940, Roosevelt announced the formation of the National Defense Research Committee (NDRC) with electrical engineer Dr. Vannevar Bush (1890–1974) as director. Since 1938 Bush had been president of the Carnegie Institution of Washington, a consortium of research institutions; his biographer tells us that he had gotten Roosevelt's uncle Frederic Delano, a Carnegie Institution trustee, to introduce him to Harry Hopkins, who brought him to Roosevelt's attention. He was a political conservative previously associated with the Liberty League. His committee, though technically an element of the NDAC, was slotted independently into the OEM and had its own budget. Even more important, Bush reported directly to Roosevelt and had regular access to him throughout the rest of his presidency.

In June 1941, Roosevelt made Bush the director of a new umbrella organization for scientific research, the Office of Scientific Research and Development (OSRD), which included the NDRC, now headed by chemist and Harvard president Dr. James Bryant Conant (1893–1978), and a new medical research organization, the Committee on Medical Research (CMR). The many successes of the Bush-Conant organization, in addition to the initial work on the atomic bomb, included the further development of radar, the proximity fuse, fire control, and many advances in military medicine. What was revolutionary was that the basic decisions about the direction of military research were made by scientists independent of the military and often in opposition to what the

War and Navy Departments wanted. The scientific story was one of the clear triumphs of the so-called mess in Washington.[37]

The NDAC expanded very quickly. By late June 1940, Donald M. Nelson (1888–1959), a Sears, Roebuck executive who would become a major figure in defense management, had been added to oversee purchasing, while other additions included W. Averell Harriman (1891–1986). Roosevelt also named two presidential assistants who served him very briefly. James V. Forrestal (1892–1949), president of the brokerage firm of Dillon, Read, who had been recommended by William O. Douglas as "the New Deal's friend on Wall Street," spent three months setting up "business and possibly espionage contacts in Latin America" before being appointed undersecretary of the navy in August, a newly created post to control the navy's expanding relations with industry.[38]

On June 20, as French representatives were being summoned to receive Hitler's terms for surrender at the same spot in the Forest of Compiègne where German representatives had accepted French terms in 1918, Roosevelt exploded a political bomb. The White House announced that he had sent nomination papers to the Senate proposing Henry L. Stimson for secretary of war and Frank Knox as secretary of the navy and accepted the resignation of Harry Woodring as secretary of war. Edison, as he and Roosevelt had discussed, resigned as navy secretary four days later, announcing that he would run for governor in New Jersey.

It is instructive that both great Allied leaders accepted cabinet members in wartime they would not have accepted in peacetime. Churchill, in a much weaker position than Roosevelt, actually shared power with Labourites like Clement Attlee and Ernest Bevin, who promptly turned him out of office in a delayed general election held after the defeat of Hitler.

Roosevelt's naming two high-profile establishment Republicans to the cabinet was a far different matter from his naming of two progressive Republicans, Wallace and Ickes, to his cabinet in 1933, as they were mavericks who had supported him in the 1932 campaign. Both Stimson and Knox had opposed Roosevelt's domestic program, but Stimson, even as Hoover's secretary of state, had been willing to collaborate on foreign policy with Roosevelt while opposing some of his domestic policies, and Knox's *Chicago Daily News* had supported the administration's foreign policy while attacking the New Deal, New Dealers, and Roosevelt himself quite severely. The move would have been thought a coup at any time, but coming just four days before the opening of the Republican National Convention it demoralized many Republicans and was a factor in Wendell Willkie's winning the Republican nomination as a dark-horse candidate. The two appointments were popular with the general public: a Gallup poll soon reported that 71 percent of those having an opinion approved them, as did 57 percent of those calling themselves Republican. And, although resented by some Senators in each party, both appointments were soon approved: Stimson by 56–28, while the vote on Knox was 66–16. In addition, it solved the long-standing problem of how to replace isolationist Harry Woodring, who supported military expansion but opposed sending frontline aircraft to the Allies. In the long run, both appointments, but particularly Stimson's, made it easier for the administration to work with some congressional conservatives in both parties.[39]

But the appointments had their price. In June 1940, Roosevelt was still insisting, verbally, with some congressional support, that he wanted no "war millionaires" created by defense spending or war spending if it came to that. Stimson was not in agreement with that view and had little sympathy for using the war to advance liberal social goals. Although his memoir claimed that he was "not eager to see business making unnatural profits," he resisted most attempts to prevent all but the worst excesses and outright fraud. As he wrote in his diary on August 26, 1940, "If you are going to try to go to war, or to prepare for war, in a capitalist country, you have got to let business make money out of the process or business won't work, and there are a great many people in Congress who think that they can tax business out of all proportion and still have businessmen work diligently and quickly. That is not human nature."

In addition, both men, as service secretaries, opposed efforts to soften segregation in the armed forces, with Knox and most admirals even more retrograde in this matter than Stimson and most generals. Both new cabinet secretaries advocated, without result, universal military training.[40]

Two days before announcing the cabinet changes, Roosevelt told his press conference that "I think we are coming to some form of universal Government service," though no details had yet been worked out. One reporter asked:

Q: How about girls?
THE PRESIDENT: Well, that is one of the things we are studying . . . one of the difficulties on the girl end of it . . . is to find enough . . . things for them to do.

This caused laughter among the overwhelmingly male reporters, and the president followed with his own joke.

THE PRESIDENT: We are going to have twenty-five miles—it is a big country—between any boys' camps and any girls' camps.[41]

The Republican National Convention in Philadelphia adopted a platform that was even more ambiguous than most. The initial fifth was largely a denunciation of the New Deal, which was dubbed a "failure" or said to have "failed" eight separate times, but much of the remaining four-fifths of the document assured voters that many New Deal benefits would not only be maintained but be improved. It promised to continue relief, extend old age security and unemployment compensation, and favor regulation of stock and commodity exchanges. While supporting the right to organize, it promised to amend the Wagner Act "in fairness to employers and all groups of employees." It pledged that "our American citizens of Negro descent shall be given a square deal" and stated that "discrimination in the civil service, the army, navy, and all other branches of the Government must cease." Two planks supported constitutional amendments: "equal rights for men and women" and "no person shall be President of the United States for more than two terms." The most contentious plank was labeled "National Defense" but was also about foreign policy, an issue that divided the party and its candidates. As finally adopted, the party was "opposed to involving this Nation in foreign war" but also called for a defense program "to defend the United States, its possessions, and essential outposts from foreign attack as well as to uphold efficiently in war the Monroe Doctrine." The plank was a result, analyst Anne O'Hare McCormick wrote, of a two-week struggle within the platform committee that threatened to disrupt the convention. It represented "a patched-up compromise between various degrees of non-interventionism and extreme isolationism."[42]

Although thirteen men were nominated, only four had significant support. With 501 votes needed for victory, New York's Tom Dewey, a limited internationalist, had 370 first-ballot votes, followed by three midwesterners: Ohio's Taft, a staunch isolationist, got 129; Indiana's Willkie, a former anti–New Deal Democrat and strong internationalist, had 107; and Michigan's Vandenberg garnered only 76. A second ballot showed a fateful decline in Dewey's vote to 338 and sizable gains for both Taft and Willkie, to 203 and 171. The convention then recessed for dinner. If, instead, at that time, the regular Republicans had been able to agree on a candidate, that man probably would have been nominated. After the third ballot, when Dewey slipped again to 315 but still led Willkie, who had moved into second with 259, and Taft improved marginally to 212, a stop-Willkie move was still possible but unlikely. Once Willkie took the fourth-ballot lead with 305, to Taft's still growing 254 and Dewey's 250, the outsider's nomination was all but inevitable. The fifth ballot did not quite do it: Dewey collapsed to 57, Taft continued to gain to 377, and Willkie surged to 429, just 72 votes short. During the sixth ballot, the other candidates withdrew and Willkie was nominated by acclamation but with much bitterness.[43]

The next afternoon, after a pro forma vote giving Oregon senator Charles McNary the second spot on the ticket, Willkie, emulating Roosevelt in 1932, became the first Republican nominee to appear before a convention. He made only brief remarks, reserving his formal acceptance for an August spectacular in Indiana. His convention appearance had been preceded by a press conference in which he told reporters that he had accepted the nomination, would resign as president of Commonwealth and Southern Corporation at once, and, asked if he planned to meet with the president should the foreign situation become critical, responded: "That depends on whether he asks me. I've been to the White House many times and done most of the talking. I will be glad to see F.D.R., any time. I think one should be courteous to his predecessor." Willkie, in 1940 and earlier, seems to have consistently underestimated Roosevelt. After first meeting him in the White House in 1934, he had telegrammed his wife: "Charm greatly exaggerated."

Earlier that day a reporter had asked Roosevelt:

Q: Do you have any thought of getting in touch with Mr. Willkie on a common approach to foreign affairs?

THE PRESIDENT: No. I would be very glad to talk about it if he wants to talk about it, naturally.

Roosevelt did not have the slightest intention of meeting, and the two met only after the election. The real news of Roosevelt's press conference was the revelation that more large appropriations would be required for weapons, coupled with a leak from the War Department that the cost would be perhaps three billion dollars more.[44]

The paramount political question remained whether Roosevelt would run. He was determined to keep the nation and particularly Democratic politicians in suspense as long as possible. This was not just a matter of his love of secrecy and of springing surprises; it was a matter of continuing control. No one will ever know just when Roosevelt decided to run for a third term. He put down a number of very public and private markers that indicated his intention of retiring in January 1941. His establishing the FDR Library; signing a January 1940 contract to write regularly for *Collier's,* a weekly magazine, at an annual salary of seventy-five thousand dollars, equaling his presidential salary; and personal statements and hints to close associates can all be cited to support his intention to retire.

But when one asks the question "What would a national leader concerned about the future of his country and party do to prepare for a good result in the 1940 election if he himself were not going to run?" one must answer that Roosevelt did none of the things one would expect him to do. The most important would have been to build up his potential successor or successors. He did encourage, for a brief period, Harry Hopkins's presidential ambitions, but one must doubt that Roosevelt ever believed that a man divorced from a Jewish wife, remarried, and often in arrears with his mandated child-support payments was a likely candidate, even before the relapse in his physical condition removed him from consideration even for the vice presidency. And Roosevelt's passive encouragement of such declared candidates as Vice President Garner, Jim Farley, and Paul V. McNutt allowed them to demonstrate only the obvious weaknesses of their candidacies.

Most informed speculation focused on the war, or the war going badly, as the most important factor in Roosevelt's decision to run. It would be the answer that Roosevelt himself eventually gave. But surely, the major setback that the nation's economy received from what was quickly dubbed "Roosevelt's Recession" must also be considered. His political opponents were quick to declare that it was proof of the essential failure of the New Deal, and a significant proportion of the electorate seemed to accept that view in the 1938 off-year elections. A major purpose of the library at Hyde Park was to celebrate what is now routinely called the presidential legacy, and Roosevelt knew all too well from his experience with the Woodrow Wilson Foundation what happens to a presidential legacy when the president is succeeded not only by the other party but by men intent on rolling back his reforms. The prospect of the nation's returning to many of the policies that produced the Great Depression must have filled him with serious concerns not only about his legacy but also for the national well-being.[45]

Although by the time of the GOP convention few doubted that Roosevelt would run, his closest advisers and even family members were uncertain about it well into 1940. Harry Hopkins, for example, had told Sherwood on January 22, 1940, that he was "virtually certain" that the president would run again, but three months later he was so unsure that he urged Sherwood, who thought it was Roosevelt's duty to run, to write Roosevelt saying just that and to get his friends who shared his sentiments to do the same. Similarly, as 1940 began, James Roosevelt felt that his father was planning to run but by April, before the German thrust into the Low Countries, believed that he intended to retire. The president had just turned fifty-eight and, apart from being a wheelchair-bound paraplegic particularly susceptible to colds and other upper-respiratory infections, seemed to be in robust health. As late as June 30, White House correspondent Felix Belair published a think piece that discussed Roosevelt's running and retiring as if they were equally plausible possibilities. Roosevelt, instead of publicly playing politics during the two weeks plus between the close of one convention and the beginning of the other, played the role of a president adapting to a changing and dangerous crisis. This was the best possible politics, while behind the scenes the party platform was being crafted in the White House and not by the platform committee in Chicago.[46]

Before recessing for the conventions, Congress had passed the Revenue Act of 1940, the first measure during the Roosevelt presidency to expand the personal income tax significantly. For a family of four, the threshold for paying federal income tax had remained at $5,000 from 1921 through 1940. The new tax bill dropped that threshold to $3,000 and lowered exemptions while raising rates slightly, creating an estimated 2.2 million new income taxpayers. On July 1, Roosevelt asked the returned Congress to pass "a steeply graduated excess profits" tax in order that "a few do not gain from the sacrifices of the many." Congress complied: the second 1940 Revenue Act, chiefly the excess-profits tax, passed in early October.[47]

In his last major action before Congress recessed for the convention, Roosevelt sent up a message calling for an additional $4.8 billion for "total defense," nearly doubling the $5.1 billion already asked for since the beginning of the year. Before making his new request, he summarized his messages on rearmament since the beginning of 1939 and followed that with a pledge that denied, falsely, that the United States was planning for offensive warfare.

> That we are opposed to war is known not only to every American, but to every government in the world. We will not use our arms in a war of aggression; we will not send our men to take part in European wars.
>
> But, we will repel aggression against the United States or the Western Hemisphere. The people and their representatives in the Congress know that the threats to our liberties, the threats to our security, the threats against our way of life, the threats to our institutions of religion, of democracy, and of international good faith, have increased in number and gravity from month to month, from week to week, and almost from day to day.

The president asked for funds in five categories, to

> continue the naval expansion program designed to build up the Navy to meet any possible combination of hostile naval forces;
> complete the total equipment for a land force of approximately 1,200,000 men;
> procure reserve stocks of tanks, guns, artillery, ammunition, etc., for another 800,000 men;
> provide for manufacturing facilities, public and private, necessary to produce critical items of equipment for a land force of 2,000,000 men;
> procurement of 15,000 additional planes for the Army and 4,000 for the Navy.

In addition, he noted that Congress was considering "a system of selective training" that would ensure that "the necessary manpower" would be on hand to use the new equipment when it became available. This was generally interpreted as support for the pending bipartisan Burke-Wadsworth bill that created the first American peacetime draft when finally enacted in September.[48]

The same day after a presidential conference with defense and treasury officials, the NDAC, and legislative leaders, the White House announced the president's approval of a plan to include in the proposed excess-profits tax bill accelerated depreciation schedules for defense-related investment in plants and equipment. This would allow such investment to be written off in five years and presaged other relaxations in what had been relatively severe limits on profits in federal contracts for airplane and ship construction. Wall Street reaction was highly favorable, as a modest rise in the securities markets the next day indicated.[49]

All American political conventions are, by their very nature, theatrical, though the performance categories differ. Frequently, as in the nomination of Franklin Roosevelt in 1932 or that of Wendell Willkie in 1940, conventions involve real drama. But the 1940 Democratic convention in Chicago was more like marionette theater than anything else, with the puppet master pulling the strings from the White House.

The best account we have of Roosevelt's behavior during the convention comes from Sam Rosenman, who was one of a very small group who lived in the White House with the president during the nine days that ended with his renomination and the nomination of Henry Wallace for vice president. Rosenman had been preparing to take his family on vacation when Missy LeHand phoned on July 5 to say that the president wanted him to spend the convention period at his side, as he had done in 1932 and 1936. His family went to Montana without him, and he reported on Wednesday evening, July 10, five days before the convention opened. That night the president presided at a dinner for five: Rosenman, Hopkins, Missy, and Grace Tully. There was "no serious conversation about the convention or anything else." Roosevelt went to bed early, and the rest played bridge. The next morning, Thursday, Hopkins, about to leave for Chicago, where he was to be a conduit for Roosevelt's instructions, briefed Rosenman on the situation. Both men "assumed, although the President was making no effort to get delegates . . . that he would be nominated [and] accept." Hopkins said that the chief possibilities discussed for vice president were Hull, Jimmy Byrnes, Speaker William Bankhead, Jesse Jones, and Henry Wallace. All but Wallace were soon eliminated. Speaker Bankhead (b. 1874) Roosevelt thought was too ill; though he was a candidate, he died in mid-September. Cordell Hull, three years older than Bankhead, apparently would have received Roosevelt's blessing, but he refused to be a candidate. Byrnes, an able conservative but a loyal supporter, had, in the president's view, a fatal disability: born a Catholic, he had formally become an Episcopalian on the eve of his marriage to a member of that church. Roosevelt feared that his selection might lose Catholic votes in an election that saw a Catholic candidate, Jim Farley, snubbed by the party. Jones was far too conservative for the president, who, despite the war, wanted social progress to continue. That left, for all intents and purposes, Henry Wallace—but that was not to be revealed until after the presidential nomination had been decided. Hopkins also told Rosenman that on the previous Monday, July 8, the president had conferred with Mayor Edward J. Kelly of Chicago, the Bronx's Ed Flynn, Frank Walker, Byrnes, and Hopkins, all of whom would have convention responsibilities. Roosevelt told them of his unsent handwritten letter to Speaker Bankhead, asking him to tell the delegates that "I have not today and never had any wish or purpose to remain in the office of President, or indeed anywhere in pubic office after next January." The assembled political leaders had all urged him not to do it, but he insisted. Hopkins showed Rosenman the letter to Bankhead that he was to hand to the Speaker and allowed Rosenman to copy it and gave him copies of rough drafts for the platform and for an acceptance speech.[50]

At Roosevelt's regular press conference the next day, the reporters, of course, wanted him to talk politics, but he would not. He did tell them that he would not go to Chicago but would take a short Potomac cruise on the weekend and that for the rest of the summer he would be going back and forth to Hyde Park more or less regularly. This produced the following:

> Q: Are those going to be your plans, regardless of what happens in Chi-
> cago, the rest of the summer?
> THE PRESIDENT: I don't know what that has to do with it. After all, I am the
> President of the United States.[51]

Early Monday morning, the day the convention opened, a series of phone calls from Chicago to Rosenman and then to Roosevelt continued the argument about the still undelivered letter to Bankhead. Rosenman, listening on an extension, wrote that he had "never seen the President more stubborn—although stubbornness was one of his well-known characteristics." The callers, not trusting Bankhead to deliver the president's vague instructions properly, wanted the message delivered by the convention's permanent chairman, the reliable Kentucky senator Alben W. Barkley, as part of his remarks on taking charge of the convention on Tuesday night. The argument that finally persuaded the president to change was that Bankhead's keynote would begin sometime after ten o'clock Chicago time and go on until close to midnight, and thus would be heard by few listeners, while Barkley's speech, beginning some two hours earlier on Tuesday, would be heard by many more. Expecting that Roosevelt would eventually relent, Rosenman had drafted a more precise statement for Barkley to read, which the president tinkered with and then approved.

In Chicago before the convention opened, dissension over what can be called the war plank seemed to threaten a floor fight the following day. Isolationists, headed by Montana's Burt Wheeler, felt that the plank, which reflected the president's recent statement, was too equivocal. The platform committee, headed by Senator Robert Wagner, referred it back to Roosevelt, who amended it by inserting the phrase "except in case of attack," so that it eventually read: "We will not participate in foreign wars, and we will not send our army, naval or air forces to fight in foreign lands outside of the Americas, except in case of attack. We favor and shall rigorously enforce and defend the Monroe Doctrine."[52]

While many journalists and historians have stressed the apparent isolationist tenor of that sentence, it was balanced by another that pledged to extend "all the material aid at our disposal" to "peace-loving and liberty-loving peoples wantonly attacked by ruthless aggressors." As Hopkins explained to reporters, the platform did not change the program of the president and secretary of state "by one jot or tittle." The revised plank satisfied many of the isolationists, including Wheeler, and no floor fight over it developed.[53]

Noteworthy in retrospect was the little-noted plank on "Our Negro citizens"—the first positive use of the word *Negro* in a Democratic platform—that matched the Republican platform's promises of ending discrimination and added a detailed recounting of the New Deal programs that aided Negroes.

Though no floor fight developed over the third term, either, there was much discussion by conservatives about trying to force the insertion of a no-third-term plank into the platform. The anti–third term tradition was particularly strong among Democrats of the generation before Roosevelt, like Speaker Bankhead, who could remember the 1896 convention, which passed a resolution, aimed at Grover Cleveland, declaring that "the unwritten law of this republic [is] that no man should be eligible for a third term in the presidential office."

In fact, even most of those who spoke of a no-third-term platform really understood that the convention would renominate Roosevelt. The headline on Anne O'Hare McCormick's think piece "Democrats Glum Facing Inevitable" caught the edgy nervousness that was not directed toward the president but reflected the uncomfortable situation in which many found themselves and their country, voting for a third term about which many of them had serious reservations but no viable alternatives. Some regretted that Roosevelt was running, others accepted it willingly, but almost all understood that only the president could bring the party victory.[54]

Back in Washington, on the afternoon of the second day of the convention, Roosevelt held his regular Tuesday press conference. Again refusing to talk politics, he read reporters statistics showing the progress of the defense program. Finally, one brave reporter asked:

Q: Mr. President, I should like to ask you very honestly and sincerely why you have refrained from making your position known on the third term question?

THE PRESIDENT: Well, I think you might get on the air tonight and listen— listen to your radio. In other words I think you can properly say that there will be an announcement in behalf of the President made by Senator Barkley tonight after his address, that being the first meeting of the Convention under its permanent organization.[55]

The announcement read:

I and other close friends of the President have long known that he has no wish to be a candidate again. We know, too, that in no way whatsoever has he exerted any influence in the selection of delegates or upon the opinions of delegates. Tonight, at the specific request and authorization of the President, I am making this simple fact clear to the Convention.

The President has never had, and has not today, any desire or purpose to continue in the office of President, to be a candidate for that office, or to be nominated by the Convention for that office.

He wishes in all earnestness and sincerity to make it clear that all the delegates to this Convention are free to vote for any candidate.

That is the message I bear to you from the President of the United States.

At this point, Barkley added, "by authority of his own word."[56]

What are we to make of all this? The sanest comment I have seen from a contemporary is in Cordell Hull's *Memoirs*. He relates a conversation with Roosevelt as they lunched alone, probably at his desk in the White House, on July 3, two days before he summoned Rosenman. After dealing with several State Department matters that Hull brought up, the president switched to politics. After saying that he had been reading George Washington's letter to James Madison complaining about criticism against his running for a second term, "Mr. Roosevelt said he had in mind to address a letter to someone like Senator George Norris and end by saying that he desired to go back to Hyde Park. Thereupon, he said, the convention would nominate me. He asked me what I thought of such a letter. I promptly replied: 'Of course such a letter would not delay your nomination by a split second.'"[57]

Hull, whose long career included a stint as chair of the Democratic National Committee, was a good judge of what the convention would do. Why Roosevelt insisted on the public charade of a seeming withdrawal from a convention that had been effectively organized to draft him is a matter for speculation, but surely his resentment about charges that he was a "dictator" was an important motivating factor.

Barkley's delivery of Roosevelt's message was supposed to set off a massive "Draft Roosevelt" demonstration, which, in the event, was far from convincing. Mayor Kelly, who controlled the building, had posted a subordinate, Thomas F. Garry, Chicago's commissioner of sewers, in the basement in control of the sound system shouting pro-Roosevelt slogans and playing martial songs at top volume for almost an hour. The "voice from the sewer" became a symbol of political manipulation, but as Freidel noted it also symbolized the fact that the Democratic big-city machines that tried to block Roosevelt's nomination in 1932 were a part of his support system by 1940.

Farley, no longer part of the president's forces and who should have known he could not win, nevertheless insisted on a roll-call vote, and the Texas delegation nominated Garner, as its instructions required. But there was really no contest. Roosevelt received 946 votes, Farley 72, and Garner 61, while noncandidates Senator Millard Tydings and Secretary Hull received 9 and 5 votes, respectively, making a total of almost 150 votes against the president. Farley then moved to make the nomination unanimous.[58] After the balloting, Mayor Kelly called the president with Rosenman in the room but not on an extension. He reports that Roosevelt for the first time insisted that Wallace be the vice presidential nominee. The mayor, though not enthusiastic, spread the word. Hopkins and Byrnes called separately, each reporting that the Wallace nomination was unpopular but that Roosevelt's wishes would be accepted by the convention. Farley also called, and Rosenman, again listening to only one side of the conversation, reports that he urged the nomination of one of three others, Jesse Jones, Speaker Bankhead, or Paul McNutt. Numerous others called or sent advice, none of it apparently favoring Wallace, though he had his supporters. At some point, before the convention's last day began, Roosevelt informed his managers that he would delay his acceptance speech until after the vice presidential nominating process was completed.

After the nomination speeches, but before the balloting for the vice presidential nominee, Eleanor Roosevelt, paralleling what Roosevelt had done in 1932, had flown to Chicago to become the first presidential spouse to address a convention. She had been sent by the president at the behest of his Chicago board of strategy, who thought that her presence might soothe ruffled feelings. She spoke after the nominating speeches for vice president had been made but before the voting began. Her ten-minute speech opened with a fulsome tribute to Jim Farley and then explained that she brought no message from the president, who would soon speak for himself. She did speak of the heavy burden of being president "in no ordinary time." Her one bit of news was that "this year the candidate who is the president of the United States cannot make a campaign in the usual sense [but] must be on his job." The remainder of her brief and effective speech was a homily on the duty of all Americans to give "service and strength to their country." Although she made no mention of the unpopular Wallace nomination, her assuring presence seemed to calm many delegates.[59]

Back in the White House, still according to Rosenman's account, the president continued his somewhat erratic behavior and acted out another charade, this one for the very small audience of White House intimates gathered in the Oval Study with him, listening to the broadcast proceedings. The candidate the president's advisers thought had the best chance to defeat Wallace, Indiana's Paul V. McNutt, announced that he would not accept nomination. Only Speaker Bankhead now opposed Wallace. Roosevelt, playing solitaire while listening to bitter speeches in favor of Bankhead, had Missy get him a pencil and a pad of paper, put aside his cards, and began to write, covering five pages while the others watched.

When he finished, he turned to Rosenman and said, "Sam, take this inside and go to work on it; smooth it out and get it ready for delivery. I may have to deliver it very quickly, so please hurry it up." Rosenman left the room, with Missy and Pa Watson following. All three read the statement. Missy, who alone of those present did not want Roosevelt to run, returned to the Oval Room, happy. Watson, appalled, wanted to tear the pages up. Rosenman refused, saying that "if Bankhead gets this nomination . . . nobody on earth is going to be able to stop him." Rosenman had a stenographer retype the statement with carbons and did some editing, as did Steve Early, who joined him. Roosevelt took their copies and made some changes and additions, and Rosenman made other changes by hand, after which the president was satisfied. "This will do; don't bother to retype it. I'll read it like this." The final document, which could have been read in about ten minutes, did not mention either Wallace or the vice presidency. Instead, it recalled his most recent Jackson Day speech and argued that Democrats could win only if they stood for liberal principles. Since the convention had been influenced by forces "pledged to reaction in domestic affairs and appeasement in foreign affairs," he could not, "in all honor, and will not, merely for political expediency, go along with the cheap bargaining and political maneuvering which have brought about party dissention in this Convention."

After more rhetoric, the never-uttered draft concluded: "I wish to give the Democratic Party the opportunity to make its historic decision clearly and without equivocation. The party must go wholly one way or wholly the other. It cannot face in both directions at the same time. By declining the honor of the nomination for the Presidency, I can restore that opportunity to the convention. I so do."[60]

Can Roosevelt have really believed, despite what his agents in Chicago told him, that Bankhead would beat Wallace? Hardly. What, then, was this closet charade about? It was, perhaps, Roosevelt's fantasy, his self-delusion that the American political struggle could be transformed into a morality play in which the forces of light and those of darkness were arrayed in uncomplicated ideological alignment. That, of course, was never the case with Roosevelt's politics. The recent appointments of conservatives Stimson and Knox, the concessions to segregationists, and hundreds of other compromises with principle testify to the fact that Roosevelt was a realistic idealist. It was apparently important, at what was a symbolic moment, to pretend for an hour or so that he was, for once, an uncompromised crusader.

When roll-call balloting began, Roosevelt, as he liked to do, kept his own running tally. It quickly became apparent that, however reluctantly and lamely, the convention was doing its nominee's bidding about a running mate, as is almost always the case. Wallace received 627 votes, Bankhead got 329, and almost 100 ballots went for scattered noncandidates or were not voted. Bankhead carried eight of the former Confederate states; the border states of Kentucky, Maryland, and Missouri; plus Arizona and Washington. Wallace carried the rest of the country, including the former Confederate states of Arkansas, Florida, and South Carolina, while Colorado went to its favorite son.

The balloting over, the hot and sweaty president was wheeled into his bedroom to wash up and change, to return in a few minutes, refreshed and jaunty, to be taken downstairs to give his acceptance speech.[61]

The speech, which had been written the previous week, began at twenty-five minutes past midnight, Chicago time, and was heard by relatively few people outside of the convention site. Unlike a typical convention address, it was delivered in a conversational Fireside Chat mode, while a spotlight focused on a huge presidential portrait, with Eleanor seated on the stage and the silent audience "huddled forward . . . fanning themselves and straining for attention." "It is very late; [he began] but I have felt that you would rather that I speak to you now than wait until tomorrow."

Speaking "with a very full heart," the president confessed "mixed feelings"— "deep personal desire for retirement on the one hand, and that quiet, invisible thing called 'conscience' on the other." He explained that because "self-appointed commentators and interpreters" would misinterpret his motives, he would speak "in a somewhat personal vein" and trust "the American people" to accept his "good faith." "When, in 1936, I was chosen by the voters for a second time as President, it was my firm intention to turn over the responsibilities of Government to other hands at the end of my term. That conviction remained with me. Eight years in the Presidency, following a period of bleak depression, and covering one world crisis after another, would normally entitle any man to the relaxation that comes from honorable retirement."

Even after war came in September, he continued, it was still his intention to retire in 1941 and to announce his intention to do so "at an early date." He soon realized, however, that "such a public statement on my part would be unwise" and that it was also "my obvious duty to preserve our neutrality, to shape our program of defense, to meet rapid changes . . . to sustain the policy of the Good Neighbor [and] to maintain to the utmost the influence of this mighty nation in our effort to prevent the spread of war, and to sustain by all legal means those governments threatened by other governments which had rejected the principles of democracy." All these factors had caused him to decide to make no announcement of his intentions "before the national Convention. It was accordingly made to you within an hour after the permanent organization of this Convention."

He went on describe how, in the recent buildup of the nation's defenses, he had "drafted" many talented men and women "into the nation's service." He then made news by endorsing the first peacetime draft in American history. Because of the millions needed for the armed forces, he argued that "most right thinking persons are agreed that some form of selection by draft is necessary and fair today as it was in 1917 and 1918." "Lying awake, as I have, on many nights, I have asked myself whether I have the right, as Commander-in-Chief of the Army and Navy, to call on men and women to serve their country or to train themselves to serve and, at the same time, decline to serve my country in my own personal capacity, if I am called upon to do so by the people of my country."

After characterizing the global conflict as "no ordinary war" but "a revolution imposed by force of arms" aiming "not to set men free but to reduce them to slavery," he returned to his own decision.

> Like most men of my age, I had made plans for myself, plans for a private life of my own choice and for my own satisfaction, a life of that kind to begin in January, 1941. These plans, like so many other plans, had been made in a world which now seems as distant as another planet. [Now] all those who can be of service to the Republic have no choice but to offer themselves for service in those capacities for which they may be fitted.
>
> Those, my friends, are the reasons why I have had to admit to myself, and now to state to you, that my conscience will not let me turn my back upon a call to service. . . . Only the people themselves can draft a President. If such a draft should be made upon me, I say to you, in the utmost simplicity, I will, with God's help, continue to serve with the best of my ability and with the fullness of my strength.

The apologia completed, he gave a spirited defense of his domestic and foreign policies, with more than an undercurrent suggesting that some of his domestic critics were essentially disloyal. He thanked the delegates for selecting Henry Wallace, sent his "most affectionate greetings" to his "old friend, Jim Farley," and spelled out, "as I think my good wife suggested an hour or so ago," that this would not be an ordinary campaign because he could not get too far away from Washington. He explained that he would continue to "report" via press conferences and radio but would "not engage in purely political debate." But he left himself an escape hatch: "I shall never be loath to call the attention of the nation to deliberate or unwitting falsifications of fact, which are sometimes made by political candidates."

The rest of the speech focused on what Roosevelt considered the primary task of the remainder of his wartime presidency, "safeguarding our institutions," which included "the processes of free elective Government—the democratic-republican form, based on the representative system and the coordination of the executive, the legislative and the judicial branches." He defined this as a dual task, one part to be done, if necessary, by the "armed defense forces" and the other by making government "responsive to the growing requirements of modern democracy." He repeated his by now familiar periodization of American history into eras of progress and reaction, and without using the term *New Deal* he praised the achievements of his administration as successful and insisted on their continuation.

I do not believe for a moment . . . that we have fully answered all the needs of human security. But we have covered much of the road. I need not catalogue the milestones of seven years. For every individual and every family in the whole land know that the average of their personal lives has been made safer and sounder and happier than it has ever been before. I do not think they want the gains in these directions to be repealed or even to be placed in the charge of those who would give them mere lip-service with no heart service.

The president admitted that much remained undone and suggested that the voters would "smile" at charges of inefficiency aimed at the "government which has boldly met the enormous problems . . . which the great efficient bankers and industrialists of the Republican Party left in such hopeless chaos in the famous year 1933."

Roosevelt insisted that American progress under freedom faced danger from European dictatorships, which some called "new and efficient." "They are not new, my friends, they are only a relapse—a relapse into ancient history. The omnipotent rulers of the greater part of modern Europe have guaranteed efficiency, and work, and a type of security." Defending his foreign policy, he declared: "The Government of the United States for the past seven years has had the courage openly to oppose by every peaceful means the spread of the dictator form of Government. If our Government should pass to other hands next January—untried hands, inexperienced hands—we can merely hope and pray that they will not substitute appeasement and compromise with those who seek to destroy all democracies everywhere, including here."

He had harsh words for unnamed domestic opponents of his foreign policy, calling them "appeaser fifth columnists" who had charged him with "hysteria and war mongering." In his peroration, he insisted that American civilization itself was at stake:

All that I have done to maintain the peace of this country and to prepare it morally, as well as physically, for whatever contingencies may be in store, I submit to the judgment of my countrymen. We face one of the great choices of history.

It is not alone a choice of Government by the people versus dictatorship.

It is not alone a choice of freedom versus slavery.

It is not alone a choice between moving forward or falling back. It is all of these rolled into one.

It is the continuance of civilization as we know it versus the ultimate destruction of all that we have held dear—religion against godlessness; the ideal of justice against the practice of force; moral decency versus the firing squad; courage to speak out, and to act, versus the false lullaby of appeasement.

But it has been well said that a selfish and greedy people cannot be free.

The American people must decide whether these things are worth making sacrifices of money, of energy, and of self. They will not decide by listening to mere words or by reading mere pledges, interpretations and claims. They will decide on the record—the record as it has been made—the record of things as they are.

The American people will sustain the progress of a representative democracy, asking the Divine Blessing as they face the future with courage and with faith.

The delegates and visitors who had remained silent throughout the speech broke into a mighty roar.[62] Back in the White House, after a few moments of mutual satisfaction with his friends, the president was taken upstairs to bed.

4 Winning an Election, Addressing the World
1940

ROOSEVELT'S REACTION TO HIS RENOMINATION was low key. He slept very late the next morning, took an extralong weekend cruise on the White House yacht, and, soon after he returned, went up to Hyde Park. A message to Congress, timed to coincide with Secretary Hull's speech at an inter-American conference in Havana, asked for expanding the lending authority of the Export-Import Bank by five hundred million dollars to help the sister republics deal with the loss of European markets because of the war. The loans were essentially an inducement to get hemispheric approval for the reassertion of the "no transfer" policy of the Monroe Doctrine, directed at the Dutch and French possessions in the New World whose status had been called into question by the latest German conquests. The Act of Havana, signed on July 30 and ratified by the Senate on October 10, was a prudent but unnecessary precaution.[1]

At his first postconvention press conference at Hyde Park, Roosevelt was asked about various "bolting" Democrats who were getting a good deal of press attention. He noted that the most prominent congressional bolter, one-term Nebraska senator Edward R. Burke, had been "bolted" by his state's Democrats, who defeated his bid for renomination in a preconvention primary, and that another organizer of "Jeffersonian Democrats" had been doing that since the 1932 election, and of the two most prominent defectors from the executive branch, former budget director Lew Douglas, and a former undersecretary of the treasury, John W. Hanes, he remarked: "Well, . . . you take good old Lew Douglas and Johnny Hanes. Lew Douglas did not vote for the democratic ticket in 1936 and I doubt very much if Johnny Hanes did. They were both in the Government and they are thoroughly honorable and amiable young gentlemen [Douglas was forty-six and Hanes fifty-three!] and I think that their slant of mind ran more to dollars than humanity."[2]

The president could afford to be casual because efforts to get a significant number of Democratic defections were going nowhere. Jim Farley, around whom an effective group might have coalesced, stepped down as national chairman but retained his post as chair of the New York state party and immediately reaffirmed his loyalty. Leading Democratic senatorial isolationists such as Montana's Burton Wheeler and Colorado's Alva Adams renounced any intention of bolting. More important, the third-term issue, much featured by the contemporary press and some subsequent historians, seems to have had decreasing traction for contemporary voters. Gallup polls over three years showed a growing majority of voters opposed to a constitutional prohibition of a third term: 52 percent in 1938, 58 percent in 1939, and 59 percent in July 1940.[3]

While at Hyde Park, Roosevelt conferred with William C. Bullitt, still his ambassador in France, who had come up on the train with him. Bullitt indicated to reporters that the policy of recognizing the government of France under Marshal Philippe Pétain (1856–1951) in Vichy would probably continue. That policy, like the parallel policy of recognizing Francisco Franco's fascist regime in Spain, would come under growing criticism from American liberals. Bullitt and Roosevelt may have discussed one of the activities recognition helped, a clandestine program that enabled American agents, acting on instructions from the president, to finance and otherwise arrange for the rescue of high-profile cultural and political refugees. They were selected from lists provided by Roosevelt's Advisory Committee for Refugees. The State Department issued some three thousand special visas for persons "of superior intellectual attainment . . . who are in danger of persecution or death." In the event, more than 1,000 such persons, almost all of them Jews, were brought out of Europe with the right to apply for American citizenship if they wished.

Roosevelt had also approved a well-publicized program in mid-July to admit temporarily an estimated 10,000 children from Great Britain. The first 104, all children of Oxford University faculty, were admitted under a new type of mass visa involving guarantees provided by a private nonprofit American committee on refugee children, which, a press release bragged, had been approved by the State Department and the Immigration and Naturalization Service (INS) in twenty-four hours. Few, if any, Jewish children were in this group. A third kind of special arrangement was made, at Roosevelt's insistence, whereby refugees who had managed to get to places outside of Germany could be granted visas that would be changed to the now largely unusable German quota. These two overt programs eventually received congressional approval. This was a far cry from the president who had refused to support a bill to allow German Jewish children admission and who did not lift a finger to allow the passengers on the *St. Louis* to land. But when asked at his press conference if there was any thought of extending the opportunity to other European children outside of Germany, the president said, "No." He later asked for and received a $125,000 appropriation for the Children's Bureau to administer the admission of refugee children; the bureau reported that the United States had admitted more that 8,000 unaccompanied children during the war, most of them British, and most of the rest domiciled in Britain. Roosevelt also directed Morgenthau and Wallace and their subordinates to assist the American Red Cross to get food to Europe, and one shipment had been delivered and distributed in Poland and another in Marseille.[4]

Behind the scenes, a struggle went on between Henry Morgenthau, whose Treasury Department was tasked by Roosevelt to expedite British war orders, and the War and Navy Departments over how many planes and plane engines could be allocated to Britain. As revealed in Morgenthau's diary, he and Arthur B. Purvis (1890–1941), director-general of the British Purchasing Commission in Washington, collaborated successfully in getting the legally required certification that materials shipped were "surplus." This July struggle ended with approval by production boss Knudsen to increase plane and engine production schedules to accommodate British needs. Morgenthau announced that "3,000 planes a month" would go to the British, who would pay for them as well as some of the costs of plant expansion. Although Morgenthau did not say so, the figure of 3,000 planes a month was very future oriented. Current American capacity was, despite everything, about 1,250 planes a month. The struggle to get materials released for the British was ongoing: as Morgenthau's biographer notes, it would soon shift to the destroyers that Churchill had been calling for since before the fall of France.[5]

Back in Washington, Roosevelt released an announcement that in the future, strategic materials, including petroleum and its products and scrap metal, could no longer be exported from the United States without a license. Many newspapers called it an embargo—"Embargo Put on Oil, Scrap Metal" was the five-column page 1 headline in the *New York Times*, though the story pointed out that it was aimed particularly at Japan but was not yet an embargo. In his press conference, Roosevelt was indignant about the inaccuracy. In response to questions, he said that the Japanese ambassador had been given prior notice and that it was not in reaction to the closing of the Burma Road, the only feasible land route for aid to China, by the British under pressure from Japan. It was, of course, a clear warning to Japan, which depended on imported oil and scrap iron for its military and war-production needs.[6]

Roosevelt began his noncampaign campaign in comfort, with a leisurely Saturday-to-Tuesday cruise to Norfolk, Virginia, accompanied by Knox, Hopkins, two senior congressional leaders, and his two military aides. A staged press conference at the Norfolk Navy Yard, where the president had not been since a 1918 visit as assistant secretary of the navy, had him questioning its commandant in front of reporters and newsreel cameras.

THE PRESIDENT: How many men do you have at the Yard all told?
ADMIRAL SIMONS: 12,000.
THE PRESIDENT: How many did you have a year ago?
ADMIRAL SIMONS: Last September we had 76 hundred.

At the private Newport News Yard, where twelve thousand were employed and an additional six or eight thousand workers were expected to be added, the company president put his finger on what would be a continuing national problem: the lack of adequate housing for the workers. At both yards, battleships and aircraft carriers as well as smaller vessels were under construction. Despite heat that approached one hundred degrees, cheering crowds jammed the streets along the president's announced route as he was driven in an open car during a long day and at one point watched a hundred-plane flyover. At the end, he pronounced himself satisfied with what he had seen and commented that "a year from now we can feel a lot better" about the defenses of the United States.[7]

While the president was in Virginia, a message went up to Congress requesting authority to call units of the National Guard into active service for up to a year in peacetime for training and service in the Western Hemisphere and in the territories of the United States, including the Philippine Islands. Roosevelt cited "the increasing seriousness of the international situation" and reminded Congress that "we know all too well the tragedy that ensues when inadequately trained men are assailed by a more skillful adversary." It was his intention, he said, to call up the guard units incrementally. If a bill to establish a draft was enacted, the press understood that the army planned to train guard units alongside drafted men. The requested authority would be granted by joint resolution at the end of August.[8]

In the president's next press conference, a reporter noted, "There is a very definite feeling, Mr. President, in Congressional circles that you are not very hot about this conscription legislation and, as a result, it really is languishing." Without responding precisely to the comment, Roosevelt embarked on a meandering disquisition about how, if he pushed for legislation, he was a "dictator," and so he did not like to do it. Then turning to the draft bill, he wound up saying:

> THE PRESIDENT: I not only hope, but definitely believe, that the Congress is going to do something about it, because it is very important for our national defense.
> Q: There is a very quotable sentence right there, if you will permit it.
> THE PRESIDENT: What is it?
> Q: That you are distinctly in favor of a selective training bill—
> THE PRESIDENT: [interposing] And consider it essential to an adequate national defense. Quote that.

Especially in an election year, the draft issue was a political hot potato; many members of Congress who favored it would have preferred to vote for it in 1941, but Roosevelt, convinced by General Marshall that it was overdue, pushed for passage before the end of summer. Marshall, in turn, in a radio address carried nationally, complained of the delay at a time that "may be the most crucial in the history of this country."[9]

Roosevelt, while not campaigning, put his party's house in order by arranging the "election" of the Bronx's reluctant Ed Flynn, the only big-city political boss Roosevelt really trusted, as Democratic National Committee chairman. He replaced Farley, whose resignation as postmaster general effective at the end of August was announced by a release of a pair of friendly letters from Hyde Park with Farley not present. Reporters were quick to note that that particular method of announcing a resignation had been used twice previously: for the resignations of Lew Douglas and Hugh Johnson, both of whom were currently campaigning against the president. Roosevelt's "Dear Jim" letter emphasized Farley's administration of the post office and their nonexistent "close personal relationship." Farley never campaigned against Roosevelt, although he did oppose his wishes in New York state politics. Roosevelt appointed his longtime man of all work Frank Walker as postmaster general on the day Farley left office. Farley, Flynn, and Walker all were Roman Catholics.[10]

The other two cabinet changes in the weeks before the election had very different causes, one representing continuity, the other change. Before beginning his campaign for vice president, Henry Wallace, following custom, submitted his resignation, effective at the beginning of the campaign season after Labor Day. Roosevelt immediately nominated as secretary of agriculture Claude Wickard (1893–1957), who had come to Washington in 1933 as assistant chief of the corn-hog section of the AAA and had become undersecretary the previous February. Accompanying his nomination was one naming Paul Appleby (1891–1963), Wallace's longtime executive assistant, to replace Wickard. Even more than the flattering letters that the president and Wallace exchanged, the appointments were a ringing endorsement of Wallace's performance as secretary.[11]

In an exchange of letters that reflected real emotions, Harry Hopkins announced his resignation and Roosevelt accepted it. The announcement took Washington by surprise. Just two weeks previously, the *Times'* White House correspondent had published a magazine piece about Hopkins that gave no hint of impending departure. The man closest to the president wrote as the German air assault known as the Battle of Britain entered its crucial phase. Hopkins's letter began with a political manifesto summarizing the response that Roosevelt directed to the German invasion of the Low Countries and all that followed:

> The experience of Britain has shown that when the national interest and security are at stake we are justified in making only the most pessimistic assumptions. To do otherwise is to be too late at every stage, to invite attack when it suits the aggressor, to face conflict half prepared. . . .
>
> We must build armaments, and because of your foresight and determination, this is being done.
>
> We must marshal our complete economic strength for the task of defense. This means that instead of retreating from our social and economic objectives,

we should push boldly forward with a program to abolish poverty from the land.

Hopkins then explained that he had wanted to resign in May, but "you indicated then that I should remain throughout the Summer in the hope that I would completely recover my strength. [Since that recovery had not occurred] I feel that I must resign as Secretary of Commerce. . . . My abiding devotion and affection for you and Mrs. Roosevelt cannot be authenticated in any exchange of letters." The president's response ignored the manifesto and spoke to the man:

> I have your letter of Aug. 22 and I fully understand all that you say and much that you left unsaid.
>
> In giving me this letter of resignation it is possible only for you to break the official ties that exist between us—not the ties of friendship that have existed so happily through the years. . . .
>
> In other words you may resign the office—only the office and nothing else. Our friendship will and must go on as always.[12]

To succeed Hopkins at Commerce, the White House let it be known that Roosevelt had chosen a person more congenial to the department's normal business constituency, sixty-six-year-old Jesse Jones, longtime RFC chairman and, since 1939, federal loan administrator with authority over a raft of lending agencies, including the RFC, the Home Owners' Loan Corporation (HOLC), and the Export-Import Bank. When a press association reporter tracked Jones down on a vacation trip in Indiana, he refused to comment. The reason soon became clear: he wanted to retain his position as loan administrator after he joined the cabinet, which would require a separate act of Congress. Two days later, Roosevelt asked Congress for that authority, and by mid-September the necessary joint resolution had been passed and Jones was confirmed for the cabinet post. Holding the two posts made Jones even more powerful than he had been. Roosevelt made a joking allusion to Jones's increased clout in an ad-libbed beginning to his speech opening the new Washington airport, which had been postponed a week because of bad weather: "The new Secretary of Commerce, who has been in office only a few days, told me proudly as he got into the car at the White House that he has discovered that the Weather Bureau is under his jurisdiction. So that explains this perfect day."[13] Jones, though not the "archconservative" he is sometimes labeled, would never insist on making social progress even in wartime, as real New Dealers did, but he was an effective fiscal manager.

While Roosevelt continued his noncampaign tours well past the traditional Labor Day opening of the campaign season, two important and controversial matters were pending, each of which had potentially negative electoral results. The first, the draft, had the president's open support and was slowly moving through Congress. The second, the overage destroyers for Britain, was pursued largely behind the scenes, with Churchill continuing to implore him to send them. For a time during the ongoing discussions with his military advisers, on the one hand, and British ambassador Lothian, on the other, Roosevelt refused to acknowledge publicly the possibility of such a deal, as in the following exchange from an early August Hyde Park press conference:

Q: Could you tell us your view, Mr. President, on the suggestion of General Pershing, that we sell fifty destroyers to the British?
THE PRESIDENT: George (Mr. Durno), there is no news on that at the present time.[14]

Roosevelt's only overt political activity in August was at Hyde Park one afternoon, when he drove up to Eleanor's cottage to speak informally to some eight hundred Democratic women from the surrounding Hudson River counties. He asked his passenger, Henry Wallace, to stand up and take a bow and spoke of "four more years." His aides made a fuss about the press calling his remark and conference with the vice presidential candidate "political," but of course everything a president does is, one way or another, political.

The next evening, he left for a tour of defense installations in New England and upstate New York. His train took him first to Portsmouth, New Hampshire, for a quick tour of its naval base. He and his party—Hopkins, Secretary Knox, his two military aides, and physician Ross McIntire, plus a changing cast of regional politicians—then boarded the *Potomac* and sailed to Boston to inspect its navy yard, after which they were driven to the Watertown, New York, arsenal where the army's new antiaircraft guns were demonstrated. The president relaxed on the yacht on Sunday and on the final day of the tour visited naval facilities at Newport, Rhode Island, and the submarine base and Electric Boat Company factory at New London, Connecticut. The on-site press conferences were uneventful, the president remarking that he was satisfied with what he had seen. He clearly was happy at being seen and photographed in martial surroundings. Neither the president nor anyone else brought up his previous embarrassment at Newport during World War I.[15]

In his August 16 press conference, Roosevelt announced three developments in what seemed a peculiar order:

THE PRESIDENT: First of all the War Department authorizes this announcement . . . Major General Delos C. Emmons, of the G.H.Q. Air Force, and Brig. General George E. Strong, Assistant Chief of Staff of the War Plans Division, are at the present time in England, as observers . . . and you also know that Admiral Chormley and several members of his staff are in England . . . and someone will ask me about destroyers so you might as well know now—

Q: (interposing) How long have they been there?

THE PRESIDENT: I can't tell you. Recently—"recently" is a very good word.

This has nothing to do with destroyers in the sense that the quid pro quo is under discussion, but I am initiating, holding conversations with the British Government for the acquisition of Naval bases and Air bases by the United States for the defense of the Americas and particularly with relationship to the Panama Canal. . . .

Furthermore . . . the United States Government is carrying on conversations with the Canadian Government, looking toward the defense of the American hemisphere.

The president authorized—and dictated—direct quotations about the bases but refused to allow any quotation about destroyers because "I do not know what the quid pro quo was going to be."[16]

The reason for what otherwise seems like unnecessary blundering by Roosevelt was that London had leaked the substance of Roosevelt's August 15 message to Churchill—"that it may be possible" to send destroyers as well as the fact of that direct communication; the fact of their previous communications was still unrevealed. While admitting that a deal was in progress, Roosevelt did not want the whole question of his correspondence with the British leader to become an issue in either the struggle over the draft in Congress or the coming election campaign. The *New York Times* reported the matter adroitly by describing the bases and the Canadian matter in Roosevelt-approved language and then saying that the president "declined to admit" that British desire for "fifty or sixty overage American destroyers" had anything to do with the case. In addition, talk of a pending deal had been all over Washington for some time. A front-page story in the *Times* on the morning of the press conference laid out much of the planned deal with reasonable accuracy.[17]

Roosevelt also insisted, falsely, that his upcoming meeting with Canadian prime minister Mackenzie King was unrelated to the nascent destroyer deal. Although there were other reasons to establish military cooperation with Canada, it was thought that if Britain fell, its fleet would be based in Canada and that having an apparatus in place would be convenient; the two men also discussed the probability of transferring the destroyers in Halifax. That meeting had been set up for Ogdensburg, in upstate New York, a border town with a ferry connection to Canada, where the president was going to attend army maneuvers the next day, August 17—not incidentally, the scheduled date of Willkie's acceptance speech in Elwood, Indiana.

Roosevelt, with Secretary Henry Stimson and Governor Herbert Lehman in his car, reviewed many of the nearly one hundred thousand troops involved in the exercise, the largest deployment in the United States since just after the Civil War. The press observed that much of the troops' equipment was make-believe. Some soldiers had to pretend that drainpipes were trench mortars and broomsticks machine guns, while trucks bore signs saying they were tanks. Army briefers explained that much of the missing equipment had been shipped to Britain, but the ersatz tanks were there because enough real ones had not yet been built. Conversely, the army had an oversupply of cavalry horses. After touring some of the maneuvers area, Roosevelt and his guests received a public briefing by a general and a colonel, each with a huge map, which made for good photo and newsreel images.[18]

Immediately after the briefing, Roosevelt and Stimson were driven to his train, where they met with Mackenzie King, who was accompanied by two minor aides and escorted by the American ambassador to Canada. After the conference, the Canadian leader dined with the president on his train, and the next morning the two leaders attended military church services together before the Canadian returned home. The public result was the creation of a minor bureaucratic organization, the Canadian United States Permanent Joint Board on Defense. But the White House treated it as a big deal and for six days made Canada the lead on its daily handouts to emphasize the hemispheric defense aspects of the story at a time when isolationists, who opposed the destroyers deal and the draft, saw the joint board as cementing a de facto alliance with Britain. Roosevelt himself referred reporters to his Kingston, Ontario, speech in 1939 when he pledged that the United States would defend Canada were it attacked.

The Canadian capital was reported as jubilant about the agreement. Instead of being protected by the United States by virtue of a presidential pledge and the Monroe Doctrine, it was now protected by mutual obligation. Members of the Joint Board were quickly appointed, with one "civilian" and four bureaucrats from each country, three of whom were military and the fourth a diplomat. The American civilian, New York mayor Fiorello La Guardia, serving as spokesman after the group's first meeting in Ottawa, announced that a joint group of the military members would inspect Canadian bases on both coasts. La Guardia's involvement served both political and bureaucratic needs: as a Republican, his appointment further underlined bipartisanship in defense, and his position as chairman of the United States Conference of Mayors was a way of folding municipal officials into the defense program. Not publicized was the fact that American and Canadian military planners had begun to have meetings in Washington.[19]

The president was meeting with Mackenzie King and did not hear Willkie's acceptance speech, which was delivered before a huge Saturday crowd of perhaps two hundred thousand persons, dozens of marching bands, and four elephants, swamping the central Indiana town of Elwood, a manufacturing center of nearly twelve thousand where the Republican candidate had been born and brought up, though he had not lived there for many years. Forty-eight years old, a decade younger than Roosevelt, he was an appealing and vigorous candidate. Anne O'Hare McCormick described him as follows: "Big, shaggy-headed, thick-shouldered, loosely built, he will always look like the over-grown, excited boy he used to be."[20] He was, hands down, the most appealing Republican presidential candidate between the first Roosevelt and Eisenhower.

His long acceptance speech (nearly fifty-six hundred words) on a very hot day (102 in the shade) was, for most of his backers, a disappointment. Written by journalist Russell Davenport, it was more a magazine essay than an appeal to partisan voters. Willkie would later demonstrate a real ability to communicate in effective, short, energetic speeches, but his campaign opener never caught fire. The only real enthusiasm came in response to Willkie's proposal near the end, "that during the next two and a half months, the President and I appear together on public platforms in various parts of the country, to debate the fundamental issues of this campaign." It was not a likely outcome—there had never been a presidential debate—and it did not become a real issue in the campaign.

Like the Republican platform, Willkie approved big hunks of the New Deal, but the platform devoted much more space to denouncing it, while Willkie hardly damned it at all. He opposed "business monopolies" and believed that "the forces of free enterprise must be regulated" and favored collective bargaining, a floor under wages and a ceiling on hours, and federal regulation of interstate utilities, security markets, and banking. He supported federal pensions and adequate old age benefits and unemployment allowances. He implied that a Willkie administration would be a less expensive New Deal: "The New Deal stands for doing what has to be done by spending as much money as possible. I propose to do it by spending as little as possible."

As Socialist Norman Thomas, who supported neither candidate, observed, "Mr. Willkie . . . agreed with Mr. Roosevelt's entire program of social reform and said it was leading to disaster. The speech was a classic example of the time honored principle of 'a stick of candy for everybody.'"

On foreign issues, Willkie supported the draft, making its passage all but ensured, praised and quoted Churchill, approved aid to Britain, and said that the loss of the British fleet would "greatly weaken our defense," though he made no mention of destroyers. Despite approving the broad goals of Roosevelt's foreign policy, he attacked the president as secretive and charged that he had "courted a war for which the country is hopelessly unprepared." After criticizing Roosevelt for "useless and dangerous" attacks on foreign powers, he went on to pledge "to out-distance Hitler in any contests he chooses in 1940 or after. And I promise that when we beat him, we shall beat him on our own terms, in our American way."[21]

Roosevelt brushed off the debate challenge: "Things are in such shape this year that it is, of course perfectly obvious that I cannot do any campaigning." He had delegated Harold Ickes to respond to Willkie even before the speech was delivered and made no comments about it himself.

Ickes's speech, best known for its characterization of Willkie as a "simple, barefoot Wall Street lawyer" and "the rich man's Roosevelt," was an effective critique of the basic inconsistencies in Willkie's support for New Deal policies while criticizing the New Deal and supporting most of Roosevelt's foreign policy decisions yet claiming that Roosevelt had overreacted. Ickes closed by reminding voters of Willkie's greatest handicap: a relative unknown, he was running against an accomplished, potent, and popular incumbent: "President Roosevelt has made America the symbol of light in a darkening world. Under President Roosevelt we are going forward to complete the mighty tasks which must be achieved if America is to be defended and democracy preserved."[22]

Roosevelt continued, as he had planned, to be presidential. He signed two bills extending the powers of the SEC to cover investment companies and advisers and in his signing statement reviewed the increasing cooperation between the SEC and the financial community. He did not hesitate to remind everyone about the progress since "the bleak days of 1929 when the market crash . . . showed all too clearly the sham and deceit which characterized [our high financiers.]"[23] Although these and other improvements to New Deal reforms were important to him, Roosevelt's major concerns in the months before the election were increasing military manpower and consummating the destroyer deal as a major aid to embattled Britain.

Late in August, Congress gave the president authority to call up some four hundred thousand men in National Guard and army reserve units for one year's peacetime federal service in the Western Hemisphere or the Philippine Islands. It passed easily and was popular with the public; a Gallup poll showed 85 percent approval. The president called some specialist units into service immediately, and reporters were told that the army planned to call up some four hundred thousand National Guardsmen and reservists in 1941 to train with draftees and regular army units.[24]

The president's major manpower concern was the draft legislation, whose eventual passage had been made easier by Willkie's support. Still, a large minority in the Senate, including such strong supporters of progressive legislation as Nebraska's George Norris and Wisconsin's Robert La Follette, were opposed and insisted on extensive debate. In addition, some senators who would support the draft tried to delay the vote until after the elections. Roosevelt would have preferred to have the draft out of the way in August, but there was no rushing the Senate. As he had explained to a reporter and later noted in his *Public Papers*: "If and when the draft bill goes through we shall need a lot of other things," including "cantonments . . . clothing, tents, and food" and "all kinds of preparations we cannot make until [the draft bill] goes through."[25]

On September 1, with the draft bill still being debated, Roosevelt left Hyde Park for a trip to one national park rather than the four planned in the spring. He made his first two speeches since the convention, dedicating a Tennessee

Valley Authority dam and the Great Smoky Mountains National Park one day and inspecting a war plant in West Virginia the next. In addition to his staff, he was accompanied by Eleanor; Secretary and Mrs. Ickes; Bernard Baruch; Paul McNutt; James L. Fly (1898–1966), former TVA chief counsel and then chairman of the Federal Communications Commission; TVA commissioner David Lilienthal; three veteran Democratic senators; and a young representative, Tennessee's Estes Kefauver (1903–63), then in his first term. Roosevelt's choice of a public power site for his major speech of the trip was widely seen as a thrust at Willkie, the private power executive who had bitterly opposed the TVA and other examples of public power development.

Reporters noted that, despite the nonpolitical nature of the trip, the president's arrival in Chattanooga resembled those of the 1932 and 1936 campaigns, with military overtones. He was greeted at the railroad station by an army honor guard, and a detachment from Fort Oglethorpe in nearby Georgia helped direct traffic. The bunting-bedecked streets were lined with cheering crowds, and fifty thousand people waited at the dam, including two governors and the rest of the TVA directors. In his speech, Roosevelt began by describing the scene when he first visited the site as president-elect: "a vagrant stream sometimes shallow and useless, sometimes turbulent and in flood, always dark with the soil it had washed from the eroding hills." He went on to describe the new dam, the sixth completed by the TVA, as "a demonstration of what a democracy at work can do" and he reminded his listeners that "there were and are those who maintain that the development of an enterprise that lies wholly within this State is not a proper activity of Government [and that I am] glad, indeed, that in spite of partisan opposition, the Congress of the United States has overwhelmingly voted the necessary funds." He went on to point out that many "new defense industries" were being built "more safe from attack in the region behind the mountains."

Later that day, the crowd witnessing the dedication of the two-hundred-thousand-acre national park astride the Tennessee–North Carolina border was much smaller. But both speeches, on Labor Day, the traditional opening of national political campaigns, went out on all three national networks and were sent abroad in translated versions by shortwave.

The president began by talking about the park as a place where there were trees that "stood before our forefathers ever came to this continent" and reminded his audience of the pioneer's dangers when the "rifle could never be far from the axe." He contrasted those dangers with the "more deadly" present threats. "The earth has been so shrunk by the airplane and the radio that Europe is closer to America today than was one side of these mountains from another [in pioneer times]. The arrow, the tomahawk, and the scalping knife have been replaced by the airplane, the bomb, the tank, and the machine gun."

"Therefore," he continued, "Congress . . . and the Chief Executive . . . are establishing by law the obligation inherent in our citizenship to serve our forces for defense through training in many capacities." Speaking at a time when the daily headlines told of ever-increasing German air attacks now centered on London, Roosevelt admitted that it was not "easy or pleasant" to ask for such sacrifices, but "we have come to realize the greatest attack that has ever been launched against freedom of the individual is nearer the Americas than ever before. To meet that attack we must prepare beforehand—for the simple reason that preparing later may and probably would be too late."

He went on to note that in developing the nation, "we committed excesses that we are today seeking to atone for." He spoke of dangers that had come from within—the destruction of both natural and human resources. "We slashed our forests, we used our soils, we encouraged floods, we overconcentrated our wealth, we disregarded our unemployed. . . . We are at last definitely engaged in the task of conserving the bounties of nature. . . . We are trying at least to attain employment for all who would work and can work, and to provide a greater assurance of security throughout the life of the family." Roosevelt then warned of "a second danger—a danger from without."

That there is a danger from without is at last recognized by most of us Americans. That such a danger cannot longer be met with pitchforks and squirrel rifles or even with the training or with the weapons of the war of 1917 and 1918, is equally clear to most of us Americans. . . .

You and I know that in the process of preparing against danger we shall not have to abandon and we shall not abandon the great social improvements that have come to the American people in these later years. We need not swap the gain of better living for the gain of better defense. I propose that we retain the one and gain the other.

But to preserve out liberties will not be easy. The task will require the united efforts of all of us. It will require sacrifices from us all. . . .

We in this hour, must have and will have absolute national unity for total defense.

Asking "What shall we be defending?" Roosevelt answered, "a way of life which has given more freedom that has ever been realized in the world before . . . a way of life that has let men hold up their heads and admit no master but God."

In closing he reflected on the pioneer spirit and the magnificent setting of the Great Smokies:

We need that spirit in this hour. We need a conviction, felt deep in us all, that there are no divisions among us. We are all members of the same body. We are all Americans.

The winds that blow through the wide sky in these mountains, the winds that sweep from Canada to Mexico, from the Pacific to the Atlantic—have always blown on free men. We are free today. If we join together now—men and women and children—to face the common menace as a united people, we shall be free tomorrow.

So, to the free people of America, I dedicate this park.[26]

In this twenty-minute speech, he had used the word *danger* twelve times.

The next morning, the president's train deposited him in South Charleston, West Virginia, for another inspection tour of defense facilities, accompanied by the governor and the state's senior senator. The first stop was an almost deserted site, a navy ordnance plant built at a cost of thirty million dollars in 1917–18 but abandoned under the terms of the 1921 naval limitation treaty. It was being restored to working order. Roosevelt told the press that it was "a sentimental pilgrimage" because he was doubly associated with the plant, first as assistant navy secretary when it was planned and built and then, in 1937, as president when he canceled a proposed sale of the plant because he had foreseen its future usefulness. An additional twenty million dollars had been appropriated to bring the plant up to date. One building on the site was being used to train three hundred NYA workers for defense jobs, and Aubrey Williams was there to explain the operation. In another, leased to Carnegie Steel, the president watched a hundred-ton hot slab of steel being forced through giant rollers as part of the armored plate manufacturing process. The president then drove through Charleston proper, most of it along a six-lane WPA-built parkway before large cheering crowds to reboard his train, which had been moved to the city's station for the trip to Washington.

Just before noon, the dozen traveling reporters were summoned to an on-board press conference in the crowded vestibule of his private car. After the usual preconference pleasantries, Roosevelt announced that in ten minutes in Washington, "the most important thing that has come for American defense since the Louisiana Purchase" would be made public. He then read from the announcement, which began:

To the Congress:

I transmit herewith for the information of the Congress notes exchanged between the British Ambassador in Washington and the Secretary of State on September 2, 1940, under which this Government has acquired the right to lease naval and air bases in Newfoundland, and in the islands of Bermuda, the Bahamas, Jamaica, St. Lucia, Trinidad, and Antigua, and in British Guiana; also a copy of an opinion of the Attorney General dated August 27, 1940, regarding my authority to consummate this arrangement.

The right to bases in Newfoundland and Bermuda are gifts—generously given and gladly received. The other bases mentioned have been acquired in exchange for 50 of our over-age destroyers.

This is not inconsistent in any sense with our status of peace. Still less is it a threat against any nation. It is an epochal and far-reaching act of preparation for continental defense in the face of grave danger.

The reference to the 1803 Louisiana Purchase, as the president later made clear, was because that purchase by Jefferson from Napoleon of what turned out to be a third of the United States before the admission of Alaska was done without prior reference to Congress. It provided the legal precedent for the chief executive to acquire territory on his own initiative, as a written opinion from Attorney General Jackson explained. That opinion also affirmed the president's right to dispose of the overage destroyers and most other military equipment.

The correspondence released with the president's message was, as he indicated, an exchange of letters between the British ambassador and Secretary Hull. There was no public mention of the exchanges between Roosevelt and Churchill, but off the record he told reporters: "There is also to be given out in Washington, simultaneously—you will have to leave this off the record as coming from me; make it just pure information—a restatement by Prime Minister Winston Churchill of what he said on the fourth of June to Parliament, and this is a restatement to the effect that the British Fleet, in case it is made too hot for them in home waters, is not going to be given to Germany or sunk."

Also off the record, Roosevelt called it "a damned good trade," and a number of polls showed that a very large majority of the population thought so, too. Wendell Willkie, trying to make space for himself, observed that "undoubtedly the country will approve" but found it "regrettable" that Roosevelt did not "secure the approval of Congress" or "permit public discussion prior to adoption." Actually, as noted below, the fact of the pending deal had been in the press for weeks, though not publicly acknowledged by any government source before the September 3 announcement.[27]

The realities of the deal were more complex than Roosevelt and most subsequent accounts have indicated. An official U.S. Army history provides illuminating details and argues: "In effect, what happened in September 1940 was that the Army and Navy were handed base sites in British possessions and were told to fit them into their plans and preparations for hemisphere defense. Potentially, the base sites were far more valuable to the United States than the destroyers for which they were exchanged, but at the moment Army and Navy officers were inclined to view their acquisition as little more than a convenient expedient to make the destroyer transfer politically acceptable to the American Congress and people."

But the first person who needed to be convinced was Roosevelt. Initially, as noted, he had decided to aid Britain, even though army planners assumed in late June that it was "doubtful that Great Britain . . . will continue to be an active combatant by the fall and winter of 1940." Even after the president was committed to a major effort to aid Britain, he felt that his hands were tied by Section 14(a), inserted into the Naval Expansion Act of June 28, 1940, by Massachusetts senator David I. Walsh (1872–1947), chair of the Committee on Naval Affairs, an isolationist who favored military expansion but not aid to

Britain. That section provided that "no military or naval equipment" could be "be transferred, exchanged, sold, or otherwise disposed of" unless either the "Chief of Naval Operations" or the "Chief of Staff" certified that it was "not essential to the defense of the United States." This was followed by a provision requiring that copies of any "contract, order or agreement" be deposited with Congress "within 24 hours of the completion of such document." There were also concerns about provisions in the Espionage Act of 1917 and the amended version of a 1794 statute largely aimed at preventing the outfitting of privateers for foreigners. Well into August, Roosevelt felt that these statutory provisions effectively tied his hands in terms of the destroyers, since many of them were currently being recommissioned for use by the U.S. Navy.

A better lawyer than he thought otherwise. Joseph Alsop (1910–89), a socially connected journalist—his mother was Theodore Roosevelt's niece—after receiving a leak from the British Embassy stressing the desperate need for the destroyers and the difficulties in getting them, took his information to Ben Cohen on July 1. Cohen passed it on to Ickes, who took the information to the president, who said he could not send destroyers without congressional action. By July 19, Cohen put together a detailed technical legal memorandum whose thrust was that neither American nor international law barred the sale of destroyers to Great Britain "if their release [would] strengthen rather than weaken the defense position of the United States."

Roosevelt was not initially persuaded by Cohen's arguments, though he did send a copy of the memo to Secretary Knox three days later, commenting, "I fear that Congress is in no mood at the present time to approve any form of sale." He suggested that Knox discuss with appropriate congressional leaders the possibility of selling destroyers to Canada with the provision that they be used only in hemispheric defense, which would release Canadian and British vessels then performing that task.

Just when the destroyers were first linked with the granting of bases by Britain is not clear. Ambassador Lothian had suggested back in May that Britain voluntarily offer to lease bases in Newfoundland, Bermuda, and Trinidad to the United States, but the British cabinet rejected the notion, in part because of Roosevelt's inability to send destroyers. We do not know if Lothian made the president aware of this then or later. By July 25, a proposal from the Century Group, an informal organization of elite New Yorkers working with William Allen White's committee, was circulating a proposal in Washington to trade destroyers for bases and on August 1 presented its proposal to Roosevelt. In an August 2 cabinet meeting, Knox proposed that Britain sell some of its possessions to the United States for fifty or sixty destroyers, but Secretary Hull objected that such an action would violate the recent agreement of Havana. Roosevelt then suggested that a leasing arrangement would be better. All agreed that Britain desperately needed the ships and that legislation was needed to permit a deal. Some speculated that Congress would not agree without a firm commitment from Britain that its fleet would not be surrendered or scuttled but sent to American waters.

On August 5, Lothian, who had talked to Hull about it the night before, sent Roosevelt a shopping list and a notion of what Britain was prepared to give up: he asked for ninety-six destroyers, twenty motor torpedo boats, fifty naval patrol bombers, some naval dive-bombers, and a quarter of a million Enfield rifles. He offered only a "continuation" of the 1939 agreement, allowing limited use of waters and shore facilities at Bermuda, St. Lucia, and Trinidad by the U.S. Navy; the U.S. Army to be allowed to use airfields on Jamaica, British Guiana, and Trinidad; Pan American Airways to be allowed to lease an area in Trinidad and build a radio station there and, acting as agent for the U.S. government, lease airfield sites in Jamaica and British Guiana; and U.S. Army aircraft be allowed to make occasional training flights to Newfoundland.

On August 8, Undersecretary of State Sumner Welles reported additional terms from Lothian to Roosevelt: the British agreed that Churchill would reiterate his pledge, made in Parliament, about the British fleet and added that its commercial airlines should have equal rights with Pan American. (As it turned out, the bases were operated as strictly military bases, and Pan American was eased out.) Sometime in the next five days, Roosevelt decided to take the advice originally proffered by Cohen and supported by others and do the destroyer deal as an executive action without formally consulting Congress. He jotted down two prerequisites:

1. Assurance on the part of the Prime Minister that in the event that waters of G.B. become untenable for British ships of war to remain, they would not be turned over to the Germans or sunk, but would be sent to other parts of the Empire for the continued defense of the Empire.
2. Agreement that G.B. will authorize use of Newfoundland, Bermuda, Bahamas, Jamaica, St. Lucia, and Trinidad and British Guiana as naval and air bases by the U.S., in the event of an attack on the Am. Hemisphere by any non-American nations. And in the meantime US to have right to establish such bases and use them for training and exercise purposes. Land necessary for above to be bought or leased for 99 years.

Impressive support for the argument that no prior congressional approval was required appeared in an extraordinary "Letter to the Editor" occupying more than three full columns of the Sunday, August 11, *New York Times* and signed by four conservative leaders of the American bar, but was, in fact, a version of Ben Cohen's memo to FDR edited to stress the urgency of the matter by Cohen and Dean Acheson.

On August 13, Roosevelt discussed his terms with some of his closest advisers and sent them on to Churchill that day, telling him that if he agreed, Roosevelt would send him fifty destroyers, some motor torpedo boats, and ten naval aircraft. On August 15, the prime minister accepted the proposal "in principle" with one modification: he offered to "reiterate" his famous June 4 declaration but not modify it with specifics about the fate of the fleet. He also noted that the Newfoundland base would have to be approved by Canada.

At a cabinet meeting on August 16, Attorney General Jackson was told to provide a legal opinion and the next day sent a letter to Knox that concluded:

> I understand that negotiations are now pending looking towards the transfer of certain old destroyers to the Canadian Government conditioned upon the granting by the British Government of certain naval and air bases in the Western Hemisphere to the United States. It is my opinion that the Chief of Naval Operations may, and should, certify under section 14(a) [of the Naval Expansion Act] that such destroyers are not essential to the defense of the United States if in his judgment the exchange of such destroyers for strategic naval and air bases will strengthen rather than impair the total defense of the United States.

(Twelve years after the fact, Jackson, by then a sitting Supreme Court justice, researched and wrote a long account of the destroyer deal with assistance from his law clerk William H. Rehnquist. After Jackson died, the account was edited by his son and his last law clerk, E. Barrett Prettyman Jr., in 1957, but was not published until 2003 in a collection of Jackson's writings about Roosevelt. In that essay, Jackson expressed admiration for both Cohen's memo and the August 11 legal opinion in the *Times*. Roosevelt, who liked to keep his multiple advisers ignorant of what their colleagues were doing, never told him that Cohen was responsible for both.)

On August 19–20, Welles drafted, at Roosevelt's instructions, two notes to be exchanged between the two countries and gave them to Lothian. The terms were quite different from anything that the British had agreed to. Welles's draft of the note to come from the British contained a pledge not to surrender or sink the fleet, an agreement for ninety-nine-year leases on the bases with the United States having the right to choose the precise locations and exercise sovereignty over them, and a statement that Britain would accept "in full compensation . . . the following naval and military material" with the specifications left blank. Welles's draft of the American note proposed that the United States turn over fifty destroyers, twenty motor torpedo boats, five Navy patrol bombers, five Army B-17 heavy bombers, a quarter-million Enfield rifles, and five million rounds of small-arms ammunition. Stimson and Marshall had approved these terms, and on August 21 Admiral Stark wrote the president that he would sign the necessary documents to permit the transfer of the destroyers and patrol bombers, but only if they were traded for bases and he was assured that funds would be available to develop them.

On August 22, Roosevelt sent a misleading "Dear Dave" letter to Senator Walsh, an old antagonist who had been an Al Smith diehard in 1932 and would soon join the America First Committee, writing him, "I do hope you will not oppose the [destroyers for bases] deal," which the president had no intention of sending to Congress. At this time, Roosevelt had made no public acknowledgment that a deal was pending, but it was all over Washington and the letter was probably intended to stop Walsh from trying to put some other monkey wrench into the statute book.

That day Roosevelt received a message from Churchill that temporarily put the whole thing on hold. The prime minister had consistently resisted spelling out details about the possible fate of the fleet that might encourage defeatism, and he did so again while bristling anew at the notion of giving up any aspect of sovereignty. He also protested against the unilateral base-selection process and argued, somewhat quixotically, that Britain had never offered any bargain or exchange. He proposed to give the bases without any compensation—what he later called a "free gift"—and said that he would do so even if the United States did not supply the destroyers and other war materials. One reason for this was surely the terms of the bargain itself: the bases were worth much more than all of the proposed military supplies, and he may have been concerned about parliamentary and public perceptions. On the other hand, getting the United States committed to almost cobelligerent status was priceless.

On August 23, Hull returned from a three-week vacation, and Roosevelt, about to leave for Hyde Park and then go to Tennessee for his Labor Day speech, told him that the talks about the destroyers had "bogged down" and asked him to "see what he could do." Hull met with Lothian and learned that one of the problems was that Churchill had made a speech in Parliament saying that bases would be given with no reference to destroyers. Hull and his aides came up with the notion that two bases, Newfoundland and Bermuda, be accepted as a gift and that the Caribbean bases be leased and exchanged for destroyers. The British agreed and added Antigua to the list. Hull also gave up the demand for unilateral choice of the base sites, and it was agreed that they would be chosen by a joint commission. Finally, Hull proposed that the statement about the British fleet, essentially a reiteration of Churchill's June statement, would be done in an exchange of brief messages between the two leaders, issued separately and not as part of the destroyer-bases deal. Churchill's cheeky response was: "You ask, Mr. President, whether my statement in Parliament on June 4, 1940, about Great Britain never surrendering or scuttling her Fleet 'represents the settled policy of His Majesty's Government.' It certainly does. I must however observe that these hypothetical contingencies seem more likely to concern the German Fleet or what is left of it than our own."

On September 1, Roosevelt's train, en route to Tennessee, paused in Washington's Union Station, where Hull boarded and got the president's signature.

At the signing ceremony on the evening of September 2, there was almost a hitch as Lothian discovered that the destroyers were specified but not the other promised military items. Hull insisted that he knew nothing about that, and Lothian, protesting, signed. (Hull makes no mention of this in his otherwise detailed memoir account.) The ambassador had known that the motor torpedo boats, which had not yet been delivered to the government by their manufacturer, could not legally be included, according to an opinion by Attorney General Jackson. The army later turned over a quarter-million Enfield rifles to the British, followed, in February 1941, by an additional fifty million rounds of small-arms ammunition. The British did not get the particular aircraft that had been promised but got an even more valuable addition. Roosevelt soon changed an existing arrangement for the allocation of B-24 bombers, which had been in part underwritten by British funds, from two planes for the United States for every one sent to Britain to an even distribution.[28]

Thus, Roosevelt's little ceremony on the train from West Virginia to Washington was to underline his formal compliance with Walsh's statute while effectively evading its intent. Some of the bases proved useful in the Battle of the Atlantic, as they effectively increased the range of American patrols; the base in Newfoundland became important in the ferrying of aircraft to England and later Europe, and, after the North African invasions of 1942, Trinidad and other southern bases were most useful in sending personnel and certain supplies to the armies there. But the assessment in Roosevelt's message to Congress that the "value to the Western Hemisphere of these outposts of security is beyond calculation" was overblown. What is noteworthy is that the political success at home of the destroyer deal with both the public and Congress undoubtedly strengthened the propensity of the president and his successors to resort to executive action for matters that might more properly be the result of joint action with the legislative branch.

Back in Washington on September 4, Roosevelt could read of broad support in the nation's press, even from such stalwart Republican organs as the *Chicago Tribune* and the *Los Angeles Times*. There was some criticism: the *Boston Post* called the deal "chicanery" and the *St. Louis Post-Dispatch* labeled it an "act of war" committed by "Dictator Roosevelt." Congressional opinion seemed more mixed, with most isolationists, like Gerald Nye, calling it "a dictatorial step." Some Republicans, like New Jersey's senator William Barbour, were pleased that the deal had been worked out, while others, like New York's representative James Wadsworth, applauded the result but criticized the means and believed that Congress would not have authorized it. A number on both sides of the aisle called it "an act of war," while New Mexico's senator Carl Hatch thought that it was "much better" done by executive agreement because if Congress had done it, it would have been "almost tantamount to an act of war." In any event, Congress's focus was on the pending draft legislation. A group of congressional leaders met with the president and expressed their pleasure with the agreement and minimized the opposition. As for the public, a Gallup poll taken in mid-August but released in early September showed three-fifths of those with opinion favoring the swap. In the face of this support, and despite the fact that assurances had been given in his name that he would not attack the deal, Willkie, speaking to farm editors, denounced the method as "the most arbitrary and dictatorial action ever taken by any President in the history of the United States."[29]

At his next regular press conference, Roosevelt ignored past controversy and complained about congressional delays in passing three pieces of legislation that were postponing full implementation of the defense program: the very large military appropriation bill, the Selective Service bill, and the excess-profits tax. As usual he refused comment on pending amendments to delay the effective date of the draft act to sometime after the election and to narrowing its age limits. That Sunday at Hyde Park, he sat quietly in his pew with his house guest, Princess Martha of Norway, listening to the pastor as part of a national day of prayer for peace that he had proclaimed. Across the Atlantic, London was undergoing the second night of the worst attacks of the war; the British responded with a massive three-hour raid on Hamburg. The next day, still at Hyde Park, the president signed the $5.25 billion arms bill, $2.7 billion of which was for current expenditures. Most of the money was for more than two hundred naval vessels of all types. Although Steve Early announced that the president's forthcoming speech to the Teamsters Union would be his first "political speech" of the campaign and serve as the labor speech, and thus the Democratic National Committee was paying for it, Roosevelt insisted, archly, that he couldn't tell whether it was political or not.

In Washington Roosevelt's day began by swearing in his replacement for Jim Farley: the new postmaster general, Frank Walker. That evening he began his talk to the Teamsters, who had unanimously and enthusiastically endorsed him that morning, even though such endorsements were against the union's constitution—by taking them through a litany of things "you can remember": when collective bargaining was rare, when employers could call on state and federal troops to break strikes and resort to labor spies, or when in 1933 "your membership dropped to 70,000" as compared to its present 500,000. Roosevelt repeatedly emphasized "the last seven years" and went on to speak of the social progress he expected in the near future: "social security benefits . . . broadened and extended," "unemployment insurance should cover a larger number of workers," and "old-age pension[s] . . . improved . . . extended . . . increased."

> Yes, it is my hope that soon the United States will have a national system under which no needy man or woman within our borders will lack a minimum old-age pension that will provide adequate food, adequate clothing and adequate

lodging to the end of the road and without having to go to the poorhouse to get it. I look forward to a system coupled with that, a system which, in addition to this bare minimum, will enable those who have faithfully toiled in any occupation to build up additional security for their old age which will allow them to live in comfort and happiness.

Noting that Congress was about to pass some form of what he styled "selective universal service" of its young men, Roosevelt argued that "no reasonable person" could object to giving the government the power to take over plants and businesses if the owners refused to make their services available for national defense.

Turning to world affairs, he declared, "I hate war, now more than ever," and repeated the pledge of the Chicago convention plank not to "participate in foreign wars . . . except in case of attack." Closing on a note of national unity, he spoke of and to all elements in the population. "The workers in the factories, the farmers on the land, the business men in plants and offices, are at last awake to the perils that threaten America. No selfish interest, no personal ambition, no political campaign, can sway the majority will of our people of America to make America strong and to keep America free."[30]

While waiting for the Selective Service Act to pass, the president took a number of executive actions. Concerned about physical fitness, he appointed John B. Kelly (1889–1960), a triple gold-medal winner in Olympic sculling, a Philadelphia businessman, and a Democrat, to create a fitness program for American men of draft age. Although press reports spoke of Kelly's articles on the subject in a Philadelphia newspaper, the president surely remembered the World War I program run by Walter Camp. He later appointed Kelly chair of the Federal Security Agency's Committee on Physical Fitness. At his press conference, he went through a general statement of principles governing defense contracts that had been adopted by the Defense Advisory Commission and that he was sending to Congress for its information. The statement began by prioritizing speed of delivery and quality. Price, "while not the sole consideration," was obviously important, but the commission, while recognizing that "competitive bidding is the better procedure," recommended that the use of "negotiated contracts be authorized where necessary." This would lead to the widespread use of the cost plus contract that insulated defense contractors against loss. The commission's principles also favored granting contracts to established firms. Although it noted the "moral responsibility" of defense suppliers to perform their tasks "without profiteering," the commission undertook no discussion of profit itself. No searching questions were asked by reporters, whose economic antennae were clearly not as well developed as their political ones.[31]

On September 14, the nation's first peacetime draft—introduced as the Burke-Wadsworth Act on June 20—finally passed comfortably by votes of 47–25 in the

Senate and 232–124 in the House. The negative votes came from both parties and from both right and left. Despite the strong support of Willkie for the bill, most Republicans voted no: 10 of 17 in the Senate and 88 of 134 in the House. In the Senate, those who voted no included conservatives such as Nevada's McCarran (D) and Ohio's Taft (R) and liberals such as California's Downey (D), Wisconsin's La Follette, and Nebraska's Norris. The only southern senator who opposed the draft was Cotton Ed Smith.

Some of the details of the draft legislation were hotly debated. After seventy-six hours of actual debate, the Senate passed its initial version on August 28. It called for the registration of men aged twenty-one to thirty-five, some of whom would be selected for one year of military service. They could not be sent outside the Western Hemisphere in peacetime; some senators had wanted to limit service to the continental United States. It also provided, in what was popularly called the conscription of industry, that the government might seize needed facilities if owners refused to make them available. The original House bill contained no such provision, but the House added one. On September 6, while police forced fifteen hundred protesting youths from the Capitol grounds but allowed them to demonstrate in adjoining streets, the House sitting as the Committee of the Whole began its amendment process.

By a non–roll call vote of 185–155, it delayed the operation of the draft for at least sixty days after the bill was passed and signed by the president. Under its terms, Roosevelt would have would have to issue a proclamation calling for four hundred thousand volunteers, the number that the War Department had said it would take in the first increment of draft call-ups. If the total number of volunteers reached or exceeded that number within sixty days, no immediate call-up would ensue. The next day, as Roosevelt urged speed in his press conference without commenting on attempted amendments, the House rejected the age limits specified by the Senate and substituted the broader range requested by the administration, twenty-one to forty-five. Although the House adopted an amendment barring racial and religious discrimination, it would have no effect on segregation in the armed forces, which was sanctioned by the Supreme Court. The final House version kept the sixty-day delay and the broader age range. A less debated difference with the Senate was that the House version would have subjected draft evaders or resisters to military courts-martial, while the Senate version called for federal court trials and inserted a procedurally different version of the industrial draft.

A two-day Senate-House conference produced a compromise bill that the House accepted but the Senate, in a rare move, rejected. The issue was the terms of the so-called industrial draft that some Senators found too weak. The conferees, using language weaker than that in either the Senate or the House version of the bill, had limited the president's authority. Crucial to the result were the votes of senators, like Norris, who opposed the draft itself but, if there was going to be one, insisted on effective language and substituted the language used in the House bill. The reconvened conference committee quickly agreed, and in a Saturday session the bill was passed and sent to the White House, which announced that the president would not sign the bill until Monday because he wanted specialists in the War and Justice Departments to check its language. But Roosevelt immediately sent a message to Congress calling for an appropriation of $1.6 billion to pay for training and equipping the eight hundred thousand men expected to be drafted in the year beginning November 15. In a little-noted draft-related move, the president created within the EOP a Health and Medical Committee headed by professionals, "to advise the Council of National Defense . . . and to coordinate health and medical activities affecting national defense." Its immediate task was to coordinate the inclusion of thousands of doctors and nurses into the armed forces. Roosevelt continued to use his emergency powers during the remainder of his presidency to swell the increasing federal effort in the health field.[32]

The accomplishment, with clear majority support from the American people and Congress, of both the destroyers-for-bases deal and the peacetime draft, remains a stunning example of Roosevelt's ability to lead public opinion and his steadfast vision of where he wanted to go. Despite all the tactical zigs and zags, the transformation of clearly isolationist public opinion between the Chicago "quarantine the aggressors" speech of October 1937 and the bold actions of the fall of 1940 was a remarkable response to his leadership. To be sure, the course of world history was a powerful persuader. But despite all the talk by contemporary pundits and later historians about a weakened presidency after the Court fight and the Roosevelt Recession, the president got from Congress in an election year all the major measures he asked for. In early October, he was able to sign an Excess Profits Tax-Amortization Bill, which was expected to raise more than one billion dollars annually as a partial offset to massive defense spending. It raised the normal corporate rate from 20.9 percent to 24 percent and added a graduated excess-profits tax ranging from 25 to 50 percent, while adopting the accelerated depreciation allowance on new defense plants and equipment. Although adopted late in the year, it was applicable to all calendar 1940 income. The bill also provided low-cost life insurance for draftees and called-up guardsmen, similar to that adopted in 1917.

In addition to giving the president the legislation he requested, Congress often gave him enhanced authority over the details. In the draft legislation, for example, Congress set the basic parameters. Draft registration was mandatory for male citizens and resident aliens twenty-one years of age and not yet thirty-six who were subjected to a draft lottery; those whose numbers were called were liable for one year's service if they were physically fit and could not receive a deferment from their draft boards. During their service, they were to be paid twenty-one dollars a month for the first four months and after that thirty dollars a month. Congress provided limited exemptions for those with dependents and for college students as well as blanket exemptions for clergy and stipulated that there should be alternative service for conscientious objectors, but Section 10 of the act provided that the president should prescribe the necessary rules and regulations to carry out the provisions of the law. On September 16, just before the president officially proclaimed the draft, the White House announced that "Negroes would have their share of the draft" and serve in all army units and that three Negro National Guard units would soon be called up and explained that Negroes were serving in all branches of the army except aviation and that the air corps would be opened to them as soon as pilots, mechanics, and other specialists could be trained "as a nucleus for the formation of colored aviation units." Sixteen and a half million men were expected to register, and four hundred thousand would be drafted by January 1; another four hundred thousand would be in the army by spring. Reporters interpreted this to mean that 9 percent of the first contingent of draftees would be Negroes. Roosevelt's proclamation set October 16 as the first date for registration and asked state governors and local officials to provide for places and personnel for registration. In a separate letter, the president asked governors to send him names of persons to be appointed to the various draft boards. After establishing these and other prosaic details, the president added rhetoric:

> America stands at the crossroads of its destiny. . . . A few weeks have seen great nations fall. . . . The terrible fate of nations whose weakness invited attack is too well known to us all.
> We must and will marshal our great potential strength to fend off war from our shores [and] prevent our land from becoming a victim of aggression. . . .
> The Congress has debated without partisanship and has now enacted a law establishing a selective method of augmenting our armed forces. The method is fair, it is sure, it is democratic—it is the will of our people. . . . On that eventful day my generation will salute their generation. . . . May we all strengthen our resolve to hold high the torch of freedom in the darkening world so that our children and their children may not be robbed of their rightful inheritance.[33]

At the end of the month, Roosevelt appointed Lieutenant Colonel Lewis B. Hershey (1893–1977) as temporary draft director and in mid-October named a high-profile director, Clarence A. Dykstra (1883–1950), president of the University of Wisconsin, who kept his university position and let Hershey do most of the work. Dykstra resigned in 1941 and Hershey took over. A former high school principal and Ph.D. student at Indiana University, he had been mobilized with his National Guard unit during World War I and became a regular army officer after noncombat service. Blinded in one eye after falling off his polo pony in 1927, he had stints at the Command and General Staff College and the War College and was assigned to army headquarters and secretary to the Joint

Army-Navy Committee on Selective Service in the EOP when the draft law was enacted. He had actually managed the process from the outset and continued to direct the Selective Service into the Nixon administration. He retired as a four-star general in 1973.[34]

While a majority of Americans approved the peacetime draft, a sizable minority, including very many young people and most of the political Left, opposed it. Folksinger Pete Seeger (1919–2014) and just eligible, wrote and performed the *Ballad of September 16*:

> Oh, Franklin Roosevelt told the people how he felt,
> We damn near believed what he said,
> He said: I hate war and so does Eleanor but
> We won't be safe till everybody's dead.

Eleanor Roosevelt, often an ally of many of those groups that now opposed the draft, spoke out sharply against two of them, her own trade union, the American Newspaper Guild, and the American Youth Congress, which she had long nurtured. In a letter published in the union's newspaper, she responded to a circular sent out by the guild's board attacking the draft bill as "anti-labor and anti-democratic" and claiming that "the very existence of the emergency" was "belied" by the failure of the draft bill to contain an excess-profits tax. Mrs. Roosevelt, writing on September 7, called the board's "sweeping statements . . . stupid beyond words" and called the objections of the American Youth Congress "claptrap." She agreed that "more democracy, not less, is needed," but the "real need," she argued, "is more unselfish willingness to serve for the good of the people" and "not a group of democratic citizens who are always asking and never giving." Two days later, when the press wanted more details, Mrs. Roosevelt, who was a multitasker before the word was coined, invited the women reporters who covered her into the fitting room where she was having her new clothes altered and answered their questions "over the heads of the busy seamstresses." She repeated her criticisms of both groups and criticized their "blanket criticisms," which she thought were "unintelligent" and "played into the hands of the people who would like to see us as unprepared as possible." The president himself took no public notice of the numerous criticisms of the draft.[35]

The not-unexpected death of Speaker William Bankhead led to his replacement by younger, abler, and more liberal Texan Sam Rayburn (1882–1961), who would become one of the truly great Speakers of the House and serve into the Kennedy administration. For Bankhead's funeral, Roosevelt and a large delegation of administration and congressional leaders went down to Jasper, Alabama, on the president's train. Typically, Roosevelt was as unobtrusive at the funeral as a sitting president can be. John W. McCormack (1891–1980), a South Boston Democrat who had been an important cog in Rayburn's team, was soon elected majority leader to succeed him.[36]

Roosevelt used the opportunity of his address at the bicentennial of the University of Pennsylvania to make a "non-political" trip on September 20 to Philadelphia, where he spent the morning inspecting various parts of the Philadelphia Navy Yard and held a brief outdoor press conference while seated in an open car. After returning to his train for lunch, he went to Convention Hall, received another honorary degree, and spoke mostly about the contrasting political philosophies of Hamilton and Jefferson—his listeners could substitute Willkie and Roosevelt. He closed by saying, "If democracy is to survive it is the task of men of thought, as well as men of action, to put aside pride and prejudice; and with courage and single-minded devotion—and above all with humility—to find the truth and teach the truth that shall keep men free."[37]

From Philadelphia the president went on to Hyde Park, where the major event was the celebration of his mother's eighty-sixth birthday. Although the president took no public notice of protests from African Americans and their supporters about being drafted into a segregated army, from Hyde Park it was announced that the president had created an advisory committee on procuring manpower in the draft composed of five white men and Dr. Channing H. Tobias (1882–1961), director of Negro work for the Young Men's Christian Association (YMCA). Back in Washington and partially in response to Japanese moves into northern French Indochina (that is, Vietnam), Roosevelt announced a complete embargo on scrap iron except to Western Hemisphere nations and Britain, effective October 16. To underline the real target, the White House provided reporters with data showing that Japan had obtained some 660,000 gross tons of scrap iron in the first seven months of 1940. That day a self-styled "flying squadron" of newspaper editors and other opinion makers, led by Chester Rowell of the *San Francisco Chronicle,* Herbert Agar of the *Louisville (Ky.) Courier-Journal,* and Lew Douglas, welcomed despite his defections, called on the president to urge him to increase aid to Britain. In their exit interview, the spokesmen reported that the president received their views with enthusiasm.[38]

That same morning, September 27, Roosevelt resumed the face-to-face discussion of segregation that had been initiated over tea with Walter White, his mother, and his wife in 1934. In April 1938 White had come to the Oval Office with a small delegation of middle-class members of the African American elite to discuss the doomed antilynching bill and received the president's sympathy and encouragement; when asked for a message for black Americans, Roosevelt told them, "Keep up the fight," but gave no promise of federal help. The precedent of receiving a delegation was important, but at that time the White House did not announce it.

The key figure in the 1940 meeting was A. Philip Randolph (1889–1979), a Socialist and founder of the Brotherhood of Sleeping Car Porters (AFL), the premier union for black workers. Randolph was already committed to supporting the president's reelection as a vice president of the organization of independents cochaired by Senator Norris and Mayor La Guardia that had been unveiled at the White House just three days previously.[39]

We know very little about how the 1940 meeting was arranged, but Eleanor Roosevelt is likely to have been involved. She had spoken at a dinner held during the annual convention of Randolph's union just eleven days before. The meeting itself was recorded surreptitiously and perhaps accidentally.

In addition to Randolph and Roosevelt, the conferees were Walter White, T. Arnold Hill of the Urban League, Assistant Secretary of War Robert Patterson, and Navy Secretary Frank Knox. The focus was on roles for Negroes in the military; unlike lynching or the poll tax, these were matters under control of the president, not Congress, so Roosevelt's former excuses did not apply. Whether it was Randolph's aggressive style, the essential weakness of the president's position, or perhaps just a bad day, Roosevelt seems inept throughout the thirty-minute meeting.

Randolph led off and despite interjections by the president—most not rendered here—simply kept on talking.

> RANDOLPH: Mr. President it would mean a great deal to the morale of the Negro people if . . . you could make some announcement on the role Negroes will play in the armed forces of the nation [and] in the whole . . . defense set-up.
>
> THE PRESIDENT: We did it the other day . . . when my staff told me of this thing.
>
> RANDOLPH: If you did it yourself. If you were to make such an announcement, it would have a tremendous effect on the morale of the Negro people . . . because I must say that . . . it is an irritating spot for the Negro people. They feel that . . . they are not wanted . . . in the various armed forces of the country, and they feel that they have earned the right to participate in every phase of the government by virtue of their [service?] in past wars of the nation.
>
> THE PRESIDENT: . . . . The main point to get across is that . . . we are not as we did . . . in the World War, confining the Negro into the non-combat services. We are putting him . . . proportionately, into the combat services.
>
> RANDOLPH: Well, we feel that's something.

Much of what Secretary Patterson said was lost because of the inadequacy of the recording system, but the main target was the navy. After a colloquy with the president in which both agreed that in some workplaces, North and South, black and white workers participated in the same unions, Randolph interrogated the navy secretary.

RANDOLPH: Colonel Knox . . . what is the position of the Navy on the integration of the Negro?

SECRETARY KNOX: Well, you have a factor in the Navy which is not present in the Army in that these men live aboard ships. And if I said to you that I was going to take Negroes into a ship's company

At this point, the recording loses key words, but it is clear that Knox was saying that it couldn't be done. The president tried to rescue his navy.

THE PRESIDENT: If you had a northern ship and a southern ship it would be different. But you can't *do* that. [Laughs].

Roosevelt then pointed out that since the Philippine Independence Act, the navy had stopped taking on Filipino messmen, so that there would be more places for Negroes. He later spoke of Negroes in the ship's bands providing "a little opportunity here, a little opportunity there."

RANDOLPH: Is there a single Negro in the Navy of officer status?

SECRETARY KNOX: There are 4,007 Negroes out of a total force of 1940 of 139,000. They are all messman's rank.

As the meeting was about to break up, Randolph gave a position paper to the president and remarked:

RANDOLPH: And these are—I'm not going to leave them here, you've got enough reading matter—petitions from eighty-five American Legion and Veterans of Foreign Wars posts from Maine to California protesting against discrimination.

After Roosevelt's comments that threatening letters to him were increasing, he said "Goodbye," and the labor leader responded:

RANDOLPH: You're looking fine Mr. President, and I'm happy to see you again. Well I'm proud to say that people don't like me too. Even in Congress.[40]

Black men confronting the president in the White House and interrogating a cabinet officer was an all but incredible event in 1940, but few white Americans learned about it. No official announcement or account of the meeting was ever issued by the administration. Various versions, however, were reported in the African American press. More than two weeks later, the White House announced a War Department policy "reiterating assurances already given" by the president that "Negroes would have equal opportunities for service under the Selective Service Training Act." The army's announcement was consistent with what Roosevelt had said: Negroes would have proportional representation in the draft, they would serve in both combat and noncombat segregated units, Negro reserve officers would be assigned to Negro units, there would be places for Negroes in officer candidate schools when established, Negroes would be given aviation training and Negro aviation units established, and Negro workers at army arsenals and posts would be afforded equal opportunity. In a point that had not been touched upon in the meeting, the War Department stated that its policy continued to be "not to intermingle colored and white enlisted personnel in the same regimental organizations.... [T]he Department does not contemplate assigning colored Reserve officers other than those of the Medical Corps and chaplains to existing negro combat units of the Regular Army." That demeaning policy would remain in effect throughout World War II except in desperate situations, most notably during the Battle of the Bulge.

Three preelection appointments of African Americans were clearly aimed at black voters. Colonel Benjamin O. Davis (1880–1970), who had become the army's first black colonel in 1930 and had been passed over for promotion on a number of occasions, was promoted by Roosevelt to brigadier general on October 25 and announced at his press conference in an aside as he went through some promotions, "Among those two colonels one is Benjamin O. Davis, who, I think . . . is the first colored man to go up to Brigadier General." Ickes's protégé, William H. Hastie, who had become dean of Howard University's law school, was named an aide to Secretary of War Stimson to advise on matters of race, and Major Campbell C. Johnson, who taught Reserve Officers' Training Corps (ROTC) at Howard, was named as an assistant to draft director Dykstra.[41]

Asked in his September 27 press conference about the treaty just signed establishing the so-called Berlin-Rome-Tokyo Axis, which was directed explicitly against the United States, the president referred reporters to the State Department. There Hull commented that the agreement did not "substantially alter" a long-standing situation.

That evening Roosevelt sent a clearly political message to the Young Democrats meeting in Miami that was delivered personally by his son Franklin Jr. The message spoke of the "inevitable struggle" waged by "the forces of liberalism and the forces of reaction." "There are two parties in this country. There always will be two parties in this country. Their names may change but the issues between them are definite." He went on to make his familiar observation that Democrats won when they were liberal and lost when they were not.[42]

The White House released a presidential letter to the two military service secretaries setting procedures to be employed under the "conscription of industry" section of the Selective Service Act. They were required to submit the details of any proposed seizure to the Advisory Commission of the Council of National Defense in the EOP for review and were instructed that no seizure was to proceed without presidential approval. The White House statement stressed that "procurement, at present, is on an entirely voluntary basis which it is hoped to maintain indefinitely."[43]

Over the last weekend in September, Roosevelt took a cruise with Assistant Secretary of War Robert Patterson, Librarian of Congress Archibald MacLeish, and their wives as guests that would land him in Baltimore Monday for an inspection of the army's Aberdeen Proving Ground, the Glenn Martin aircraft plant, and Fort Meade. The "nonpolitical" nature of the trip did not prevent Maryland's governor, Herbert O'Connor, and other state Democrats who had thwarted the 1938 purge attempt from assuring reporters that the president would carry Maryland again. At the proving ground, Roosevelt saw the whole range of artillery pieces and the new semiautomatic Garand rifle demonstrated. At the Martin plant, he saw bombers and at Fort Meade newly constructed barracks and other facilities for an expected increment of twenty-five thousand draftees and National Guardsmen by February 1.[44]

By the beginning of October, the pattern of the presidential campaign had become established. On most days, Willkie made several speeches, while Roosevelt adhered to his policy of ignoring his opponent. As noted, he campaigned by not campaigning but by showing himself as a very public president going about his business to make America safe. Willkie struggled vigorously against the man he often called "the Champ," but his effort suffered from the apparent disconnect between the liberal who supported almost all of the New Deal and whose basic foreign policy was indistinguishable from Roosevelt's and the bulk of the Republican Party that opposed most of the New Deal and was strongly isolationist, as the congressional vote on the draft had demonstrated.

In addition, Willkie was very much an amateur—that was part of his appeal—but he kept making beginner's blunders. Unused to extensive public speaking, he often got too far away from the stationary microphones, so that audiences could not always hear what he was saying. He also ad-libbed so much that reporters found his advance texts unreliable. In his post–Labor Day campaign tour, Willkie spoke so much that after two days, his voice was badly strained and remained so until after election day. He ignored medical advice to stop talking; one of the specialists called in to treat him told reporters that the candidate needed a "policeman" rather than a physician. Willkie named House minority leader Joe Martin, a symbol of isolationism, as chair of the Republican National Committee.[45]

Willkie's specific attacks on Roosevelt's policies often boomeranged. At Joliet, Illinois, on September 14, he charged that the president had "telephoned Mussolini and Hitler and urged them to sell Czechoslovakia down the river"; his press secretary had to admit that he had misspoken, but the candidate continued to try to link Roosevelt to Munich. He warned Kansans that if they reelected Roosevelt, "you will be living under an American totalitarian government before the long third term is up." In San Diego, he endorsed Hiram Johnson, the archisolationist, as a "true liberal." In Portland he repeated his support for all "the social gains that labor has made" and in Seattle charged that "the New Deal candidate does not believe that there are any more jobs, whereas I know there are," a curious claim to make in a region already showing signs of the boom times to come with continuing expansions of Boeing plants and shipyards. In Pittsburgh, aiming for the labor vote, he promised that his secretary of labor would come from trade union ranks, but his thoughtless ad-lib—"and it won't be a woman either"—clearly undermined his efforts to attract women's votes.

The Democratic response was managed quietly by Ed Flynn along lines laid down by the president: Willkie was attacked by various Roosevelt supporters, most of whom were better known than the challenger. The attack that had begun with Ickes's demolition of Willkie's acceptance speech continued ceaselessly. In the Midwest, Henry Wallace campaigned hard and effectively, especially in agricultural areas. Fiorello La Guardia, who favored "Roosevelt with his known faults" over "Willkie with his unknown virtues," led the campaign directed at independents abetted ably by George Norris, who hit repeatedly at Willkie as the enemy of public power.[46]

Willkie, as he began to campaign in industrial states, encountered hostile crowds for the first time. When objects were thrown at Willkie in Pontiac and elsewhere in Michigan, Roosevelt in his press conference called it reprehensible, but did not utter his opponent's name. Despite incessant attacks from Willkie in October, largely designed to label him as a warmonger eagerly waiting for conflict, Roosevelt continued to make inspection trips and refrained from overt political campaigning. His carefully worded "escape clause"—deliberate or unwitting falsifications of fact by the opposition—could have been legitimately invoked anytime after Willkie began to campaign, but Roosevelt bided his time. He surely always intended to campaign actively. Sam Rosenman reports being called back from a West Coast vacation in the first week of September for the speech to the Teamsters and being kept on hand for the nonpolitical speeches as well as the political speeches to come; Harry Hopkins was his chief collaborator for the September speeches, but in early October, for the first time, Rosenman and newcomer Robert E. Sherwood worked together. Rosenman called the award-winning playwright his favored collaborator. One or both of them, often assisted by Hopkins, were responsible for the drafts of every major speech in the campaign after that.

Sherwood (1896–1955) had dropped out of Harvard in June 1917 to enlist and, when rejected by the army and navy as too tall—he was six foot seven—went to Montreal, enlisted in a Canadian regiment, was gassed twice, and was wounded in both legs by shrapnel, ending the war in a military hospital. Back home in 1919, he became one of the first serious motion-picture critics and then took up playwriting. By the time he wrote the ad for the White committee, he had won three Pulitzer Prizes for Drama. Sherwood relates that he had been drawn into Hopkins's network in the spring of 1940 and that Hopkins brought him into the White House circle.[47]

Before leaving for Hyde Park in early October, Roosevelt talked to congressional leaders about the Gallup poll and predicted: "Next Sunday in the Gallup poll, we'll have a great many—too many—votes handed to us. . . . And my judgment is that they are going to start Willkie—pickin' up! pickin' up! pickin' up! [giving] people the idea that this fella can still win." That turned out to be an amazingly accurate prediction of how Gallup reported the polls in the press.[48]

The president went up to Hyde Park to dedicate a three-school complex, the Franklin D. Roosevelt High School and two grade schools. He used the event to highlight New Deal accomplishments, pointing out in his nationally broadcast speech that the schools had "been paid for, in part by the [local] taxpayers [and by] the Federal Government to give work to many Americans who otherwise could find no work." He went on to speak about how the government through elected representatives in the legislative and executive branches had assumed the responsibility to "alleviate the suffering of their fellow beings and to stimulate recovery." He spoke of schools built "in almost every one" of the nation's thirty-two hundred counties and added, "There is not a single person in the United States who has not seen some new useful structure—a hospital, or a bridge or a town hall or an airport or a dam or a new water works or a sewage disposal system . . . the results of giving employment on useful projects. . . . In terms of dollars and cents no sounder investment could be made for the American people." But even more important than the material return was "a development of morale, a new hope, a new courage, a new self-respect among the unemployed. . . . In building for the well-being of America, I think we have built for the defense of America as well."[49]

After a celebration of Eleanor's fifty-fourth birthday joined by Harry Hopkins, whom Roosevelt described as his "permanent house guest," Franklin and Eleanor left the next day for an upstate inspection trip. Their train stopped in Albany to pick up Governor Lehman, who joined the party that included Pa Watson, Ross McIntire, and General Frank T. Hines, head of the Veterans Administration (VA). At the nearby federal arsenal at Watervliet, he saw large artillery pieces being forged, held a brief press conference at which he spoke of the expanding labor force at Watervliet, and then made his first visit to the Revolutionary War battlefield at Saratoga that Congress, at his suggestion, had made a national park in 1938. While there he approved plans to move a highway out of the park proper and selected the site for its visitors center, not completed until 1962. He proceeded to the Saratoga Springs spa, which had undergone a renovation begun in his gubernatorial administration and completed during his presidency with the help of the RFC, and looked chiefly at the new Roosevelt Baths, which adjoined those named for Washington and Lincoln. One of the reasons for having the VA's Hines along is that Roosevelt wanted veterans with psychiatric problems to be treated there. Along the route of his motorcade, "extraordinarily large crowds" were encountered in every town and village. The party stopped to have dinner at the home of Earl Miller, the former state trooper who had been one of his bodyguards. On the return to Albany's railroad station for the trip to Washington, the president received "an old-time mass ovation." Roosevelt was quite content in performing these mundane tasks of the institutional presidency, feeling confident that his planned late counterattack would seal another victory.[50]

Back in Washington, a two-day tour of Pennsylvania and Ohio was announced with a series of nonpolitical events as well as scheduled stops for local politicians to board the train and meet briefly with the president. After a day with stops from Johnstown, Pennsylvania, to Akron, Ohio, Charles Hurd wrote in the *Times* that "persons who habitually accompany the President worked today for the first time this year in the atmosphere of a political campaign." Enthusiastic crowds were everywhere, and perhaps a quarter of a million persons saw Roosevelt. Moving quickly, Roosevelt inspected a number of steelworks, looked at engineering projects, and dedicated a United States Housing Authority (USHA) public housing project in Pittsburgh where he met the hundred thousandth family to benefit from this program. A large part of his day was "devoted to shaking hands with State leaders who streamed through his car in relays" and got into his motorcade. At the end of the day in Akron, a crowd of twenty-five thousand who jammed the rail yards demanded a speech. The president, complying, spoke from the rear platform, explaining, "I have had a very interesting day. I have been trying to learn at first hand how this great defense program of ours is going." He argued that "the best way to avoid an attack is to be ready to meet one," and thus he urged everyone to "hurry up."

The following day began in Columbus with the president visiting Fort Hayes, named for the nineteenth president, which was to become a processing center for draftees, and a USHA housing project for Negroes. Since Roosevelt was traveling as president and not as a candidate, his procession in what was Republican territory was more subdued than in Pittsburgh or Youngstown: Republican officeholders Governor John W. Bricker and Mayor Floyd F. Green rode in the open car with the president, while Democratic officials and candidates were in following vehicles. At Dayton that afternoon, the president first visited a soldiers' home and then inspected the army air force facility at Wright Field, today's Wright-Patterson Air Force Base. He was accompanied by James M. Cox, his running mate in the 1920 election, and Orville (1871–1948), the surviving Wright brother, and was joined by his son Elliott, a recently commissioned air force captain who was stationed there. After a private dinner at the Cox home, the president returned to his train for the only real speech of the trip, which had been described by Steve Early as a "fireside chat to the Western Hemisphere."

The venue was the dining car of Roosevelt's train, set up as a broadcasting facility with bright lights for the motion-picture cameras filming the entire speech, which was translated into Spanish, Portuguese, French, and German. On a day when Nazi and Soviet troops were beginning a takeover of Romania, Roosevelt's speech was a clear statement of American foreign policy that reiterated support for Britain and other free peoples, denounced appeasement, proclaimed inter-American unity, and pledged a hemispheric defense.

Noting that it was Columbus Day, he praised the Italian navigator and "the groups of Italians who have come in welcome waves of immigration to this nation" without mentioning the narrow quota that had been imposed on contemporary Italians. He then spoke of the "first settlers, the first refugees from Europe . . . who formed here in the Western Hemisphere . . . a new human reservoir, and into it has [flowed] the masses yearning to be free. . . . [They came] not for economic betterment alone, but for the personal freedoms and liberties which had been denied to them in the old world." Although he had just come from a housing project for what the naturalization statutes called "persons of African descent," he uttered not a word about the hundreds of thousands of Africans who had been brought to North America in chains or the millions who had been brought to the Caribbean or Central and South America.

In speaking of defense, he stressed the unity of the hemisphere and warned of the danger to it "from overseas." "Why should we accept assurances that we are immune? History records that not long ago these same assurances were given to the people of Holland and Belgium and Norway. It can no longer be disputed that forces of evil which are bent on conquest of the world will destroy whomever and whenever they can destroy. . . . We know now that if we seek to appease them by withholding aid from those who stand in their way, we only hasten the day of their attack on us."[51]

In Washington again, Roosevelt broadcast his usual annual appeal for support of private charity. On draft registration day, he was up and dressed in time to make an 8:00 a.m. broadcast from the White House, an hour after registration had begun in the East. The brief message—about six minutes—stressed that the "duty of this day has been imposed upon us from without" and that the registrants were "obeying the first duty of free citizenship." The president composed a briefer personal message to registrants, which seems not to have been delivered. In it he wished that he "could personally talk to each one of you" and "welcome you as one whose name has been inscribed on the roll of honor of those Americans ready, if need be, to join in the common defense of all." When the time came to be called for induction, draftees received greetings not from the president but from the "friends and neighbors" of their local draft board. Unlike the experience of 1917, when significant antidraft riots occurred in many parts of the country, the process went smoothly, as some fourteen million young men registered on the day.[52]

On the morning of October 15, Steve Early announced that the DNC had purchased time for the president to make political broadcasts on October 23 and 30. That afternoon in his press conference, Roosevelt pooh-poohed the notion that they were political speeches but said that the DNC was paying for them just in case "I mention that my great-grandfather fought in the Revolutionary War." He also wasn't sure where he would be on those dates, but thought that he would be on another inspection trip fairly close to the capital. In New York two days later, Ed Flynn announced five political speeches by the president and gave dates and places. Whether this represented another case of the left hand not knowing what the right hand was doing, a quick change of plans, or perhaps a deliberate attempt to keep his opponent off balance is not clear. The following morning, with some seeming disarray, Roosevelt read from a typed statement that had been "liberally edited"—it was already 10:40 a.m.—with the promise of a mimeographed copy later.

> In the speech of acceptance to the Democratic National Convention on July 14, 1940, the President said:
>
> > "I shall not have the time or inclination to engage in purely political debate. But I shall never be loathe to call the attention of the nation to deliberate or unwitting falsifications of fact."
>
> There has been in this campaign, however, a systematic program of falsification of fact by the opposition. The president does not believe that it has been an unwitting falsification of fact. He believes it a deliberate falsification of fact.
>
> He has, therefore, decided to tell the American people what these representations have been and in what respect they are false. With that purpose in mind the President will make five speeches between now and election day.
>
> Q: Mr. President, are you ready at this time to give us some indications of what these misrepresentations are?
> THE PRESIDENT: You will have to wait until the five speeches. . . .

The first speech was scheduled for October 23, five days later, and the last at Hyde Park on election eve, November 4.[53]

The president left that evening for Hyde Park, where the governor-general of Canada, the Earl of Athlone, and his wife, Princess Alice, were to be weekend guests. Despite two front-page stories, the visit produced no news, and the president was seen only at the railroad station and at church. At New York's World's Fair, Postmaster General Walker read a letter from the president hailing "all that has been achieved by Negroes" since the Thirteenth Amendment and unveiled a commemorative postage stamp to celebrate the seventy-fifth anniversary of its adoption before a largely black crowd addressed by the NYA's Mary McLeod Bethune, heavyweight champion Joe Louis, and other celebrities.

Monday morning the president was back in Washington, where Rosenman and Sherwood, with a lot of help from their friends, had been gathering material for the five speeches.[54]

What most distinguished Roosevelt's public speeches from those of his opponents, apart from his oratorical virtuosity, was the intensive preparation involved in most of them, preparation that Roosevelt directed and played a vital part in. When the time came to give the speeches, he was thoroughly familiar with them. Neither of his first two presidential opponents was an accomplished speaker, but Wendell Willkie was very good. He bragged, falsely, that he "rolled his own," but Willkie's writers sometimes gave him speeches that he had barely read before delivery, and many of his statements, sometimes blurted out, were ill-considered. As the campaign continued, he seemed to back away from his own internationalism and attacked Roosevelt as headed toward war and dictatorial powers. Above all, he made too many speeches—better than one a day—and was a tired man with a damaged voice during much of the campaign. Roosevelt concentrated on his five speeches—spread over thirteen days—and appeared fresh and vigorous. His speeches probably did not change the result, but they changed the mood of the campaign and of other campaigners and surely added something to Roosevelt's electoral margin.

On the eve of leaving for the first of the five speeches, the president, asked about his traditional election prediction, said that he had put it in an envelope "about three weeks ago" and saw no need to change it. At noon the next day, he boarded his train in Washington and later gave a brief rear-platform talk in Wilmington, Delaware, to a crowd of the thousand that probably did not need his reminder that the town had been the home of the Liberty League. They cheered his prediction that the issue of liberty would be settled in 1940 as it had been settled in 1936.

Greeted by a "huge fanfare" and assorted Democrats at Philadelphia's Twenty-Fourth Street Station, his motorcade crossed the Delaware to Camden, New Jersey, where he inspected a shipyard and looked at a seaplane tender and what would become the thirty-five-thousand-ton battleship *South Dakota*. Speaking briefly to its nine thousand workmen, he thanked them for their labor and assured them that the ships were "not being built to go to war but to keep us at peace." He then went back to Philadelphia to look at a large shipyard, closed and derelict since just after World War I, which was about to be rehabilitated and resume operation. Then he made his last inspection stop at the Frankford Arsenal, where he spoke briefly to ten thousand workers and guests before boarding his train, which had been moved to the arsenal's siding, for dinner and a little relaxation.

He was driven to the Convention Center "by a circuitous route" through streets lined with spectators. He began by reminding listeners of his convention pledge to deal with "falsifications" and that the "time had come to do just that." He would on "this . . . and four other nights . . . point out to the American people the most fantastic" campaign misstatements. "I emphasize the words 'most fantastic,' because it would take three hundred and sixty five nights to discuss all of them."

Arguing that "truthful discussion of public issues" was essential in a democracy, he gave as examples of "falsifications"

> that the President of the United States telephoned to Mussolini and Hitler to sell Czechoslovakia down the River;
> that the unfortunate unemployed of the nation are going to be driven into concentration camps;
> that the social security funds of the Government of the United States will not be in existence when the workers of today become old enough to apply for them;
> that the election of the present Government means the end of American democracy within four years.
> I think they know, and I know we know that all these statements are false.

Then, after a long discussion of economic conditions, including a litany about what it was like "back in 1932" with a lot of factual statements about economic conditions but no mention of unemployment, the president provided one of those light touches that so often punctuated his serious speeches.

> Last Sunday morning I had a good laugh, when I read the following in the financial section of The New York *Times*—a paper which is reputed not to love me too much.
>
> This is what a writer on the financial section of the New York *Times* said, I quote: "The Federal Reserve Bank in the week added another point to its index of production for September and the figure now stands at one hundred and twenty-five or thirteen and a half per cent above the 1929 average"—mind you, not the 1932 average, but the 1929 average. I quote further: "Dreams of business 'flat on its back' must come from smoking campaign cigars or else the speakers are talking about some other country."
>
> Wouldn't it be nice if the editorial writers of the New York *Times* could get acquainted with its own business experts?

(The paper had endorsed Roosevelt in both 1932 and 1936 but was backing Willkie in 1940. Charles Hurd's front-page story quoted what the president said about his paper in toto and without comment; the paper's editorial that day, "Mr. Roosevelt in Rebuttal," ignored it.) The President obviously enjoyed himself, and let everybody know it: "I am an old campaigner, and I love a good fight."[55]

The next day at the White House, Roosevelt, who slept on his train, which spent most of the night idle on a siding close to Washington, did not see reporters the next day. He gave a pointedly nonpartisan radio address to the *New York Herald Tribune* Forum focused on Lincoln's famous Cooper Union speech of 1860. The speech paralleled the challenge to American democracy in Lincoln's time with the present challenge to British democracy and closed with Lincoln's words: "Let us have faith that might makes right, and in that faith let us to the end dare to do our duty as we understand it."[56]

The big political news of October 25 came not from the White House but from the headquarters of the United Mine Workers (UMW), where John L. Lewis, in an address carried by the major networks, echoed many Republican attacks by denouncing Roosevelt as a dictator intent on war. Speaking as a private citizen, he pledged that if Roosevelt were reelected, it would be "the equivalent of a vote of no confidence and [I] will retire as president of the C.I.O. at its convention in November." In addition to attacking Roosevelt's foreign policy, Lewis hit at the president's failure to solve unemployment, claiming that even after all of the announced defense spending there would still be five million unemployed.

Roosevelt, typically, did not comment, but Steve Early announced that the president did not hear the speech and left any response to its foreign policy aspects to Secretary Hull, who denounced Lewis's charges as "baseless." The immediate fallout included much disarray among CIO leaders, none of whom had been apprised of Lewis's intentions, though his growing hostility to Roosevelt was quite apparent. At the convention of his miners that January, Lewis had predicted that the president would not run and that if he did, he would be defeated—after which "speaker after speaker" expressed confidence in both Roosevelt and Lewis. The AFL's William Green jeered at Lewis as "a general without an army." Despite its professed nonpartisan stance, most AFL unions supported Roosevelt, some of them, like Tobin's Teamsters, vociferously. The relatively few AFL unions that supported Willkie, such as Bill Hutchinson's Carpenters, were highly conservative, while most of the CIO unions who aligned with Willkie were led by left-wingers influenced by the Soviet Union's alliance with Germany. "White House sources" soon attributed Lewis's action to the president's rejection, in two recent meetings with the CIO chief, of several demands, including the removal of Sidney Hillman from his position as labor's representative on the NDAC, a position analogous to one held by Samuel Gompers during World War I.[57]

Roosevelt's second overtly political speech, in New York's familiar Madison Square Garden, was in many ways the bravura performance of the campaign. It was the final scheduled event of a fourteen-hour day in the Greater New York area, made more hectic by breaking news of the further expansion of war in Europe by the Italian invasion of Greece. On four occasions, Roosevelt paused to take telephone calls from Hull and Undersecretary Welles in the State Department as they prepared the documents that Roosevelt was required by the Neutrality Act to sign personally. The president was greeted by a crowd of fifty thousand on arrival in Newark just before nine after an overnight train trip from Washington. He soon proceeded to Staten Island via the Bayonne Bridge to begin his fifty-eight-mile journey through all five New York boroughs. The seat of honor next to the president in the open car was most often filled by Mayor La Guardia, who several times relinquished his place to various Democrats and once to New York's archbishop Francis J. Spellman (1889–1967). A ferry escorted by two of the new torpedo boats took the president to Brooklyn, where Roosevelt participated in the groundbreaking for the Brooklyn-Battery Tunnel; other major stops were for dedications of public Hunter College in Manhattan, the almost completed Thirty-Eighth Street Tunnel to Queens, and La Guardia Field, all federally funded. The final stop was at Catholic Fordham University in the Bronx, after which the president went to his train parked in the nearby New York Central yards for dinner and a rest. In a demonstration of party loyalty, Jim Farley went to Roosevelt's train and along with his successor in the party, Ed Flynn, rode in the president's car and appeared onstage with him at the Garden.

Roosevelt spoke for about forty-five minutes to twenty-two thousand, while another twenty thousand listened to an amplified version outside. He improvised a paragraph in which he spoke of his telephone conversations with "the Department of State and with the Secretary of State, Cordell Hull," about the new war and was "quite sure that you will feel the same sorrow in your hearts that I feel—sorrow for the Italian people and the Grecian people." Then he began his attack: "Tonight I take up . . . the far from disagreeable duty of answering major campaign falsifications with facts. Last week . . . I nailed the falsehood about some fanciful secret treaties. . . . I now brand as false the statement being made by Republican campaign orators, day after day and night after night, that the rearming of America is slow, that it is hamstrung and impeded, that it will never be able to meet threats from abroad." After defending the administration's rearmament program and praising by name Knudsen, Stettinius, and others of the NDAC, he began to criticize individual Republican leaders—but never mentioning Willkie—indicting them "out of their own mouths" by comparing what they said about defense "in the days before this election year" and what they were presently saying. He began by quoting the ranking House Republican on its Committee on Foreign Affairs, Hamilton Fish, who said, "The facts are that we have the largest and most powerful Navy." He then quoted "the only living ex-President" in 1938, "We shall be expending nine hundred million dollars," and followed that with similar quotations from "Republican leader Senator Vandenberg" in the same year and "Republican leader Senator Taft in February 1940." "Until the present political campaign opened, Republican leaders, in and out of the Congress shouted from the house-tops that our defenses were fully adequate. Today they proclaim that this administration has starved our armed forces, that our Navy in anemic, our Army puny, our air forces perilously weak. Yes, it is a remarkable somersault. I wonder if the election could have anything to do with it." The president then talked at length about the party votes in Congress on a number of defense and foreign policy matters, and then came what he clearly regarded as the line of the speech. Speaking about the vote repealing the arms embargo that allowed arms to be shipped to embattled Britain: "The Act was passed by Democratic votes but it was over the opposition of Republican leaders. And just to name a few, the following Republican leaders, among many others, voted against the Act: Senators McNary, Vandenberg, Nye, and Johnson; now wait, a perfectly beautiful rhythm—Congressmen Martin, Barton, and Fish." (In uttering the first two names of the trio the president parodied his own broad *a* by stressing it and followed with the terse utterance of the third name. The audience laughed.) After a paragraph of explaining that "now at the eleventh hour they have discovered what we knew all along"—that it was good American defense policy—Roosevelt added: "Great Britain and a lot of other nations would never have received one ounce of help from us—if the decision had been left to [here the pause was longer and the emphasis even more pronounced] Martin, Barton, and Fish." The audience roared.

The rest of the speech was largely a defense of the administration's defense program. Roosevelt listed what he had done and not done in his successful efforts to keep America out of war, ending on his customary religious note: "We guard ourselves against all evils—spiritual as well as material—which may beset us. We guard against the forces of anti-Christian aggression which may attack us from without, and the forces of ignorance and fear which may corrupt us from within. We go forward with firm faith. And we shall continue to go forward in peace."[58]

It can be argued, with some justice, that to make fun of a person's name is vulgar, unworthy of a president. But real humor is so rare in politics that when a candidate can use it successfully to get voters to laugh at the opposition, electoral success is, if not guaranteed, made more likely. When Roosevelt used the phrase—once—in the speech at Boston in Martin's state two nights later, the audience, having heard the New York speech, chanted the three names along with him.

The evening's triumph in New York was marred by an ugly incident. After the speech, Steve Early, prevented by police from boarding the president's train, parked in an underground siding in Penn Station, drove his knee between the legs of James Sloan, a forty-two-year-old African American uniformed New York City police officer, injuring him badly enough for him to take sick leave. He had undergone a hernia operation four months before. As Early first recounted it, he had been stopped by two white officers, and when Sloan joined them he said that "his knee came against the man's body." Democrats were concerned about the possible harm done to their campaign, and Republicans tried to make political hay.

Joe Louis, campaigning for Willkie, arrived with reporters at Sloan's bedside three days after the incident and was disappointed to learn that Sloan was a Democrat who would vote for Roosevelt. The policeman told reporters, "If anyone thinks they can turn me against our great President who had done so much for my race because of this thing, they are greatly mistaken." Roosevelt never commented publicly on the incident, though Eleanor made excuses for Early, blaming his temper.

Early insisted that he had done nothing wrong and got several members of the lily-white presidential press corps who allegedly witnessed the affray to depose statements of support. Almost a month later at a White House press conference, as part of his preconference banter with reporters, Roosevelt discussed a painting that, he said, was supposed to represent a fighting Irish Democrat.

> Q: I see a picture of Steve (Mr. Early) coming out of the station, Mr. President. (Prolonged laughter)
> MR. EARLY: Knee Action. (More laughter)[59]

Of course, not a word of the byplay was published.

Roosevelt might have gone straight to Boston, where he would speak in less than forty-eight hours, but he headed right back to Washington, where the first draft numbers were to be drawn the next day. At noon in the War Department auditorium, draft director Dykstra introduced the president with cabinet members, members of Congress, and other civilian and military officials in attendance. In his brief broadcast remarks, Roosevelt said that there was "no fanfare—no blowing of bugles or beating of drums" because it was a "solemn occasion . . . mustering all our resources, manhood, and industry and wealth" to defend the nation." He noted the "tragic circumstances" overseas that had "forced . . . our nation . . . to take measures for total defense."

After crediting Congress with the decision for "selective service" as both the "most democratic" and "most efficient" method, he described the process, noting that "less than 5 per cent" of the 16.4 million registered would be called. He then read endorsing paragraphs from three national religious leaders, a Protestant, a Jew, and a Roman Catholic, none of whom referenced the Sixth Commandment, though the Protestant expressed thanks that the law recognized "the rights of sincere conscientious objectors."

The process began when a blindfolded War Secretary Stimson picked a small capsule from a huge bowl containing nine thousand capsules and handed it to Roosevelt. He opened it, took out the slip, and read the numbers "1–5–8." Other cabinet members each drew one number, and then lesser officials took over and a draft officials made the announcements in a process that continued through the night and into the next morning. Roosevelt spent much of the day and evening in conferences and consultations with Hull and Welles, and before he left on his train for New England shortly before midnight he heard, or heard about, Ambassador Joe Kennedy's broadcast from New York branding as false the charge that Roosevelt had made any secret agreements with Churchill and endorsing his reelection.[60]

In southern New England the next morning, Roosevelt spoke in New Haven and Hartford, Connecticut, and Worcester, Massachusetts, and inspected Hartford's Pratt and Whitney aircraft engine plant. His talks in all three places focused on the false fears that Republican orators were raising. More than once, he repeated and referred to his famous phrase about fear from the 1933 inaugural. In Hartford Roosevelt made what the *Times*' White House correspondent called "one of the sharpest statements of his campaign." The president, noting that the city was "the great insurance center of the United States," charged that "many insurance company executives were spreading fear [among] policy holders in every part of the United States," which he called "the most dastardly and the most unpatriotic action of any Americans I know of."

He spoke to large crowds everywhere and to occasional hecklers. In Boston, when the president's car arrived at the apartment building where his son John was living and with whom he would have dinner, students in a Massachusetts Institute of Technology (MIT) fraternity house next door set off a "We Want Willkie" chant.[61]

The speech in the Boston Garden was controversial before it was given, and it has remained so. Sherwood described a typical speech-revision scene on the campaign train: "Roosevelt . . . sat in a low-backed armchair in his private car, the latest draft of the speech on his lap, with Missy LeHand, Grace Tully, Hopkins, Rosenman and me, all working with carbon copies." At a crucial point in the discussion of a passage meant to reassure mothers about the treatment their drafted sons might receive, Hopkins handed the president a telegram from Ed Flynn, repeating earlier requests that assurances be given that "their boys" were not going to fight a war. Sherwood wrote:

> "But how often do they expect me to say that?" Roosevelt asked. "It's in the Democratic platform and I've repeated it a hundred times."
> Whereupon I remarked, "I know it, Mr. President, but they don't seem to have heard you the first time. Evidently you've got to say it again—and again—and again."
> So it was put in as follows.
> "And while I am talking to you mothers and fathers, I give you one more assurance.
> I have said this before, but I shall say it again and again
> and again.
> Your boys are not going to be sent into any foreign wars."

Rosenman reminded them that the Democratic platform included the words *except in case of attack,* but the president brushed that off as unnecessary. "'It's not necessary,' he said. 'It's implied clearly. If we're attacked it's no longer a foreign war.'"[62]

The Boston speech was a long one, revealing new defense plans, attacking Joe Martin's record at great length, and criticizing Republican agricultural politics. But the passage about "your boys" would become a favorite for anti-Roosevelt speakers and writers and is frequently commented upon by historians, sometimes quoting a purported Willkie statement made while listening to the speech on the radio: "That hypocritical son of a bitch. This is going to beat me."[63]

If Willkie said that, it was he who was the hypocrite. The GOP candidate had made the same promise, in the same city, just nineteen days earlier, saying that if he were elected, "Our boys shall stay out of European wars," and other anti-Roosevelt orators, including John L. Lewis, had quoted that statement with approval. Willkie's biographer Steve Neal writes that when he switched from supporting Roosevelt's foreign policies to attacking them, he "buckled to expediency." When asked during his 1941 testimony in favor of Lend-Lease before the Senate Foreign Relations Committee about his charge that if Roosevelt won, the United States would be at war by April 1941, Willkie sloughed it off as "a bit of campaign oratory."[64]

The question that Roosevelt's remarks at Boston raise is to what degree the president was deliberately misleading the American people about his foreign policy intentions. Rosenman, a devoted supporter, argues legalistically that "the promise in the Boston speech . . . was oversimplified, but even that promise was kept. Certainly no one can say that the Japanese war was a 'foreign' war after Pearl Harbor, or that the European war was a 'foreign' war after Germany declared war upon us."[65]

Nothing better demonstrates the deliberately duplicitous nature of many of Roosevelt's political statements about war and peace after the fall of France exposed the weakness of the Western democracies than the tortured language necessary to support the Boston statement. If, instead of making the question whether Roosevelt broke a promise or "lied to the American people," one asks, "Did Roosevelt deliberately mislead the American people about the likelihood of his various foreign policy actions involving aid to the Allies embroiling the United States in combat?" the only possible answer is, "Yes, he did." Whether that duplicity was justified is the kind of question that Dutch historian Pieter Geyl said involves not an answer but "a debate without end."

Had he survived to create his own version of history, Roosevelt might have argued that if he had not misled the American people about the eventual likely results of his policies, it would have been impossible to gain majority popular support for such executive decisions as the destroyer-for-bases deal or congressional support for the draft and would most likely have led to his defeat in 1940 and the creation of a Republican majority in Congress unlikely to take many of the measures that won the war. One lesson that his presidential successors seem to have drawn is that it is permissible to mislead the American people as long as one can argue that it is for their own good.

Probably none of the events in the final six days between the Boston speech and election day greatly affected the result. Roosevelt went straight back to Washington, where he conferred with Hull about the Italian invasion of Greece and went out to Bethesda to dedicate the new National Institute of Health building, where he spoke about the role of health in the nation's defense: "We cannot be a strong nation unless we are a healthy nation." He anticipated and went on to speak of a coming mobilization of the nation's "medical and health resources . . . to serve" both the civilian and the military sectors. He tried to protect this expansion of the federal health role from political attack by going out of his way to deny any intent to socialize medicine: "Neither the American people nor their Government intends to socialize medical practice any more than they plan to socialize industry. In American life the family doctor, the general practitioner, performs a service which we rely upon and which we trust as a nation."[66]

At his regular Friday-morning press conference, he laid out his hectic schedule for the last four days of campaigning: major addresses in Brooklyn and Cleveland, with a lot of whistle-stops, and a final talk on election eve from Hyde Park. Later that day, he left to give his traditional last-Saturday-before-election speech in Brooklyn's Academy of Music. With Farley again in his entourage, Roosevelt made another attack speech, referring, without mentioning names, to the spectacle of radicals and union-hating industrialists united in support of Wendell Willkie, which he twice called an "unholy alliance." As he had done at Hartford, he attacked the insurance companies but made his charge against them clearer. "As an example of [their] doctrine of fear, certain insurance companies are sending letters to their policyholders warning them that if this administration stays in office, their policies will shrink in value. . . . The fact is that the very existence of most of these insurance companies I speak of was saved by this Administration in 1933. They are today more solvent than they ever were before."

After quoting a prominent Philadelphia lawyer's Republican campaign speech: "'The President's only supporters,' he said, 'are paupers who earn less than $1,200 a year and aren't worth *that*, and the Roosevelt family.'" (The minimum wage in 1940 was 30 cents an hour, which could provide an annual wage of $600. The average "full-time employee" earned $1,291 that year.) Roosevelt commented, "'Paupers' who are not worth their salt—there speaks the true sentiment of the Republican leadership in this year of grace. Can the Republican leadership deny that all this all-too-prevailing Republican sentiment is a direct, vicious, unpatriotic appeal to class hatred and class contempt? That, my friends, is what I am fighting against with all my heart and soul." He then proceeded, in seven parallel sentences, to say what he was fighting for:

> . . . for a country in which all men and women have equal rights. against the revival of Government by special interests.
> . . . for the rights of the little man as well as the big man—for the weak as well as the strong, for those who are helpless as well those who can help themselves.
> . . . to keep this Nation prosperous and at peace.
> . . . to keep our people out of foreign wars.
> . . . for these great and good causes.
> . . . to defend them against the power and might of those who now rise up to challenge them.

To conclude his speech, he added: "And I will not stop fighting."[67]

After his speech, the president went directly to his train for the run to Cleveland and the fifth and final speech. At a pause in Rochester, New York, he told the crowd at the station that he was glad it was raining because it had rained when he was there in 1936. He pointed out that in four years as governor and seven and a half years as president, he had never called out troops to quell disturbances, adding that "it seems to me that a fellow with that kind of record . . . must have his feet on the ground rather than his finger on the trigger." At Buffalo he left his train for two hours, inspecting two aircraft plants and the Bethlehem Steel works in Lackawanna, and spoke to a crowd of forty thousand in the city center. After complaining about Republican misrepresentations of his intentions, he said flatly, "Your President says this country is not going to war."

The Cleveland speech, though it contained attack elements, was of a somewhat different nature than the other four, perhaps because his writers were working from a draft provided by journalist Dorothy Thompson. She had originally supported Willkie but abandoned him when he began attacking the president's foreign policy. Rosenman later judged the resulting speech the best he heard in seventeen years of Roosevelt's speeches: "Although it was a campaign speech it was pitched on a level far above the political battle."

In packed Convention Hall, Roosevelt made a direct appeal for reelection. "For the past seven years I have had the high honor and the grave responsibility of leadership of the American people. In those seven years, the American people have marched forward, out of a wilderness of depression and despair. They have marched forward right up to the very threshold of the future—a future which holds the fulfillment of our hopes for real freedom, real prosperity, real peace. I want that march to continue for four more years. And for that purpose, I am asking your vote of confidence."

In the attack phase of the speech, the president made specific the main elements of the "unholy alliance" he had warned of in Brooklyn, "the forces of dictatorship in our land—on one hand, the Communists, and on the other, the Girdlers." Cleveland was steel magnate Tom Girdler's hometown, and many in the audience worked in his plants.

In his positive peroration, Roosevelt projected a vision of America with a repeated Whitmanesque phrase, "I see an America":

> . . . where factory workers are not discarded after they reach their prime, where there is no endless chain of poverty from generation to generation, where impoverished farm hands do not become homeless wanderers, where monopoly does not make youth a beggar for a job.
> . . . whose rivers and valleys and lakes . . . are protected as the rightful heritage of all the people.
> . . . where small business really has a chance to flourish . . .
> . . . of great cultural and educational opportunities for all . . . where the wheels of trade and private industry continue to turn . . .
> . . . with peace in the ranks of labor.
> . . . [where] the workers are really free and—through their great unions undominated by any outside force, or by any dictator within—can take their proper place at the council table with the owners and managers of business.
> . . . [where] those who have reached the evening of their life shall live out their years in peace and security.

Then, for the only time on the campaign trail, he referred to the "third term," a phrase never far from the lips of his opponents, but did not use those words.

> There is a great storm raging now, a storm that makes things harder for the world. And that storm, which did not start in this land of ours, is the true reason that I would like to stick by these people of ours until we reach the clear, sure footing ahead.
> We will make it—we will make it before the next term is over.
> We will make it; and the world, we hope, will make it, too.
> When that term is over there will be another President, and many more Presidents in the years to come, and I think that, in the years to come, that word "President" will be a word to cheer the hearts of common men and women everywhere.

In that passage, Roosevelt gave a first overt glimpse of his vision of American world leadership. Returning to domestic concerns, he proclaimed, "Our future belongs to us Americans. It is for us to design it; it is for us to build it. . . . Always the heart and soul of our people will be the heart of the common man—the men and women who never have ceased to believe in democracy, who never have ceased to love their families, their homes and their country. The spirit of the common man is the spirit of peace and good will. It is the spirit of God. And in His faith is the strength of all America."[68]

The president's train took him to Washington, where he conferred with Hull and Welles, presumably about the situation in Greece, where the British were now assisting the Greeks against the Italians. He also issued a nonpartisan statement directing that all "federal employees be given sufficient time from their duties to" vote and urged that "all other employers grant the same privilege." He left that night for Hyde Park, where he toured his old three-county senatorial district, speaking briefly in Rhinebeck, Kingston, Newburgh, Beacon, and Poughkeepsie, and made a ten minute election-eve address from his home. He was introduced from Washington by Secretary Hull as "the President" whose "continued leadership" was necessary "in the critical days and months which lie ahead."

Speaking from the small study where he had done his homework as a boy and with Sara, Franklin Jr., his wife, and Harry Hopkins as audience, he spoke "not of partisan politics but of the Nation."

> As I sit here tonight with my own family, I think of all the other American families. . . . They have eaten their suppers. . . . [T]hey will be able to sleep in their homes tonight. . . . Tomorrow . . . they will be free to choose their own leaders. . . . And I cannot help but think of the families in other lands . . . living in homes like ours. On some of these homes bombs of destruction may be dropping even as I speak to you. Across the seas life has gone underground. . . . We thank God that we live in . . . peace, that we are not in war and that we propose and expect to continue to live out our lives in peace—under the peaceful light of heaven.

He then spoke of voting and its importance. "Dictators have forgotten—or perhaps they never knew—the basis on which democratic Government is founded: that the opinion of all the people, freely formed and freely expressed. . . . The service of democracy is the birthright of every citizen. The white and the colored; the Protestant, the Catholic, the Jew; the sons and daughters of every country in the world." Apart from urging participation—"a free election is of no use to the man who is too indifferent to vote"—the president made no appeal for votes, saying only that "after the ballots are counted, the United States of America will still be united." He ended his talk with a rather long old prayer, asking "the guidance of God for our nation." He had found it in a late-nineteenth-century prayer book.

There was one last-minute "falsification" to be countered. The White House staff in Poughkeepsie issued a statement that "the President had been informed" that "circulars have been given to State and municipal employees" about a "bill pending in Congress" that would take away their pensions and those of school-teachers. This was denounced as "another unethical and deliberate misrepresentation of fact," and Roosevelt stated "categorically" that "no federal law" would endanger any state pension.[69]

On election day, the president, along with his wife and his mother, voted in the town hall a little after noon, posed for pictures, and returned home. Just before midnight, Roosevelt, accompanied by Sara, Eleanor, his youngest son, and two of his daughters-in-law, came out on the porch of his mother's home to greet a traditional torchlight parade that had come down from the village to celebrate what was already a clear victory, even though the West Coast results were not yet in. "We are facing difficult days in this country," he told the crowd, "but I think that you will find me in the future the same Franklin Roosevelt you have known a great many years."

A few minutes later, at his headquarters in Manhattan's Hotel Commodore, Wendell Willkie appeared briefly before campaign workers and told them not to quit, adding, despite convincing evidence to the contrary, that victory would come. At 1:30 a.m., he sent down word that he was going to bed and that there would be no statement until morning. That morning he sent the president a cool congratulatory telegram. But by Armistice Day, Willkie, in a radio address aimed at the millions who supported him, called upon them to be a "loyal opposition." He generally supported Roosevelt's foreign policy, while calling for reduced spending on everything but defense and for higher taxes. Speculation that he would openly work with the president to support such policies soon came to pass.[70]

The election results were startling. Rather than the relatively close election that almost everyone expected, Roosevelt carried thirty-eight of forty-eight states, won 449 electoral votes to only 82 for Willkie, and captured almost 5 million more votes, receiving 27.3 million to 22.3 million for Willkie. In terms of percentage of votes, the president received 54.3 percent to Willkie's 44.5 percent. As the prognosticator in chief admitted in his postelection press conference, he badly underestimated his appeal. He told the press that "I never was as worried as some people were." He had sealed a prediction of 340 electoral votes in an envelope in August, "and I saw no reason at any time in the campaign to change it."

Q: Mr. President what State surprised you?
THE PRESIDENT: Well, about one hundred and ten votes did.
Q: Would you care to identify them further?
THE PRESIDENT: No.

The two major preelection polls reported quite different results. The Gallup poll, as of noon on November 3, gave Roosevelt 52 percent of the vote, "not considered enough for certain victory." This conclusion was supported by some fictitious history. "Political history indicates that when a Democratic candidate has 52 per cent of the popular vote it is an even race because of the surplus Democratic popular majorities in the South." But no previous Democratic presidential candidate had ever received 52 percent of the vote, although Gallup published false figures for Wilson in 1916 and Cleveland in 1888 to back up his theory. Neither of those two-term Democrats ever received even 50 percent of the vote, despite four victories between them.

The *Fortune* poll, directed by Elmo Roper (1900–1971), a loyal Democrat except for a defection to Norman Thomas in 1932, was very close to the actual result, reporting 55.2 percent for Roosevelt as of October 31, but added that a trend toward Willkie was gaining. It declared that the range of possibilities ran from "a substantial but not landslide victory for Roosevelt" to "a narrow victory for Willkie in the Electoral College, without a popular majority."[71]

Democrats were also overwhelming winners in the congressional elections, gaining seven seats in the House as Republicans lost two, while in the Senate Republicans picked up three seats. Thus, Democratic majorities remained robust: they outnumbered Republicans 268–162 in the House and 66–28 in the Senate.

Many, perhaps most, recent historians, writing within a tradition of late–New Deal decline and decay, have failed to accord Roosevelt the kudos he deserves for a brilliantly conceived and almost flawlessly executed election strategy. David M. Kennedy, for example, within a chapter titled "The Agony of Neutrality," stresses Willkie's amateurish blunders and the fact that Roosevelt's majority was reduced from the 1936 landslide. But Roosevelt's clear triumph in a comfortable victory was achieved despite his flaunting the third-term tradition and pushing through two potentially unpopular measures that he deemed necessary, the destroyers-for-bases deal and the institution of a peacetime draft. One respected British scholar goes so far as to say that Roosevelt's margin was "only 55 percent," even though only one other Democrat, Lyndon Johnson in 1964, has ever reached that mark.[72] The 1940 triumph was the most impressive of Roosevelt's four presidential victories not only because of the circumstances but also because it was the only time he faced a presidential opponent who was a potential winner. Many of Willkie's blunders were forced errors; desperately anxious to meet his rival head-on, he was clearly discomfited when Roosevelt ignored him. His resulting overexposure and eventual exhaustion—the *Times'* Jim Hagerty had counted 550 speeches near the end of the campaign—were encouraged by the president's strategy and tactics; he was not dubbed "Champion Campaigner" for nothing.

Roosevelt returned to Washington Thursday morning to be greeted at Union Station by Eleanor, who had come the day before; Henry and Ilo Wallace; and a host of lesser officials. The president and the vice president-elect were driven to the White House in an open car, seated side by side with their wives in front of them. A crowd estimated at two hundred thousand lined Pennsylvania Avenue, and a large crowd on the White House lawn persisted in cheering until both couples had made two appearances on the North Portico of the White House. The president held an informal reception for all employees of the White House and its executive offices. He received just two official visitors, Joe Kennedy, who came to congratulate him, and Arthur Purvis, the British purchasing agent, who came to say good-bye before flying to London. He had his weekly lunch with Henry Morgenthau and met with the NDAC in the afternoon.

At his Friday press conference, postponed until just after noon because the president slept late, in addition to his remarks on the election, Roosevelt announced that he had established a "rule of thumb": for most items needed by both Britain and the United States, current production would be fifty-fifty.[73]

In the days and weeks that followed, while he undertook relatively routine activities—authorizing an expansion of the lending authority of the Federal Housing Authority (FHA) by a third, which would allow an additional 250,000 homes to be financed; laying a wreath at Arlington; sending greetings to the AFL Convention and urging labor unity; and signing the required proclamation of neutrality in the war between Italy and Greece. Privately, Roosevelt was contemplating future steps to aid Britain. Churchill sent him an eloquent plea for more help as soon as the election results were known, telling him that he sought "the full, fair, and free play of your mind on the world issues now at stake. . . . We are entering upon a somber phase of what must evidently be a protracted and broadening war. . . . Things are afoot which will be remembered as long as the English language is spoken in any quarter of the globe."[74]

The president was in no hurry to respond. With a new mandate from the people, he could now consider bolder options. In a statement thanking the large number of persons who sent him congratulations on his victory, he took a dig at the newly formed isolationist America First Committee by pledging "to work shoulder to shoulder with all who place true Americanism above all other considerations." He told reporters that on an impending four-day cruise on the *Potomac* he intended to catch up on his sleep and read official documents. The cruise took him down to the York River in Virginia, where he fished for striped bass and let eleven days pass between press conferences. He had canceled the usual Thanksgiving in Warm Springs because it was too far from Washington and spent a quiet private holiday at Hyde Park instead.[75]

Although Roosevelt had been aware for some time that Britain would soon not have the funds to finance its war orders in the United States, it was the British ambassador who thrust the topic into the public domain. While the president was still at Hyde Park, Lord Lothian, flying back from London via Lisbon after a month's stay in Britain, said bluntly in a press conference at La Guardia Field that Britain, which had spent four billion dollars for war supplies in the United States since 1939, was running out of dollars. It would need financial aid during 1941 if it was to continue its purchases. Lothian's otherwise optimistic report on Britain's prospects included the flat statement, given in an answer to a question, that "England definitely does not need men." Lothian thus put in play what would become the great American political question of 1941: how to enable the stream of American aid to Britain to continue when the embattled nation could no longer adhere to the cash-and-carry policy required not only by the amended Neutrality Act but also by the Johnson Act of 1934, which barred loans to nations in default on their World War I debts? (Those who read to its end the *New York Times* story on Lothian's press conference on an inside page learned that four of the eleven passengers on his plane were American army air force and navy officers returning from temporary observer duty in Britain.)

After Lothian met with Roosevelt in the White House, both denied that they had discussed financial aid. Roosevelt, of course, was aware of the problem and realized that it would require legislative approval, but he had not yet come up with a method for solving it.[76]

Other matters on the president's to-do list included the matter of paying, at least in part, for defense costs, which meant new taxes, about which preliminary end-of-November conferences with Morgenthau and congressional leaders were scheduled. In addition, there was the usual end-of-year work on the budget and the annual message, plus the preparation of the third inaugural address.

In his press conference at Hyde Park, Roosevelt had set out some principles for the next budget. His general policy would to be to cut nonmilitary public works "down to the bone" and to have many approved and fully planned projects "on the shelf." That way, when defense employment "comes to an end . . . we will be able . . . to take projects . . . off the shelf" and employ "laid-off defense workers to build them . . . preventing a serious depression." To that small group of regulars, he revealed, off the record, his increasing concern about sabotage in industrial plants from Communist workers. He explained the unobtrusive methods the government would use to help employers remove persons regarded as security risks without resorting to prosecutions in cases where there was not enough evidence to obtain convictions. At his very next conference, however, when asked to comment on a bill introduced in the House by conservative Howard Smith (D-VA) mandating life imprisonment for anyone convicted of industrial sabotage, Roosevelt's response was a quizzical "Only life imprisonment?" producing the expected laughter.[77]

After his brief Hyde Park Thanksgiving, the president spent less than a week in Washington before heading for warm weather. Some pieces of old business were taken care of, and staff work for the New Year was proceeding: he met with Norman Davis of the American Red Cross and New York banker Thomas W. Lamont about possible food relief for some nations on the European continent and with Knudsen about defense matters, and he approved lending another one hundred million dollars to China to aid in its war against Japan. He left on December 2 by train for Miami, where he boarded the cruiser USS *Tuscaloosa* for a twelve-day Caribbean cruise and inspection trip of some of the base sites gained in the destroyer deal.[78]

After an absolutely newsless press conference on the train going down, when for security reasons he did not reveal his itinerary but spoofed that he was "going to Christmas Island to buy Christmas cards and then . . . to Easter Island to buy Easter eggs," the president's train reached Miami. Roosevelt and his only guest, Harry Hopkins, plus Pa Watson, his naval aide Captain Daniel J. Callaghan, and Dr. McIntire went immediately aboard the *Tuscaloosa*, as did the president's newly acquired Scotch terrier, Fala. They sailed in the early afternoon of December 3, stopping at Guantánamo, then an American naval base, and then visited or observed base sites on the British islands of Jamaica, St. Lucia, Antigua, and Mayaguana in the Bahamas. The ship paused off French Martinique to receive a report from the American consul and the American naval officer stationed there to monitor French naval vessels, including the aircraft carrier *Bearn*, stagnating there, safe from German seizure.

In a touch of glamour, the former king of Great Britain, now Edward, Duke of Windsor and Governor of the Bahamas, was flown in a U.S. Navy flying boat for a conference and a lunch with the president aboard the *Tuscaloosa*. The two had met previously in 1919, when Edward, then Prince of Wales, visited Annapolis and Roosevelt was assistant secretary of the navy. Just before the duke left the *Tuscaloosa*, the president began a press conference with the three wire-service reporters who covered the trip from one of the accompanying destroyers. After Edward's departure, Roosevelt used a large chart to give the trio a mostly off-the-record briefing about the importance of the newly acquired bases. The next day, in harbor at Charleston, South Carolina, he held a brief press conference and invited the left-behind reporters to get trip details from their pool colleagues. Although Roosevelt seemed to deny having any notions about further aid to Britain in his postvoyage press conference at Charleston, this was not the case. The important and unreported event of the cruise was that Roosevelt had arrived at a solution for the problem of how to continue massive aid to a dollarless Britain. Hopkins later told Sherwood how Roosevelt devised the program known as Lend-Lease: "I began to get the idea that he was refueling, the way he so often does when he seems to be resting and carefree. . . . Then one evening, he suddenly came out with it—the whole program. He didn't seem to have a clear idea about how it could be done legally. But there wasn't a doubt in his mind that he'd find a way to do it."[79]

Roosevelt returned to Washington via Warm Springs, where he spent the day driving around in his little car. At a luncheon for the patients and guests, after Basil O'Connor introduced him saying that it was like a "third Thanksgiving," Roosevelt in a jocular mood commented casually that perhaps a third Thanksgiving was a "good idea" and that if turkey had not been served, he would have carved O'Connor. He went on to say that he hoped to come back in March, "if the world survives." The *New York Times* and other papers turned this into a front-page headline: "Roosevelt Hints of Crisis in Saying 'If World Survives.'" Wire-service editors, starved of real news about the president, sent reporters scampering through the halls of Congress asking congressmen what they made of the statement, even though the president's leisurely return to Washington was clear evidence that there was no crisis. Leaving from the Warm Springs station that evening, he qualified his return more moderately, saying that he would return in March, "if things go all right."

On the morning after the president's return, Morgenthau testified before a House committee that British officials had told him their country could not order any more war materials in the United States unless it received financial assistance. (Hull and Knudsen had previously made similar statements.) Morgenthau then went to his customary weekly lunch with Roosevelt. In his regular press conference late that afternoon, Roosevelt observed that "a very overwhelming number of Americans" believed "that the best immediate defense of the United States is the success of Great Britain in defending itself." Thus, "from a selfish point of view . . . we should do everything to help the British Empire to defend itself."

In the especially long briefing of some forty-three hundred words, most of which were in presidential monologues about what came to be called Lend-Lease,[80] although Roosevelt did not then use the phrase, he voiced some form of *lend* five times, *loan* twice, *borrow* twice, and *lease* once. The president reduced the complex problems of getting war materials to the British into homely terms that most people could understand, insisting the whole time that it was not a matter of money when in fact that was precisely the problem.

> Suppose my neighbor's home catches fire, and I have a length of garden hose four or five hundred feet away; but, my Heaven[s], if he can take my garden hose and connect it up with his hydrant, I may help him to put out his fire. Now, what do I do? I don't say to him before that operation, "Neighbor, my garden hose cost me $15; you have to pay me $15 for it." What is the transaction that goes on? I don't want $15—I want my garden hose back after the fire is over. All right. If it goes through the fire all right, intact, without any damage to it, he gives it back to me and thanks me very much for the use of it. But suppose it gets smashed up—holes in it—during the fire; we don't have to have too much formality about it, but I say to him, "I was glad to lend you that hose; I see I can't use it any more, it's all smashed up." He says, "How many feet of it were there?" I tell him, "There were 150 feet of it." He says, "All right, I will replace it." Now, if I get a nice garden hose back, I am in pretty good shape.

Since the conference was "off the record," that passage could not be quoted but was paraphrased, and the words *garden hose* or just *hose* were generally used by the press. Roosevelt's thoughts were on page 1, his treasury secretary's on page 10.[81]

At his Friday-morning press conference on December 20, the president insisted, "There *isn't* any news. In other words I am not ready on anything." A reporter who had good information asked whether a "change of defense setup" would be announced later in the day and got the reply, "I can't make any promises: I don't know." A conference with congressional leaders produced agreement that Congress would take up the problem of financing aid to Britain at the start of the new session. After an afternoon meeting with the NDAC, Roosevelt was able to call another press conference at five o'clock to announce that he would create in the Office of Emergency Management—the body provided for in the 1939 Reorganization Plan and placed in the EOP but not previously activated—a new body, the Office of Production Management (OPM), and put it at the apex of the defense establishment. But it was run by four old familiar faces: Knudsen as director, the two cabinet-service secretaries Stimson and Knox, plus Hillman. The issue holding up agreement had been whether Hillman would be in the top group. That two immigrant workingmen, the Danish-born Knudsen and the Lithuanian-born Hillman, could rise to such positions of power was an extreme example of the kind of mobility that sometimes happened in Roosevelt's America.

While much stayed the same (the NDAC remained in existence and Knudsen and Hillman were both still on it), Roosevelt explained that "from now on the responsibility . . . the three important things—production, purchasing and priorities—will be in the Office of Production Management." But the real motive for the change was political. Roosevelt laid it out early in the conference before mentioning any of the names of the appointees. He railed—off the record—at "editorial writers who don't know a thing about government business but are willing to write about it. . . . As I said before, it is impossible to find any one 'Czar' or 'Poobah' or 'Akhoond of Swats.' . . . Therefore, the amateurs who talk about sole responsibility in one man, prove their ignorance. Nobody ever found that paragon yet, and as I explained the other day, nobody did in the World War either."

There was, of course, one person who *did*, in the final analysis, have the last word. Just before the conference ended, a reporter asked:

Q: Mr. President, you don't have to give the final approval?
THE PRESIDENT: No, no, but believe me, if they make some kind of a decision which goes wrong and I say that it is contrary to the national interest, I will probably call them in and say, "Here, here, what is this?"

At the time the president spoke, final details of the OPM had not yet been worked out. Only at the end of the first week of the new year were the necessary orders issued.[82]

In a Christmas Eve ceremony on the Ellipse behind the White House before a crowd of five thousand who had come to see the lighting of the national Christmas tree, the president spoke informally before his broadcast began. For next Christmas, he said, "if we are here," he and Mrs. Roosevelt had spoken that morning about moving the ceremony to the South Lawn of the White House and having "you good people" come into the White House grounds so he could speak from the White House porch.

In his brief broadcast Christmas message, Roosevelt spoke of the difficulties of celebrating Christmas with much of the world at war and testified to his own belief in the idea of progress.

> Sometimes we who have lived through the strifes and the hates of a quarter century wonder if this old world of ours has abandoned the ideals of the Brotherhood of Man. Sometimes we ask if contention and anger in our own midst in America are a portent of disunion and disaster. Sometimes we fear that the selfishness of the individual is more and more controlling in our lives. . . . We must keep on striving for a better and a more happy world. . . . Compared with the days when Charles Dickens wrote the Christmas Carol, we see a definite betterment. We do not claim attainment, and we recognize that there is much—oh, so much—to do.

Yet for large numbers of Americans with more money in their pockets than at any time since the Depression set in, it was a Christmas marked by "an orgy of spending."[83]

The day after Christmas, Rosenman and Sherwood moved into the White House, where they worked with Harry Hopkins on a Fireside Chat to be delivered on Sunday evening, December 29. The preparation for the chat was intensive, and it was preceded by an unusual amount of planted news about its contents. Steve Early told reporters that it would be comparable in importance to the first chat, on banking, in 1933. Before the fact, the *New York Times* estimated the president's radio audience at eighty million, some three-fifths of the population, and in a postspeech story New York theater owners reported that their normal Sunday-night audiences were down 50 percent. Even the venue and audience were special: President Roosevelt broadcast from the Diplomatic Reception Room before friends, government officials, and Hollywood's most glamorous couple, Carole Lombard and Clark Gable.

Roosevelt began what he said was a talk on "national security" by assuring his listeners that his "purpose" was "to keep you now, and your children later, and your grandchildren much later, out of a last-ditch war for American independence." Playing off the advance publicity, he reminded them of his talk on the banking crisis "eight years ago." "I had before my eyes the picture of all those Americans with whom I was talking. I saw the workmen in the mills, the mines, the factories; the girl behind the counter; the small shopkeeper; the farmer doing his spring plowing; the widows and the old men wondering about their life's savings." He reminded them that they had met that crisis with "courage and realism" and would meet the new crisis the same way: "Never before since Jamestown and Plymouth Rock has our American civilization been in such danger as now."

The source of the danger he identified as "three powerful nations, two in Europe and one in Asia," but as he would not in a domestic campaign name his antagonist, in this foreign campaign he did not use Hitler's name but spoke of "Nazis" and of him as "the leader of the Nazis." "Only three weeks ago their leader stated this: 'There are two worlds that stand opposed to each other. . . . With this world we cannot ever reconcile ourselves. . . . I can beat any other power in the world.' So said the leader of the Nazis." Having established the threat, he turned to those who would deny it. "Some of our people like to believe that wars in Europe and in Asia are of no concern to us. But it is a matter of most vital concern to us that European and Asiatic war-makers should not gain control of the oceans which lead to this hemisphere." Turning to the purpose of the talk, he asked:

> Does anyone seriously believe that we need to fear attack anywhere in the Americas while a free Britain remains our most powerful naval neighbor in the Atlantic? Does anyone seriously believe, on the other hand, that we could rest easy if the Axis powers were our neighbors there?
>
> If Great Britain goes down, the Axis powers will control the continents of Europe, Asia, Africa, Australasia, and the high seas—and they will be in a position to bring enormous military and naval resources against this hemisphere. It is no exaggeration to say that all of us, in all the Americas, would be living at the point of a gun—a gun loaded with explosive bullets, economic as well as military.
>
> We should enter upon a new and terrible era in which the whole world, our hemisphere included, would be run by threats of brute force. To survive in such a world, we would have to convert ourselves permanently into a militaristic power on the basis of war economy.

After pointing out, as he had done before, the vulnerability of the United States to attack by air, he heaped scorn on those he called "the American appeasers" who

> ignore the warning to be found in the fate of Austria, Czechoslovakia, Poland, Norway, Belgium, the Netherlands, Denmark, and France. They tell you that the Axis powers are going to win anyway; that all this bloodshed in the world could be saved; that the United States might just as well throw its influence into the scale of a dictated peace, and get the best out of it that we can.
>
> They call it a "negotiated peace." Nonsense! Is it a negotiated peace if a gang of outlaws surrounds your community and on threat of extermination makes you pay tribute to save your own skins?

Such a dictated peace would be no peace at all. It would be only another armistice, leading to the most gigantic armament race and the most devastating trade wars in all history. And in these contests the Americas would offer the only real resistance to the Axis powers.

With all their vaunted efficiency, with all their parade of pious purpose in this war, there are still in their background the concentration camp and the servants of God in chains.

On the crucial question of America's going to war, joining what he now called a "war against an unholy alliance," Roosevelt retreated significantly from his campaign statements. He now said, a month and a half after the election, "there is far less chance of the United States getting into war, if we do all we can now to support the nations defending themselves against attack by the Axis than if we acquiesce in their defeat, submit tamely to an Axis victory, and wait our turn to be the object of attack in another war later on." Admitting that "there is risk in any course we may take," the president argued that his course, arming Britain, "involves the least risk now and the greatest hope for world peace in the future."

That admission, absent from his campaign utterances, was followed by a demonstrable falsehood. "There is no demand for sending an American Expeditionary Force outside our own borders. There is no intention by any member of your Government to send such a force. You can, therefore, nail any talk about sending armies to Europe as deliberate untruth." American military planners, including their civilian masters, had long assumed that eventually, the United States would become involved in a war with some or all of the Axis powers and hoped that the fighting would take place as far from the United States as possible.

After a long discussion of the effort and sacrifice that was needed to build and deliver the various implements of war, Roosevelt arrived at the key passage. "We must be the great arsenal of democracy. For us this is an emergency as serious as war itself. We must apply ourselves to our task with the same resolution, the same sense of urgency, the same spirit of patriotism and sacrifice as we would show were we at war."

Despite the attempt to invoke the spirit of the first Fireside Chat, this "Arsenal of Democracy" speech was really more like the first inaugural, when Roosevelt promised "to wage a war against the emergency [as if] we were in fact invaded by a foreign foe." Unlike most Fireside Chats, this talk was essentially oratorical rather than conversational. It marks the beginning of the successful fight to provide more aid to Britain on an unprecedented scale and a much clearer commitment of the United States to an aggressive interventionist position in world affairs, to which it still adheres.[84]

5 Sailing toward War
1941

ROOSEVELT WAS QUICK OFF THE MARK. In his first 1941 press conference, three days before Congress met, he announced that so many ships were being sunk that "we have begun taking the first steps toward" building two hundred merchant ships, which would cost between $300 and $350 million. To get the program started, he would use $36 million of his $200 million contingent fund. He mentioned that he expected to announce his new ambassador to Britain in the next week and added, "but in the meantime I am asking Harry Hopkins to go over as my personal representative for a very short trip to the other side, just to maintain—I suppose that is the best word for it—personal contact between me and the British government."

Asked whether Hopkins had "any special mission," the president said "NO, no, no!"; any title?, "No, no!" Asked if Hopkins would be the new ambassador, Roosevelt answered, "You know Harry isn't strong enough for that job." Noting that Hopkins had "no status" and "no power," and would receive only expenses, he finally ended the colloquy by saying, "No, you can't get anything exciting. He's just going over to say 'How do you do?' to a lot of my friends."[1]

Hopkins, on the other hand, was very excited. Sometime in late December, Roosevelt remarked that if he and Churchill could talk face-to-face, a good many matters could be settled quickly. Hopkins volunteered that he could go and talk to him, but Roosevelt said no and continued to do so for some days. Even though Hopkins recruited both Justice Frankfurter and Missy LeHand to intercede for him, it was apparently to no avail. Immediately after the January 3 press conference, Steve Early phoned upstairs to congratulate Hopkins. When Harry asked why, he was told that "the boss" had just announced that Hopkins was going to London. Two days later, he was airborne. Thus began Hopkins's final government career as a presidential emissary-administrator. From the time of his graduation from Grinnell in 1912 until he went to work for Governor Roosevelt's Temporary Emergency Relief Administration, Hopkins had been a social worker and later a social work executive. In his final social work position as head of the New York Tuberculosis and Health Association, his salary was twenty-five thousand dollars; during all but a few months of his federal career, his salary was ten thousand dollars. In five-plus years as director of federal relief—*Time* once called him the

New Deal's "almoner"—he ran huge programs, including the WPA, which cost some $9 billion, and enabled millions of American families to survive with dignity. Many wondered, however, if his blunt, no-nonsense approach was appropriate in delicate international relations. Churchill's announcement of the appointment of Lord Halifax, a ranking member of his war cabinet, as Britain's ambassador to the United States within a week of Roosevelt's announcement of Hopkins's mission can be viewed as complementary to that move.

Hopkins was curious and somewhat skeptical about Churchill, saying sarcastically, in Felix Frankfurter's presence, that Churchill regarded himself as "the greatest man in the world." The justice rebuked him, saying that if he kept that "chip on his shoulder," he ought to cancel his passage. Whether the chip came off then or later is not clear, but Hopkins and Churchill, who spent entire days together, clearly hit it off, and Hopkins became his—and Britain's—advocate. Churchill later gave him the mock title of "Lord Root of the Matter."[2]

In his annual message, Roosevelt noted that he was speaking "at a moment unprecedented in the history of the Union. I use the word 'unprecedented,' because at no previous time has American security been as seriously threatened from without as it is today." Roosevelt warned that

> the democratic way of life is at this moment being directly assailed in every part of the world—assailed either by arms, or by secret spreading of poisonous propaganda by those who seek to destroy unity and promote discord in nations that are still at peace.
>
> During sixteen long months this assault has blotted out the whole pattern of democratic life in an appalling number of independent nations, great and small. The assailants are still on the march, threatening other nations, great and small. . . .
>
> As your President, performing my constitutional duty . . . I find it, unhappily, necessary to report that the future and the safety of our country and of our democracy are overwhelmingly involved in events far beyond our borders.

Roosevelt granted that "as long as the British Navy retains its power," there was no danger of invasion, but if there "were no British Navy that was another matter."

> The first phase of the invasion of this Hemisphere would not be the landing of regular troops. The necessary strategic points would be occupied by secret agents and their dupes—and great numbers of them are already here, and in Latin America.
>
> As long as the aggressor nations maintain the offensive, they—not we—will choose the time and the place and the method of their attack. . . . That is why the future of all the American Republics is today in serious danger. . . . The need of the moment is that exclusively—to meeting this foreign peril. For all our domestic problems are now a part of the great emergency.

In three consecutive paragraphs, he argued that "by an impressive expression of the public will and without regard to partisanship":

> ... we are committed to all-inclusive national defense.
>
> ... we are committed to full support of all those resolute peoples, everywhere, who are resisting aggression and are thereby keeping war away from our hemisphere.
>
> ... we are committed to the proposition that principles of morality and considerations for our own security will never permit us to acquiesce in a peace dictated by aggressors and sponsored by appeasers. ...

Therefore, the immediate need is a swift and driving increase in our armament production.

After a discussion of current war production that admitted some shortcomings, and stating his intention to ask Congress for more money and authority, he declared that "our most useful and immediate role is act to as an arsenal" for nations resisting aggression "as well as for ourselves." "They do not need man power, but they do need billions of dollars worth of the weapons of defense. The time is near when they will not be able to pay for them all in ready cash. We cannot and we will not tell them that they must surrender, merely because of present inability to pay." After pointing out that these foreign needs could be blended into American defense orders, the president touched again on the question of repayment. "For what we send abroad, we shall be repaid within a reasonable time following the close of hostilities, in similar materials, or, at our option, in other goods of many kinds which they can produce and which we need."

It is highly dubious whether Roosevelt, even at that early stage, believed that there would be significant postwar repayment in kind or other merchandise. But he was unwilling to state what surely had to be the case, that in all likelihood there would no significant repayment for "billions."

He went on to reaffirm his commitment to maintaining and expanding democracy at home, including "equality of opportunity for youth and for others. Jobs. ... Security. ... The preservation of civil liberties." He listed things that "call for immediate improvement": expanding "old age pensions and unemployment insurance ... widen[ing] the opportunities for adequate medical care." Calling for sacrifice, the president noted that taxes would rise and said that "no person should be allowed to get rich out of this program."

Then came the passage that would help establish Roosevelt's bid for world leadership, a passage Rosenman tells us Roosevelt dictated in almost its final form.

> In the future days, which we seek to make secure, we look forward to a world founded upon four essential human freedoms.
>
> The first is freedom of speech and expression—everywhere in the world.

The second is freedom of every person to worship God in his own way—everywhere in the world.

The third is freedom from want—which, translated into world terms, means economic understandings which will secure to every nation a healthy peacetime life for its inhabitants—everywhere in the world.

The fourth is freedom from fear—which, translated into world terms, means a world-wide reduction of armaments to such a point and in such a thorough fashion that no nation will be in a position to commit an act of physical aggression against any neighbor—anywhere in the world. That is no vision of a distant millennium. It is a definite basis for a kind of world attainable in our own time and generation. That kind of world is the very antithesis of the so-called new order of tyranny which the dictators seek to create with the crash of a bomb.[3]

Roosevelt's Four Freedoms are often grouped with Wilson's Fourteen Points, but the two are as different as the two men. Wilson's fourteen were largely crafted by the professors and pundits who made up his "Inquiry" and were mostly legalistic and specific. Roosevelt's four were his creation, vague and all encompassing. There was no way to popularize Wilson's points; Roosevelt's were turned into cultural icons in 1943 by America's most popular illustrator, Norman Rockwell, whose four paintings personifying them became war-bond posters.[4]

Immediate congressional reaction was largely favorable on both sides of the aisle, including even some Republican former isolationists such as Michigan's Vandenberg. The most trenchant criticism came from a Democrat, Montana's Wheeler, who said the speech was meant "to frighten the American people to a point that they would surrender their liberties and establish a wartime dictatorship in this country." He did like "the two minutes the president devoted to . . . social and economic gains." Republican critics in the Senate included Taft of Ohio, who thought that Roosevelt was "asking for unlimited personal authority to loan abroad as much as he sees fit," while Kansas's Arthur Capper (1865–1951) complained that Roosevelt "was still making war speeches."[5]

The president's budget message was filled with figures that were almost unimaginable. Its first numbers, summarizing defense program appropriations, authorizations, and as-yet-unapproved recommendations from June 1940 to the end of 1942, came to $28.5 billion. The estimated addition to the deficit for 1941 and 1942 came to $15.4 billion. Taxes would have to be raised, and cuts in such programs as the WPA enabled a slight reduction in nondefense spending, from almost $7.1 billion in 1941 to almost $6.7 billion in 1942. Roosevelt did not believe it was possible to avoid greater debt. He was confident that "we can meet the demands of armament because we are a people with the will to defend and the means to defend. The boundaries of our productive capacity have never been set. The whole program set forth in this Budget has been prepared at a time when no man could see all the signposts ahead. One marker alone stands out all down the road. That marker carries not so much an admonition as a command to defend our democratic way of life."

The budget message sparked the expected critiques from economizers in both parties. Particular outrage centered on the president's questioning the utility of the statutory debt limit, which had first been enacted in 1919 as part of the postwar reaction to Wilson's war. Virginia's Harry Byrd called Roosevelt's attitude "dangerous," an "incentive to extravagance."[6]

At his press conference at the end of the first week of the new year, after announcing that Sherman Minton (1890–1965), a one-term New Deal Democratic senator from Indiana who had just lost his seat, had been appointed "as Administrative Assistant to act as legs for me," he then explained at some length the just-issued orders governing the OPM that he had talked about in the Fireside Chat on national security.

> THE PRESIDENT: I suppose the easiest way to put it is that these four peo-
> ple—the [OPM]—fix the policy, and then Knudsen and Hillman carry it
> out, just like a law firm . . . there are two partners. . . .
> Q: Are they equals?
> THE PRESIDENT: That's not the point; they're a firm. Is a firm equals? I don't
> know? . . . Roosevelt & O'Connor was a law firm in New York. I don't
> know whether we were equals or not. . . .
> Q: Mr. President, is this the firm of Roosevelt, Hillman, and Knudsen?
> THE PRESIDENT: I have nothing to do with this.
> Q: What about the clause 'under the direction of the President'?
> THE PRESIDENT: That's only to conform with the law. I have nothing to do with
> it, whatsoever. There may be a question of policy, and they may say, What
> does the President think of this question with a pro and con on it? They
> may come in and ask what I think of it. That will happen very rarely.

Roosevelt loved to spin elaborate fairy tales, and this was one of them. There was no question of who was the boss. As he had told Knudsen at the first NDAC meeting, it was the president. One of the purposes of this tale was to make it seem that Knudsen and Hillman, capital and labor, had equal power. The simple fact of their titles—Knudsen was director general and Hillman associate director general—shows that the claim was bogus. In addition, as a quick glance at the organizational chart in the executive order will confirm, it is clear that considerable authority would be exercised by persons subordinate to both Knudsen and Hillman, such as Donald Nelson, the Sears, Roebuck executive who headed OPM's Division of Purchases.[7]

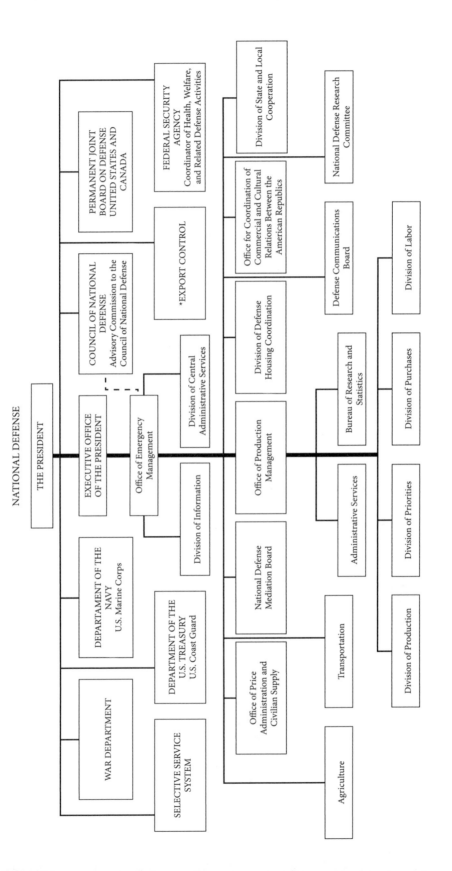

NATIONAL DEFENSE

THE PRESIDENT

WAR DEPARTMENT

DEPARTMENT OF THE NAVY
U.S. Marine Corps

DEPARTMENT OF THE TREASURY
U.S. Coast Guard

SELECTIVE SERVICE SYSTEM

EXECUTIVE OFFICE OF THE PRESIDENT

COUNCIL OF NATIONAL DEFENSE
Advisory Commission to the Council of National Defense

PERMANENT JOINT BOARD ON DEFENSE UNITED STATES AND CANADA

FEDERAL SECURITY AGENCY
Coordinator of Health, Welfare, and Related Defense Activities

Office of Emergency Management

*EXPORT CONTROL

Division of Information

Division of Central Administrative Services

Office of Production Management

Division of Defense Housing Coordination

Office for Coordination of Commercial and Cultural Relations Between the American Republics

Division of State and Local Cooperation

National Defense Research Committee

Defense Communications Board

Office of Price Administration and Civilian Supply

National Defense Mediation Board

Administrative Services

Bureau of Research and Statistics

Division of Labor

Agriculture

Transportation

Division of Production

Division of Priorities

Division of Purchases

Source: Samuel I. Rosenman, comp., *The Public Papers and Addresses of Franklin D. Roosevelt,* 1940 volume, *War and Aid to Democracies,* 701.

The Knudsen-Hillman law firm lasted barely a year and would be replaced by the War Production Board. To describe and analyze all of the variations and permutations of the various special defense and war agencies that Roosevelt created would require a volume much larger than this one. Almost all were created by executive, administrative, and military orders and placed within the administrative ambit of the Office of Emergency Management, located within the Executive Office of the President. This meant that they could be created, modified, and abolished without referral to Congress, except for appropriations. In some instances, organizations could be funded from money that Congress had appropriated for the discretionary use of the president. And while he delegated that authority, he always had the ability to snatch it back and redelegate it, sometimes to essentially the same persons clustered in different alignments.

In his Tuesday-morning press conference, Roosevelt initiated a two-month struggle for the passage of his Lend-Lease Bill, which was introduced in the House symbolically labeled H.R. 1776 later that day. Curiously, there was no presidential message about it, but he described it to reporters, on the record, as a "blank check."

Instead of a presidential message, the two majority leaders, Barkley and McCormack, after a conference with the president, issued a brief official interpretation whose key paragraph read: "The bill simply translates into legislative form the policy of making this country the arsenal for the democracies, and seeks to carry out President Roosevelt's pledge to [send] these countries 'in ever-increasing numbers ships, planes, tanks, guns.'"

Titled "An Act to Promote the Defense of the United States," the bill was an exceedingly broad grant of authority to give weapons and other war materials to "the government of any country whose defense the President deems vital to the defense of the United States." It had been drafted in Morgenthau's Treasury Department, which oversaw Allied purchases in the United States. Roosevelt wanted the bill passed by March 1; he actually signed it on March 11. The only serious limitation on his authority in the original draft was that most of the materials had to be purchased with appropriated funds, though the president did have the authority to give away "defense articles" to which the government already had title. Before the congressional debate began, Roosevelt told Barkley and Rayburn that he would accept four amendments they thought necessary for comfortable passage: a time limit on the bill, periodic reports to Congress, consultation with senior military officials before transferring materials, and a meaningless one stating that nothing in the bill authorized U.S. Navy convoying Lend-Lease materials, meaningless because the president as commander in chief already had the power to order that. As passed the act ran until June 30, 1943, and required presidential reports every ninety days. A later amendment put a $1.3 billion cap on army and navy property released under the program. No dollar cap was placed on material manufactured for the British and other clients. Roosevelt refused, then or later, to accept any limitation on his power to decide what nations could receive Lend-Lease materials.

The expected protests against the bill were immediate and vituperative. Hiram Johnson, describing himself as "neither an appeaser nor a Hitlerite" and wanting to see "Hitler whipped and Britain triumphant," called the bill "monstrous." Its enactment would make the United States "a member of the totalitarian states." But the realistic hopes of the opposition were described by an unidentified isolationist senator who predicted no more than a dozen no votes in his chamber. National Republican leaders old and new quickly sounded off. Asked for a comment, Hoover, in strangled language, claimed that the powers requested would threaten democracy in the United States. Alf Landon went further, describing it "as the first step toward dictatorship by Mr. Roosevelt." Tom Dewey, while strongly favoring "every possible aid to Great Britain short of war," charged that the bill "would bring an end to free government in the United States" and for all practical purposes would abolish the Congress. He had a ten-worst list of things that Roosevelt could do under the bill, including giving away "the whole Navy," "every gun in the Army," and "every American airplane."[8]

Willkie, though under pressure from other Republicans to attack the bill, kept silent for two days and then issued a statement not only backing the bill but predicting that "appeasers, isolationists, or lip-service friends of Britain will seek to sabotage the program of aid to Britain and its allies behind the screen of opposition to the bill."

Willkie did have one reservation: he thought that there ought to be a time limit on the grant of power to the president. He revealed that he was planning "a trip to England . . . to see what conditions are over there." These sentiments did not sit well with most Republican leaders and probably killed whatever chances Willkie might have had for party leadership. Roosevelt was delighted and invited him to the White House on the eve of the third inaugural. He facilitated Willkie's trip in a number of ways, including giving him a handwritten note to Churchill.

To a Certain Naval Person:
Dear Churchill:
Wendell Willkie is taking this to you. He is being a true help in keeping politics out of things. I think this verse applies to your people as well as to us:
"Sail on, O Ship of State!
Sail on, O Union strong and great!
Humanity with all its fears,
With all the hopes of future years
Is hanging breathless on thy fate."

FRANKLIN D. ROOSEVELT[9]

In a speech on February 9, Churchill read the verse, explained how it came to him, and asked, "What is the answer that I shall give . . . to this great man . . . ? Here is the answer I will give to President Roosevelt. Put your confidence in us. . . . Give us the tools and we shall finish the job."

But even as Churchill gave the ultimate testimonial for Lend-Lease, the king's and the president's commanders were making secret plans in Washington to send millions of American soldiers abroad to complete a victory that British leaders knew they could not achieve alone. While Congress debated and enacted Lend-Lease, American, British, and Canadian military officials were planning the joint strategy to be pursued when the United States would be drawn fully into the war. The conference, called ABC-1, which met from January 29 to March 27, 1941, is discussed later in this chapter.

The congressional struggle over Lend-Lease, marked by extreme bitterness, went through three dramatic acts to an all but preordained result. There were hearings, then debates, and finally votes in each house, accompanied by public meetings and intense coverage in print and on the air. The most celebrated remark was Burton Wheeler's charge on a radio program before the hearings had begun that Lend-Lease was "the New Deal's triple A foreign policy: it will plow under every fourth American boy." Roosevelt made it famous in his January 14 press conference by denouncing "those who talk about plowing under every fourth American child, which I regard as the most untruthful, as the most dastardly, unpatriotic thing that has ever been said. Quote me on that. That really is the rottenest thing that has been said in public life in my generation." Contemporary accounts of the press conference indicate that the president was quite angry; the *Times* correspondent wrote of a "wrathful" president whose words "burst forth" as his voice "rose."[10]

The congressional hearings—January 16–28 in the House, January 27–February 12 in the Senate—proceeded in the best parliamentary tradition. Witnesses were called by the committee chairs and by an opposition member. Cabinet members Hull, Stimson, Knox, and Morgenthau plus Knudsen all spoke at great length and were questioned by committee members. In addition, some elite members of the public added their favorable voices, including Harvard president James Bryant Conant, Mayor La Guardia, and theologian Reinhold Niebuhr (1892–1971). The arguments put forth were generally those of the administration, and care was taken not to call any of the growing number of "hawks" who wanted a declaration of war, but the next-to-last witness, Harvard's Conant, backed the bill and said that as a "last resort" he favored sending troops to Europe to defend the democratic way of life. The final supporting witness, Wendell Willkie, who cut short his stay in Britain in order to testify, was the most dramatic. While he had some suggestions for change, his prescription was captured in a headline: "Send Britain Bombers, More Destroyers."

The public figures who testified in opposition had varying views. The most celebrated such witness, Charles Lindbergh, believed that there was no way to avoid a German victory and favored a negotiated peace and did not believe that either a German-dominated Europe or America could invade the other without a prior internal collapse. Norman Thomas thought that England should be aided but argued that the bill gave Roosevelt too much power: "No man, not even an angel from heaven, who asks such breath-taking powers of war or peace with such vague limitations should be trusted with them." Sears, Roebuck & Co.'s Robert E. Wood, head of the newly formed America First Committee, said that he feared war "within ninety days" if the bill passed and that his committee favored some unspecified aid to Britain but only after all its assets in American securities had been liquidated. Historian Charles A. Beard characterized the measure as "a bill for waging undeclared war.[11]

The passage of the bill through Congress, given the passions involved, was reasonably rapid. The votes were not even close. The House vote on February 8 was 61 percent favorable, 260–165. Just 25 of 261 Democratic votes were opposed, and only 24 of 159 Republican votes were favorable. Sixty-two of 95 senators favored the bill, 65 percent; 14 of 65 Democrats were opposed, as were 18 of 28 Republicans. (The bill the Senate passed on March 8 was different from the measure passed by the House a month earlier and required a second House vote on March 11, which passed by a much larger margin, 317–71, 82 percent.)

Public opinion seems to have been even more favorable to Lend-Lease than Congress was: four separate Gallup polls between February 9 and March 8 showed that of those with settled opinions, 71, 73, 73, and 68 percent favored the bill. Even more striking is that in a March 11 poll, Gallup found that 72 percent of those with opinions approved of Roosevelt as president, his highest rating up to that time. These numbers suggest that the long and well-publicized debate, despite its bitterness, solidified Roosevelt's popularity. The highest rating Gallup had found before 1941 had been 69 percent in 1934 as Roosevelt's first year in office was coming to an end.[12]

Great pains had been taken to give the appearance of urgency; since the House was acting under a rule that barred amendments, an engrossed copy was ready to be attested to and hand-carried to the White House by the chair of the House Committee on Enrolled Bills. The show of haste was a sham: no Lend-Lease aid had reached Greece by the time it surrendered at the end of April. But the appearance of urgency was useful in pushing through the $7 billion request for the first installment of Lend-Lease aid, which the president sent to the House the next day. Despite threats of delaying tactics from some congressional diehards, the funding request got relatively prompt action. The House appropriated the full amount by a vote of 337–55 a week after receiving the request, and the Senate followed suit, 67–9, five days later. The appropriation included the $1.3 billion to replace transferred army and navy property as well as goods made and purchased for Lend-Lease.[13]

The president was admittedly tired by his exertions over the Lend-Lease Bill and had been troubled by a particularly persistent cold since the end of February. The *Times'* White House correspondent had noted that on March 4, as he began his ninth year as president, Roosevelt had not come downstairs to his office until just before the four o'clock press conference and that, though he joked with reporters as usual, "he did not seem to radiate the cheerfulness and hope that marked his accession in 1933. He spoke in such a low voice . . . that it was difficult for those in the back of the room to hear his brief remarks. . . . Even his exceptional Vitality and ability to laugh off cares have been challenged of late and all bits of evidence seem to indicate that after his wearing service he President is finding it less easy to bound back full of vigor after a period of intense activity."

Frank Kluckhohn concluded his Sunday think piece with the perceptive observation that "Roosevelt meditates, as well as rests, on [his vacation] trips, talking quietly with Harry Hopkins and others. Action usually is the after-result."[14]

Hopkins had returned from Britain in mid-February. In reporting to the president, he persuaded him to send the millionaire New Dealer Averell Harriman, who had worked with him in the Commerce Department, to London to coordinate Lend-Lease matters. He flew to Britain the day before Roosevelt signed the Lend-Lease Bill so he would be in place when the appropriation act passed and the flow of materials began. He communicated with Roosevelt—and thus Hopkins—by coded navy radio, bypassing the American Embassy; Roosevelt and Churchill also used him to send messages one or the other did not want to be seen by others.[15]

Hopkins again joined the president's party during a late-March Gulf of Mexico fishing trip and with Attorney General Robert Jackson helped their boss work out the details of Lend-Lease administration. It was generally understood that Hopkins would oversee Lend-Lease, but it was not clear what his title or rank would be. Roosevelt put Hopkins back on the public payroll by a presidential letter dated March 27, "to advise and assist me in carrying out [my] responsibilities placed upon me by the Act of March 11, 1941, entitled 'An Act to Promote the Defense of the United States' at an annual salary of $10,000." Hopkins's authority over materials for Allied purchasing commissions had come to him from Morgenthau almost two weeks before that. Hopkins's authority stemmed from his appointment as secretary of the four-man committee of cabinet officers—Hull, Morgenthau, Stimson, and Knox—which was originally referred to as Roosevelt's special war committee but was eventually named the President's Liaison Committee. It met with him mostly in the evening. Stimson suggested making it an administrative apparatus, with one of his aides, General James H. Burns, as secretary to run things. Roosevelt accepted his war secretary's suggestion with one crucial change: Hopkins would be the secretary. This meant that instead of the War Department having the dominant role, the White House would. General Burns was assigned to what became known as the "Hopkins shop" along with two top Treasury officials, Oscar Cox, who had drafted the Lend-Lease Bill, and Philip Young; Rear Admiral Ray Spear acted for the navy. They worked in the Federal Reserve Building, while Hopkins continued to live and work in the White House, often from his bed. Only in early May did an executive order regularize what was called the "Hopkins shop." It was established as part of the Office of Emergency Management in its Division of Defense Aids, and four days later, by military order, General Burns was appointed its executive secretary.

By late summer Lend-Lease had become more complex: Russia was about to become a major aid recipient, and Roosevelt had signed a second appropriation bill, bringing the total to almost $13 billion. He then issued another executive order, establishing the Office of Lend Lease Administrator in the Office of Emergency Management in the EOP and abolishing the Division of Defense Aids Reports. He had already appointed Edward R. Stettinius Jr. as Lend-Lease administrator. Stettinius, the liberal son of a Morgan partner, had been a protégé of U.S. Steel's Myron C. Taylor, who appointed him president of U.S. Steel as his successor when Stettinius was only thirty-eight years of age. He had become friendly with Hopkins during Harry's brief stint as secretary of commerce and after service on the NDAC came to Washington to work as a dollar-a-year man in the OPM in 1940. Stettinius describes how he learned of his Lend-Lease appointment, in effect replacing Hopkins, who had done the job without the title. Summoned to the White House by Hopkins, Stettinius found him in bed with piles of papers on the covers.

> HOPKINS: Ed, the President wants you to take over the administration of the Lend-Lease program. He thinks there is nothing more important now for the country than getting this Lend-Lease show moving at top speed. We stayed up late last night talking over the whole situation and he feels that you are the man to do it.
> STETTINIUS: I'm here in Washington to serve wherever the President feels I can be most useful and if he wants me to run the Lend-Lease show, I'll take it and do my best.

In appointing Stettinius, Roosevelt endowed him with all of his powers under the Lend-Lease Act, including the right to appoint personnel, except that Roosevelt reserved to himself the power to determine which nations could receive Lend-Lease, and the responsibility of negotiating Lend-Lease agreements with other nations was vested in the State Department.[16]

The reasons for the subterfuge about Hopkins's role after he resigned as secretary of commerce are several. The main ones were Hopkins's undeserved reputation as a reckless spender and the fact that many in Washington, including both New Dealers and opponents of the administration, mistrusted him. In addition, Roosevelt loved to camouflage his behind-the-scenes actions. But many administration insiders knew that the frail, post-1938 Hopkins—Roosevelt once referred to him as a "half man"—was a vital force in the wartime White House. Crusty Henry Stimson wrote in his diary after Hopkins returned from his first visit to Churchill's Britain: "The more I think of it, the more I think it is a godsend that he should be at the White House."

As different as Hopkins's relief and Lend-Lease jobs were, there was a certain similarity between them. As both Federal Emergency Relief Administration (FERA) administrator and presidential assistant, he oversaw funds and projects that were conceived and executed at the discretion of the president. In each circumstance, Roosevelt ran his eye over the lists of projects but could not possibly be responsible for them all. He delighted in finding items he could talk about in his press conferences, as when he discovered that his metaphorical "garden hose" had an actual existence in the Lend-Lease program:

> THE PRESIDENT: The last three items are for 900,000 feet of garden hose. (*Laughter*) Not garden hose but fire hose—actually fire hose—at a total cost of about $300,000. I thought it was a rather nice little coincidence.

Although the cost of Lend-Lease dwarfed that of federal relief—some $62 billion as opposed to $9 billion for work relief—each was a massive expenditure for its time.[17]

Parallel to the assignment of Harriman to London was the replacement of Joe Kennedy as ambassador there by John G. Winant. There could not have been a greater contrast between Joe Kennedy and his successor. Kennedy, a man of the right center, had favored appeasement and consorted largely with those who had similar views. Winant (1889–1947), the new ambassador, was an important but little-known figure of the Roosevelt era. He became personally friendly with Anthony Eden and had numerous contacts with Labour Party figures such as Ernest Bevin, many of whom he knew through years of service as the leading American figure in the Geneva-based International Labor Organization (ILO), the only League of Nations body with which the United States was affiliated. As its head after the Germans overran the Low Countries and France in 1940, he brought its headquarters from Geneva to Montreal. Because of his wide European experience, he was one of those on whose opinion Roosevelt relied in overruling the judgment of his military advisers that Britain was not likely to survive.

Born into an upper-middle-class New York City family that moved to New Hampshire in his youth, Winant was educated at St. Paul's in Concord, a prep school consonant with Groton, and at Princeton. He taught history at St. Paul's until 1917, when, unable to get into aviation training in the United States, he went to Paris and was accepted by the nascent American air units there, enlisting as a private. He flew dangerous observation missions ending the war and ended the war as a captain commanding an observation squadron. After returning to teach at St. Paul's, he entered politics as a Republican and served three terms as New Hampshire's governor; he and Roosevelt were fellow governors during Roosevelt's last two years in New York, and both took extraordinary anti-Depression measures. Winant, who never left his party, supported many early New Deal measures and accepted Roosevelt appointments to a commission to settle a textile strike, to the NRA, and to the ILO. In 1935 the president named him the first chair of the Social Security Board. When during the 1936 election campaign Landon attacked Social Security, Winant felt that it was appropriate to resign and take the stump to refute him. After the election, Winant submitted to Roosevelt's "draft" and returned to the SSB and made its first report to Congress before resigning in late January 1937 and returning to the ILO in Geneva.

The Washington and London embassies were of particular importance throughout the war. When Halifax arrived aboard the huge new battleship HMS *King George V* to take up his post in Washington, Roosevelt, who understood the impression a gesture could create, was driven to Annapolis followed by two cars of alerted reporters. There he boarded the *Potomac* and sailed out to meet the *George V* off Annapolis. After Ambassador and Lady Halifax were transferred to the yacht, the president hosted a small formal lunch with the British chargé d'affaires and his wife, Secretary Knox, Admiral Stark, and Roosevelt's naval aide Captain Dan Callaghan. Ashore, the ambassadorial couple were driven with the president in his car from Annapolis to the steps of the British Embassy. To say that the welcome broke precedent is an understatement.

In his memoir, Winant described his later, parallel, reception in Britain. The Duke of Kent, the king's brother, met his plane at Bristol and on the train toward London told him that the king would meet his train at Windsor. "When the train stopped at Windsor station, the King was standing directly in front of the carriage door. He took me up to the castle in his car."

It is not too much to say that Roosevelt's gesture, and the British reciprocation of it, symbolized the formation of the informal but potent Anglo-American alliance, the "special relationship" that has been a major, if declining, factor in world affairs since that time.[18]

Winant's London embassy, even if bypassed by direct and indirect contacts between Roosevelt and Churchill, and by Harriman's mission, was a powerhouse throughout the war under his direction, with a staff of a thousand. At his request, Ben Cohen was appointed counselor to the embassy and accompanied him on the flights to London. Later Winfield Riefler, Roosevelt's consulting economist from early New Deal days, came to serve as minister for economic warfare, and, particularly during the period before the United States entered the war, the embassy smoothed the way for American military liaison officers.

Winant himself, at Roosevelt's behest, spent much of his time talking to people all over Britain. Clement Attlee's tribute, that Winant "brought a feeling of warmth, confidence, and courage to the British people in their time of greatest need," attests to how Winant responded to his instructions. He was notable among ambassadors in not only eschewing striped pants but also appearing almost invariably in rumpled trousers. During the war, he gave just two formal dinners: one for Eleanor Roosevelt, the other for General Eisenhower. Despite the kudos Winant received, Roosevelt's habit of bypassing him on such matters as Lend-Lease and relations with the USSR caused him to feel, from sometime in 1943 on, that he had been superseded. "I have been bypassed continually," he complained in a telegram to Hopkins, which itself bypassed the secretary of state.[19]

As opposed to the abundant, open aid to Britain, aid to embattled China was skimpy and quasi covert. In late January, the White House announced that Lauchlin Currie, who had lost enough of his anonymity to be identified by the Associated Press as "Roosevelt's personal economics advisor," was being sent to Chungking to gain firsthand information about China's economic situation. Currie at that time had no special knowledge about Chinese affairs. The mission, as everyone knew, was really about aid. As it happened, Currie returned after three weeks in Chungking and several meetings with Chiang Kai-shek—with American-educated Madam Chiang interpreting—just as Roosevelt was signing the Lend-Lease Bill. A reporter asked the president:

Q: Will there be aid to China?
THE PRESIDENT: Oh, I guess so.
Q: Would it depend, sir, on the report that Lauchlin Currie makes to you?
THE PRESIDENT: That might have something to do with it; I wouldn't say it would depend on it.[20]

There already had been some assistance to China, chiefly in the form of Export-Import Bank loans totaling $120 million to purchase American trucks, tires, gasoline, metals, machinery, and electrical equipment. That move was widely and correctly interpreted in the press as a counter to Japan, though that nation was not mentioned in the statement. Four days after his casual press conference remark, Roosevelt, in an important speech on the broader implications of Lend-Lease, made an unambiguous commitment to "a policy of unqualified, immediate, all-out aid for Britain, for Greece, for China, and for all the Governments in exile whose homelands are temporarily occupied by the aggressors. And from now on that aid will be increased—and yet again increased—until total victory has been won. . . . China likewise expresses the magnificent will of millions of plain people to resist the dismemberment of their historic Nation. China, through the Generalissimo, Chiang Kai-shek, asks our help. America has said that China shall have our help."

That commitment, thanks to the terms of the Lend-Lease Act, was Roosevelt's alone to make: on May 6, he made the necessary declaration that the defense of China was "vital to the defense of the United States." Much of the early aid to China was to maintain the Burma Road, then the only effective route to deliver aid into China.

Also important was the training of Chinese aviators in the United States and the covert but widely publicized Flying Tigers, formally the American Volunteer Group (AVG). It was composed of civilian pilots led by Claire L. Chennault (1893–1958), a former army air corps pilot who had retired with the rank of captain in 1937 and was employed by Chiang's government to reorganize the Chinese air force. The group was not ready for action until after Pearl Harbor and would be incorporated into the United States Army in April 1942. Currie, who had been appointed as Lend-Lease coordinator for China in April 1941, served as the chief White House advocate for Chennault's group.[21]

From late January to the end of March 1941, high-level American, British, and Canadian military planners met secretly to map joint strategy in a conference given the code name ABC-1, for "American British Conversations." Although he did not personally participate, just before the conference began Roosevelt set down two basic principles to guide the American planners: first, "our military must be very conservative until our strength [has] developed," and second, "we must be ready to act with what is available."[22]

Among the propositions agreed upon were that defeating Germany should be the first priority and that Japan should be held in check without war if possible, but if the United States and Britain were at war with both Germany and Japan, defeating Germany remained the first priority. The British government quickly approved the plan; President Roosevelt, who liked to keep his options open, never approved it, but later, at a crucial moment, insisted that its "Germany first" doctrine be adhered to. Roosevelt did intervene by vetoing a British proposal to station units of the American fleet at Singapore. As General Marshall pointed out, he had not disapproved the ABC-1 policy guidelines, and American planners acted as if he had approved them, and Roosevelt knew that they had done so. The ABC meetings began a process by which wary American and British military planners learned to work together despite pervasive and continuing mutual suspicions.[23]

In April the war expanded significantly and unfavorably for the British. In late 1940 and early 1941, the Royal Navy had considerable success against the Italians in the Mediterranean, while British armies were decisively defeating

Italian forces in the North African desert west of Cairo and in Italian Somali-land—part of today's Eritrea—in the Horn of Africa. In mid-February German forces under General Erwin Rommel began to assemble in Tripoli and soon advanced toward Cairo, forcing the British to retreat. In Greece, where the Greek army was successfully pushing the Italian invaders back into Albania, the British sent troops from North Africa to Crete and to Greece itself in early March to help the Greeks repel an expected German attack. That attack came early in April, soon running over the Greeks and British, and before the month was out Greece surrendered. In North Africa, the British, weakened by the loss of troops sent to help the Greeks, retreated eastward toward Cairo in the face of Rommel's attacks. A stunningly successful German airborne invasion of Crete using both parachute- and glider-borne troops conquered the island in an eleven-day campaign that ended with the surrender of the British troops, largely New Zealanders, on June 1. Crete remained an unsinkable aircraft base for the Germans for the rest of the war.

With Lend-Lease enacted, concern shifted to the problem of getting the supplies to the British. In the Battle of the Atlantic, the combination of German submarines, operating mostly from French ports like Lorient and Brest with direct access to the Atlantic, and the occasional forays of German surface ships were sinking merchant ships faster than Britain could replace them.

Roosevelt's moves toward joining the Battle of the Atlantic evolved slowly. In a press conference on January 21, questioned about "convoying ships"—which opponents of Lend-Lease claimed he intended to do—the president stressed on "background, as long as you don't attribute it to anybody," that he "had never even considered [convoying] in any way at all." He expounded on how dangerous convoying would be:

> THE PRESIDENT: Obviously when a nation convoys ships, either its own flag or another flag, through a hostile zone, just on the doctrine of chance there is apt to be some shooting—pretty sure that there will be shooting—and shooting comes awfully close to war, doesn't it?
> Q: Yes, sir.
> THE PRESIDENT: You can see that is about the last thing we have in our minds. If we did anything it might almost *compel* shooting to start.

But the denial shows that he had been thinking about it and he continued to do so.[24]

Some weeks after he had secretly authorized sending a team to Greenland to survey possible airfield sites, Roosevelt announced on April 10 that he had signed an agreement with the prewar Danish minister in Washington to include "Greenland in our system of cooperative hemispheric defense." (The Danish government protested, but after liberation in 1945 the Danish Parliament ratified it.) The U.S. occupying forces established airfields and other bases in Greenland that were useful as emergency landing fields for aircraft being flown to Britain from Canada and New England. In addition, Julianehaab on Greenland's southwest coast, midway between Newfoundland and Iceland, was ice-free most of the year. On the same day, Roosevelt sent a message to Congress asking authority to "requisition" foreign ships interned in American ports as a way to ease the acute shipping shortage. Congress complied in early June; eventually, this added 105 ships, amounting to nearly seven hundred thousand tons of shipping, about a tenth of what the Germans were then sinking each month. The president revoked his proclamation making the Red Sea a war zone the next day, which meant that American ships could deliver supplies to the British in Egypt. He also signed a Senate Joint Resolution opposing the transfer of any territory in the New World from one non-American power to another. Roosevelt referenced Greenland to the press, but it could also cover French Martinique.[25]

On the economic front in April, Roosevelt faced the problem of inflation arising from the massive defense spending. Roosevelt took to the airwaves to urge purchase of newly created Defense Savings Bonds and Stamps, later War Savings Bonds and Stamps. Roosevelt's pitch, directed at individuals, was "for financial support to pay for our arming," but the real purpose of the program was to soak up as much spending power as possible to reduce inflation. In what he called a "homey" touch, he told his listeners. "I am buying not one stamp but ten stamps, each to go into a little book for each of my ten grandchildren."

Although there were later variations, the standard E-series bonds in denominations of $25, $50, $100, and $1,000 sold at three quarters of their face value and matured in ten years, resulting in an interest rate of about 2.9 percent compounded semiannually. The stamps, in denominations of 10, 25, and 50 cents and $1 and $5, earned no interest until they were redeemed for a bond and were popular for schoolchildren, who typically brought dimes and quarters to school weekly and exchanged them for a $25 bond when they had accumulated $18.75 in stamps. Petty as all these amounts seem, they soaked up almost $45 billion of personal income by the end of the war. Defense bonds were not a great investment, but they were better than World War I Liberty Bonds, which, by the time they matured, had lost almost a fifth of their face value. The World War II bonds were guaranteed to be redeemed at face value. In each instance, inflation had decreased their real value.[26]

In another anti-inflation move seeking controls on both capital and labor, Roosevelt created what would evolve into one of the most effective and unpopular of his wartime economic agencies, the Office of Price Administration (OPA). He appointed as price administrator economist Leon Henderson. Now very much a Hopkins man, Henderson, after administering last rites to the NRA, had gone to the SEC and was also on the NDAC, where he was in charge of its Office of Price Stabilization, which the president abolished. The OPA was slotted into the OEM. Although the president's executive order cited the national emergency and a number of statutes, including the Selective Service Act, which gave him various emergency powers, there was no statute specifically empowering price fixing. Asked by a reporter:

Q: Mr. President, . . . will [Henderson] have the authority to enforce [his decisions]?

THE PRESIDENT: As far as the laws go.

Beyond that he would not go. Henderson, in a press conference the next day, said that he would use economic sanctions such as withholding supplies against any efforts to raise the price of basic commodities. He specifically mentioned the price of steel. His focus at this time was on producer rather than consumer goods.[27]

A strike of bituminous coal miners that had begun on April 2 despite a plea from the president threatened steel production. Both John L. Lewis's United Mine Workers and most of the coal companies had come to an agreement, but the traditional division of the industry between northern and southern mines, and an agreement between the operators not to consummate agreements until both groups had settled, produced a walkout. The chief bone of contention was the traditional 60-cents-a-day differential between northern and southern mines. The northern owners had agreed to a dollar a day raise, bringing the basic daily wage to $7; the southern operators agreed to a similar raise, bringing their daily wage to $6.40. The union wanted the same rate, North and South. Despite efforts of the Department of Labor, including Secretary Frances Perkins and John R. Steelman of its Conciliation Service and of the National Defense Mediation Board (NDMB), no settlement had been reached. Informed that a long day's negotiations conducted in New York and Washington had been without positive results, the president issued a statement at 10:45 p.m., April 21, saying that it was "imperative that there be no shortage now, or at any other time, of coal for defense production purposes."

But the president had no power to compel the parties to agree; he could only "recommend and urge," a process that came to be known as "jawboning." In this instance, the process worked. Six days later, a panel of the National Defense Mediation Board, a minor, powerless branch of the NDAC, recommended unanimously that the president's terms be accepted by both sides. The following day, the southern operators, who met with Commerce Secretary Jones acting for the president, agreed to a $1 raise and to negotiate about the 60 cent differential, so four hundred thousand miners returned to work. The southern mine workers eventually got the 60 cents. A little-remarked feature of the contract was the provision for annual paid vacations. Such fringe benefits would become an increasingly important part of wartime collective bargaining as the government placed limits on wage increases. The result was both a triumph for the president and an illustration of the limits of his power.[28]

In late April, Roosevelt, reviewing events since the war in Europe began, contended in an extended press-conference colloquy that the difference between patrolling, which the navy had been doing since the war began, and convoying, which the navy was not doing, was as clear as the difference between "a horse and a cow" and acknowledged that some patrols were a thousand miles east of the Maryland shore.

> THE PRESIDENT: Now this is a patrol, and has been a patrol for a year and a half, still is, and from time to time it has been extended, and is being extended, and will be extended—the patrol—for the safety of the western hemisphere.
>
> Q: Could you tell us, sir, how far it could possibly go?
>
> THE PRESIDENT: That is exactly the question I hoped you would ask. (he laughs) As far on the waters of the seven seas as may be necessary for the defense of the American hemisphere.[29]

A less poetic version of those limits was contained in a secret navy document, Western Hemisphere Defense Plan #2, edited by the president himself and promulgated four days earlier. It defined the Western Hemisphere as extending from "the International Date Line" in the mid-Pacific to the twenty-sixth meridian in the Atlantic, which "included Greenland and all of the Azores" but not Iceland. Belligerent warships or planes found within the hemisphere were to be tracked and their position broadcast in clear language, supposedly to warn other American nations but actually to inform British forces. Any approach of such planes and warships within twenty miles of Western Hemisphere territory, except the Azores, was to be regarded as evidence of an intended attack. American armed forces were to warn the intruders; if the intruders ignored the warning, they were to be attacked.[30]

We now know that both Roosevelt and Hitler, with their memories of the Great War, assumed that an incident in the Atlantic might be the ultimate spark setting off the second German-American war that each expected. Thus, each, at times, reined in hawkish naval commanders. In a late May conference, Hitler spoke of his desire to move southwest into Iberia to take Gibraltar and close the western entrance to the Mediterranean as well as to take the Azores "in order to be able to operate long-range bombers from there against the United States." But since he had decided to go east, he refused to give permission for attacks on U.S. Navy ships, but hoped to return to those projects after Russia had been smashed in the fall (!). Hitler, who sometimes liked to give multiple reasons for his actions, believed that Roosevelt was still undecided about full participation in the war, and under no circumstances did he wish to create incidents that would lead to American entry into the war before he conquered Russia, "especially since Japan will probably come in only if the United States is the aggressor."[31]

With Lend-Lease functioning, at the beginning of May Roosevelt began discussing with Congress the new taxes he had called for in his January budget message. Following up on Morgenthau's recommendations, he urged North Carolina's Robert L. Doughton (1863–1954), a small-town banker who had chaired the powerful House Ways and Means Committee since 1933, to "act favorably" on his treasury secretary's goal of new taxes amounting to $3.5 billion. The president stressed that the new taxes should not "make the rich richer and the poor poorer" but be based on "the principle of ability to pay." He insisted that "the tax liabilities of individuals and corporations" could not be established with equity "as long as the tax base is defined to exclude substantial and significant elements of income." This set off a struggle in Congress that would not be settled until the president signed the 1941 Revenue Act in late September.[32]

During May war news from the Mediterranean and the North Atlantic continued to worsen: official military historians later wrote of the "Crisis of May 1941." Roosevelt tried to focus public attention on future plans rather than present difficulties by releasing a letter to War Secretary Stimson—a strong airpower advocate—calling for "a substantial increase in heavy bomber production" because "command of the air by the democracies must and can be achieved." The mid-April promotion of Wall Street lawyer Robert A. Lovett (1895–1986) to the newly created post of assistant secretary of war was but another of the incremental steps by the president in his transformation of the place of airpower in the military establishment.[33] In other preparatory moves, he requested funds to train NYA workers for defense work and to build the "Big Inch" pipeline to bring Gulf Coast oil to the Northeast. He created the Office of Civilian Defense (OCD) in the OEM and appointed Fiorello La Guardia to head it part-time. In addition to being mayor of New York City, normally considered a full-time job, La Guardia chaired the American section of the Permanent Joint Board on Defense with Canada and had long been president of the United States Conference of Mayors. Perhaps the key phrase in the EO appointing him and describing his manifold duties was "utilizing the operating services and facilities of [existing government agencies] as much as possible."[34]

The president's military advisers were becoming increasingly concerned about Hitler's possible moves into Iberia and the Atlantic. They were planning what they hoped would be preemptive responses into Iceland, the Azores, and Brazil. Secretary Stimson, often privately critical about Roosevelt's means rather than his ends, wrote with some exasperation in his diary on May 23 that "the President shows evidence of waiting for the accidental shot of some irresponsible captain on either side to be the occasion of his going to war."

That interesting perception is well worth considering in any attempt to understand why Roosevelt refused to take the bolder steps toward war that some of his military advisers—particularly Stimson, Secretary Knox, and Admiral Stark—kept urging. Stimson tended to attribute Roosevelt's reluctance to his fears about getting too far ahead of public opinion, something that Roosevelt was clearly concerned about. There is also considerable evidence that Woodrow Wilson's experience was often in his thoughts. Early in May, he had taken time to go down to Staunton, Virginia, to dedicate Woodrow Wilson's birthplace. The highlight of the speech was his statement that "we are ever ready to fight again" for "the freedom of democracy in the world." But later in his brief remarks, he may well been thinking of his own posthumous reputation when he said of Wilson: "That selfish men did not share his vision of a world emancipated from the shackles of force and the arbitrament of the sword in no wise detracts from its splendor. Rather does the indifference of hostile contemporaries enhance the beauty of the vision which he sought to build."[35]

On May 24, as Roosevelt's speechwriters were beginning to work on what the president had decided would be a major speech, came the startling news that the German battleship *Bismarck,* then the largest warship afloat, had slipped through the British blockade and in a brief but deadly engagement in the Denmark Strait between Greenland and Iceland had sunk the British battle cruiser *Hood,* had damaged the battleship *Prince of Wales,* and was loose in the North Atlantic, headed God knows where. Sherwood remembered Roosevelt in his shirtsleeves in the Oval Study speculating casually about the *Bismarck,* suggesting that it might be headed toward Martinique. If that happened and a navy submarine managed to sink it, he asked, "Do you think the people would demand to have me impeached?" They soon learned that the *Bismarck,* damaged by the British ships, was headed east, toward the French coast, and later that it had been spotted by a PBY Catalina seaplane and then, on the day of the president's speech, that it had been sunk by the Royal Navy. The information that the seaplane had been flown by one of seventeen U.S. Navy pilots flying those planes in Royal Air Force (RAF) Coastal Command squadrons was kept secret even from cabinet officers such as Harold Ickes.[36]

The president's speech indicated that he did not seem to have advanced his polices beyond what he had laid down in the Arsenal of Democracy and Four Freedoms speeches of early winter. As Lawrence and Cornelia Levine note, its "ideological center" was this statement: "We will not accept a Hitler dominated world. And we will not accept a world, like the post-war world of the 1920s, in which the seeds of Hitlerism can again be planted and allowed to grow."

The president laid out more clearly than before that both capital and labor must accept restraints in the name of national defense. "All of us know that we have made very great social progress in recent years. We propose to maintain that progress and strengthen it. When the Nation is threatened from without, however, as it is today, the actual production and transportation of the machinery of defense must not be interrupted by disputes between capital and capital, labor and labor, or capital and labor. The future of all free enterprise—of capital and labor alike—is at stake."

The "news" in the speech was Roosevelt's announcement upgrading the "limited national emergency" he had declared in September 1939 to an "unlimited national emergency." The precise difference in presidential power between the two is not clear. Roosevelt said only: "I have tonight signed a proclamation that an unlimited national emergency exists and requires the strengthening of our defense to the extreme limit of our national power and authority."

But the message of the speech was that Hitler was bent on world domination and that the United States would do anything necessary to stop him. The real clue was Roosevelt's reasserting the traditional doctrine of "freedom of the seas." He used the phrase five times—one of them adding it to the four freedoms he had espoused earlier. It was ancient and traditional—and Wilson's exercise of it had led to a declaration of war, as Roosevelt knew well. He had deliberately refused to use the phrase earlier. A computerized search reveals no use by Roosevelt in a public statement before the unlimited-emergency speech and that he used it in eight subsequent speeches, all but one of them in 1941. Clearly, the president was laying the groundwork for reinstituting convoys, as had been the case in 1917–18. Queried by reporters just after the speech, Steve Early "explained" that the president did not mean convoying "in the old sense of the term," but "it probably means a strengthening, a better and more efficient patrol, with more ships patrolling."

Anticipation about what the president might say had been intense on both sides of the Atlantic, particularly on the East Coast, where speculation about the *Bismarck* and what it might do was intense. A night baseball game at the Polo Grounds between the Giants and the Boston Braves was paused for forty-five minutes while seventeen thousand spectators and both teams sat in silence and listened to a live broadcast of the speech and then resumed. In Ottawa a parliamentary session was ended prematurely so the members could listen, while in Britain hundreds of thousands were up at 4:30 a.m., listening to a shortwave broadcast transmitted by the BBC nationwide.[37]

When Sherwood went to Roosevelt's bedroom to say good night, he found the president in bed, "surrounded with telegrams . . . a thousand or more." Roosevelt, always conservative about such things, told him: "'They're ninety-five percent favorable!' he said. 'And I figured that I'd be lucky to get an even break on this speech.'"

The Hooper rating service estimated a record audience of eighty-five million. The first Gallup poll taken in the week after the speech showed a distinct uptick in those favoring convoying: in April only a minority, 41 percent, favored convoying, while 50 percent opposed; in two May polls, 52 percent favored convoying, and in the June poll 55 percent approved while only 38 percent opposed.[38]

At an overflow press conference the next afternoon, the president's remarks frustrated reporters and disappointed some hawks within the administration, including Hopkins, as seeming to retreat from the implications of his speech. He denied that he planned to convoy or that there would be any attempt to make additional changes in the Neutrality Act. The conference ended with the following exchanges:

Q: You said there were some eight pages of statutes that confer upon you various powers in an emergency. Could we possibly obtain access to those eight pages?

THE PRESIDENT: No, because you might misconstrue them.

Q: Mr. President. Could you tell us if naval patrol ships are to resort to any new measures, as yet, beyond signaling?

THE PRESIDENT: That is one thing Hitler wants to know.

Q: Mr. President, are we to assume from these answers that all of the steps that you may take from now on of a naval and military character are secret?

THE PRESIDENT: I wouldn't say everything . . . I have answered directly, without using that method, about three-quarters of all the questions that you have asked today. There are some things that I am not going to tell you about, and you will get accustomed to not asking them after a while.

Q: No, we won't.[39]

Actually, though Roosevelt didn't know it, an American destroyer had already fired what a naval historian called "the first shot" of the undeclared Atlantic war some seven weeks earlier. On April 11, the USS *Niblack,* while rescuing torpedoed Dutch seamen off Iceland, picked up a sonar contact that could have been a U-boat and dropped three depth charges without visible result. At the end of April, back in port, its commander reported the incident to his admiral, who assumed that it had been a false contact—which postwar examination of German records confirmed—and did not pass the information on to the Navy Department.

But as soon as the crew of the *Niblack* got shore leave, word began to spread in the navy about a "U-boat encounter." Eventually, the naval high command heard about it and began an investigation. It also reached the ears of journalists, one of whom published an item about it in his column in mid-June. Other accounts, many of them made of whole cloth, followed. Secretary Knox gave a detailed and accurate account to Congress, which was widely disbelieved. There is no evidence that this incident influenced Roosevelt's cautious Atlantic policy, though historians have long made that assumption. By the time Roosevelt learned of it, he was already planning to expand the scope of naval patrolling.[40]

The largely symbolic declaration of an unlimited national emergency was followed by a succession of incremental, tangible steps, both public and secret, all of which could have been accomplished without it. In rapid succession, Roosevelt appointed Ickes "petroleum coordinator for national defense" and secretly gave tentative approval to a military plan for a friendly occupation of the Azores, perhaps assisted by Brazilian troops. He withdrew that approval when he learned from the British, who as allies of the Portuguese had been asked to inquire if such a move would be welcomed, that the answer was no.

On June 6, the president secretly directed an occupation of Iceland—which none of his military planners wanted—eventually replacing British forces there. It took a month to execute. The move effectively expanded the Western Hemisphere a degree of latitude eastward, simplified the escorting of ships that far, and made conflict with German submarines more likely.

Backing up his tough talk in the May 27 speech, Roosevelt, for the first time, used federal troops in a labor dispute and at the same time used his emergency powers to seize the Los Angeles aircraft plant involved. The plant had two hundred million dollars in military contracts. The dispute had been "settled" by an agreement mediated by the National Defense Mediation Board and accepted by management and the national leadership of the United Automobile Workers (UAW). But the local union, which was led by antiwar left-wingers, some of them Communists, rejected the settlement and closed down the plant. Roosevelt's order specified his powers as "President . . . and Commander in Chief" and ordered the secretary of war "to take possession of and operate" the plant, employing persons of his choice to do so. Two thousand soldiers were sent to the plant, and newspaper headlines featured "Bayonets," but the only serious violence had occurred between strikers and police attempting to allow nonstriking workers into the plant before the troops arrived. Production resumed almost immediately, as many workers went back to work from the picket line.

This episode set a pattern for worst-case labor problems during the emergency and war periods. The president's statement assured workers that their rights would be respected and that the terms of the eventual settlement would be retroactive to May 1. Most labor leaders supported such procedures. Within the administration, there was a range of reactions: Attorney General Jackson found the situation more like an "insurrection" than a strike, the OPM's Sidney Hillman blamed the strike on "a small band of irresponsibles," while many others ascribed the problem to Communists. General Hershey, following World War I draft precedents, wired Los Angeles draft boards to "reconsider" any occupational deferments given to workers who went on strike. In Congress, particularly in the House, antilabor rhetoric reached new heights. After less than a month, on July 2, the president ordered the plant returned to private ownership, and the troops and government appointees left.[41]

Only on June 10 did Washington learn of the loss of the American freighter *Robin Moor* on May 21 in the South Atlantic; happily, all the crew and passengers were rescued. They testified that a German U-boat was the culprit. It was the kind of incident Hitler had feared. Roosevelt could have used it to ratchet up tension, but he did not choose to do so. He refused for almost two weeks to say anything significant about it. While he was waiting, Sumner Welles in the State Department announced in a press conference that "at the direction of the president" and because of "subversive activities" by German officials in the United States, all twenty-six German consulates were ordered closed, along with a number of semiofficial organizations. But diplomatic relations were not broken. The Germans naturally reciprocated.

When Roosevelt had full reports from Brazil ten days later, he issued a statement to Congress and sent it to the German Embassy. He laid out the facts showing that the Germans had violated international law and then denounced "German plans for universal conquest—a conquest based upon lawlessness and terror on land and piracy at sea." He argued further that "we must take the sinking of the *Robin Moor* as a warning to the United States not to resist the Nazi movement of world conquest. It is a warning that the United States may use the high seas of the world only with Nazi consent. Were we to yield on this we would inevitably submit to world domination at the hands of the present leaders of the German Reich. We are not yielding and we do not propose to yield."[42]

Many of the administration's hawks, including Hopkins, expected the president to escalate the stakes, either by arming merchant vessels or by instituting convoys or both, but Roosevelt, who had set the occupation of Iceland in motion, made no such move. As for the *Robin Moor,* it was all but forgotten in the press of more important matters. Although Germany did not respond publicly to Roosevelt's charges about the sinking, Hitler had secretly barred attacks on U.S. merchant and naval vessels outside the war zone.[43]

Hitler's Operation Barbarossa, the invasion of the Soviet Union, did not surprise world leaders, except for Joseph Stalin (1879–1953). Acting on intelligence reports, Roosevelt had sent the Soviet premier warnings as early as March 1941, which he ignored. Once it began, in the early hours of June 21, everyone knew that a change had come in the war. War Secretary Stimson wrote Roosevelt that his view of the situation, and that of General Marshall and the War Plans Division, was that "Germany will be thoroughly occupied in beating Russia for a minimum of one month and a possible maximum of three months."

Stimson and Knox both urged Roosevelt to use the brief window of opportunity when German forces would be tied down to strike major blows in the Atlantic. The British military similarly predicted that "the occupation of Moscow and the Ukraine might take as little as three or as long as six weeks, or more."

Fortunately, the political leaders in each country were willing to consider giving aid to Russia. The prime minister and the president soon coordinated their responses. Churchill wrote, "We shall of course give all encouragement and any help we can spare to the Russians, following the principle that Hitler is the foe we have to beat." He added his hope that his statement would not cause Roosevelt "any embarrassment." The president assured him via Ambassador Winant that he would publicly support any such statement.[44]

Churchill spoke to the British people on the evening of the day after the invasion. The White House helped arrange nationwide live coverage on the major America radio networks. Borrowing from his own rhetoric, the Briton asserted, "We are resolved to destroy Hitler and every vestige of the Nazi regime. . . . We shall fight him by land; we shall fight him by sea; we shall fight him in the air, until, with God's help, we have rid the earth of his shadow, and liberated its people from his yoke. Any man or State who fights against Nazism will have our aid. Any man or State who fights with Hitler is our foe."[45]

Roosevelt, in different circumstances, orchestrated a more measured response, but as the proprietor of the Arsenal of Democracy it was his response that mattered. It came, first, in a formal statement by Sumner Welles, which he made clear came from Roosevelt. The statement denounced both Russia and Germany as powers that did not recognize the free exercise of religion, but insisted that "Hitler's armies are today the chief dangers of the Americas." Welles made no commitment about aid to Russia but noted that the Lend-Lease law empowered the president to provide aid to any nation deemed vital to the defense of the United States. In his press conference the following afternoon, Roosevelt endorsed Welles's statement and added that "we are going to give all the aid we possibly can to Russia." But he refused to say precisely what because no requests had been received. He did say that he had ordered the Treasury to unfreeze forty million dollars of Soviet funds. The next day, he announced that he would not enforce the Neutrality Act against the USSR, which had the practical effect of leaving the Pacific port of Vladivostok open to receive shipments from the United States.[46]

Initial congressional reactions revealed substantial resistance to assisting the Russians by isolationists regardless of party and from some interventionists. Among the former in the Senate, Democrat Bennett Clark of Missouri felt that "Stalin was as bloody minded as Hitler. I don't think that we should help either one," Wisconsin Progressive La Follette predicted that "interventionists" would stage "the greatest whitewash act in history" to get the country into war, while Ohio's Taft opposed aid to Russia because "the victory of communism in the world would be far more dangerous to the United States than the victory of fascism."

Even a then obscure New Deal Democrat, Missouri's Harry Truman, could sound off in what one of his biographers calls his "Captain Harry" mode: "If we see that Germany is winning we ought to help Russia and if Russia is winning we ought to help Germany and in that way let them kill as many as possible, although I don't want to see Hitler victorious under any circumstances. Neither of them think anything of their pledged word." Herbert Hoover, while continuing to support aid to Britain and China, denounced any aid to a Communist power as a "gargantuan jest" that betrayed American ideals.[47]

However, Roosevelt could take solace from the polls. In Gallup's initial sampling after Hitler's invasion, 72 percent of respondents to the question of whom they wanted to see win the war opted for Russia, a mere 4 percent favored Germany, 17 percent said it made no difference, and 7 percent answered "don't know." Relatively few, 22 percent, thought Russia would win; 47 percent believed Germany would win; 8 percent expected a stalemate, and 23 percent had no opinion. An earlier June poll gave the president a resounding 76 percent approval rating.[48] In addition, Roosevelt knew that the attack on Russia would mean that American Communists and their supporters in the labor movement would no longer be instigating strikes in defense industries.

Significant aid to Russia would take a long time to generate, because of the logistical difficulties, mutual suspicions, and Roosevelt's habitual caution. He did later agree to Hopkins's suggestion that he go to talk to Stalin; only after his mission was completed did detailed plans for aid began.[49]

But the president's immediate focus remained on the North Atlantic. He would not go as far as Admiral Stark, who pressed him to institute transatlantic convoys, but he gave his hawkish subordinates license to go beyond what he was willing to authorize. When, for example, he was asked about a public speech in which Navy Secretary Knox said that "the time to use our Navy to clear the Atlantic of the German menace is at hand," he refused comment. He later said that he continued to "hope" that the United States could stay out of the war, but would not say, as he once had, that he expected it to be able to do so.[50]

On July 7, the occupation of Iceland went off without challenge, as Hitler's instructions for restraint were followed. The navy landed a brigade of some four thousand Marines escorted by a small armada of warships ready to fight if necessary. As it was progressing, Roosevelt sent a message to Congress announcing the action, suggesting falsely that there had been an immediate likelihood of a German occupation. Included in the message was the announcement that American troops would take up posts at bases secured in the 1940 destroyer deal in British Guiana and Trinidad. Both moves, the president claimed, were "to forestall any pincers movement undertaken by Germany against the Western Hemisphere." He also described the arrangements made with the Icelandic government, which was promised recognition and given some favorable trade terms. Eventually, the British garrison would be removed for service elsewhere. Twelve days later, the U.S. Navy issued orders "to escort convoys of United States and Iceland flag shipping, including shipping of any nationality which may join

United States or Iceland flag convoys, between United States ports and bases, and Iceland." What this meant, in effect, was that the American navy, with help from Canadian and Free French frigates and destroyers, was convoying ships that took the northern route to Britain roughly halfway, allowing the British to intensify their efforts in the eastern half of the Atlantic. In each convoy the U.S. Navy guarded, there was supposed to be at least one American vessel bound for Iceland. Most vessels went on to Britain.

In the press conference following Roosevelt's announcement of Iceland's occupation, a reporter queried:

> Q: Mr. President, the last time you gave us the imaginary line, it ran be-
> tween Iceland and Greenland. Has there been a shift in that line?
> THE PRESIDENT: That is, as I say, depending on the geographer I had seen the
> previous night.[51]

After it was clear that the Iceland move was a success, Roosevelt and Hopkins had a long talk about the war on Friday evening, July 11. As a result, Hopkins went off on his second mission to Churchill. He was to look into how Lend-Lease was operating and to set up a meeting between Roosevelt and the prime minister. Instead of accompanying the president on his weekend cruise, Hopkins

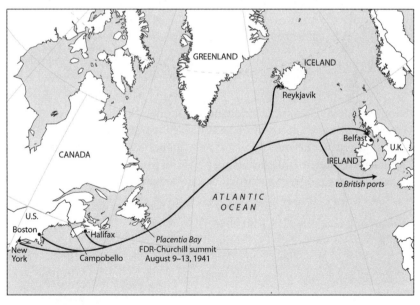

Major convoy routes in the North Atlantic, where American naval and air forces were increasingly engaged with German submarines during the twenty-seven months of American neutrality. After Pearl Harbor, German submarines had great success sinking unescorted merchant ships along the American east coast.

had a whirlwind trio of conferences with Welles, with the head of the Maritime Commission, and with Lend-Lease administrator General Burns. He then dined Saturday night with Ambassador Halifax and flew out Sunday morning on commercial flights to Montreal and Gander, Newfoundland. From Gander he flew in a Lend-Lease B-24 bomber being ferried to Prestwick, Scotland. Unlike his previous trip aboard a luxurious Pan American clipper, whose seats converted to beds as on a Pullman car, military flying was in frigid, unpressurized aircraft that were uncomfortable for young pilots and agony for a middle-aged semi-invalid. Hopkins was invariably ill by the time such journeys ended. Churchill had him brought straight to Chequers, his country house.

Hopkins achieved his goals and invented a new assignment for himself. After a week and a half in England, he was asked by Ambassador Winant if he thought it a good idea for him to ask the president's permission to fly to Moscow to encourage the Russians. Hopkins responded positively, and, according to Winant, "after a moment of silence, he said, 'What would you think of my going from here?'" Winant thought that it would be even more effective because of Hopkins's well-known closeness to Roosevelt and role in Lend-Lease. They drafted a cable "For the President only," signed "Harry," which made a case for Hopkins making the trip. The following night at Chequers, Hopkins received Roosevelt's cable that "highly approved" the trip. Churchill arranged for Hopkins to be flown from Scotland to Archangel in the Russian Arctic in a PBY. He carried with him only a handwritten visa from the Soviet ambassador in London and a cable from Welles beginning:

> The President asks that when you see Mr. Stalin you will give him the following message in the President's name: "Mr. Hopkins is in Moscow at my request for discussions with you personally and with such other officials as you may designate on the vitally important question of how we can most expeditiously and effectively make available the assistance which the United States can render to your country in its magnificence resistance to the treacherous aggression by Hitlerite Germany. . . . I ask you to treat Mr. Hopkins with the identical confidence you would feel if you were talking directly with me."

As had been the case in London, Hopkins made a strong positive impression in Moscow and received a level of cooperation and relative openness not shown to other envoys. Both leaders accounted his mission a success.

The arduous journey was made worse for Hopkins as he forgot the medicines he needed to take every day. He returned to Scotland, quite ill, in time to be bundled aboard the *Prince of Wales* a day before it sailed to take Churchill to his first meeting with the president, though the two had met in London during World War I.[52]

The meeting, called in retrospect the first summit, involved some danger to its principals. Churchill simply disappeared; Roosevelt staged a hoax, a false fishing trip aboard the *Potomac* along the New England coast, which had taken him from his embarkation point, the submarine base at New London. Once at sea, Roosevelt spent a day actually fishing off Martha's Vineyard and then was transferred to the cruiser USS *Augusta,* along with his personal staff—Pa Watson, Dr. McIntire, and naval aide Captain John Beardall—and for his first long sea voyage Roosevelt's Scotch terrier, Fala. An accompanying cruiser, the USS *Tuscaloosa,* carried Generals Marshall and Arnold, Admirals Stark and King, and staff officers who had secretly boarded in New York. With escorting destroyers, the little flotilla headed for the rendezvous with Churchill and his staff, plus Harry Hopkins on the *Prince of Wales,* in Placentia Bay, adjacent to the American base at Argentia. Undersecretary of State Welles and Averell Harriman had flown in from Boston on August 9. And, perhaps without Roosevelt's prior knowledge, his sons Elliot and Franklin Jr., serving naval officers, were ordered to visit with him.

As the *Potomac* continued to cruise off New England, with a crewman sometimes fishing as if he were the president, the navy sent false messages describing the president's fishing. It did not fool the press, which was immediately suspicious because the "three musketeers," the wire-service pool reporters, were not accommodated. From London came rumors of a Churchill trip when it was announced that he would not be present for an important session of the House of Commons. By the morning of August 6, three days before the summit began, the *Times'* White House correspondent, Frank Kluckhohn, had put most of the pieces of the puzzle together. Admitting that he was speculating, he guessed that Roosevelt, Hopkins, and Churchill "had met or would meet at sea or in some New World port."[53]

The meeting of the two Western leaders on August 9–12, 1941, was an extraordinary event that began their physical collaboration. By the time of their last meeting in Egypt on February 15, 1945, they would spend some four months—133 days—in each other's company. In World War I, Wilson had not met with other Allied leaders until the Peace Conference. That flawed and fateful meeting might have turned out better if he had.

Roosevelt had been talking about such a meeting since December. Each leader was curious about the other. They came with different agendas. Churchill wanted, above all, to get the United States into the war; Roosevelt was most interested in setting forth the principles on which their joint struggle was based. As Churchill put it in a cable to his cabinet sent from the conference, Roosevelt attached great "importance to the Joint Declaration which he feels will affect the whole movement of United States opinion . . . I fear the President will be very much upset if no Joint Statement can be issued and grave and vital issues might be affected."

Many American and British writers speak of Roosevelt and Churchill as if they were comparable leaders, but that was not the case. First of all, Roosevelt was a head of state, Churchill the chief of a cabinet; Roosevelt didn't even tell many of his cabinet officers that there had been a conference until after it was over. And while Churchill cut a great figure on the Anglo-American stage, Roosevelt could capture the imagination of Asian and African leaders in a way that the staunch imperialist Briton never could. Churchill envisaged a world very much like the past; Roosevelt was trying to create a new one.

The military leaders, apart from getting to know one another, accomplished nothing new. They did ratify naval arrangements already agreed upon, which assigned the responsibility of convoying in the western Atlantic to the American navy, thus freeing some fifty British destroyers and corvettes for duty elsewhere. The convoying was expected to produce armed encounters with U-boats, which all concerned thought likely to trigger a German-American war, as in 1917. Churchill's report to his war cabinet that "the President had said that he would wage war but not declare it, and that he would become more and more provocative. If the Germans did not like it, they could attack the American forces." That may not be an accurate quotation—it sounds more like Churchill than Roosevelt—but is probably a good gloss on the president's real intentions. Both leaders agreed that the priorities on the Pacific front were the same as in ABC-1: try to neutralize Japan without war, but if Japan came in, defeat Germany first.[54]

On the political side, a joint statement was, as Churchill's message to his cabinet indicated, adopted only at Roosevelt's insistence, though Churchill in his memoirs tried to make it seem that it was done at his initiative. Roosevelt, seconded by Welles and Hopkins, and Churchill, seconded by Alexander Cadogan (1884–1968), permanent undersecretary of the Foreign Office from 1938 to 1946, were able to agree upon a text in meetings in Roosevelt's "office" aboard the *Augusta*. The eight points they drafted aggregated a mere 319 words in a document titled "Joint Statement by President Roosevelt and Prime Minister Churchill, August 14, 1941." That document was a press release, and, somehow, no one thought to have it signed or even initialed. Its eight points provided:

First, . . . no aggrandizement, territorial or otherwise.

Second, . . . no territorial changes that do not accord with the freely expressed wishes of the peoples concerned.

Third, . . . the right of all peoples to choose the form of government under which they will live . . . sovereign rights and self-government restored to those who have been forcibly deprived of them.

Fourth, . . . the enjoyment by all States, great or small, victor or vanquished, of access, on equal terms, to the trade and raw materials of the world.

Fifth, [to secure] for all, improved labor standards, economic advancement, and social security.

Sixth, after the final destruction of the Nazi tyranny . . . a peace which will afford to all nations the means of dwelling in safety [that all] men . . . may live out their lives in freedom from fear and want.

Seventh, such a peace should enable all men to traverse the high seas and oceans without hindrance.

Eighth, . . . all of the nations of the world, for realistic as well as spiritual reasons must come to the abandonment of the use of force.

This utopian document, with its touches of a New Deal for the world, was a piece of propaganda like Roosevelt's Four Freedoms, which it partially echoed. It was released in both Washington and London on August 14 while both leaders were still at sea. In Washington, after Steve Early gave reporters the release just before nine in the morning, Secretary Hull held a news conference but made no comments apart from a denunciation of "uncivilized behavior" by unnamed nations. Congressional comment was generally favorable, as was the editorial reaction of the nation's press. Criticism by the shrinking isolationist minority was sharp, with emphasis on the president's exceeding his constitutional powers. The *Chicago Tribune* argued that Roosevelt, in pledging himself to the defeat of Hitler, overstepped his authority: "He was more than outside the country. He was outside his office."

In London the Foreign Office was doubly disappointed, having hoped for an American declaration of war and upset by many elements of the declaration that one unnamed spokesman styled "piteous platitudes." But a different London voice, the Labour Party's organ, the *Daily Herald,* understood that the statement was "a matchless weapon for our cause" and called it an "Atlantic charter." Neither Roosevelt nor Churchill had used that term or would use it in the following days and weeks, but the name had legs, and by January 1, when the United States, Great Britain, the USSR, China, and twenty-two other United Nations signed a joint declaration, it was officially described as a subscription to "a common program of purposes . . . known as the Atlantic Charter."[55]

While the two leaders were still at sea, a message from Roosevelt and Churchill was delivered to Stalin by their ambassadors, suggesting that "we prepare for a meeting . . . in Moscow [to plan] for the future allocation of our joint resources" and that looked forward to "complete victory." The Soviet leader immediately agreed to the proposal.[56]

Roosevelt returned to the United States on the *Potomac.* Before he came ashore at Rockland, Maine, he invited waiting reporters aboard for his first press conference in fifteen days. After saying that he had no news, welcoming them, and pointing out Harry Hopkins "just back from Moscow," he took the expected question.

PRESS: Could you tell us where this conference with Mr. Churchill was held?

THE PRESIDENT: I cannot, for obvious reasons. I had better make one or two things clear in the beginning. Names of ships are out. I suppose it has been published. The Prime Minister was there on the *Prince of Wales* and I was there on the AUGUSTA, but outside of that, nothing about ships, nothing about times, dates, and nothing about locations. All those things for perfectly obvious reasons, which I don't have to explain. *Just for example, I wanted to slay a gentleman that said I was coming to Rockland today because it's merely an invitation.*

Things of that kind cause trouble, if you make known the exact location on the high seas of the President and the Prime Minister. However, it was foggy between North Haven and Rockland, and while it's open season out there, no submarine fired a torpedo at us as far as we could see, and we are here safely.

The president spoke about what impressed him the most on the trip—"a very remarkable religious service on the quarterdeck of the PRINCE OF WALES last Sunday morning"—went through the names of the American conference participants, refused to say how long Churchill was with him, played down the conference as an "interchange of views, that's all. Nothing else," and generally gave meaningless answers.

On one topic, however, he was forthcoming: the fact that news came out of London that was not available from Washington. Steve Early, who had been kept in the dark like almost everyone else, had radioed him the day after the conference ended that "London is leaking" and that pictures of Roosevelt and Churchill were being offered to the American press in London. Early later urged him to have a conference in Maine. So when asked, Roosevelt was ready.

THE PRESS: One thing, Mr. President, were any steps taken to document this
　　meeting for history, from the American point of view?
THE PRESIDENT: I will have to talk off the record—not for use, literally, not
　　for use. There is no reason why you fellows shouldn't know. The reason
　　I can't use it is that it would be discourteous. The whole point of the
　　original arrangement was, as you know, secrecy, for perfectly obvious
　　naval reasons, and I didn't take you three fellows or anyone else. Neither
　　did I take any cameramen. But when we got there we found that there
　　was a moving picture man who goes around with Mr. Churchill. . . .
　　On the question of writing . . . the Ministry of Information in England,
　　at the last minute, had sent two gentlemen who they insisted were not
　　newspapermen, they were people who wrote books. . . . If I had known
　　I would have done it too. . . . I can't say "Mea culpa." Because it was the
　　other fellow's "culpa."

Despite the president's protestations, it was his culpability in insisting on the secrecy and his delight in putting one over on everybody. Had Early been told that a conference was afoot, he might have been able to persuade his boss to have the three musketeers and a picture person or two placed aboard the *Augusta*. It was an error not repeated.[57]

After the press conference, the president boarded his train to return to the capital; on Roosevelt's arrival, Hull, who had been told of the conference beforehand, was waiting on the platform, and they rode back to the White House together and conferred for more than two hours. Later, the president announced a plan to ferry aircraft to the British in Egypt via a route that went through U.S. bases in the Caribbean, eastern Brazil, West Africa, and the Sudan. Despite press reports that it was the "first fruit" of the Atlantic meeting, the army had been developing the plan for some time; it actually went into operation in November. Roosevelt described it as delivering "aircraft from the 'arsenal of democracy' to a critical point in the front against aggression." Initially, the ferrying was done by civilian pilots working for Pan American Airways, which would also operate a service in its own planes, taking spare parts to the British and bringing ferry pilots back; later, it was taken over by the army's Ferrying Command. This and later cooperation from most Latin American nations was surely another fruit of the Good Neighbor policy. After Hull had given tacit approval to joint British-Soviet occupation of Iran to control a new railroad running from the Persian Gulf to the USSR and forestall a feared move by Germans from French-mandated territory in the Middle East, informed sources in Washington pointed out that this would be a less remote and troublesome route to send Lend-Lease supplies to the USSR than using Vladivostok, which received its first shipments of American gasoline at the end of August.[58]

While Roosevelt was away, Congress had passed a much-debated bill extending the term of service for draftees and mobilized National Guardsmen and reservists whose original term of service had been one year. The legislation passed, but only after a one-vote decision in the House of Representatives, 203–202. After Pearl Harbor, and for years after that, Democrats belabored Republicans for almost destroying the army, and most historians who have written about it have echoed the charge, not understanding what the vote was about.[59] In fact, there was never a danger of the army melting away. A great deal of muttering about it could be heard in army camps, and "OHIO," an acronym for "over the hill in October," army slang for desertion, had been chalked in latrines and on walls in many of them. In the event, no wave of desertions occurred.

The issue was never the continuation of the draft but how long the service of nonvolunteers already in the service would be extended. Back in July, the original joint resolution authorized the president to extend such service "for such periods of time as may be necessary," the kind of authority Roosevelt liked but did not always expect to get. He knew that a majority in the country supported a draft extension of some kind; a Gallup poll released just before the Senate began to vote showed 51 percent in favor of an extension of the time those drafted would serve, 45 percent opposed, and just 4 percent with no opinion.

The congressional opposition that arose was, first, against giving the president such authority and, second, over how long the terms were to be extended.

The major fight in the Senate, after the Democratic leadership abandoned the blanket grant of authority, was over the length of the additional service. The leadership opted for an eighteen-month extension; an amendment by Senator Taft cutting the extension to six months was defeated 50–27; a one-year extension was defeated 50–21 after the leadership flexed its muscles. At the same time, some of the sting was taken out of the bill by separate legislation allowing those over twenty-eight years of age, the upper limit of the draft, to be released from the army if they wished, and adding a monthly increase of ten dollars in pay of all who would be extended. The Senate passed the eighteen-month increase by 45–30.

Since it was a joint resolution, the House measure contained the blanket grant of authority to the president, but the leadership quickly substituted the Senate bill, and the single House vote was on that. While some hard-core isolationists like Missouri's Dewey Short (1898–1979) hoped to stop the draft altogether, more realistic opponents tried to trim the length of the extension. Had they succeeded in defeating the eighteen-month extension, there would have been votes on shorter extensions, and any temporal change in the Senate bill would have faced a hostile conference committee. The narrow House victory was achieved, as had been the case with the original draft legislation in 1940, without the direct intervention of the president. Roosevelt had spoken favorably about the extension in a July press conference, but it was General Marshall who told Congress that the army would face "disintegration" if draftees and others had to be released. Roosevelt signed the legislation shortly after he returned to the White House and issued the necessary proclamation to put the new law into effect four days later. At a September press conference when asked to comment on suggestions that "the draft be limited" or perhaps done away with, his response was emphatic: "No. I would like to know who suggested it. I would like to send him to St. Elizabeth's," the federal mental institution.[60]

In the Senate, Virginia's Harry Byrd was making a detailed attack on the administration's management of war production, stressing its inefficiency and the delays caused by strikes and calling for a revamping of the structure of war production under a czar, something he knew that the president would continue to resist.[61]

Before leaving for a Hyde Park weekend, Roosevelt, responding to criticism that two of his four freedoms—religion and information—had been left out of the joint statement with Churchill, allegedly out of deference to Stalin, sent a formal message to Congress reporting on his meeting, with a very brief explanation he had written out in his own hand the night before.

> The Congress and the President having heretofore determined through the Lend-Lease Act on the national policy of American aid to the democracies

which east and west are waging war against dictatorships, the military and naval conversations at these meetings made clear gains in furthering the effectiveness of this aid.

Furthermore, the Prime Minister and I are arranging for conferences with the Soviet Union to aid it in its defense against the attack made by the principal aggressor of the modern world—Germany.

Finally, the declaration of principles at this time presents a goal which is worthwhile for our type of civilization to seek. It is so clear cut that it is difficult to oppose in any major particular without automatically admitting a willingness to accept compromise with Nazism; or to agree to a world peace which would give to Nazism domination over large numbers of conquered Nations. Inevitably such a peace would be a gift to Nazism to take breath— armed breath—for a second war to extend the control over Europe and Asia to the American Hemisphere itself.

It is perhaps unnecessary for me to call attention once more to the utter lack of validity of the spoken or written word of the Nazi Government.

It is also unnecessary for me to point out that the declaration of principles includes of necessity the world need for freedom of religion and freedom of information. No society of the world organized under the announced principles could survive without these freedoms which are a part of the whole freedom for which we strive.[62]

At a Hyde Park news conference, Roosevelt told reporters that since many persons had contacted him about Senator Byrd's criticism of war production he had asked the army to check Byrd's figures, and it had been reported to him that, except for the senator's statements about airplane production, which came from a published OPM report, "all of the figures . . . are completely inaccurate." Byrd had charged that "not a single tank had gone to Europe." Roosevelt answered that hundreds had been sent to the British in Egypt and were performing with excellent results. Byrd had said that only four 90mm antiaircraft guns were being made monthly, but the army reported that current production called for 61 monthly and was on schedule. Byrd said that monthly production of 81mm mortars was 15, but the army said that July production had been 72 and that production schedules called for 160, 260, and 320 for subsequent months. Roosevelt concluded, "Somebody sold him down the river on the figures." Byrd's rebuttal, carried in the same day's paper, stood up for the accuracy of his plane figures—which the president had granted—and admitted that 200 tanks had been sent to Egypt. He failed to respond to the rest of Roosevelt's rebuttal and reiterated his call for a thorough overhaul of war production. Further checking indicated that both Byrd and the president had significantly understated the total number of tanks delivered.[63]

On the following day, still in Hyde Park, the president caused a series of executive orders to be issued. The first directed Secretary Knox to take over and operate a New Jersey shipyard with $493 million in government contracts where production had been halted by a long strike. This second government takeover of a private company was agreeable to both management and labor, so that, unlike the Los Angeles strike situation, the use of troops was unnecessary. The second order authorized the construction of a petroleum pipeline from Louisiana refineries to North Carolina so that southeastern states would be less dependent on tankers, which were increasingly needed for military use. A third order authorized the secretary of commerce to allow the employment of "alien masters, officers, and crew on American flag ships" despite long-standing laws requiring that U.S. citizens fill such roles. Bill Hassett, increasingly assuming Early's tasks when the president was out of Washington, explained that this would allow British crews to man ships and was largely intended for interned foreign vessels whose seizure and use had been authorized by Congress.[64]

In another move demonstrating how Lend-Lease dominated American defense strategy, Roosevelt announced a military mission to help China use its Lend-Lease materials effectively "in the interest of the United States, of China, and of the world effort in resistance to . . . conquest by force." He said that a similar mission would soon be sent to the USSR. In Tokyo a source close to the Foreign Office called sending the mission to China "an unfriendly act."

The mission was headed by Brigadier General John Magruder, who had done two tours of duty in China as an attaché. His late-October report would express alarm over an impending Japanese drive to cut off the Burma Road and irritated General Marshall by urging support of Chennault's AVG group, which Marshall persistently opposed in the face of White House support.[65]

China's low place in Roosevelt's aid pecking order can be seen in the importance given to the parallel mission to the Soviet Union at a time when Hitler's forces were still advancing deeper into Stalin's empire almost every day. That mission was headed by W. Averell Harriman, a participant in the Argentia meeting, who carried a letter to "My Dear Mr. Stalin" from the president. It introduced "my friend Averell Harriman" and added: "Harry Hopkins has told me in great detail of his encouraging and satisfactory visits with you. I can't tell you how thrilled all of us are because of the gallant defense of the Soviet armies. I am confident that ways will be found to provide the material and supplies necessary to fight Hitler on all fronts, including your own. I want particularly to take this occasion to express my great confidence that your armies will ultimately prevail over Hitler and to assure you of our great determination to be of every possible material assistance."

Others on the mission included Major General Burns, who had served as Hopkins's deputy in Lend-Lease operations; Major General George H. Brett, chief of the air corps under Arnold; Admiral William H. Standley (retired), a former chief of naval operations; and William H. Batt, a dollar-a-year man who was director of the materials division of the OPM and perhaps a dozen others.

The parallel British mission was headed by Beaverbrook, another Argentia participant.[66]

Just before the president left for the meeting with Churchill, he had summoned Rosenman, still a New York judge, to the White House and instructed him to interview what we would call today the chief government stakeholders in war production as a prelude to yet another reorganization. After a number of such conferences, facilitated by the Budget Bureau, Rosenman, assisted by Wayne Coy (1904–57), another of Roosevelt's anonymous assistants then assigned as liaison with OPM and budget director Smith, drafted a variety of executive orders reflecting the widely conflicting views. The advantage for the president in using Rosenman, who then held no federal job, was that the whole process could be kept within the larger White House.

At the end of the month, Roosevelt made his decisions and created the Supply Priorities and Allocations Board (SPAB). The one new element was placing Vice President Wallace as its chairman. Otherwise, it was a rearrangement of the usual suspects who had been directing war production all along. A seeming difference was that what Roosevelt had called the law firm of Knudsen and Hillman now had four additional partners, none of them new to the scene: the two service secretaries, Stimson and Knox, representing the two biggest consumers; Harry Hopkins, representing the foreign consumers of military aid; and Leon Henderson, as price administrator, to represent the civilian consumers. To manage the caseload, SPAB was given an executive director, Donald M. Nelson, former vice president of Sears, Roebuck. Nelson, who had been the OPM purchasing director, was now called OPM priorities director. In his dual role, he was expected to oversee the distribution of the twenty thousand applications for priorities that arrived weekly. Other changes included the Stettinius appointment as Lend-Lease administrator, as noted above, and John D. Biggers (1888–1973), president of Libby-Owens-Ford Glass Company, who had been OPM production director, was sent to London as minister to replace Averell Harriman, with Knudsen adding OPM production director to his other tasks.

The White House spin on this was that the reorganization stemming from Rosenman's report was "a voluntary agreement" between OPM, the Office of Price Administration and Civilian Supply, and the War and Navy Departments, but it was a lot more than that. It was, for Roosevelt, a matter of keeping control of defense production within the EOP, another attempt to deflect the constant demands for an economic czar, and a way to continue to ignore publicly, for a time, the elephant in the room: the fact that the largest single consumer of steel and other vital commodities was the automobile industry, which was enjoying its best sales since the onset of the Great Depression and was reluctant to begin retooling its plants. Roosevelt did recognize that converting existing plants to military production could involve a considerable short-term increase in unemployment by as much as two million persons.[67]

Before leaving for Hyde Park, the president indicated that his Labor Day address, normally about domestic politics, would contain something of importance about the war, since it fell on the second anniversary of Hitler's attack on Poland. Roosevelt, as part of a radio program devoted to labor organized by the OPM, told a worldwide audience that "American labor now bears a tremendous responsibility in the winning of this most brutal, most terrible of all wars." "In our factories and shops and arsenals we are building weapons on a scale great in its magnitude. To all the battle fronts of this world these weapons are being dispatched, by day and by night, over the seas and through the air. And this Nation is now devising and developing new weapons of unprecedented power toward the maintenance of democracy. Why are we doing this? Why are we determined to devote our entire industrial effort to the prosecution of a war which has not yet actually touched our own shores?" Sounding more like a president at war than ever before, he began five successive paragraphs with the words *These enemies* and then warned, "Those who think that Hitler has been blocked and halted are making a dangerous assumption." His peroration stressed future dangers.

> Yes we are engaged on a grim and perilous task. Forces of insane violence have been let loose by Hitler upon this earth. We must do our full part in conquering them. For these forces may be unleashed on this nation as we go about our business of protecting the proper interests of our country.
>
> The task of defeating Hitler may be long and arduous. There are a few appeasers and Nazi sympathizers who say it cannot be done. They even ask me to negotiate with Hitler—to pray for crumbs from his victorious table. They do, in fact, ask me to become the modern Benedict Arnold and betray all that I hold dear—my devotion to our freedom—to our churches—to our country. This course I have rejected—I reject it again.
>
> Instead I know that I speak the conscience and the determination of the American people when I say that we shall do everything in our power to crush Hitler and his Nazi forces.

The words seem to call for a declaration of war, but the president closed, after urging "all of us together . . . to build a democratic world on enduring foundations," with the hope that "on some future Labor Day . . . some future President of the United States [will say] that we did our work faithfully and well."[68]

We know very little about the genesis of this speech in which Roosevelt, in the words of the *Times'* White House correspondent, "went further than ever before to make clear that the United States was determined to insure Hitler's downfall." The president wrote the ten-minute message that weekend with only Hopkins for assistance. Neither Rosenman nor Sherwood had any part in it, and historians have not paid much attention to it. The only direct account of its purposes comes from what Hopkins wrote in a memo dated the day after the speech: "The president indicated that he wanted to make a straight forward speech about Hitler. It seemed to me that the drafts prepared were not taking the line that the president had in mind." Certainly, some, if not all, of the drafts came from the State Department, but Hopkins's remark does not deal with what seemed to be the most striking innovation of the speech, its warning to Americans about the likelihood of a German attack.[69]

To understand what Roosevelt was trying to convey on Labor Day, we must remember that he fully expected his actions in the North Atlantic to result, sooner or later, in either a German declaration of war or, more likely, an action against the United States so outrageous that public opinion would insist on his declaring war. As the official army history of hemispheric defense puts it, "Before a full state of war could develop in the Atlantic Japan struck in the Pacific."[70] Roosevelt's chief actions after Labor Day would be calculated to provoke hostilities in the North Atlantic.

6 The Last Days of Peace
1941

WHILE EXPECTING FURTHER ESCALATION IN the North Atlantic, what Wilson had called watchful waiting, Roosevelt continued his preparations for a global war. The most monumental of those projects was the construction of the army headquarters building that became the Pentagon, the largest single building project of his administration. In mid-July, sure that war and previously undreamed-of military expansion were bound to occur, War Secretary Stimson and his aides tasked the Corps of Engineers to design a very large building as soon as possible. A brilliant, arrogant, and often unpleasant engineer officer, Brehon B. Somervell (1892–1955), ramrodded the project through in record time. Somervell, then a brigadier general, was already known to Roosevelt as an effective WPA administrator who had taken over in New York City after Hugh Johnson resigned and was believed to enjoy the patronage of Harry Hopkins. He began preliminary work on the project on July 17, 1941, quickly decided that the place for it was across the Potomac in Virginia, and received the president's approval a week later. Ground was broken on September 11, the first bureaucrats began to move in to a partially completed building on April 30, 1942, and Stimson and Marshall moved into their suites in mid-November 1942.

The one major glitch came after Roosevelt returned from the meeting at Argentia and found a note from his uncle Fred, who was concerned about the building's location. Since 1924 he had been the unpaid chair of the National Capitol Park and Planning Commission and pointed out to his nephew that the huge building would spoil the views of Washington from Arlington Cemetery and otherwise degrade the ambience of that hallowed ground.

Roosevelt convoked a small motorcade on August 29 to conduct a personal inspection of the sites. Somervell was seated on one side of Roosevelt in his limousine, and Gilmore D. Clarke (1892–1982), chair of the congressionally chartered United States Commission on Fine Arts, an outspoken opponent of the project whom Somervell had persistently snubbed, was on the other. As they proceeded, Somervell persisted in trying to persuade the president not to make any changes, until, as reported by Clarke, Roosevelt said, "My dear general, I'm still commander-in-chief of the Army." When they got to a new site, still in Arlington but well away from the cemetery as the president and Clarke had discussed, Roosevelt said, again according to Clarke, "Gilmore, we're going to put the building over there, aren't we? Yes, Mr. President. Did you hear that general?"

When they returned to the White House grounds, Roosevelt, before leaving them, asked Somervell, "General, you're going to show the plans for the proposed building to the Commission on Fine Arts, are you not?"

When Somervell replied with an emphatic negative, Roosevelt instructed, "Well, General, you show the plans to the Commission on Fine Arts, and when they've approved of them, show them to me. That done everything should go ahead at full speed."

Four days later, the president announced that the project would go ahead and that it would be smaller and thus less expensive than the original proposal. In fact, it turned out to be larger—a fifth aboveground floor was added—and the cost, constantly covered up, was many billions above the estimate of thirty-five billion dollars given the president. In addition, Roosevelt had what seems today the quaint notion that once peace returned to the world, the Pentagon would be a great place to store the constantly increasing mass of records that the government was generating.[1]

Other arrangements involved getting the newly created board to manage priorities up and running and strengthening the American health care system. After meeting with Vice President Wallace after his appointment as SPAB director, the president told reporters there would be a greater emphasis on converting existing defense plants and less on building new ones. In a parallel statement, Wallace, after meeting with the president, provided details and said that production for civilians would be cut to provide more for the military. Ever the administrative innovator, Roosevelt had invented a task for vice presidents beyond presiding over the Senate and inquiring after the health of the president, something most of his successors have tried to emulate.[2]

Health care, which the president had meant to be in the disallowed new department Congress had refused to approve, now naturally fell to the subdepartment Federal Security Agency headed by Paul V. McNutt. But when Roosevelt created the Office of Defense Health and Services by executive order, he placed it also into the EOP, where it was relatively immune to congressional interference. He later used it to improve federal health services in many ways that Congress was unlikely to approve and fund, including, eventually, a large day-care program for war-worker mothers and improved medical care in areas with significant defense and war industry.[3]

Roosevelt's immediate legislative goal was to get a new tax bill passed shortly after the House returned from a Labor Day recess in midmonth. After meeting with the president, a congressional leader quoted him as being "particularly satisfied" with the pending provisions lowering the tax threshold from $2,000 to $1,500 for married persons and from $800 to $750 for single persons. Such an expanded tax base was expected to produce from $4.5 to $5 billion, covering perhaps a third of all projected current-year expenditures.[4]

The shooting war that Roosevelt expected began even before convoying resumed. On the morning of September 4, the recommissioned World War I destroyer USS *Greer,* out of Argentia and headed for Iceland some 125 miles southwest of Reykjavik, with a cargo of mail, freight, and a few army officers, was signaled by a British patrol plane that a German submarine had submerged some ten miles ahead. The *Greer's* skipper, obeying standing instructions not to attack but to track and broadcast the position of German vessels, sped toward the indicated area. After sonar picked up echoes of the German U-652, the destroyer followed the slower submerged vessel and signaled the British pilot that there would be no attack. The patrol plane, low on fuel, dropped four ineffective depth charges and flew away. Several hours later, U-652 decided to attack the still-tracking American ship, which managed to evade two torpedoes. *Greer* subsequently dropped nineteen depth charges in two attacks without major effect. In early evening, it ceased searching and proceeded toward Iceland.[5]

That night the Navy Department released an accurate but incomplete report: "The USS Destroyer *Greer,* en route to Iceland with mail, reported this morning that a submarine had attacked her by firing torpedoes which missed their mark. The *Greer* immediately counter-attacked with depth charges. Results are not known."[6]

In his morning press conference, Roosevelt began on the offensive:

THE PRESIDENT: You will all be asking about the attack of yesterday, so we might as well clear that up first. There is nothing to add, except that there was more than one attack, and that it occurred in daylight, and it occurred definitely on the American side of the ocean. . . . Then he recounted what "perhaps we might call an allegory."

Once upon a time, in a place I was living at, there were some schoolchildren out in the country who were on the way to school, and somebody undisclosed fired a number of shots at them from the bushes. The father of the children took the position that there wasn't anything to do about it—search the bushes, and take other steps—because the children hadn't been hit. I don't think that that's a bad illustration, in regard to the position of some people this morning.

The destroyer—it is a very fortunate thing that the destroyer was not hit in these attacks. And I think that is all that can be said on the subject today.

But he said a good deal more during a longish press conference, including, about halfway through, amending his allegory to include a "schoolteacher," with whom he identified, who "is searching the bushes," that produced this dialogue:

MR. GODWIN: Mr. President, what is the schoolteacher going to do if they find this marauder? What can be done? Seriously, can you discuss that?

THE PRESIDENT: I suppose eliminate him. Try to.

The final exchange in the conference was:

Q: Mr. President, a while ago, in connection with what might be done to the attacker of the *Greer*, you used the word "eliminate." Can we quote that one word?

THE PRESIDENT: I think so.

The result was headlines such as "FLEET TO 'ELIMINATE' ATTACKING SUBMARINE" on front pages all over America, even though the search for the U-652 had been broken off hours after the initial attack.[7]

The same day's papers carried an American reporter's story from Reykjavik saying that unidentified "officers and crew" of the *Greer* had told him that they were sure that their depth charges had at least damaged and may have sunk the submarine and that the *Greer* "was assisted by British aircraft in repelling the attack."[8]

Some hours after the press conference, Roosevelt left for a Hyde Park weekend, planning to give a Fireside Chat about naval policy in the North Atlantic on Monday evening. But the death of his mother postponed that for three days. Sara, who would have been eighty-six on September 21, had spent much of the summer in Campobello, where she had required the presence of a nurse, and suffered a sudden circulatory collapse late Saturday night and died shortly after noon on Sunday without regaining consciousness. Franklin had spoken with her on Saturday, and he and Eleanor sat with her until her death. She died in the bed in which she had given birth to her son.

We can only imagine the effect of his mother's death on Franklin; he never spoke of such matters. Eleanor's terse "It was a great sorrow to my husband" says as much, and as little, as can be said. Sara's funeral on Tuesday was private, with a service at her home with only family, personal friends, neighbors, and tenants in attendance. No reporter was allowed to attend. Her pallbearers—the eight oldest male employees of her estate, as had been the case in her husband's funeral four decades earlier—took her to a grave site beside her husband in the village churchyard.

With Sara's death, Springwood and its grounds passed to Franklin under the terms of his father's will. Her will, executed in October 1928 and not amended, after leaving five thousand dollars to the village church and to each of her three trustees, one of whom was her son, left 90 percent of her estate to Franklin; the other tenth was divided into six equal parts, one each for Eleanor and the five grandchildren who had been born before she made her will. Eleanor received the income from her share in trust for her lifetime; it then reverted to Franklin or his children. The grandchildren got the accrued income at age twenty-one and the principle and further income of the trust at age thirty.[9]

While still at Hyde Park, Roosevelt issued orders delaying a threatened nationwide railroad strike, which would have crippled the defense effort by invoking the sixty-day cooling-off period provided in the Railway Labor Act. He created a special fact-finding board headed by Dean Wayne L. Morse (1900–1974) of the University of Oregon Law School. Similar procedures would be a hallmark of Roosevelt's wartime labor policy.

He began his return to the capital Wednesday afternoon and summoned Hopkins and Rosenman, who had been working on the postponed Fireside Chat at the White House, to meet his train in Manhattan's Mott Haven yards, so they could polish the speech on the train. Their version was significantly stronger than any of the four versions from the State Department. A little after nine, the train arrived at Union Station in Washington, where Hull was waiting, and all four went to the White House, where Stimson and Knox had been summoned for a meeting that went on until almost midnight. Roosevelt read them the new draft, which had been expanded from fifteen to twenty-five minutes, some thirty-three hundred words. After the meeting, the two speechwriters—Sherwood was in Europe—made minor revisions, and in the morning the president read it to congressional leaders of both parties. On the eve of his chat, many in Congress expected the president to call for repeal of the Neutrality Act to permit arming of American merchant ships. The fact that congressional leaders, after meeting with the president, sent word that members of the recessed House should return early to be present by Tuesday only heightened the tension.[10]

Roosevelt spoke from the White House's Diplomatic Reception Room before a small audience of advisers and family, a mourning brassard on his left arm. He opened with a factual but misleading account of the *Greer* incident, omitting mention of the destroyer's collaboration with British aircraft and its airborne depth charges, which enabled him to characterize the incident as "piracy legally and morally." "It was not the first nor the last attack of piracy which the Nazi Government has committed against the American flag in this war. For attack has followed attack." The president then recounted four other incidents, going back to the torpedoing of the *Robin Moor* and including two submarine sinkings of American-owned vessels, one flying the Panama flag, since the *Greer* incident. He made it clear that these attacks were not to be considered as a reason to go to war.

> Our type of democratic civilization has outgrown the thought of feeling compelled to fight some other Nation by reason of any single piratical attack on one of our ships. . . . It would be unworthy of a great Nation to exaggerate an isolated incident, or to become inflamed by some one act of violence. But it would be unexcusable folly to minimize such incidents in the face of

evidence which makes it clear that the incident is not isolated, but is part of a general plan . . . the Nazi design to abolish the freedom of the seas and to acquire absolute control and domination of these seas for themselves.

For with control of the seas in their own hands, the way can obviously become clear for their next step—domination of the United States—domination of the Western Hemisphere by force of arms. . . . Hitler's advance guards—not only his avowed agents but also his dupes among us—have sought to make ready for him footholds and bridgeheads in the New World, to be used as soon as he has gained control of the oceans. His intrigues, his plots, his machinations, his sabotage in the New World are all known to the Government of the United States. Conspiracy has followed conspiracy . . . His intention has become clear. The American people can have no further illusions.

No tender whisperings of appeasers that Hitler is not interested in the Western Hemisphere, no soporific lullabies that a wide ocean protects us from him—can long have any effect on the hard-headed, far-sighted, and realistic American people.

After reminding his listeners that "one peaceful nation after another" had fallen to "the Nazis," he vowed, "No matter what it takes, no matter what it costs, we will keep open the line of legitimate commerce in these defensive waters." Then came lines that, at the last minute, Hull and the State Department wished to remove. "We have sought no shooting war with Hitler. We do not seek it now. But neither do we want peace so much, that we are willing to pay for it by permitting him to attack our naval and merchant ships while they are on legitimate business." After noting the indifference of "German leaders" to diplomatic niceties, he delivered the punch lines of the speech. "When you see a rattlesnake poised to strike, you do not wait until he has struck before you crush him. These Nazi submarines and raiders are the rattlesnakes of the Atlantic. They are a menace to the free pathways of the high seas. They are a challenge to our sovereignty. . . . Their very presence in any waters which America deems vital to its defense constitutes an attack."

After a brief recourse to history, noting that both John Adams and Thomas Jefferson had used the navy to defend American commerce, Roosevelt claimed:

My obligation as President is historic; it is clear. It is inescapable.

It is no act of war on our part when we decide to protect the seas that are vital to American defense. The aggression is not ours. Ours is solely defense.

But let this warning be clear. From now on, if German or Italian vessels of war enter the waters, the protection of which is necessary for American defense, they do so at their own peril.

The orders which I have given as Commander in Chief of the United States Army and Navy are to carry out that policy—at once.

The sole responsibility rests on Germany. There will be no shooting unless Germany continues to seek it.

In closing, the president insisted that his action was "my obvious duty . . . the clear right of this sovereign nation . . . the only step possible. . . . I have no illusions about the gravity of this step. I have not taken it hurriedly or lightly. . . . [I]t cannot be avoided." After expressing confidence in the wisdom and resolve of Americans, he closed by invoking "that inner strength that comes to a free people conscious of their duty, and conscious of the righteousness of what they do, they will—with Divine help and guidance—stand their ground against this latest assault against their democracy, their sovereignty, and their freedom."[11]

Reactions in the capital and in the national press were decidedly mixed, but public opinion about the president and his foreign policy continued to be highly favorable. Wendell Willkie gave unequivocal approval, saying that Roosevelt "spoke as he should have spoken" and calling for "all Americans to rally to his support." Republican congressional leaders were cautious: Senator McNary called it "a candid statement . . . without any attempt to involve Congress," and Representative Martin agreed with the president to the extent that his action moved the country "closer to the shooting." Most Democrats supported the president with varying degrees of enthusiasm, while isolationists in both parties condemned his action. Nevada's McCarran called it "nothing short of an unauthorized declaration of war," while Senator Nye said that "we are nearer to a shooting war by presidential proclamation."

Many newspapers that often opposed Roosevelt supported his actions in this instance. The *New York Herald Tribune,* Republican and internationalist, found the president's speech based on "the broadest and firmest of all possible grounds—the historic American policy of freedom of the seas." Some southern newspapers, such as the *Montgomery (Ala.) Advertiser,* seemed almost eager for war: "We will follow our destiny, and if need be blaze the path with blood, new blood to refresh old marks."[12]

The loudest single voice of opposition came from Charles Lindbergh, acting as the America First Committee's spokesman. He spoke at its rally in Des Moines, timed so that his remarks immediately followed the president's speech, which had been piped into the hall live. Lindbergh included a statement that many of his supporters regretted: "The three most important groups that have been pressing this country toward war are the British, the Jewish and the Roosevelt administration."

In a clumsy attempt to shield himself from the inevitable charge of anti-Semitism, the famous aviator affirmed that "no person with a sense of the dignity of mankind can condone the persecution of the Jewish race in Germany." But he followed this with advice that seemed more like a warning, arguing that "instead of agitating for war, the Jewish groups in this country should be opposing it in every possible way, for they will be among the first to feel its consequences." He capped his discussion of the Jews by claiming that "their greatest danger to this country lies in their large ownership and influence in our motion pictures, our press, our radio, and our government."[13]

Roosevelt never responded to Lindbergh publicly. Since he was winning the public relations war, he didn't have to. A whole series of late September Gallup polls made clear, as the friendly *New York Times* wrote, that "the vast majority of Americans are with the President, not against him." A Gallup question asked voters if "Lindbergh, Wheeler, Nye and others" formed a "Keep-Out-of-War" party that ran candidates in the 1942 congressional elections, "would you vote for such a candidate?" Only 16 percent of those answering were positive. In a second poll asking whether respondents approved "having the United States shoot at German submarines and warships on sight," 56 percent approved, 34 percent disapproved, and 10 percent had no opinion. Two days later, Gallup reported that 60 percent of those who had voted Republican in 1940 favored their party "supporting the administration's foreign policy," 23 percent favored opposing it, and 17 percent were undecided. At the end of the month, as administration leaders in Congress prepared to push through a repeal of the Neutrality Act, Gallup reported that although in April voters had been against arming American merchant ships carrying war materials to Britain by two to one, by late September a majority of those with opinions favored changing the Neutrality Act "to permit American merchant ships with American crews to carry war materials to Britain"—46 percent for, 40 percent against, 14 percent no opinion. Counting only those with opinions gives a 53 percent positive result.[14]

Obviously, that polar change resulted from several factors: the American public's reactions against Hitler's aggression, sympathy for Britain's plight, and responses to Roosevelt's leadership. That leadership was, by design, meandering. Roosevelt was not so much the leader of a parade as he was a shepherd with a sheepdog moving an unruly and seemingly purposeless flock back and forth, left and right, but eventually pushing it to the place he had in mind.

Emboldened by the obvious success of his political strategy and tactics, the president, who had arranged to get advance copies of Gallup and other polls, used his September 23 press conference to kick off his campaign against the last bulwark of congressional isolationism, the once-sacrosanct, much-amended Neutrality Act, which had been on the books since 1935. The American-owned *Pink Star* had recently been sunk by a German submarine at the southern end of the Denmark Strait between Greenland and Iceland, the first such sinking since the so-called shoot-on-sight speech. Roosevelt used the incident as a way to talk about how John Adams and Jefferson had employed armed merchant-men, which elicited a "softball" question: "Mr. President, do you think that these ships that are being sunk so—er—rapidly, should be provided with some measure of self defense?" This set off an extended colloquy, ending with:

Q: Mr. President, if we are going to arm merchant ships, we have got to amend the present Neutrality law, that is right?

THE PRESIDENT: Yes, that is right.

Q: Then is it going to be piecemeal repeal on that from now on, or are you going -

THE PRESIDENT: (Interposing) Well that's the thing that is under consideration . . . the problem is how much we will ask in the way of repeal.[15]

On October 9, a little more than two weeks later, the president sent a formal message to Congress asking for revision of the Neutrality Act to permit the arming of American merchant ships and indicated that other aspects of the act needed revision. In actuality, the arming of merchant ships was a symbolic rather than a practical matter. The armaments a merchant vessel might carry were no real danger to submerged submarines, though light antiaircraft guns could be a deterrent to low-flying aircraft. Much more crucial were the provisions that kept American ships out of war zones.

Referring to Lend-Lease, Roosevelt noted that "since the American people, through the Congress," had resolved to send aid to "nations actively fighting against Nazi-Fascist domination," the government should not be limited by the restrictions of the Neutrality Act.

The revisions which I suggest do not call for a declaration of war any more than the Lend-Lease Act called for a declaration of war. This is a matter of essential defense of American rights.

[Changing the act] will not leave the United States any less neutral than we are today. . . .

I say to you solemnly that if Hitler's present military plans are brought to successful fulfillment, we Americans will be forced to fight in defense of our own homes and our own freedom in a war as costly and as devastating as that which now rages on the Russian front. . . .

We cannot permit the affirmative defense of our rights to be annulled and diluted by sections of the Neutrality Act.[16]

Eight days later, while the joint resolution to amend the Neutrality Act percolated through congressional committees, a five U-boat attack on a convoy protected by American and British warships produced the first American military deaths of what became World War II. A little after midnight on October 17, the new destroyer USS *Kearny*, part of the escort for a large eastbound convoy west of Iceland, was hit by a torpedo from an attacking U-boat. Badly damaged, it managed to get to safety in Reykjavik; eleven of the crew were killed, the first of nearly three hundred thousand American combat deaths in the war.

In Washington the Navy Department was quick off the mark, issuing a terse statement about the attack and providing a file photo of the *Kearny* early on the morning of the attack; the House was scheduled to vote on amending the Neutrality Act that afternoon and, as expected, approved arming merchant ships by a vote of 258–138. A reportedly "grim" Roosevelt, at Hyde Park, was given the information by telephone from Admiral Stark but had little to contribute in that day's and subsequent press conferences, except to say that the attack took place within his prescribed "defense zone."[17]

Roosevelt's comment on the *Kearny* came in his Navy Day address almost two weeks later and while the Senate was still debating what to do about the Neutrality Act. Delivered before a heavily military audience in a Washington hotel and broadcast nationally and internationally, it is usually described as Roosevelt's most militant speech before Pearl Harbor. It is interesting not only for what it said but also for what it did not say. The president began by pointing out that it was exactly five months since his declaration of an unlimited national emergency, and he recounted much that had happened since then.

> Our Army and Navy are temporarily in Iceland in the defense of the Western Hemisphere.
>
> Hitler has attacked shipping in areas close to the Americas in the North and South Atlantic.
>
> Many American-owned merchant ships have been sunk on the high seas. One American destroyer was attacked on September fourth. Another destroyer was attacked and hit on October seventeenth. Eleven brave and loyal men of our Navy were killed by the Nazis.
>
> We have wished to avoid shooting. But the shooting has started. And history has recorded who fired the first shot. In the long run, however, all that will matter is who fired the last shot.
>
> America has been attacked. The *U.S.S. Kearny* is not just a Navy ship. She belongs to every man, woman, and child in the Nation.

By the standards that existed at the outbreak of war in 1939, such a scenario would surely have meant a declaration of war. But Hitler and Roosevelt had so changed the rules of engagement that not only was there no war declaration, but both nations continued to maintain limited diplomatic relations! Left to their own devices, no one can say what it would have taken for either leader to declare war on the other. Roosevelt did not even think that it was any longer necessary for him to mention the possibility of a war declaration or even a rupture of relations.

Roosevelt responded to the protests of "some Americans—not many—[who] continue to insist that Hitler's plans need not worry us," by asserting, "Very simply and very bluntly—we are pledged to pull our own oar in the destruction of Hitlerism." He then defined the nation's "primary task": "producing and providing more and more arms for the men who are fighting on actual battlefronts.

. . . And it is the Nation's will that these vital arms and supplies of all kinds shall neither be locked up in American harbors nor sent to the bottom of the sea. It is the Nation's will that America shall deliver the goods. In open defiance of that will, our ships have been sunk and our sailors have been killed. I say that we do not propose to take this lying down."

Then, using for the first time publicly the three words headline writers had put in his mouth, he avowed "That determination of ours not to take it lying down has been expressed in the orders to the American Navy to shoot on sight. Those orders stand."

Noting that the House had already voted to amend an "outmoded" part of the Neutrality Act and that a Senate committee had recommended eliminating further "hamstringing provisions," the president, for the first time, urged specifically that American ships be authorized to deliver materials directly into war zones, which is "the course of honesty and of realism." "Our American merchant ships must be armed to defend themselves against the rattlesnakes of the sea. Our American merchant ships must be free to carry our American goods into the harbors of our friends. Our American merchant ships must be protected by our American Navy."

In closing, after denying the claims of those who "say that we have grown fat and flabby, and lazy—and that we are doomed," Roosevelt insisted: "Today in the face of this newest and greatest challenge of them all we Americans have cleared our decks and taken our battle stations. We stand ready in the defense of our Nation and in the faith of our fathers to do what God has given us the power to see is our full duty."[18]

Domestic reactions to the president's speech were predictable. Steve Early announced that messages to the White House were running eight to one in favor. By the second day of Senate debate on amending the Neutrality Act, opponents were resigned to the passage of the ship-arming provision approved by the House but retained a "modicum of hope" that they could prevent the repeal of the provisions that kept American ships out of the war zones.[19]

While the pros and cons of Roosevelt's speech were still being discussed and considered on both sides of the Atlantic, the destroyer USS *Reuben James,* a World War I four-stacker, was torpedoed while on convoy duty in the dark early-morning hours of October 31, west of Iceland. The single missile tore into the ship, causing the forward magazine to explode. The stricken vessel sank quickly; 115 of the crew of 150, including all officers, were killed.

Roosevelt's reaction—more properly lack of reaction—seems curious and callous. He opened his press conference on the morning of the sinking with a terse announcement and went on to other matters: "You have had the Navy announcement a little while ago. (On the sinking of the U.S. destroyer *Reuben James.*) There has been no further news since that time."

Later in the conference:

Q: Mr. President, is there any possibility of a severance of diplomatic relations with Germany as a result of these sinkings?
THE PRESIDENT: I hadn't heard a thing about it until you asked the question.
Q: Mr. President, now that one of our own warships has now—has been sunk, is there any difference in our international situation?
THE PRESIDENT: I don't think so. Carrying out the duty assigned.

Still later in the conference:

Q: Have you any information that German submarines have been sunk, or any that you could give out?
THE PRESIDENT: I wouldn't tell you if I did.

Well into his next press conference at Hyde Park three days later a reporter asked

Q: Is there any more on the REUBEN JAMES, Mr. President?
THE PRESIDENT: No. Nothing. There wasn't last night. I haven't talked this morning.

The matter of the sinking never came up again, and the president did not mention those and other American deaths in the North Atlantic in his remarks at Arlington National Cemetery on Armistice Day. In fact, the public record does not reveal that the words *Reuben James* ever crossed the president's lips until almost a year after the event.

The militant commander in chief of the Navy Day speech seemed to have been replaced by a cautious politician, perhaps afraid that popular anger might force him to call for war. That he did not wish to do so he had made clear in his November 3 press conference at Hyde Park.

Q: Mr. President . . . Lots of people who think just as you do on this war issue, also think that a continuance of diplomatic relations with Germany is a form of dishonesty. Could you elaborate your thoughts for background?
THE PRESIDENT: No. Only off the record. I would have to make it completely off the record. . . . We don't want a declared war with Germany because we are acting in defense—self-defense—every action. And to break off diplomatic relations, why, that won't do any good. It might be more useful to keep them the way they are.[20]

Robert Sherwood, the hawk of hawks among Roosevelt's inner circle, writing in 1948, explained Roosevelt's seemingly flat behavior in the days after the loss of the *Reuben James,* and many scholars have echoed him: "[Roosevelt] had said everything 'short of war' that could be said. He had no more tricks left. The hat from which he had pulled so many rabbits was empty. The President was now the creature of circumstance which must be shaped not by his own will but by the unpredictable determination of his enemies."[21]

Of course, that is the circumstance that any brink-of-war president must face, and Roosevelt knew that both Lincoln and Wilson had faced it. He had been very much in a one-step-at-a-time mode since the outbreak of war in 1939, and perhaps the prospect of emasculating the Neutrality Act *and* breaking relations seemed too precipitous.[22]

The *Reuben James* quickly faded from American memory as larger and more threatening tragedies occurred, leaving only Woody Guthrie's mournful wail as its only lasting marker.

Tell me what were their names?
Tell me what were their names?
Did you have a friend on the good Reuben James?[23]

Roosevelt was waiting for two distinct legislative steps. On November 7, the eleventh day of a bitter debate, the Senate voted 50–37 not only to repeal Section 6 of the Neutrality Act, which had forbade the arming of merchant ships, as the House had done three weeks earlier, but also to repeal Sections 2 and 3 as well, which barred merchant ships from belligerent ports and from presidentially declared war zones. The amended measure then moved to the House, where it met an unexpected snag: the demand by some House members, mostly prowar conservative southern Democrats, for assurances that something would be done about what seemed to them an unreasonable number of strikes, with the Lewis-led coal strike the chief point of complaint.

At a White House conference between the president and the two chief leaders of the House, Speaker Rayburn and Majority Leader McCormack, an exchange of letters was arranged. The two leaders wrote the president: "A number of members have asked what effect failure on the part of the House to take favorable action on the Senate's amendments would have upon our position in foreign countries and especially in Germany. Some of these members have stated that they hoped that you would make a direct expression upon this matter."

As agreed, the president answered immediately. He began by saying that he had had no thought of making such a statement, but "in view of your letter, I am replying as simply and clearly as I know how."

In the British Empire, in China, and in Russia . . . the effect of failure of the Congress to repeal Sections 2 and 3 of the Neutrality Act would be definitely discouraging. I am confident that it would not destroy their defense or morale, though it would weaken their position from the point of view of food and munitions.

Failure to repeal these sections would, of course, cause rejoicing in the Axis nations. . . .

Our own position in the struggle against aggression would be definitely weakened. . . . Foreign Nations, friends and enemies, would misinterpret our own mind and purpose. I have discussed this letter with the Secretary of State and he wholeheartedly concurs.

May I take the opportunity of mentioning that in my judgment failure [to repeal Sections 2 and 3] would weaken our great effort to produce all we possibly can and as rapidly as we can. Strikes and stoppages of work would become less serious in the mind of the public. I am holding a conference tomorrow in the hope that certain essential coal mines can remain in continuous operation. This may prove successful.

But if it is not successful, it is obvious that this coal must be mined in order to keep the essential steel mills at work. The Government of the United States has the backing of the overwhelming majority of the people of the United States, including the workers.

The Government proposes to see this thing through.

At the conclusion of eight hours of debate spread over two days, Majority Leader McCormack summed up. He first read a letter from Secretary Hull and statements from General Marshall and Admiral Emory S. Land, chair of the Maritime Commission, all emphasizing the importance of repeal for "the defense of the United States."

Then, speaking for himself, McCormack insisted that the question was "whether or not we of this generation are going to go down in history as . . . the first generation of Americans that failed to perform their trust." He called it "foolish, unfair, and dangerous" to vote against a vital defense measure because one disliked the administration's labor policy.

Finally, in a rare move, Speaker Rayburn left his chair and spoke from the well of the House. He first revealed and read Roosevelt's letter and added his own pledge that he was "ready to follow, or to lead in any move by legislation, or sanely otherwise, that will keep defense production going in the United States of America."

The vote that followed agreed to the Senate provisions, 212 to 194; the administration's majority had shrunk from 120 on the bill that permitted ship arming to just 26 in a little less than a month. Persons on both sides of the debate agreed that without Roosevelt's letter and Rayburn's intervention, the measure would have been more narrowly decided, if not defeated.[24]

Gallup polls showed a decided switch in public opinion brought about by events in the North Atlantic and the president's interpretation of them. Polling between October 22 and November 1 showed a nine-point increase on the already high percentage supporting arming merchant ships to 81 percent, with 14 percent opposed and 3 percent undecided. On the more controversial change—to allow American ships with American crews to deliver war material to Britain—Gallup showed a reversal of opinion since April, when only a third of those with opinions had favored that change: by early November, two-thirds of those with opinions favored it. Fifty-nine percent of Republican voters favored the arms change that would be opposed by 86 percent of House Republicans. The change in public opinion on intervention short of outright war—Roosevelt's stated foreign policy goal—was clearly a significant achievement. It put Roosevelt in the position he had been maneuvering toward since the crisis brought about by Hitler's successes in the spring of 1940. To be sure, it left him and the nation in the position of waiting for their enemies to make the next move, but that had always been an inherent implication of his policy.[25]

During the last months of the struggle over North Atlantic strategy and tactics, two other major matters were occupying Roosevelt's attention: the threat of a strike by John L. Lewis's United Mine Workers and increasing tension with Japan. They will be treated in separate narratives.

*   *   *

Roosevelt was reluctant to interfere with the right to strike both as a matter of principle and of practical politics: on the one hand, trade union support was an important part of his electoral coalition, and, on the other, public and congressional opinion was adamantly against strikes in defense industries. Polls since April 1940 showed persistently that about three quarters of the population thought there should be no right to strike in defense industries, and only about a fifth favored permitting such strikes. An early November poll asking, "Do you think that John L. Lewis was justified in calling this strike [against the captive mines]?" reported that only 8 percent answered yes, 60 percent said no, 14 percent were undecided, and 18 percent had not heard of the strike. A majority of trade union members in the poll also favored limiting the right to strike.[26] It is no coincidence that the first successful postwar rollback of a major New Deal achievement would be the 1947 Taft-Hartley Act, which significantly impaired but did not destroy the 1935 Wagner Act. Roosevelt's hopes that the firm of Knudsen and Hillman at OPM would provide a model for labor-management cooperation were unrealistic, and he had yet to construct an effective labor policy for a national emergency.

The UMW strike, of major importance in its own right, was also a part of the even larger question of the right to strike in defense industries. The period of the defense emergency—that is, between the fall of France and Pearl Harbor—was marked by continuing economic recovery that saw the unemployment rate drop below 10 percent for the first time since 1930. It was also a period of major gains for organized labor: perhaps a million and a half members were added to trade unions, and many former bastions of the open shop joined what was becoming a near consensus of major firms recognizing trade unions for the first time. At the same time, the number of defense plant strikes grew. Between July 1, 1940, and October 1, 1941, such strikes involved almost two million workers and resulted in twenty-four million lost man-days of work. By March 1941, the incidence of such strikes was serious enough for Roosevelt to create by executive order the National Defense Mediation Board and slot it into the OEM in his EOP. The chief advantage of this tactic was that he did not have to go to Congress, but the offsetting weakness was that the board did not have the power to enforce its findings or even subpoena documents or persons. Its eleven members served pro bono and were fully employed. The chair and three members represented the public, and four each represented labor and management. As critics immediately pointed out, the NDMB, as constituted, would be unlikely to settle fundamental disputes. This quickly proved to be the case in the southern coal strike in April, which Commerce Secretary Jones had to settle, and would be the case in an even more acrimonious coal dispute in the fall.[27]

That strike's prime issue was the status of the fifty-three thousand miners toiling in the so-called captive mines owned and operated by the major steel companies. Any prolonged interruption of production in these mines would have a major effect on defense production. The dispute was over the union's demand for a "union shop," which would require anyone hired by management to join the union. A union shop was already in effect in the other coal mines of the region under the so-called Appalachian Agreement. Only 5 percent of the captive miners were not members of the United Mine Workers, but both union and management saw the union shop as a key issue because the companies feared and the unions hoped that if a union shop were established in the steel companies' mines, it would provide a precedent for union shops in their steel mills, which were as yet only partially organized.

When the strike began on September 15, the NDMB asked the miners to return to work pending a hearing before it. Both sides agreed to a thirty-day truce while the board deliberated and the miners went back to work. More than a month later, John L. Lewis gave notice that the miners would walk out again in four days. On the Friday before the slated Monday strike, the NDMB told the president that its panel could not agree, even in the face of Lewis's promised Monday strike. The board's chair, William H. Davis (1879–1964), suggested alternative courses. The OEM, speaking for the president, proposed that Myron C. Taylor, the former head of U.S. Steel and now Roosevelt's representative at the Vatican, and Lewis negotiate a settlement. Lewis and Taylor were compatible negotiators who had settled a 1934 captive mine strike and the 1937 recognition of the steelworkers union in 1937. The OEM asked the two men to negotiate immediately and for work in the mines to continue.

Lewis replied to the president immediately, agreeing to meet with Taylor, but would not call off the strike. He disparaged Davis and all his works. He complained that the NDMB had been "casual and lackadaisical to the point of indifference [and] dumps its own sorry mess into the already overburdened lap of the chief executive."

The president's Saturday response dealt only with Lewis's refusal to again postpone the strike. "I must ask you to reconsider this decision. . . . [I]n this crisis of our national life there must be uninterrupted production of coal for making steel, that basic material of our national defense."

Roosevelt went on to note that Lewis and Taylor had agreed to meet on Wednesday "to see if you and he in private and personal conference can work out a solution" and insisted that while the talks went on, "the production of coal for steel-making [and] the established wage scales of the Appalachian agreement should continue." He closed by asking Lewis and his colleagues "to come now to the aid of your country."

On Monday, after the walkout began, Lewis replied to the president, insisting there was not yet any "question of patriotism or national security involved" because the steel companies, in preparation for the strike, had been stockpiling coal. After defending the patriotism of his miners, he characterized the dispute as "only between a labor union and a ruthless corporation—the United States Steel Corporation." He raged eloquently and irrelevantly against Wall Street: "My adversary is a rich man named Morgan who lives in New York." He told the president that he and Taylor would meet on Wednesday.

In that case, he claimed, no "impairment of defense production" would occur. But if more coal were needed to replace that lost in the brief stoppage, he would recommend that the miners work extra days to do so. In a closing comment, he offered to meet with the president and "my adversary, Mr. J. P. Morgan, for a forthright discussion of the equities of this problem."

Although Roosevelt knew there had to be some kind of accommodation with Lewis, he could not afford to allow the union leader's defiance to go unchallenged. In an immediate response Monday afternoon, the president, after saying that he was "sorry" that Lewis had not properly replied and ignoring his argument about the short-term adequacy of the coal supply, wrote, "Whatever may be the issues between you and Mr. Taylor or you and Mr. Morgan, the larger question of adequate fuel supply is of greater interest to the national welfare. There is every reason for continuance of negotiation. There is no reason for a stoppage of work. It is, therefore, essential that the mining of coal should go on without interruption. For the third time your Government through me asks you and the officers of the United Mine Workers to authorize an immediate resumption of mining."[28]

That evening, in his militant Navy Day address, Roosevelt made a deft ad-lib in his prepared text that transformed an almost pro forma balanced denunciation of a "small but dangerous minority" of both "industrial managers" and "labor leaders" into an attack on John L. Lewis. Instead of calling for greatly increased production "from every assembly line," the president used the words "from every coal mine." According to the *Times'* White House correspondent, the ad-lib drew the "longest and loudest" applause from the affluent audience in a Washington hotel ballroom.

Lewis's defiance of the president evoked all too typical congressional hyperbole from both friends and foes of Roosevelt. Texan Tom Connally, who was shepherding the Neutrality Act revision through the Senate, dubbed Lewis the "fourth member of the Axis," and his colleague Virginia's Harry Byrd claimed that he knew of "no more humiliating and disgraceful episode in American history" than Lewis's shut down of the captive mines. Although Roosevelt in his press conference refused to be specific about what he might do if the coal strike remained unresolved, the word went out on Monday and Tuesday that the president had told congressional leaders that he was ready to approve strong labor legislation limiting labor's right to strike in defense-related matters and claimed that a House bill by Georgia's Carl Vinson, modeled in part on the pre–New Deal Railway Labor Act mandating a compulsory cooling-off period and stressing arbitration of major strikes, could be passed in a few days if the president asked for it. On Tuesday evening, while sound and fury about punitive legislation—what the *New Yorker* magazine regularly labeled "wind on Capitol Hill"—continued to blow, the president met for thirty minutes with Myron Taylor, who reported acceptance by U.S. Steel of the mediation offer. The next morning, Taylor and Lewis had their meeting in a Washington hotel suite at ten and emerged a little after three. Taylor told the press they would continue the conference at the White House and was driven there with Davis.

After an hour and a half with the president in his study—the first time Lewis and Roosevelt had come face-to-face since before the miners' leader had endorsed Willkie—the negotiators emerged. Copies of a three-sentence letter from Roosevelt describing the results were given to the press. The president wrote that he had asked the parties to "immediately re-open the mines, on the understanding that [the NDMB] will proceed in full session to consider the merits of the dispute and make its final recommendations." The president specified that neither side was bound to accept the result.

After the White House meeting, Lewis told reporters that he would consult with the appropriate union leaders and probably have a back-to-work decision by "noon tomorrow or a little later." Taylor said only that "personally," he agreed with the president's decision.[29]

A little before noon the next day, Lewis announced that the men would go back to work. He warned that if no agreement were reached, he had approval to call the miners out again after November 15, just over two weeks away. He praised Taylor as "an industrial statesman of far-seeing vision" and even had a positive word about Roosevelt's "gracious approval" of a settlement that Lewis said was entirely due to the efforts of Taylor and himself.

Two days of public hearings opened before the NDMB on November 3, with Lewis and steel company executives presenting the same opinions they had held before the strike began. Davis announced that closed board meetings would begin the next day and promised a decision soon. Five days before Lewis's November 15 deadline, the board issued a nine-to-two decision against the union shop. The four industry members had been joined by the three public members and, surprisingly, the two labor members representing the AFL. The two CIO representatives, both UMW members—Philip Murray (1886–1952), a former Lewis lieutenant and his successor as CIO president, and Thomas Kennedy, secretary-treasurer of the UMW—resigned from the NDMB the next day, and it was clear that the usefulness of the board was at an end. Neither Roosevelt nor Lewis made any immediate public response.[30]

Most of the speculation about what the president would do if the board failed to settle the dispute and the miners walked out again discussed two possibilities: that he would either use the army to seize the mines or ask Congress for new "tough" labor legislation. Roosevelt, who had refrained from significant comment on the most recent phases of the dispute, did neither. On Wednesday the president called for union and management representatives to meet with him in the White House at 11:15 on Friday morning, knowing that Lewis would meet with the national policy committee of the UMW a few blocks away at 10:00 a.m. Assistant press secretary Bill Hassett, who announced the president's decision, speaking on the record in response to a question, denied that the dispute was a personal one between the president and Lewis: "If there is any quarrel it is between the United Mine Workers and the United States Government."

Roosevelt, as usual, held his cards close to his chest. On the very eve of the conference, in his previously quoted public letter to Rayburn and McCormack urging passage of amendments to the Neutrality Act, he also informed them of the impending conference for which he had hopes of success, writing, "But if it is not successful, it is obvious that this coal 'must be mined in order to keep the essential steel mills at work. The government of the United States has the backing of the people of the United States, including its workers. The government proposes to see this thing through."[31]

The next morning, six negotiators were ushered into the president's study promptly at 11:15: Lewis, Murray, and Kennedy for the UMW and steel company presidents Benjamin Fairless of U.S. Steel; Eugene R. Grace of Bethlehem Steel, the second-largest producer; and Frank Purcell of Youngstown Sheet and Tube, who represented the smaller owners of captive mines. Grace, Purcell, and most of the companies they represented had never before negotiated directly with a CIO union.

Although the negotiators had been invited to what Hassett referred to as a "joint conference," what they got was a brief lecture of fewer than seven hundred words, which the president read from a text that was distributed to the press immediately afterward. "I have asked you gentlemen here," he began, "to give you certain facts" and "when I have finished to withdraw . . . to confer in a final effort to insure continued production of coal for the manufacture of steel."

Most of what followed was a recitation of the facts of the matter—the national emergency, the vital role of coal in the production of steel, the key role of steel in the major implements of warfare—which the conferees knew and was intended for Congress and the public. Having established that "a cessation" of coal production would "create a further danger to American defense," Roosevelt argued that it was "the indisputable obligation of the president" to see that coal production continued. In a strange aside aimed perhaps at Lewis, he commented, "In spite of what some people say, I seek always to be a constitutional President."

Then Roosevelt switched what had been an Economics 101 lecture into a slightly more advanced treatise on practical politics. "If legislation becomes necessary" to continue production, he assured them that Congress would pass it, adding that "as some of you know, the pressure on me to ask for legislation" had been constant and heavy. He insisted that this was not a threat but "a simple fact." He hoped, therefore, "that you will work out some method for the continued production of coal."

About the "collective bargaining" that he was asking them to resume, he offered "two suggestions." The first was reasonable and practical: if they could not come to an agreement, "you will submit the point, or points, at issue to an arbiter." The second was that they "consider some other method of employment," the nub of the dispute.

> I tell you frankly that the Government of the United States will not order, nor will Congress pass legislation ordering, a so-called closed shop. It is true that by agreement between employers and employees in many plants of various industries the closed shop is now in operation. This is a result of legal collective bargaining, and not of Government compulsion on employers or employees. It is also true that 95 percent or more of the employees in these particular mines belong to the United Mine Workers Union. The Government will never compel this 5 percent to join the Union by a government degree. That would be too much like the Hitler methods toward labor.

In this passage, the longest in his lecture, Roosevelt was grandstanding. The closed shop was not an issue, the notion that Congress might order a closed shop was fantastic—in fact, bills had been dropped into the congressional hoppers to outlaw it—and the inaccurate reference to Hitler's methods was gratuitous. Roosevelt's closing, however, was strictly business. After reiterating that mining coal to make steel was "a national necessity," he concluded, "And so I am asking you—I never threaten—. . . please talk over this problem of continuing coal production. If you can't agree today, please keep on conferring tomorrow and

Sunday. I don't want any action that is precipitate. I want every chance given. And let me have some kind of report on Monday next—a report of agreement, or at the least that you are making progress." The two trios of participants left the White House separately, spoke briefly to reporters, and began joint negotiations in a Washington hotel after lunch.[32]

On Saturday, November 15, after the second day of direct negotiations, Lewis told reporters that there had been "no progress," while Fairless insisted that "much progress had been made." Lewis noted that the truce expired at midnight and reminded them of the UMW's standing policy that miners did not work without a contract or other agreement, though the talks would continue on Sunday. When Monday morning came, miners, getting no word to continue to work, set up picket lines at the coal pits, shutting down the captive mines. Later that morning, the parties met briefly and in separate letters informed the president that they could not reach an agreement. Lewis's letter rejected the management offer because, he said, it would jeopardize the union shop agreed to in the Appalachian Agreement covering the other mines. He had his letter delivered to the president and went off to give a fiery speech to the large UMW policy committee, on hand to ratify any agreement.

Lewis told his listeners that there had been no agreement because the steel companies expected Roosevelt to use the army. He painted a lurid picture of the military marching "into mining communities . . . terrifying, intimidating and breaking the morale of the mine workers, to crush the strike, with accompanying bloodshed." He also claimed that Bethlehem Steel's Grace had kept the other two executives from agreeing to the union shop, an allegation that the three later denied, specifically, in a joint letter to the president. In talking to reporters, however, Lewis calmly described what he thought would happen if the troops were sent: "If the soldiers come, the mine workers will remain peacefully in their homes, conscious of the fact that bayonets in coal mines will not produce coal."

While Lewis spoke, the executives went to the White House to deliver their response to the president. It said that they were ready to agree to a contract conforming to the decision originally handed down by the NDMB—which meant that they, like Lewis, had not moved an inch during two and a half days of conference. Their letter did quote with approval that part of Roosevelt's lecture that attacked the closed shop.

Roosevelt made no immediate response and clearly did not wish to use the army in this instance. Each of the three such uses of troops by Roosevelt had involved individual urban plant sites and had been essentially peaceful.

In addition, the CIO, now five million strong, in its annual convention in Detroit was backing the miners' demands at the same time as it formally separated itself from Lewis's isolationism and supported aid to Britain and other aspects of Roosevelt's foreign policy. Roosevelt appreciated that, but he also released telegrams between him and his AFL ally, the Teamsters' Dan Tobin. Tobin had wired that a wage dispute in the Midwest involving 225,000 drivers would be submitted to the NDMB "because of the serious, disturbed conditions confronting our nation and the world." Roosevelt replied, "You express to me the spirit of fair play and patriotism which I have always believed existed in hearts and minds of American labor and unionism. What a fine Thanksgiving it would be for us all if leaders in other fields of labor would but follow your example."[33]

Responding to a question about the coal strike in his Tuesday-afternoon press conference, Roosevelt gave his opinion that Lewis's interpretation of the Appalachian Agreement was wrong and did not jeopardize the existing union-shop contracts. The belief was widespread in Washington that Roosevelt would use troops or ask Congress to pass an antistrike bill, or both. However, in a letter to both sides, dated on Tuesday but not delivered or released until the next day, Roosevelt took an unexpected tack. After a long preamble rehashing the course of the dispute and its issues, and stressing his insistence that the coal must be mined, he offered two alternatives: the first would leave the matter of the 5 percent of nonunion miners "in status quo" for the period of the emergency, with all other parts of the Appalachian Agreement continuing; the second would "submit the matter of non-union miners to binding arbitration," also for the period of the national emergency. Roosevelt surely knew that Lewis would not accept the first; he must have believed that there was a chance that he would accept the second, and he apparently was assured that the steel executives would accept either. A telegram from Fairless accepted "either alternative." Roosevelt's letter was hand-delivered by a White House messenger to Lewis in his office while the UMW chief was being interviewed by a reporter. Lewis allowed the letter to remain unopened on his desk for "at least fifteen minutes" while he continued to reminisce about the coal strike of 1922. He made a lengthy reply to the president later that day, Wednesday, November 19. He explained that Murray, Kennedy, and most of the members of his national policy committee were in Detroit at the CIO convention and that a meeting to consider the two proposals would begin at 10:00 a.m. on Saturday, November 22.

He then gave the president his personal opinion of the two proposals. The first, which he judged to be for an "open shop," was one that "no officer or representative" of the UMW could accept. He did not denounce the principle of arbitration but pointed out, "Your recent statements on this question, as the Chief Executive of the nation, have been so prejudicial to the claim of the mine workers as to make uncertain that an umpire could be found whose decision would not reflect your interpretation of government policy, Congressional attitude and public opinion."

Although headlines spoke of Lewis defying the president and the generally negative attitude of his long letter, Lewis was, as Roosevelt would understand, not rejecting arbitration but questioning the possible arbitrator.[34] On Saturday morning, just before the 10:00 meeting was about to start, Lewis is widely believed to have received a telephone call from Labor Secretary Perkins, asking him to delay his meeting until he received a letter from the president. Lewis left the UMW building and did not return until 11:15. Refusing to tell reporters where he had been, he went upstairs to his office, where he waited with a few close associates until a little after noon when a White House messenger arrived with a letter from Roosevelt. In it the president, after some preliminaries rehashing the dispute that had been going on for almost four months, named the arbitrator after noting that "the steel companies have advised me of their acceptance of my [arbitration] proposal, and you have advised me that the matter would be considered by your national policy committee today. [To complete] this arrangement, I am appointing a board of three members . . . Dr. John R. Steelman, as the public representative [plus Fairless and Lewis]. I am suggesting that this Board begin its work immediately and remain in continuous session until this task is completed. May I request an immediate reply and acceptance from your national policy committee?"

Lewis soon came downstairs and recommended that the waiting committee approve the president's proposal, which it did unanimously. Lewis sent a brief letter of acceptance to the White House.

The appointment of Steelman (1900–99) was the key. He was a native Arkansan with a Ph.D. from the University of North Carolina whom Secretary Perkins had met when she spoke in 1934 at the small Alabama college where he taught sociology and economics. She soon brought him to Washington as a member of her department's conciliation service and in 1937 made him its director. He had conducted many successful mediations, including the Appalachian Agreement governing the noncaptive mines, and was a known supporter of the union shop embedded in it. No one challenged Roosevelt's description of him as a person of unquestioned integrity. For the purposes of the captive-mine arbitration, he was given "temporary leave" from his post at the Labor Department and became a "public member" so that, if he found for the union shop, as every knowledgeable observer expected, it would not contradict Roosevelt's pledge that the government would not force any worker to join a union.

Washington was stunned by dénouement, but it had a certain logic. It is almost impossible not to believe that Roosevelt had long been keeping the arbitration option open, but there is no direct evidence for this.[35]

The striking miners returned to work immediately, and an important UMW district leader, William (Billy) Hynes, expressed views consistent with the behavior of most miners, who followed Lewis's lead in union matters but voted overwhelmingly for Roosevelt: "In this situation two of the best men in America was on the spot—John L. Lewis and Roosevelt, and I'm for both of 'em."

The three arbiters met amid press reports that three of the larger steel firms would not accept the arbitration, but soon an industry spokesmen announced that all companies were expected to accept the arbitration award, and that turned out to be the case. The expected two-to-one decision, with Lewis and Steelman voting for the union shop, came early in the afternoon of December 7, before the board learned of the Pearl Harbor attack. U.S. Steel's Fairless, though he had always known the likely result, bitterly spoke of Hitlerian tactics. Lewis simply said that the decision justified his union's actions.

Steelman explained that the nine-to-two vote against the union shop by the NLRB had reflected a policy not to impose union membership by government order, but he reasoned that the arbitration board did not have to take that into account because "our decision is binding on the parties only by reason of their agreement that it be so."[36]

For the next few years, the captive-mine arbitration would be an influential precedent in favor of the union shop. As the headlines indicated, it was a victory for Lewis. But it was also a victory for Roosevelt. Without losing his labor support, he had appeared strong in the eyes of the public, continued the flow of coal to the steel-mill furnaces, and upheld the principle that, in national emergencies, both labor and capital must bow to the national interest as conceived by the president.

* * *

Despite Roosevelt's long-held notion that some kind of naval incident in the North Atlantic would bring the United States into the war, throughout most of 1941 he continued to take small steps that made conflict with Japan more likely. Chief of these were increasing the not very effective support for China, Japan's enemy and, probably more influential, the slow cutting off of the flow of oil and other war materials that resource-poor Japan needed to support its war machine. The resulting pressure on Japan was enormous. Its leaders understood that their oil reserves were shrinking at a rate of twelve thousand tons a day. One of them likened Japan to a fish in a pond that was being drained.

Thus, in early January 1941, Japan's most brilliant naval strategist, Admiral Isoroku Yamamoto (1884–1943), began the detailed preparations for a desperate gamble: a carrier-based air attack on Pearl Harbor with twin goals of sinking as much of the American fleet anchored there as possible and then destroying its shipyards and other naval installations.[37]

The conflict between the two Pacific powers originally arose from colliding imperialisms. The United States' annexation of Hawaii and the Philippines at the end of the nineteenth century forestalled similar Japanese ambitions. When Japan established a protectorate over Korea in 1905 and annexed it in 1910, the United States failed to protest, but later it opposed Japanese attempts to seize Chinese territory. As the student of imperialism V. I. Lenin observed in 1920, "War is brewing" between Japan and America who "cannot live in peace on the shores of the Pacific . . . three thousand versts apart."

A secondary issue between the two nations had been immigration. In 1924, when the United States broke the Gentlemen's Agreement between the two nations by making Japanese ineligible for immigration, politically aware Japanese felt humiliated. As George F. Kennan noted in 1951, the "long and unhappy story" of U.S.-Japanese relations in the first half of the twentieth century was constantly worsened by the fact that "we would repeatedly irritate and offend the sensitive Japanese by our immigration policies and the treatment of people of Japanese lineage . . . in specific localities in this country."[38]

Neither Roosevelt nor Churchill had any real awareness of the desperation that drove Japanese leaders. Both men continued to favor the Germany-first doctrine laid down in ABC-1. The Briton's comment in his first message to the president as prime minister—that he expected the United States to keep "that Japanese dog quiet in the Pacific"—was typical of the way that each man underestimated Japanese military capabilities, a failure not unrelated to their common notions of white, Anglo-American supremacy.

Churchill had only peripheral contacts and concerns with Japan, even though between 1902 and 1922 Britain and Japan had been allied by the Anglo-Japanese naval treaty. Roosevelt, of course, as assistant secretary of the navy, had been steeped in the navy notion of Japan as "the most probable enemy," though as a Democratic Party spokesman in the 1920s he had argued against the notion of an inevitable Pacific conflict. Japan's annexation of Manchuria in 1931 and its defiance of the League of Nations probably caused his attitudes toward Japan to harden. His postelection, preinauguration endorsement of the Stimson doctrine effectively limited his options vis-à-vis Tokyo without any compensating gain. Early in the New Deal, he used PWA funds to launch a naval building program toward the limits set by the international naval agreements. The deliberate Japanese bombing of the gunboat *Panay* in 1937 provided the president with an opportunity for saber rattling, but he accepted Tokyo's apologies and indemnification, even if he did not believe the former. Japan's continuing aggression against China prompted him to begin aid to Chiang Kai-shek, and Japan's increasing adherence to the Anti-Comintern Pact of European fascism in 1937, and what became known as the Rome-Berlin-Tokyo Axis in 1940, made any rapprochement between the two Pacific powers highly unlikely. Despite the growing tensions between the United States and Japan, Roosevelt continued until very late in the day to hold the false belief—a belief he shared with Hitler—that some kind of a North Atlantic naval incident would be the ultimate casus belli.

Tokyo saw the outbreak of each world war in Europe as an opportunity to gain advantage in Asia. In World War I, allied to Britain, Japan made war on Germany in the Pacific, seizing and retaining the German concession in China and the few German-held islands in the Pacific while aiding the British in suppressing German naval raiders. Toward the end of that war, Japan occupied much of far-eastern Russia but failed to annex the territory. In 1938–39 in an undeclared war on the Manchurian-Mongolian border, Soviet forces led by General Georgi J. Zhukov (1896–1974) eventually inflicted a serious defeat on invading Japanese forces, which was a factor in Japan's decision to go south rather than northwest. Western leaders, civilian and military, paid little attention. After the outbreak of World War II, allied with Germany, Japan pressured French governments to allow an expanding occupation of French Indochina—today's Vietnam—and made demands for raw materials, especially oil, from the Netherlands' colonies in Southeast Asia, today's Indonesia. The conquest of the Netherlands and France by Germany in 1940 and the weakened position of beleaguered Britain made their Asian colonies likely targets for Japanese expansion southward. Hoping somehow to deter the Japanese, in June 1940 Roosevelt ordered that major elements of the fleet be kept at Pearl Harbor, even though his military advisers thought that this was bad strategy.[39]

In his January 1941 State of the Union message, the president did not even mention Japan, but his strong statement of support for China surely caused added concern in Tokyo. His emphasis, as has been shown, was clearly on aid to Britain and eventually the USSR, but in May, again against the advice of his military advisers, he authorized Lend-Lease for China. For the first six months of the year, Roosevelt never mentioned Japan in any of his public papers and said little about it in his press conferences, except on February 11, when, after referring to the incoming Japanese ambassador, Admiral Kichisaburo Nomura (1877–1964), as "an old friend of mine," he was asked, "Do you think there is danger of war" in the Pacific? He answered directly, "No, I do not." The answer about Nomura was a stretch: Roosevelt knew him when he was Japan's attaché in its Washington embassy in 1916–18; the answer about war was, as he would admit later, not truthful. A real show was made of Nomura; when he came to the White House to present his credentials, Secretary Hull, for the only time during his tenure, personally escorted an ambassador to see the president.[40]

Only in late July, as south-moving Japanese convoys were landing troops at Cam Ranh Bay in Indochina, was Roosevelt's growing concern about Japan revealed to the public. First, Sumner Welles at the State Department denounced the incursion as a threat to American "national security," condemned Japan's action, and made it clear that he was speaking for the president. Later that day, Roosevelt used a scheduled first meeting of the volunteer participation committee of Fiorello La Guardia's Office of Civilian Defense to make extemporaneous remarks explaining why he was cutting Japan off from oil and other war materials and giving his spin on why, over the objections of hawks like Ickes and the *New York Times,* he had not done so earlier. He did not tell them that the move was opposed by his military advisers. The language suggests that he may have been using a large map as a teaching aid.

Now the answer is a very simple one. There is a world war going on. . . . One of our efforts from the very beginning was to prevent the spread of that world war in certain areas where it hadn't started. One of these areas is a place called the Pacific Ocean—one of the largest areas of the earth. There happened to be a place in the South Pacific where we had to get a lot of things—rubber—tin—and so forth and so on—down in the Dutch East Indies, the Straits Settlements [today's Malaya], and Indo-China. And we had to help get the Australian surplus of meat and wheat, and corn, for England.

It was very essential from our own selfish point of view of defense to prevent a war from starting in the South Pacific. So our foreign policy was—trying to stop a war from breaking out down there. At the same time, from the point of view of even France at the time—of course France still had its head above water—we wanted to keep the line of supplies from Australia and New Zealand going to the Near East—all their troops, all their supplies that they have maintained in Syria, North Africa, and Palestine. So it was essential for Great Britain that we try to keep the peace down there in the South Pacific.

All right. And now here is a Nation called Japan. Whether they had at that time aggressive purposes to enlarge their empire southward, they didn't have any oil of their own up in the north. Now if we cut the oil off they probably would have gone down to the Dutch East Indies a year ago, and you would have had war.

Therefore, there was—you might call—a method in letting this oil go to Japan, with the hope—and it has worked for two years—of keeping war out of the South Pacific for our own good, for the good of the defense of Great Britain, and the freedom of the seas.[41]

The next public move came two days later, July 26. Roosevelt issued an executive order freezing Japanese assets in the United States and a military order placing land and sea forces of the Philippines under U.S. command. He took former chief of staff Douglas MacArthur, who had been in Manila since 1935 as military adviser to the Philippine Commonwealth, off the retired list, promoted the sixty-one-year-old officer to lieutenant general, and named him commander of U.S. troops in the Philippines as well as all military forces of the Commonwealth of the Philippines, but all naval forces were under the commander of the U.S. 16th Naval District, at Cavite, in the Philippines. Tokyo retaliated to the freeze order by freezing American and British assets in its banks while continuing to move troops into Indochina, a move forced on the hapless Vichy government of Marshal Pétain.

The appointment of MacArthur, which was accompanied by an unannounced order to reinforce American forces in the Philippines, was part of a reversal by the president of a long-held basic American military assumption that those islands could not be defended successfully against Japan, a change that was opposed by his military advisers.[42]

Early in August, while Roosevelt was secretly on his way to the "first summit" with Churchill, Prince Fumimaro Konoye (1891–1945), who had been Japan's prime minister since July 1940, instructed Nomura to propose what would have been a "Pacific summit" between himself and Roosevelt. The ambassador presented the idea to Hull on August 8. After Roosevelt returned from the meeting with Churchill, he intended to tell Nomura that if Tokyo agreed not to send any more troops south, and to do so "specifically and not contingently" (Tokyo had previously said that it would consider withdrawing from Indochina after the "China incident" was settled), he would be willing to explore the possibilities of restoring the flow of oil. But he would warn Nomura that if Japan refused and took further military action, his government would have to react with various steps that might result in war between Japan and the United States. He estimated to colleagues that if Tokyo agreed, it would delay the outbreak of hostilities for at least thirty days.

Hull and his advisers were horrified by Roosevelt's distinctly undiplomatic approach and suggested softening it, lest it seem to the Japanese that he was challenging them. Roosevelt, perhaps thinking of his historical reputation should his language provoke an immediate armed response, agreed to tone down his remarks. He allowed the State Department to divide their substance into two "oral statements," with written versions handed to Nomura, which was done in a meeting at the White House on August 17. Nomura was misled by Roosevelt's cordiality—his manner rather than his words. Those, despite Hull's weakening, held little real hope for what Tokyo was insisting on. Nomura reiterated the proposal of a Konoye-Roosevelt meeting in Honolulu, to which Roosevelt responded that Juneau, Alaska, might be better. The meeting never occurred, as it became clear to both sides that neither could accept the preconditions of the other. The replacement of Konoye as prime minister by General Hideki Tojo (1884–1948) on October 18 was clear evidence that the military was in complete control in Tokyo. Robert Butow writes that the defiant ending of a new patriotic song reported in the *Japan Times* on the morning of the Konoye government's fall was somehow appropriate:

> Enemy planes are only mosquitoes or dragon flies.
> We will win, we must win.
> What of air raid?
> We know no defeat.
> Come to this land to be shot down.[43]

In mid-November, immediately after the successful change in the Neutrality Act, Roosevelt revealed his growing concern about the danger of war in Asia in a press conference during which much of the discussion and almost all the press coverage was about the Japanese threat. The fact that a special envoy from Japan, Saburo Kurusu (1886–1954), a senior Japanese diplomat who, as Tokyo's ambassador to Germany had signed the tripartite alliance with Germany and Italy, had just flown into San Francisco and was expected in Washington the next day to join Nomura in a continuing discussion of a possible agreement with the United States heightened a growing sense of a crisis in the Pacific.

In his November 14 press conference, Roosevelt answered a hypothetical question—the kind that he usually brushed off or refused to answer—that shows he wanted reporters to publicize what would seem to be a change in his views.

Q: Mr. President . . . could you tell us how you think war between Japan and the United States could be avoided?

THE PRESIDENT: I could—If I said No on that, someone might use what they call interpretation, and if I said yes on it, it would be pure guess, absolutely pure guess. I don't know. You don't know. No interpreter knows.

He knew that the press would, without further prompting, contrast this answer with his mid-February statement that he did not think that there was a danger of war in the Pacific. Variations of the two-column *New York Times* headline, "President Indicates Dangerous Situation in Far East Might Lead to War," appeared in many American newspapers. Roosevelt had opened the conference by postponing his traditional Thanksgiving visit to Warm Springs and later announced that the 970 Marines stationed in Shanghai and two other Chinese cities were being withdrawn. These moves only elevated the tension.[44]

Kurusu arrived in Washington on November 15. Two days later, with Ambassador Nomura, he met first with Hull and then for an hour with Roosevelt and Hull at the White House. Kurusu's mission created much excitement in the press, but, according to the State Department's account, "It became clear at the outset of the meetings that Mr. Kurusu had brought no new material or plans or proposals." A similar report on the U.S. position could have been issued in Tokyo. After the Japanese occupation of Indochina, neither side was willing to make a single significant concession.

After Kurusu's arrival, the American code breakers' ability to read his coded instructions from Tokyo—the famous Magic intercepts—made it clear that Japan planned to move soon. A crucial Tokyo message on November 22 informed the envoys that a previous deadline for the conclusion of negotiations, set for the twenty-fifth, could be extended to the twenty-ninth, but "this time we mean it, that the deadline cannot be changed. After that things are automatically going to happen."

Knowing this, on November 24, Roosevelt ended a cable to Churchill describing the most recent negotiations: "This seems to me a fair proposition for the

Japanese but its acceptance or rejection is really a matter of internal Japanese politics. I am not very hopeful and we must all be prepared for real trouble, possibly soon."

The two envoys met again with Roosevelt and Hull in the White House on the twenty-seventh. The president's contribution was to compliment the efforts of peace forces in Japan and insist that most Americans wanted a peaceful settlement. He had not given up hope, he said, but insisted that the situation was serious and that the United States could not relax its economic restrictions on Japan unless Japan manifested peaceful intent. He also said that his government was convinced that mirroring Hitlerite aggression was against Japan's best interests and went on to say that at a minimum, Japan should begin to withdraw from China and detach itself from the Axis. He, like Kurusu, had nothing new to offer.[45]

Despite the obvious impasse, conversations between the Japanese envoys and the secretary of state continued. During the entire period since the July 26 embargo, Japanese forces in Indochina had been increasing. Toward the end of November, reports of a buildup on the Gulf of Siam suggested further movement toward the Burma Road, Siam (today's Thailand), or Singapore, and a report from Australia suggested a buildup around Palau, in Micronesia, that threatened Indonesia.

Franklin and Eleanor had but two guests in the White House for Thanksgiving dinner, Jimmy Roosevelt and his wife. After the second meeting with Kurusu, the president felt free to go to Warm Springs, where he carved a huge turkey and gave his traditional talk. Referring to the millions of people at war, he said, "I think we can offer up a little silent prayer that these people will be able to hold a Thanksgiving more like an American Thanksgiving next year. That is something of a dream, perhaps. In days like these it is always possible that the boys in the military and naval academies may actually be fighting in defense of these American institutions of ours."

Immediately after dinner, a telephone call from Hull reporting threatening statements made by Premier Tojo in Tokyo caused Roosevelt to order his train to be made ready to take him back to Washington the next day. As the *Times'* White House correspondent commented: "When he gets back to Washington Mr. Roosevelt will have travelled forty hours to have a twenty-six hour vacation of sorts. As he boarded the train to return trip he said plaintively to a friend, 'at least I had a drive.'"

On December 2, Roosevelt instructed Hull to ask the envoys to explain the continuing increase of Japanese forces in Indochina, and the envoys said that they would inquire.[46] Reporters learned of these inquiries from the State Department, and at a press conference that afternoon they asked Roosevelt about their nature. Roosevelt gave the press an apparently extemporaneous five-paragraph summary of the eight months of negotiations with Japan that was his fullest prewar public account.

As you know, since last April we have been discussing with the Japanese government some method to arrive at an objective. The objective was permanent peace in the whole area of the Pacific. It seemed at times as if progress was being made toward that objective. And during that whole period up to I think it was the end of June, we assumed that as both nations were negotiating toward that objective, that there would be no act which would be contrary to the desired end of peace.

We were therefore somewhat surprised, the end of June, when the Japanese government sent troops—I think to a specified overall total, in other words a number that would not be exceeded—into Indo-China, after very brief negotiations with the French Vichy government; the conclusion of which arrangement the Vichy government let it be understood rather clearly that they had agreed to this number of troops, principally because they were powerless to do anything else.

Sometime thereafter, after the troops had gone there, the conversations were resumed between Japan and the United States, and for a while they seemed to be making progress. But again we made it perfectly clear that the objective that we were seeking meant the taking of no additional territory by anybody in the Pacific area. And the other day we got word from various other sources that already, in Indo-China, there were large additional bodies of Japanese forces—various kinds of forces—naval, air, and land—and that other forces were on the way; and that even before these other forces had arrived, the number of forces there had already exceeded, in Indo-China, the original amount the French government had agreed to, and that the forces that were on the way would greatly exceed the original number.

And the question was asked this morning of the Japanese government, at my request, very politely, as to what the purpose of this was—what the intention of the Japanese government in doing this was, as to the future; and eliminating, of course, which was an exceedingly peaceful spot beforehand.

And we hope to get a reply to that very simple question shortly.

He was asked in his next press conference:

Q: Have you any word as to the Japanese reply yet, Mr. President?
THE PRESIDENT: They are going to see the Secretary of State at 11:15 this morning [who] is coming around here to lunch with me at one o'clock. And until he comes around for lunch I won't know anything about it.[47]

At the State Department, Nomura, having queried Tokyo, replied that the latest troop movements were defensive measures because of Chinese activity along the northern border of Indochina. Since most of the buildup was in the southern part of the colony, Nomura's report did not inspire confidence.

The next day, Saturday, December 6, Roosevelt sent a message to Emperor Hirohito (1901–89), something he had planned to do for some time as a last resort. He modified a draft that Hull had previously supplied and ordered it dispatched in the most expeditious manner. Hull sent it out at 9:00 p.m. to Ambassador Joseph Grew in Tokyo. Roosevelt's letter was an appeal for peace that ignored most of the contentious issues between the two nations and broke no new ground.

He began by talking about the near century of peaceful relations between the two Pacific powers and went on to speak of the desire for peace of the American people, who have "eagerly watched the conversations between our two governments." He spoke of the American wish for an end to "the present conflict between Japan and China" and a "peace of the Pacific" in which all nations could "live without fear of invasion," with "the unbearable burdens of armament lifted," and that "all peoples would resume commerce without discrimination." After describing the continuing movement of large numbers of Japanese troops into Indochina, and the fears of future aggression that those moves had caused, the president made a specific proposition to the emperor. "There is absolutely no thought on the part of the United States of invading Indo-China if every Japanese soldier or sailor were to be withdrawn therefrom. I think that we can obtain the same assurance on the part of [the Netherlands East Indies, Malaya, and Thailand]. I would even undertake to ask for the same assurance on the part of the Government of China. Thus a withdrawal of the Japanese forces from Indo-China would result in the assurance of Peace throughout the whole of the South Pacific area." Roosevelt concluded his appeal with the "fervent hope" that "Your Majesty" may, as I am doing, "give thought in this definite emergency to ways of dispelling the dark clouds. I am confident that both of us, for the sake of the peoples not only of our own great countries but for the sake of humanity in neighboring territories, have a sacred duty to restore traditional unity and prevent further death and destruction in the world."[48]

For a variety of reasons, having largely to do with deliberate delays in the Tokyo cable office, the emperor learned of the message only as Japanese planes were taking off from their aircraft carriers northwest of Pearl Harbor. It is all but inconceivable that timely or even slightly earlier dispatch would have produced a different result.[49]

What did Roosevelt hope to gain from this eleventh-hour endeavor? It is highly doubtful that he expected it to dissuade Japan from doing whatever it was that it planned to do with its massive southern troop movements. He may have thought that it might cause some delay while a response was crafted, as he knew that reinforcements were on their way to American forces in the Philippines. But he asked a lot of the emperor and offered little in return. It seems much more likely that he was concerned not only about his historical reputation but also about being able to claim that he tried to avert war if it turned out, as he and his advisers expected, that further aggression by Japan would create a situation that would oblige him to ask Congress to declare war. Like Lincoln before him, he wanted his adversary to fire the first shot. His message sent, he could only sit and wait.

Roosevelt did not have to wait for long. At 9:30 that evening, shortly after he had sent his letter to Hirohito, as he and Harry Hopkins were sitting in his upstairs study in the White House, a young naval officer, Lieutenant Lester R. Schulz, on the staff of Roosevelt's naval aide, brought the president a so-called Magic transcript, the name for the system that was able to decipher Japanese codes. It was the first thirteen parts of a fourteen-part message from Tokyo to Nomura and Kurusu that they were directed to present to Hull at 1:00 p.m. on December 7. The navy handled these messages, and its cumbersome protocol allowed for only one copy of the translation to exist. That copy had to be transmitted in a locked pouch by a naval officer who took it around to a handful of high-ranking officials, one at a time. A naval officer had to remain present while the recipient read the message. Recipients were not permitted to copy the documents or to take notes. The officer eventually left with the documents, and they were then taken to the next recipient or back to the Navy Department. In this instance, the courier, a navy captain, was waiting across the street in what is now the Executive Office Building.

In February 1946, Schulz, then a lieutenant commander on sea duty, was called to testify before the congressional Pearl Harbor attack hearings. The heart of his testimony, in response to the questioning by committee counsel Seth W. Richardson, follows:

RICHARDSON: Whom did you find in the study when you arrived there?
SCHULZ: The President was there seated at his desk and Mr. Hopkins was there. . . . To the best of my recollection I took . . . perhaps fifteen type-written pages . . . out of the pouch and handed them to the President personally. . . . I did not read the message. . . . The President read the papers which took perhaps ten minutes. Then he handed them to Mr. Hopkins [who] then read the papers and handed them back to the President. The President then turned toward Mr. Hopkins and said in substance—I am not sure of the exact words but in substance—"This means war." Mr. Hopkins agreed, and they discussed then, for perhaps 5 minutes, the situation of the Japanese forces, that is, their deployment and—
RICHARDSON: Can you recall what either of them said?
SCHULZ: In substance I can. There are only a few words that I can definitely can say that I am sure of, but the substance of it was that—I believe that

Mr. Hopkins mentioned it first—that since war was imminent, that the Japanese intended to strike when they were ready, at a moment when all was most opportune for them. . . . That is, when their forces were most properly deployed for their advantage. Indochina in particular was mentioned, because the Japanese forces had already landed there and there were indications of where they should move next.

The President mentioned a message he had sent to the Japanese Emperor concerning the presence of Japanese troops in Indochina, in effect requesting their withdrawal.

Mr. Hopkins then expressed a view that since war was undoubtedly going to come at the convenience of the Japanese, it was too bad that we could not strike the first blow, and prevent any sort of surprise. The President nodded and then said, in effect, "No, we can't do that. We are a democracy and a peaceful people." He then raised his voice, and this much I remember definitely. He said, "But we have a good record."

The impression that I got was that we would have to stand on that record, we could not make the first overt move. We would have to wait until it came. During this discussion there was no mention of Pearl Harbor. The only geographic name I recall was Indochina. The time at which war might begin was not discussed, but from the manner of the discussion there was no indication that tomorrow was necessarily the day. I carried that impression away because it contributed to my personal surprise when the news did come.[50]

Schulz's testimony is compatible with everything we know: it was clear to Roosevelt from both overt and covert intelligence reports that the Japanese were itching to expand to the south. He went to bed that Saturday night wrestling with the problem of what to do if the Japanese attacked Malaya, or Singapore, or the Dutch islands. He apparently did not believe that the Japanese would attack the Philippines. Not one of the president's top advisers, civilian or military, had ever suggested that the United States needed to be concerned about a direct attack from Japan.

Readers familiar with the historical literature on Pearl Harbor will have noted that my narrative ignores the notorious "The question was how we should maneuver them into the position of firing the first shot without allowing too much danger to ourselves" sentence from Secretary Stimson's diary entry, describing what Roosevelt said at a White House meeting on November 25 with Hull, Knox, General Marshall, and Admiral Stark also present. The quote does not comport with everything else we know about Roosevelt's attitude at that time. All the other evidence we have indicates that Roosevelt was sure the Japanese would attack at least one Western power's possessions in Southeast Asia and that he thought that he would have to respond with a declaration of war. He did not want to maneuver the Japanese into attacking, but rather had consistently tried to delay the attack he expected as long as possible. The Stimson diary quotation has been a staple of historical literature since Charles A. Beard's *President Roosevelt and the Coming of War* (1948). Beard scrupulously quoted the diary correctly in his text, but morphed it into "Maneuvering the Japanese into Firing the First Shot" as a chapter title and running head, and that is the way it has often been used by later writers. Although Stimson used no direct quotation marks, the words, in one form or another, are often put into Roosevelt's mouth. As we know from Lieutenant Schulz's comments—and many other sources—Roosevelt was concerned about the first shot, but there is nothing else to suggest that he wanted to manipulate the Japanese into attacking. It seems much more likely that Stimson got it wrong.

7 A War Presidency, Pearl Harbor to Midway
1941–42

ROOSEVELT TOOK NO SPECIAL ACTIONS in the sixteen hours between reading the Magic intercept Saturday night and learning of the Pearl Harbor attack at lunch Sunday afternoon. Among his first reactions Saturday night was to phone Admiral Stark. But when the White House operator told him that Stark was attending the theater, the president told the operator to place the call after he had left the theater, not wanting to cause any public alarm by having the admiral summoned from his box.[1] He eventually spoke to Stark, but no new action resulted from their conversation or was meant to. At heart a navy man, it apparently did not occur to the president to phone General Marshall. All the evidence we have strongly suggests that Roosevelt went to bed Saturday night even more convinced than he had been when he got up that morning that a Japanese attack *somewhere* was coming soon. The appropriate commanders had been warned days before. All he could do was wait.

As Harry Hopkins describes it in a note he wrote before going to bed after midnight on Pearl Harbor Sunday, he and the president were having lunch upstairs in the Oval Room, "talking about things far removed from the war," when "at about 1:40" Roosevelt took a call from Secretary Knox telling him that a radio message from Hawaii had been picked up saying that an air raid was in progress and that it was "no drill." "I expressed the belief [Hopkins wrote] that there must be some mistake and that surely Japan would not attack in Hawaii. . . . The president thought the report was probably true and thought that it was just the unexpected sort of thing the Japanese would do."

Roosevelt "discussed at some length . . . his earnest desire to complete his administration without war," but that if the report was true, "the Japanese had made the decision for him." At "five minutes after two," it occurred to him to call Hull to tell him of the report. He instructed him not to mention the news to Nomura and Kurusu, but to receive their reply "formally and coolly and bow them out."

Hull, who was the antithesis of cool, told the envoys off in no uncertain terms. But he denied, in his memoirs, that he "'cussed out' the Japanese envoys in rich Tennessee mountain language," as rumor quickly had it.[2]

At 2:28 Admiral Stark phoned the president to confirm the attack, saying that it was "very severe" and that "some damage had been done" as well as causing "some loss of life." Roosevelt told him to "execute the agreed orders" to commence hostilities. The president then reached Steve Early at home and dictated a brief statement of the known facts for immediate release.

By 3:00 Roosevelt had convoked a meeting of Hull, Stimson, Knox, Marshall, and Stark. Hopkins observed, "The conference met in not too tense an atmosphere because I think that all of us believed that in the last analysis the enemy was Hitler and that he could never be defeated without force of arms; that sooner or later we were bound to be in the war and that Japan had given us an opportunity. Everyone, however, agreed on the seriousness of the war and that it would be a long, hard struggle."

The order of Hopkins's notes suggests that a transatlantic telephone call from Ambassador Winant was taken by the president during the conference with the so-called war cabinet. After Roosevelt confirmed the news of the attack, Winant, who had been dining with Churchill, told the president that he had a friend who wanted to speak to him—"You will know who it is as soon as you hear his voice"—and put the prime minister on the line. Roosevelt told him that "we are all in the same boat now," and they told each other that war would be declared the next day. Churchill was exultant, telling the president, "This certainly simplifies things," and writing, years later, that he "went to bed and slept the sleep of the saved and the thankful." The two may have agreed then that Churchill should come to Washington as soon as possible. He was on his way by December 12.[3]

The war-cabinet meeting went on until about 4:30. Among other things, the president outlined his plan to address Congress the next day and deliver a brief message and submit a longer account later. Hull argued then, and at the full cabinet meeting later, that a longer account detailing the negotiations with Japan ought to be in the message to Congress, but Roosevelt was adamantly opposed. Hopkins suggested and Roosevelt agreed that there should be two additional conferences that evening, the first with the cabinet and the second with selected congressional leaders. Throughout the day and evening, additional reports from the Pacific—Hopkins noted that "the phone was ringing constantly"—gave the increasingly depressing details of the Pearl Harbor attack. Roosevelt "handled the calls personally." Sometime that afternoon, he issued a presidential proclamation to begin the planned roundup of Japanese nationals from the lists compiled by the Justice Department.[4]

After the war-cabinet meeting broke up, Roosevelt dictated the first draft of his war message to Grace Tully. The president, Hopkins, and Tully had dinner in the Oval Study and then worked over the draft speech. The full cabinet met at 8:30, not in the cabinet room but in the Oval Study, where "they formed a ring completely around the President, who sat at his desk." A solemn Roosevelt told the group that "this was the most serious cabinet session since Lincoln met with his cabinet at the outbreak of the Civil War" and read his speech to them.

Vice President Wallace and nine congressional leaders from both parties came in about 9:30; with two exceptions, they were the leaders of both houses and both Foreign Affairs Committees. One exception was the absence of Hamilton Fish, ranking Republican on the House Foreign Affairs Committee whom Roosevelt refused to have in the White House; the other was the presence of archisolationist Hiram Johnson, who was added by Roosevelt to show that isolationism was not a factor in a war against Japan. Roosevelt did not read his message to the delegation or even tell them that he was going to ask for a declaration of war in his address to them because, as Hopkins put it, it was "perfectly footless ever to ask a large group of Congressmen to keep a secret."[5]

Hopkins closed his note by recording that after the congressional delegation left, "waiters brought in beer and sandwiches and at 12:30 the President ordered everybody out and said he was going to bed." But Hopkins did not record that "everybody" included CBS correspondent Edward R. Murrow, who had assumed that his scheduled appointment was canceled until Roosevelt sent word that he should come. After asking Murrow a few questions about the bombing in England, Roosevelt told him what he knew about the bombing in Hawaii, at one point pounding the table as he spoke of American planes destroyed "on the ground, by God, on the ground!"[6]

The president, "as ever," according to a Hopkins note, "had a good night's sleep, although someone woke him up at 7:30."[7] After a quiet morning in the White House, taking in more and more bad news and putting some of it into the draft speech, the president was driven to the Capitol with extraordinary police and Secret Service protection, past cheering crowds lining Pennsylvania Avenue. He waited in the Speakers' Room until just before 12:30, when he entered the House chamber, which was filled by the Congress, the Supreme Court, and the cabinet. Unlike Wilson, whose address asking for a declaration of war from a bitterly divided Congress and nation was a long and argumentative document of nearly 3,700 words, Roosevelt, addressing a united Congress and nation, needed only 503 words. It is the shortest major address by an American president; even Lincoln's magnificent second inaugural required nearly 1,400.

The speech was essentially what the president had dictated the night before. The copy on display at his Hyde Park library shows two handwritten corrections by Roosevelt on the first page. The crucial one lined through *world history* and inked in *infamy*, while the other substituted *suddenly* for *simultaneously.*

> Yesterday, December 7, 1941—a date which will live in infamy—the United States of America was suddenly and deliberately attacked by naval and air forces of the Empire of Japan.
>
> The United States was at peace with that Nation and, at the solicitation of Japan, was still in conversation with its Government and its Emperor looking toward the maintenance of peace in the Pacific. Indeed, one hour after

Japanese air squadrons had commenced bombing in the American Island of Oahu, the Japanese Ambassador to the United States and his colleague delivered to our Secretary of State a formal reply to a recent American message. And while this reply stated that it seemed useless to continue the existing diplomatic negotiations, it contained no threat or hint of war or of armed attack.

It will be recorded that the distance of Hawaii from Japan makes it obvious that the attack was deliberately planned many days or even weeks ago. During the intervening time the Japanese Government has deliberately sought to deceive the United States by false statements and expressions of hope for continued peace.

The attack yesterday on the Hawaiian Islands has caused severe damage to American naval and military forces. I regret to tell you that very many American lives have been lost. In addition American ships have been reported torpedoed on the high seas between San Francisco and Honolulu.

Yesterday the Japanese Government also launched an attack against Malaya.

Last night Japanese forces attacked Hong Kong.

Last night Japanese forces attacked Guam.

Last night Japanese forces attacked the Philippine Islands.

Last night the Japanese attacked Wake Island.

And this morning the Japanese attacked Midway Island.

Japan has, therefore, undertaken a surprise offensive extending throughout the Pacific area. The facts of yesterday and today speak for themselves. The people of the United States have already formed their opinions and well understand the implications to the very life and safety of our Nation.

As Commander in Chief of the Army and Navy I have directed that all measures be taken for our defense.

But always will our whole Nation remember the character of the onslaught against us.

No matter how long it may take us to overcome this premeditated invasion, the American people in their righteous might will win through to absolute victory. I believe that I interpret the will of the Congress and of the people when I assert that we will not only defend ourselves to the uttermost but will make it very certain that this form of treachery shall never again endanger us. Hostilities exist. There is no blinking at the fact that our people, our territory, and our interests are in grave danger.

With confidence in our armed forces—with the unbounding determination of our people—we will gain the inevitable triumph—so help us God.

I ask that the Congress declare that since the unprovoked and dastardly attack by Japan on Sunday, December 7, 1941, a state of war has existed between the United States and the Japanese Empire.[8]

In just over half an hour, both bodies had done what Roosevelt asked by joint resolution: the overwhelming unity of Congress and the nation was somehow enhanced by a lone negative vote of conscience by Montana Republican Jeannette Rankin. Her similar vote in 1917 had been one of fifty-six congressional negatives. By 4:10 p.m., the engrossed copy had been delivered to the White House and signed by Roosevelt.[9]

Roosevelt made no mention of Germany, but based on a number of factors, including intercepted messages from Hitler to Tokyo in late November that he would attack the United States if Japan did, the president ordered proclamations issued providing that since "an invasion or predatory incursion is threatened upon the territory of the United States" by Germany and Italy, German and Italian nationals were "alien enemies." He authorized the beginning of a selective roundup, even though the European powers had not yet declared war. On December 9, the Justice Department announced that twelve hundred enemy aliens were already in custody: nearly four hundred Germans and Italians along with almost nine hundred Japanese.[10] During the entire war, perhaps thirty-one thousand of the roughly one million enemy aliens were interned, including several thousand whom the United States rendered from Latin America. Those left at liberty were subjected to a wide variety of restrictions.[11]

Getting a Fireside Chat ready for delivery Tuesday evening was a rush job. Rosenman and Sherwood, who had been in New York on Sunday, called the White House that afternoon and were told by Grace Tully that the president wanted them right away. They flew in that night, came to the White House early Monday morning, and waited to be put to work. Eventually, Mrs. Roosevelt called to invite them to go to the Capitol with the presidential party to hear his speech. When they returned, the two writers joined Hopkins and Tully for lunch in the upstairs study with the president. There was no "small talk." The president insisted that Hitler was the major enemy but understood that many Americans would want to put more or most emphasis on the war with Japan. He wanted it made clear in the talk, Rosenman reports, "that for more than a year we have been trying to prevent war in the Pacific . . . that we were not appeasing Japan, but that the longer we could prevent war with Japan the stronger we could become and the more help we could send to the people fighting Hitler."

After lunch the two writers returned to the cabinet room and were given a draft by Sumner Welles, mainly about prewar diplomacy—a version of the speech Hull and Welles had wanted the president to give earlier. Rosenman and Sherwood were the chief writers with significant contributions made by the president. Grace Tully took dictation, and relays of typists created successive drafts. The president worked with them after dinner Monday night until 11:30 and then went to bed while the two writers and Tully continued. Sometime after midnight, Archibald MacLeish joined them and insisted that the public had a right to know the details of the disaster. Rosenman and Sherwood believed otherwise, holding that the Japanese could not know how much damage had been done and that no details should be given out. They called it a day at 3:00 a.m., leaving a draft for the president when he got up.

Rereading their work Tuesday morning, both writers found their draft dull. Having read it in bed, Roosevelt concurred, and though airtime was just hours away, they tried a fresh approach. Instead of a chronology of failed diplomacy—which would be done later as a state paper—the objective was to make it a call to arms, like Churchill's "blood, toil, tears, and sweat" of May 13, 1940. Roosevelt told them, "Suppose you try to get up something else; let me have it by lunch, and we can all eat together and talk about it." After the lunch dishes had been cleared away, Roosevelt "made some suggestions and dictated a few paragraphs," but soon had to leave for other business."[12]

Tuesday afternoon, as the bad news continued to pour in, the president held his first wartime press conference, largely taken up with reporters' complaints about the difficulty of getting information and the president's discussion, without specifics, about the need for restraint in the release of news that might give "aid and comfort to the enemy."[13]

The writers were not able to get back to him with a new draft until 5:30 p.m.; the chat was to begin at 10:00 p.m., with mimeographed copies given to the press beforehand. Roosevelt was, as he had been since learning of the attack, calm and patient, with the angry outburst to Murrow the only recorded exception.[14]

Unlike what is most often referred to as the "Date of Infamy speech," the chat contained no particularly memorable passages or watchwords and is not well remembered. It did, however, allow Roosevelt to reach and reassure a large part of the population and merge the three Axis nations into one common threatening entity.

"The sudden criminal attacks perpetrated by the Japanese in the Pacific," he began, were quickly likened to those of "powerful and resourceful gangsters ... banded together to make war on the whole human race. . . . The course that Japan has followed for the past ten years in Asia has paralleled the course of Hitler and Mussolini in Europe and in Africa. [The Axis collaboration has turned] all the continents of the world, and all the oceans [into] one gigantic battlefield."

He then ticked off, as he liked to do, a list of sixteen attacks, all "without warning," in the 1930s and 1940s, perpetrated by one or another of the Axis partners. The president was frank about the overall picture without revealing details, many of which he himself did not yet know.

So far, the news has been all bad. We have suffered a serious set-back in Hawaii. Our forces in the Philippines, which include the brave people of that Commonwealth, are taking punishment, but are defending themselves vigorously. The reports from Guam and Wake and Midway islands are still confused, but we must be prepared for the announcement that all of these three outposts have been seized.

The casualty lists of these first few days will undoubtedly be large. I deeply feel the anxiety of all of the families of the men in our armed forces and the relatives of people in cities which have been bombed. I can only give them my solemn promise that they will get news just as quickly as possible.

Roosevelt was willing to acknowledge that "our enemies have performed a brilliant feat of deception, perfectly timed and executed with great skill. It was a thoroughly dishonorable deed, but we must face the fact that modern warfare as conducted in the Nazi manner is a dirty business. We don't like it—we didn't want to get in it—but we are in it and we're going to fight it with everything we've got." After stressing that guerrilla warfare against the Germans "in, let us say, Serbia or Norway helps us; that a successful Russian offensive against the Germans helps us; and that British successes on land or sea in any part of the world strengthen our hands," and pointing out that "Germany and Italy, regardless of any formal declaration of war consider themselves at war with the United States," the president concluded with quiet confidence:

The true goal we seek is far above and beyond the ugly field of battle. When we resort to force, as now we must, we are determined that this force shall be directed toward ultimate good as well as against immediate evil. We Americans are not destroyers—we are builders.

We are now in the midst of a war, not for conquest, not for vengeance, but for a world in which this Nation, and all that this Nation represents, will be safe for our children. We expect to eliminate the danger from Japan, but it would serve us ill if we accomplished that and found that the rest of the world was dominated by Hitler and Mussolini. We are going to win the war and we are going to win the peace that follows.

And in the difficult hours of this day—through dark days that may be yet to come—we will know that the vast majority of the members of the human race are on our side. Many of them are fighting with us. All of them are praying for us. For in representing our cause, we represent theirs as well—our hope and their hope for liberty under God.[15]

The next day, Roosevelt had to make a crucial decision about Pacific strategy. As part of the plan to reinforce the Philippines, a five-ship convoy carrying some four thousand troops, fifty-two dive-bombers, eighteen pursuit planes, and other supplies on a circuitous route had put into Suva, Fiji, on the news of Pearl Harbor to await instructions. On December 9, the Army-Navy Board had decided to order it to return to Hawaii to bolster its defenses. The great fear was that a second air attack there might destroy vital dock and repair facilities. Had that occurred, the

American naval counterattack would have had to be conducted from the West Coast of the United States and been significantly delayed. That night General Marshall had second thoughts, and in the morning he shared them with Stimson, who went to the White House to ask the president to intervene. Roosevelt "asked" the board to reverse itself and send the convoy to Australia, which it did. While pious hopes were expressed about possibly getting some of the men and weapons to the Philippines, both the original and revised decisions represented an abandonment of the forces in the Philippines. That day there was more bad news from the Far East: two large and powerful British warships, HMS *Prince of Wales* and *Repulse,* newly based in Singapore, foolishly sortied, without air cover, north along the Malaysian east coast, seeking a Japanese convoy to attack, and were destroyed by Japanese dive- and torpedo bombers.[16]

On December 11, both Hitler and Mussolini declared war on the United States, one before the Reichstag and the other from a Roman balcony. Roosevelt simply sent a message to Congress asking that it "recognize a state of war between the United States and Germany . . . and Italy." He noted that Germany was "pursuing its course of world conquest" and that "the long known and the long expected has thus taken place." Warning that "the forces endeavoring to enslave the entire world now are moving toward this hemisphere," Roosevelt insisted that "never before has there been a greater challenge to life, liberty, and civilization."

Congress acted quickly, first by passing two separate joint resolutions stating that "the state of war . . . thrust upon the United States, is hereby formally declared." The vote in each chamber was unanimous: Jeannette Rankin voted "present" twice. Just after 3:00 p.m., Roosevelt signed both documents in the presence of the same group of congressional leaders who had brought him the Japanese declaration three days before, noting that "I've always heard that all things come in threes. Here they are."[17]

Congress also undid some isolationist legislation, repealing the ban on sending draftees anywhere other than U.S. territory and extending the terms of service of all in the armed forces to what became the familiar "duration plus six months." Soon after learning the magnitude of American losses, Roosevelt sent Navy Secretary Knox to Honolulu.[18]

Knox's press conference and accompanying brief statement after his return on December 15 contained blunt truths, calculated disinformation, and outright falsehoods. He made no bones about the unprepared state of the defenders. Under the circumstances, he gave a reasonably accurate casualty report, admitting the deaths of 91 naval officers and 2,368 seamen. He stated that responsibility would be determined by a commission that the president would appoint. His disinformation, aimed largely at the enemy, included downplaying the ship losses, claiming that only one battleship had been sunk and another capsized. In fact, none of the eight battleships present at Pearl Harbor were then capable of combat. The USS *Arizona, California,* and *West Virginia* had been sunk, the *Oklahoma* capsized, the *Nevada* grounded, and the others damaged, but all not sunk eventually returned to the fleet. The outright falsehoods included the statement that one reason for the attack's success was what he called "the most effective fifth column work that's come out of this war except in Norway." That charge, featured by the press, was not in Knox's formal statement. Such rumors were rife in Hawaii, but they were false. For the next six months, Knox would lead the arguments for mass incarceration of all Japanese persons in the islands. The *New York Times* reporter editorialized that Japanese born in Hawaii were "technically" American citizens."[19]

On December 18, the White House announced that a commission headed by Supreme Court justice Owen J. Roberts would go to Honolulu "to ascertain and report the facts relating to the attack" on Pearl Harbor and "to provide bases for sound decisions whether any derelictions of duty or errors of judgment on the part of United States Army or Navy personnel contributed to such successes as were achieved by the enemy." The press pointed out that Roberts had investigated Teapot Dome for the Coolidge administration, but what was crucial for Roosevelt was that he, like Knox, was a Republican.[20]

The next day, the expected relief of the three senior Pearl Harbor commanders was announced. The major change was Roosevelt's choice of Rear Admiral Chester W. Nimitz (1885–1966) to replace Admiral Husband E. Kimmel as commander in chief of the Pacific fleet (CINCPAC). The president had known Nimitz during his service since 1938 as chief of the Bureau of Navigation and had offered him the Pacific command in January 1941, but Nimitz thought it inappropriate for the chief personnel officer to be promoted over some four dozen more senior admirals, and he declined. There was no question of refusing in wartime. Nimitz would direct all naval action in the Pacific throughout the war.

The two senior army officers removed had only local responsibility and were replaced by General Marshall's choices. The more important, Lieutenant General Delos C. Emmons (1889–1965), a pioneer army aviator who was the ranking army air force officer at Washington general headquarters replaced Lt. General Walter C. Short as commander of the Hawaii Department and military governor of Hawaii, since martial law had been declared there shortly after the attack.[21]

Four days after Emmons took command, he made a public statement, published in the local newspapers, that there had been no sabotage on Oahu, but under the martial law existing in Hawaii the statement did not appear in the mainland press.

In a move that was in part triggered by the Hawaiian disaster, Admiral Stark, who as chief of naval operations (CNO) had done so much to shape the Germany-first strategy, suffered a two-step removal from a central role in naval command. On December 18, all of his command functions were passed by Roosevelt to Admiral Ernest J. King (1878–1956), who became commander in chief of the U.S. fleet (COMINCH). King had been in command of the Atlantic fleet during the undeclared naval war with Germany. Stark retained the title of CNO until March, when he was shifted to a largely administrative post in Britain, and King assumed the role of CNO as well. Despite an acerbic personality, King is described by Samuel Eliot Morison as "undoubtedly the best naval strategist and organizer in our history." These appointments, along with the earlier ones of Marshall and Arnold, demonstrate Roosevelt's remarkable ability to select outstanding commanders without regard to seniority.[22]

With the military high command now largely in place, Roosevelt created an Office of Censorship that he put into professional civilian hands. He named Byron Price (1891–1981), who had been executive editor of the Associated Press since 1937, to head it and made him directly responsible to the president. At his press conference announcing the new arrangement, Roosevelt explained that it could not go into effect until he signed a pending War Powers Act similar to one passed in 1917, permitting, among other things, suspension of the First Amendment for the duration.

The president also told reporters, off the record, that the statement he was about to read had been written for him by Price. Beginning with the disarming "All Americans abhor censorship, just as they abhor war," it emphasized that it was essentially self-censorship, as the government was calling upon "a patriotic press and radio to abstain voluntarily from [publishing news about things such as] the movements of vessels and troops." The armed forces continued to censor news emanating from combat areas, including Hawaii. In addition, Price had control of "the mails, radio . . . cable" or any other medium. When asked for details of mail censorship, Roosevelt responded, "I don't know. You will have to ask Byron that. I suppose, off-hand, it would be a censorship of outgoing and incoming mail. Not domestic." As the system developed, postal censorship was the largest single aspect of the office's work. About a million letters a day were taken out of the flow of mail, opened, read, and replaced, usually within twenty-four hours.

Arthur Krock, head of the *New York Times* Washington Bureau, pointed out in his column that the first result of the new law to cross his desk was a curt directive from the Navy Department: "At the request of Justice Roberts, head of the inspection board, there shall be no publicity on the departure of or stopovers of the board en route to Hawaii." Once it got set up, Price's office was more subtle, but the effect was the same.

By mid-January, a set of guidelines was issued and published. In addition, a number of specific prohibitions—including an unpublished standing order that the physical presence or absence of the president was a military secret unless it was announced by the White House—were sent to some twenty-five thousand media outlets. There followed a continuing stream of special or general prohibitions. In an early example, the spring 1942 visit of Soviet foreign minister

Vyacheslav Molotov to Washington was not to be mentioned until after he had returned to the USSR. An extreme case was the June 28, 1943, message requesting the nonpublication of anything relating to atom smashing or atomic energy. The request included the term *uranium* but added as a smoke screen a number of other elements, including ytterbium and polonium, which few editors would have even heard of.[23]

On the evening of December 22, Roosevelt went across the Potomac to Washington National Airport to greet Winston Churchill and bring him and his personal staff to the White House. They had arrived at Hampton Roads, Virginia, aboard the HMS *Duke of York* that afternoon after a ten-day transatlantic dash through sub-infested waters. The prime minister was accompanied by Beaverbrook plus his military and naval chiefs of staff and their aides. The official statement spoke of discussions of "all questions relevant to the concerted war effort" and of "one primary objective . . . the defeat of Hitlerism throughout the world."

The public aspects of Churchill's visit were a triumph. The next day, Roosevelt presented him to an overflow and enthusiastic press conference. After a few preliminary remarks, the president, noting that an amphitheater was needed, asked Churchill, who sat slumped in a chair beside him, to stand, so those in the back could see. The prime minister complied and then, to loud cheers, stood on a chair and waved. He blithely answered a variety of questions.

Q: Do you think the war is turning in our favor in the last month or so?
THE PRIME MINISTER: I can't describe the feelings of relief with which I find Russia victorious, the United States and Britain standing side by side. It is incredible to anyone who had lived through the lonely months of 1941.

Asked how long it would take to "lick them":

THE PRIME MINISTER: If we manage it well, it will take only half as long as if we manage it badly.
Q: How long, sir, would it take if we managed it badly?
THE PRIME MINISTER: That has not been revealed to me at this moment. We don't need to manage it badly.
Q: How long if we manage it well, sir? . . .
THE PRIME MINISTER: Well, it would be imprudent to indulge in a facile optimism at the moment. . . .
Q: Mr. Minister, do you have any doubt of the ultimate victory?
THE PRIME MINISTER: I have no doubt whatever.

On Christmas Eve, Churchill joined Roosevelt on the South Portico of the White House for the annual lighting of the national Christmas tree. After the president announced a National Day of Prayer for January 1, he insisted that "our strongest weapon in this war is that conviction of the dignity and brotherhood of man which Christmas Day signifies—more than any other day or any other symbol." Churchill, for his part, offering a "pendant" to Roosevelt's "necklace of Christmas good will and kindliness," went on to acknowledge ties of blood, friendship, and "comradeship in the common cause of great peoples who speak the same language, who kneel at the same altars. . . . I cannot feel myself a stranger here."

The day after Christmas, Churchill went up Pennsylvania Avenue to address Congress. Some in the administration worried about the reception he might get from Anglophobes and isolationists. Their fears were groundless. Churchill's oration was an enormous success.

He began by reminding the legislators of his American mother and speculated that had his father been American and his mother British, he might well have found his way to Congress on his own and not have to be invited. Most of the speech hurled defiance at their common foes and confidently predicted victory. The most striking passages came at the end. Speaking in the building in which Wilson's dreams of an American-led League of Nations had been smashed and where mere months before Roosevelt and his supporters had been hard-pressed to get many measures of defense passed, he called confidently for an Anglo-American alliance.

> Twice in a single generation the catastrophe of world war has fallen upon us. . . . If we had kept together after the last war, if we had taken common measures for our safety, this renewal of the curse need never have fallen upon us. . . . Duty and prudence alike command, first, that the germ centers of hatred and revenge should be constantly and vigilantly curbed and treated in good time and that an adequate organization should be set up to make sure that the pestilence can be controlled at its earliest beginning before it spreads and rages throughout the entire earth.

After suggesting, without naming him, that God's will was "being worked out here below," he closed with: "It is not given to us to peer into the mysteries of the future. Still I avow my hope and faith, sure and inviolate, that in the days to come the British and American people will for their own safety and for the good of all, walk together in majesty, in justice and in peace."[24]

The closed aspects of the visit involved parallel sets of formal conferences as well as ongoing conversations between the two leaders, with Hopkins often the only other person present. At least eight meetings took place in the White House with Roosevelt, Churchill, Hull, Stimson, Knox, Beaverbrook, Hopkins, and the British and American chiefs of staff participating, while in the nearby Federal Reserve Building the two sets of chiefs of staff with their aides met twelve times.

The meetings, code-named the Arcadia Conference, extended from December 23 to January 14, served, first of all, to quench British fears that events in the Pacific would override the Germany-first strategy agreed upon during ABC-1 almost a year earlier. Marshall and Stark opened the military meetings by stating that "our view remains that Germany is still the prime enemy and her defeat is the key to victory."

That apart, both sets of meetings revealed basic differences, previously somewhat masked, that would continue throughout Roosevelt's presidency. Churchill's private remark to aides during preparations for the conference about the appropriate way to treat America after Pearl Harbor, as reported in the diaries of Lord Alanbrooke, General Marshall's British opposite number, speaks volumes: "Now that she is in the harem, we talk to her quite differently."

Those who write about the Roosevelt-Churchill relationship as if it were like a Hollywood buddy movie fail to understand that while the two prima donnas enjoyed their relationship and matching wits with one another, each was a relatively hard-boiled national leader seeking to gain both long- and short-term advantages. Perhaps the most fundamental difference was their attitudes toward colonialism. The Briton wished to maintain and restore the British Empire, much of which was falling apart under the pressure of Japanese advances and glaring military and political ineptitude by Britain's colonial administrators. The American, although in his small talk capable of grossly inappropriate comments, had in the final analysis become an anti-imperialist who understood that colonialism had run its course and that China and even India would play a larger role in the postwar world. It can be argued that Churchill strove vainly to restore the past, while Roosevelt dreamed of creating a better future.

Both men understood that in the wartime crisis, the appearance of Anglo-American unity was paramount. They and their military planners agreed to set up a joint command of American, British, Dutch, and Australian (ABDA) forces to manage the resistance to the southward push of Japanese forces toward Singapore, the Dutch East Indies, and Australia and to make the British lieutenant general Sir Archibald Wavell its commander. The military chiefs had agreed in the ABC-1 meetings to create a coordinating military committee once war came. This was now done and misleadingly called the Combined Chiefs of Staff (CCS); it sat in Washington. It was a joint body of the American and British chiefs, not an all-powerful body superior to them. From then on, the use of the word *combined* in an organizational title indicated a joint operation. After the conference, Roosevelt created three additional joint boards to manage raw materials, munitions, and shipping. These decisions ensured that the war would be run from Washington, not London, and that the United States was the senior partner.

In discussing provisional strategy against what Hitler was to call *Festung Europa* (Fortress Europe), the chief strategic difference between the Allies was that the British, haunted by their appalling loss of manpower in World War I, wanted to avoid a direct assault as long as possible. They would consistently argue for peripheral attacks in the Middle East, North Africa, the Mediterranean, and eventually on what Churchill called the "soft underbelly" north of the Adriatic. For their part, the Americans wanted a direct cross-Channel approach. Somewhat naively, they even talked about landing troops on the European continent in 1942. As Allied forces crumbled before persistent winter-long Japanese attacks on a broad arc from the Philippines to Burma, overrunning the British bastion of Singapore with relative ease, overwhelming the Dutch East Indies, destroying the ABDA naval forces in the process, and threatening Australia, the Germany-first doctrine would be modified but not abandoned. Relatively large numbers of American troops had been sent to reinforce the Philippines before Pearl Harbor, and after that others were quickly diverted or sent not to the fighting fronts but to the West Coast of the United States, Australia, and to a lesser degree India, making impossible even the beginnings of a second front in Europe. The only U.S. troops that went to Europe in 1942 were those sent to Northern Ireland and Great Britain, beginning at the end of January.[25]

Roosevelt's comments on the military planning during the Arcadia Conference, made in a press conference in November 1942, after the successful landings in North Africa, are worth noting.

> THE PRESIDENT: We discussed at that time the desirability of an offensive. And there were various offensives considered, especially the possibility of a very large frontal attack across the English Channel. . . . And the military opinion at that time was that it would be feasible. . . . The more it was studied, however, the more it became apparent that . . . an offensive along the coast of France or Belgium could not be carried out with a reasonable chance of success in the year 1942.[26]

Churchill came to Washington hoping to deal only with military matters, but pressure from Roosevelt and the course of events caused him to follow the American political lead. Roosevelt, unable to send more than token aid to the Philippines, sent a message to its people on December 28, calling them "loyal Americans" and giving them "my solemn pledge that their freedom will be redeemed and their independence established and protected. . . . I count on every Philippine man, woman, and child to do his duty."

Churchill made a brief trip to Ottawa, where he delivered a rousing speech to the Canadian parliament praising Roosevelt—"that great man whom destiny has marked for this climax of human fortunes"—and describing the ongoing conference in Washington as "concerting the united pacts and resolves of more than thirty states and nations to fight on in unity together."

On his return, Churchill joined Roosevelt in observing the National Day of Prayer in Mount Vernon, where the two leaders prayed together in George Washington's pew. That afternoon in the White House, they and Maxim Litvinov for the USSR and T. V. Soong for China signed the war-aims document that Roosevelt had wanted. Twenty-two representatives of other nations signed the next day at the State Department: five represented British dominions, eight were conquered European governments in exile, and nine were Central American and Caribbean states. No South American nation was, as yet, directly involved in the war.

The nations pledged adherence to the principles embodied in the Atlantic Charter; to defend life, liberty, independence, and religious freedom; "and to preserve human rights and justice in their own lands." Each agreed to wage war with all its resources, to cooperate with other signatories, and to make no separate peace. Provision was made for other nations to sign later. The White House announced that Roosevelt had personally inked in the last change in the document at 2:30 a.m. on New Year's Day. To avoid using the terms *Allied Powers,* or simply *Allies,* which had been widely used in World War I, or *Associated Powers,* which the United States had used in World War I to show that it was not formally aligned with any other nation, Roosevelt coined the term *United Nations* by titling the document "DECLARATION BY UNITED NATIONS."[27]

Critics immediately pointed out that the Soviet Union was hardly a protector of human rights at home or anywhere else, and even Litvinov had boggled at signing a document pledging his government to "religious freedom," but Roosevelt insisted that religious freedom included the right to have no religion. The fact that the Caribbean and Latin American signatories were no paladins of liberty, and three of them—the Dominican Republic, Haiti, and Nicaragua— were particularly oppressive dictatorships—was ignored by Roosevelt and little noted in the media.

Even during the Arcadia Conference, Roosevelt's attention was demanded by dozens of other matters, chief of which was preparing the annual and budget messages. Roosevelt noted that although rationing was not yet necessary, it soon would be, as part of an "integrated program, including direct price controls, a flexible tax policy, allocations, rationing, and credit controls," and estimated, in a year-end press conference that in fiscal 1943 (July 1, 1942–June 30, 1943), perhaps half of government expenditures would be war related. The pre–Pearl Harbor estimate had been that defense expenditures might be as high as 27 percent. He pointed out that the conversion of auto plants to making tanks and planes would result in temporary unemployment of thousands of workers. (The automobile makers, who were raking in huge profits, resisted retooling for war work as long as they could.)

Because of the war, Congress now met virtually throughout the year. Its 1941 session adjourned on Friday, January 2, 1942, only to reconvene on Monday,

January 5. Roosevelt sent a budget message up on that day and delivered his State of the Union message the next. Although the war news was bad, the president, described as "grim and resolute," was upbeat: "I am proud to say to you that the spirit of the American people was never higher than it is today—the Union was never more closely knit together—this country was never more deeply determined to face the solemn tasks before it." He could not resist an I told you so. "Exactly one year ago today I said to this Congress: 'When the dictators . . . are ready to make war upon us, they will not wait for an act of war on our part. . . . They—not we—will choose the time and the place and the method of their attack.'" Although it was Japan's attack, he pointed at the main target: "We know their choice of the method: the method of Hitler himself." Tracing the history of past Axis aggression, he claimed that "when Hitler organized his Berlin-Rome-Tokyo alliance, all these plans of conquest became a single plan."

He admitted losses. "It was bitter, for example, not to be able to relieve the heroic and historic defenders of Wake Island. It was bitter for us not to be able to land a million men in a thousand ships in the Philippine Islands. But this adds only to our determination to see to it that the Stars and Stripes will fly again over Wake and Guam. Yes, see to it that the brave people of the Philippines will be rid of Japanese imperialism; and will live in freedom, security, and independence."

Insisting that the "United Nations"—he used the new term eight times in the speech—must have "overwhelming superiority" in arms and the other materials of war and that these would be produced by the United States, he set challenging production goals: 60,000 planes for 1942, 125,000 for 1943; 15,000 tanks in 1942, 75,000 in 1943; 6 million tons of shipping in 1942, 10 million tons in 1943. Few of his auditors had any notion that these were arbitrary goals based not on careful professional estimates but upon notions of need.

Roosevelt began his peroration with a question. "Many people ask, 'When will this war end?' There is only one answer to that. It will end just as soon as we make it end, by our combined efforts, our combined strength, our combined determination to fight through and work through until the end—the end of militarism in Germany and Italy and Japan. Most certainly we shall not settle for less."

He then paid tribute to Churchill: "All in our Nation have been cheered by Mr. Churchill's visit. We have been deeply stirred by his great message to us. He is welcome in our midst, and we unite in wishing him a safe return to his home." There followed a florid statement of what "we of the United Nations are fighting for":

> We are fighting today for security, for progress, and for peace, not only for ourselves but for all men, not only for one generation but for all generations. We are fighting to cleanse the world of ancient evils, ancient ills. Our enemies

Production of Selected Munitions Items, July 1, 1940–July 31, 1945

Item	July 1, 1940 through December 1941	1942	1943	1944	January 1, 1945 through July 31, 1945	Cumulative July 1, 1940 through July 31, 1945
Military airplanes and special-purpose aircraft	23,228	47,859	85,930	96,359	43,225	296,601
Naval ships (new construction, excluding small, rubber, and plastic boats)	1,341	8,039	18,431	29,150	14,099	71,060
Displacement tonnage of above new naval construction	270,000	846,000	2,569,000	3,224,000	1,341,000	8,250,000
Total Maritime Commission ships	136	760	1,949	1,786	794	5,425
Deadweight tonnage of above maritime construction	1,551,000	8,090,000	19,296,000	16,447,000	7,855,000	53,239,000
Machine guns	126,113	666,820	830,384	798,782	302,798	2,724,897
Tanks	4,258	23,884	29,497	17,565	11,184	86,388

Source: Samuel I. Rosenman, comp., *The Public Papers and Addresses of Franklin D. Roosevelt,* 1942 volume, *Humanity on the Defensive,* 61.

are guided by brutal cynicism, by unholy contempt for the human race. We are inspired by a faith that goes back through all the years to the first chapter of the Book of Genesis: "God created man in His own image." . . . That is the conflict that day and night now pervades our lives. No compromise can end that conflict. There never has been—there never can be—successful compromise between good and evil. Only total victory can reward the champions of tolerance, and decency, and freedom and faith.

By all accounts, the reception of the speech was overwhelmingly favorable. *New York Times* reporters could find no member of Congress willing to criticize the president; even Hamilton Fish acknowledged that it was "a good pep talk." Despite an "undercurrent of skepticism" about the feasibility of reaching the production goals that Roosevelt had set, foreign policy critics like Wheeler, Taft, and Vandenberg were complimentary: the Montana Democrat was particularly pleased with remarks about plane and tank production, while the Ohio Republican thought that the president had described American war aims "in an incomparable manner", and his Michigan colleague hailed the speech as "a tremendous dedication to victory." Administration leaders gushed with superlatives with the palm going to Majority Leader McCormack, who hailed it as "one of the greatest speeches of all times. . . . [W]e can all thank God that in this crisis he gave us our leader Franklin D. Roosevelt."

Gallup released no poll evaluating the president's speech, but a late January poll showed that Roosevelt's approval had hit a new high: 84 percent, up 12 percentage points since just before Pearl Harbor and the highest rating since the poll began in 1936. Particularly illuminating was a mid-December poll that asked, "Which country is the greater threat to America's future, Germany or Japan?" Nearly two-thirds, 64 percent, opted for Germany, 15 percent said that they were equal threats, and only 15 percent thought the greater danger came from Japan; 6 percent could not decide. This was another indication of the degree to which Roosevelt's view of the world had been absorbed by the general population.[28]

Churchill, who had spent five days at Ed Stettinius's Florida beachfront villa, headed home on January 13 to face a confidence vote. After a debate airing serious and well-founded criticisms of British strategy, tactics, and leadership in Malaya and elsewhere, he drew only one negative vote. Roosevelt faced no such challenge. Most in Congress had confidence in the military leadership and were more likely to question the president's role as "final arbiter of war production." He governed largely by executive orders rather than statutes.

The only statutory component of the major home-front actions in the early wartime months was the enactment of the Emergency Price Control Act at the end of January. Its signing ended a months-long debate with the farm bloc in Congress and was an important development in the relatively successful fight against inflation. Its passage involved a struggle between Roosevelt and some Democratic leaders who sought to exempt farmers from most price controls. Roosevelt managed the removal of the most damaging part of the bill, which would have placed all controls on farm prices in the Department of Agriculture, but he accepted clearly inflationary aspects of the bill, the most harmful of which prohibited price control of any farm product that had not reached 110 percent of parity.

The president's point man on inflation would continue to be the farsighted Leon Henderson, who, with Isador Lubin, had helped Lauchlin Currie in tutoring Roosevelt about Keynesianism. Henderson's involvement with defense and war economic policy began with his appointment as price stabilization commissioner on the National Council of Defense in May 1940; in April 1941, when Roosevelt established the OPA by executive order, he made Henderson its chair. In that period, the chief concern was industrial prices, and since there was no price control statute Henderson could only jawbone. The new statute gave him authority to fix prices for almost anything civilians could buy and set the price of rental housing. John Kenneth Galbraith, his deputy at OPA, judged his boss to be "one of the greatly innovative figures of World War II." His relatively brief wartime career will be discussed in the next chapter.[29]

The president also wrote in a "personal" letter to Judge Kenesaw Mountain Landis, the baseball commissioner, that "it would be best for the country to keep baseball going." He argued, among other things, that "5,000 or 6,000 players . . . are a definite asset to at least 20,000,000 of their fellow citizens."[30]

The Roberts Commission Report on the Pearl Harbor attack was released in time for the Sunday papers on January 25. Its major finding was that responsibility for the unprepared state of Hawaii's defenses was due mainly to the failures of Admiral Kimmel and General Short to take effective joint action to defend the Hawaiian Islands. The report also stated, falsely and without supporting evidence, that the attack was greatly abetted by Japanese spies, some of whom were described as "persons having no open relations with the Japanese foreign service," though sworn secret testimony assigned the blame to unregistered agents of the Japanese consulate. Roberts had presented his report to the president personally and spent two hours with him. We have no information about what he told Roosevelt, but the justice also met with Stimson, who reported in his diary that Roberts told him that Japanese in the islands "posed a major security risk through espionage, sabotage, and fifth column activities." Only espionage was discussed in the report, and the investigating board had received sworn testimony that neither sabotage nor fifth-column activities had occurred in Oahu before, during, or after the attack.[31]

Not surprisingly, the 1942 Birthday Balls had a United Nations flavor, with balls in London and many Latin American capitals. Incredibly, the fiction writers at MacArthur's headquarters sent a greeting to the president, signed by the general: "Today, Jan. 30, the anniversary of your birth, smoke-begrimed men, covered with the marks of battle, rise from the foxholes of Bataan and the batteries of Corregidor to pray reverently that God may bless immeasurably the President of the United States."

We know that the troops in the Philippines had no such notions. Their self-evaluation was:

We're the battling bastards of Bataan;
No mama, no papa, no Uncle Sam.
No aunts, no uncles, no cousins, no nieces,
No pills, no planes, no artillery pieces.
. . . And nobody gives a damn.[32]

By the beginning of February, important new elements had clearly emerged in the day-to-day structure and functioning of the Roosevelt presidency. Most immediate and obvious was increased security: the unobtrusive Secret Service was supplemented by uniformed troops. Armed soldiers manned the White House gates, antiaircraft weapons were manned on its roof, a cordon of soldiers separated the president from the public at outdoor events, and when Roosevelt and Churchill went to Mount Vernon to pray, those inside the church could see "soldiers with fixed bayonets [march] past the windows." At Hyde Park, the protection was largely covert; a detachment of 170 military police permanently stationed there patrolled Springwood and adjoining properties as unobtrusively as possible, and when Roosevelt was in residence a Coast Guard cutter constantly patrolled the Hudson and would meet and escort his train some ten miles below Hyde Park, all apparently unmentioned in the press.[33]

Inside the White House in the days after Pearl Harbor, Roosevelt's naval aide Captain John Beardall fixed up a makeshift map room in a ground-floor room adjacent to the Oval Office, placed a number of maps on easels around the room, and had safes brought in for classified messages. When Churchill came in mid-December, he had his own portable map room—better developed and more sophisticated than the president's—brought to the White House, and it was installed in a second-floor bedroom across from the suite he was using. Roosevelt and Churchill often went there together. The president told Beardall, "Fix up a room for me like Churchill's."

The new Map Room faced the elevator that brought the president down from the living quarters to the Oval Office, so he could look into it first thing in the morning, the last thing at night, and at his convenience during the day. The walls were overlaid with soft wallboard to which appropriate maps were attached. Desks, filing cabinets, and a safe for classified documents were in a central island so Roosevelt could roll right up to the maps in his wheelchair. It was staffed around the clock by at least one of six junior officers, three from each service, who provided security and posted incoming information on the appropriate maps and set aside for the naval aide messages that the president might want to see.

It was also the place where presidential messages to and from the other major Allied leaders—Churchill, Stalin, and Chiang—were archived. Outgoing messages were entrusted to the navy, while incoming messages came through the army's messaging system. The Map Room was the only place in Washington where a complete file of those messages was kept. Roosevelt knew that control of information was an element of power. The downside was that sometimes key officials, even at the cabinet level, did not have all available information in a timely manner. Entrance to the Map Room was extremely limited. Its other important "customers" were Harry Hopkins, who sometimes got room service; Admiral Leahy; and, during his White House visits, Churchill.[34]

The appointment of William D. Leahy as chief of staff to the commander in chief in July 1942 was the last key piece in the administrative structure that Roosevelt created to control the machinery of military command. They had known each other since the Wilson administration when Leahy was an aide to Roosevelt's chief, Josephus Daniels. Shortly after Roosevelt became president, he appointed Leahy chief of the Bureau of Navigation and in 1937 made him CNO; he served until his mandatory retirement in 1939, when Roosevelt named him governor of Puerto Rico. In December 1940, he sent the admiral as ambassador to the French government in Vichy, hoping that a military man might be effective in communicating with its leader, Marshal Pétain. Keeping the American Embassy open there also provided a listening post within Nazi Europe. Leahy was ordered home only in May 1942. Like most of Roosevelt's ranking military advisers and not a few of his diplomats, Leahy was very much a man of the Right, as his memoir comment on Mussolini's 1943 ouster illustrates: "Il Duce . . . brought about an improvement in conditions which previously verged on anarchy. [He] made his fatal mistake when he joined Hitler in 1940." It is not surprising that he and Pétain got along.

Roosevelt's announcement of Leahy's appointment puzzled reporters and not a few historians.

Q: Mr. President, can you tell us what the scope of Admiral Leahy's—
THE PRESIDENT: (Interposing) Chief of Staff.
Q: (Continuing) position will be?
THE PRESIDENT: Chief of Staff. I think that's all that's necessary.
Q: Will he have the staff of the Army, Navy, and Air Force under him?
THE PRESIDENT: I haven't got the foggiest idea; and it has nothing to do with the "price of eggs."
Q: Well, sir, will he be Chief of Staff of the United Nations strategic command?
THE PRESIDENT: He will be Chief of Staff to the Commander in Chief.

After several other topics were discussed:

> MR. J. M. MINIFIE: Mr. President, does the appointment of Admiral Leahy as Chief of Staff to the Commander in Chief mean that the Commander in Chief will take a more active direction of the strategic conduct of the war—world war?
>
> THE PRESIDENT: That will be almost impossible. (loud laughter).
>
> Q: Could you tell us any more of the Admiral's duties as Commander—as Chief of Staff to the Commander in Chief?
>
> THE PRESIDENT: Well, whatever—put it this way: whatever's necessary from the point of view of the Commander in Chief. Now, as a matter of fact, I wouldn't go guessing around about things, in assigning more importance to this than it really deserves.
>
> I have—the reason I asked—I answered brother Minifie's question that way was that, of course, I do spend an awful lot of time on it, from an American point of view. And at the same time, in so doing, there are all kinds of opinions that I have to read, all kinds of opinions I have to get, and do get, and it takes a very long time. It takes a great deal of time, which after a pretty careful survey for 7 months, I should say could—I should be helped to save, by somebody else doing an awful lot of leg-work, and indexing work, and summarizing work, and at the same time somebody in whose judgment I have a good deal of real confidence. And it is going to save me a great many hours of work—
>
> Q. (INTERPOSING): Mr. President—
>
> THE PRESIDENT: (Continuing)—and all kinds of tasks—instead of doing them myself, finding out about things—if I can get somebody else to do the leg-work.[35]

Leahy's job description is familiar. It is essentially that of one of Roosevelt's presidential assistants. Of course, one cannot describe a four-star admiral as a presidential assistant, even if he is rendering that kind of service, and there was no question of anonymity. In addition, Leahy was more than that. He also met with the Joint Chiefs of Staff (JCS), serving as its chair, and on the Combined Joint Chiefs as well. He attended all subsequent summit conferences and as a good military bureaucrat tried to ensure a greater sharing of information within the government.

Wars cause any presidency to become less public, but Roosevelt used the war emergency to provide private space for himself. The regulation about the secrecy of presidential travel meant that his frequent trips to Hyde Park—some forty of his two hundred presidential visits there were in wartime—were not covered by the press, and his various absences were announced, if at all, only after his return.

Early in the war, after two successive press conferences had been canceled and a third had lasted "barely three minutes," some reporters feared that Roosevelt might discontinue press conferences, as Wilson had done after the sinking of the *Lusitania*. That never happened, but their number was significantly reduced. From 1933 through 1941, Roosevelt's press conferences averaged about ninety a year. During 1942 there were seventy-five, in 1943 fifty-eight, and in the final sixteen months of his presidency another fifty-eight. The fact that there were no press conferences at Hyde Park after Pearl Harbor was a factor in their decreased frequency.[36]

After the 1940 election, an increasingly stressed Steve Early had stopped traveling with the president, and his chore of tending the press away from the White House fell largely to his longtime assistant, William D. Hassett, a veteran newspaperman who had come to the White House in 1935.[37] Hassett, who had a literary bent, also composed minor "personal" letters for the president, who came to call him the "the Bishop."

On January 6, 1942, just before entraining with Roosevelt on the first wartime trip to Hyde Park, Hassett purchased a "journal" to "jot down a few notes of a unique trip to Hyde Park with the President." There are many New Deal "diaries"—the best known, by Morgenthau and Ickes, are consolidated compilations—and countless memoirs, but Hassett's diary is the only one by a key White House insider, and it reveals an aspect of Roosevelt's presidency that was largely unknown before its 1958 publication. In July 1944, Roosevelt wrote a public letter announcing that he would accept a draft for a fourth term that included the following: "All that is within me cries out to go back to my home on the Hudson River, to avoid public responsibilities, and to avoid also the publicity which in our democracy follows every step of the Nation's Chief Executive."

Although the press and most of his political friends and enemies smiled or scoffed at the idea that Roosevelt yearned for a quiet life, the tales told in Hassett's diary lend it verisimilitude. Only a few persons on his staff, some Secret Service personnel, and a number of his friends and neighbors in and around Hyde Park had any notion that from January 1942, the president of the United States played hooky from his duties on numerous occasions, mostly weekends, puttering with some of his papers and memorabilia at his new presidential library, bird-watching at sunup, and paying occasional calls on a few old friends and relatives. The diary is also useful for giving us a concerned layman's account of the president's health in persistent comments, including the last days at Warm Springs. The first of these occurs in a May 1942 entry: "He was as fit as a fiddle and full of enthusiasm."[38]

February was another terrible month of military defeats for the United States and its allies in the Pacific, the Mediterranean, and American coastal waters. Japanese forces pushing west had entered Burma in mid-January and by the end of February were in the outskirts of Rangoon. On February 8, the Japanese southbound thrust through Malaya gained a foothold on the island of Singapore, the main British bastion east of India. Churchill instructed commanders there to battle to the last man and that senior officers should die with their troops, but on February 15 the British commander, Lieutenant General Arthur Percival surrendered Singapore and 130,000 British, Australian, and Indian troops to General Yamashita, who commanded 35,000 soldiers. In the Philippines, American forces on the Bataan Peninsula were being ground down by superior Japanese forces with command of the air. Farther south, Japanese troops had landed on many of the islands of the Dutch East Indies and, farther southeast, in the Solomon Islands. On February 18, Japanese aircraft made their first attack on Australia with a heavy air raid on its northern port at Darwin, the point through which meager assistance was being sent to help the Dutch. Farther east, a small positive note was struck as planes from the aircraft carrier USS *Enterprise* bombed long-held Japanese installations in the mandated Gilbert and Marshall Islands and on newly captured Wake Island.

In the Mediterranean, British successes against Italian troops in North Africa came to an end as German forces, the soon-to-be-famous Afrika Korps led by General Erwin Rommel, checked the British advance in late January and began to push the Eighth Army back toward Egypt. And beginning in mid-January along the North American Eastern Seaboard, from the mouth of the St. Lawrence to the South Florida coast, and later in the Caribbean, German submarines wreaked havoc on unconvoyed coastal shipping for the first five months of 1942. It was a period that U-boat commanders would later remember as the "happy time" and that the German admiralty labeled Operation Paukenschlag (Drumbeat). The highly successful U-boat attacks, a few of them in full view of bathers on American beaches, sank hundreds of thousands of tons of shipping at little cost. Typically, the submarines would lurk at periscope depth at night just beyond the normal shipping lanes near heavily populated areas so that passing vessels would be backlit by the lights of coastal communities. Refusals to extinguish or dim commercial and residential lighting—except during air-raid drills—became a national scandal, as was the failure of Congress or the administration to force communities to comply with naval requests. Only in April and May were dim-out—not black-out—regulations put into effect and enforced.[39]

Under these deteriorating conditions, Roosevelt struggled to maintain American morale, fight complacency, and insist on the need for unity. It was in this atmosphere that Roosevelt authorized the most blatant mass federal violation of the freedom of American citizens by signing an executive order, drafted by military lawyers in the War Department with the reluctant cooperation of their colleagues in the Department of Justice. Intended primarily to corral American-born persons of Japanese ancestry and their alien parents, it was broad enough to ensnare anyone living in the United States.[40]

These events began to unfold in the early afternoon of February 11, when Stimson telephoned Roosevelt in the White House and received from him approval to remove as-yet-unspecified numbers of Japanese Americans, both aliens and citizens, from their West Coast homes. As assistant secretary of war John J. McCloy (1895–1989) described it in a telephone conversation with a subordinate officer in San Francisco's Presidio later that afternoon, "We talked to the President and the President, in substance, says go ahead and do anything you think necessary. . . . [I]f it involves citizens, we will take care of them too. He says there will probably be some repercussions, but it has got to be dictated by military necessity, but as he put it, 'Be as reasonable as you can.'"

It is not clear to what degree Roosevelt was then aware of an ongoing struggle between Stimson and Attorney General Francis Biddle (1886–1968) over how much of the civil liberties of Japanese American citizens it was appropriate to curtail. Somewhat overawed by the imperious Stimson, who had been a cabinet officer in the year that Biddle was graduated from law school, the junior member of Roosevelt's cabinet had grudgingly agreed to a series of escalating demands for such things as warrantless searches of Japanese American homes and businesses, but when it came to locking up what the army's provost marshal general Allen W. Gullion called "Jap citizens," Biddle drew the line. In a letter to Stimson on February 12, Biddle wrote, "No legal problem arises when Japanese citizens are evacuated, but American citizens of Japanese origin could not, in my opinion, be singled out of an area and evacuated with other Japanese." But the attorney general—unaware of Roosevelt's verbal approval the day before—went on to advise his cabinet colleague that he might get his desired result by "evacuating all persons in the area and then licensing back" everyone except the Japanese Americans and any others the military wanted to keep out, an expedient that army lawyers had considered. Five days later, at almost the eleventh hour, Biddle wrote the president, making clear his objections, but never saying that it was repugnant to the spirit of the Constitution. In a formal "MEMORANDUM TO THE PRESIDENT," Biddle included what he probably knew was a useless caveat:

> To evacuate the 93,000 Japanese in California over night would materially disrupt agricultural production in which they play a large part and the farm labor now is so limited that they could not be quickly replaced. Their hurried evacuation would require thousands of troops, tie up transportation and raise very difficult questions of resettlement. Under the Constitution 60,000 of these Japanese are American citizens. If complete confusion and lowering of morale is to be avoided, so large a job must be done after careful planning. The Army has not advised me of its conclusion in the matter.[41]

It never occurred to Biddle or the few other civil libertarians among the New Deal elite who were concerned about what was being done to the Japanese

Americans to resign in protest. Roosevelt was, they reasoned, the father of the nation and knew best.

Roosevelt, as was his habit, did not simply accept Stimson's advice. He seems to have relied upon a memorandum written primarily by Benjamin V. Cohen that, like his previous efforts about such matters as economic regulation, assigned almost unlimited power to the executive. Accordingly on February 19, 1942, a date that has increasingly become infamous for those concerned with civil liberties and the post–World War II evolution of the national security state, Roosevelt signed Executive Order 9066. In an extreme delegation of assumed presidential power, it authorized

> the Secretary of War, and the Military Commanders whom he may from time to time designate to prescribe military areas . . . from which any or all persons may be excluded . . . subject to whatever restrictions the Secretary of War or the appropriate Military Commander may impose in his discretion. The Secretary of War is hereby authorized to provide for residents of any such area who are excluded therefrom, such transportation, food, shelter, and other accommodations as may be necessary, in the judgment of the Secretary of War or the said Military Commander, and until other arrangements are made, to accomplish the purpose of this order.

The text was printed in the *New York Times* two days later, and its front-page story provided a good account of what was to come by a well-briefed reporter.[42]

Why did Franklin Roosevelt decide, seventy-four days after the Pearl Harbor disaster, to sign an order, on the grounds of "military necessity," that resulted in the expulsion and eventual incarceration of some 120,000 Japanese Americans, men, women, and children, more than 70 percent of them native-born U.S. citizens? Since the president never once discussed publicly or, as far as we know, privately why he agreed to oust Japanese Americans from their homes and imprison them, any answer to that question must be in part speculative. But we do have a great deal of evidence about his willingness to make pragmatic compromises about other matters of principle in civil rights. As has been shown, when it came to advancing the civil rights of African Americans or attempting to amend immigration regulations to admit refugee children, he had often refrained from taking actions that he said he favored on the grounds that doing so might interfere with congressional and popular support for aspects of his program he deemed more pressing. As he told his press conference on February 13, "I have been opposed to the poll tax all my life," but he never gave substantive support to congressional efforts to outlaw it. Similarly, he refused to comment on rioting by whites in Detroit protesting the opening of a federal housing project for African Americans.

While, as noted, Roosevelt was concerned about fifth columnists, he did not ask FBI director Hoover for his opinion. Of course he was concerned about the threat of invasion, but his military advisers had assured him that, apart from the possibility of the odd hit-and-run raid, there was no immediate threat to the West Coast. His chief domestic concern, as he clearly indicated, was wartime unity, not only to prosecute the war but to ensure a lasting peace, not another long armistice. The request from Stimson, the chief symbol of wartime bipartisanship, had been dramatically seconded two days later by a resolution signed by all the senators and representatives of the three West Coast states, which had been organized by California's Hiram Johnson and released to the press. It called upon the president to order "the immediate evacuation of all persons of Japanese lineage and all others, aliens and citizens alike, whose presence shall be deemed dangerous or inimical to the defense of the United States from all strategic areas [in] the states of California, Oregon, and Washington and the territory of Alaska."[43]

The available evidence suggests to me that political motives, not military necessity, were paramount in shaping Roosevelt's decision. Although Roosevelt was confident of eventual military victory, the war news was terrible, and he knew that it would get worse before it got better. He had one eye on the off-year election, less than nine months away; with his vivid memory of the Democrats' loss of control of Congress in the 1918 off-year elections, and the disastrous results of that loss for Wilson's hopes for a long-lasting peace, the demand from the West Coast delegation must have given Roosevelt pause. It seems to me likely that the president's fear of the possible political consequences of not taking drastic steps against the West Coast Japanese Americans was more significant in shaping his dreadful decision than any fears he had of invasion or sabotage. And, as will be shown, when it came to relaxing the restrictions on the incarcerated people in the closing weeks of 1944, domestic political calculations were even more clearly paramount.

In mid-March, Roosevelt issued an executive order establishing the War Relocation Authority (WRA) to run the camps built by the Corps of Engineers to imprison West Coast Japanese Americans. Most of them were still in their homes because the government had no place to put them. Their organized removal would begin only on March 31 and continue, piecemeal, under army auspices until late June. Although the WRA was slotted into the Executive Office of the President, he kept it at arm's length. The first WRA director, Milton S. Eisenhower (1899–1985), a longtime Department of Agriculture official, quickly regretted that he had taken the job. On April 1, he wrote his former boss agriculture secretary Claude Wickard that "I feel most deeply that when the war is over and we consider calmly this unprecedented migration of 120,000 people, we as Americans are going to regret the avoidable injustices that may have been done." But in his June 18 letter of resignation to the president, he made no reference to "avoidable injustices." He did tell the president that "public attitudes have exerted a strong influence in shaping the program and charting its direction. In a democracy this is unquestionably sound and proper." Eisenhower's successor, a fellow agricultural bureaucrat, Dillon S. Myer (1891–1982), served from June 1942 until the agency was disbanded in 1946. As had been the case with the February order that authorized the mass exile of Japanese Americans, Roosevelt made no statement about it for more than a year.[44]

While Roosevelt's executive order needed no statutory approval, something had to be done to provide a penalty for anyone violating the military orders. There was no way civilians could be judicially punished for violating a general's order if martial law had not been declared, something that Roosevelt was willing to allow in the Territory of Hawaii but not in the United States itself. Congress accordingly passed Public Law 503, drafted by military lawyers, which made it a federal crime for anyone ordered to leave a military area to refuse to do so. On the Senate floor, Ohio's Taft commented that it was the "sloppiest" criminal law he had ever seen, but since it would affect only Japanese he would vote for it. It passed both houses without a single negative vote and was signed by Roosevelt on March 21.[45]

With that law on the books on March 24, Lieutenant General John L. DeWitt (1880–1962), in charge of the Western Defense Command and the only commander delegated to execute Executive Order 9066, issued his initial Civilian Exclusion Order, the first of 108, which directed the 257 "persons of Japanese ancestry, both alien and non-alien," then living on tiny Bainbridge Island, a short ferry ride from Seattle, to report to the island's dock six days later for "evacuation," bringing with them "only what they could carry." The regular island ferry took the men, women, and children, under armed guard, to Seattle, where they were placed on a train to the camp being constructed at Manzanar, California, where nearly a thousand "volunteer" Japanese American citizens were already domiciled.

By June the army had removed the Japanese from the communities in which they had lived and confined them in nearby temporary facilities, including racetracks and livestock pavilions in which some of the exiled people had to live in stalls still reeking with the odors of their former occupants. By November all were in purpose-built camps from eastern California to southeastern Arkansas. Neither of the WRA directors would admit that they were concentration camps; Dillon Myer actually issued a directive to his staff forbidding them to use the term.

In an October 29 press conference, Roosevelt announced the beginnings of what became known as the Bracero Program. It would bring in supposedly temporary Mexican workers outside of the normal immigration process. In discussing the farm-labor crisis, he mentioned:

THE PRESIDENT: In some cases, like the Montana beet fields, they are already moving some of the Japanese labor into the Montana beet fields. . . . .

Q: Mr. President, will some of the Mexicans replace the Japanese in the truck gardens in California?

THE PRESIDENT: That I don't know.

Q: Where did the Japanese come from who are being shipped to Montana, sir?

THE PRESIDENT: Concentration camps.

Asked if they got paid, the president affirmed that they did, but he didn't know at what rate. A reporter then chimed in: "The Japs don't pay our boys over there."[46] No journalist asked a question about the incarceration of the Japanese Americans in any of the president's 1942 press conferences. Ironically, a disaster for one generally despised minority provided an opportunity for another.

Despite his failure to discuss the fate of the Japanese Americans, Roosevelt had, nevertheless, proved amenable to certain positive modifications in the conditions of confinement for some of the citizen Nisei. The first of these began in mid-May 1942, when he agreed to a suggestion made by California governor Culbert Olson (1876–1963), acting on a suggestion from the University of California's Robert G. Sproul (1891–1975), that Nisei students be released to attend universities and colleges outside of the forbidden West Coast zone that would accept them. Urged on by a number of New Dealers, Roosevelt, after consultation, agreed, writing Olson that "qualified American-born Japanese students will be able to continue their education in inland institutions." Despite complications and difficulties, some four thousand Nisei students gained release from the concentration camps beginning in mid-1942 and received limited WRA financial support to attend college. Alan W. Austin, the historian of the wartime college Nisei, argued recently that they were the "precursors of the 'over-representation' of Asian American students" on university campuses today and thus "harbingers" of a trend toward multiculturalism.[47]

Feeling that the nation needed a pep talk, Roosevelt scheduled a Fireside Chat for February 23 and asked newspapers to print maps. The *New York Times* called attention to the speech on its front page and printed an eight-column world map covering more than a third of the page under a caption, "Clip and Save This Map for Use during the President's Speech Tonight."

Roosevelt began by praising George Washington's "moral stamina" during eight years of war and calling for the same kind of resolve in "a new kind of war," different from all other wars of the past, not only in its methods and weapons but also in its geography. It is warfare in terms of every continent, every island, every sea, every air lane in the world.

Speaking as if he were a professor of geography, Roosevelt invited his listeners "to take out and spread before you a map of the whole earth" and follow "with me" as he spoke of "the world-encircling battle lines of this war." He noted that the "broad oceans [once] our protection from attack have become endless battlefields on which we are constantly being challenged by our enemies." He explained that the objective of "the Nazis and the Japanese" was "to separate and to isolate" the United States, Britain, China, and Russia, "the old familiar Axis policy of 'divide and conquer.'"

Then came the map exercise: "Look at your map. Look at the vast area of China, with its millions of fighting men. Look at the vast area of Russia, with its powerful armies and proven military might. Look at the British Isles, Australia, New Zealand, the Dutch Indies, India, the Near East, and the continent of Africa, with their resources of raw materials, and of peoples determined to resist Axis domination." Attacking the now discredited isolationists, he argued that "those Americans who believed that we could live under the illusion of isolationism wanted the American eagle to imitate the tactics of the ostrich. Now, many of those same people, afraid that we may be sticking our necks out, want our national bird to be turned into a turtle. But we prefer to retain the eagle as it is—flying high and striking hard."

The president admitted losses and warned that there would be more, but he insisted that increasing American war production meant that Allied strength would grow, while that of the Axis would fade. He did not discuss problems of internal security or mention what was planned for Japanese Americans. He did continue to mention the United Nations—eleven times—most importantly in a paragraph near the close: "We of the United Nations are agreed on certain broad principles in the kind of peace we seek. The Atlantic Charter applies not only to the parts of the world that border the Atlantic but to the whole world; disarmament of aggressors, self-determination of Nations and peoples, and the four freedoms—freedom of speech, freedom of religion, freedom from want, and freedom from fear."[48]

As Roosevelt was speaking, a large aircraft-carrying Japanese submarine, the I-17, surfaced near Santa Barbara, California, and from a range of perhaps twenty-five hundred yards fired thirteen rounds from its 5.5-inch deck gun that failed to hit any of the large oil storage tanks that were the presumed target and did negligible damage. The next night, a phantom air raid alarm in Los Angeles, set off by a presumed radar image, caused antiaircraft guns all over the county to fire some fourteen hundred shells skyward after a gun based in Santa Monica fired at what was later believed to be a weather balloon. That, and later fears that Japanese forces would attempt to retaliate for the April 1942 Doolittle raid on Tokyo, prompted the dispatch of even more forces, badly needed elsewhere, to be sent to the panicky West Coast.[49]

Meanwhile, Roosevelt had to make decisions about Douglas MacArthur and the Philippines. The debacle in the Philippines was even more egregious than that at Pearl Harbor. Although the commanders in the Philippines had long expected to be attacked, raiding Japanese planes had destroyed half of the military aircraft in the Philippines on the ground in attacks that began nine hours after officers there learned of the attack in Hawaii. Losses included eighteen of the thirty-five B-17 Flying Fortresses, fifty-three P-40 fighters, and most of the installations at the two main Luzon airfields. Eighty air force personnel were killed and 150 wounded. The Japanese lost seven fighters and no bombers. The three senior officers—MacArthur; his chief of staff, General Richard K. Sunderland; and the air force commander, General Lewis H. Brereton—each gave a different account of the command decisions or nondecisions on the first day of the war. They all cannot be accurate; perhaps none was.[50] Given the consequences, each of the three merited being relieved of duty as much as Admiral Kimmel or General Short did, but all three later received, and may have earned, decorations and promotions.

Major unopposed Japanese landings north and south of Manila on December 22 and 24 were the other decisive strokes in the conquest of the Philippines. The day after the first landing, MacArthur decided to withdraw to Bataan and to the island fortress of Corregidor in Manila Bay. He declared Manila an "open city," and Japanese forces occupied it on New Year's Day. After a harrowing month in which the American forces were badly battered, the War Department received messages on February 8 from both MacArthur and Philippine president Manuel Quezon. Quezon's, addressed to Roosevelt, proposed that the islands immediately be given the independence promised for 1945 and then neutralized by the mutual withdrawal of American and Japanese troops and the disbanding of the Philippine army. MacArthur's supporting message told Washington, for the first time, that his troops had suffered a casualty rate of 50 percent, and that his divisions were now regiments, his regiments battalions. "There is no denying," he told General Marshall, "that we are near done."

An immediate negative came from Roosevelt in personal messages to each man. He told Quezon that the United States would never agree to such a solution. He offered sympathy to the Philippine leader and promised American support, "whatever happens to the present American garrison. . . . We shall not relax our efforts until the forces we are now marshalling . . . return to the Philippines and drive the last remnant of the invaders from your soil."

In answering MacArthur, Roosevelt had to face something no other American president has encountered: the impending surrender of an entire army. He authorized MacArthur to surrender the Filipino troops, if necessary, but forbade the surrender of American troops "so long as there remains any possibility of resistance." He insisted that "the duty and the necessity of resisting Japanese aggression to the last transcends in importance any other obligation now facing us in the Philippines." He went on to explain that "as the most powerful member" of "a globe-circling opposition" to the Axis, "we cannot display weakness in fact or spirit anywhere." After recognizing the difficulty of the assignment, Roosevelt closed by saying, "I particularly request that you proceed rapidly to the organization of your forces and your defenses so as to make your resistance as effective as circumstances will permit and as prolonged as humanly possible."

Both Quezon and MacArthur accepted, without demur, the president's directive. The general informed the president on February 11 that he and his family would remain in the Philippines "and share the fate of the garrison." Four days later, the disgraceful British surrender at Singapore took place. A week later, Roosevelt secretly directed MacArthur to leave the Philippines. Quezon, his family, a few officials of his government, and U.S. High Commissioner to the Philippines Francis B. Sayre had already been evacuated in the submarine USS *Swordfish.*

In his Valley Forge chat the next day, the president, after praising "the defense put up by General MacArthur [that] has magnificently exceeded the previous estimates of endurance . . . he and his men are gaining eternal glory," went on to explain that "it has been said that Japanese gains in the Philippines were made possible only by the success of their surprise attack on Pearl Harbor. I tell you that this is not so. Even if the attack had not been made your map will show that it would have been a hopeless operation for us to send the fleet to the Philippines through thousands of miles of ocean, while all those island bases were under the sole control of the Japanese."

However reassuring this may have been for most of the general public, according to official army historian Louis Morton, it was a "huge blow" to knowledgeable officers in the islands, as "no prospect of relief could be found in the president's message," which undermined the basic theme of the propaganda broadcasts from Corregidor's "Voice of Freedom" that "help was on the way."

On February 23, the same day he gave the chat, Roosevelt sent a second directive to MacArthur, informing him that his eventual destination was Australia, where he was to direct the American buildup as allied commander of the Southwest Pacific theater, which stretched north as far as the Philippines. MacArthur, with his wife, four-year-old son Arthur, Chinese nurse Ah Cheu, and sixteen staff officers, including a public relations specialist and one master sergeant, embarked from Corregidor about midnight on March 12 in four PT boats. They headed for Mindanao, which American forces still controlled. After a daylight layover on an uninhabited island, they concluded the six-hundred-mile journey just before daylight on March 14. From there a B-17 flew the party to Australia. By the time MacArthur arrived in Australia, Wavell's ABDA command had been dissolved after the Japanese victory in the Battle of the Java Sea. As Samuel Eliot Morison put it, this defeat "doomed" the Dutch Empire in Asia. On arrival MacArthur announced, "I came through, and I shall return."

Once the news was out, Roosevelt read a formal announcement during his press conference: "I know that every man and woman in the United States admires with me General MacArthur's determination to fight to the finish with his men in the Philippines. But I also know that every man and woman is in agreement that all important decisions must be made with a view toward the successful termination of the war. Knowing this I am sure that every American, if faced with the question as to where General MacArthur could best serve his country, could come to only one answer."[51]

Left behind were the rest of MacArthur's forsaken forces, whom Roosevelt placed under the command of Major General Jonathan M. Wainwright (1883–1953), whom he promoted to lieutenant general after MacArthur reached Australia. MacArthur had planned to retain personal command of the Philippines and had left one of his staff officers in charge, but Roosevelt and Marshall put an end to that. On April 8, Roosevelt withdrew his no-surrender order. Eventually, he told Wainwright, after the surrender of the Bataan forces, that "whatever decision you have made has been dictated by the best interests of your troops and of the country." He added that he hoped that Corregidor could hold out, but gave Wainwright "complete freedom of action" and expressed "full confidence" in whatever decisions he made. Wainwright declared his "heartfelt gratitude" for Roosevelt's confidence in his judgment. The final surrender was not consummated until June 9, as the Japanese command refused to grant the Corregidor garrison prisoner-of-war (POW) status unless Wainwright obtained the surrender of all American forces in the Philippines, which took time. The fear was that, if resistance continued elsewhere, some eleven thousand Americans who had destroyed their weapons would be executed. Although a few small units carried on guerrilla warfare, Wainwright's forces were granted the promised status. As is notorious, the treatment that they and most other Euro-American captives of Japanese military forces received was significantly below the standards prescribed in the Geneva Convention of 1926.

Roosevelt sent a valedictory message to Wainwright that said, in part:

> During recent weeks we have been following with growing admiration the day-by-day accounts of your heroic stand against the mounting intensity of bombardment by enemy planes and heavy siege guns. In spite of all the handicaps of complete isolation, lack of food and ammunition, you have given the world a shining example of patriotic fortitude and self-sacrifice. The American people ask no finer example of tenacity, resourcefulness, and steadfast courage. The calm determination of your personal leadership in a desperate situation sets a standard of duty for our soldiers throughout the world. . . . You and your devoted followers have become the living symbols of our war aims and the guarantee of victory.

While the message clearly pleased the general, it was at best cold comfort for those who lived through the horrible "death march" and years of brutal captivity from which survivors emerged undernourished and disease ridden.[52]

A final question remains. How was it that Roosevelt, who had a history of issues with MacArthur dating back to the earliest years of his presidency, continued to promote and otherwise favor him despite a distinctly subpar military performance in the Philippines? The most satisfactory answer is that it was the politically expedient thing to do. MacArthur, whatever the reality, cut a heroic, larger-than-life figure at a time when the nation needed heroes. And it was good politics to send him to Australia, and although Roosevelt and Marshall both thought it inappropriate, neither demurred when mostly Republican congressmen wanted the general awarded the Congressional Medal of Honor. Eventually, Wainwright got one too.[53]

While Roosevelt's concern with purely military matters was never more intensive than in the seven months after Pearl Harbor, he devoted much attention to creating and rearranging various government agencies to manage more effectively the civilian economy necessary to support the war effort. Sam Rosenman, who in addition to his speechwriting chores had been overseeing various aspects of reorganizing government to expedite defense and war mobilization, lists seventeen different government bodies Roosevelt created or reorganized in the first six months of 1942, roughly one every eleven days. Only the more significant can be treated here.

The creation of the National War Labor Board (NWLB) in mid-January stemmed directly from a labor-management conference convoked by the president in late December. After five days, the conferees had agreed to a no-strike pledge and the peaceful settlement of disputes. They recommended that the president should establish a War Labor Board, but they were deadlocked over whether to give the board authority to establish a closed shop, which labor insisted on and management rejected. Labor Secretary Perkins relates that as a last resort she arranged for a midafternoon meeting of the conferees with Roosevelt. "I preceded them to tell the President about the dispute over the closed shop and prepare him for disappointment. 'Oh well,' he said, 'I can handle that. We can't expect perfection. I'll accept the three important points they *have* agreed to with thanks. I'll promise to appoint the board promptly.' His right eyebrow lifted quizzically. 'We'll let the board make its own rules and regulations and determine its jurisdiction.'"

Roosevelt did just that and, with that combination of authority and charm he knew how to apply, managed to avoid the closed-shop issue. In neither his talk with the conferees nor his formal statement did he mention the board's jurisdiction. The executive order establishing the NWLB called for twelve members—four each from labor, management, and the public—and provided that it "shall have the power to promulgate rules and regulations appropriate for the performance of its duties." It was placed it in the Office of Emergency Management, with working links to the Labor Department. William H. Davis was carried over as chair from the phased-out NDMB as one of four public members. In signing the executive order, Roosevelt asserted that "the national interest demands that there shall be no interruption of any work that contributes to the effective prosecution of the war."

As Roosevelt expected, the NWLB had to deal with the union security question. In cases where there was a contractual provision for either a closed or a union shop, there was no problem. In disputes where there was no such provision, the board tended to provide for "maintenance of membership," which approached a union shop. In many instances, this provided unions with security against raiding by a rival.

From its inception until V-J Day in August 1945, the NWLB closed 17,650 disputes. Forty-six cases that it could not settle were referred to the president and were usually followed by a presidential seizure order or a threat of one. Such disputes, particularly those involving John L. Lewis and Sewell Avery of Montgomery Ward, came to dominate press, congressional, and eventually the public view, but they were atypical of the nearly fifteen thousand wartime strikes. Most of these were wildcat walkouts, like the prewar dispute at North American Aviation, against the wishes of national union leaders. All told some 6.7 million workers walked out, resulting in more than 36 million worker-days of idleness. That was a mere 11/100ths of 1 percent of available working time, but even such minuscule figures could prompt even a sensible NWLB public member like Oregon law professor and later U.S. senator Wayne L. Morse to threaten to "apply the laws against treason" against anyone who would promote a jurisdictional dispute. The case in question involved who should paint a building at a former Frigidaire plant in Dayton, Ohio, being converted to war production; the dispute had idled 252 AFL members for five working days when the foolish threat was made. Despite such outbursts, the NWLB generally promoted relative industrial peace during the war years.[54]

Like the NWLB, the War Production Board (WPB), established two days later, was fundamentally a reshuffle of an existing institution rather than a new departure. Roosevelt transferred to it the duties previously handled by the SPAB and the OPM, thus dissolving what he had called the law firm of Knudsen and Hillman. Knudsen was—to the disgust of many army officers—made a lieutenant general and put in charge of War Department production, thus giving Stimson and Marshall more direct control of the supply of crucial military hardware. Hillman was named director of the Labor Division of the WPB and later got the added title of a special assistant to the president. Donald Nelson, but not the board of eight officials who were shifted from SPAB to help him run the WPB, was charged with overall supervision of production, subject only to review by the president. From then until August 1944, Nelson was the most important civilian charged with managing the economy.[55]

In January and February, a rescue operation was necessary to avoid a congressional clampdown of the Office of Civilian Defense. The agency, and its part-time head, New York's Mayor La Guardia, drew much criticism. Consistent with his delight in racing to fires, La Guardia concentrated solely on protective measures, but failed to provide stirrup pumps and other specialized equipment for the air raids that never came. When Eleanor Roosevelt joined in by criticizing him for not supplying opportunities for other citizen participation, Fiorello quickly invited her to become his assistant director.

Despite the obvious risks—she would be a target for the president's enemies—Mrs. Roosevelt accepted the mayor's challenge at the end of September 1941. This gave the agency two part-time high-profile heads, neither of whom drew federal pay. The president also recognized the risks, but according to management expert Anna Rosenberg, who often advised Roosevelt, "He was glad to channel [Eleanor's] energies into one area so that she would leave him alone in other areas. He knew that she felt frustrated because many of the liberal programs had to be put aside."

Although the mayor and the first lady made a joint journey to the West Coast in the immediate aftermath of Pearl Harbor, they worked in separate spheres, he concentrating sporadically on protection, she focusing steadily on her Voluntary Participation Program. Mounting congressional criticism directed at the two-job mayor and moves to cut off funding or transfer civil defense to the War Department (or both), which neither it nor the White House wanted, forced the president to act. In early January, he appointed Harvard Law School dean James M. Landis (1899–1964) executive director to "assist" La Guardia. After the mayor resigned in an exchange of letters, the president appointed Landis, a Felix Frankfurter protégé who had previously served on the Federal Trade Commission and succeeded Joe Kennedy as chair of the SEC, as OCD director. Eleanor Roosevelt consoled the mayor, thanking him "for letting me organize a part of the work in which you did not believe."

By this time, Eleanor herself was under attack. Two Associated Press stories that seemed to be the result of OCD press releases sparked congressional criticism: one announced the appointment of movie actor Melvyn Douglas as arts director for the OCD; the other made known that Mayris Cheney, described as a "dancer protégé of Mrs. Franklin D. Roosevelt," had been named head of children's activities in OCD's physical fitness division. The next day, the AP dug up a four-year-old picture of Cheney demonstrating a new dance called the "Eleanor Glide" before her smiling patron in a New York hotel. A howl about both appointments went up from chronic New Deal baiters in the House, some calling Cheney a "fan dancer." Virginia's Harry Byrd, chair of the Senate Budget Committee, complained, with more gravitas, about "frills and furbelows." No complaints were made about the appointment of Olympic star Jesse Owens as OCD athletic director.

Douglas, who after all was somebody, as was his wife, Helen Gahagan Douglas, the Democratic National Committeewoman from California, was defended by several congressmen and the Screen Actors Guild, and he defended himself ably, pointing out that rather than his reported salary of eight thousand dollars as arts director, he was taking only per diem. Cheney, who was literally nobody, had no defenders beyond her patron and quickly resigned. Even the president took a cheap shot at her in his press conference. Commenting on the fact that Landis, unlike La Guardia, would be paid, he added, "Off the record, whether he does a Sally Rand act or not." (Sally Rand was a famous fan dancer; Cheney's performances were fully clothed.) The president, who did not pay attention to those who sat below the salt, was probably unaware that Cheney had recently been a guest at a White House dinner for Winston Churchill or that she had been Eleanor's guest aboard his 1936 campaign train.

The real target, Eleanor Roosevelt, asked for but did not receive a hearing from Congress. She soon resigned, saying, "By remaining in the Office of Civilian Defense I would only make it possible for those who wish to attack me for my beliefs, to attack an agency which I consider can prove its usefulness so completely to the people that it should be free of attack in order to render its maximum service."

On her Sunday radio program, she went further, probably too far. Claiming that since she had resigned she was "free to speak her mind as a private person," she called her critics a "small and unenlightened group of men" making "the age old fight for the privileged few against the good of the many." Admitting that she had "suggested Miss Mayris Cheney's name," she said that "the fact that she was a friend of mine had no bearing on the decision" to hire her. This flies in the face of the facts that as assistant director of the OCD, she had surrounded herself with friends, including her unpaid assistant Elinor Morgenthau and her young friend Joseph Lash.

Although the OCD was a prime target for all-out foes of the New Deal, there was some substance to charges of the inappropriateness of many of its activities. Modeled on the British experience that hundreds of government officials had observed once war came, the OCD was essentially preparation for a war that never came to America. Landis, in his defense of the OCD after he took over, pointed out that it was overseeing some five million volunteers. Many performed useful public services, but a budget of one hundred million dollars meant that it cost twenty dollars to supervise each volunteer, which seemed to many serious critics not to be cost-effective.[56]

By April a growing awareness of labor shortages caused Roosevelt to create the inappropriately named War Manpower Commission (WMC) to ensure "the most effective mobilization and utilization" of the nation's "manpower." Later data would show that while unemployment shrank steadily—from about 6.2 million persons in September 1940 to some 1.5 million two years later—the size of the armed forces grew in the same period from 500,000 to 4.6 million, and employment by federal war agencies ballooned from 100,000 to 1.1 million.

Roosevelt's executive order showed that, once again, while seeming to take decisive action to solve what would continue to be a serious problem, the president was actually ensuring that no one person or body would control such an important function. The order itself described the composition of the commission in terms of representatives of four existing departments (War, Navy, Agriculture, and Labor) and five lesser government bodies (the War Production Board, its Labor Products Division, the Selective Service system, and the Civil Service Commission, with the federal security administrator as chairman). That the FSA administrator was Paul V. McNutt (1891–1955) suggests how little real power Roosevelt intended the WMC to have. The son of an Indiana judge, McNutt had always wanted to be president and grew up to become a handsome six-foot-two politician who looked like a president. He parlayed a World War I army career that involved no overseas service into election as national commander of the American Legion and conservative leadership in the Indiana Democratic Party. The head of its delegation to the 1932 Democratic National Convention, he switched its vote to Roosevelt only after the nomination was clinched. His subsequent election as Indiana governor, constitutionally limited to one term, was his only elective success. Roosevelt named him high commissioner to the Philippines in 1937 and made him federal security administrator in 1939. McNutt was an overt candidate for the Democratic presidential nomination in 1940 until Roosevelt made himself available, so the party's national convention that year was both the acme and the nadir of his national political ambitions. A strong contender for the vice presidential nomination until Roosevelt chose Henry Wallace, he received a twenty-minute ovation from rebellious delegates while standing, helpless, at the podium, waiting to withdraw his name.

Perhaps the major achievement of the WMC was due to the skills and insights of its New York regional director, Anna Rosenberg (1902–83), who developed the so-called Buffalo Plan. It inhibited the stockpiling of skilled workers by placing numerical limits on the numbers of workers in any given plant, assigned workers found surplus to other plants, and emphasized providing child care for working mothers and hiring African American workers. Both management and labor complained that Rosenberg's plan interfered with their rights. Later elements of the plan were applied to West Coast war plants from San Diego to Seattle."[57]

In his 1942 annual message, the president had acknowledged that "war costs money. So far, we have hardly even begun to pay for it." Almost four months later, that was still the case. To underline the seriousness of the economic aspects of the war, Roosevelt sent a seven-point stabilization message to Congress in late April and followed it up the next evening with a Fireside Chat. It is worth pointing out that Roosevelt acted similarly during the two greatest crises of his presidency. In both 1933 and 1942, he deferred levying most new taxes and reported often to the people. The first three Fireside Chats in 1933 were within 134 days; the first three after Pearl Harbor were within 109 days. In each of 1933, 1942, and 1943, there were four chats. All the intervening years had two, except 1939, which had one.

The message to Congress was blunt, but it contained little that was new, calling rather for legislative reinforcement of the goals he had been working toward by fiat. His seven points focused on taxes, price ceilings, wages, farm prices, war bonds, rationing, and restrictions on credit. The attention-grabbing proposal was a somewhat populist call for an income cap: "Discrepancies between low personal income and very high personal incomes should be lessened. . . . No American citizen ought to have a net income, after he has paid his taxes, of more than $25,000 a year. It is indefensible that those who enjoy large incomes from State and local securities should be immune from taxation."

The president repeated the call for the $25,000 limit verbatim in his Fireside Chat the following evening. The proposal about tax-exempt bonds, though hardly radical—Andrew Mellon had proposed it in the 1920s—was also repeated. One has to wonder whether either was a serious as opposed to a rhetorical goal. Similarly, Roosevelt had previously refused to push legislation designed to take the profit out of war after endorsing the principle.

The Fireside Chat began by describing the main military events in nearly five months of war. While the president did not fail to note again defeat at Pearl Harbor and admitted that in the Far East, "we have passed through a phase of serious defeat," his emphasis was on the positives of the American military buildup overseas. He spoke of "several hundred thousand" soldiers and sailors serving "thousands of miles from home" and of "American warships . . . now in combat in the North and South Atlantic, in the Arctic, in the Mediterranean, in the Indian Ocean, and in the North and South Pacific. American troops have taken stations in South America, Greenland, Iceland, the British Isles, the Near East, the Middle East, and the Far East, the continent of Australia, and many islands of the Pacific. American war planes, manned by Americans, are flying in actual combat over all the continents and all the oceans."

The president praised the "great armies of Russia" who "have destroyed and are destroying more armed power of our enemies . . . than all the other United Nations put together." Noting the rise of Nazi puppet Pierre Laval to power in Vichy France without naming him, he pledged, if necessary, to prevent the use of French territory anywhere by "Axis powers."

In the middle portion of the chat, Roosevelt spoke of what was required on the home front. Noting that the government was spending "about $100,000,000 every day" and that by year's end, "that almost unbelievable rate of expenditure will be doubled," he explained that money in the pockets of Americans combined with a shortage of consumer goods was creating a danger. "You do not have to be a professor of mathematics or economics to see that if people with plenty of cash start bidding against each other for scarce goods, the price of those goods goes up."

The president then summarized the seven points of his stabilization program and pointed out that they would affect "every person in the United States." "As

I told the Congress yesterday, 'sacrifice' is not exactly the word to describe this program of self-denial. When, at the end of this great struggle, we have saved our free way of life, we shall have made no 'sacrifice.' The price for civilization must be paid in hard work and sorrow and blood. The price is not too high. If you doubt it, ask those millions who live today under the tyranny of Hitlerism." He followed with one of his iterated litanies: "Ask the workers of France . . ., ask the farmers of Poland and Denmark . . ., ask the businessmen of Europe . . ., ask the women and children whom Hitler is starving whether" a number of the president's proposed measures—stabilization of wages, parity prices, limitation of profits and personal income, rationing of tires, gasoline, and sugar—"is too great a sacrifice."

Roosevelt devoted the final third of the chat to describing a few recent examples of heroism by individual American fighting men. He closed by saying:

They are the United States of America.
That is why they fight.
We too are the United States of America.
That is why we must work and sacrifice.
It is for them. It is for us. It is for victory.[58]

Roosevelt would have liked to be able to talk about a stunning American exploit—the Doolittle raid on Tokyo ten days earlier—but he was constrained by notions of security, although Tokyo had announced the fact of the raid as it happened and American newspapers of April 18 and 19 were filled with news stories about the raid.[59]

Only when the raid's commander, Brigadier General James H. Doolittle (1896–1993), had returned to Washington more than a month after the raid were the details revealed to accompany a ceremony in which the president presented the aviator with the Congressional Medal of Honor in the Oval Office. Roosevelt, who sometimes took more credit than he deserved, said nothing about his initiative in getting the raid attempted. As air force commander Arnold wrote later, "From the start of the war, Franklin Roosevelt wanted a raid on Japan proper. . . . As I remember it, Admiral King came to me and said he had been talking with the President and he wanted to know if I thought it would be advisable for B-25s to take off from one of the Navy's carriers. From that time on it was just a matter of King and me arranging the details and keeping the President informed."

The raid itself did little actual damage but boosted American morale at a time of few victories. In Japan it caused a significant reallocation of scarce resources into air-raid defense and may have been a factor in impelling Admiral Yamamoto to risk so much of Japan's navy at Midway a few weeks later.[60]

Throughout this dark period in American history, Roosevelt's leadership continued to enjoy a very high level of popular support. Gallup polls repeatedly showed his job approval rating at around 80 percent. When asked if there were things they didn't like about the president's role, about three in ten of the approvers—roughly a quarter of all voters—mentioned policies they didn't like. The chief complaints were ones that Republican leaders had long harped upon—too much favoritism to unions and a failure to delegate power.[61]

Roosevelt's mid-May executive order establishing the Woman's Army Auxiliary Corps (WAAC) was a cautious step toward bringing women into the American armed forces. It provided for enrolling not more than 25,000 women. The impetus seems to have come from General Marshall, who, perhaps impressed by what he had seen in Britain, where a quarter million women were in uniform, pointed a finger at a subordinate, saying, "I want a women's corps right away and I don't want any excuses." A draft bill worked out between Stimson and Marshall for the army and Edith Nourse Rogers (1881–1960), a Maine Republican who had entered the House in 1925 via "widow succession," passed both chambers easily, 249–86 in the House and 38–27 in the Senate. Senate opposition was led by an obscure Connecticut Democrat who opposed it as an attack "on the sanctity of the home," echoing a charge made by some Catholic bishops. An attempt to limit WAAC service to the continental United States failed.

Initially, members of the WAAC remained civilians, serving with the army but not in it. They received lower pay for comparable service than male soldiers and could be released from service but not court-martialed. Soon a navy bill to create its own female unit, to be called WAVES, making them members of the naval reserve and thus in the navy with full pay and allowances, passed the House with no dissenting votes. Marshall went to the Senate committee and requested an amendment to the army's bill that had already passed the House to treat WAACs in the same manner. When that failed, Roosevelt tried, without success, to get the navy's bill to conform with the army's. Other aspects of the navy bill barred WAVES from serving overseas or aboard ships.

The army had preselected the first head of the WAAC: Oveta Culp Hobby, a thirty-seven-year-old mother of two and wife of a former Democratic governor of Texas, who had a law degree and had been the publisher of the *Houston Post*, owned by her husband. She would have the title of director and receive the pay of a major. She had been hired by the War Department in 1941 on a per diem basis as head of a newly created women's interest section of its Bureau of Public Relations and had been planning for the WAAC for some time.

At her swearing-in ceremony, attended by Stimson and Marshall, Hobby, whose pending appointment had been protested by African Americans because of her Texas heritage, announced that at least "40 Negro women" would be among the first group of officer candidates and that "two of the first companies would be Negro units."

The WAAC and the other women's units in the navy, marines, and coast guard quickly demonstrated their worth in freeing male personnel for combat roles and by the excellence and seriousness of their performance in jobs that many draftees had filled indifferently. In November 1942, an additional executive order raised the limit on WAAC numbers to 150,000. On the first anniversary of the corps, which then numbered in the 60,000s, Roosevelt spoke of its women writing "a new page" in the nation's military history. He noted that "many . . . smiled and [others] violently opposed . . . women serving with our armed forces," but "they have justified magnificently the faith that was placed in them." A month and a half later, he signed a new law that made the corps a part of the army and renamed it the Women's Army Corps, which meant that its members were now soldiers who were paid the same as other soldiers, and, when discharged, they would be veterans, eligible for all veterans benefits, including medical care and educational opportunities and housing provided by the so-called G.I. Bill of Rights. In a rare rush of enthusiasm, Marshall spoke of a goal of 600,000 WAACs.[62]

Actually, the WAAC never had more than 100,000 members at any one time, and the combined peak numbers of women in all branches of the armed services never reached 300,000, even when one includes the 75,000 army and navy nurses who had traditionally been commissioned officers. Why the United States, which had been among the pioneering nations to adopt woman suffrage, lagged in military utilization of "womanpower" is a complex question, but surely part of the answer is that the United States did not face the kind of direct threat that Britain did. But another part of the answer is that despite the enthusiastic support of some top military leaders, including Marshall, Arnold, and later Eisenhower, most army officers were, at best, lukewarm supporters of women in the military, and most noncommissioned officers were its vociferous opponents. Training camp cadres taught troops demeaning cadence chants such as "The Wacs and Waves will win the war, so what the hell are we fighting for," and slanderous campaigns about the general sexual promiscuity of military women seeped from the training camps to the general public. Roosevelt, it must be noted, provided some support for the principle of women in the military; whether his more active support, along with that of lesser military and civilian leaders, could have changed the conservative American social mores is at least dubious.[63]

Although Roosevelt made no public acknowledgment of them until August and September, two naval engagements in the Southwest and central Pacific during May and June mark a clear turning point in the nature of American participation in World War II. The Battle of the Coral Sea in May, though not a clear victory for either side, blunted the Japanese advance southward and significantly reduced the available Japanese strength in aircraft carriers. In the crucial Battle of Midway in the first week of June, American carrier- and land-based aircraft not only sank all of Admiral Yamamoto's carriers but also killed the cream of Japan's very small crop of trained carrier pilots, a loss that was irreplaceable. Crucial to the victory was the American ability to read Japanese naval codes and Admiral Nimitz's nerve and daring by basing his strategy on the accuracy of those intercepts. Thus, Nimitz positioned his forces where they could strike the first blow at Yamamoto's superior fleet and ignored the Japanese feint into the Aleutian Islands, which was supposed to draw off some of Nimitz's forces.[64]

Before those battles, despite a commitment to "Germany first" and planning for American landings on the European and African continents, the American army was overwhelmingly deployed in the defense of the United States and the rest of the Western Hemisphere. As late as early July 1942, of the 800,000 soldiers "assigned to active theaters and defense commands"—that is, not in training or assigned to Washington and other domestic garrisons—about 75 percent were divided about equally between continental U.S. defense commands and outposts within the hemisphere. The lion's share of each group was facing Japan, chiefly in the Western Defense Command and in Hawaii.[65] A confident president and his military planners had been preparing for offensive land warfare in Africa and Europe since the ABC-1 conferences of early 1941, but had Yamamoto rather than Nimitz won at Midway, the execution of those plans would surely have been delayed.

8 Taking the Offensive
1942

THE GREAT QUESTION TO BE DECIDED IN June 1942 was whether the
United States and Britain would create a second front in the West against Germany in 1942, and, if so, where it would be. At the end of May, Vyacheslav M.
Molotov (1890–1986), Soviet commissar of foreign relations and the second
most powerful person in the USSR, came to Washington to lobby for a second
front, after having failed to get such a commitment in London. Molotov stayed
in the White House for three nights, moving to nearby Blair House on June 1 for
the rest of his eight-day stay when the president left for a secret meeting with
Churchill at Hyde Park. Although much of what has been written about the
Molotov visit is taken up with the loaded revolver and partially eaten sausage
the White House butler found while unpacking the old Bolshevik's suitcase, it
was an important encounter. In addition to meetings with the president, the
commissar met with Hull, Marshall, King, Hopkins, and others. Roosevelt kept
the congressional leadership in the loop by having the chairs of the Foreign
Relations Committees, Senator Tom Connally and Representative Sol Bloom,
attend a small lunch for Molotov. A joint statement, dated June 11, contained
a sentence that was almost a public commitment to military action in 1942.
It had been written by Molotov and accepted by the president, even though
Marshall had wanted *1942* removed: "In the course of these conversations full
understanding was reached with regard to the urgent tasks of creating a second
front in Europe in 1942." As Sherwood remarks, "The exact meaning of those
words . . . provoked interminable and often violently acrimonious discussions
for a long time thereafter."

Other results of the visit included an extension of the Lend-Lease agreement
and a statement by Roosevelt that "these conversations have been most useful in establishing a basis for fruitful and closer cooperation between the two
Governments in the pursuit of the common objectives of the United Nations."
Hopkins noted that during a small White House cocktails-and-dinner gathering in the Oval Study, Molotov evinced "a somewhat unexpected frankness
and amiability," which led Hopkins to believe that Stalin had told him "to be
somewhat more agreeable than is Mr. Molotov's custom." The Russian's letter to
Roosevelt on leaving the country was almost gracious. Roosevelt commented

to Churchill, "Molotov warmed up more than I expected and I feel sure that he now has a much better understanding of the situation than he had previously. I must confess that I view the Russian front with great concern."[1]

Toward the end of May, Winston Churchill arranged to "flip over" to talk to Roosevelt about the "second front," which both had discussed with Stalin via Molotov. For this third meeting of the two leaders, Churchill had arrived at Bolling Field, Washington's military airport, and left his advisers in Washington. With only a small personal staff, he was flown in a U.S. Navy plane to the small New Hackensack airport, south of Poughkeepsie, an airport Roosevelt never used. The president himself picked him up and drove him to Hyde Park in his little hand-controlled Ford. Churchill spent a relaxed day and a half in Roosevelt's home. Hassett reports him walking "barefoot" on the lawn early in the morning and that at dinner, with the president in "a black tie and white dinner coat," Churchill came down in his one-piece zippered "siren suit," which was "O.K. with the Boss." Roosevelt took him to see his library and to tea with his cousin Laura Delano, and the two had several conferences, some of them with Hopkins, whose room at Hyde Park was adjacent to Churchill's. In their conferences, Churchill stressed that "no responsible British military authority" could see any chance of success of a cross-Channel invasion in September 1942. He argued that the second front should be established by joint landings on the Atlantic and Mediterranean coasts of French North Africa. Roosevelt accepted this view. They also reached an agreement, the details of which were worked out later, for a joint effort, code-named "Tube Alloys," to create an atomic bomb, with most of the research centered in the United States. Even before the two left Hyde Park, news of Churchill's opposition to a landing on the Continent had been leaked to the press in both London and Washington, but their atomic decision remained secret.[2]

Although a large number of staff conferences had to take place before the details of the North African landings could be worked out, the joint decision by two political leaders, made with no military officials present, set the terms of the coming struggle for Europe.

Invading North Africa in the fall of 1942 precluded a cross-Channel attack in 1943 and made the subsequent invasions of first Sicily and then Italy in that year logical moves. The Hyde Park decisions did not ensure a cross-Channel attack in 1944; that was still to be decided. It is tempting to speculate, as some have, that a successful landing in France in 1943 would have meant a meeting of Western and Soviet forces somewhere on the plains of eastern Europe rather than at the Elbe, with all that might have meant for the ensuing Cold War. It will not be pursued here.[3]

The two leaders returned to Washington on the president's train. Shortly after they arrived at the White House, Roosevelt was given and handed to Churchill two messages from his Map Room, announcing the surrender of the British garrison of thirty-three thousand at Tobruk to Rommel's Afrika Korps. The Briton was stunned. After a few moments, Roosevelt turned to him and asked, "Is there anything we can do to help?" Churchill later wrote that he had been "the unhappiest Englishman in North America since Burgoyne."

In response to the president, Churchill said that he needed tanks. Roosevelt spoke to Marshall about it, and three hundred new Sherman tanks, intended for training divisions that were still using trucks with signs on them saying "tank" during maneuvers, were instead shipped to Egypt along with, at Marshall's suggestion, a hundred self-propelled 105mm guns.

All parties realized the implications of the loss of Tobruk and the thirty-three thousand soldiers taken prisoner there. The great fear was that Rommel would sweep through Egypt, close the Suez Canal, and invade Asia Minor and eventually link with German forces invading the Soviet Caucasus. Two weeks later, as the situation worsened, Roosevelt sent a message to Stalin: "The crisis in Egypt with its threat to the supply line to Russia has led Prime Minister Churchill to send me an urgent message asking whether forty A 20 bombers destined for Russia and now in Iraq can be transferred to the battle in Egypt. It is impossible for me to express a judgment on this matter because of limited information here. I am therefore asking that you make the decision in the interest of the total war effort." Two days later, Stalin responded, "In view of the situation in which the Allied forces find themselves in Egypt I have no objection to forty of the A 20 bombers now in Iraq en route to the USSR being transferred to the Egyptian front."[4]

The joint statement with Churchill, released after Churchill returned to London, did not use the phrase "second front" but did offer assurance that "coming operations"—which they and their military advisers had discussed—"will divert German strength from the attack on Russia." For the Pacific, the announcement spoke only of discussions about "methods to be adopted against Japan."

Less salient parts of the brief fifteen-sentence message noted that the "transportation of the fighting forces, together with the transportation of munitions of war and supplies, still constitutes the major problem of the United Nations," admitted that submarine warfare still "takes a heavy toll," and observed that there was "no doubt in their minds that "the over-all picture is more favorable to victory" than at the times of their previous meetings.[5]

Back in England, as had been the case in January, Churchill faced another vote of confidence. The bitter debate began on July 1, the day Rommel reached El Alamein, just outside Cairo. Churchill carried this vote of confidence too, 475–25,[6] but had Rommel taken Cairo it is not inconceivable that Churchill's government might have gone down.

In mid-July, Roosevelt sent Hopkins, Marshall, and King to London with a remarkably detailed formal set of instructions "to reach immediate agreement on joint operational plans between the British and ourselves along two lines":

2. . . . (a) Definite plans for the balance of 1942.
   (b) Tentative plans for the year 1943 which, of course, will be subject to change. . . .
3. (a) The common aim of the United Nations must be the defeat of the Axis Powers.
   (b) We should concentrate our efforts and avoid dispersion.
   (c) Absolute coordinated use of British and American forces is essential.
   (d) All available U.S. and British forces should be brought into action as quickly as they can be profitably used.
   (e) It is of the highest possible importance that U.S. ground troops be brought into action against the enemy in 1942.
4. British and American materiel promises to Russia must be carried out in good faith. . . .

Points 5 and 6 were about SLEDGEHAMMER, the code name for a 1942 cross-Channel invasion, designed to take the pressure off Russia. In point 5, Roosevelt wrote that "every reason calls for the accomplishment of it," but he followed that with

6. Only if you are completely convinced that SLEDGEHAMMER is impossible of execution with reasonable chances of serving its intended purpose, inform me.

If Roosevelt had intended his men to make an all-out fight against the determined resistance of Churchill and his men, the memorandum would have ended there. Instead, it was immediately followed by this:

7. If SLEDGEHAMMER is finally and definitely out of the picture, I want you to consider the world situation as it exists at that time, and determine upon another place for U.S. troops to fight in 1942.
   It is my present view of the world picture that:
   (a) If Russia contains a large German force against her, ROUNDUP [combined American-British offensive against continental Europe] becomes possible in 1943. . . . If Russia collapses . . . ROUNDUP may be impossible in 1943.
8. The Middle East should be held as strongly as possible whether Russia collapses or not.

There followed a list of seven very bad consequences of losing the Middle East, concluding with:

8. You will determine the best methods of holding the Middle East. These methods include definitely either or both of the following:

(a) Sending aid and ground forces to the Persian Gulf, to Syria and to Egypt.

(b) A new operation in Morocco and Algiers intended to drive in against the backdoor of Rommel's armies. The attitude of French Colonial troops is still in doubt.

Point 9 was a paragraph-long reiteration of the Germany-first argument. (American negotiators, particularly King, had a way of threatening to increase forces in the Pacific when the British seemed loath to take action in the West.) "I am opposed," the president stressed, "to an American all-out effort in the Pacific." His final remark here—"Defeat of Germany means defeat of Japan, probably without firing a shot or losing a life"—seems to suggest that Roosevelt still did not understand the nature of his Japanese enemy.

10. Please remember three cardinal principles—speed of decision on plans, unity of plans, attack combined with defense but not defense alone. This affects the immediate objective of U.S. ground forces fighting against Germany in 1942.

11. I hope for total agreement within one week of your arrival.

The document was signed, "Franklin D. Roosevelt, Commander-in-Chief."[7]

No one reading this document, even without knowing Churchill's predilections, which were shared by his generals, should be surprised that the 1942 second front was in North Africa or that the cross-Channel attack was eventually deferred until 1944. Although Marshall and his planners waged a bureaucratic delaying action, Roosevelt made sure that the decision went forward, specifying that the North African operation begin by October 30, just four days before the off-year election.[8]

On the home front, the big issue in June was rubber. In the immediate aftermath of Pearl Harbor, it became clear that the supplies of natural rubber from Southeast Asia were no longer accessible, and although some stockpiling of rubber by Jesse Jones's RFC had taken place, a crash program to create an adequate supply of synthetic rubber had belatedly begun. In late December 1941, a system for rationing the existing stocks of tires was put into place, and the newly established Office of Defense Transportation, which was primarily concerned with rail transport, established regulations governing the use of commercial trucks and buses. But the vast majority of the nation's thirty-three million motor vehicles were the cars and small trucks of private persons, and keeping those vehicles in continuing but reduced operation was a necessity, especially for those living in small towns and the countryside.

Only in March did the president ask state governors to reduce speed limits to forty miles per hour. As the rubber crisis deepened, Roosevelt made a mid-June radio appeal for old rubber in any form, specifying tires, garden hoses, shoes, bathing caps, gloves. "If you think it is rubber," he said, turn it in "to your nearest filling station." In addition, he urged everyone to "cut the use of your car—save its tires and drive it less."

The scrap drive, originally announced for fifteen days, had to be extended a further ten, but eventually 450,000 tons of scrap rubber were collected for the production of lower-grade automobile tires and retreading. An estimated million tons would have been necessary to re-tire all private vehicles. Collectors were paid a penny a pound on the spot, with the RFC repaying the filling stations.[9]

As the scrap drive was winding down, WPB boss Donald Nelson attacked what the press called the Farm Rubber Bill, which gave the highest priority to the increased use of grain alcohol in the manufacture of synthetic rubber and took the authority to control rubber production from his board. Nelson called the bill unnecessary and harmful because "it would take out of the hands of the president the right to control priorities." Despite this and other evidence of administration displeasure, farm-bloc leaders, emboldened by their victories in the fight over parity, pushed the bill through a Congress diminished by the absence of many members fleeing the capital's heat. Over the opposition of Majority Leader Barkley, the bill passed by voice vote at a time when only nine senators were present. Two days later, a House with just over a third of its members present passed an identical bill, 104–18.

Even before the expected veto, informed observers thought it could not be overridden. Roosevelt delivered more than the expected veto; he made a "move" along with it to ease real concerns about the rubber program. The long veto message—nearly twenty-three hundred words—in early August 1942 attacked Congress's violation of the principle previously established that "in order to carry on a unified, integrated, and efficient program of war production it is necessary to centralize the power to determine the priorities of materials not only between military and civilian needs, but also among competing military needs."

In short, if enacted, the bill would have undone much of the structure that the president had been authorized to create. In addition, he took a shot at the end product, pointing out that the bill "provides that even civilian needs of rubber—for pleasure driving, joy riding—must be given consideration . . . irrespective of the relationship of such civilian needs to winning the war."

In an unusual step, as part of the veto message itself, Roosevelt first explained that the War Production Board was already constructing new plants to produce synthetic rubber, some of which used grain as its basic raw material, while others used petroleum. He granted that "it may well be that serious mistakes have been made in the past [or] that the present program of the War Production Board is not the best solution. If so, the facts should be ascertained and made public."

To get those facts, he announced the formation of a special committee of three chaired by Bernard Baruch, with two university presidents—Harvard's James B. Conant and MIT's Karl T. Compton (1887–1954), the one a chemist, the other a physicist—"to investigate the whole situation, and to recommend such action as will produce the rubber necessary for our total war effort, including essential civilian use, with a minimum interference with the production of other weapons of war," and report "at the earliest possible moment." The president made it clear that, pending the committee's report, the WPB's programs for synthetic rubber would continue but that decisions on some related matters, such as nationwide gasoline rationing, would wait.[10]

After five weeks, the Baruch Committee, with a staff of about twenty-five engineers and technicians, plus clerical help, produced a twenty-thousand-word report that recommended a nationwide rationing program for both tires and gasoline, a national speed limit of thirty-five miles per hour, and appointment of a rubber administrator within the WPB to have broad authority "to bull the present program through." The report gave little joy to the farm bloc, putting most of its technical recommendations behind petroleum-based processes. The report was critical, without naming names, of both prewar and wartime mishandling of stockpiling and production and revealed that, though the USSR had been successfully producing synthetic rubber for ten years, its February 1942 offer to send over Russian plans and engineers had been ignored. Not surprisingly given its membership, no mention was made of prewar cartel arrangements with German industry by firms like Standard Oil, which inhibited production of synthetic rubber. Something of the committee's imperial outlook can be gained from this paragraph in its report: "How much rubber we shall get from South America . . . depends on the shifting of half a million natives—it would be one of the great population moves of history—and on how many of them succumb to sickness and disease."

In releasing the report, Roosevelt called it "excellent" and said that its recommendations would be effected "as rapidly as arrangements can be made." In the wake of the report, the Senate subcommittee charged with responding to the veto message lamely recommended that action to override be deferred pending the rubber program's process, but the president's veto was clearly going to prevail.[11]

On September 15, WPB director Nelson, with the express approval of the president, named William M. Jeffers (1876–1953), president of the Union Pacific Railroad, as what the press called the "Rubber Czar" ignoring the Baruch Committee's injunction that the director be a "manufacturing executive, preferably with experience in the rubber industry." Jeffers, a lifetime employee of the railroad, was a surprise choice and may have been suggested by W. Averell Harriman. In an executive order two days later, Roosevelt gave the rubber director unusual power, making him independent of Nelson, who had appointed him. He was also given power over Jesse Jones's rubber reserve.

Apart from its programmatic effects, the Baruch report, through recommendations for rationing and conservation, made those measures politically possible, although gas rationing was eventually one of most unpopular wartime measures with a public largely sheltered from the harsh realities of war. Roosevelt had adroitly turned what could have been a clash with Congress into a temporary consensus and proceeded with a reorganization that soon resulted in an adequate supply of rubber for military needs and by 1944 some tires for civilians as well.[12]

Other significant midyear actions included the creation of two more wartime agencies, the Office of War Information (OWI) and the Office of Strategic Services (OSS), the one public and democratic, the other largely secret and a keystone of the emerging national security state. Considered together, they illustrate some of the inevitable contradictions involved when a democracy plans and fights a war.[13]

Shortly after war broke out, Roosevelt began creating centralized agencies to provide information as opposed to the publicity bureaus attached to almost every federal organization during the New Deal. Under the 1939 Reorganization Plan, he had created the Office of Government Reports and placed it within the EOP under the direction of Lowell Mellett (1884–1960), the former editor of the *Washington Daily News* who had been a White House aide since 1938. The OGR's five stated purposes were: to provide a "central clearing house" to receive and transmit information; to assist the president in managing information; to collect and distribute information about the activities of the executive branch; to keep the president informed about the "opinions, desires, and complaints" of citizens and state and local governments about the work of the federal government; and to report on the basis of information received on ways to reduce the operating costs of the federal government. Many Washington insiders believed that Mellett would become a kind of information czar—and Mellett may have thought so too—but he attracted a great deal of negative attention from the press and Congress, and his quickly built new six-hundred-thousand-dollar headquarters building became known as "Mellett's Madhouse."

As late as February 1941, Roosevelt seemed willing to leave information policy to others, but in March, with the OGR still in existence, he established a Division of Information within the OEM to provide information about defense activities, and in July he named William J. Donovan (1883–1959) as "coordinator of information" with a brief to "collect and assemble information and data bearing on national security" and "analyze and collate such materials for the use of the President." Roosevelt thought that the recently established Office of Civilian Defense should not only engage in civilian protection activities but also sustain morale, so he sent the mayor a memo suggesting that La Guardia's

OCD should handle domestic morale while Donovan's organization handled broadcasts to other nations, but the mayor read it with a blind eye.

Donovan was a Republican lawyer who had been in Roosevelt's class at Columbia and commanded a battalion of New York's famed "Fighting 69th" in the American Expeditionary Force, winning the Medal of Honor and other laurels. He also acquired the nickname Wild Bill, though it was, as a biographer noted, "the opposite of his personality and character." Despite the caveat that his work should not impinge on a variety of existing institutions, including the general staff, the regular intelligence services, and the FBI, Donovan was being set up as the nation's first spymaster. Roosevelt had already sent him on information-gathering missions to wartime England, the Mediterranean, and the Balkans.

Donovan's operation also had responsibility for overseas propaganda, and Robert Sherwood organized and ran the Foreign Information Service within it. The liberal Sherwood clashed with Donovan, who, impressed with what the Germans had done, believed that with war surely coming, the United States ought to engage in unorthodox operations and counter Axis propaganda. Sherwood, conversely, wanted to promote what he saw as the "truth" and believed that American credibility would be damaged by the use of lies or even half-truths. Roosevelt ignored Sherwood's argument that "it is all right to have rabid anti–New Dealers or even Roosevelt haters in the military establishment or in the OPM, but I don't think it appropriate to have them participating in an effort which must be expressive of the President's own philosophy."

In October 1941, the president created in his EOP yet another organization, the Office of Facts and Figures, to facilitate "the dissemination of factual information to the citizens of the country." Knowing that he would appoint Librarian of Congress Archibald MacLeish (1892–1982), Roosevelt provided that the director would receive no salary. The eloquent MacLeish proclaimed a "strategy of truth" as opposed to a totalitarian "strategy of terror," but he soon found that he had neither the staff nor the authority to effect significant change.

As noted, in the immediate aftermath of Pearl Harbor, Roosevelt had put Byron Price in charge of censorship, but he kept the group of information agencies separate. Sometime after Pearl Harbor, the president realized that these overlapping units were not functioning effectively, and he decided to create a single liberally oriented wartime information agency. Typically, he assigned several persons to design such an agency—budget director Smith in February and Rosenman in March among them—but there were many other more pressing problems, so results came only after six months of increasing confusion about wartime information policy.[14]

The executive order creating the Office of War Information began by establishing it in the EOP and transferring to it the existing information agencies plus the information aspects of Donovan's office. It gave the director, who was responsible only to the president, authority over dissemination of all official news and propaganda everywhere except for Latin America. He would also "coordinate the war informational activities and agencies" and "review, clear and approve" all proposed films and radio programs sponsored by the government. The order also provided for collaboration between the OWI director and the director of censorship. All should be "consistent with the war information policies of the president [and] the foreign policy of the United States." Although not mentioned in the executive order, the major players in the former agencies received assignments in the OWI: Sherwood would head its overseas branch, MacLeish became vice chairman, and Mellett became head of its motion-picture bureau.

Roosevelt chose journalist Elmer Davis (1890–1958), a fifty-two-year-old Rhodes scholar from Indiana who began a nightly commentary for CBS ten days before war came in 1939. After a March 1942 broadcast in which he urged the formation of a single organization to control war information, E. B. White in the *New Yorker* quoted Davis with approval and said "he is the man to sit on the desk." That and other recommendations resulted in Roosevelt talking to him and persuading him to take on the job. At his press conference following the announcement creating the OWI, Roosevelt, asked for details, would reply only that "you had better ask Mr. Davis." He went on to add, "You had better let [him] operate."

Davis in fact operated with great difficulty. He faced problems in getting information released from military sources and from internal ideological disputes caused by Sherwood and others in his overseas branch who, in essence, wanted to alter U.S. foreign policy as well as report on it. Despite continuing problems, almost all authorities, then and later, have agreed that the OWI improved the quality and consistency of the dissemination of government information. Davis, who stayed on until the end of the war, became an important and trusted presidential adviser as well as a department head.[15]

The rearranged circumstances of Donovan's organization were described in a terse military order, which, unlike most such, was printed in the *New York Times* but without other comment. It subtracted "foreign information activities" given to the OWI, charged its name from "Office of Coordinator of Information" to "Office of Strategic Services," and transferred it to "the jurisdiction of the United States Joint Chiefs of Staff," that is, into the EOP, and it continued to report directly to the president. Donovan himself was named as director of strategic services. Nothing was said, officially, about its so-called cloak-and-dagger activities, but they were part of the talk of Washington, as frequent exchanges from Roosevelt's press conferences suggest. During the months after its creation, there were a number of press releases announcing appointments within the OSS, mostly of academics who were taking on public roles, without reference to its darker side.[16]

As summer approached, and the presidential yacht deemed unsafe except for cross-river trips, a nearby cooler retreat was sought for the president. A site in Maryland's Catoctin Mountain Park was approved by Roosevelt. Its existence was known, but its location was a wartime secret. It came to be known as Shangri-La. It was significantly cooler than Washington, had a swimming pool, and could be reached in a two-hour drive from the White House. Additions to the president's quarters and facilities had to be provided for the Secret Service and for the Filipino messmen from the *Potomac* who did the catering and cleaning. The redesigned seventeen-by-twenty-four-foot camp lodge had four bedrooms, two baths, and a dining/living room, a kitchen, and a screened-in porch. Sam Rosenman reports that the president's bedroom looked "out through the woods over a beautiful valley. To it was attached one of the two bathrooms. The other three bedrooms [had only] two simple metal beds, a dresser, and a chair."

Churchill, a guest there for three nights in May 1943, wrote that it was "in principle a log cabin with all modern improvements." Altogether, Roosevelt made twenty-one trips to Shangri-La between mid-1942 and July 1944.[17]

* * *

The front pages of June 28 morning newspapers reported the capture of two four-man teams of trained German saboteurs who had been landed from German submarines on New York and Florida beaches and "were promptly swept into the net of the F.B.I." The truth was that the men had been landed on June 13 and 17 and that those from Florida had gotten as far as Cincinnati and Chicago. One from New York had gotten as far as Washington and checked into its Mayflower Hotel, a few minutes' stroll from the White House, eventually phoning the FBI to give himself up, having been at large in America for a week; his information enabled the FBI to arrest the others. Attorney General Biddle telephoned the news of the captures to Roosevelt; it is not clear how many of the details he revealed. By June 27, authorities knew from what the informer had told them that all eight men had lived in America and been members of the German American Bund and that two of them were American citizens.

Three days later, in a memo to Biddle, Roosevelt made it clear that he wanted death sentences for all eight. "The two citizens were guilty of high treason. This being war-time it is my inclination to try them by court martial. . . . [T]he death penalty is all but obligatory." The other six, who the president assumed were German citizens and part of the German military, he likened to Nathan Hale and Major André "in the revolution. Both of them were hanged."

On July 2, five days after the final apprehension, Roosevelt issued a military order and a proclamation. The order named a military commission of six army officers, all generals, to try the case: Biddle and the army's judge advocate general (JAG), Myron Cramer, to prosecute the case and two military officers, Colonels

Cassius M. Dowell and Kenneth Royall (1895–1971), as defense counsel; later, other officers were added. Royall, a Harvard Law School graduate with extensive experience as a trial lawyer, became the dominant figure in the defense. The commission was to meet on July 8 "or as soon thereafter as is practicable to try" the eight named defendants "for offenses against the Law of War and the Articles of War." The order further provided that the commission should make its own rules and decide what evidence should be admitted and that only two-thirds of the members were necessary to approve any sentence.

Not satisfied with naming the judge, the jury, and the special rules for the trial, Roosevelt issued a proclamation declaring that the defendants and any others in their situation "shall be subject to the law of war and to the jurisdiction of military tribunals" and "shall not be privileged to seek any remedy . . . in the courts of United States . . . except as the Attorney General, with the approval of the Secretary of War may . . . provide." Intended to apply to the saboteurs, whose actions had taken place before the proclamation was issued, it was clearly an ex post facto decree, something specifically forbidden by the Constitution.

What concerned Roosevelt and Biddle was a well-known 1866 Supreme Court decision, *Ex parte Milligan,* striking down the decision of a military commission appointed by Abraham Lincoln. His commission had convicted Indiana Confederate sympathizers of conspiracy to seize munitions from federal arsenals and use them to liberate Confederate POWs held in midwestern camps and sentenced them to be hanged. An appeal to the Supreme Court, which Lincoln's government did not try to prevent, resulted in release of the prisoners. Arguing that the Constitution provides "a law for rulers and people, equally in time of war and peace," the 1866 Court voided the military commission's decision because such a trial of civilians by a military tribunal violated the constitutional guarantee of trial by jury as long as the civilian courts remained open. The reason that Roosevelt's government did not want to try the saboteurs in a federal court was that they had conspired only to commit sabotage and had actually done nothing that could, as the law then stood, result in anything but a relatively minor sentence.

On July 6, just before the trial began, Royall and Dowell wrote Roosevelt that there was "a serious legal doubt" about the constitutionality of his order and proclamation. They asked him if, as serving officers, they could act contrary to the orders of the commander in chief so that they or someone else could appeal, and they requested a personal meeting with him. Biddle immediately advised Roosevelt that it would be a "mistake" to deny them access to a civil court, because it "might tend to give the public impression that the prisoners are not being given a fair trial." Biddle drafted a letter for Roosevelt that told the officers, in essence, to use their own judgment.

Roosevelt would neither meet with defense counsel nor communicate with them directly, but he did have his secretary Marvin McIntyre phone them almost immediately and tell them that they should act according to their own judgment. This meant that, though he never admitted it, he was wisely retreating from the arrant tyranny of his proclamation while leaving it on the record for possible use by him or one of his successors. The officers wrote the president on July 7 that they would arrange for an appeal by civilian counsel or do it themselves unless ordered not to. They heard nothing more from the White House.

The trial began on July 8, eleven days after the last saboteur was captured. It was almost totally secret, to the despair of the OWI's Davis, who appealed to the president, without avail, to at least allow three press-association reporters to view the trial. Only regular sanitized summaries were issued. On July 11, eleven journalists were allowed into the court—actually a lecture room deep in the Justice Department building on Pennsylvania Avenue—for about a quarter of an hour to see the prisoners in their places, ask questions and take pictures, but not witness any part of the proceedings.

At the beginning of the trial, Royall, the lead defendant's counsel, gave the court notice that he might appeal to a civil court. He stated that he thought that Roosevelt's military order was "invalid and unconstitutional" and, using language from the *Milligan* decision and noting that the civil courts in the District of Columbia were open, challenged the commission's jurisdiction.

Twelve days later, Royall advised the court that he had been unable to arrange for defense counsel, had prepared the necessary papers to apply for a writ of habeas corpus, and now presented them to the court. The other defense counsel announced that they would not join him. The commissioners retired to confer; when they returned, Royall was told that "the commission does not care to pass on that question."

Since the Supreme Court was in its summer recess, Royall went to see Justice Hugo Black at his local home. On July 23, the two went with defense counsel Dowell, Biddle, and JAG Cramer to confer with Justice Owen J. Roberts at his farm in southeastern Pennsylvania while the trial was in a one-day recess. After a discussion, Roberts phoned Chief Justice Harlan Fiske Stone, who decided that the Court would meet in a rare special session on July 29 to hear oral argument. This was announced by the Court's clerk on July 27, even though no petition had yet been presented to any regular federal court. The commission recessed while Royall pursued his appeal on July 28. After a brief proceeding in the District of Columbia Federal District Court, Judge James W. Morris, a Roosevelt appointee of 1939 and a former assistant attorney general, ruled at 8:00 p.m. that Roosevelt's proclamation blocked the appeal and that he did not consider *Milligan* relevant.

Seven associate justices answered Stone's call on July 29, but Frank Murphy, who was a reserve officer, had been on maneuvers and was still on active duty; he recused himself on that account. Justice Douglas was en route from the West Coast and missed the first of two days of oral argument, which because the justices had no briefs beforehand, went on for an unprecedented nine hours. In one sense, it was a charade, because no justice had the slightest intention of ordering the prisoners turned over to the civil courts. Whether the president and Congress would have allowed this is another matter. Stone, at least, surely knew that such a decision might well set off another Court fight, one that Roosevelt would surely win and one that might result in a significant diminution of the Court's power.

The Court first heard, and grilled, Royall on July 29. He argued that Roosevelt's procedure was unconstitutional and that the prisoners should be tried in civil courts. The next day, it was Biddle's turn. With Cramer, he argued that the defendants had "no capacity to sue in the Court or any other court" because they were enemies of the United States. They made the extreme claim for presidential authority: "The President's power over enemies who enter this country in time of war, as armed invaders intending to commit hostile acts, must be absolute."

In answer to the direct question from Stone, "Does the Attorney General challenge the jurisdiction of this Court?" Biddle replied, "No, I do not, Mr. Chief Justice." But the simple answer was misleading. As Louis Fisher puts it in his brilliant study *Nazi Saboteurs on Trial*: "Basically, [Biddle] consented to the court reviewing the petition, as long as it rejected it."

On July 31, knowing that the commission had resumed its proceedings, Stone authorized an announcement at noon that the Court had denied the saboteurs' petition and would issue an opinion later. That opinion was not forthcoming until October. It distinguished the saboteurs' case from *Milligan* by noting that its defendants were not enemy belligerents.

Arguments by the prosecution and defense at the resumed military tribunal ended on August 1, and the judges retired to issue their verdict. On August 3, its still secret verdict—all eight defendants had been found guilty and sentenced to death, with a recommendation of a partial commutation for two saboteurs who had cooperated—went to the president, still secret. In his press conference the next afternoon, Roosevelt would say only that he had received the trial record and the verdict and would announce his decision within two or three days. In answer to a question about how much time the trial took, the president claimed that "the press comment has pointed out that this is a nation of laws and . . . that so far this very serious case, happening in a time of war, has been carried out through the processes which we call the American process of justice."

Only after six men had been executed in the District's electric chair on August 8 did the White House issue a brief statement of the facts and report that one man had received a life sentence and the other a thirty-year term. Roosevelt never spoke publicly about the case again. Rosenman tells us that he had "worked over the evidence and recommendations of the Military Commissioners almost continuously for two days before discussing them with the President. I then went over the record with him fully and in detail."

Apart from the bare public record, there are seven separate references to Roosevelt's comments or knowledge about the case in Hassett's diary. At the very beginning, he probably learned from his Secret Service chief that J. Edgar Hoover was claiming credit for the FBI for things done by other agencies. When he signed the order establishing the military commission, he explained that it "does not suspend the writ of habeas corpus, but it does deny access to the civil courts to certain persons." He hoped that the trial verdict would be unanimous and asked Hassett, "Should they be shot or hanged?" Roosevelt said, as the trial was ending, that he hoped the commission would recommend death by hanging and indicated that he believed that it was governed by the rules of court-martial, apparently forgetting that his proclamation had told it to make its own rules. His hopes for a short and simple report were dashed when an army officer was flown up to Hyde Park with what Hassett described as "a veritable bale of papers." There is no reason to believe that approving the death sentences gave him any pause.[18]

* * *

Despite the prevailing Germany-first strategy and the blunting of the Japanese drive east by the victory at Midway, continued Japanese advances in the southwest Pacific into New Guinea and the Solomon Islands demanded an American counter. American planners were particularly concerned by the news that Japanese forces on Guadalcanal, the largest of the Solomons, were constructing an airfield. If completed and supplied, its planes could threaten the major American supply line to New Zealand and Australia.

Roosevelt was not involved in the initial decisions about Guadalcanal, but he was responsible for the divided command in the two Pacific theaters, Nimitz at Pearl Harbor and MacArthur in Australia, which would plague American efforts in the Pacific, successful though they were. The army's history of Guadalcanal, subtitled "The First Offensive," makes it clear that the operation originated as an effort to block further Japanese progress southward with little notion that a bloody six-month struggle would ensue.

A successful surprise landing by Marines on August 7 overpowered the outnumbered original Japanese forces on Guadalcanal and quickly captured the almost completed airfield. But shortly after midnight on the night of August 8–9, divided U.S. and Australian ships were surprised by an adept Japanese naval and air attack illuminated by flares and searchlights, which Morison describes as "probably the worst defeat inflicted on the United States Navy in a fair fight." The results of the battle—three American and one Australian cruiser sunk with negligible Japanese losses—and even the fact that there had been a battle, were not revealed by the Navy Department for more than a month.

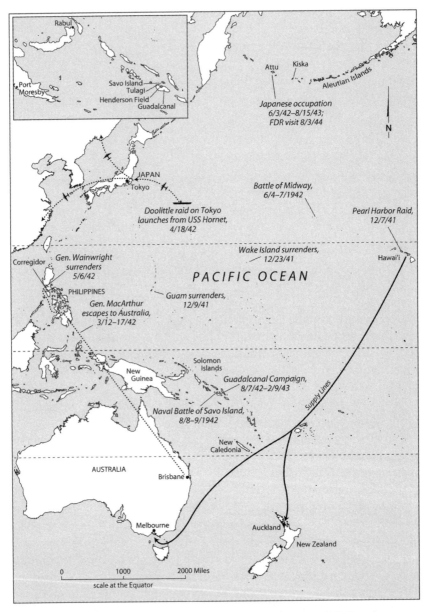

Western Pacific Theater, 1941–42, where, after the attack on Pearl Harbor, Japanese forces quickly seized Guam and other mid-Pacific outposts and wore down outnumbered forces in the Philippines. General MacArthur escaped to Australia, leaving General Wainwright ultimately to surrender the remaining American and Filipino forces. The final Japanese thrust was turned back by the American victory at Midway, the turning point of the Pacific War. The Japanese feint into the Aleutian Islands was abandoned before American forces were able evict them. The token bombing of Tokyo on April 19, 1942, had raised American morale, but the long American counter-attack began in November 1942 with the landing on Guadalcanal.

Roosevelt, who of course had the results almost immediately from his Map Room, was disturbed by the overoptimistic press reports and admonished his press conference without breaking security.

I am a little bit worried this morning, and yesterday, and the day before, lest the press of the country lead the country to believe that we have had a great, smashing major victory in the Southwest Pacific. Well, for instance, one of the papers this morning (*The Washington Post*) "Japanese Offensive Smashed." Well, I wouldn't call it an offensive. There have been only two things that have happened since we occupied Tulagi and Guadalcanal. . . . The first was a combination of the landing of 700 Japs on Guadalcanal, which was wiped out, and a series of—small attacks by Japanese planes. As you know, in that we have done pretty well, knocking down about—I don't know, what?—30 or 32 of them, at a cost to us of about 4 planes. But those were all minor operations."

While Roosevelt was quite ready, as he had admitted, to dissemble in order to deceive the enemy, he was generally careful, unlike many leaders, not to claim too much and was concerned about overconfidence and confusion.

He had underlined his concerns about confusion three days earlier in an extraordinary letter to "the responsible head of each department and agency of the Federal Government," admonishing them to cease making "public criticism of other agencies of the government." The president who had seemed to delight in public controversies between his cabinet officers now maintained that "this is inadvisable at any time. But in times of war it is particularly contrary to public policy."

As the fighting on Guadalcanal continued, Roosevelt on October 24, some two weeks before the inception of the North African invasion, ordered the Joint Chiefs to hold Guadalcanal at all costs, even if it meant deferring specific aid items promised to Britain and others.[19]

On the home front, Roosevelt had stressed in a post–Labor Day message to Congress the still pending economic measures he had urged in April. A headline encapsulated his message: "PRESIDENT TO CONGRESS: CURB PRICES OR I WILL." He set an October 1 deadline, saying that if Congress had not passed needed legislation by then, "I will act [to ensure] that the war effort is no longer imperiled by threat of economic chaos."

Many expected the president's Fireside Chat that evening to be an all-out attack on a dilatory or obstructive Congress. Roosevelt did devote about three-fifths of his time to a discussion of the high cost of living and Congress's failure to do the right thing, and in the process he made his broadest claim of executive power. But he surrounded the central message of his text with a discussion of individual heroism at the beginning and a discussion of the possibility of losing the war at the end, whose combined emotional impact was calculated to carry all before it.

The president began by wishing that "all the American people could read all the citations for heroism" that he received. "I am picking out one," he told them, "which tells of the accomplishments of Lieutenant John James Powers, United States Navy, during three days of the battles with Japanese forces in the Coral Sea."

During the first two days, Lieutenant Powers, flying a dive bomber in the face of blasting enemy anti-aircraft fire, demolished one large enemy gunboat, put another gunboat out of commission, severely damaged an aircraft tender and a 20,000-ton transport, and scored a direct hit on an aircraft carrier which burst into flames and sank soon after.

The official citation then describes the morning of the third day of battle. As the pilots of his squadron left the ready room to man their planes, Lieutenant Powers said to them, "Remember, the folks back home are counting on us. I am going to get a hit if I have to lay it on their flight deck."

He led his section down to the target from an altitude of 18,000 feet, through a wall of bursting anti-aircraft shells and swarms of enemy planes. He dived almost to the very deck of the enemy carrier, and did not release his bomb until he was sure of a direct hit. He was last seen attempting recovery from his dive at the extremely low altitude of 200 feet, amid a terrific barrage of shell and bomb fragments, smoke, flame and debris from the stricken vessel. His own plane was destroyed by the explosion of his own bomb. But he had made good his promise to "lay it on their flight deck."

I have received a recommendation from the Secretary of the Navy that Lieutenant John James Powers of New York City, missing in action, be awarded the Medal of Honor. I hereby and now make this award.

The central message of the chat reprised his congressional message in more personal and emotive language. "You and I," the president began, "are 'the folks back home'" for whom Lieutenant Powers had fought. After asking if "we" were "playing our part 'back home' in winning the war?" he answered, "We are not doing enough." He explained at some length about "inflation" and the "cost of living," defining them as "essentially what a dollar can buy." He talked about what he had asked Congress to do in April and why it was important—from "January 1, 1941, to May of this year . . . the cost of living went up about 15 percent." At that time, "We undertook to freeze the cost of living." But we could not do a complete job of it, because Congress had raised many farm prices from 100 percent of parity to 110 percent, an "act of favoritism" that raised "the cost of food to everybody." He then called for Congress to roll parity back to 100 percent and raise taxes as necessary steps toward winning the war: "Failure to solve this problem . . . now" would make winning the war "more difficult."

Repeating what he said to Congress—if it did not act, he would—Roosevelt gave the following justification for his hypothetical action. "The President has the powers, under the Constitution and under Congressional Acts, to take measures necessary to avert a disaster which would interfere with the winning of the war. . . . If we were invaded, the people of this country would expect the President to use any and all means to repel the invader."

The claim and language were somewhat familiar; in his 1933 inaugural he had put it: "But in the event that the Congress shall fail to take one of these two courses, and in the event that the national emergency is still critical, I shall not evade the clear course of duty that will then confront me. I shall ask the Congress for the one remaining instrument to meet the crisis—broad Executive power to wage a war against the emergency, as great as the power that would be given to me if we were in fact invaded by a foreign foe."

In 1942, after assuring farmers that in addition to reducing the parity level he would seek legislation to put a floor under farm prices to avoid "the collapse of farm prices that happened after the last war," and again calling for the twenty-five-thousand-dollar limit on after-tax income, he noted that in 1943, "global war" would cost the nation nearly a hundred billion dollars.

Roosevelt devoted the final section of the chat to a fuller report on the conduct of the war than he had previously given. Confident but cautious, he divided his discussion into four fronts, insisting they were not in order of importance because "all are vital and . . . interrelated."

About Russia, he reported that the Germans still had not won "the smashing victory" Hitler claimed "almost a year ago." The "Russians are killing more Nazis . . . destroying more airplanes and tanks" than "on any other front." "Russia will hold out," Roosevelt predicted, and "with the help of her allies will ultimately drive every Nazi from her soil."

In the Pacific, "We have stopped one major Japanese offensive . . . inflicted heavy losses on their fleet. But they still possess great strength. . . . We must not overrate the importance of our successes in the Solomon Islands. . . . At the same time, we need not underrate the significance of our victory at Midway. There we stopped the major Japanese offensive."

In the Mediterranean and Middle East, "The British together with the South Africans, Australians, New Zealanders, Indian troops and others . . . including ourselves, are fighting a desperate battle with the German and Italians. . . . The battle is now joined. We are well aware of the danger, but we are hopeful of the outcome."

In the European area, he could only speak of the future: "The aim is an offensive against Germany [whose] power . . . must be broken on the battlefields of Europe." The president gave assurance that "certain vital military decisions have been made. In due time you will know what these decisions are—and so will our enemies. . . . Today, exactly nine months after Pearl Harbor, we have sent overseas three times more men than we transported to France in the first nine months of the First World War."

And, he assured his listeners, "reinforcements" would continue, and the war would finally be won by the military forces of "all the United Nations operating in unison." He reminded them that "several thousands Americans have met death in battle" and warned that "other thousands will lose their lives."

It was immediately clear that Congress would pass the necessary legislation, though a few Republicans, led by Robert Taft, complained of Roosevelt's attempt at dictatorship. Gallup polls found increasing support for wage and price controls: some two months before Pearl Harbor 61 percent of voters had favored wage and price controls; 71 percent were in favor in a poll released two weeks after Roosevelt's chat, with only 11 percent opposed, and midwestern farmers favored controls as strongly as the general public.[20]

Roosevelt sent letters opposing the boost in parity to key congressional chairs—arguing that 100 percent of parity "was a good standard for peacetime—it is a good standard for war."

The president's intervention was successful; the raised parity was not in the final anti-inflation bill, which was completed almost within Roosevelt's deadline. Each house had passed an acceptable bill by October 1 but needed to work out the differences in conference and then pass the revised bill. Roosevelt grumbled about the delay in his press conference but was happy to sign the results after the completed bill was sent to him on the evening of October 2 and signed immediately. Although the debate had been bitter in both houses, the final votes were lopsided: 82–0 in the Senate and 257–22 in the House.[21]

The next day, Roosevelt appointed James F. Byrnes, whom he had appointed to the Supreme Court less than fourteen months before, as director of economic stabilization. Byrnes, who would serve in that and successor posts, became the second most powerful civilian in Washington until Truman appointed him secretary of state in 1945 and would often be called "assistant president," but never by Roosevelt.

The president issued a statement saying, "The Congress has done its part. . . . The new legislation removes exemption [of many agricultural products from price control] with the result that I have today taken action to stabilize 90 per cent of the nation's food bill. It leaves the parity principle unimpaired. It reaffirms the powers of the Executive over wages and salaries. It establishes a floor for wages and for farm prices." The president went on to predict that "from now on this substantial stabilization of the cost of living will assist greatly in bringing the war to a successful conclusion, will make the transition to peace conditions easier after the war."

Neither in his statement nor in the executive order did Roosevelt try to define Byrnes's duties. Byrnes himself, in a statement after meeting with the president, made it clear that he had an office in the Executive Wing of the White House. Otherwise, he was cautious. "That power to determine policy does not mean that I would be called on to administer it. Price control involves many organizations and] conflicts will arise. My duty would be . . . to resolve the conflicts and relieve the President of that determination. In time of peace I would not resign from the Supreme Court to accept any office. In the situation now confronting the nation I could not decline to serve wherever the Commander in Chief requests." Included in the executive order were two obscurely worded provisions that seemed to put in place a version of the controversial twenty-five-thousand-dollar salary cap. The president, as he had threatened to do, had in essence levied a tax by fiat, using as authority emergency war powers granted to him by Congress.

At the same time, Roosevelt sent two letters to price administrator Leon Henderson, gently instructing him, "I wish [you to] consult with the Secretary of Agriculture and immediately establish ceiling prices for eggs, chickens, butter, cheese, potatoes, flour, and such other foods as can be controlled under existing laws" and "immediately issue appropriate orders to prevent price increases on urban and rural dwellings. . . . In such areas as you deem appropriate to reduce current rents, I am sure you will proceed to take such action as may be necessary."[22]

The passage of the stabilization legislation and its effective administration were not only a victory for the president and his policy, but, by taming inflation and at the same time providing a postwar floor under wages and agricultural prices, it also provided a foundation for postwar economic policy. The April 1942 price controls were quite effective, but the Consumer Price Index (CPI) for food, which was largely uncontrolled, climbed steadily, from 122 in May to 130 in October (1935–39 = 100). The overall price index for the same months rose only from 116 to 119, and the index for most controlled items was nearly flat. Congress's response to Roosevelt's ultimatum allowed the OPA to control food prices. For 1943 the CPI averaged 124, in 1944 it averaged 125.5, and by the end of 1945 it stood at 128. It was a truly remarkable achievement, effected by Keynesian economic administrators Leon Henderson and his successors John Kenneth Galbraith and Paul A. Porter (1904–75) but achieved because Roosevelt faced down Congress. The president's success in this and many other wartime matters calls into serious question the conventional wisdom that he had, somehow, lost his touch with Congress during the closing years of his presidency. In addition, the appointment of Byrnes provided a stability in day-to-day economic management in a period when Roosevelt would have long absences from Washington.

For the tax bill, the wait was a little longer, but there was never the same kind of urgency about it as long as the statute was on the books before the new year. Roosevelt had underlined the necessity of increased taxes to finance the war in both of his January messages and again in both the stabilization messages to Congress and the Fireside Chat. Although he accurately called the 1942 Revenue Act that Congress passed on October 20 adding $9 billion to the annual tax bill the "greatest in American history," Treasury Secretary Morgenthau considered it "inadequate." He and his experts were already planning for additional taxes in revenue acts in 1943 and 1944. Its rates will seem breathtaking to early-twenty-first century American taxpayers, but they were well below what British taxpayers were then facing. The individual basic income taxes and surtaxes applied to all calendar 1942 earned income and were payable by March 15, 1943. Rates were increased and most deductions decreased. Normal tax, which had been 4 percent, rose to 6 percent. Surtax, which had been at 6 percent on the first $2,000 of taxable income and increasing to 77 percent of all income over $5 million, was increased to 13 percent on the first $2,000 of taxable income and rising to 82 percent of all income over $200,000. The previous personal exemptions of $1,500 for married persons, $750 for single persons, and $400 for dependents were reduced to $1,200, $500, and $350, except for enlisted men in the armed forces. A novelty in the 1942 bill was the first deduction for medical expenses, including health and accident insurance premiums; such expenses in excess of 5 percent of net income were deductible, but could not exceed $2,500. On top of all this was the Victory Tax, the first federal income tax to be deducted from pay envelopes and paychecks; the 1 percent Social Security tax had preceded it. The Victory Tax was a flat 5 percent of wages over $12 a week to be taken out starting on January 1, 1943.

The normal tax rates for corporations were maintained at 15 percent for the first $5,000, rising to 19 percent for those earning up to $25,000, with a flat rate of 24 percent after that. But the surtax and the excess-profit tax went up. The previous rates of 6 percent below $25,000 and 7 percent above it were replaced by 10 percent and 15 percent. The excess-profits tax rates, ranging from 35 to 60 percent, were replaced by a flat 90 percent rate. (Too often omitted from a discussion of wartime taxes was a provision limiting the maximum paid in all income taxes to 80 percent of net corporate income.)

Many new excise taxes were added, and existing ones were increased. The rates on estate and gift taxes were retained, but deductions and exemptions were reduced. All told, the federal tax bill was estimated at $25 billion for 1943. Since spending was at more than $100 billion, about a quarter of federal costs were covered, with the rest being added to the soaring deficit.[23]

While Congress debated stabilization, Roosevelt had made his first extensive wartime, and therefore secret, inspection trip. His train left Washington on the evening of Thursday, September 17 and took him as far west as Seattle and as far south as New Orleans, inspecting military bases and larger defense plants. The president had logged 8,764 miles, and although workers and soldiers saw him and surely told their friends, the nation, to use one of his frequent phrases, knew nothing about it because of the wartime secrecy about the whereabouts of the president. He had been accompanied only by the three familiar wire-service reporters who filed daily stories—mere squibs—that could not be printed until

Roosevelt was back in Washington. The *New York Times* printed one for each working day of the trip on page 15 of its October 2 paper. Much more information was in the bare itinerary it published the next day. A trade union weekly, the International Association of Machinists' *Auto Mechanic,* had to destroy a run of thirty-thousand copies because it featured a story about Roosevelt's visit to the Boeing plant.

Just after five o'clock on the day of his return, the president opened his first press conference in sixteen days before a packed crowd of angry reporters. Thirty-five of them, after failing to get a satisfactory response from either Byron Price, Elmer Davis, or Steve Early, sent a letter of protest to the president, complaining that no adequate explanation had been given for the ban and that the complete suppression of news was neither wise nor necessary since so many thousands of people saw the president. It was never formally answered.

The first half of the nearly hourlong press conference was largely a presidential monologue, as Roosevelt recounted details of the trip, stop by stop. The president was obviously more than pleased by what he had observed at some of the nation's most important war plants, including the Kaiser shipyards and the Douglas aircraft facility in Los Angeles. He referred more than once to the increasingly important work being done by "the large number of women that were employed in machine work [on] big machines that are operated largely by push-buttons."[24]

Although much of his attention must have been occupied by the impending North African invasion that he and Churchill had authorized, much of Roosevelt's public activity in October focused on postwar problems. He issued a statement on October 7 whose key passage read: "I now declare it to be the intention of this Government that the successful close of the war shall include provision for the surrender to the United Nations of war criminals." The audacity of this proposal at that time—when the United States Army had yet to engage with its European enemies and the United Nations was just a collection of signatures—reflects Roosevelt's firm conviction that an effective global organization must emerge from the war. He had made two earlier wartime statements about Nazi barbarity. In October 1941, he denounced the execution of "scores of innocent hostages in reprisal" for attacks on Germans in occupied countries, and in August 1942, taking notice of a communication from nine of the European governments in exile about continuing atrocities in occupied countries, Roosevelt spoke of the "barbaric crimes of the invaders" and warned that "they shall have to stand in courts of law in the very countries in which they are now oppressing and answer for their acts." His press-conference comments indicate that he was concerned about possible postwar acts of vengeance.

But just two months later—October 1942—he announced that "this Government is prepared to cooperate with the British and other Governments in establishing a United Nations Commission for the Investigation of War Crimes.

... It is our intention that just and sure punishment shall be meted out to the ringleaders responsible for the organized murder of thousands of innocent persons and the commission of atrocities which have violated every tenet of the Christian faith."

An agreed British parallel statement was of a different sort and caliber. Leading a rambling discussion in the House of Lords, the Churchill government's lord high chancellor, John Simon, suggested that the composition of international courts would present difficult problems and commented favorably on a member's observation that military courts were quicker. Churchill and his government, as Warren Kimball puts it, "disliked the idea of lengthy war crimes trials" and "proposed immediate execution of Nazi Leaders." It is clear from Roosevelt's comments that, unlike the wartime secrecy he had favored for the Nazi saboteurs, he expected war criminals to be tried in some kind of open court.[25]

After issuing a brief Columbus Day statement in which he celebrated most of the myths about American immigrants—"people who sought liberty, democracy, religious tolerance, the fuller life"—he went on the air that evening for the fourth Fireside Chat of the year. He began by talking about his recent trip and reported that he found the American people "united as never before in their determination to do a job and do it well." He went out of his way to praise women workers, as he had done in his press conference, and suggested that they were more diligent. "I noticed, frequently, that when we drove unannounced down the middle aisle of a great plant full of workers and machines, the first people to look up from their work were the men—and not the women. It was chiefly the men who were arguing as to whether that fellow in the straw hat was really the President or not."

In a talk that was overwhelmingly positive and prosaic, Roosevelt touched lightly on employment discrimination. "In some communities, employers dislike to employ women. In others they are reluctant to hire Negroes. In still others, older men are not wanted. We can no longer afford to indulge such prejudices or practices."

Leading up to what was the major news in the chat, he spoke of his inspections of military training camps where "young strong men" get "thorough training." He pointed out that an army division with an "average age of 23 or 24 is a better fighting unit" than one whose "average age is 33 or 34." "Therefore, I believe it will be necessary to lower the present minimum age limit for Selective Service from twenty years down to eighteen. We have learned how inevitable that is—and how important to the speeding up of victory."

Confident of victory even before American forces were fully committed to battle against the European Axis, the president closed with a warning about the recurrence of isolationism, although that word was left unspoken: "There are a few people in this country who, when the collapse of the Axis begins, will tell our people that we are safe once more . . . that the future of civilization can jolly well take care of itself insofar as we are concerned."

After scoffing at such notions—"It is useless to win a war unless it stays won"—he closed with a simple statement of American war aims. In addition to a total defeat of Germany, Italy, and Japan, "We are united in seeking the kind of victory that will guarantee that our grandchildren can grow and, under God, may live their lives, free from the constant threat of invasion, destruction, slavery, and violent death."[26]

Congress responded immediately to the president's call for lowering the draft age, something the military leadership had always wanted. Within five days, the House passed a bill that suited the army, 345–16, and a week later the Senate followed suit, 58–5. But the Senate bill contained a provision prohibiting sending anyone under twenty into combat without a full year of training, even though first General Marshall and then Roosevelt objected. Typically, new recruits received sixteen weeks of basic training and were then assigned to a division for further training. The law would have required stripping a division of many younger soldiers before it went overseas. After the House removed the Senate restriction and repassed the bill, a conference committee adopted the House version, and on the heels of the successful North African invasion the Senate passed the bill by a face-saving voice vote. Roosevelt immediately signed the bill and in his signing statement took note of the fact that many young men would have their education interrupted and announced that "I am causing a study to be made [of how to] enable the young men whose education has been interrupted to resume their schooling and afford equal opportunity for the training and education of other young men of ability after their service in the armed forces has come to an end. Some useful action along this line was taken at the end of the last war. This time we are planning in advance."

This was the first public statement about what became the most important federal involvement in higher education since the Morrill Act of 1862, which created the land-grant colleges. The president's creation, the Armed Forces Committee on Post-War Educational Opportunities for Service Personnel, sent him a report in October 1943 that became the basis of the G.I. Bill of Rights enacted in June 1944.[27]

Roosevelt's overt participation in the third off year of his presidency was minimal. He endorsed only two candidates: a democratic candidate to succeed Governor Lehman in New York and George Norris in Nebraska for reelection. Both lost. Those endorsements and a call for all Americans to vote and for employers to give workers time off to vote "without any loss of wages," plus his own appearance at the Hyde Park polling place, were his only overt involvements.

As is usually true in off-year elections, the president's party lost seats. The new Senate would divide 58 to 37, with eight fewer Democrats and nine more

Republicans. La Follette, the remaining Senate independent, usually supported the president. The new House would be startlingly close, as the Democrats lost 50 seats to reduce their majority to just 10 seats, with a split of 218–208, although the four independents usually voted with the Democrats.

There was no overriding issue and a great deal of apathy. The Democrats were hurt by low voter turnout—soldiers had difficulties in getting absentee ballots, and many workers had migrated to war jobs and were not yet eligible to vote in their new locations. An understandable impatience with the lack of positive results in the war against the European Axis encouraged apathy. One factor that Roosevelt had hoped for when he set the date of the North African invasion to take place by October 30 was a patriotic "bounce," but shipping difficulties delayed the landings from four days before the election to five days after it.

Tom Dewey, by ending the twenty-year run of Democratic governors in New York, established himself as the front-runner for the GOP presidential nomination in 1944.[28]

Undoubtedly, Roosevelt understood that if he had chosen to campaign, he might well have changed the results in a few close races. But given his oft-stated goal of national unity, and with the example of the disastrous postwar results of Wilson's call for a Democratic Congress in the 1918 election ever before him, he abstained from campaigning, even though his instincts were always for political combat, in which he reveled.

In the week after the election, Roosevelt had real combat to talk about. He opened his postelection press conference by commenting on the British Eighth Army in Egypt driving Rommel's Afrika Korps back toward Libya in what the president called "a victory of major importance." In the early hours of Sunday morning, November 8, American and British troops invaded the French North African colonies of Algeria and Morocco with landings on Mediterranean and Atlantic beaches in the operation that Churchill and Roosevelt had agreed to at Hyde Park in June.

On the U.S. side, the decision was purely Roosevelt's. As the official army history describes it, in a section headed "The President Commits the United States to Operation TORCH," the Combined Chiefs, meeting in London, agreed conditionally on July 25 to the operation, with the important proviso that it be reconsidered later.

But the president disregarded the conditional nature of the Combined Chiefs' decision and on the same day informed Secretary of War Stimson, Admiral Leahy, and Generals Arnold and Joseph T. McNarney, when they met him at the White House, that he had already committed the United States uncondi-tionally to the North African operation. After General Marshall and Admiral King returned from London, the former apparently still believing that the final decision to mount the North African invasion was to be reached on September

15, the President repeated "very definitely" to a special conference of representatives of the Joint Chiefs of Staff at the White House that "he, as Commander in Chief, had made the decision that TORCH should be undertaken at the earliest possible date. He considered that this operation was now our principal objective, and the assembling of means to carry it out should take precedence over other operations."[29]

Attacking a former ally was a ticklish business. The United States, but not Great Britain, maintained diplomatic relations with Vichy France. In the fall of 1940, Roosevelt summoned to Washington Robert D. Murphy (1894–1978), who had been counselor in Bullitt's Paris embassy and then chargé d'affaires in Vichy. Sumner Welles brought him to the White House and introduced him to the president, who grilled him about French North Africa—which Murphy had never seen fit to visit. Roosevelt made him his personal representative who would report to him, not the State Department. As Murphy writes, "The French African policy of the United States Government thus became the president's personal policy. He initiated it, he kept it going, and he resisted pressures against it, until, in the autumn of 1942 French North Africa became the first major battleground where Americans fought Germans."

Murphy's testimony is important. Marshall, and Marshall's biographer Forrest Pogue, was convinced that it was the wiles and persuasiveness of Winston Churchill that seduced Roosevelt to agree to what they regarded as a misadventure in North Africa. Roosevelt had been working toward such a result on his own. That he did not inform his chief military advisers of his thoughts and plans can be criticized, but that was Roosevelt's style.

Murphy returned to Vichy and went to French North Africa, where, on Roosevelt's instructions, he arranged for nonmilitary supplies to be sent to French military units there. He and an augmented group of consuls remained in both Algeria and Morocco after Pearl Harbor. In the run-up to the invasion, he was again summoned to Washington and flown in an army plane to Hyde Park, where he met with Roosevelt and Hopkins, both, Murphy notes, "tieless and in shirtsleeves," for a second consultation. The president then sent him to London to consult with Dwight Eisenhower (1890–1969), who would command the North African invasion and added the diplomat to his staff.

Murphy openly and General Mark W. Clark (1896–1984) and other military officers covertly were present in Algiers at the time of the invasion. The hope was that French forces would not resist. Roosevelt himself had prerecorded an appeal in French that was broadcast to France and North Africa by the BBC as the invasion began. After noting his own personal experience in France in 1918 and speaking of the long history of "friendly ties," the president told the French, "We come among you to repulse the cruel invaders. . . . We come among you solely to defeat and rout your enemies. . . . Do not obstruct, I beg of you, this great purpose."

Roosevelt also launched a diplomatic offensive by sending a message to Pétain, telling him of the invasion by "indomitable American forces . . . equipped with massive and adequate weapons of modern warfare which will be made available for your compatriots in North Africa." Without actually asking him to do anything, Roosevelt clearly hoped that Pétain would at least turn a blind eye to what Roosevelt hoped would be cooperation with the United States by Vichy forces in North Africa. Pétain curtly rebuffed the president, saying, "France and her honor are at stake. We are attacked; we shall defend ourselves; this is the order I am giving."

For Pétain, whose government collaborated in deporting French Jews to concentration camps and other French citizens to German factories, to speak of honor was fatuous. Pierre Laval, chief of government at Vichy, formally ended diplomatic relations with the United States the following day. Roosevelt's other diplomatic initiatives, letters to Spain's Francisco Franco, the president of Portugal, and such marginal figures as the sultan of Morocco and the bey of Tunis, had the desired calming effect.[30]

Despite the best efforts of Roosevelt and Murphy, French military forces resisted for up to forty-eight hours, most strenuously around Oran on the Mediterranean and Casablanca on the Atlantic. Murphy, with the help of Mark Clark, then persuaded Admiral Jean Darlan (1881–1942), commander of all Vichy

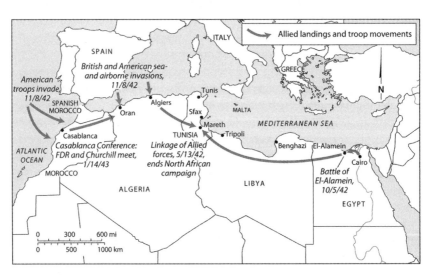

The North African campaign inflicted the first major defeat of German military power by the western allies. The British drive west from the very gates of Cairo and the American and British drive east from their landings on Atlantic and Mediterranean beaches eventually met in Tunisia and expelled Axis forces from Africa. Even before that, Roosevelt and Churchill staged the conference at Casablanca, then hundreds of miles removed from the front lines.

armed forces, who was privately in Algiers with his wife because their adult son had been stricken with polio, to issue orders that ended French military resistance in Algeria and Morocco. About five hundred American soldiers had been killed and twice that number wounded.

The use of Darlan to stop the fighting was surely appropriate, but making him, in effect, their chief administrative officer was a serious error in judgment by Eisenhower and Murphy. They hoped, naively, that he might be able to add significant numbers of French forces, including those in Tunisia, to the Allied cause and even help them gain control of French naval vessels in Toulon. Another error in judgment, attributable largely to Murphy, was the importation of Henri Giraud, a French general with an impeccable anti-German pedigree, who had demonstrated personal heroism but little political understanding, in the belief that he could influence French officials. The politically shrewd Darlan told the Americans, "He's not your man," and called him a political "child."

Hitler's reaction to the invasion of North Africa was twofold: he violated his armistice agreement with Pétain by sending German troops into what had been unoccupied Vichy France and began sending German air and ground forces into Tunisia, where they had not been, while Italian forces seized Corsica. These moves frustrated British and American hopes for an easy occupation of Tunisia and a quick linkup with British forces driving west into eastern Libya.[31]

But the larger failure of American policy can be laid to Roosevelt and Hull, who adamantly refused to have anything to do with the emerging leader of the free French, Charles de Gaulle (1890–1970), who had been recognized and supported by the British and whose forces were actually fighting against Vichy and the Germans. The French leader had gotten into Hull's—and to a lesser degree Roosevelt's—bad books when his men successfully seized the last remnants of France's once vast North American empire, the two small islands of St. Pierre and Miquelon at the mouth of the Gulf of St. Lawrence, just south of Newfoundland, on Christmas Eve 1941. It certainly made sense not to embrace de Gaulle's movement publicly as long as there was advantage to be gained from cooperation with Vichy. Churchill had wanted to inform de Gaulle about the invasion of North Africa the day *before* it happened, but Roosevelt adamantly refused and ordered his planners in London to tell de Gaulle nothing. A wiser policy would have been somehow to find a way to bring de Gaulle's movement into the new arrangements being made in Africa. The failure to do so created short-term embarrassment and long-term difficulties for the United States, although many of the latter might well have resulted under any circumstances.

Roosevelt had a clearer vision of the future than any of his contemporary world leaders: Churchill, Stalin, Chiang Kai-shek, Hitler, and Mussolini, each in his own way, sought a world that would never be, while many of Roosevelt's dreams came true. It would be unfair to blame him for not seeing in the gangling, bumptious, and arrogant French brigadier a major world leader of the second half of the twentieth century, but he can be faulted for not utilizing the free French leader earlier.

Within a week, the "Darlan deal," as the press called it, began to stink: Darlan had been a key figure in the profascist forces in France. Roosevelt, who made no public criticism of Eisenhower, tried to distance himself from Darlan. He publicly accepted Eisenhower's "political arrangements for the time being" but insisted that "no permanent arrangement should be made with Admiral Darlan." More trenchant was his "not to be made public" message to Eisenhower:

> You should know and have in mind the following policies of this Government:
> 1. That we do not trust Darlan.
> 2. That it is impossible to keep a collaborator of Hitler and one whom we believe to be a fascist in civil power any longer than is absolutely necessary.
> 3. His movements should be watched carefully and his communications supervised.

How long was absolutely necessary? We will never know. Darlan was still exercising administrative power in North Africa on Christmas Eve when he was assassinated by a young French monarchist, who was executed the day after Christmas. He was replaced by Giraud, the political child, who, as Darlan had warned, was a leader without followers.

While the American Left from liberal Republicans like Wendell Willkie to the American Communist Party bitterly condemned any dealing with Darlan as a betrayal of democracy, it is striking that Stalin justified the Darlan deal. Sherwood quotes the Russian dictator telling Churchill: "It seems to me that the Americans used Darlan not badly in order to facilitate the occupation of Northern and Western Africa. The military diplomacy must be able to use for military purposes not only Darlan but, 'Even the Devil himself and his grandma.'" Stalin had earlier written Roosevelt directly that "we here are all highly gratified by the brilliant successes of American and British armed forces in North Africa. Allow me to congratulate you on this victory. With all my heart I wish you further success."

Roosevelt, in his press conference on the day he backed Eisenhower's use of Darlan, had also—very much off the record—invoked the devil, telling reporters about an old Balkan proverb he claimed was approved by the Orthodox church: "My children, you are permitted in time of great danger to walk with the devil until you have crossed the bridge."[32]

The sordidness of the Darlan affair, which demonstrates what is likely to happen when presumed "military necessity" is allowed to dictate political decisions, should not be permitted to diminish our awareness of what Roosevelt and his lieutenants achieved in North Africa in 1942. Not one American in a thousand is aware of November 8, 1942, as a significant date in history, while the date of the other crucial European D-Day—June 6, 1944—ranks, in what the Library of Congress calls the American Memory of World War II, second only to Pearl Harbor.

While not nearly as massive, bloody, or protracted as the Normandy invasion, the 1942 landings were, in many ways, more difficult to achieve. The troops came from farther away, chiefly from England and Virginia; had limited air support from a few small escort carriers; and were planned by men who had never participated in a combat landing. There had never been anything remotely like it in the history of warfare. As General Thomas T. Handy, chief of the Operations Division of the War Department, told a White House conference, "Torch was the most complex operation in military history."

Roosevelt felt at the time, as he told the *New York Herald Tribune* Forum in a nationally broadcast speech nine days after the North African landings, and just twenty days short of the first anniversary of Pearl Harbor, "During the past two weeks we have had a great deal of good news and it would seem that the turning point of this war has at last been reached. But this is no time for exultation. There is no time now for anything but fighting and working to win." (Churchill had said, the week before, that it was, "perhaps, the end of the beginning.")

The president also spoke of the victory in the just-ended naval battle around Guadalcanal that had raged from the afternoon of November 12 to just past midnight on the fifteenth and had to announce the death of "my close personal friend" and former naval aide Rear Admiral Daniel J. Callaghan on the bridge of his cruiser. He might well have also mentioned the ongoing Battle of Stalingrad in which a million additional Russian soldiers had just been thrown into the battle. The total Allied force in western Africa numbered sixty-five thousand.[33]

Noting that a grueling overseas trip awaited him, Roosevelt took it easy from late November until the new year, spending much time as squire at Hyde Park, quietly visiting friends and relatives, and working in his library. There was no trip to Warm Springs for Thanksgiving.

Hassett, writing in his diary about a quiet last Sunday in November, noted that Roosevelt was "calm and composed, always at his best, as the first year of the war draws to a close. Still unruffled in temper, buoyant of spirit, and, as always, ready with a wisecrack or a laugh, and can sleep anywhere wherever opportunity affords—priceless assets for one bearing his burdens, which he never mentions. No desire to be a martyr, living or dead."

A month later, the squire and his wife hosted Christmas parties for the troops who were protecting them; there were two so that the whole guard contingent could be accommodated. The parties were held in the library and included its staff and their families and others who worked on the estate. At the parties, the president, with his half-brother's widow seated beside him, received all visitors, including fifty young women from Poughkeepsie in army trucks. All gathered around a Christmas tree and sang carols, and then Christmas presents for everyone were passed out, with Grace Tully acting as assistant Santa. Eleanor organized a set for a Virginia reel, which the president called and which many of what Hassett called "the boys and girls" were dancing for the first time. A more impressive first occurred when "the soldiers and girls sat in a circle" before the commander in chief, "who told stories of his experiences in the First World War."[34]

In an appointment that was a harbinger of things to come, during a small White House ceremony on December 5, Roosevelt named Herbert Lehman as the first director of the State Department's Foreign Relief and Rehabilitation Operations. It was created to manage aid in liberated areas of Africa and eventually Europe until some kind of international agency could be created. In addition to his government experience, Lehman had been closely associated with the Joint Distribution Committee, the major American Jewish nonprofit group dealing with immigrants and refugees since the World War I era. Lehman's new organization provided food, clothing, and medical supplies to needy civilians and refugees in North Africa, the Middle East, and Europe during 1943. When the United Nations Relief and Rehabilitation Administration (UNRRA) was created in November 1943, Lehman soon became its first director general.

The creation of this office in the State Department was the first formal federal acknowledgment of American responsibilities to poor nations. Speaking about the appointment at a late November press conference, Roosevelt showed his understanding of the problem and its political consequences.

> THE PRESIDENT: You will begin to find in the United States quite a group of people that will say, in regard to the appointment of Governor Lehman . . . "Is the United States going to shell out our food and our clothing? Are we going to spend our good money to—to rehabilitate other nations? What's the big idea?" Now you will find that an increasing—from now on—slogan. It will be put out all over the United States.
>
> Q: *Are* we going to, Mr. President?
>
> THE PRESIDENT: What? Sure, we are going to rehabilitate them. Why? All right. Not only from the humanitarian point of view—you needn't stress that unless you want to—there's something in it—but from the point of view of our own pocketbooks, and our own safety from future attack—future war.[35]

By the end of the first year of war, it had become apparent that instead of the endemic surpluses that had plagued American agriculture since the end of World War I, the nation now faced certain food shortages. A combination of factors, including the loss of imports, higher consumption by soldiers and by better-paid workers and their families, a reduced agricultural workforce, plus the necessity of shipping vast amounts of American food as part of Lend-Lease and to feed our growing overseas forces as well as the expected task of wartime and postwar relief and rehabilitation caused growing concern in the government and among industry leaders.

Many of the latter called for the appointment of a food czar, who might play a role comparable to the one Herbert Hoover performed during World War I, but that was the last thing that Roosevelt wanted. Instead, he issued an executive order centralizing control of food production within the Department of Agriculture and created the position of war food administrator to oversee it. The initial appointee was longtime New Deal bureaucrat Chester C. Davis, who served six months and was replaced by Marvin Jones (1886–1976), an eleven-term Democratic congressman from Texas who had chaired the House Agriculture Committee throughout the New Deal and had served as an assistant to economic stabilization director James Byrnes. He ran the War Food Administration until the end of the war.

By early 1945, some 1.6 million farm boys were in military service, and 3.5 million farm men and women of working age had left the farms for industrial and commercial jobs. Despite these massive losses of farm workers, American agriculture during 1943–45 produced more than ever before, thanks in part to Mexican and other "temporary" immigrant laborers, many of them brought in by the government under the Bracero and similar smaller programs for agricultural workers from the Caribbean.[36]

As part of the anniversary reflections, the Navy Department finally allowed a fairly full account of the disaster at Pearl Harbor to be published. Nowhere in either the OWI account or the official navy report is there any reference to the sabotage and espionage in Hawaii that Secretary Knox and Justice Roberts spread around Washington in its immediate aftermath, nor was there any reference to the existence of such officially spread falsehoods. The papers, the airways, and the nation's pulpits overflowed with praise for American resilience. Roosevelt's letter to the *Army and Navy Journal* for a special issue emphasized a familiar theme: "The dominant note in our common war effort is unity, unity of our people, and unity of the United Nations. That is the hard fact which is the spearhead of victory. I am happy in the knowledge that it exists with us."[37]

Although Roosevelt and Hopkins had long wanted to make the WPA a regular part of the federal establishment, Congress had consistently refused to do so, and its existence had always depended on emergency regulations. But Roosevelt and budget director Smith decided that there need not be a WPA line in the fiscal 1943 budget they were preparing, and the White House released a formal statement of its abandonment. The "Works Projects Administration," the president wrote, "has asked for and earned an honorable discharge." Stating that "a national work relief program is no longer necessary," the president said that some of those still on the rolls might have to be given aid by the states, though most would be able to find work. He continued, "This government accepted the responsibility of providing useful employment for those who were able and willing to work but who could find no opportunities in private industry. [The WPA] reached a creative hand into every county . . . has added to the national wealth, . . . repaired the wastage of the depression, and has strengthened the country to bear the burden of war."

WPA officials reported that WPA employment, which had reached a peak of 3,334,594 in 1939, had dropped to 354,619 by the end of November 1942. They summarized the seven years of the WPA's existence: it gave employment to 8.5 million persons with 30 million dependents at a cost of $10.5 billion. Tangible results included the construction of 644,000 miles of roads and 77,000 bridges, creation or improvement of more than 800 airports and 700 miles of runways, 878 million hot lunches for schoolchildren, and operation of 1,500 nursery schools.

All of this was accomplished, Roosevelt said, "in the face of uninformed criticism." The WPA experience, he concluded, "will be of great assistance in the consideration of a well-rounded public works program for the postwar period." But sadly, that experience has been ignored by all but one of his successors, who have failed to acknowledge what Roosevelt took as a given: "Every employable American should be employed at prevailing wages."[38]

President Roosevelt and Ambassador Josephus Daniels at a 4-H Club camp for boys and girls in West Potomac Park, Washington, D.C., June 14, 1940.

Eleanor Roosevelt on Manhattan's Fifth Avenue, December 20, 1940, perhaps Christmas shopping. She preferred not to have Secret Service protection.

President Roosevelt's sixtieth birthday portrait, January 30, 1942. He closed his traditional Birthday Ball broadcast that evening by saying, "The lives of all of us are now dedicated to working and fighting and, if need be, dying for the cause of a better future—that future will belong to the little children of our beloved land."

President Roosevelt with naval aide Captain John McCrea, welcoming the exiled president of the Philippines, Manuel Quezon; his wife, Maria Aurora Quezon; and their son, Manuel Quezon Jr., to Washington, D.C., in June 1942. Roosevelt vowed that Quezon would be returned to his homeland, but he would die in exile during 1944.

President Roosevelt makes conversation with French general Henri Giraud while Prime Minister Winston Churchill and French general Charles de Gaulle stare at the cameras during the photographic prelude to the only press conference at the Casablanca Conference, January 24, 1943. A later photo showed the two generals shaking hands, but apparently they did not exchange a single word with each other. They were ushered offstage before the two principals spoke.

Eleanor Roosevelt, shown here with War Relocation Authority director Dillon S. Myer inspecting the Gila River Relocation Center in Arizona on April 23, 1943, was the only important political figure to visit any of the ten concentration camps established for Japanese Americans. While her visit showed her concern, and was so viewed by many Japanese Americans, she never denounced the wartime incarceration.

President Roosevelt and Fala in the family quarters in the White House in 1943. Fala was given to FDR as an early 1940 Christmas present from his cousin Margaret Suckley when the Scotch terrier was almost a year old. He traveled almost everywhere with the president. When the dog died, in 1952, he was buried near his master at Hyde Park.

Prime Minister Winston Churchill waiting to go on the air during the first Quebec Conference, August 1943. Among the things he said of the conference was that "on the whole things are very much better than they were when we met at Casablanca."

President Roosevelt flanked by Marshall Stalin and Prime Minister Churchill at the long-awaited first meeting of the Big Three, Tehran, November 29, 1943. Although rightist politicians, publicists, and some scholars have overemphasized the Yalta Conference, the agreements reached at Tehran were more critical to the outcome of the war.

President Roosevelt broadcasting a Fireside Chat from his study at Hyde Park, December 24, 1943. Although it was Christmas Eve—and he did end with a Christmas message—it was largely about the Cairo and Teheran Conferences and his hopes for the postwar world. "I believe that we are going to get along with [Stalin] and the Russian people—very well indeed."

President Roosevelt signing the agreement establishing the United Nations Relief and Rehabilitation Administration in the East Room of the White House on November 9, 1943. He addressed representatives of forty-four nations before him and the peoples of the world by radio. Speaking almost two years before the United Nations organization was formally established, he stressed that "nations will learn to work together only by actually working together."

President Roosevelt and Prime Minister Churchill in animated conversation at the second Quebec Conference on September 12, 1944. Decisions made there led to the second Big Three meeting at Yalta.

President Roosevelt, with Prime Minister Churchill on his left and Canadian premier William Lyon Mackenzie King on his right, leads the press conference on the parapet of the Citadel at the second Quebec Conference on September 16, 1944. The confident president declared that after "the surrender of Germany . . . the Allies are going to start in to do as fast a job as they possibly can in the war against Japan."

Army Chief of Staff General George C. Marshall and Army Air Force Commander H. H. Arnold pose at the second Quebec Conference in September 1944. They were but two of the many top commanders personally chosen by President Roosevelt to direct the American armed forces before and during World War II.

President Roosevelt flanked by General Douglas MacArthur and Admiral
William D. Leahy, while Admiral Chester W. Nimitz explains strategy using a very
large map of the central and western Pacific on July 28, 1944, in Honolulu. The
conference effected no changes in Pacific strategy.

This White House portrait of President Roosevelt, taken in August 1944, a month before the speech to the Teamsters in which the president noted that he was twelve years older than when first elected, shows a man in his sixty-second year with thinning hair and in apparent good health.

President Roosevelt broadcasting from the White House for the Sixth War Loan Drive, November 19, 1944. The day before, Dr. Howard G. Bruenn, his cardiologist, recorded that "the president looked tired." The war-loan drives were important as part of the successful attempt to combat inflation, but Roosevelt stressed patriotic duty: "in the name of our wounded and sick, in the name of our dead, and in the name of future generations of Americans. I ask you to plow out this furrow to the end." The drive raised more than twenty-one billion dollars, 151 percent of its stated goal.

Soviet premier Joseph Stalin and Foreign Minister Vyacheslav Molotov in the Livadia Palace, Crimea, during the Yalta Conference, February 1945. As had been the case at Tehran, both were relatively cooperative. This would not be the case in postwar meetings.

Three members of the American delegation at the Yalta Conference in the Livadia Palace, February. Harry Hopkins (left), although ill, was Roosevelt's key personal adviser. Charles Bohlen (right), a diplomat who served as Roosevelt's interpreter in all of Roosevelt's meetings with Stalin at Tehran and Yalta, is a key witness of those events. Stephen Early (center), Roosevelt's original press secretary, had to deal with frustrated correspondents who, as had been the case at previous wartime conferences, were denied access to the leaders until the final press conference, at which no questions were permitted.

President Roosevelt and King Ibn Saud of Saudi Arabia conversing aboard the USS *Quincy,* Bitter Lakes, the Red Sea, February 14, 1945. The man bending forward is the American minister to Saudi Arabia, Lieutenant Colonel William A. Eddy of the Marine Corps, who interpreted for both men. Roosevelt later told Congress, in an ad-lib, that "on the problem of Arabia, I learned more about that whole problem—the Moslem problem, the Jewish problem—by talking with Ibn Saud for five minutes, than I could have learned in the exchange of two or three dozen letters." However that may be, it did not affect his continuing support for a Jewish homeland in Palestine.

9 Advancing on All Fronts
1943

ROOSEVELT'S TENTH STATE OF THE UNION MESSAGE has been little appreciated. His two collaborators, Rosenman and Sherwood, had wanted a fighting speech to confront the increased Republican minority and were less than enthusiastic about the result. It was, however, an effective effort, well characterized by the banner in the *New York Times:* "ROOSEVELT SEES ALLIES ON THE ROAD TO VICTORY; URGES A POST-WAR AMERICA FREE FROM WANT." It fell into three parts, reviewing first the global military situation, then surveying domestic production and its direction, and finally looking forward to what the postwar world might look like.

The president told Congress that it was meeting at "one of the great moments in the history of the Nation. The past year was perhaps the most crucial for modern civilization; the coming year will be filled with violent conflicts—yet with high promise of better things."

He did not shy away from giving credit to Stalin's soldiers: "By far the largest and most important developments in the whole world-wide strategic picture of 1942 were . . . the implacable defense of Stalingrad [and the recent] offensives by the Russian armies . . . which still roll on."

Claiming that the "Axis powers knew that they must win the war in 1942—or eventually lose everything," the president went on to speak of the Pacific, where "our most important victory . . . was the air and naval battle off Midway." Reporting that "Japanese strength in ships and planes is going down and down, and American strength in ships and planes is going up and up," he promised "to bomb [the Japanese people] constantly from the air."

Turning to the European theater, Roosevelt pointed out that "our first task was to lessen the concentrated pressure on the Russian front by compelling Germany to divert part of her manpower and equipment to another theater of war." Justifying the North African expedition as performing that task, Roosevelt went on to argue that it also "opened to attack what Mr. Churchill well described as 'the under-belly of the Axis.'" He promised more action in the European theater in 1943: "Day in and day out we shall heap tons upon tons of high explosives on [Axis] war factories and utilities and seaports."

As for the war at home, Roosevelt described "the miracle of production:" "[In 1942] we produced 48,000 military planes—more than the airplane production of Germany, Italy, and Japan put together. Last month, in December, we produced 5,500 military planes and the rate is rapidly rising. We produced ten and a quarter billion rounds of small-arms ammunition, five times greater than our 1941 production and three times greater than our total production in the first World War. . . . I think that the arsenal of democracy is making good."

While all this was being achieved, Roosevelt noted that "during the past year our armed forces have grown from a little over 2,000,000 to 7,000,000. In other words, we have withdrawn from the labor force and the farms some 5,000,000 of our younger workers. And in spite of this, our farmers have contributed their share to the common effort by producing the greatest quantity of food ever made available during a single year in all our history."

Addressing his critics, the president observed, in words reflecting a reality that many historians have ignored, "It is often amusing, and it is sometimes politically profitable, to picture the City of Washington as a madhouse, with the Congress and the Administration disrupted with confusion and indecision and general incompetence. However—what matters most in war is results. And the one pertinent fact is that after only a few years of preparation and only one year of warfare, we are able to engage, spiritually as well as physically, in the total waging of a total war."

Before dealing with the postwar world, Roosevelt, obviously thinking about the ongoing furor about the Darlan deal and the Vichyites still in power in North Africa, insisted that "we should never forget the things we are fighting for. But, at this critical period of the war, we should confine ourselves to the larger objectives and not get bogged down in argument over methods and details." Those larger objectives included an enduring peace abroad and economic security at home. As Roosevelt put it, "I have reason to know that our boys at the front are concerned with two broad aims beyond the winning of the war. They know, and we know, that it would be inconceivable—it would, indeed, be sacrilegious—if this Nation and the world did not attain some real, lasting good out of all these efforts and sufferings and bloodshed and death. . . . And, equally, they want permanent employment for themselves, their families, and their neighbors when they are mustered out at the end of the war."

Again employing his now familiar four-freedoms metaphor, Roosevelt invoked the third freedom—Freedom from Want.

When you talk with our young men and our young women, you will find they want to work for themselves and for their families; they consider that they have the right to work; and they know that after the last war their fathers did not gain that right.

When you talk with our young men and women, you will find that with the opportunity for employment they want assurance against the evils of all major economic hazards—assurance that will extend from the cradle to the grave. And this great Government can and must provide this assurance.

The phrase "cradle to the grave" came from the already famous British Beveridge Report, which set a living standard below which no one should be allowed to fall, introduced only a month before, and became an inspiration if not a blueprint for the postwar British welfare state. We can be sure that those words produced a chill on the Republican side of the House chamber. Roosevelt spoke of the horrors of future wars, inspired, Sherwood tells us, by his knowledge that, just a month earlier, a team led by Enrico Fermi had successfully split an atom of uranium 235.

Victory in the peace . . . means striving toward the enlargement of the security of man here and throughout the world—and, finally, striving for the fourth freedom—freedom from fear.

It is of little account for any of us to talk of essential human needs, of attaining security, if we run the risk of another World War in ten or twenty or fifty years. That is just plain common sense. Wars grow in size, in death and destruction, and in the inevitability of engulfing all Nations, in inverse ratio to the shrinking size of the world as a result of the conquest of the air. I shudder to think of what will happen to humanity, including ourselves, if this war ends in an inconclusive peace, and another war breaks out when the babies of today have grown to fighting age.

Roosevelt struck from the text a suggestion that the war might end during the term of the present Congress—that is, by January 1, 1945—and instead ended the speech by saying:

I do not prophesy when this war will end.

But I do believe that this year of 1943 will give to the United Nations a very substantial advance along the roads that lead to Berlin and Rome and Tokyo. . . .

Therefore, let us all have confidence, let us redouble our efforts.

A tremendous, costly, long-enduring task in peace as well as in war is still ahead of us.

But, as we face that continuing task, we may know that the state of this Nation is good—the heart of this Nation is sound—the spirit of this Nation is strong—the faith of this Nation is eternal.[1]

The annual budget message for fiscal 1944 (July 1, 1943–June 30, 1944) had been discussed with reporters at the budget press conference on January 9. The numbers seemed fantastic: the total of $109 billion (of which $100 billion was in the category of war expenditures) was slightly more than the federal government had spent from its inception through fiscal 1932. Roosevelt justified the huge sums: "Last year I called the budget an instrument for transforming a peace economy into a war economy. This Budget presents the maximum program for waging war. We wage total war because our very existence is threatened. Without that supreme effort we cannot hope to retain the freedom and self-respect which give life its value. Total war is grim reality. It means the dedication of our lives and resources to a single objective: Victory. . . . In total war we are all soldiers, whether in uniform, overalls, or shirt sleeves."[2]

Roosevelt left for Africa two days before the budget message was read in Congress. Under wartime security rules, the press could not report his absence, and the White House kept sending new business to Congress, so all but the most astute and careful readers and listeners were unaware of Roosevelt's absence. Among the business sent to Congress were the nominations of Wiley B. Rutledge (1844–1949) to replace Byrnes on the Supreme Court and Prentiss M. Brown (1889–1973) to replace Leon Henderson at the OPA. Rutledge was an Iowa law professor who had supported the 1937 Court-packing plan and received a 1939 appointment to a U.S. Court of Appeals. The last of Roosevelt's eight Supreme Court appointees, he immediately made an impact by changing the balance on the Court in the flag-salute cases. Brown, a Michigan Democrat who had served two terms in the House and one in the Senate before losing in 1942, was a less confrontational OPA administrator who continued Henderson's policies.[3]

The trip to Casablanca began with a rail journey—two nights and a day—from Washington to Miami, followed by a Pan American clipper flight of nearly eleven hours to Trinidad, where the president, Hopkins, Admiral Leahy, Dr. McIntire, his naval aide Captain John L. McCrea, Secret Service men, and supervising army officers spent the night.

It was Roosevelt's first flight as president. He told newspaper editors after the trip, "I *don't* like flying! Not one bit. The more I do of it, the less I like it." And, as Hopkins noted, "Dr. McIntire was worried about the President's bad heart." Sixty-seven-year-old Admiral Leahy became ill in Trinidad and was left there as the clipper took the others on to Belem, Brazil, where the army had established a 250-man Ferry Command base through which planes destined for Africa were routed. On that leg, McIntire became more concerned as they flew at nine thousand feet, and Hopkins noted that the president "appeared to be very pale at times." Roosevelt's repeated flying in unpressurized aircraft over the next two years cannot have been beneficial to his health.

After a night in Brazil, the clipper took them to a British base in Bathurst, Gambia, the other end of the air force air ferry route, where they spent the night on the cruiser USS *Memphis*. From there two army C-54 four-engine transports flew the party to Casablanca, where they arrived on January 14, almost five full days after leaving Washington. Members of the Joint Chiefs and their staffs and their British opposite numbers had been there for three days before their leaders.[4]

Roosevelt himself described the origins of the Casablanca Conference at his press conference there: "We began talking about this after the first of December and at that time we invited Mr. Stalin to join us at a convenient meeting place. Mr. Stalin very much wanted to join us, but he was precluded from leaving Russia as he was conducting the new Russian offensive." If Stalin had come, the proposed meeting place was Khartoum. Had that meeting come off, Roosevelt might well have gone to North Africa, as he was anxious to meet with troops at war.[5]

The major tasks of the conference were to plan the next operation after Axis forces had been driven from North Africa and to decide whether and when the cross-Channel invasion of Europe would begin. At Casablanca General Marshall made what military historian Maurice Matloff called his "last stand" for a cross-Channel invasion of France in 1943, though it can be argued that the decision to invade North Africa had already made a major cross-Channel invasion improbable if not impossible.

Alanbrooke, for the British chiefs of staff, argued that no major landing in France could occur before late-summer 1943 and would be limited in size and suffer from a lack of landing craft. He proposed, instead, further action in the Mediterranean. If successful, it would not only offer additional opportunities to attack but also shorten supply lines and help ease the endemic shipping shortage. He did say that an invasion of Germany should take place in 1944. Churchill fully supported the British staff's position.

Roosevelt saw merit in both cases. He had always supported an attack on Germany as soon as possible, but he also wanted American troops to see more action in 1943. In the end, Marshall gave way. There was a commonsense aspect of the British argument: after all, battle-tested troops would be in place on the south shore of the Mediterranean with a variety of targets in range. It was agreed that Sicily, the closest target, would be invaded with "the favorable July moon" if not sooner, in an operation code-named Husky. The stated strategic objectives were to make the Mediterranean more secure, divert German pressure on the USSR, and intensify pressure on Italy. Eisenhower was to be theater commander, and when the British Eighth Army united with his forces, its leader, General Sir Harold R. L. G. Alexander, would become his deputy and command the Allied forces in Tunisia and the preparations for the invasion of Sicily.

Other global decisions followed. There would be a continued air bombardment of Germany. While the British argued that any real assault against Japan could wait until Germany was defeated, Marshall, while adhering to the long-established Germany-first decision, insisted that perhaps 30 percent of the American effort should be in the Pacific, including offensives in the southwestern and central Pacific, with the latter's purpose being the acquisition of bases for the bombing of Japan.[6]

After all the hours of detailed and often intense debate over a variety of issues, the military decisions were dwarfed by a two-word phrase from the president in the postmeeting press conference. Although it was a joint conference—the president and the prime minister were seated side by side on a grassy lawn— Roosevelt dominated. Not only did he make the opening and closing statements, but Churchill's one statement began with "I agree with everything the president has said . . ."

The most important thing that the president said, as was often the case with Roosevelt, was wrapped in an anecdote. He ended his opening statement with the following passage:

> I think that we have all had it in our hearts and heads before, but I don't think that it has ever been put on paper by the prime minister and myself, and that is the determination that peace can come to the world only by the total elimination of the German and Japanese war power.
>
> Some of you Britishers know the old story—we had a General called U. S. Grant. His name was Ulysses Simpson Grant, but [often] called "Unconditional Surrender" Grant.
>
> The elimination of German, Japanese, and Italian war power means the unconditional surrender of Germany, Italy, and Japan. That means a reasonable assurance of future world peace. It does not mean the destruction of the population of Germany, Italy, or Japan, but it does mean the destruction of the philosophies of those countries which are based on conquest or the subjugation of other people. While we have not had a meeting of all of the United Nations, I think that there is no question—in fact we both have great confidence that the same purposes and objectives are in the minds of all of the other United Nations—Russia, China. And all the others.

From the first press reports to the present, the words *unconditional surrender* characterize the meeting.

In the second part of Roosevelt's talk—it was a press conference with no questions—he spoke of the presence of "General Giraud and General de Gaulle. The Frenchmen had come out with the two leaders at the beginning of the conference, sat beside them in silence while still and motion-picture photographers did their work, and at Roosevelt's request stood up and, obeying his instructions in French, stiffly shook hands for the camera, with the president commenting "a historic moment" as the generals left without a word. Roosevelt explained that the meeting provided an opportunity "for those two gentlemen to meet one another."

While the official communiqué mentioned two dozen military and civilian participants, it is striking that neither the president nor the prime minister mentioned the name of a single member of the Joint Chiefs. Naturally, the censorship had blocked all news of the conference. Somewhat surprisingly, the news embargo was lifted on January 26, just two days after the press conference and before either leader had returned home.[7]

During his eleven days in Morocco, Roosevelt left the conference villa twice. He visited and reviewed troops; the nearest German soldier was hundreds of miles away. He and his party drove to Marrakech, at the foot of the Atlas Mountains, some 150 miles away. Churchill wanted Roosevelt to see the mountains at sunset from a certain tower. Roosevelt had to be carried up the sixty steps for the view, over which he and Churchill lingered. That evening they and Hopkins composed a message to Stalin describing the tenor of the conference decisions.

The next morning, Roosevelt flew back to Bathurst, where he gave the governor of Britain's West African provinces "an earful, telling him flatly that wise administration commanded that more attention be given to the health and well-being of the native population."[8]

Despite McIntire's concerns, Roosevelt flew three times the next day. A C-54 took him to Liberia for a lunch with its president, a review of black American troops who had been sent there in October, and a tour of a large Firestone rubber plantation whose output helped meet American needs.

The next day, he boarded the clipper and flew to Natal, Brazil, to meet his ally President Getúlio Vargas (1882–1964). Vargas had been flown up from Rio in an American transport the night before and spent the night on an American destroyer anchored in the harbor, which was the site of most of the next day's conference. Roosevelt joined Vargas on the destroyer after his early-morning arrival, and they conferred on board for much of the day and then went ashore to inspect an American air base. The key passage in their brief joint statement was that "West Africa and Dakar [must] never again become a blockade or invasion threat against the two Americas." The next day, Roosevelt was flown to Trinidad, where he found Admiral Leahy waiting for him. A flight to Miami and a train brought him to Washington without ceremony on January 31. The previous day had been Roosevelt's sixty-first birthday, and Eleanor and Basil O'Connor made the traditional broadcast in the president's place. She read a brief message from him, and O'Connor spoke about the national foundation's work. Again, Birthday Balls and other celebrations took place across the nation and in London and Latin America.[9]

Interest about the Casablanca meeting was intense. On the afternoon of his first day back, Roosevelt met for an hour and a half with eleven congressional leaders, including four Republicans, who were pledged to secrecy, though one doubts that they were told anything not revealed in the press conference the next morning. The president said that he "could not tell them where" the next blows would fall on Germany, encouraging speculation that the decision had been made, and denied that there was dispute between the two French generals.

Ten days later, he told a different and more accurate story to the American Society of Newspaper Editors, explaining that he and Churchill called Giraud "the bridegroom" and de Gaulle "the bride" and that their purpose at Casablanca was to force them into a "shotgun wedding." He revealed that the two Frenchmen had to be cajoled into so simple a matter as shaking hands for the camera. What really mattered, he told the editors, was support for General Eisenhower.[10]

That evening the president broadcast a report to the people on the state of the war and his trip. He emphasized what he had seen, the state of the forces overseas, and what was in store for them. "I have seen our men—and some of our American women—in North Africa. Out there it is war. These men know that before this war is over, many of them will have given their lives to their nation. But they know also that they are fighting to destroy the power of the enemies of this country, that they are fighting for a peace that will be a real and lasting peace and a far better world for the future."

He spoke not of divisions but of Frenchmen united "in one great paramount objective—the complete liberation of France." Roosevelt closed by expressing his faith that future "generations will come to know that here, in the middle of the twentieth century, there came a time when men of good will found a way to unite, and produce, and fight to destroy the forces of ignorance, and intolerance, and slavery and war."[11]

Of course, while Roosevelt concentrated on Casablanca and the forces in North Africa, the war went on elsewhere and problems at home continued. The Russian front continued to be of chief importance: on February 4, the president sent a public message to Stalin congratulating him on the "brilliant victory at Stalingrad."

But secret exchanges showed that all was not sweetness and light; there were open dissatisfactions on both sides. In what was in effect a joint message, the Western leaders informed Stalin on February 9 of the decisions at Casablanca: "We hope to destroy or expel [a quarter of a million Germans and Italians in Eastern Tunisia] during April if not earlier. [Then] we intend in July or earlier if possible, to seize Sicily . . . to be closely followed by an operation in the eastern Mediterranean, probably against the Dodecanese."

After a paragraph describing the difficulties of getting sufficient shipping and landing craft and mentioning that they intended to "press any advantages gained to the utmost," there followed an inaccurate paragraph about the possibilities of a cross-Channel invasion. "We are also pushing operations to the limit of our resources for a cross-Channel operation in August in which both British and United States units would participate. Here again, shipping and assault landing craft will be limiting factors. If the operation is delayed by weather or other reasons, it will be prepared with stronger forces for September. The timing of this attack must of course be dependent on the condition of German defensive positions across the Channel at that time."

Even with the hedging, this was, to say the least, disingenuous. An official U.S. Army historian described the situation after Casablanca as follows: "Casablanca had opened with the hopes of the U.S. staff centered on an invasion of the Continent in force in 1943. It was obvious from the discussions that such an invasion of the Continent was not to take place, but Sir Alan Brooke reassured the Americans, 'we should definitely count on reentering the Continent in 1944 on a large scale.'"

Stalin may have understood what the situation really was, but his response on February 16 took his Allies' statement at face value. After complaining about the delay of the Tunisian operation until April, he said of their later plans, "As regards the opening of a second front . . . in France . . . scheduled only for August or September . . . the present situation demands that this date should be brought nearer as much as possible." Later, Stalin would add that the Sicily invasion was no substitute "for a second front in France."[12]

While Stalin had reason to be disappointed with his Western allies, they had complaints of their own. In mid-April 1943, the German government announced that it had discovered a mass grave of thousands of Polish army officers whom it said had been murdered by the Russians sometime after they occupied eastern Poland in 1939. We now know that Stalin and his secret police carried out the murder of almost all the twenty thousand Polish officers it had captured. The Soviet government insisted for almost half a century that the Nazis had killed them. When in 1943 the Polish government in exile based in London persisted in demanding an international inquiry by the Red Cross, Stalin used it as an excuse to break relations with the London Poles, accusing them of "collusion" with Hitler. He set up a rival Polish government based in Moscow, which the Soviets later installed in power. Roosevelt tried to restrain Stalin, telling him that while the London Poles had "made a mistake" in appealing to the Red Cross, they were not, he thought, acting "with the Hitler gang." He closed his communication by noting, "Incidentally, I have several million Poles in the United States, very many of them in the Army and Navy. They are all bitter against the Nazis, and knowledge of a complete diplomatic break between you and Sikorski would not help the situation."

Despite this and other admonitions from Western leaders, Stalin went ahead with his design. Warren Kimball's analysis—"The realities of war, Polish intransigence, and the need to maintain the Grand Alliance and extend it to Japan prevented the Anglo-Americans from giving the Poles anything more than private and empty reassurances"—is astute. The episode was a grim harbinger of the future.[13]

At home there were challenges from Congress around the edges of domestic policy just as there was a consensus about its major thrust, greater production to win the war. One continuing skirmish involved the putative salary cap of twenty-five thousand dollars that the president had "legislated" by executive order in October. In early February, responding to a note from House Ways and Means chair Robert Doughton telling him of a pending rider to the bill raising the national debt limit to $210 billion from $125 billion, which would also nullify his executive order, Roosevelt wrote "Dear Bob" a public letter, expressing his "earnest hope" that the bill would pass without "amendments not related to [its] subject matter." He told reporters to ask Doughton to show it to them. Some committee members, speaking of "a revolt against government by directive," offered to propose legislation to effect the salary cap, but it seemed highly unlikely that such a measure could pass Congress, which was why the president had done it by executive order in the first place.

Roosevelt's follow-up letter to Doughton rehashed the whole controversy over salaries in wartime, recalling 1924 Republican and Democratic convention planks that pledged to take the profit out of war. He noted that in April 1942, he had asked Congress to legislate a salary cap of twenty-five thousand dollars, and after it had failed to do so the attorney general had advised that his October executive order imposing it was legal and limited to the war period.

He stressed the "gross inequity" for the president of a war plant "to receive a salary and bonus of $500,000 a year," while the plant workers "were denied an increase in wages by my executive order." If Congress passed legislation that appropriately taxed the rich, he promised to revoke his order.

Congress refused to pass such legislation and did attach the rider canceling the executive order to the Public Debt Act. Roosevelt explained, "I should veto the bill," but said that the "Treasury has advised me" that "the Public Debt Act must become effective without further delay" for war financing to continue. This meant, as both Roosevelt and Congress knew, that the bill was veto proof. Therefore, Roosevelt wrote, "I am accordingly allowing the bill to become law without my signature."

His message went on to assail Congress on both substance and procedure. On substance he took the high ground, pointing out that "two or three thousand persons" could continue to receive salaries "in excess of $67,500," that about "750 persons will be able to receive Salaries in excess of $100,000," that "about 30 persons, salaries in excess of $250,000," and "3 or 4 persons, salaries in excess of $500,000." In contrast, "One hundred and thirty million Americans can make the stabilization program work even though a relative handful of persons are not obligated to cooperate as they should. The exemption accorded these excessively high salaries does not help morale, but American morale is too strong to be permanently injured by this ill-considered action."

On procedure, however, Roosevelt wanted to have it both ways. Although both he and Congress had deviated from traditional procedure—he by using an executive order to accomplish what he could not get by statute, Congress by using a rider to avoid a veto that almost certainly would be upheld—Roosevelt called the latter a foul. But he ignored his executive order, which was just as clearly a foul.[14]

Roosevelt clearly lost that skirmish, but he had won a major battle in his war against inflation four days before. On April 8, he issued what he called a "hold the line" executive order, the final piece in the complicated structure of wage and price controls he had begun to build the previous April. The order forbade wage increases above the level of the Little Steel formula and empowered manpower commissioner Paul McNutt to issue regulations that would freeze most war workers in the jobs they currently held. Because the order was largely directed against workers, many of Roosevelt's opponents in Congress supported it. Immediate comments by Senators Byrd, Wheeler, and Vandenberg were highly favorable. New OPA director Prentiss Brown said the order gave assurance "to the man on the street that the current level of prices will be maintained," while George Meany of the AFL gave cautious support and unnamed labor leaders told reporters that if the order "clamped a lid on living costs the result would be wholesome." In retrospect cost-of-living data show that Roosevelt's April 8 order began a period of relative stability that lasted into early 1946, when the Truman administration began to relax controls.[15]

This was the centerpiece of Roosevelt's economic policy in 1943, achieved, like so much of his wartime management, without much congressional action apart from forbearance. Other aspects of the home-front struggles included continuing static from various congressional elements, most prominently the House Committee on Un-American Activities, which had been authorized by a coalition of Republicans and southern Democrats in 1938 with a mandate to investigate "the extent, character, and object of Un-American propaganda activities in the United States." Congress had indulged in such investigations since the success of the Bolshevik Revolution in 1917. Like its predecessors and successors, the 1938 version, headed by Martin Dies (D-TX), produced no legislation and thrived on the willingness of the press to print their often baseless charges as if they were serious news. Kenneth O'Reilly has calculated that in its first month of existence, the committee received five hundred inches of news coverage from the *New York Times,* which largely regurgitated its reckless charges. J. Parnell Thomas (R-NJ), senior minority member during the Roosevelt years, once defined un-American activities as including "the four horsemen of autocracy . . . Fascism, Nazism, Bolshevism, and New Dealism," though the committee's focus was almost always on the latter two, and it emitted a flow of racism and occasionally attacked birth control.

Many New Dealers, especially the always combat-ready Harold Ickes, wanted to confront the Dies committee, but Roosevelt thought it better to ignore it until early December 1940, when, against the advice of Ickes, he had a private meeting with Dies that seemed to have a moderating result. Without fanfare or formal structure, the Justice Department and the Civil Service Commission had routinely handled personnel investigations. For 1941 Attorney General

Biddle had announced that thirty-six federal employees had been discharged for subversive activities and noted that only two of them had been on a list of eleven hundred names furnished by the Dies committee. In early February 1943, Roosevelt created an interdepartmental committee to investigate any charges of subversion brought against a federal employee, with the proviso that it could look at charges brought against army and navy employees only with the consent of the service secretary. The president named five senior civil servants to the committee. Rosenman reports that in the next thirty-two months, the committee looked at 671 cases: 24 of them resulted in discharge, and 143 others were ended by resignation or other disposition.[16]

As a further correction to the growing labor shortage, the president decreed in mid-February that, although the War Manpower Commission could make exceptions, the forty-eight-hour week would become standard in industry and that the provisions of the Fair Labor Standards Act and any additional contractual provisions about overtime wages would remain in effect. This would not only increase war production, which was its major thrust, but also increase the production of civilian goods and reduce inflationary pressures in that way, though the increased hours would put substantially more money into the weekly wage packets of the affected workers.[17]

*   *   *

After Roosevelt learned that Madame Chiang Kai-shek (1898–2003) wanted to come to the United States for spinal surgery, he had Harry Hopkins arrange a military flight from Chungking in late November, 1942. Under wartime rules, her comings and goings were not to be reported, and she got Secret Service protection. Hopkins met her and her entourage of ten—which Bill Hassett called her "horde"—and checked her into Harkness Pavilion in New York, where Eleanor paid her a visit. She would remain in the country a good half year. Her attractive appearance, idiomatic American English, and quick intelligence made her a most effective public advocate for China. In talks with Hopkins, she made clear her criticisms of American policy; she and the generalissimo favored a Japan-first strategy, which made her more than welcome to Roosevelt's political enemies such as Henry and Clare Boothe Luce. Her visit helped cement the so-called China Lobby, which distorted post-Roosevelt American China policy well into the Nixon administration. Jonathan Daniels reports that Lauchlin Currie told him that "when Madame Chiang Kai-shek came here and found out that liberalism, as represented by Currie and [Owen] Lattimore, was not really in power any more, she went like a homing pigeon to Willkie and Luce, who are really her type."

On several occasions, she was a house guest of the Roosevelts at both Hyde Park and the White House, and the president's staff was soon fed up with what Hassett and Daniels called her "arrogant and overbearing" ways. A Chinese-born American academic reported that she traveled with a supply of silk sheets that had to be changed after each use. Even Roosevelt, who took genuine pleasure in hosting a variety of royal visitors, found her a chore.

Judging from press reports, Madame Chiang kept her arrogance masked during public appearances, and her first official visit to Washington in mid-February was a triumph. The Chinese "first lady" was met in Union Station by Mrs. Roosevelt and the Chinese ambassador, who walked with her to the automobile in which the president was waiting. The White House announced three public events, a separate address to each house of Congress, the second to be broadcast nationally, and a joint press conference with both Roosevelts to which women reporters accredited to Eleanor's press conferences would be admitted.

In her brief, informal speech to the Senate the next day, Madame Chiang began by speaking of her American education and claimed that "coming here today I also feel that I am coming home." She went on to speak of the common aspirations of the Chinese and American people.

Her formal address to the House was, in essence, an appeal for an abandonment of the Germany-first strategy by the United States. As she had done in conversations with Hopkins, she challenged "the prevailing opinion" that defeating Hitler was the "first concern" and claimed that Japan had more resources at its disposal than Germany, implying that it offered the greater threat to America. Press accounts indicated that the applause that greeted that part of her speech began on the Republican side of the chamber.

The press conference the next morning was a double lovefest. One hundred seventy-two reporters crowded into the president's office to find Madame Chiang in the central of three chairs, with Mrs. Roosevelt on her right and the president on her left. Mrs. Roosevelt, normally thought of as loquacious, was silent throughout. The president opened with a brief introduction, ending with "I am going to ask her . . . just to say a few words. And afterwards . . . perhaps she will be willing to answer a few questions of the 'non-catch' type."

Her four-paragraph opening statement contained mostly pleasantries and an incredible assertion that no one challenged: "I want to say one thing to you, and that is that we in China have always had social democracy throughout these thousands of years." There was no trace, in either her opening remarks or in any of her answers to questions, of the criticism of American war priorities and strategy she had raised with Hopkins and in her speech to the House. The questioning began.

Q: Are you here . . . on an official mission or on a personal visit . . . ?

MADAME CHIANG: This is a personal visit. . . . I came here for my health.

Q: At the same time, you made quite an impression with your speech yesterday, which might percolate into official mentality?

MADAME CHIANG: That is for you to judge.

An ill-phrased and initially misunderstood question, what "the people of this country" can do "to help China," was answered:

THE PRESIDENT: (Interposing) I can answer that: with more munitions. We are all for it. That is unanimous.

MADAME CHIANG: The President is right.

The only question that seemed hostile asked whether China was utilizing its vast manpower properly.

MADAME CHIANG: We are using as much manpower as there are munitions to be used. We can't fight with bare hands. . . . But it is not true . . . that China is not supporting the front with her manpower, because we are. . . .

Q: Madame Chiang, would you care to speak about the American air force in China. . . .

MADAME CHIANG: I can't pay sufficiently high tribute to the American volunteer air force—the American Volunteer Group—when they first came out to us. . . . But I think the greatest help was the feeling on the part of our Chinese people that we have not fought and died alone, and that America was helping us, and that America is really our ally. . . . .

Now the present American air force—as the President has just said, we need munitions. We need munitions, We have got manpower. We have even got trained pilots. But we haven't got the planes, nor have we the gasoline. And the point is, how are we going to get them? But the president has solved so many difficult problems, he has come through so many great crises with flying colors, I feel that I can safely leave that answer to him.

At this point Roosevelt took control of the press conference.

Q: Madame Chiang,—

THE PRESIDENT: (Interposing) Madame Chiang, you are absolutely one hundred percent right on what we want to do, and what we are trying to do, and I might even say what we are beginning to do. . . .

He went on to explain the logistical difficulties of getting equipment into China, insisted that "we are just as keen to knock out Japan as China is," and summed up by saying, "If I were a member of the Chinese government, I would say 'But when?' 'How soon?' 'Why not a little more?'; and I say that as a member of the American government too. Just as fast as the Lord will let us."

Asked in a final question if she had any suggestions for speeding up the aid, she responded:

MADAME CHIANG: The President said that "as soon as the Lord will let us."
. . . Well, I might say—add on to that, the Lord helps those who help
themselves.

THE PRESIDENT: Right.

It should be noted that no questions were asked about the corruption endemic in China, or the struggle with the Chinese Communists, or the role of
the American commander in China, General Joseph W. Stilwell. She was asked
how to pronounce her name.[18] It was not a great day in the history of American
journalism.

Roosevelt's interventions, designed as damage limitation, may have been a
short-term success but did nothing to educate the public and his successors about
the realities behind his China policy. Getting aid to China had then, and would
continue to have, a relatively low place on the American priority list. At most
China was seen as an eventual base for bomber raids on the Japanese home islands,
a difficult proposition at best, which was made unnecessary by the development
of the B-29 long-range aircraft and the capture of unsinkable air bases on Saipan
and Iwo Jima in bloody battles in the summer of 1944 and the winter of 1945. The
president's strategic notions about the liberation of China never contemplated the
use of large American armies, but concentrated on the ill-fated Stilwell mission
and the successful efforts to get Stalin's commitment to use Soviet forces to liberate Manchuria by defeating the large Japanese armies there. Despite the attention
focused on Madame Chiang and her embattled homeland, the real Pacific news
in February was the successful end of the six months of naval, air, and land battles
for Guadalcanal. Its consequences were several. First of all, the Japanese advance
in the Southwest Pacific had come to an end at a cost that the U.S. Army historian
had judged not to have been "prohibitive." Of some 60,000 Marine and army
troops involved, about 1,600 were killed and 4,245 wounded. Japanese manpower
losses were more severe. Of 36,000 troops landed on Guadalcanal—many were
killed at sea trying to get there—more than 14,800 were killed or missing, and
9,000 died of disease. About 1,000 were taken prisoner. Each side lost twenty-four
major vessels, but the Japanese loss of six hundred planes and their pilots would
hamper their subsequent operations. As would often be the case, the president
made no direct public comment about the victory, but he awarded Major General
Alexander A. Vandegrift of the Marine Corps, who commanded during the most
crucial stages of the battle, the Congressional Medal of Honor in a ceremony in
his office.[19]

In Africa the February military news was not good. The slow initial Allied
movement into Tunisia, hampered by poor organization, a lack of appropriate vehicles, and poor weather and road conditions, had allowed German and
Italian reinforcements to become firmly established there, frustrating hopes of

a rapid link with British forces moving east from Egypt. An attack on poorly organized American forces by battle-hardened veterans of Rommel's Afrika Korps produced a short-lived German victory in the Battle of Kasserine Pass in mid-February, which revealed serious deficiencies in army training and equipment: its tanks were too small, and G.I.s soon learned to call the 75mm half-track gun carriers "Purple Heart Boxes."

The War Department was prompt and frank about the setback: Secretary Stimson, in his weekly report to the press, admitted "a sharp defeat" but insisted that it was "not unexpected" and predicted, correctly, that there would be a relatively speedy recovery. In a retrospective account of the North African campaign, A. J. Liebling (1908–63), perhaps the most astute of the correspondents who covered the war and surely the best writer, noted that Rommel's short-lived offensive was "the last flurry of the hooked and dying fish." Perhaps most unsettling to the military authorities was that in a little over a week, the German forces took more than 4,000 prisoners, most of them Americans who had borne the brunt of the counterattack, and seized large amounts of American equipment and supplies, including forty-five tons of ammunition. The pass was quickly retaken, and after another two and a half months of fighting the Axis was driven out of Africa. The American losses were considerable. Of 18,221 casualties, 2,715 were killed, 8,978 wounded, and 6,528 missing, almost all of whom were POWs.

We have to judge Roosevelt's opinions from his actions. According to a Hopkins memo, during the Casablanca Conference, General Marshall had urged the president to promote Eisenhower to "full General" so he would have equal rank with his British counterparts. Roosevelt refused. Saying that it was difficult with Eisenhower's "army mired in the mud," he told the chief of staff that "he would not promote Eisenhower until there was some damn good reason for doing it" and "that he was going to make it a rule that promotions should go to people who had done some fighting." He relented some two weeks later.[20]

With the legislative session well under way, Roosevelt held an unusual White House evening reception for the 117 new members of Congress, many of them hostile to his domestic program, and every one of them came. They were seated at small tables in the State Dining Room and offered soft drinks, beer, cheese, crackers, cigars, and cigarettes. Speaker Sam Rayburn, acting as master of ceremonies, brought them over to where the president was seated and introduced them in small groups. Reporters were told that the president spoke to them mostly about war and told anecdotes about the Casablanca Conference. The evening ended with Roosevelt making brief informal remarks about how the war had changed his working days. They give us insights about the president's self-knowledge.

Well, all you "freshmen"—some of whom are older than I am!—it's grand to make your acquaintance. You know, during the last Congress things were pretty busy at the White House, and I honestly believe there were thirty to forty of the new Congressmen in the last session whom I never met at all.

I know perfectly well that you realize some of my problems. You don't really get the truth from the columnists, because they say that I am overburdened and overworked. I am not working as hard, so far as appointments go—so far as seeing people goes—as I did before the war started, nothing like it.

Now I haven't an excess of "gray matter," but I do have to have a little bit more time to think and to read. The amount of literature that I get from the General Staff, the needs of the Army, and manpower, the size of the Army and Navy, and things like that, the amount of stuff that I have to read today does take an awful lot of time. And it limits my schedule in the morning when I see people—to about five or six people—five or six different appointments in the course of the morning, instead of the ten or fifteen, or twice as many as I used to put in before the war. And that honestly is the only reason that I can't see you people of the Senate and House as much or as often as I used to. It isn't because of any greater burden on me, but it's the necessity of doing more reading. In some ways I feel as if I had gone back to school. As far as the work goes, it isn't any heavier, but it's a little bit different character of work.

And so I know that you will bear with me and be lenient, if it takes any of you who want to see me about something important a long, long time before you can get in. You will have to take the will for the deed. I am doing the best I can. I do wish to goodness that I had more time, as I did before, to see personally the members of the House and Senate.

I think that part of it is my fault, so my secretaries tell me. When somebody comes in on a ten-minute appointment, I start to do the talking. I get enthusiastic, and the result is that at the end of ten or fifteen minutes my visitor hasn't had a chance to get in a word edgewise. And that is something I am trying to school myself to omit, to try to let the other fellow talk, instead of my doing it. And that is about the hardest thing I have to do in this life, because as some of you who have been here before know, I love to talk. It's an unfortunate characteristic.

So I say, please bear with me, and if you do come in, say to me quite frankly, "Now listen, before you talk, Mr. President, let me have my say." I think it would be a grand thing.[21]

There is no evidence that anyone ever tried that suggested frank approach to the president, or was intended to. Earlier that day, Roosevelt had sent a massive report from the National Resources Planning Board to Congress. Although a House committee had, in effect, killed the board by striking it from the bill funding federal offices, he told reporters that "I don't care how planning is done. They can abolish the National Resources Planning Board if they set up some other organization to do the work." His message merely pointed out the general thrust and importance of the report: "We can all agree on our objectives and in our common determination that work, fair play, and social security after the war is won must be firmly established for the people of the United States of America." His support for the report and its principles was consistent with what he had been saying since the war tide had begun to turn.

The report outlined the major long-range objectives of the larger program:

Government provision of work for all adults who are willing and able to work, if private industry is unable to provide employment.

Appropriate measures to equip young persons beyond the compulsory school attendance age for assuming the full responsibilities of citizenship.

Assurance of basic minimum security through social insurance, as far as possible.

Establishing of a comprehensive underpinning general public-assistance system providing aid on the basis of need, to complete the framework of protection against economic insecurity.

Expansion of social services which are essential for the health, welfare, and efficiency of the whole population; this expansion should be as wide and as rapid as possible.

In addition, the report laid out the need for $7 billion in public works to cope with expected unemployment resulting from end-of-war and postwar reconversion.

Immediate reactions from Congress were predictable: New Dealers like Robert Wagner and Claude Pepper praised it, while Republicans and conservative Democrats attacked it as "socialism" or "too expensive." At the same time, many once hotly debated war and foreign policy questions were now a matter of course: the House approved a fully funded third year of Lend-Lease by a vote of 407–6.[22]

Roosevelt also spoke of continuing shortages of farm labor and spot shortages of all sorts of foodstuffs, each caused in part, judging from the remedies he suggested, by military hoarding and stockpiling. To help get a needed fifty thousand workers onto dairy farms, the army had been ordered to release most soldiers over thirty-eight and to return some twelve million cases of canned goods for resale in grocery stores to ease the food shortages. A White House statement spoke of utilizing conscientious objectors and, without resorting to a draft of labor that many had called for, described what the War Manpower Commission and local draft boards were being instructed to do to persuade the released soldiers to take those unattractive, low-paying dairy jobs.[23]

Food shortages were felt even by the president and his top aides. On his first trip to Hyde Park since Casablanca, Roosevelt, on boarding the train, asked that orange juice be served to his party, which included Harry Hopkins, Grace

Tully, and the Morgenthaus, only to be informed by the porter that doing so would leave none for the president's breakfast. Once rationing had set in, the White House had to supply the food for the train, and, as Hassett explains, "La Nesbitt" sent only ten oranges, so "all went without." The president spent four quiet days at Hyde Park, but left behind him a long veto message.

The vetoed bill would have raised farm prices considerably, changing the method by which parity was calculated. Roosevelt warned that its passage would set off an "inflationary tornado" and made his case in a paragraph.

> If by this bill you force an increase in the cost of the basic foodstuffs, and as a result the National War Labor Board increases wages, no one can tell where increases will stop or what those increased wages will ultimately cost the farmers and all people of the Nation. If the price of food goes up, if wages rise, it will necessarily result in increasing the cost of our armaments, ships, and planes. We should have to borrow even greater sums to meet the increased cost of the war, and after the war an excessive burden of debt would have to be borne by all the people, including those now in uniform.

But his veto message went on for some twenty-seven hundred words because it was part of the preparation for the "hold the line" stabilization program that would be unveiled in a week's time. The practical politics of the matter were that there was no chance of his veto being overridden: in fact, many Democratic stalwarts, including Majority Leader Barkley who had originally voted yea, immediately backed off and supported the president's veto. One suspects that at least some of the original majority wanted to be able to tell their constituents of that vote. Shortly after returning to Washington, the president issued his "hold the line" stabilization order noted earlier.

While at Hyde Park Roosevelt learned that Sam Rosenman was experiencing severe eyesight problems and would have to be hospitalized for some time. As Rosenman, who had just turned forty-seven, explains in his memoir:

> Since Pearl Harbor I had been commuting weekly between Washington and New York, taking care of my judicial duties and spending all vacations and weekends in Washington. As a result [of the stress] one of my eyes became temporarily blind. [After six weeks of hospital treatment] sight in the eye was completely restored [but his doctor told him that to avoid a recurrence he should give up one of his jobs]. When I told this to the President, he said that he would prefer to have me resign from the Court and come down to Washington for the duration of the war. I complied with his request.

Rosenman resigned from the New York State Court of Appeals in September and was appointed the first counsel to the president, another Roosevelt innovation that has become permanent. Rosenman did not mention that his new job involved a pay cut from twenty-five to ten thousand dollars.[24]

That evening the president and a large party left Washington for a sixteen-day inspection tour that under the now familiar wartime secrecy rules took him as far west as Denver and included six military installations and three war plants. But since the tour also included a trip to Mexico, where secrecy could not be enforced, Mexican papers were full of news about it. A *New York Times* stringer there reported being "approached by acquaintances and strangers" seventy-two hours before the event, asking where, exactly, it would be celebrated.

As the train neared Mexico, Roosevelt explained in an onboard press conference that a planned January 1942 meeting with Mexican president Manuel Ávila Camacho had been canceled because of Pearl Harbor and that this was only the second such meeting. In 1909 William Howard Taft and Porfirio Díaz shook hands at the midpoint of the international bridge at El Paso–Ciudad Juárez. He also noted that "last fall . . . aircraft factories employed from 25 to 30 percent women," and this spring it was "about one-half. . . . [The] girls are doing well . . . another reason why the manpower problem is not as serious as Washington [!] made it out to be."

For the entry into Mexico, the president's party had been reinforced by the presence of Eleanor Roosevelt and Undersecretary of State Sumner Welles. The Mexican foreign minister and the American ambassador to Mexico, George Messersmith, greeted the party at the border and traveled with the Americans to Monterrey, where they introduced the American visitors to President Ávila Camacho and his wife. Monterrey, a state capital and manufacturing center in northern Mexico of some 350,000, gave the presidents a rousing welcome as they drove through the streets in an open car. It had been the site of a bloody Mexican War battle, something neither president mentioned in his speech.

Roosevelt, who began with six words of Spanish, spoke about their common revolutionary heritages—"Hidalgo and Juarez . . . Washington and Jefferson"—and the shedding of blood on "December 7, 1941 and May 14, 1942" "of citizens of the United States and Mexico alike." Often speaking directly to his counterpart, Roosevelt closed by proclaiming, "Let the meetings between the presidents of Mexico and the United States recur again and again and again."

The next day, the two presidents held a joint review of air cadets at Corpus Christi, Texas. which included a group of young Mexican officers being trained for the Mexican air force. Roosevelt went a little over the top in his brief remarks, claiming that the "perfectly magnificent reception" he had received in Mexico "was one of the high points of my life."

In a grim statement announced in Washington as coming from Corpus Christi, the president revealed what the government had known for more than a month, that the Japanese government had executed some of the eight captured airmen who had participated in the Doolittle Raid the previous April. "With a feeling of deepest horror," Roosevelt denounced the action of the Japanese government and promised, again, that the perpetrators would be brought to justice after the war. The reason for the delayed statement was that the details of the Tokyo bombing—including the fact that "Shangri-La" was the aircraft carrier USS *Hornet*—had been released only the day before, the raid's first anniversary. The eight captured airmen were tried by a Japanese military commission in Shanghai and condemned to death. The sentences of five were commuted; the other three were shot. In February 1946, four responsible Japanese officers were tried, convicted, and given prison sentences by an American military commission sitting in Shanghai.

Roosevelt returned to the capital on April 29, having traveled some seventy-six hundred miles, and immediately held a brief press conference largely taken up with reading a telegram that had been sent to John L. Lewis, demanding that he call off an impending work stoppage in the soft coal mines.[25]

The coal settlement forced by the president in December 1941 resulted in a two-year contract that had expired on March 31, 1943. As the date approached, the president had asked that bargaining continue; the parties agreed, extending the contract to April 30. Roosevelt planned his return to the White House for April 29. The dispute had been certified to the War Labor Board, but the union had refused to participate. As had been the case in 1941, Lewis wanted more in wages than the NWLB, bound by the president's stabilization guidelines, was able to give. As a mine shutdown loomed, Roosevelt telegrammed Lewis, warning that "strikes and stoppages in the coal industry . . . are in clear violation of the 'no-strike' pledge. . . . They are strikes against the United States Government itself. These strikes are a direct interference with the prosecution of the war." Then, still in the telegram addressed to Lewis, Roosevelt spoke over Lewis's head to the miners themselves.

> Not as President—not as Commander in Chief—but as the friend of the men who work in the coal mines, I appeal to them to resume work immediately, and submit their case to the National War Labor Board for final determination. . . .
>
> The enemy will not wait while strikes and stoppages run their course. Therefore, if work at the mines is not resumed by ten o'clock Saturday morning [May 1, 1943], I shall use all the power vested in me as Commander in Chief of the Army and Navy to protect the national interest and to prevent further interference with the successful prosecution of the war.

As the 10:00 a.m. deadline passed without a positive response from Lewis, Roosevelt issued an executive order seizing the mines and ordering Secretary Ickes, who was also solid-fuels coordinator, "to take possession of and operate the coal mines for the United States Government." In an accompanying statement, he called upon "all miners who may have abandoned their work to return immediately to the mines and work for their Government." (Although the press, most members of Congress, historians, and sometimes Roosevelt himself referred to coal strikes, in this and most instances there was no strike. Lewis would always insist that the miners "do not work without a contract." This gave him a flexibility in negotiations: since there had been no strike, a work stoppage could be started and stopped by him without a time-consuming ratification process.) The president's statement accompanying the order ended by saying that he would "talk over the radio with the miners of the nation on Sunday at 10 p.m."

Unlike most previous seizures, the army was not directly involved. Ickes, following Roosevelt's instructions, immediately informed mining companies by telegram that they had been seized, instructed them to hoist American flags over their properties, to swear by return telegram, to operate the mine in the interest of the government, and to be prepared for men to come back to work on Monday morning. If the "maintenance of order" was threatened, Ickes instructed mine officials to get in touch with the appropriate regional officials, who would presumably contact the military.

Twenty-two minutes before the president was to go on the air Sunday evening, Lewis, who had spent most of Sunday negotiating with Ickes and Labor Department conciliator John R. Steelman in Washington, announced at a New York hotel that he had just concluded a meeting of the UMW's three-hundred-man negotiating committee that had unanimously approved a fifteen-day temporary agreement with the government while a contract for a new mining agreement was worked out. "The mine workers recognize [Lewis said] that they have a new employer who has not yet had time to face the immediate problems facing the industry. It is our desire to cooperate with the government and to relieve the country from the confusion and stress of the existing situation."

Roosevelt learned of Lewis's statement just as he "was being wheeled from his study" to go downstairs to make the broadcast. He cannot have been surprised by Lewis's getting his acquiescence on the record before he could speak to the people, but he made the speech without mentioning that the coal mining crisis had, for the moment, passed.

The Fireside Chat was unusual in that Roosevelt directed much of it to a select audience: "I am talking tonight to the American people," he began, "and in particular to those of our citizens who are coal miners." The president spoke first of the broader crisis: "This war has reached a critical phase. After the years we have spent in preparation, we have moved into active and continuing battle with our enemies. We are pouring into the world-wide conflict everything that we have—our young men and the vast resources of our nation."

He then spoke of his just-completed trip and the progress in training and production that he had witnessed, observing that the "American people have accomplished a miracle." He insisted that "the United States and the United Nations cannot be stopped by our enemies" and "must not be hampered by any one individual or any one group here back home." Most of the rest of the speech—some three-fifths of it—was about coal mining, coal miners, their families, and their union. As was almost always the case with Roosevelt's major domestic opponents, neither John L. Lewis nor the United Mine Workers was mentioned.

> I want to make it clear that every American coal miner who has stopped mining coal—no matter how sincere his motives, no matter how legitimate he may believe his grievances to be—every idle miner directly and individually is obstructing our war effort. We have not yet won this war. We will win this war only as we produce and deliver our total American effort on the high seas and on the battle fronts. And that requires unrelenting, uninterrupted effort here on the home front.
>
> A stopping of the coal supply, even for a short time, would involve a gamble with the lives of American soldiers and sailors and the future security of our whole people. It would involve an unwarranted, unnecessary, and terribly dangerous gamble with our chances for victory. Therefore, I say to all miners—and to all Americans everywhere, at home and abroad—the production of coal will not be stopped.
>
> Tonight, I am speaking to the essential patriotism of the miners, and to the patriotism of their wives and children.

And he continued to talk directly to miners, even discussing—without using names—individual miners' sons who had been wounded while fighting for their country. After saying, "I know that the American people will not tolerate any threat offered to their government by anyone," the president closed on a positive note: "I believe the coal miners will not continue the strike against their Government. I believe that the coal miners as Americans will not fail to heed the clear call to duty. Like all other good Americans, they will march shoulder to shoulder with their armed forces to victory. Tomorrow the Stars and Stripes will fly over the coal mines, and I hope that every miner will be at work under that flag."[26]

Some miners were back on Monday, and most of the others were back on Tuesday. What had changed? As *New York Times* labor journalist Louis Stark reported, Ickes, with his several sets of powers, could guarantee the miners a six-day week, with the sixth day at a wage of $10.50, making a weekly pay packet of $318.50 as opposed to the $249 for five days. The coal operators could not do that easily, as the price of coal, like everything else, was supposed to be frozen. But Ickes, as solid-fuels administrator, could authorize a price raise based on increased production. Thus, each leader could claim victory: Lewis's men got more money; Roosevelt got more coal.[27] But the gains had both short- and long-range costs. In the short run, as both men soon discovered, a Congress enraged at Lewis's defiance passed restrictive labor legislation and enacted it over Roosevelt's veto. And the long-term decline in the legal position of American labor unions is not unrelated to the animosities heightened during the war years.

On May 9, Roosevelt sent congratulatory messages to General Eisenhower and General Giraud on the conclusion of the campaign in Tunisia, which actually continued for four more days. Axis forces had been driven out of North Africa and more than 275,000 German and Italian troops taken prisoner, most of whom would be sent to POW camps in the United States. This made it imperative that further detailed military plans be made, and Winston Churchill and a large staff were scheduled to arrive in Washington on May 11 for what was known as the Trident Conference.

Partly overlapping Trident, and overshadowed by it, was a United Nations conference on food and agriculture in Hot Springs, Virginia, at a fashionable mountain resort. The conference was attended by delegations from forty-four nations, meeting two years before there was a formal United Nations organization. Roosevelt, in a letter that was read to the delegates by war food administrator Marvin Jones, who chaired the U.S. delegation and was elected president of the conference, shared his vision of the postwar world.

> We know that in the world for which we are fighting and working the four freedoms must be won for all men. We know, too, that each freedom is dependent upon the others; that freedom from fear, for example, cannot be secured without freedom from want. If we are to succeed, each Nation individually, and all Nations collectively, must undertake these responsibilities:
>
> They must take all necessary steps to develop world food production so that it will be adequate to meet the essential nutritional needs of the world population. And they must see to it that no hindrances, whether of international trade, of transportation, or of internal distribution, be allowed to prevent any Nation or group of citizens within a Nation from obtaining the food necessary for health. Society must meet in full its obligation to make available to all its members at least the minimum adequate nutrition. . . .
>
> In this and other United Nations conferences we shall be extending our collaboration from war problems into important new fields. Only by working together can we learn to work together, and work together we must and will.

The conference issued a seven-point declaration on the postwar tasks of the United Nations: to prevent future wars, greatly expand food production all over the world, expand and balance the international economy to provide full employment and abolish poverty, and see that all peoples got the best possible diets. An interim committee was set up to begin planning for a permanent international organization. It is remarkable that in the midst of Trident, devoted to tactical and strategic plans for the prosecution of the war, Roosevelt could focus so precisely on fundamental postwar problems and set the agendas for international bodies that did not yet exist except in his mind.[28]

In the run-up to the Trident Conference, Roosevelt made what the official U.S. Army history calls "one of the most far-reaching decisions of the war." Beginning with a series of White House meetings to prepare for Trident, attended by the president, Hopkins, and the Joint Chiefs of Staff on May 2, 6, and 8, Roosevelt took a position close to one that General Marshall had advocated. He now fully supported an early cross-Channel invasion. By the third meeting, the Americans had decided that their chief objective for Trident would be to get a firm British commitment to a cross-Channel invasion at the earliest feasible date in 1944 and to make full preparations for the operation by the spring of 1944. In case that was not agreed to, they were prepared to propose shifting more resources to the Pacific theaters.

As is often the case, it is not possible to document precisely the evolution of Roosevelt's strategic shifts, but the basic facts are clear. Roosevelt had supported the North African campaign when that was, in essence, the only real choice if there were to be any American troops engaged in fighting Hitler's forces in 1942. Whether he then understood that this might well mean no cross-Channel invasion in 1943 is unclear. Now, with American troops blooded and successful, he threw his weight behind the American staff's insistence that the absolute top priority be given to preparations for a 1944 cross-Channel invasion.

The president sent Harry Hopkins to New York harbor to meet Churchill, who, with his military staff, had crossed the Atlantic aboard the *Queen Mary* with several thousand German and Italian POWs confined belowdecks. Hopkins escorted Churchill and a staff of perhaps a hundred persons on a special train that brought them to Washington on the evening of May 11. They were met by the president and the JCS. The secrecy that had prevailed about such visits and meetings was largely abandoned. Although Roosevelt told a press conference that wartime secrecy applied, some two and a half hours later the White House announced that Churchill and his party had arrived, but did not reveal that they had come by train. The Trident Conference began the next morning; it was the largest assemblage of Anglo-American brass so far in the war.

As in past such conferences, there were two sets of meetings: the Combined Joint Chiefs met with Roosevelt, Churchill, and Hopkins six times in the White House during the fourteen days of the conference, while both sets of chiefs and their staffs met almost continuously in the conference room of the Federal Reserve Board on nearby Constitution Avenue. The White House meetings followed a pattern: the members of each team of Joint Chiefs would state their views in an ongoing debate in which Churchill joined freely, while Roosevelt largely listened, as if considering which argument he preferred. His final weigh-in, which was bound to be decisive, did not differ significantly on the main points from what he had agreed to in earlier meetings with his own advisers.

The major decision at Trident was a firm commitment to a cross-Channel invasion in the spring of 1944 with an initial target date of May 1, 1944, accompanied by corollary decisions to pursue a joint American-British bombing offensive to soften up German defenses, communications, and production. The decision about whether to invade Italy, which the British would have made a primary objective, was left to be decided after Husky, the invasion of Sicily, was successfully completed. Seven divisions of the troops assembled in North Africa were to be transferred to Britain for further training and use in the spring 1944 invasion; the British had wanted to keep these troops in the Mediterranean for other operations there. Decisions made about Asian and Pacific theaters were of little positive moment.

On June 2, after spending a long weekend at Hyde Park recuperating from, essentially, two weeks of Winston, Roosevelt sent a message to Stalin informing him of the Trident decisions. Stalin's reply rehearsed previous Anglo-American promises about a second front, concluding, "Now, in May 1943 you and Mr. Churchill made the decision postponing the British American invasion of Western Europe until spring of 1944. That is the opening of the second front in Europe which was postponed already from 1942 to 1943, is being postponed again, this time until spring 1944. This decision creates exceptional difficulties for the Soviet Union."[29]

Churchill's two weeks in the White House had, as usual, disrupted normal routines. He liked to talk, and work, and drink, into the wee hours of the morning and take long naps in the middle of the day. Roosevelt, who normally went to bed before midnight, was kept up long past midnight to share the talk, but he drank very little after dinner—an occasional scotch and soda but more often a nonalcohol "horse's neck."

During the conference, Churchill made a broadcast to Britain on the third anniversary of the establishment of its Home Guard, offering the initial firsthand report of what was being discussed at Trident. Later, in a fifty-minute oration ranging over the whole history of the war, he told a joint session of Congress what it wanted to hear: after endorsing the Germany-first strategy, which many in Congress opposed, he spoke of the "necessary and desirable" duty "of laying the cities and other munitions centers of Japan in ashes." Before departing for home—where no vote of confidence awaited him—he deftly fielded questions at Roosevelt's press conference for forty minutes. As Trident came to an end, Roosevelt issued a meaningless but requisite announcement: the staffs had reached "complete agreement on future operations in all theaters of the world."[30]

Two of the often unremarked differences between the wartime roles of Roosevelt and Churchill are that Churchill, as prime minister and minister of defense, largely left it to others in his coalition government to handle domestic policy matters. Roosevelt had to deal with such matters continuously and also had to be concerned with electoral politics. Churchill, while he had to manage Parliament, did not have to worry about elections. There was no general election in Britain between November 1935 and July 1945, while in the United States the election schedule went on without interruption. In addition, as head of state, Roosevelt continued to have ceremonial duties hosting foreign dignitaries. The continuing management of the wartime economy plus planning for the postwar world were among his most important concerns. But with war production beginning to meet its goals, Roosevelt was ready to pass off more of his responsibilities.

On May 14, in the midst of the Trident Conference, Jimmy Byrnes, concerned that his job as head of the Office of Economic Stabilization (OES)—which he was handling well—did not offer him enough scope for his talents and ambitions, sent a letter of resignation down the hall to the president. He claimed that Roosevelt was being hurt politically by having someone "so closely associated with you" making unpopular decisions about wages and prices and argued that he could be doing more important things, even though he was managing to get involved in a lot of matters. Over trays in the Oval Office, Roosevelt and Byrnes reached an agreement that an enlarged role would be created for Byrnes, who worked out an executive order with budget director Smith that was issued on May 27.

It created the Office of War Mobilization (OWM) and made its director (Byrnes) the chairman of a new committee consisting of the secretaries of war and navy, the chairman of the Munitions Assignments Board, the chairman of the War Production Board, and the director of economic stabilization.

The three functions of the OWM, "subject to the direction and control of the president," were specified as:

(a) To develop unified programs and establish policies for the maximum use of the Nation's natural and industrial resources for military and civilian needs. . . .

(b) To unify the activities of Federal agencies and departments engaged in or concerned with [war and civilian production, procurement and distribution] and to resolve and determine controversies between such agencies or departments, except those to be resolved by the Director of Economic Stabilization

(c) To issue such directives on policy or operations to the federal agencies as may be necessary to carry out the programs developed, the policies established, and decisions made under this order.

Roosevelt's announcement that he had created the OWM "to unify more clearly the work of the war agencies . . . under the direction of Justice James F. Byrnes" made it sound like just another supervisory agency. *New York Times* White House correspondent Bill Lawrence was closer to the mark, writing that Byrnes's new powers "exceeded those previously given to Donald M. Nelson . . . or those given to Bernard M. Baruch in the First World War." Unlike many of his colleagues, Lawrence understood that the other five members of what the

Times headline writer called a "6-Man Board" had advisory powers only and that direction came from Byrnes.

Like other Washington journalists, Lawrence had gotten into the habit of designating various administrators of this and that—Czar Nelson of production, Czar Ickes of fuel, Czar Jeffers of rubber, and so forth—so now he had to describe the president as having "subordinated to Mr. Byrnes all the other 'czars.'" Byrnes did have a lot of power—including the power to act when Roosevelt was away—but to talk of multiple czars, or "Super-Czar," as the *Times*' subhead had it, deprives the term of real meaning. Real czars had no fellows and were known by their first names: if there were a czar in World War II Washington, it was Czar Franklin.

To replace Byrnes as OES director, Roosevelt named Fred M. Vinson (1890–1953), a seven-term Kentucky congressman and a key figure in tax policy until Roosevelt appointed him to the Circuit Court of Appeals for D.C. in 1937. Vinson, like Byrnes, gave up a tenured judgeship to serve Roosevelt. Vinson got Byrnes's title but not his office. Byrnes, who wanted not only power but all its trappings, kept his office in the East Wing; Vinson, and the OES, was shunted to the Federal Reserve Building. Byrnes also had the White House announce that he would give a major address from his hometown Spartanburg, South Carolina.[31]

Although Byrnes's letter to Roosevelt resigning the OES job had insisted that "I have no political ambitions," and in his memoir he would claim that only in June 1944 did he find himself thinking "seriously" about the vice presidency, it is clear that his speech was the opening gun in his campaign to become president. That speech, "America Mobilizes for Victory," broadcast nationally, was Byrnes's attempt to establish himself as an authority not only on the home front but about the battlefronts as well. The topic was truly presidential and his account of mobilization convincing, but his discussion of military matters was lame.

In June 1943, Byrnes's game plan called for him to supplant Wallace on the ticket in 1944 and win the presidential nomination in 1948 when Roosevelt, having won the war, would surely not run again. There was no particular reason in 1943 to be concerned about the president's health—Byrnes was barely three months younger—but those hoping for the office do follow the old vice presidential precept and inquire regularly after the health of the president. On his record as an effective administrator—and he would add to it in the OWM post—Byrnes was by far the ablest of the putative candidates. But there were two impediments to his candidacy, each possibly fatal, but in tandem surely so. Born and baptized a Catholic, he converted to a Protestant denomination with his marriage, and, although not one who constantly played the race card, he was an implacable foe of full citizenship for black Americans and an opponent of any meaningful change in the color bar in the South. While still in the Senate in 1938, he had filibustered against the antilynching measure. Somewhat less strident segregationist views had not kept Garner off the ticket in 1932 and 1936, but by 1944 black votes in many northern cities made them a crucial element in the Roosevelt coalition that could not safely be ignored.[32]

The well-publicized executive order that gave more power to Byrnes, who had already been dubbed "assistant president"—a term the president never sanctioned—was one of two executive orders issued on May 27. The other reestablished and strengthened the Fair Employment Practices Committee, originally set up in June 1941. Yet in the long sweep of American history, the FEPC order is the more important of the two, the modest beginning of the first effective federal action against race discrimination since Reconstruction. Had Byrnes been wise as well as smart, he could have become the patron of what was an orphan agency and perhaps nullified or minimized much of the opposition to him, but it clearly never occurred to him until it was too late that anything as inconsequential as the opinions of black voters could have any effect on his presidential ambitions. He persistently refused to have anything to do with the FEPC. As his biographer points out, when anything concerning it reached his East Wing office, he redirected it to Jonathan Daniels (1902–81), by 1943 the presidential assistant to whom racial matters were assigned.

The first FEPC had come about in the wake of the September 27, 1940, meeting of African American leaders with Roosevelt and his military advisers in which some concessions were gained and promises made about the place of black Americans in the nation's armed forces. The most militant and effective of those leaders, A. Philip Randolph, began to talk about and then to organize a black march on Washington to demand jobs and at least the trappings of equality. Using locals of his union of sleeping car porters as a base, he organized chapters of a March on Washington Movement (MOWM) across the nation. By spring he was writing the president of his plans and inviting him and other officials to address the march at its goal, the Lincoln Memorial, on Tuesday, July 1, 1941.

Alarmed lest the marchers be attacked by angry whites and about the effect such a march would have on Congress, the president summoned NYA chief Aubrey Williams to the Oval Office and dispatched him to New York to organize a meeting on June 13 with Randolph, Eleanor Roosevelt, Anna Rosenberg, and Mayor La Guardia at city hall to persuade Randolph to call off the march. He refused. Rosenberg phoned Pa Watson, saying that she, Eleanor, and the mayor all agreed that only a meeting with the president could stop the march. Finally, Roosevelt invited Randolph to the White House to discuss it on the afternoon of June 18, 1941, just thirteen days before the march was scheduled. Randolph brought with him the National Association for the Advancement of Colored People's (NAACP) Walter White, one of the staunchest supporters of the MOWM, and two other black labor leaders, Virgin Islander Frank R.

Crosswaith (1892–1965) and the most prominent black woman in the American labor movement, Layle Lane (1893–1976), a vice president of the American Federation of Teachers. Roosevelt called in an array of government officials, including Knox, Stimson and his deputy Patterson, the Knudsen-Hillman law firm from the OPM, La Guardia, and others.

Unfortunately, we have no tape recording or other record of the 1941 meeting and must rely chiefly on the memories of the two leading black participants, Randolph and White. The most artful reconstruction, by Doris Kearns Goodwin, depicts Randolph in full charge, cutting off a Roosevelt monologue with:

Mr. President, time is running out. You are quite busy, I know. But what we want to talk to you about is the problem of jobs for Negroes in defense industries.

Well, Phil, what do you want me to do.

Mr. President, we want you to issue an Executive Order making it mandatory that Negroes be permitted to work in these plants.

Well, Phil, you know I can't do that. [Then, after further negative comments conceding] In any event I couldn't do anything unless you called off this march of yours. [Followed by more negatives.]

I'm sorry, Mr. President, the march cannot be called off.

How many people do you plan to bring?

One hundred thousand, Mr. President.

At this point, according to Walter White's memoir, Roosevelt turned toward the NAACP leader and asked him how many would "really march." White, who makes this moment the key to the meeting, repeated Randolph's figure. Roosevelt then, as he often did to end such meetings, told them to go to the cabinet room and work out the details. Although nothing was decided that day, it seems apparent that both Roosevelt and Randolph came to the meeting prepared to compromise, and that is what happened.

The next morning, Joseph L. Rauh Jr. (1911–92), who was counsel to Harry Hopkins's Lend-Lease organization, got a hurry-up call to report to the White House, where he was told to draft an executive order doing what Randolph demanded. The MOWM leader found more than one of Rauh's drafts unacceptable, but signed off on the final version, telling Eleanor Roosevelt in a phone call to Campobello that it was "just great." The president signed and issued it on June 25, 1941, and then Randolph made a series of calls to the more important figures of his MOWM, all but two of whom endorsed his decision to cancel the march.[33]

The very brief order announced that "it is the policy of the United States to encourage full participation in the national defense program by all citizens of the United States, regardless of race, creed, color, or national origin [and given that needed workers had been denied employment in defense industries] solely because of consideration of race, creed, color, or national origin [that it was] the duty of employers and of labor organizations . . . to provide for the full and equitable participation of all workers in defense industries, without discrimination because of race, creed, color, or national origin."

There followed three specific orders. The first mandated that government employment and training programs comply with the nondiscrimination policy, the second provided that all future defense contracts have nondiscrimination provisions, and the third created within the OPM the Committee on Fair Employment Practice, initially with a chairman and four others who were presidential appointees without pay. The committee had the authority to investigate, and to recommend actions to others, but no authority to act or even to subpoena persons or documents; it was given a small paid staff.

In 1941 the nation's major newspapers largely ignored both Randolph's MOWM and the FEPC. Randolph complained that "the white press maintained a dreadful conspiracy of silence"—he made an exception for Marshall Field's New York tabloid *PM*. A computerized search of the *New York Times* via the ProQuest search engine failed to find a single mention of the march during 1941, and the White House meeting that canceled it was noted only in a routine listing of the president's appointments. The paper did print a brief page 1 story about the committee's creation, and probably as a result of Early's guidance the *Times* limited its analysis to a passive-voice assertion that the order had been issued "principally because the government's attention had been called to cases of discrimination against Negroes in some defense industries and labor unions."

On the other hand, the black press, which had covered the plans for the proposed march, went over the moon at the signing of the executive order, often likening it to a latter-day Emancipation Proclamation. But the efforts of the first FEPC were limited. Probably most effective was its focus on discrimination within the federal government. At the end of August, the committee met with the president for the first time and presented him with its report, done in collaboration with the federal Council of Personnel Administrators, documenting the continuing discrimination within the federal government. In early September, Roosevelt released a letter he had sent to all department heads that month insisting on "immediate steps" to implement the nondiscrimination policy and promising his ongoing interest.

In the months after Pearl Harbor, the president did not pay much attention to either racial discrimination or the FEPC. By June 1942, disappointed by what he saw as a lack of progress, Randolph spoke publicly—and got press coverage—about a new campaign and march, but that came to naught.

On July 30, 1942, Roosevelt approved the request of Paul McNutt that the FEPC be transferred to his War Manpower Commission, which had a certain administrative logic. It is not clear that Roosevelt intended this to be a diminution of the committee's effectiveness, but it was so seen by most of the committee and some of its supporters, and public protests resulted. Roosevelt responded that he had read the criticisms about the transfer of the FEPC and "regretted that the reasons for it had been so widely misunderstood." "It is the intention to strengthen—not to submerge—the committee, and to reinvigorate—not to repeal—Executive Order 8802. At the same time, as the President said in his letter of transfer . . . 'the committee shall be preserved as an organizational entity.' It will carry on its receipt, investigation, and redress of complaints of discrimination in employment in war industries, and in the departments of the federal government. . . . ' Moreover the committee will continue to refer to the President all matters which, in its judgment, require his decision." The committee's relationship with McNutt and the WMC remained uncomfortable. Its budget was reduced, but it was still able to plan and conduct hearings, which were a principal means of gathering information.[34]

A final crisis in that relationship began in early January 1943 when McNutt asked that the committee cancel its already scheduled hearings into the employment practices of railroads, set for the end of the month. The committee members denied the request, and on Monday, January 11, McNutt announced that he had canceled the hearings. He gave reporters to understand that the administration was considering a new approach to the problem of discrimination against Negroes and minorities. As it happened, Roosevelt had left for Casablanca late on January 8, but under the wartime secrecy rules his absence was not revealed for seventeen days. McNutt may have been aware of his absence, but whether Roosevelt had any knowledge of what McNutt was going to do is unknown. Thus, during January almost everyone concerned had to assume that McNutt's action had at least the passive approval of the president, and most scholars treating the FEPC have shared that assumption.

When Roosevelt returned to the White House on February 2, he found the resignation of the FEPC chairman in his in-basket, and he immediately began damage control. In a public statement released the next day, he addressed both short- and long-term aspects of the FEPC crisis. He promised that, after a strengthening of the committee, "the hearings in the railroad case and in any other cases which may have been temporarily postponed will be continued." As for the future of the FEPC, it was explained that Roosevelt had directed McNutt to call a conference to consider revising and strengthening the powers of the FEPC and that McNutt and the committee would meet to plan the conference the following Monday. He said that the FEPC "and its executive director have done an excellent piece of work" but "have been handicapped by the fact that the members of the committee" were part-time volunteers without the power or personnel "commensurate with their responsibilities."

That was undoubtedly the case, but those were the conditions the president had insisted on some twenty months before. What had changed? By early 1943, an increasingly broad constituency for positive change in race relations was evolving, and at the same time interracial conflicts in northern and western cities and war plants were on the rise. What had seemed a bold forward step in mid-1941 was now palpably inadequate.

The meeting of officials that Roosevelt had ordered resulted in a conference of some two dozen activists, including Randolph and White, with government officials on February 19. It recommended a larger, better-financed, and more powerful FEPC. It took three months for meaningful action to occur. On May 19, Monsignor Francis J. Haas (1889–1953), dean of Catholic University's School of Social Science and a longtime mediator for the Department of Labor, told reporters on leaving a White House meeting with Roosevelt that although "much opposed," he had accepted appointment as FEPC chairman since "we [are] in war."

Finally, on May 27, a new executive order removed the FEPC from McNutt's control and gave it greater prestige by slotting it into the catchall OEM in the president's EOP. Its chairman received the ten-thousand-dollar salary that was tops for those who worked directly for the president, while the other members remained volunteers receiving only per diem. The staff was increased significantly, and more funds were made available to it. In a direct slap at McNutt, the order provided that the committee "shall also recommend to the Chairman of the War Manpower Commission" measures to improve its training programs and to "conduct such measures and hearings as may be necessary." But without the statutory powers that Congress was unwilling to grant, its orders lacked teeth and it had no authority over nonwar production or in the service sector where many black workers were employed. Black employment in wartime in the higher-paying manufacturing sector was certainly increased by the committee's efforts, and it generated increasing support for the FEPC.

During the 1944 election campaign, not only did Roosevelt endorse making the FEPC permanent in his speech at Chicago's Soldier Field, but the Republican Party platform had done the same thing previously. Those historians—and they are legion—who insist that New Deal–type reform died in 1937–38 and that Roosevelt did not advance Negro rights significantly have either belittled or ignored the FEPC. Without in any way diminishing the courage and vision of A. Philip Randolph and other black pioneers, it was Roosevelt who inserted into the national consensus the concept that the responsibility of government was not only to provide an equal administration of justice but also to prevent discrimination.[35]

Defense- and war-related migration drew millions of white and black workers to urban centers of war production like Los Angeles and Detroit, where they competed for housing and control of urban spaces. Not surprisingly, these conflicts erupted into violence on many occasions, continuing a long and disgraceful history of race riots. Although the White House was not often directly involved with concerns about what was happening, fears about what might happen along the troubled racial frontiers of urban America can never have been far from Roosevelt's mind and alternatively spurred and inhibited his inclination to bring about racial accommodation.

In 1943 the most conspicuous flash points were in Los Angeles, Detroit, and New York. In Los Angeles early in June, a kind of serial pogrom against Mexican American young men—misnamed by the press the "Zoot Suit Riots"—in central and East Los Angeles by gangs of servicemen on leave was abetted by the city police and sheriff's departments that often arrested the victims and said, falsely, that the servicemen had to be left to the military police who were not initially deployed in significant numbers. The local press responded with headlines—and stories to match—demonizing the young Mexican Americans: "44 Zooters Jailed in Attacks on Sailors," "Zoot Suit Chiefs Girding for War on Navy," "Zoot Suiters Learn Lesson in Fight with Servicemen." Only after several days of rioting—no deaths were reported—did military authorities led by the navy declare much of Los Angeles off-limits. Although the rioting received national press coverage, none of it landed on the front page of the *New York Times,* and the president took no public notice, even after CIO president Philip Murray publicly asked him to do so.

Roosevelt could not avoid involvement in the twenty-four-hour bloody race riot that broke out in Detroit on Sunday evening, June 20. Amid a great deal of ineptitude and indecision by state and federal officials in the region well into Monday, the governor of Michigan appealed to the White House for assistance. Roosevelt, at Hyde Park, worked out over the telephone with the Pentagon the terms of a proclamation that, without invoking martial law, sent six thousand federal troops and armored cars into the city Monday evening, and shortly thereafter the rioting ceased.

The riot had occurred largely in a black neighborhood, Paradise Valley, where, before the army arrived, thirty-four persons had been killed—twenty-five blacks and nine whites—and some seven hundred injured. The Detroit police killed most of the blacks, many of them for allegedly looting stores in Paradise Valley.

A riot in New York's Harlem that began on August 1—another Sunday night—was contained by the New York Police Department (NYPD) without calling for either state or federal troops. It, too, lasted about twenty-four hours. Six persons, all black, were killed and perhaps two hundred wounded. Unlike the situation in Detroit, where almost all commentators agree that police and public officials were negligent or worse, there is general agreement that the preparation and efforts of Mayor La Guardia and the NYPD contained the riot and limited its effects.

Although Roosevelt was urged, before, during, and after these riots, by persons inside and outside of the government, to make a public response to them, he never said or issued a public word, apart from his Detroit proclamation, about race riots.

Roosevelt was never asked a single question about race riots in his press conferences. Given the lily-white attendees in the Oval Office, operating under the eye of Steve Early, that is not surprising. Some insight into Roosevelt's views can be gained from the precedent-breaking special press conference held for some fifteen members of the Negro Newspaper Publishers Association the following winter. After an exchange of pleasantries, the president heard a prepared statement of the group's views declaring that the "second class citizenship now imposed on . . . Negro Americans violates the principles of the Declaration of Independence and the Constitution. . . . We maintain that the Federal Government should begin now to use its authority to end abridgment of the Negro's citizenship."

Specific objectives included equal opportunity in employment and education, unrestricted suffrage, all civil rights and liberties established by law, government should not impose or sanction segregation, and the Atlantic Charter applied to all colonial and exploited peoples.

THE PRESIDENT: I think it's an awfully good statement.

Roosevelt then listened to a detailed complaint about mistreatment of Negroes in the military, a matter, he was told, that "is causing the colored people lots of concern."

THE PRESIDENT: I am glad you brought that up because I have been in touch with it. It is perfectly true, there is definite discrimination in the actual treatment of the colored engineer troops, and others. And you are up against—you know perfectly well—I have talked about it—I had the Secretary of War and the Assistant—I had everybody in on it. The trouble lies fundamentally in the attitude of certain white people—officers down the line—

MR. IRA LEWIS [PITTSBURGH COURIER]: (Interjecting) That's right.

THE PRESIDENT: (Continuing)—who haven't got very much more education, many of them, than the colored troops and the Seabees and the engineers, for example. And they—well you know—you know the kind of person it is. We all do. We don't have to do more than think of a great many people we know. And it has become not a question of orders—they are repeated fairly often, I think, in the camps of colored troops—it's a question of the personality of the individual. And we are up against it, absolutely up against it. I always think of the fact that it probably is improving. I like to think that mere association helps things along.

One of the publishers might well have asked, "Mr. President, it is all very well to say that to us—and we agree—but why don't you say it to the American people?" But none did. Instead, after the president told some stories, the conference ended with three voicings of "Thank you, Mr. President" and a presidential "Good-bye."[36]

*   *   *

At the end of June, the president vetoed the Smith-Connally bill (the War Labor Disputes Bill), which Congress had passed overwhelmingly. His veto message insisted that the bill would make its stated purpose—the prevention of strikes in wartime—more difficult. Stating, "I am unalterably opposed to strikes in wartime," he added that it was "the will of the American people" that in wartime labor disputes should be settled by "regular procedures" and that "no war work be interrupted by strike or lockout." He praised the "no strike, no lockout" pledge that he said had been well kept, "except in the case of the leaders of the United Mine Workers." He noted that during 1942, "only 5/100 of 1 percent" of total man-hours had been lost due to strikes. The president praised the first seven sections of the bill, which largely made many of executive actions in the labor field statutory. But two sections of the bill, he said, "foment slow-downs and strikes." Section 8, which introduced the "cooling-off" concept into national labor legislation, he argued, ignored the no-strike pledge and "would stimulate labor unrest and give Government sanction to strike agitations."

Section 9, which barred political contributions by labor organizations, was, according to Roosevelt, irrelevant to the bill's purpose. Of course, as everyone knew, it was relevant to the next presidential election. His analysis done, he said what he would do and recommend. "I intend to use the powers of government to prevent the interruption of war production by strikes." He then recommended a cure for which there was not yet a disease: amending the Selective Service Act "so that persons may be inducted into non-combat military service up to the age of 65 years." This would be meted out to "all persons who engage in strikes or stoppages or other interruptions of work in plants in possession of the United States." That had not yet occurred and did not occur.

Congress overrode the veto the next day by a comfortable 249–108 in the House and a narrower 56–25 in the Senate. Philip Murray blamed the Democratic absentees in the Senate, which included Majority Leader Barkley, for the successful override, and that may have been the case. It is more likely that some of the absent and not-paired Democrats did not wish to oppose the president or their constituents. In was only the eighth overriding of a Roosevelt veto in more than ten years. The defeat was significant as an indicator of increasing congressional impatience with organized labor in general and John L. Lewis in particular.

More significant in the short run was Roosevelt's continuing ability to keep Congress in check during the repeated struggles with the farm bloc and its allies in his efforts to control inflation. The 1943 battle involved what should have been a routine reauthorization of the Commodity Credit Corporation, but

Congress had prohibited using its funds to conduct sales of stored food crops at a loss to keep prices down. Roosevelt's veto was sustained, and the subsequent reauthorization was by immediate joint resolution, as Roosevelt had suggested in his veto message.[37]

At a state dinner for General Giraud in Washington on July 9, Roosevelt had the kind of opportunity to surprise his audience that he relished. "I have just had word," he began, "of the first attack on the soft under-belly of Europe."

> I am going to ask you not to say anything about it after you leave here, until midnight ends.
> American and British forces and some French observers, have attacked and landed in Sicily. The operations have just begun, and we won't get definite news until later in the day but the news will be coming on from now on.
> There are a great many objectives, and of course the major objective is the elimination of Germany—that goes without saying—the eliminating of Germany out of the war. And as a result of this step which is in progress at this moment, we hope it is the beginning of the end.

The next day, he sent a message to the pope, assuring him that "the neutral status of Vatican City as well as the papal domains throughout Italy will be respected."

Six days later, he and Churchill broadcast a joint message to the Italian people and had it printed on millions of leaflets that were dropped by American bombers all across Italy. Its message was for Italy to leave the war.

> The sole hope for Italy's survival lies in honorable capitulation to the overwhelming forces of the United Nations.
> If you continue to tolerate the Fascist regime which serves the evil power of the Nazis, you must suffer the consequences of your own choice.
> The time has come for you, the Italian people, to consult your own self-respect and your own interests and your own desire for a restoration of national dignity, security, and peace. The time has come for you to decide whether Italians shall die for Mussolini and Hitler—or live for Italy, and for civilization.

Three days later, some of the same planes dropped bombs on Rome's railroad marshaling yards in an attempt to inhibit the southward movement of German arms and equipment. This raised the whole question of possible damage to the Vatican and of making Rome an "open city."[38]

In domestic matters, an exasperated Roosevelt had to deal with an internal quarrel too big for the so-called assistant president to deal with. Unlike earlier disputes between dedicated New Dealers like Ickes and Hopkins, who, despite their battles over turf and style, agreed on most of the basic issues, the difficulties between Vice President Henry Wallace and RFC boss and Secretary of Commerce Jesse Jones were between men of vastly different temperaments and beliefs. It was Wallace's role as chairman of the Board of Economic Warfare that created the most explosive conflict between the two.

A long-smoldering feud between Wallace and Jones burst into flame in late June 1943 when Wallace publicly accused Jones of having failed, in the months before Pearl Harbor, to amass an adequate stockpile of vital materials and that after the BEW was created he had "thrown a great many obstacles in the way" of obtaining materials necessary for the war effort. Jones responded that Wallace's charges were "filled with malice and misstatements."

The president brought what Hassett called a "vendetta" to a sudden halt with a veritable thunderbolt, considering the extraordinary reluctance he had shown throughout his presidency to silence anyone. Frequently, those out of favor were given face-saving roles. Without apparently any warning to either man, he sent and had Steve Early release a curt letter to each, addressed "Gentlemen," that began:

> I have come to the conclusion that the unfortunate controversy and acrimonious public debate which has been carried out between you in the public press concerning the administration of foreign economic matters make it necessary in the public interest to transfer these matters to other hands.
>
> In the midst of a war so critical to our national security and to the future of all civilization there is insufficient time to investigate and determine where the truth lies in your conflicting versions as to transactions that took place over a year and a half ago.
>
> My action today in not intended to decide that question. The important thing is to clear the decks and get on with the war at once. To do this requires a fresh start with new men, unencumbered with interagency dissension and bitterness.
>
> I am persuaded that the present controversy indicates that future cooperative action between your two agencies is impossible, and that without full cooperation between you the program of economic warfare cannot be carried out.

The president issued an executive order on the subject as well as a separate letter to all department and agency heads with which he enclosed a copy of his letter of August 21, 1942, stipulating that "disagreements as to either fact or policy should not be publicly aired but are to be submitted to me." The 1943 letter went on to add, "I cannot overlook any further violations of my Instructions [but if] when you have a disagreement with another agency [that] you feel you should [release] to the press, I ask that when you release the statement for publication, you send me a letter of resignation. If any subordinate of yours violates my instructions in this regard, I shall expect you to ask for his immediate resignation."

Apparently, no such resignation ever took place, but the president's words were designed to get the attention of administrators. Apart from these statements, the president refused to comment on the Wallace-Jones conflict when asked in press conferences before and after the statements, though he did admit that Wallace's charges surprised him.

The accompanying executive order "terminated" the Board of Economic Warfare and put in its place the Office of Economic Warfare with similar powers and funding, headed by a director to be appointed by the president. Three corporations and the Export-Import Bank of Washington and their "functions, powers, and duties, together with the functions, powers, and duties of the Reconstruction Finance Corporation and of the Secretary of Commerce with respect to them," were transferred to the OEW. In addition, the order provided that until Congress furnished other means of financing, "the Secretary of Commerce and the Reconstruction Finance Corporation are authorized and directed to supply necessary funds" to the transferred corporations, "using for this purpose all the borrowing powers and unobligated funds" of the RFC. "Such funds shall be supplied" at "times" and in "amounts," "manner," and on "terms and conditions . . . as the Director of War Mobilization . . . may from time to time determine." These and other provisions gave Jimmy Byrnes supervisory power over all the activities of the new agency, as well as control of the finances and financing powers of Jesse Jones's RFC. He was given authority to "utilize the facilities of other departments and agencies, including the machinery for the coordination of foreign economic affairs established in the Department of State."

If Byrnes was the big winner in the controversy he could not quell, Wallace was the big loser, as the episode removed him from any active role in the operation of the government apart from his constitutionally mandated duties to preside over the Senate. It surely helped to keep him off the national ticket in 1944. Jones lost some authority and had his feelings hurt, but saw his enemy badly damaged.[39]

On Sunday, July 25, as Rosenman and Sherwood were working with Roosevelt at Shangri-La, putting the final touches on a Fireside Chat scheduled for Tuesday, a phone call from the White House told them of a broadcast announcement from Rome that Mussolini had resigned. (Actually, a vote of the Fascist Grand Council ousted him, and the Italian king, Victor Emmanuel III [1861–1947], had named as premier Marshal Pietro Badoglio [1871–1956], whom Mussolini had fired as chief of staff after the Italian army's debacle in Greece.) Although Roosevelt and his writers could not get any immediate confirmation or details, they penciled in a paragraph to be revised later.

As matters turned out, the Allies did not have a plan in place to get troops into central Italy or the initiative to try to improvise one. The German high command reacted quickly by rushing troops there and treating Italy as an occupied country and began committing atrocities on the general population and rounding up Jews for extermination.

When Roosevelt delivered the Fireside Chat, he had no clear idea of what, exactly, had happened in Rome, except that Mussolini was out of power. He began by reminding listeners that he had predicted victory and that now, "the first crack in the Axis has come. The criminal corrupt Fascist regime in Italy is going to pieces. . . . Mussolini came to the reluctant conclusion that 'the jig was up'; he could see the shadow of the long arm of justice. But he and his Fascist gang will be brought to book, and punished for their crimes against humanity. No criminal will be allowed to escape by the expedient of 'resignation.' So our terms to Italy are still the same as our terms to Germany and Japan—'unconditional surrender.'"

The speech also had a special, unstated subtext. Earlier in the year, as noted, Congress had refused to provide funds for the continuance of the National Resources Planning Board despite Roosevelt's requests. The very word *planning* conjured up for many members of Congress, whom Keynes would describe as "badly brought up," visions of socialism, fuzzy-minded professors, regimentation, and unnecessary taxation, none of which they wanted any part of. The president never mentioned the NRPB in his chat, but the words *plan, plans,* or *planning* occurred fifteen times, referring to both already demonstrated military successes and as-yet-unconsummated postwar plans.

> It is a little over a year since we planned the North African campaign. It is six months since we planned the Sicilian campaign. I confess that I am of an impatient disposition, but I think that I understand and that most people understand the amount of time necessary to prepare for any major military or naval operation. We cannot just pick up the telephone and order a new campaign to start the next week.
>
> The same kind of careful planning that gained victory in North Africa and Sicily is required, if we are to make victory an enduring reality and do our share in building the kind of peaceful world that will justify the sacrifices made in this war.
>
> The United Nations are substantially agreed on the general objectives for the postwar world. They are also agreed that this is not the time to engage in an international discussion of all the terms of peace and all the details of the future. Let us win the war first.

Roosevelt was willing to be quite specific about the kinds of things he was planning to do for returning veterans after the war. "Among many other things we are, today, laying plans for the return to civilian life of our gallant men and women in the armed services. They must not be demobilized into an environment of inflation and unemployment, to a place on a bread line, or on a corner selling apples. We must, this time, have plans ready—instead of waiting to do a hasty, inefficient, and ill-considered job at the last moment."

The president spoke of the need to plan for all Americans in the postwar era and argued what few would deny that members of the armed forces should have special consideration. "The least to which they are entitled" included enough mustering-out pay to cover a reasonable period of time before getting a job, unemployment pay for those who could not find a job, an opportunity for further education or trade training at government expense, Social Security credit for time spent in the armed forces, improved and liberalized provisions for hospitalization and medical care, and sufficient pensions for disabled veterans. And there was, he assured them, more to come: "Within a few weeks I shall speak with you again in regard to definite actions to be taken by the executive branch of the Government, and specific recommendations for new legislation by the Congress."

Although the president did not attempt to say how long the war would last, he did caution that predictions of its ending in 1943 were too optimistic and that those saying that it would be going on in 1949 were too pessimistic. He closed with the following:

> We still have to defeat Hitler and Tojo on their own home grounds. But this will require a far greater concentration of our national energy and our ingenuity and our skill.
>
> It is not too much to say that we must pour into this war the entire strength and intelligence and will power of the United States. We are a great Nation—a rich Nation—but we are not so great or so rich that we can afford to waste our substance or the lives of our men by relaxing along the way.
>
> We shall not settle for less than total victory. That is the determination of every American on the fighting fronts. That must be, and will be, the determination of every American here at home.[40]

At his press conference two days after the chat, Roosevelt began a strategic withdrawal from the notion of unconditional surrender for the special situation that seemed to be developing in Italy:

> THE PRESIDENT: There are rumors that Mussolini and members of his Fascist gang may attempt to take refuge in neutral territory. One day Hitler and his gang and Tojo and his gang will be trying to escape from their countries. I find it difficult to believe that any neutral country would give asylum to or extend protection to any of them. I can only say that the Government of the United States would regard the action by a neutral Government in affording asylum to Axis leaders or their tools as inconsistent with the principles for which the United Nations are fighting and

that the United States Government hopes that no neutral Government will permit its territory to be used as a place of refuge or otherwise assist such persons in any effort to escape their just deserts.

After Roosevelt finished what was essentially a long monologue, the third question was as follows:

Q: Mr. President, there has been some discussion as to whether we ought to deal with the Badoglio Government, or with the King, and so forth; and I wonder whether you might think it useful to clarify the point?

THE PRESIDENT: Steve said you would ask that question. (Laughter) I said to him it reminds me a good deal of the old argument—I could go on and have an argument about that—as to which came first, the chicken or the egg. When a victorious army goes into a country, there are two things— two essential things that they want to meet, in the first instance. The first is the end of armed opposition. The second is—when that armed opposition comes to an end—to avoid anarchy. In a country that goes into a state of anarchy, it is a pretty difficult thing to deal with, because it takes an awful lot—it would take an awful lot of our troops.

I don't care who we deal with in Italy, so long as it isn't a definite member of the Fascist government, so long as they get them to lay down their arms, and so long as we don't have anarchy. Now his name may be a King, or a present Prime Minister, or a mayor of a town, or a village. You will also remember that in the—I think it was the Atlantic Charter, something was said about self-determination. That is a long-range thing. You can't get self-determination in the first week after they lay down their arms. In other words, common sense. And I don't think that any controversy is either called for or advisable. . . . .

Q: Mr. President, you wouldn't consider General Badoglio as the Fascist, then?

THE PRESIDENT: I am not discussing personalities. It was only a columnist who went on the air the other night who did that. Gave his own opinion.

Q: Thank you, Mr. President.

Thus, without explicitly saying so, Roosevelt was backing away from the unconditional-surrender formula in the Italian situation; in effect, the military was in charge. The papers that morning were filled with General Eisenhower's message to the Italian people, which was signed, imperially, "Eisenhower." The *New York Times* headlined "Eisenhower Offers Italy Peace Terms."

That such a change was coming had seemed clear for some days. The comment about the columnist at the end of the press conference referred to a high-minded writer for the liberal *New York Post*, Samuel Grafton (1907–87), who, in an OWI broadcast beamed overseas, had attacked government policy, insisting that fascism remained in power in Italy and had only "put on a new face." He went on the attack: "The moronic little king who has stood behind Mussolini's shoulder for twenty-one years has moved forward one pace. This is a political minuet and not the revolution we have been waiting for."

Grafton spoke for many American liberals, normally the president's supporters, who saw this, like the long recognition of Vichy, the use of Darlan in North Africa, and the refusal to have much to do with de Gaulle, as a watering down of America's professed liberal war aims. Many of them also feared the influence of Churchill, who would have been happy to restore kings to their thrones and perhaps some pretenders along with them, as opposed to the social democracy that most American liberals preferred.[41]

10 Waiting for D-Day
1943–44

IN MID-AUGUST 1943, WITH ALLIED TROOPS still fighting in Sicily and the Quebec Conference, code-named Quadrant, about to begin, Roosevelt, after joshing about his fishing, had some real news.

> THE PRESIDENT: I've have just had a telephone message from Mr. Mackenzie King [that Churchill and his staff were in Canada and] I think you can assume that I will probably see him. . . . I can't tell you the time, date or anything else.
>
> Q: Will there be any Russian participation in these talks in Canada?
>
> THE PRESIDENT: I don't think so. That doesn't mean that we wouldn't be awfully glad to see them. It's just British and American, that's all.

The president's casual tone was disingenuous. He had been urging Stalin to meet with them—and sometimes just with him—and Stalin's definitive refusal, with the lame excuse that he needed to be close to the front, had been received just two days before. Thus, the coming leaders meeting would be a duet, not a trio.

The president did not reveal that he was about to host Churchill on his second visit to Hyde Park, now accompanied by his daughter Mary. Although the White House later styled it "personal," the two again did business, much of it atomic business. A formal signed agreement about atomic weapons provided that they would never use "this agency" against each other or "against third parties without each other's consent," or give atomic information to anyone else. Meeting without scientific advisers, they seem to have foolishly imagined that they could maintain a two-power monopoly. On a more immediate matter, Roosevelt held that the nation that provided the greater number of troops for the invasion of France—which would be the United States—should name the supreme commander. Churchill, although he had offered the post to General Alanbrooke, saw the force of the argument and agreed.

Averell Harriman, overseer of Lend-Lease in London and Moscow, had traveled with the prime minister and would later attend the Quebec Conference. He reports that at the Roosevelts' Hyde Park dinner party for the Churchills, a conversation between Eleanor and Winston prefigured positions they would take during the Cold War. Churchill favored perpetuating the Anglo-American relationship, a "loose association" rather than a treaty. According to Harriman, "Mrs. Roosevelt seemed fearful this might be misunderstood by other nations and weaken the UN concept." Churchill insisted that "any hope of the UN working would be in the leadership" of the Anglo-Americans. The president, as he often did in such situations, listened. After dinner Roosevelt took the Churchills to the train for their return to Quebec.[1]

August 14, the day the Churchills left Hyde Park, the American and British military staffs' meetings opened Quadrant. During preparatory meetings in Washington, the American planners' extreme mistrust of the British was expressed in an eloquent letter to Roosevelt that Secretary Stimson presented to and discussed with him in a White House meeting on August 10:

> We cannot now rationally hope to be able to cross the Channel and come to grips with our German enemy under a British commander. His Prime Minister and his Chief of Imperial Staff are frankly at variance with such a proposal. The shadows of Passchendaele and Dunkerque still hang too heavily over the imagination of these leaders of his government. Though they have rendered lip service to the operation, their hearts are not in it and it will require more independence, more faith, and more vigor than it is reasonable to expect we can find in any British commander to overcome the natural difficulties of such an operation carried on in such an atmosphere of his government.

Stimson did not say what Roosevelt surely knew: that the American planners were also concerned lest he would again, as they saw it, be seduced by Churchill's arguments for multiple fronts. Although Roosevelt assured Stimson—in what the war secretary later wrote in his diary was one of his "most satisfactory" conferences with the president—that he agreed with and would support his planners' views, they left for Quebec still concerned that more seduction would follow.

These fears were not assuaged during the first three days of military meetings in Quebec. General Marshall opened for the Americans, making the case that the cross-Channel invasion, now code-named Overlord, receive overriding priority over other operations in the European theater. Responding for the British, General Alanbrooke expressed agreement that Overlord should be the main 1944 operation in Europe, but went on to insist that three preconditions had to be met first:

1. A reduction in German fighter strength
2. The restriction of German strength in France and the Low Countries and of German ability to bring in reinforcements in the next two months
3. The solution of the problem of beach maintenance

In addition, Alanbrooke, with that emphasis on the centrality of the Mediterranean that dominated British military thinking, went on at some length about how vital to the accomplishment of his first and second conditions was a successful campaign in northern Italy. The military planners also discussed the other war theaters, but the crucial military decision for Roosevelt and Churchill was about Overlord.

Roosevelt, Churchill, and their immediate staffs and map rooms were housed in the Citadel, a residence of the governor-general of Canada, which had been fitted with ramps for Roosevelt's convenience, and meetings involving him were held there. The other meetings were held in the more luxurious Château Frontenac, the Canadian Pacific Railway hotel where the other participants were housed. The arrangements were so convenient that the second Quebec Conference, a year later, replicated them.

The major military planning results of the conference, ratified by the two political leaders, represented a vindication of American planning and resolve:

1. A commitment to a cross-Channel invasion in May 1944, supplemented by a secondary invasion of Mediterranean France
2. Invasion of Italy to be a decision of the theater commander; Corsica and Sardinia to be occupied
3. The supreme commander in Europe to be an American
4. Creation of a Southeast Asia Command with Lord Louis Mountbatten (1900–1979), with General Stilwell to be his deputy; although both men had been brought halfway around the world, that was largely for show: this theater continued to receive very few resources and was a bone of contention

Although the results of Quadrant represented a victory for the American military planners, they continued to wonder whether the British would remain steadfast. In the event, Churchill kept urging various southern and eastern European sideshows, but the cross-Channel invasion decision was irrevocable.[2]

The major political accomplishment at Quebec was paving the way for a joint meeting with Stalin; lesser results included an agreement to work for a four-power declaration that there would be a new international organization after the war and secret agreements about atomic research and any weapons resulting from it. Churchill and Roosevelt were unable to agree on a common policy toward the French Resistance leaders: Churchill remained, essentially, a friend of the bride, Roosevelt of the groom; two days later, they issued similar but not identical statements recognizing the French Committee of National Liberation, of which both Giraud and de Gaulle were members, "as administering those French overseas territories which acknowledge its authority," which did "not constitute the recognition of a government of France or of the French

Empire." They dabbled with the question of a possible Italian surrender, but left the details to Eisenhower.

The official statement over the names of both leaders was deliberately bland. The "conference . . . has now completed its work," and the two leaders "were able to receive and approve the unanimous recommendations of the Combined Chiefs of Staff" and had reached agreement on "the political issues." Then, misleadingly, it claimed that "the discussions of the Chiefs of Staff turned very largely on the war against Japan and the bringing of effective aid to China." It discussed the possibility of a "tripartite meeting" and stated that reports of the decisions about the war against Germany and Italy "will be furnished to the Soviet Government."[3]

The end-of-meeting press conference, the only contact some 170 reporters had with the two leaders, had a dramatic setting—the Terrace of the Citadel three hundred feet above the St. Lawrence—but was otherwise without excitement. Roosevelt and Churchill were seated on either side of Mackenzie King, with Britons Anthony Eden and Brendan Bracken (1901–68), Churchill's information minister, seated with Harry Hopkins and Steve Early on the parapet behind them. As at Casablanca, there was not a military man in sight. The Canadian premier, who had been given no part in the meeting itself, acted as host and master of ceremonies. Churchill and Roosevelt did all the serious talking during what was really a joint lecture, as no questions were permitted.

After a brief interval in which still and newsreel photographers were allowed to take pictures, Churchill, who noted that he had expected to follow Roosevelt, who "tells me that he wants me to begin," spoke about their meetings but said nothing about their private talks or voluminous correspondence.

This is the sixth conference I have had with the President and I know there are some people who say, "Why is it necessary to have all these conferences?" But I think that a much more reasonable way of looking at it would be to say, "How is it they are able to get on with such long intervals between the conferences?" . . .

A great advantage is achieved by personal contact. I assure you it would not be possible to carry on the complicated warfare we are waging, without close, intimate, friendly, personal contacts, and they have been established at every level in the very large organizations which have been brought together here at Quebec.

I must tell you that I have found the work very hard here—very hard. I have hardly had a minute to spare, from the continuing flow of telegrams from London to the necessity of dealing with a number of great questions which cannot be hurried in their consideration; and a great many minor decisions, some of which take just as much time and trouble. . . . Well, we have got to the end of the task. We have reached very good—very sound—I hope very good conclusions. They are certainly unanimous, and most extreme cordiality prevails. . . . I never felt more sure about anything than I do about the fact that these conferences are an indispensible part of the successful conduct of the war

[He then summarized the military situation.]

Well, on the whole things are very much better than they were when we met at Casablanca.

They are even better than when we met in Washington last. Now, great operations have been successfully accomplished. All Sicily is prostrate under our authority. . . . I do look forward to great steps being taken to beating down our antagonists one after another.

Roosevelt, for his part, opened by apologizing for a lack of real news. Following Churchill's example, he recounted some history: "[In] June, 1942, when we were meeting in Washington things looked pretty dark—to the days of Tobruk, to the days of a lack of an offensive on our part. We were still on the defensive, clearly, in almost every part of the world. . . . And so, what was planned in June of 1942 didn't go into effect until November, 1942. And the things that were planned at Casablanca have only just gone into effect, which we realize through the capture of Tunis, and then Sicily."

As we know, the greatest decision of the war had just been made, but could not be discussed. Unlike the situation after Casablanca, when a slogan (unconditional surrender) and a dramatic photo (the de Gaulle–Giraud handshake) in an unknown locale captured the imagination of the Anglo-American public, Quebec, in box-office terms, laid an egg.[4]

Roosevelt, before returning to Washington, went to nearby Ottawa to make a brief speech to the Canadian Parliament. As American secrecy rules did not apply there, a large crowd was at the station, and thirty thousand greeted him on Parliament Hill. The speech's most interesting passage, which surely did not go down well with many members, concerned the postwar world. "It is no secret that at Quebec there was much talk of the post-war world. . . . There is a longing in the air. It is not a longing to go back to what they call the 'good old days.' I have distinct reservations as to how good 'the good old days' were. I would rather believe that we can achieve new and better days." Placing his plans in august company, he went on: "I am everlastingly angry only at those who assert vociferously that the four freedoms and the Atlantic Charter are nonsense because they are unattainable. If those people had lived a century and a half ago they would have sneered and said that the Declaration of Independence was utter piffle. . . . A thousand years ago they would have laughed uproariously at the ideals of Magna Charta. . . . Several thousand years ago they would have derided Moses when he came from the Mountain with the Ten Commandments."

In a bow to Canadian bilingualism, he closed with two sentences in French, hailing its "union of two great races" as an example for "all humanity." He then went to the governor-general's residence for a formal luncheon at which he toasted the king and complimented Canada and then returned to his train to go home. While he was traveling, Churchill let it be known that he would be joining Roosevelt in Washington.[5]

After a brief stay at Hyde Park, Roosevelt returned to a capital filled with rumors about the State Department and its two leading figures, Cordell Hull and Sumner Welles. Secretary Hull's resentment of his number two who was Roosevelt's confidant went all the way back to the earliest days of the New Deal. As the Quebec Conference was winding down, many papers printed, as matters of fact, stories about Welles's resignation. Thus, on Roosevelt's first morning back in the White House, he read in the *New York Times* and other papers an account of Hull's press conference the previous day in which the secretary had denounced the syndicated columnist and radio commentator Drew Pearson (1897–1969) for saying that Hull and other State Department officials were hostile to the Soviet Union and wished it to be bled white. These, Hull said, "were monstrous and diabolical falsehoods." The president knew, or quickly learned, that Pearson was reacting to the attacks on Welles, although neither the columnist nor Hull had publicly mentioned Welles's name.

What seems to have happened is that Welles's enemies within the State Department had amassed evidence about his homosexuality, including an episode involving his drunken sexual advances to porters on the presidential train returning from Speaker Bankhead's funeral in 1940, and presented it to Secretary Hull. Then, according to historian Irwin Gellman, Hull lunched with the president in the Oval Office on August 15, presented some evidence of Welles's sexual behavior, and insisted that Welles must go. Welles came to the White House that afternoon, and Roosevelt told his friend that he could not remain as undersecretary but urged him to accept a roving commission in Latin America; the next day, Welles presented a letter of resignation effective on September 30. Roosevelt had not acted on it for almost six weeks, apparently hoping to work out something that would keep Welles in his service.

Many in Washington saw Hull as representing "reaction" and Welles as representing "progress" within the State Department, and a smaller number, including Pearson, believed that Welles's unannounced but widely believed resignation was causing Soviet uneasiness about its future relations with the United States.[6]

In none of this was Welles's sexual orientation mentioned, as had been true in the Newport, Rhode Island, naval base scandal after World War I. Such matters were simply not yet discussed in family newspapers, and Roosevelt never referred to them publicly. But as early as 1941, William Bullitt, who spearheaded much of the opposition to Welles, had given the president affidavits attesting to Welles's conduct, which J. Edgar Hoover told Roosevelt were apparently accurate. According to an anecdote related by Eleanor in her 1949 memoir, soon after she returned from a trip to the South Pacific on September 24, 1943, Franklin told her of his dismissal of William Bullitt, who had come to see him asking to be appointed as Welles's replacement. She wrote, substituting X for *Bullitt* and Y for *Welles,* that Franklin told Bullitt: "X if I were St. Peter and you and Y came before me, I would say to Y, 'No matter what you may have done, you have hurt no one but yourself. I recognize human frailties. Come in.' But to you I would say, 'You have not only hurt another human being, but you have deprived your country of the services of a good citizen; and for that you can go straight to Hell!'"[7]

Some notion of the attitudes toward homosexual behavior that prevailed in wartime Washington may be seen in this incident in Roosevelt's Map Room, described by George Elsey, a participant.

One morning, the Army lieutenant colonel who served as executive officer for army matters under Admiral Brown failed to show up. Admiral Brown gave us no explanation for his absence, nor did General Watson. . . . The mystery deepened when his tight-lipped brother, a colonel on duty at the War Department, came by to pick up personal possessions such as a pair of reading glasses and to drive away the missing officer's car, which had been left in a White House parking area. Leahy, ordinarily so talkative, had "no information." Only many weeks later did we learn that the lieutenant colonel had been arrested by military police for homosexual activity with an employee of the Mayflower Hotel where he had been living. We found that he was being held incommunicado in a psychiatric ward at Walter Reed Hospital and would be held there until all future operations of which he had knowledge had taken place. This was the military's mind-set at the time—homosexuals were automatically regarded as security risks. A court-martial to throw him out of the army was ruled out—too great a chance of publicity that would embarrass the White House.

My map room associates and I were dumbfounded when we heard the facts. We were naïve about homosexuality. A West Point graduate! That it existed in all areas of society was not generally known in those days. We were saddened; I think all of us liked that man and had seen a bright future for him. He had been selected for promotion to full colonel and was a prospect for an important post in the forthcoming invasion of Normandy. The event sobered and matured us.[8]

Thus, when Roosevelt began his post-Quebec press conference on August 31, he knew that both Welles's status and Hull's extraordinary attack on Pearson were sure to come up. After some insider persiflage about high jinks in Quebec, Roosevelt announced that General Eisenhower was being promoted to the permanent rank of major general (he had been a colonel and held the temporary rank of general) because of "his outstanding services as Commander in Chief of the Allied forces in North Africa" and that while General Marshall's four-year term as chief of staff was expiring, "he of course would continue [because of] outstanding service." The first question was:

Q: Mr. President, could you tell us whether you have accepted the resignation of Under Secretary of State . . .

THE PRESIDENT: (Interposing) I haven't got any news on that. And when there is news, you will probably be informed.

Q: Then there will be news on it?

THE PRESIDENT: What?

Q: Then there will be some news on it?

THE PRESIDENT: I said—*if* and when, I should have said,—(laughter)—

Q: (Interjecting) I'm glad to hear you use that word, sir.

Q: (Interposing) Mr. President,—

THE PRESIDENT: (Continuing)—but the *when* will be decided by me and by nobody else.

Nothing else was said in the August 31 press conference about Welles, although the president did associate himself will Hull's attack on Pearson, so that, uncharacteristically, papers could print headlines like "President Brands Columnist a Liar."

More than three weeks later, on September 25, the White House issued a statement in the president's name announcing three appointments: the dollar-a-year man Edward R. Stettinius to replace Welles as undersecretary of state, Leo R. Crowley (1882–1972) to have the job of foreign economic administrator, and Herbert Lehman to become special assistant to the president to plan for the creation of the United Nations Relief and Rehabilitation Administration in November, which he was expected to head. Of Welles, the president said that he accepted his resignation "with deep and sincere regret" and that Welles had told him that his "wife's health" had caused him to resign. Roosevelt praised Welles, saying that he had "served the Department of State and this government with unfailing devotion for many years." Reporters noted that the standard practice of releasing the letter of resignation and the president's response to it was not followed. In a later press conference the following exchange occurred:

Q: Mr. President, there have been reports that Sumner Welles might be given an important post. Is there anything on that?

THE PRESIDENT: No news at all.

That was the last mention of Welles in the public record of Roosevelt's presidency.[9]

Apart from the Welles matter, much of Roosevelt's attention after he returned from Quebec was focused on managing the war and getting Stalin's agreement to meet and then making arrangements for two separate conferences. He also had to deal with a Congress returning from a two-month recess and with the negative aspects of some of its previous actions. As the National Youth Administration, which Congress had killed by failing to appropriate money for it, would be out of business by year's end, Aubrey Williams resigned with regret at the circumstances. In the customary exchange of letters, the president praised him and the NYA, noting that "while Congress [ended] the NYA . . . nothing can end the long results of its usefulness." He told reporters that he expected "to call on [Williams] for some other services" because "he did a remarkable job."

Roosevelt gave a very brief Fireside Chat—fewer than fifteen minutes—to kick off the third in an escalating series of war-bond campaigns. While most of the nontax funding of the war came from the sale of bonds and Treasury notes, great emphasis was placed on the sale of the lower-interest rate bonds and non-interest-bearing stamps to the general public. Although the theme was on patriotism and raising money for weapons of war, the real purpose was to attract cash that would otherwise be spent on consumer goods and services and contribute to inflation. The first drive in November–December 1942 raised $12.9 billion, $7.7 billion of it not from commercial banks; the second, in April–May 1943, brought in $18.6 billion, $13.5 billion of it not from banks; and the third, which ran into November and from which banks were barred, would raise $18.9 billion. The greater proceeds were due more to the increasing national payroll as the war proceeded and the economy approached full employment than to a measurable increase in patriotism. Concerned that victories in the Mediterranean might lead to overconfidence—Italy had just surrendered—Roosevelt stressed the individual responsibility of Americans on the home front.

> The great news you have heard from General Eisenhower does not give you license to settle back in your rocking chairs and say, "Well, that does it. We've got 'em on the run. Now we can start the celebration."
>
> The time for celebration is not yet. . . .
>
> Success on the Third War Loan will be the symbol that America does not propose to rest on its arms—that we know the tough bitter job ahead and will not stop until we have finished it.
>
> Now it is your turn!
>
> Every dollar that you invest in the Third War Loan is your personal message of defiance to our common enemies—the ruthless savages of Germany and Japan—and it is your personal message of faith and good cheer to our allies and to all the men at the front. God bless them![10]

The president had paid little attention to Japanese Americans since he had issued the orders that resulted in their mass incarceration in early 1942. In February 1943, he made his second partial mitigation of his orders; in a public letter to War Secretary Stimson, the president gave his "full approval" to the army's plan to form an "all-Japanese" unit of volunteers, which eventually became the vaunted 442nd Regimental Combat Team. In support of this, Roosevelt issued a strong egalitarian statement: "No loyal citizen of the United States should be denied the democratic right to exercise the responsibilities of his citizenship regardless of his ancestry. . . . Americanism is not, and never was, a matter of race or ancestry."

At that moment, there were some seventy thousand Japanese American citizens in the concentration camps he had established to confine them and some fifty thousand Japanese American aliens. Many of the incarcerated Japanese Americans, while pleased by the president's statement, raised an interesting question: "If what the president said is true, why are we in concentration camps?"

From the inception of the draft in late 1940 until shortly after the Pearl Harbor attack, more than a thousand Japanese American young men had been drafted without any official discrimination and assigned to units throughout the army. The original Selective Service Act had contained a statutory prohibition against discrimination because of "race, creed or color" or political opinion. In the months immediately after Pearl Harbor, some army commanders discharged Nisei soldiers by transferring them to the enlisted reserve; others were given menial assignments, while still others remained in training or on active service. Most West Coast draft boards simply reclassified all Nisei registrants as "IV-F," physically unfit for duty. On March 20, 1942, the Selective Service system ordered all registrants of Japanese ancestry classified as "IV-C," a category reserved for aliens. For almost a year afterward, while the draft status of mainland Japanese Americans remained unchanged, they could again enlist in the army. Almost all were assigned to a segregated unit that would be heavily involved in combat, the 442nd Regimental Combat Team. In that period, more than a thousand mainland Japanese Americans voluntarily enlisted in the army, as did thousands more in the Territory of Hawaii.[11]

After hearings investigating conditions in the WRA camps held by a subcommittee of its Military Affairs Committee, the Senate, just before its long recess in early July, passed a resolution asking the president to issue an executive order directing the segregation of "disloyal" Japanese Americans in the camps from those who were loyal and to arrange for a report on conditions in the camps and procedures for release. The subcommittee was concerned not about the civil liberties of American citizens but with the alleged "luxuries" that the prisoners were enjoying.

In a mid-September letter to the Senate, Roosevelt responded, "I find that the War Relocation Authority has already begun a program of segregation . . . train movements began in early September." He sent on to the Senate a brief report over James Byrnes's signature—largely written by the WRA and the army—that assured Congress that the incarcerated people were served only "third grade" beef and "no fancy cuts," and their food was "nourishing but definitely below Army standards" at an average cost per person of "34 to 43 cents a day." The president's letter concluded with a strong positive paragraph about Japanese Americans, while offering no explanation of why they were imprisoned. "Americans of Japanese ancestry, like those of other ancestries, have shown that they can, and want to, accept our institutions and work loyally with the rest of us, making their own valuable contribution to the national wealth and well being. In vindication of the very ideals for which we are fighting this war it is important to us to maintain a high standard of fair, considerate, and equal treatment for the people of this minority as of all other minorities."

The program of segregation was the result of an unwise questionnaire devised by the WRA, whose results it and the army authorities used to establish the first large-scale federal loyalty test since the Civil War. To effect a segregation program, the WRA transferred those whose loyalty it questioned plus others regarded as troublemakers to the camp at Tule Lake in northeastern California. The result there was a calamity within a disaster. Although Roosevelt had been assured that "their treatment in all respects will be fair and humane," the camp director soon called in military police units, which imposed martial law for some two months between mid-November 1943 and mid-January 1944. The army brought in tanks—which never fired—to cow the resisters and built a special prison stockade within the camp in which several hundred inmates were held without hearings for as long as nine months during which brutality and what inmates claimed was torture was common. In mid-February 1944, without changing its leadership, the president issued an executive order transferring the WRA from his EOP to the Interior Department, where it was supervised by Harold Ickes, the cabinet officer most sympathetic to Japanese Americans, and his deputy Abe Fortas (1910–82).[12]

Roosevelt also sent Congress a long message about the progress of the war. Rosenman tells us that the president spent a great deal of time on it and that it went through six drafts. Beginning with a brief discussion of the invasion of southern Italy, which was just beginning, he noted that it had been planned at Casablanca, and he revealed what everyone assumed, that he and Churchill had planned further operations at Quebec. He warned again that the war would be long and involve much sacrifice and that Japan would be "literally pounded into the dust." He recited mind-boggling details: the war had already cost $128 billion, and the cost was going up $250 million a day; in addition to vast numbers of planes, ships, tanks, and guns, "In the two and a half years between January 1, 1941, and July 1, 1943, the power plants built for installation in Navy vessels had a horsepower equal to all the horsepower of all hydroelectric plants in the United States in January, 1941."

After praising the heroism of the armed forces, and the productivity of American workers, and stressing the need for everyone to work together, he ended with a utopian vision of the postwar world that would follow undoubted victory. "Finally, as the war progresses, we seek a national cooperation with other Nations toward the end that world aggression be ended and that fair international relationships be established on a permanent basis. The policy of the Good Neighbor has shown such success in the hemisphere of the Americas that its extension to the whole world seems to be the logical next step."[13]

During early September, Roosevelt was involved with Churchill both in Washington and at Hyde Park. Churchill came to the White House on September 3, now accompanied by his wife, Clementine, as well as his daughter, plus staff, and spent five days there. Sir Alexander Cadogan (1884–1968), permanent undersecretary of Britain's Foreign Office, wrote that he spent a long day at the White House: "I was there till 8," helping to draft a message to Stalin, "running between the PM in bed and the President in his study." He complained that Churchill's sleep habits "have now become quite promiscuous. He talks with the president until 2 a.m., and consequently spends a large part of the day hurling himself violently in and out of bed, bathing at unsuitable moments and rushing up and down corridors in his dressing gown."

Churchill went off to Boston to make a speech and pick up an honorary degree from Harvard and was back at the White House before Roosevelt left on the ninth to spend most of rest of the month at Hyde Park. He told the Briton to make himself at home, have anyone he liked in for meals, to feel free to "summon any of my advisers with whom you wish to confer," and to stop off at Hyde Park on his way to Halifax, where HMS *Renown* would pick up his party and take it home. Churchill made full use of the White House facilities for two hectic days and nights, culminating in a command appearance by the American Joint Chiefs on September 11, during which, as the Americans anticipated, he resumed his push for an expansion of activities in the Mediterranean and a consequent lessening of support for Overlord. To the relief of White House personnel, he left that night for Hyde Park. We don't know what the two leaders talked about during the daylong visit, but they apparently reached no new decisions.[14]

Meanwhile, in Europe, although Eisenhower had decided to invade Italy in mid-July, a week before Mussolini's ouster, no Allied troops actually invaded southern Italy until September 3: the largely unopposed British troops landed across the Straits of Messina at the toe of the Italian boot and moved north up its eastern side very slowly, seizing important airfields around Foggia only on September 28. They gave no support to the American landing on the west

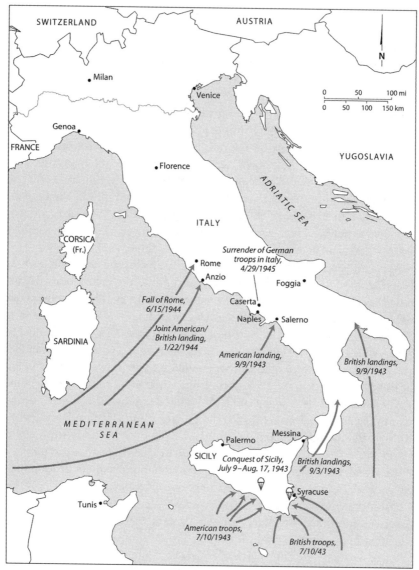

Mediterranean Theater, 1943–45. The invasion of Sicily, agreed to at the Casablanca Conference, went off almost like clockwork, although many Axis troops escaped to Italy. Whether to invade Italy was left undecided until the surprising ouster of Mussolini on July 25, 1943, triggered a response that was too slow. The resulting multiple invasions of Italy were, as the contemporary complaint put it, "too little and too late," and were met by effective and more timely German response. The Italian campaign was the least effective aspect of the successful allied counter attacks of the final years of the war.

coast at Salerno, below Naples, on September 9, which faced stiff resistance at the beachhead from German armored troops. The Salerno landing was delayed because it required the same landing craft used by the British. With the help of offshore naval gunfire and Allied command of the air, the beachhead was held and the American Fifth Army, under the command of Mark Clark, took Naples by October 1 and five days later was on the south bank of the Volturno River, north of the city. The whole operation was a clear military success, but it was also another set of opportunities lost.

Whether Roosevelt thought so is not clear. He was not given to intervening in tactical matters, and his known comments, both on and off the record, were uniformly positive. But the hopeful note that he and Churchill had sounded, telling the Italian people in a September 10 message that "now is the time for every Italian to strike his blow" and assuring them that "the German terror in Italy will not last long," was tragically overoptimistic. German war crimes against the Italian people continued for the rest of the war.[15]

Apparently to compensate for the lack of meaningful additional support for Pacific allies, Roosevelt made moves aimed at bolstering their morale. He directed Sam Rosenman to take care of a request from the exiled Philippine president Quezon that the islands' independence, which the 1935 Tydings-McDuffie Act had scheduled for July 4, 1946, be advanced. Roosevelt not only wanted to boost Philippine morale but also hoped that his actions, including the eventual grant of independence, would serve as a model for the postwar behavior of the British, French, Dutch, and Portuguese toward their Asian colonies. Both Stimson and Ickes had serious objections and wanted to substitute "independence after the Japanese have been expelled" for Quezon's "immediate independence." During negotiations Rosenman conducted at Quezon's bedside—the island leader was seriously ill with tuberculosis and died in August—a compromise was reached: Roosevelt would ask Congress to authorize him to proclaim independence as soon as feasible, and Congress eventually agreed.[16]

The morale boost for China, which had been preceded by a joint Anglo-American surrender of extraterritoriality there in February, was a message to Congress, urging passage of a bill repealing the 1882 Chinese Exclusion Act. This followed a nationwide campaign by the Citizens Committee to Repeal Chinese Exclusion and Place Immigration on a Quota Basis, which had begun in late May. Its key figure was New York publisher Richard J. Walsh, the husband of novelist Pearl S. Buck, and its letterhead listed 150 prominent Americans, from Roger Baldwin of the American Civil Liberties Union and Broadus Mitchell, an academic socialist, on the Left, to publisher Henry Luce and retired admiral Henry R. Yarnell on the Right. The rationale of the committee, some of whose members had met with the president, was that this was important for the sake of China and ignored its significance for Chinese Americans, not one of whom was on the committee. The president told Congress that he regarded the proposed legislation "as important in the cause of winning the war and establishing a secure peace. . . . China is our ally. We owe it to the Chinese . . . to wipe from the statute books those anachronisms in our law which forbid the immigration of Chinese into this country and which bar Chinese residents from American citizenship. Nations, like individuals, make mistakes. We must be big enough to acknowledge our mistakes of the past and to correct them."

Aware of the traditional nativist arguments for exclusion, Roosevelt pointed out that the Chinese quota would be only about a hundred a year and that "any such number" could not cause unemployment. After hearings in which favorable testimony far outweighed in both quality and quantity that of the bill's opponents, it passed the House easily and the Senate without a recorded vote. Madame Chiang cabled thanks to both the House and the Senate. Roosevelt, in signing the bill, spoke of it as lifting "an unfortunate barrier between allies" and claimed that the "war effort in the Far East can now be carried on with a greater vigor and a larger understanding of our common purpose."

It is usually the case that politicians and statesmen claim a greater impact for their actions than sober reflection allows. The repeal of Chinese exclusion is a rare opposite, a major achievement deliberately downplayed by its author. Chinese exclusion, as Roosevelt well knew, was no minor anachronism. Its enactment in 1882 was the hinge on which American immigration policy turned: after its barring of "Chinese laborers," what Emma Lazarus called a "golden door" had been reduced to a narrow gate by 1924. During the New Deal, no policy inherited from the old order seemed more permanent than the national origins system installed in the era of Harding, Coolidge, and Hoover.

The bill repealing Chinese exclusion also made Chinese—but no other excluded Asians—eligible for naturalization, which had become in 1924 a prerequisite for immigration. Roosevelt had acknowledged this anomaly in his message asking for repeal—"It would give the Chinese a preferred status over certain other Oriental people"—but he understood that such an inequity would be impossible to defend in a postwar world. Thus, in the Truman years, a series of statutes granting the right of naturalization to Filipinos and "natives of India" made it possible for Korean and Japanese war brides to join their husbands and in 1952 dropped all ethnic barriers to naturalization. Thirteen years later, Roosevelt's protégé Lyndon Johnson widened what was still a gate quite considerably. Thus, it can be argued the repeal of Chinese exclusion marked another hinge on which American immigration turned. We cannot know how well the president foresaw the future course of events, but it seems clear that he understood the possibilities. By the time he signed the repeal bill in mid-December, Roosevelt had just returned from the Tehran and Cairo conferences; the latter was intended as an even more important morale builder for China and her leaders.[17]

The process by which those meetings were arranged was a long one. After being informed of the results of the Quebec meeting, Stalin cabled Roosevelt on September 8, proposing a foreign ministers meeting in Moscow in October and expressed a desire to meet with the president and Churchill "as soon as possible" and suggested that they meet in Iran. The Moscow meeting was quickly agreed to, and Hull departed to meet with Eden and Molotov on October 7 for what was a successful if tedious negotiation in which he was aided by the new American ambassador Averell Harriman. Hull returned from Moscow to find traditional roles momentarily reversed: Roosevelt was waiting for him at the airport, what the secretary called "an unanticipated honor." The formal results, announced from Moscow while Hull was still there, included China, even though China was not a participant in the conference. Roosevelt had long wanted this, but it was only Hull's persistence that achieved it. China was named as one of four signatories along with Britain, the Soviet Union, and the United States. Thus, China became one of what Roosevelt would call "the four policemen" and eventually become one of five permanent members of the United Nations Security Council.

The seven-point Moscow declaration of November 1, 1943, pledged that the four nations would continue "united action" after the war, act together about surrender and disarmament, take "all measures" necessary to enforce surrender terms, establish "a general international organization" for "peace-loving States . . . large and small," "consult with one another" and others to maintain the peace, not use their military forces in peacetime "except for the purposes envisaged in this declaration," and cooperate in the reduction of armaments. Three separate protocols dealt with the Italian surrender, the reestablishment of an independent Austria, and a statement on "Atrocities" that promised punishment for their perpetrators. The last statement was considered so important that it alone was signed by the three leaders and issued separately from each capital.

Roosevelt, concerned about the postwar world, fearful of a recurrence of isolationism—Sherwood speaks of him as haunted by Wilson's ghost—and wanting to get Congress, including Republicans, on the record favoring postwar international cooperation before it became a campaign issue, was quite pleased that the Senate overwhelmingly endorsed his policy by passing the so-called Connally Resolution. By a vote of 85–5 just after the results of the Moscow meeting were announced, the resolution endorsed a postwar international organization in terms all but identical with those of the Moscow declaration. A September 21 vote in the House on a similar resolution by Arkansas freshman J. William Fulbright (1905–95) had passed by a 360–29 margin. Congressional isolationism, which never won a major battle with Roosevelt, was now a spent force.[18]

While Hull was coming home, the last snag in the arrangements for the first meeting of the three leaders was cleared. They had quickly agreed on starting dates—either November 20 or 25—but Stalin insisted that because he had to be in constant touch with Moscow, he could meet no farther away from his borders than Tehran. Roosevelt's stated objection to Tehran was constitutional. As he explained to Stalin by cable on October 14—and later had Hull, in Moscow, do it in person on October 25 with a second letter reiterating the earlier objection—"Congress will be in session. New laws . . . must be acted on by me after their receipt and must be returned to the Congress physically before ten days have elapsed." He explained that with the difficulties of flying in and out of Tehran—weather sometimes closed the airport for three or four days—it might not be possible to make the round-trip in ten days.

Stalin rejected each request, responding to the second message on November 5 by excluding any meeting place "farther than Tehran" and offering to send Molotov, his "first deputy," who "according to our Constitution" would have "all the powers of the Soviet Government." Roosevelt agreed to go to Tehran, saying that if necessary, "I will fly to Tunis [to sign papers] and then return to the Conference."

Roosevelt had no intention of making such a side trip. Rosenman explains that the president interpreted the constitutional requirement as meaning that the counting of the "ten days" should begin only when he actually received the bill and got an opinion from Attorney General Biddle supporting that view. While the president was at Tehran, and later at Yalta, the receipt given to the congressional clerk who brought the bill to the White House read "For forwarding to the President."

The Americans and British had already arranged to meet with Chiang Kai-shek in Cairo before meeting with the Soviet leader, and Roosevelt, to the distress of Churchill and his staff, invited Stalin to send Molotov to that meeting, not mentioning that Chiang would be there. Stalin accepted but canceled Molotov's appearance when he learned that the Chinese leader would be present, lest it serve as a spur to a Japanese attack on the Soviet Far East.[19]

Before leaving for the conferences, Roosevelt spoke to the representatives of forty-four nations assembled in the East Room in a twelve-minute radio talk after they had signed the agreement creating the United Nations Relief and Rehabilitation Administration. The president emphasized that this new agency "will help to put into effect the high purposes set forth" in the creation of the United Nations almost two years before. Linking it to the just-signed Moscow declaration, he said that it "shows that we mean business in this war in a political and humanitarian sense just as surely as we mean business in a military sense." He pointed out that the relief that had been administered for almost a year in North Africa, and now in Sicily and Italy, had been the responsibility of just two nations; now it and later operations would be the responsibility of forty-four. "Nations will learn to work together only by actually working together. Why not? We Nations have common objectives. It is, therefore, with a lift of hope, that we look on the signing of this agreement by all of the United Nations as the means of joining them together still more firmly."

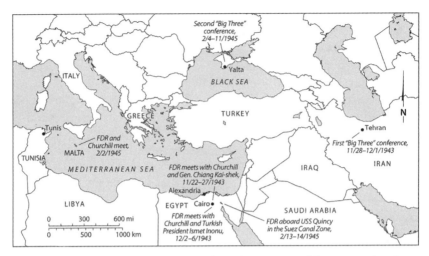

Second "Big Three" conference, 2/4–11/1945

Yalta

BLACK SEA

ITALY

TURKEY

GREECE

Tunis

FDR and Churchill meet, 2/2/1945

MALTA

TUNISIA

MEDITERRANEAN SEA

FDR meets with Churchill and Gen. Chiang Kai-shek, 11/22–27/1943

Alexandria

LIBYA

EGYPT Cairo

FDR meets with Churchill and Turkish President Ismet Inonu, 12/2–6/1943

0   300   600 mi

0   500   1000 km

Tehran

First "Big Three" conference, 11/28–12/1/1943

IRAN

IRAQ

SAUDI ARABIA

FDR aboard USS Quincy in the Suez Canal Zone, 2/13–14/1945

N

The Tehran and Yalta Conferences were the only meetings of the wartime big three. The less-written-about Tehran meeting was the more important. Each involved compromises with Stalin about his conquests in Eastern Europe. Myths about Yalta were an important aspect of the postwar attack on Roosevelt's legacy. Each was a victory for his policies, triumphs which took an incalculable toll on his lessened physical resources.

The delegates reassembled in Atlantic City and during almost three weeks of meetings ratified the choice of Herbert Lehman as first director, created an organizational structure, and set out a tentative budget of two billion dollars, with three-quarters of it to come from the United States.[20]

On Friday, November 13, Roosevelt left the White House and boarded the USS *Iowa*, a new forty-five-thousand-ton battleship at Hampton Roads. Since he shared the old sailor's superstition that it was bad luck to begin a voyage on a Friday, the departure was delayed until just after midnight. Thus, he began what would be a grueling journey with a relaxing cruise. His party of about fifty included the Joint Chiefs, who held a series of onboard conferences. The president and his personal staff—Hopkins, Leahy, Pa Watson, Admiral Brown, and Dr. McIntire—took their meals in the captain's quarters, which Roosevelt took over; there were drinks before dinner—the navy's no-alcohol rule was ignored by its commander in chief—and a movie afterward. There was one disturbing incident: on the second day out, in the midst of an air-raid drill in which antiaircraft guns were fired, one of the escorting destroyers accidentally fired a torpedo directly at the *Iowa*. Roosevelt, who was topside to see the drill, insisted on being pushed to the other side to see the torpedo that the *Iowa* evaded. The presidential party debarked at Oran in Algeria on the morning of November 20 and was met by General Eisenhower, who took them to his headquarters in Tunis. The military had seen to it that two of Roosevelt's sons, Elliott and Franklin Jr., and Hopkins's son Robert were on hand.

Roosevelt spent much of the next day with Eisenhower, who took him on a tour of some of the recent battlefields and the ruins of Carthage. Although Roosevelt had not yet decided who would command the cross-Channel invasion, he let Eisenhower believe that Marshall was going to get the job and that he would be called back to the Pentagon to take his place. "Ike, you and I know who was the Chief of Staff during the Civil War but practically no one else knows, although the names of the field generals—Grant, of course, and Lee and Jackson, Sherman, Sheridan and the others—every schoolboy knows them. I hate to think that 50 years from now practically nobody will know who George Marshall was. That is one of the reasons why I want George to have the big command—he is entitled to establish his place in history as a great General."

But Admiral Ernest King, who, like all the American Joint Chiefs, wanted Marshall to continue as chief of staff, made Eisenhower aware that the final decision had not yet been made. On the evening of the second day in North Africa, the entire presidential party made a night flight to Cairo, arriving on the morning of the twenty-second, and Churchill, Chiang, and Madam Chiang were waiting for them.

Roosevelt spent five full days in Cairo. His chief purpose there, to establish more firmly China's status as one of his "four policemen," was accomplished by the mere fact of the meeting. In addition, several military decisions were made there, including expanded offensives in Burma and an amphibious invasion of the Andaman Islands in the Bay of Bengal. If the generalissimo and his wife believed everything they had been told, they should have left Cairo well satisfied that their political and military objectives had been obtained. But within two weeks, the Andaman operation had been scrubbed, the mainland operations had been downsized, and Southeast Asia would remain a backwater for the American military until the fall of Dien Bien Phu in May 1954.

The staff talks with the British consisted largely of the continuing attempts by Churchill's men to shift resources to the eastern Mediterranean and southeastern Europe and the determined resistance by the Americans to any operation that might use assets intended for Overlord. On Thanksgiving Day, after the British presented what Leahy called "an alarming proposal" to delay the cross-Channel landing to exert more effort in the Aegean area, the Americans followed the instructions from Roosevelt not to allow any subtraction from or delay of Overlord. After that the British arranged a "polite gesture" of a Thanksgiving service in the All Saints Cathedral in Cairo. "One of our skeptics," Leahy reports, called this an example of "reverse lend-lease." (Roosevelt had recently used that term to describe such substantial contributions as Australia's feeding American troops there, thus saving shipping space.)

In a distinct change in public relations policy, the brief official conference communiqué was released from Cairo only three days after the president left for Tehran and while he was still out of the country. A four-paragraph document announced war aims that were all but axiomatic but had never been officially articulated. The key paragraphs read:

> The Three Great Allies are fighting this war to restrain and punish the aggression of Japan. They covet no gain for themselves and have no thought of territorial expansion. It is their purpose that Japan shall be stripped of all the islands in the Pacific which she has achieved and occupied since the beginning of the first World War in 1914, and that all the territories Japan has stolen from China, such as Manchuria, Formosa, and the Pescadores, shall be returned to the Republic of China. Japan will also be expelled from all other territories which she has taken by violence and greed.
>
> The aforesaid Three Great Powers, mindful of the enslavement of the people of Korea, are determined that in due course Korea shall become free and independent.[21]

As Roosevelt approached his first meeting with Stalin, so long pursued that the staff had code-named it Eureka, he had a clear notion of what he wanted to achieve and how he proposed to do it. Roosevelt had both short- and long-term objectives. Had the meeting taken place in 1942 or even early in 1943, his concerns would have included ensuring Soviet survival and forestalling the possibility of a separate German-Soviet peace as had occurred in 1917. His maps now showed him that Soviet armies were nearing the Polish border. He could expect that their advance westward would continue and, assuming a successful cross-Channel invasion and advance eastward, that the invading armies would meet somewhere in central Europe, probably in Germany. He wanted, first of all, no relaxation of Soviet military pressure on Germany, which might allow shifting of German forces from east to west. Second, he wanted some assurance of Soviet assistance in subduing Japan. There was a large Japanese army in Manchuria that he did not want to have to dislodge with American forces, though he had already broached with Stalin the possibility of establishing American air bases in Soviet Asia for bombing Japan. Third, with eventual victory—which he had apparently never doubted—now in sight, he was more and more concerned, as we have seen, with the postwar world. He wanted to start postwar planning earlier and do it better than in the Wilson years. Talking to reporters in March, he likened the American preparations for the Versailles Peace Conference after World War I to "a lady trying to pack for a month's trip in three hours." As a tactic to gain Stalin's confidence, he decided to do a little needling of Churchill and, when possible, to side, or seem to side, with the Soviet leader rather than the Briton.

Unlike Churchill or de Gaulle, Roosevelt envisaged a postwar world very different from the world they had known. Most striking in that regard was his insistence that China, weak, divided, and hopelessly corrupt, should be one of his four policemen. In the wake of Hull's achieving China's inclusion in the Moscow agreement, Roosevelt wrote "Dickie" Mountbatten how "very useful it will be twenty-five or fifty years hence" to have "the four hundred and twenty five million Chinese" on their side, despite their present weakness. He very much wanted real, not pro forma, Soviet participation in the postwar international organizations, and in that regard the reports coming from the UNRRA organizing meeting in Atlantic City were encouraging.

Much of Roosevelt's advice about Russia came from Harriman, newly installed as ambassador in Moscow. In the run-up to the Tehran meeting, he had cabled Roosevelt from Moscow, pointing out that the Russians did not like to face "Anglo-American decisions already taken." He urged "strongly" that Molotov be invited to Cairo, with the result already noted.

In Cairo, invited by General Marshall to brief the American chiefs of staff, Harriman delivered the same message, warning that it would be "unfortunate" if the Soviet military was given the impression that they were being presented with "*faits accomplis*" and recommended that the Americans should adopt an attitude of "perfect frankness." While in Cairo, Harriman gave the president a two-page memorandum, "Notes for the Impending Conference," urging "complete frankness" in dealing with Stalin and warning him that the fate of Poland "would probably go by default" unless he intervened.

The president's party left Egypt at seven on the morning of the twenty-seventh and flew over the Holy Land and the Tigris and Euphrates Valleys, landing without incident in Tehran that afternoon. As Roosevelt had insisted, there was no official reception. The shah had offered him a royal palace, and Stalin had offered a separate building with a newly installed bathroom in the large, well-guarded Russian embassy compound, about a mile away and cheek by jowl with the British compound, but Roosevelt had declined the offer.

Around midnight, what had been an afternoon and evening of settling in at the American legation in Tehran turned into melodrama. After his return to Washington, Roosevelt told the improbable tale to reporters reasonably accurately, but making it seem that he and Stalin had direct discourse on the matter, which was not the case. In the course of complaining about the security arrangements when he traveled, and prefacing it with "I don't set much stock in this," he later told the tale.

And that night, late, I got word from Marshall Stalin that they had got word of a German plot.

Well, no use going into details. Everyone was more or less upset. Secret Service, and so forth. And he pleaded with me to go down to the Russian Embassy—they have two or three different buildings in the compound—and he offered to turn over one of them to me, and that would avoid either his, or Mr. Churchill's, or my having to take trips through the streets, in order to see each other.

So the next morning I moved out, down to the Russian compound. I was extremely comfortable there, and it was just another wall from the British so that none of the three of us had to go out on the street for example.

Although one would expect that the president was exaggerating—and none of the reporters, who came with their own agendas, asked for further details—the reality as reported by Harriman and in the memoir by the head of the Secret Service White House unit was much more dramatic. Almost without exception, the president's advisers, though skeptical and concerned about the possibility of hidden listening devices, thought it a good idea to move to the Russian embassy compound, and the president approved the move. It seemed a good way to demonstrate trust. The move itself involved a heavily guarded convoy that did not include the president; he was whisked away in a private car under the personal supervision of the Secret Service's Mike Reilly, which got him safely to the Russian compound along back streets before the convoy arrived. As Reilly wrote in his memoir, "The Boss, as always, was vastly amused by the dummy cavalcade trick and other cops-and-robbers stuff. I was glad it amused him, because it did not amuse me."

Roosevelt, Hopkins, and Leahy moved in, along with a dozen Secret Service agents, an unspecified number of U.S. soldiers, plus the Filipino kitchen staff from the *Potomac*, which also serviced Shangri-La; most of the other members of the delegation were quartered in an American army camp outside the city. Maids, cleaners, and other Russians were all NKVD (People's Commissariat of Internal Affairs) agents, heavily armed, which made Reilly nervous. (He claims that during de Gaulle's interview with Roosevelt at Casablanca, he waited out of sight with a drawn revolver.) Harriman reports that after he returned to Moscow, he asked Molotov "whether the plot in Tehran had been a German plot or a Molotov-Harriman plot?" Molotov answered that they were aware of German agents in Tehran but had no knowledge of a particular plot. Stalin, he said, thought Roosevelt would be safer in the Soviet compound.

Stalin made his scheduled visit at 3:00 p.m. Roosevelt had annoyed Churchill by refusing to have lunch with him because he didn't want Stalin to think they were ganging up on him. The Soviet dictator came with only his interpreter, V. N. Pavlov, while Roosevelt used a Foreign Service officer whom Harriman brought from Moscow.

Charles E. Bohlen (1904–74), who had translated successfully for Hull, was on hand for every minute that Roosevelt and Stalin conferred at both the Tehran and the Yalta conferences. In the few minutes before Stalin walked into the room where Roosevelt was waiting for him, Bohlen suggested that the president try to speak no longer than two or three minutes at a time and then let him translate, explaining that this made it easier for him to be accurate and for his non-English-speaking listener to stay alert. Roosevelt understood and, according to Bohlen, "was an excellent speaker to interpret for," while Churchill, who would speak for as long as seven minutes, "was much too carried away by his own eloquence" to pay attention to his interpreter's needs. Bohlen, who prior to Tehran had only perfunctory contact with the president, so impressed both Roosevelt and Hopkins that he was later brought into the White House to provide the close connection with the State Department that had been missing since Welles's departure. The interpreter, a self-styled realist who thought that Roosevelt was overly optimistic about possible postwar relations with the Soviet Union, felt that the president "was the dominating figure at the conference."[22]

The pattern of the conference was similar to that established at the Anglo-American meetings: one set of meetings for the leaders, each supported by only a handful of aides; at Roosevelt's insistence, there was no formal agenda or official record, and, as the only formal head of state, Roosevelt more or less presided. A parallel set of military meetings was more structured and better recorded. At both sets of meetings, topic A, of course, was the much-delayed second front.

On that issue, British planners eventually gave up their formal reservations, although the American planners expected continued attempts at troop diversions in the eastern Mediterranean. Stalin, anxious for the cross-Channel invasion to begin, commented that until a supreme commander was named, he could not be certain it would occur. Roosevelt assured him that this would be done in a matter of days. On a second issue, the nature of the postwar international organization, Stalin conceded more than his Western allies expected. He also indicated a willingness to enter the war against Japan after Germany's defeat. Only on the question of eastern European boundaries did Stalin reveal Soviet ambitions.

Roosevelt tried to explain to Stalin some things about ethnic politics in the United States, telling him what apparently he had said to no one else, that unless the war was over, he would run for reelection in November 1944 and had to consider the sensitivities of a large number of Polish American voters. Thus, he let Stalin and Churchill come to an agreement about the borders of Poland at a meeting he refused to attend; the result allowed Stalin to keep what he had gained after his 1939 pact with Hitler and compensated Poland with territory to the west of the Polish border established by the Versailles Treaty. He did tell

Stalin that he would not go to war for the Baltic republics, which had been incorporated into the USSR.

Apart from this issue, Stalin generally spoke softly and recognized the American contribution to Allied victory in a way that he would never do in public: "The most important thing in this war are machines. The United States has proven that it can turn out from 8,000 to 10,000 airplanes a month. Russia can turn out, at most, 3,000 airplanes a month. . . . The United States, therefore, is a country of machines. Without the use of those machines, through Lend-lease, we would lose this war."

Only once did Stalin show what the world has come to know as his true face, though some chose not to recognize it. When he suggested that fifty or perhaps one hundred thousand German military officers should be liquidated—to which Churchill reacted strongly—many assumed that he was joking. In his 1973 memoir, Bohlen wrote, "Actually Stalin made the remark in quasi-jocular fashion, with a sardonic wave of the hand, and meant this as a gibe at Churchill. I cannot believe that he had any intention of putting it into effect."

Of course, we now know that Stalin had already arranged to have some twenty thousand captured Polish officers murdered and buried in mass graves. By 1973 Bohlen should have at least been aware of the possibility. He is also critical of Roosevelt's suggested "compromise"—forty-nine thousand—but understands that it was a bad joke.[23]

Instead of a communiqué, the Tehran meeting closed with a "Declaration of the Three Powers" signed with last names—Roosevelt, Churchill, Stalin. Although differences abounded, the brief statement, just over three hundred words, feigned total unity, ending with "We came here with hope and determination. We leave here friends in fact, in spirit, and in purpose." Before that, the statement contained two basic propositions, one military, one political.

The military proposition—"The common understanding that we have here reached guarantees that victory will be ours"—was a realistic assessment. The political proposition—"We are sure that our concord will win an enduring peace"—was certainly Roosevelt's hope but probably not shared by either of his partners, though all could at least give it lip service.

As host at a final dinner, Roosevelt was holding forth on possible arrangements for postwar Germany, Bohlen, sitting next to him and translating, reports: "Roosevelt was about to say something else when suddenly, in the flick of an eye, he turned green and great drops of sweat began to bead off his face; he put a shaky hand to his forehead. We were all caught by surprise. The president had made no complaint, and none of us had detected any sign of discomfort."

Typically, Hopkins took charge, had the president wheeled to his bedroom, accompanied him, and soon returned, repeating assurances from Dr. McIntyre that it was only "a mild attack of indigestion"; some four months later, Dr. Bruenn would discover gallstones, which are a most likely cause of the president's distress. Roosevelt did not return that evening, and Churchill and Stalin continued their conversation. The next day, Roosevelt reappeared in full vigor and remained so for the remainder of the trip.

Before flying back to Cairo, he went to the American base outside of Tehran, where some three thousand troops expedited the passage of supplies to the Soviet Union. He spent the night of December 2 there and in speaking briefly to the troops gave a thumbnail account of what he thought had been accomplished.

> I got here four days ago to meet with the Marshal of Soviet Russia and the Prime Minister of England, to try to do two things. The first was to lay military plans for cooperation among the three Nations, looking toward the winning of the war just as fast as we possibly can. And I think we have made progress toward that end.
>
> The other purpose was to talk over world conditions after the war—to try and plan a world for us and for our children when war would cease to be a necessity. We have made great progress in that, also.

He was back in Cairo the next day for three days of Anglo-American talks with Turkey's president, İsmet İnönü, and his foreign minister, looking to get them to enter the war. This was a pet project of Churchill's in which neither Roosevelt nor Stalin set much store. American military planners feared that if Turkey entered the war, scarce assets might have to be employed in rescue operations if it got into trouble. In the event, the Turks stayed neutral. It was during this meeting that Roosevelt cabled Chiang that the planned operations against the Andaman Islands and Burma had to be canceled because decisions at Tehran involve "us in combined grand operations on European continent."[24]

While in Cairo, spurred by Stalin's expressed concern, Roosevelt made the fateful decision to appoint Eisenhower as commander of the cross-Channel invasion. General Marshall later wrote Sherwood that in Cairo, Roosevelt explained his decision by telling him, "I feel I could not sleep at night if you were out of the country."

In a note to Stalin on December 6, the president wrote, "The decision has been made to appoint General Eisenhower immediately to command of cross-Channel operations." The next day, in Tunis, Roosevelt told Eisenhower, "Well, Ike, you are going to command Overlord." (The decision was not officially revealed until Roosevelt announced it in a Christmas Eve broadcast to the nation.)[25]

The president's trip home included brief stops at Malta, to pay tribute to the island and its defenders, and Sicily, where he reviewed troops and informed an admonished General George S. Patton that he considered the incident of his slapping a shell-shocked soldier closed. The president was flown to Dakar on the Atlantic, where a French escort vessel took the party out alongside the *Iowa* for the long voyage home, with the president boarding via a bos'n's chair.

While at sea, he received word of the death of his secretary Marvin McIntyre, who had been ill for three years and many of whose duties had been assumed by Pa Watson. Roosevelt's statement spoke of "another faithful servant . . . lost to the public service" who "despite frail health . . . could not be persuaded by any consideration of self-interest" to retire. "To me personally his death means the severing of a close relationship of a quarter of a century."

Just before leaving the *Iowa* on December 16, in Hampton Roads, he spoke to the crew, and after some pleasantries tried to give some notion of what he thought was being accomplished.

> One of the reasons I went abroad . . . was to try, by conversations with other Nations, to see that this war that we are all engaged in shall not happen again. We have an idea—all of us, I think—that hereafter we have got to eliminate from the human race Nations like Germany and Japan, eliminate them from the possibility of ruining the lives of a whole lot of other Nations. . . . [W]e made real progress. . . . [W]hen we win the war [we want] to make the possibility of a future upsetting of our civilization an impossible thing. I don't say forever. None of us can look that far ahead. But I do say as long as any Americans and others who are alive today are still alive. That objective is worth fighting for.[26]

At his December 17 press conference, the first since Armistice Day, reporters found Roosevelt "tanned and healthy," while news from London told of Churchill, who was some five years older than Roosevelt, recovering from pneumonia in an undisclosed overseas location, Clementine flying to his side. The big news of the press conference was that the president would save most of the news about the trip for his Christmas Eve Fireside Chat and January report to Congress.[27]

Triumphant abroad, Roosevelt returned to face domestic problems from almost every point of the political compass. In addition to growing resistance from congressional conservatives in both parties, new attacks on his policies came from the Left. His natural allies in the labor movement were preparing to violate their no-strike pledge, as Lewis and his miners had done repeatedly. The most immediate threat was a nationwide rail strike, set for December 30. The chaos that could result if freight and passenger trains, including troop trains, were simply halted at the next sizable station meant that any effective seizure would have to take place before the strike was actually called. The day after his return, Roosevelt called for representatives of both management and the railroads to meet at the White House the next day, December 20. A five-hour conference, with Roosevelt participating for three hours and Byrnes and Vinson participating throughout, produced some movement. The administration held to a 4-cents-an-hour raise; the unions wanted 37.5 cents, but, in what became a pattern, pushed for increasing other benefits, in this instance time and a half for overtime, which rail workers—not covered by the Wagner Act—did not enjoy, and paid vacations. (In wartime workers got the monetary equivalent and kept working.) Meetings continued with some presidential participation, but nothing had been finalized when Roosevelt left for Hyde Park on the evening of the twenty-third. He instructed Attorney General Biddle to prepare the documents necessary for seizure in conjunction with the army, which would be in charge.

Watching the president at a party for the troops who guarded Hyde Park, the current *New York Times* White House correspondent crafted a verbal snapshot of the president. Noting that the Roosevelts had last celebrated Christmas at Hyde Park in 1932, John Crider wrote:

> Since then his hair has become much whiter and, as he remarked to the photographer yesterday, has thinned out almost to baldness. Lines are deeper in his face and a slight nervousness also bears testimony to the tremendous strain of eleven [*sic*] years in office.
>
> But for all the passing of the years, with their domestic emergencies and foreign wars, the President retains his flair for buoyant conversation, his sharp humor and his quick smile. Thanks to his recent trip abroad, on which he had opportunity for some rest in the midst of much work, he looks much healthier than he did a few months ago.[28]

The big news of the Fireside Chat from his library was the announcement that Eisenhower would lead the combined American and British forces in their attack on Germany "from other points of the compass." Perhaps the trickiest part of his talk was how to describe his relations with the Russian dictator. Roosevelt could safely use encomiums to describe Chiang Kai-shek ("a man of great vision, great courage, and a remarkably keen understanding") but was somewhat more circumspect in describing Stalin ("a man who combines a tremendous, relentless determination with a stalwart good humor"). He reported that he "got along fine" with Stalin and said he believed that "we are going to get along very well with him and the Russian people—very well indeed." What would be crucial in the postwar world, Roosevelt declared, was the continued unity of Britain, Russia, China, and the United States. "But those four powers must be united with and cooperate with all the freedom-loving peoples of Europe, Asia, Africa, and the Americas. The rights of every nation large and small, must be respected and guarded as jealously as are the rights of every individual within our own Republic. We are agreed that if force is necessary to keep international peace, international force will be applied—for as long as may be necessary."

The president promised that there would be more details in his forthcoming message to Congress and closed by noting that "less than a month ago," he had flown "over the little town of Bethlehem, in Palestine."

> Tonight, on Christmas Eve, all men and women everywhere who love Christmas are thinking of the ancient town and of the star of faith that shone

there more than nineteen centuries ago. American boys are fighting today in snow-covered mountains, in malarial jungles, on blazing deserts; they are fighting on the far reaches of the sea and above the clouds, and fighting for the thing for which they struggle. I think it is best symbolized by the message that came out of Bethlehem. On behalf of the American people—your own people—I send this Christmas message to you who are in our armed forces. . . . God bless us all. Keep us strong in our faith that we fight for a better day for humankind—here and everywhere.[29]

Before Roosevelt went to Hyde Park, the railroads and two of the operating brotherhoods had agreed to his personal arbitration, while three had rejected it. By nightfall all but three of the twenty brotherhoods had agreed to arbitration, but Roosevelt issued the planned seizure order, explaining that "I cannot wait until the last moment to take action. . . . [M]ajor military offensives now planned must not be delayed by the interruption of vital transportation facilities. If any employees of the railroads now strike, they will be striking against the Government of the United States."

Unlike the World War I situation in which the government seized and operated the railroads, the current seizure was planned to be temporary. And, profiting from Ickes's experience with the oft-seized coal mines, the government made no attempt to manage railroad operations. Instead, Secretary Stimson had the presidents of seven large railroads commissioned as colonels who were each appointed director of one of seven regions established by the government. Two ranking officials of the brotherhoods were taken on as consultants. Existing railroad personnel, management and labor, continued to do their jobs. Some nine hours before the strike was due to start, the three holdout brotherhoods rescinded their strike orders. No strike took place. Wage adjustments similar to those awarded to the operating brotherhoods were made for the others. The government relinquished control of the railroads at midnight on January 18, 1944, after nineteen days of putative ownership.[30]

The steel dispute, though it was an actual strike, was dealt with more simply, partly because it involved just one union. The largely regional walkout on Christmas Day was triggered by a deliberately provocative announcement by bitterly antiunion Ohio steel companies that they would follow a recent War Labor Board ruling and not make any future settlement retroactive to the expiration of their contracts, which were expiring on Christmas Day. Informed of the strike while still at Hyde Park, Roosevelt, before leaving for Washington on December 26, sent telegrams to the steelworkers' Philip Murray and a number of company executives, asking that the strike be called off. He stated, in contradiction of what the War Labor Board had just ruled, that any wage increases finally agreed to would be retroactive to the expiration date of the previous contract. On the next day, while Roosevelt was trying to head off the rail strike, the NWLB, or more precisely its four public members, reversed themselves by voting for retroactivity, changing an eight-to-four negative decision into an eight-to-four positive one. Informed of the change, Murray wired union leaders to resume work without further interruption, and most of the workers were back at work on December 28.[31]

Roosevelt opened the year's final press conference by discussing the measures being taken to operate the railroads; the steel strike was ignored. After some questions about details, a new topic was broached:

MR. DOUGLAS CORNELL (ASSOCIATED PRESS): (Interposing) Mr. President, after our last meeting with you, it appears that someone stayed behind and received the word that you no longer liked the term "New Deal." Would you like to express any opinion to the rest of us?

THE PRESIDENT: Oh, I supposed that somebody would ask that.

Both the *New York Times* and *Time* had published stories relating that Cleveland Unitarian pastor Reverend Dilworth Lupton (1884?–1972) had written in his newspaper column that Roosevelt told him that the New Deal slogan was out of date and needed to be replaced by something like "win the war." Republican politicians had had a field day. Indiana's Charlie Halleck (1900–1986), a future House majority leader, claimed that Roosevelt was admitting that "the New Deal's mixing of social pipe dreams with the realism of war . . . breeds confusion on the home front."

Roosevelt ruefully admitted that the column was "accurate reporting" and that he would have to be "terribly careful" about what he said after press conferences. After sloughing off the reactions as "puerile and political," he launched into a monologue of some fifteen hundred words, long even for him, summarizing the various programs of his presidency. In the process, he created an allegory that has beguiled historians ever since. The problems of 1933 required an internal medicine specialist, "Dr. New Deal," who prescribed cures for such matters as unemployment, bankrupt banks, and closed factories, but two years ago his patient had suffered an "accident" and "old Dr. New Deal" called in his partner, "Dr. Win-the-War," an orthopedic surgeon who specialized in things like broken bones. Leaving his allegory, Roosevelt closed the monologue by noting that, after victory, the old doctor, or someone with his specialization, would be back in business.

THE PRESIDENT: But it seems pretty clear that we must plan for, and help to bring about, an expanded economy which will result in more security, in more employment, in more recreation, in more education, in more health, in better housing for all of our citizens, so that the conditions of 1932 and the beginning of 1933 won't come back again.

Now, have those words been sufficiently simple and understood for you to write a story about?

MR. BERT ANDREWS (NEW YORK HERALD TRIBUNE): Does that all add up to a fourth term declaration?

Roosevelt, adding a third *P* word, found the question "picayune," but of course it was all politics. The run-up to the election had clearly begun: unlike the situation four years earlier, hardly anyone doubted that the president would seek reelection.[32]

The president's 1944 began with Roosevelt "indisposed" with what seemed to be minor ailments that he had suffered throughout his adult life, as Josephus Daniels had noted years before. A fuller discussion of his health will follow later in this chapter. Although the president's handlers, led by Steve Early and Dr. McIntire, played down his illnesses, they were not secret and were described as colds, flu-like, and eventually bronchitis. For the first time, the president did not brief the press on the budget, but left it to Harold Smith.

As was always the case during the war, the bureaucracy around Roosevelt released presidential statements as if he were, in fact, doing business in the White House. During this period of incapacity, it issued the president's brief New Year's message, which called attention to the formation of the United Nations two years before when they "were on the defensive in every part of the world" and contrasted it with the current "gathering for new and greater assaults which will bring about the downfall of the Axis aggressors." Noting "the different kind of struggle that must follow the military phase . . . struggle against disease, malnutrition, unemployment, and many other forms of economic and social distress," he emphasized, as he had done in his talks during and after the trip to Tehran, "final victory on the battlefield" and "establishing an international organization of all peace-loving Nations to maintain peace and security in generations to come." The annual message was read by clerks, but Roosevelt broadcast it from the White House as a prime-time Fireside Chat.[33]

The classic account of the 1944 annual message by James M. Burns in 1970 called it "the most radical speech" of Roosevelt's life and tended to downplay the conservative elements within it. The *New York Times* headline, "President Asks Civilian Draft to Bar Strikes, Realistic Taxes, Subsidies, New Bill of Rights," is a more accurate account of the contemporary ordering of the elements. Roosevelt set great store by the speech as a kind of manifesto for the election only ten months away. He had been particularly insistent that it be kept absolutely secret and that "only us boys"—the president and his two speechwriters—"and Grace" (Tully) should be privy to it; Hopkins had been rehospitalized at the New Year and would not be available until shortly before the election. Rosenman reports that he was aghast that "assistant president" Byrnes was to be kept out of the loop. And even on the eve of the speech, the president gave congressional leaders no clues about its contents; leaving the White House, blunt Sam Rayburn told the press that he expected a "general" message.

The president began with assurances that neither Hull at Moscow nor he at Tehran had made any "secret treaties or political or financial commitments" apart from those necessary for military victory. "The one supreme objective for the future [was] Security," not just "physical security" but also "economic security, social security, moral security—in a family of Nations."

There followed an appeal for continued unity at home. Roosevelt contrasted "the overwhelming majority of our people have met the demands of this war with magnificent understanding" with the "many evidences of faulty perspective here in Washington." He complained about "people who burrow through our nation like unseeing moles," spreading false beliefs about international cooperation, and denounced the "pests who swarm through the lobbies of Congress and the cocktail bars of Washington," seeking "special favors for special groups."

He also warned about "overconfidence and complacency" and complained that after last spring's victories—he specified Stalingrad, Tunisia, and "against the U-boats"—war production had dropped, not from strikes but because people believed that "the war's in the bag."

Therefore . . . I recommend that the Congress adopt:
(1) A realistic tax law. . . .
(2) A continuation of the law for the renegotiation of war contracts. . . .
(3) A cost of food law. . . .
(4) Early reenactment of the stabilization statute [which] expires June 30, 1944.
(5) A national service law—which for the duration of the war, will prevent strikes, and, with certain appropriate exceptions, will make available for war production or for any other essential services every able-bodied adult in this nation.

A good portion of the rest of the speech was devoted to a detailed explanation of why national service was essential to winning the war, ending with "I hope that the Congress will recognize that, although this is a political year, national service is an issue that transcends politics."

The president had one more specific measure to advocate: an effective national statute to allow soldiers, particularly those serving overseas, to vote. He argued that it was a congressional responsibility to see that a national statute was passed to remove "this unjustifiable discrimination against the men and women in our armed forces."

Just before the end came the radical passage setting forth an agenda not yet completed early in the twenty-first century, what the president called a "second Bill of Rights." He prefaced his discussion by echoing the second inaugural of 1937: "It is our duty now to begin to lay the plans and determine the strategy for the winning of a lasting peace and the establishment of an American standard of living higher than ever before known. We cannot be content, no matter how high the general standard may be, if some fraction of our people—whether it be one-third, or one fifth, or one tenth—is ill-fed, ill-clothed, ill-housed, and insecure."

The president asked for no specific legislation to bring about any aspect of this new bill of rights, but laid down eight specific rights to be protected.

The right to a useful and remunerative job . . . ;
The right to earn enough to provide adequate food and clothing and recreation;
The right of every farmer to raise and sell his products at a return [providing] a decent living;
The right of every businessman . . . to trade [free] from unfair competition and domination by monopolies . . . ;
The right of every family to a decent home;
The right to adequate medical care . . . ;
The right of adequate protection from the economic fears of old age, sickness, accident, and unemployment;
The right to a good education.

Observing that "America's own rightful place in the world" was contingent on maintaining prosperity at home, he warned that if "we were to return to the so-called 'normalcy' of 1920s . . . we shall have yielded to the spirit of Fascism here at home."

After an oft-repeated statement about the inseparability of the war front and the home front, he ended with a benediction: "Each and every one of us has a solemn obligation under God to serve this nation in its most critical hour—to keep this nation great—to make this nation greater in a better world.[34]

Little of what the president proposed was enacted in anything resembling the terms he suggested. The national service proposal drew the broadest rejection, including not only the president's regular opponents in Congress and a short-lived united front of often divided labor leaders, but also elements of the business community, civil libertarians, and many within his own administration. Although the CIO's Philip Murray, first off the mark for labor, could wisecrack to his executive board that Dr. Win-the-War was prescribing "quack medicine," his prior public use of that epithet blamed the malpractice on a two-year campaign for national service by "administrative and executive agencies." The AFL's William Green said that national service "would not add a single bullet" to existing production, and John L. Lewis's organ saw it as "the high-road to Fascism." Two major management bodies, the National Association of Manufacturers and the United States Chamber of Commerce, objected on the grounds that satisfactory production results could be jeopardized if worker morale suffered. Initial surveys of congressional opinion suggested, correctly, not only that the national service proposal had little chance of enactment but also that, of the other specific proposals, only the renewal of the wage-stabilization proposal had much likelihood of success. The day after the annual message, Green and Murray set aside their differences and went to the White House together with a joint statement opposing what they called a "labor draft" and spent an hour and a half discussing the proposal with the president. Some left-wing CIO unions, such as the National Maritime Union and Harry Bridges's West Coast longshoremen, soon supported national service, echoing a line taken by American Communist leaders. Most labor leaders in 1944 who supported a draft for civilian workers had opposed a military draft before the invasion of the USSR in 1941.

No one has satisfactorily explained why Roosevelt, after resisting various proposals for national service from Stimson for a good two years, switched to support it. A working group he had set up—Baruch, Byrnes, Admiral Leahy, Hopkins, and Rosenman—advised against it in late July 1943. Faced with continuing demands from Stimson, with support from the navy's Frank Knox and Admiral Emory Land of the Maritime Commission, Roosevelt had a national service bill drawn up in the fall but took no action. According to Rosenman, the president came back from Tehran determined to push for national service. His failure to get it through Congress in 1944 did not stop him from making a second unsuccessful attempt in 1945, despite the splendid record of war production in the interim.[35]

Roosevelt sent a message to the United States Conference of Mayors, promising "great national programs to aid veterans, to create employment for those leaving war industries, and to meet new problems of the post-war world," and added that additional programs should be added by states and cities.

We can get more than an inkling of what one of those programs would have been. Back in February 1938, after talking with a senator about his bill for an interstate highway system, Roosevelt summoned the commissioner of the Bureau of Public Roads (BPR), Thomas H. MacDonald (1881–1957) to the White House to discuss the concept.

"The President drew lines on a United States map—three east-west lines and five north-south lines—and asked MacDonald to study the feasibility of building a network of toll superhighways in those corridors." MacDonald, a dominant figure who ran the bureau under seven presidents from 1919 to 1953, had long favored an expanded highway system. In two months, he submitted an internal report, *Proposed Direct Route Highways,* which held that "a national system of direct route highways designed for continuous flow of motor traffic, with all cross traffic on separated grades, is seriously needed and should be undertaken." The year 1938 was no time for proposing vast projects to Congress. In that year, Congress did ask the BPR for a report on a toll "superhighway" system of three east–west and three north–south routes. Roosevelt sent the completed report,

Toll Roads and Free Roads, to Congress at the end of April 1939. Like its predecessor, it argued that traffic tolls on many of the routes could not generate enough revenue to pay off the expenses of building them. But the report was otherwise positive, as was Roosevelt, who, however, made no proposal to build any of it. He did appoint an Interregional Highway Committee in April 1941, chaired by MacDonald, and made his uncle Fred, because of his role on the National Planning Commission, one of its seven members. He received their report later that year, but did not release it. On July 13, 1943, Congress called for a report in six months. Thus, on January 12, 1944, Roosevelt sent the report he had been holding for more than two years to Congress with his endorsement. The report called for an annual appropriation of $750 million for ten or twenty years to build some thirty-four thousand miles of superhighways, which would create some two million jobs. Roosevelt never proposed actual construction, but presumably he was prepared to do so at an appropriate time. The project remained in limbo until the Eisenhower years.[36]

In the annual budget message, Roosevelt estimated war expenditures at $92 billion for the current year and $90 billion for the year beginning July 1, 1944. Thus, total "war expenditure" since 1940 totaled $300 billion. Just five years before, when Americans learned that Harry Hopkins, in his five years as relief administrator, had spent a total of $9 billion, it seemed an incredible sum.

"In this budget," Roosevelt said, "I have outlined the financial requirements for victory." He held out the possibility that there could be "victory on one front" during the life of the budget, which would entail significant demobilization and contract cancellation. He was highly critical of provisions of the tax bill working its way through Congress. He spoke of the need to rehabilitate liberated areas and to plan for postwar prosperity. His closing paragraphs concentrated, as had much of the message, on the postwar world.

> Military victory is not enough. We shall not have completed the defense of our way of life until we also solve the second task, the reconstruction of an economy in which everyone willing to work can find for himself a place in productive employment. The enemy, though beaten on the battlefields, may still rise in our midst if we fail in the task of reconstruction.
>
> Victory will be not only a cause for joy over an accomplishment but at the same time a challenge to another great undertaking. You and I have the responsibility to prepare for victory and for peace. Let us make sure that the Budget, the Government's work plan, serves both ends.[37]

On January 16, Morgenthau brought to the president a devastating document meticulously prepared by his staff. Its opening lines were uncompromising:

> One of the greatest crimes in history, the slaughter of the Jewish people in Europe, is continuing unabated. This Government has for a long time main-

tained that its policy is to work out programs to serve those Jews of Europe who could be saved.

I am convinced on the basis of the information which is available to me that certain officials in our State Department, which is charged with carrying out this policy, have been guilty not only of gross procrastination and willful failure to act, but even of willful attempts to prevent action from being taken to rescue Jews from Hitler.

Even in the so-called Morgenthau diaries, there is no good firsthand account of the president's reactions except that he was loath to believe that Assistant Secretary of State Breckinridge Long (1881–1958), a longtime associate, had deliberately worked to sabotage any attempts to rescue Jews. Nevertheless, the president acted decisively by sending Morgenthau to consult with newly appointed Undersecretary of State Stettinius, who ably abetted Morgenthau's plans.

The first fruit of Morgenthau's efforts was the creation, just six days after his meeting with Roosevelt, of the War Refugee Board (WRB) by executive order. Nominally directed by Hull, Morgenthau, and Stimson, it was placed in the EOP and was actually run by John W. Pehle (1909–99), a Treasury lawyer, and its expenses paid for by a combination of the president's contingency funds and money donated by American Jewish organizations. Despite the bold language of the executive order—"It is the policy of this government to take all measures within its power to rescue the victims of enemy oppression who are in imminent danger of death and otherwise to afford such victims all possible relief and assistance consistent with successful prosecution of the war"—the fact is that the WRB was never empowered to bring even a single refugee to the United States. It did rescue many thousands and resettled them in temporary camps in the Middle East, North Africa, and Europe. Roosevelt and his subordinates continued to be blocked by fear of congressional reaction if the WRB violated the immigration statutes, whether they approved of them, as Stimson did, or opposed them, as Morgenthau did. At some time, then or a little later, Roosevelt decided to act independently of the law when he thought that the time was ripe.[38]

The Birthday Balls, held a day early because the birth date fell on a Sunday, were similar to those that had gone before. The most striking novelty was a ball in Moscow hosted by Ambassador Harriman. The president's broadcast remarks focused on research to defeat polio as well as on palliative care. In his conclusion, he moved from "this war against disease" to the war against the Axis. After speaking about the current fourth war-bond campaign, he reminded his listeners that "every one of us has a chance to participate in victory by buying war bonds."[39]

In February three separate, long-simmering disputes with Congress about the soldier vote, farm prices, and taxation came to a head. The Senate had passed a deliberately ineffective soldier vote bill, 42–37, in December. The southern Democrats who sponsored the bill—Mississippians James Eastland in the Senate and John Rankin in the House—were the two of the three most blatant racists then in Congress, but talked about "states' rights" and were concerned about the administration bill, which called for forty-eight simple federal ballots, one for each state, listing only candidates for president and the appropriate congressional candidates. These would be issued to all soldiers, whether they were registered or not, and returned and delivered to the states by the army. This meant mass black suffrage in states that had long successfully subverted the Fifteenth Amendment, which supposedly forbade the denial or abridgment of the right of citizens to vote on account of "race, color, or previous condition of servitude." Had Roosevelt's message stressed the Constitution, that might have made it impossible for many Republicans, like Ohio's Taft, to support the southerners' bill and allowed an effective soldier vote bill to pass. But Roosevelt did not take that course, which might have put unbearable strains on the Democratic Party apparatus.

In September 1942, he had reluctantly approved a similar soldier vote bill for the off-year congressional elections. As he later noted, of some 5.7 million in the armed forces then, only 28,000 had been able to take advantage of it. However, in a presidential year, with 9 million in the armed forces, 5 million of them overseas, who, it was assumed would vote overwhelmingly for their commander in chief, the stakes were higher. Roosevelt seemed to believe that though his support of a strong soldier vote bill would cost him some congressional support, by election day traditional loyalties would prevail. To help ensure that result, his message did not mention the Constitution or Negroes. He was correct. The 1944 election was the last in which a solid South supported a Democratic candidate. In the event, Roosevelt could have won in the electoral college without a single southern electoral vote, but that result might have made Congress even less receptive to the president's postwar plans.

After a long and bitter struggle, the House passed a slightly revised soldier vote bill on March 15, 273–111, and Roosevelt allowed the still unsatisfactory measure to become law without his signature on April 1. A somewhat conciliatory statement of his reasons called the bill "wholly inadequate" and urged, vainly, the adoption of improving amendments. He also, as will be discussed in the next chapter, began a campaign to make individual state absentee-ballot laws more effective in an effort to increase the soldier vote significantly.[40]

In February a House vote of 249–118 extended the life of the Commodity Credit Corporation, which funneled federal funds to farmers, but it included a rider that prohibited using any of its funds as a subsidy on any agricultural product. This was essentially a reprise of the president's struggle with the farm bloc over control of farm prices, which had resulted in a veto that was sustained. The president's almost immediate veto, sent the next day, described in homey terms what would happen to grocery store prices: "10¢ more for a pound of butter . . . 7¢ more for a ten pound bag of flour. . . . Hamburger would go up 4¢ a pound. . . . Round steak would go up 5¢ a pound." Roosevelt concluded his veto message: "The Bill presented to me would destroy the stabilization program. I cannot accept responsibility for its disastrous consequences. I hope the Congress will not compel these consequences."

As had been the case in July, enough House members switched, or refrained from voting, or added their votes in support of the president to sustain the veto by a vote of 226 to 151, a comfortable margin. Since failure to renew the life of the corporation would cut off various payments to farmers, farm-bloc members quickly introduced a renewal bill without the rider that sailed through.[41]

Although Morgenthau and other Treasury officials had called for a tax bill that would provide $10.5 billion in additional taxes, Congress provided a bill that increased taxes by a little more than $2 billion. The president said it actually added less than a billion to annual receipts. Although no general tax bill had been vetoed in the twentieth century, congressional leaders had expected one, but its vehemence startled and angered them. The message, Rosenman tells us, was written in Byrnes's office, and Roosevelt "signed it pretty much in the form in which it had come to him." Having important messages written without his active participation is an example of how Roosevelt loosened his supervision in the months after his return from Tehran.

The veto message called the bill "wholly ineffective" and "providing relief not for the needy but for the greedy." He criticized specifically:

elimination of increases in the Social Security law . . .

[increased use of] depletion allowances . . . [special exemptions for] the lumber industry . . . natural gas pipelines [and] commercial airlines. . . .

The Nation will readily understand that it is not the fault of the Treasury Department that the income taxpayers are flooded with forms to fill out that are so complex that not even Certified Public Accountants can interpret them. . . . Taxpayers, now engaged in an effort to win the greatest war the nation has ever faced, are not in the mood to study higher mathematics.

The president also criticized the congressional failure to provide graduated withholding rates, as the Treasury had suggested, which would have relieved millions of the lowest wage earners from withholding. He suggested that, after sustaining the veto, Congress by joint resolution could simply reimpose the existing excise taxes to protect the revenue stream. But most observers, and almost certainly the president himself, expected the veto to be overridden.

In what seems to have been an act of arrogance, Roosevelt after sending his veto to Congress early enough to have it read immediately made no mention of it in his Tuesday-afternoon press conference. He left for Hyde Park that evening instead of his normal Friday. In Congress on Tuesday and Wednesday, members from both sides of the aisle denounced what seemed to them as an unjustified attack on the integrity of Congress.

Majority Leader Barkley's forty-five-minute Senate speech on Wednesday, which occupied the better part of a page in the *New York Times,* was a point-by-point challenge of the president's veto. In an emotional conclusion, he announced that he would resign as majority leader at a meeting he had called for 10:30 the following morning, which is a senator's notion of an early start. His boast was: "There is something more precious to me than any honor. . . . That is the approval of my own conscience and my own self-respect."

After talking to Byrnes, Roosevelt composed a conciliatory telegram to Barkley and had Steve Early deliver it personally to Barkley's home and release it to the press.

> As I am out of the city [the president's telegram began] I am unable to have a personal talk with you. . . . I regret to learn that that you thought I had in my message attacked the integrity of yourself and other members of the Congress. Such you must know was not my intention. You and I may differ, and have differed on important measures, but that does not mean we question one another's good faith. . . .
>
> When on last Monday I read to you portions of my tax message and you indicated your disagreement, I made certain changes as a result of our talk. You did not however try to alter my basic decision. . . . While I did not realize how very strongly you felt about that basic decision, had I known, I should not have tried to dissuade you from exercising your own judgment in urging the overriding of the veto.
>
> I sincerely hope that you will not persist in your announced intention to resign as Majority Leader of the Senate. If you do, however, I hope that your colleagues do not accept your resignation, but if they do so I sincerely hope that they will immediately and unanimously reelect you.
>
> With the many serious problems daily confronting us, it is inevitable that at times you should differ with your colleagues and differ with me. I am sure that your differing with your colleagues does not lessen their confidence in you as leader. Certainly your differing with me does not affect my confidence in your leadership nor in any degree lessen my respect for you personally.
>
> Very sincerely yours,
>
> Franklin D. Roosevelt

The president knew his man and his colleagues. At the Thursday meeting, Barkley resigned and was immediately reelected by a unanimous vote of the Senate's Democrats.

Barkley responded in an equally conciliatory public letter, thanking the president for his "disavowal of any intention to reflect on my own or the integrity of other members of the Congress." He assured Roosevelt of his "personal affection" and commented that the language of the message was "abundantly susceptible" to the interpretation that he and other senators had made. He acknowledged that Roosevelt "was burdened with a responsibility that no other president has ever borne" and told him that "faith in you endures in me today and will continue to endure." He stressed the need for unity in "this great crisis." Insisting that "you have my utmost confidence and affection," he recounted the bare details of his resignation, reelection, and his continuance as majority leader, despite "my own personal preference to yield" because of his colleagues' "earnest and unanimous action" and "your own generous and manly statement to me." He closed by voicing his trust that "this incident" would bring "the executive and legislative departments closer together" in winning the war and establishing the peace.

The exchange of letters could not mend an irreparable breach between the president and Congress, and no serious person thought it could. But it did make it possible for most Democratic politicians to maintain a facade of unity with a presidential nominating convention less than five months away. Unlike his rigidity during the 1937 Court fight, Roosevelt realized that he had over-reached and responded quickly and effectively, making it easier for the minor-ity of Senate Democrats unswervingly loyal to him and his principles to work with the majority. The president's veto was easily brushed aside: in the House, Democrats voted ninety-nine to eighty-nine to override, as did all but three Republicans, while in the Senate only thirteen Democrats voted to sustain the president, while thirty-nine voted to override, as did all but one of three dozen Republicans.[42]

As winter turned into spring, it was difficult to tell just how well or ill Roos-evelt was. He seldom appeared in public. The *New York Times* reported late in March that "President Roosevelt went over to the Executive Office this morning after four days of confinement to his White House Quarters with a head cold."

Correspondents attending the March 24 press conference noted the appar-ent effects of his illness in his voice and appearance. He had no color, and his voice was out of usual pitch. "The illness from which he is now recovering is his second this year. Earlier, he was confined for two weeks with the grip[pe], from which he recovered slowly. He was reported to have lost ten pounds at that time."

At his next conference, on March 28, Roosevelt seemed most forthcoming in answering the inevitable question.

Q: Mr. President, in view of a lot of stories that have appeared, would you like to tell us how you feel?

THE PRESIDENT: How do I feel?

Q: Yes.

THE PRESIDENT: You mean personally?

Q: Yes.

THE PRESIDENT: I got bronchitis.

Q: But otherwise?

THE PRESIDENT: But otherwise—fine. I was out to the naval hospital this afternoon—went out after lunch, to get a thing called X-rays taken; and I have—I have had for probably a couple of weeks—between two and three weeks—a touch of bronchitis. It isn't very—(coughing involuntarily) serious, but I catch like that. That's about it.

Q: You don't view yourself with as much alarm—

THE PRESIDENT: (Interposing) No,—

Q: (Continuing)—as has been—

THE PRESIDENT: (Continuing)—except—(Again continuing)—I suppose bronchitis in one case out of 48 thousand 5 hundred develops into pneumonia. So I have one chance, according to the prognosis—I think that's the word—pneumonia. But I wouldn't use it as a headline, because there's rather a slim chance, especially as I have had it about three weeks.

There were no follow-up questions on health in the conference. Crider's front-page account in the *Times* described the president's "jovial mood" and said that he was "looking much better than he did last Friday. . . . Not only were the President's color and voice better than at Friday's press conference, when most correspondents thought he looked bad, but his spirits were good, too." Crider reprinted, without comment, Dr. McIntire's late-January assessment that "the Chief Executive was in better health than at any time since he entered the White House."[43]

What seemed to be a relatively frank statement from McIntire about the president's health was in fact a deception based on seeming frankness. It is a pattern of official concealment of presidential illnesses that goes back at least to Grover Cleveland in 1893 and continues into our own time.

The catalyst for a much-needed change in the president's health care seems to have been his daughter, Anna. With her husband, John Boettiger, serving overseas, she had come to the capital in early December 1943 with her three children, two teenagers and four-year-old John, intending to stay for the holidays. Unexpectedly, and to her everlasting delight, Anna became, without title or pay, an aide and hostess for her father, as she and her younger son lived in the White House for the rest of his presidency, while the teenagers went back to boarding schools.

Like others in the president's circle, Anna became increasingly concerned about his health in early 1944. Hassett, who had recently been promoted to secretary, taking Marvin McIntyre's slot, noted in his diary that Roosevelt was "not looking so well in his bedroom this morning, nor later when he held a press and radio conference—voice husky and out of pitch. The latest cold has taken lots out of him. Every morning, in response to inquiry as to how he felt, a characteristic reply has been 'Rotten' and 'Like hell.'"

Anna seems to have been instrumental in persuading or bullying Dr. McIntire into arranging a full physical examination of the president with the participation of other physicians, something that may not have been done since the celebrated 1932 examination for the insurance policy to demonstrate the health of the presidential candidate. We do not know when this 1944 examination was arranged, but Roosevelt told Hassett about it the evening before.[44]

The crucial part of the examination was conducted by Lieutenant Commander Howard G. Bruenn (1905–95), a cardiologist with an elite education— B.A. Columbia, M.D. Johns Hopkins, residency at Manhattan's Columbia Presbyterian—who was commissioned shortly after Pearl Harbor and soon assigned to the Navy Hospital at Bethesda, Maryland, just outside of the capital. He was a consultant in cardiology to the hospital and to the Third Naval District and head of the hospital's Electrocardiograph Department. Twenty-six years later, he published "Clinical Notes on the Illness and Death of President Franklin D. Roosevelt," beginning with the March 28, 1944, physical examination, in a professional medical journal. Since Roosevelt's medical chart, maintained and kept by Dr. McIntire, "could not be found" after Bruenn recorded the president's death on it, those notes plus Bruenn's unpublished diary provide the best documented record of Roosevelt's physical condition as president. Bruenn writes, "The President . . . was brought to the office in his wheel chair and lifted to the examining table by attendants. . . . He appeared to be very tired, and his face was very grey. Moving caused considerable breathlessness. He was in good humor but obviously moved with difficulty. He coughed frequently during the examination but produced no sputum."

Bruenn had Roosevelt give him a history of his post-Tehran illnesses and learned from the chart that he had developed a severe iron anemia deficiency in May 1941, evidently due to bleeding hemorrhoids that responded quickly to treatment. There were no cardiac symptoms reported at that time. Bruenn's own examination, which included an electrocardiogram, fluoroscope, and X-ray, showed "a temperature of 99 F by mouth, pulse of 72/min, and respiration of 24/min [and] Blood pressure was 186/108 mm Hg." Based on his reading of the cardiogram, X-rays, and fluoroscope observations, Bruenn arrived at the following "completely unsuspected" diagnosis and presented it to McIntire. "In view of the continued low-grade pulmonary infection and cough and dyspnea on effort, it appeared that these symptoms might well be due to early left ventricular failure. Accordingly, a diagnosis was made of hypertension, hypertensive heart disease, cardiac failure (left ventricular), and acute bronchitis."

On receiving this, McIntire requested a memorandum of recommendations, which Bruenn provided.

The patient should be put to bed for 1 to 2 weeks with nursing care.

Digitalization should be carried out: 0.4 grains of digitalis every day for 5 days; subsequently 0.1 grain every day.

A light easily digestible diet. Portions were to be small, salt intake was to be restricted. Potassium chloride in a salt shaker could be used as desired for seasoning.

Codeine, ½ grain, should be given for control of cough.

Sedation should be taken to ensure rest and a refreshing night's sleep.

A program of gradual weight reduction.

Bruenn reports that his advice was rejected by McIntire "because of the exigencies and demands on the President," and instead Roosevelt was placed on "modified bed rest and given a cough syrup with ammonium carbonate and codeine."[45] Bruenn protested, and under the hospital's protocols a series of meetings with medical staff and outside consultants occurred during the last three days of March. Bruenn's continuing challenge to McIntire—who was not only a vice admiral but also surgeon general of the navy—jeopardized his naval career. He made it clear that if his recommendations were not followed, he would withdraw from the case. His view eventually prevailed, and he became, in his words, "the attending physician to President Franklin D. Roosevelt from 1944 to the day of his death." McIntire, however, retained the title of personal physician to the president, and Bruenn was, almost literally, kept invisible until April 12, 1945, when he signed the president's death certificate.

In addition to blocking Bruenn's prescriptions for a time, McIntire continued his campaign of disinformation about the president's health that continued even after Roosevelt died. McIntire was acting not as a physician—several of his actions violated the Hippocratic Oath—but as a loyal member of Roosevelt's official family. Although forced to accept Bruenn's views about treatment, he publicly continued to maintain that Roosevelt's condition was not serious. In an unprecedented on-the-record news conference in Steve Early's office a week after the president's examination at Bethesda, McIntire told reporters, "I can say to you that the check-up is satisfactory. The only thing that we need to finish up on is just the residuals of bronchitis and one of his sinuses, and they are clearing very rapidly. He is feeling quite well this morning. In fact I think he will be getting out today. The greatest criticism we can have is the fact that we haven't been able to provide him with enough exercise and sunshine."

This statement, made at a time when Bruenn had been dosing the president with the powerful heart stimulant digitalis for five days, cannot be described as anything other than a lie. Similar statements are made in McIntire's memoir published the year after Roosevelt died. In his discussion of Roosevelt's final days, McIntire would have us believe that the president was never really sick until the unexpected massive cerebral hemorrhage occurred about two and a half hours before he was declared dead.

Perhaps the most shocking feature of McIntire's care, which can only be inferred in the absence of the president's chart, is his lack of interest in Roosevelt's blood pressure. Bruenn recorded, from the chart, a series of increasingly elevated blood-pressure readings beginning with 136/78 in 1935 and rising steadily to 188/105 in February 1941, after which no others were recorded until Bruenn got a reading of 186/108 on March 28, 1944. This makes it seem that McIntire did not want to know what his patient's blood pressure was. McIntire's views about Roosevelt's health were generally accepted until the 1970 publication of Bruenn's article.[46] The first book to utilize Bruenn's information was James M. Burns's second volume, *Roosevelt: The Soldier of Freedom* (1970).[47] All subsequent discussion of Roosevelt's health will be based on Bruenn's account and his later comments on it in an interview.

What Roosevelt thought of all this is difficult to say. Bruenn tells us that after he began to make almost daily visits to examine Roosevelt in the White House, "at no time did the President comment on the frequency of these visits or question the reasons for the electrocardiograms and the other laboratory tests that were performed from time to time; nor did he ever have any questions as to the type or variety of medications that were used."

Thus, while it may well be that his "I got bronchitis" remark at the March 28 press conference represented what he believed at that moment, he could not have been unaware that the repeated hookups to the cardiograph and frequent chest X-rays after the bronchitis had been cured meant that his doctors were concerned about his heart. Bruenn had been ordered not to volunteer information, so the "don't tell if he doesn't ask" policy meant that the president and his attending physician never spoke about his heart, although Bruenn always asked him how he was feeling, if he had slept well, and what his appetite was like. We can speculate that the reasons for this silent stoicism about his health were similar to his expressed views about assassination: since there was nothing he could do about it, he put it out of his mind.

Bruenn's regimen produced fairly rapid positive results; two weeks after the dosing of digitalis began, X-rays "showed a definite decrease in the size of the heart and marked clearing of the lung fields." But he indicated in both his essay and later interviews that, after the effects of the digitalis and other aspects of his prescriptions took effect, Roosevelt remained a patient with "heart failure" and at great risk of a fatal attack.

It may well be, as political historian Robert H. Ferrell argues in his lugubrious *The Dying President: Franklin D. Roosevelt, 1944–1945*, that a December–January illness marks the beginning of a long decline that led to Roosevelt's death fifteen months later. But as one layman criticizing another, it seems to me that as far as we *know,* the president was first diagnosed as having a serious heart condition in March 1944 and died in April 1945. Describing him as "dying" during that period and thus calling into question his decisions and directions during those crucial months in world history is a political and not a medical description.

On April 7, Roosevelt held the only White House press conference of the month. The *Times* again took Crider's description of the president's health out of his press conference story, but this time put both stories on the front page. The health story noted that the president had been "confined to his quarters by order of Vice Admiral Ross T. McIntire, his personal physician, because of a stubborn cold and sinus complications." Crider added that "correspondents thought he looked better than when they last saw him a week ago Tuesday. . . . He had been hoarse for some time, but today his voice sounded about normal, and he appeared to be in his customary good humor."

Not a word about Dr. Bruenn appeared in the *Times* until the stories about Roosevelt's death. In the busy wartime White House traffic, it was easy not to notice one more khaki-uniformed middle-grade officer. Bruenn told an interviewer, "They gave me a car and I would drive [to the White House] in the morning to see him then go back to work in the hospital." At the April press conference, strangely, there were no questions about Roosevelt's health or how he felt; perhaps reporters had been warned off by Early."[48]

That night, with no public announcement, Roosevelt left by train for a planned two-week vacation that lasted a month at Bernard Baruch's secluded twenty-three-thousand-acre estate, Hobcaw Barony, largely a hunting preserve on the South Carolina coast, near the small port city of Georgetown, population twelve thousand. The president had wanted to go to Guantánamo, which would have given him even more privacy and better weather and fishing, but security concerns and inconvenience of access ruled that out. For Baruch, Margaret Coit has argued, the "presidential visit marked a crowning achievement"; Baruch himself wrote that "I spent many hours with F.D.R. during that sojourn," but it is doubtful if they were often alone.

The president's party consisted of the regulars—Admiral Leahy, military aides Pa Watson and William Brown, and Dr. McIntire—plus Dr. Bruenn, who would accompany Roosevelt on all his trips outside of Washington for the remainder of his life, and assistant naval aide Lieutenant William Rigdon, who acted as Roosevelt's traveling secretary, as he would do on many later occasions. As usual the Secret Service had reconnoitered the plantation and its surroundings as well as modifying the house and grounds for the president: ramps and railings built, an escape chute installed from a second-floor bedroom, and portable telephones linked to the White House switchboard, as Baruch deliberately refused to have telephone service in the house.

The morning after Roosevelt arrived, in a departure from previous wartime practice, the White House announced that the president "has left Washington for the South" and would be away for about two weeks, "unless some unexpected emergency" compelled his return, but did not reveal where in the region the president was staying. It mentioned the presence of three wire-service reporters whose stories would be embargoed until after his return.

United Press (UP) reporter Merriman Smith recounts in his memoir the frustrating experience of "covering" a president whom he didn't even lay eyes on for twenty days. He makes it clear that the presidential presence was not a secret locally, something that Roosevelt understood. Smith's notes for the fourth day of the visit claim that "about every living soul in Georgetown and the surrounding county knows that 'He' is here. . . . Ladies in the grocery stores say that not only the President, but Churchill and Stalin are out fishing."

It took the death of a cabinet member—Navy Secretary Knox from the effects of a series of heart attacks—for Roosevelt to convoke a late-evening press conference for the three wire-service men to express regret and get a tribute on the record. Among the president's comments was one that may have reflected his hopes about his own situation: "that it was the Lord's great will that the Secretary had been spared to do the great work that he had done toward the nation's victory." The White House ignored the conference but issued a statement in the president's name.

The best inside report on the vacation is a long paragraph from Bruenn's essay.

> At Hobcaw the weather was excellent, although a little cool, and the President followed a very simple regimen. He usually awakened about 9:30 AM. He had breakfast in bed, and I attended him shortly thereafter.
>
> He spent most of the morning reading newspapers and going over his correspondence. Lunch was usually attended with the group. . . . After lunch the President usually retired for a nap, and later he either went fishing in a Coast Guard patrol boat . . ., motoring, or on occasion visiting with [Baruch's daughter] Belle . . . occasional visitors including Mrs. Roosevelt . . . daughter Anna, Mrs. Rutherford, Miss Suckley, and various important dignitaries. In the late afternoon and early evening the President would go over the contents of the "pouch" . . . and sign the necessary papers. Dinner was at 7 PM, preceded by cocktails of which the president had one or two dry martinis. Rarely did the president give the signal for rising from dinner before 8:30 or 9 PM. The conversation was animated with the President playing the dominant role. It ranged from reminiscences [sic] with Mr. Baruch over earlier contemporaries and incidents to a discussion of recent and current events.

The president remained "asymptomatic until April 28," Bruenn reports, when periods of sometimes acute abdominal pain began. This eventually kept him in bed for two days in the first week of May, but by the time of departure (May 6), that pain "had entirely subsided." Roosevelt "looked well . . . lungs were entirely clear . . . heart remained enlarged . . . electrocardiogram remained unchanged . . . blood pressure taken twice daily [April 9–June 14] averaged about 196/112 mm Hg on awakening and 194/96 mm Hg in the evening."

Asked during the second three-man press conference on departure day about how he had spent his stay:

> THE PRESIDENT: Very little. Just been sitting around on the dock and riding around on the plantation. I have been to the jut of this peninsula. Have seen the old fort there, and the old graveyard. The majority of the graves there are of British officers. It was there that the main traffic artery, the King's highway—north to south—came down from Myrtle Beach to the south, ferried across the river to Belle Isle and another fort. These two forts guarded the river.

Roosevelt also said that he very much wanted to come back.[49]

A "tanned, rested" president was greeted at Union Station by Secretary Hull, who rode with him to the White House. Dr. McIntire told reporters that "it is my feeling that we gained everything we expected from a four-weeks rest and I am perfectly satisfied with his physical condition." The physician's remarks complemented nicely the prediction made in New York by the new Democratic national chairman, Robert E. Hannegan (1903–49), at a Jefferson Day Dinner, that Roosevelt, "fit and ready for the fight" despite "malicious rumors to the contrary," would run and defeat Dewey in November, even though the president had not announced his candidacy and neither man had been nominated. Unlike 1940, when the questions of whether Roosevelt should or would run dominated the preconvention period, in 1944 it was largely assumed by friends and foes alike that the president would run for a fourth term, and Dewey was strongly favored to win the GOP nomination.

The next day, the president met with his secretaries in his bedroom just before ten in the morning and told them that at Hobcaw, he had worked four hours a day and that since, in Hassett's words, "the nation got along . . . he thought he owed it to the country to continue that schedule." The president said he would spend two hours in the mornings on appointments and told Pa Watson to minimize them, eat lunch alone, rest for an hour and a half, and then spend two hours on paperwork. Hassett commented in his diary, "This is too good to be true. We shall see." When asked about the reduced schedule, Early confirmed that the president was taking it a little easier and said that Dr. McIntire did not want him to return to "a killing pace."

In retrospect, it seems apparent that for the next few weeks, Roosevelt was largely quiescent, resting himself for the exertions that were on his agenda. At the first of four May press conferences, on May 9, the first question was whether he had "heard of the Montgomery Ward case." The question was not really about the "case," a labor dispute between the giant mostly mail-order retailer and its workers, which had resulted in a federal seizure. It was about what was already a famous photograph published in the morning papers of April 28 of Ward's chairman, Sewell L. Avery (1874–1960), obviously angry, being carried from his building by two military policemen while still seated in his office chair. The seizure occurred because of the firm's refusal to obey a unanimous NWLB order to continue a union contract pending a recertification election. This provoked a strike that interrupted the shipment of war materials ordered by the government.

Roosevelt, aware of a Gallup poll report that 61 percent of those with opinions thought that the government had made a "mistake," talked about "the law" and complained of the failure of the press to explain the issues. At his next press conference, the president ignored the fact that the Senate had refused to invoke cloture to end a filibuster on anti–poll tax legislation. It was the fourth and final attempt to end debate in the Senate during the entire Roosevelt presidency. Each involved what we would call today a civil rights measure and failed, with none receiving more than forty-two positive votes. If all Senators voted, the rules then provided that sixty-four votes were necessary to end debate.[50]

After his return to the White House on the morning of May 25, the president began a fuller but still reduced schedule, holding, for the first time in more than two months, consecutive press conferences on May 26 and 30. Reporters found him more forthcoming and reflective. A keen sense of anticipation pervaded much of Washington and the nation. All knew that a cross-Channel invasion was in the works, but only a very few knew exactly where or when. The president and many governors, including New York's Dewey, had already suggested that civilians go to their homes or churches for prayers when D-Day was announced. Several of the minor baseball leagues announced that there would be no games on D-Day, but both major leagues announced that scheduled games would not be canceled but suggested to the clubs that if D-Day was announced prior to a game, it should be started with prayer, and that if a game was under way, it should be interrupted for a prayer and the national anthem and then resumed.

The press conference on May 26 was so packed with information that four separate page 1 stories in the *Times* resulted from it, one of which was manufactured. The president parried the inevitable questions about his candidacy in November, ending with a good-natured "Time will tell." Someone later asked:

Q: Mr. President, do you anticipate a meeting with Mr. Churchill this summer?

THE PRESIDENT: Oh, I hope some time, but I don't know when. This summer, or autumn—or late spring—something like that.

From this one correspondent wrote a page 1 story that began, "A press conference remark by President Roosevelt that he might meet Prime Minister

Churchill . . . late next spring," and went on to claim that this was "the clearest public indication . . . that he expects to run." Although Roosevelt was not bashful about complaining about newspaper misrepresentation, he simply qualified his remarks in the next conference, admitting that he had made "an unfortunate slip." He amended it to "like to see Mr. Churchill . . . between now and next January 20th" and that "I'd like to see him next spring, regardless."

Roosevelt had begun the conference by announcing the details of the forthcoming monetary conference at Bretton Woods, New Hampshire, whose details had been accurately leaked the day before. This meeting laid the foundations for the International Monetary Fund and the other international arrangements and institutions that still dominate international economic institutions. Roosevelt's stress on such matters was another example of his increasing focus on postwar problems since the Tehran meeting and even before the great battles of the war had been joined. He remarked that in December 1918, when Wilson went to Europe for the Peace Conference, "there had been practically no discussion of postwar–first World War terms with the other allies." He contrasted this with the present concerns and recent conferences such as the one on food and the very recent ILO meeting and with the Casablanca, Cairo, and Tehran meetings.

He demonstrated this more fully in the next press conference when asked a pair of "softball" questions about his original support for Wilson's League of Nations and how he felt about a League of Nations today; his response might have been affected by his awareness of Memorial Day. After a White House military aide had placed a Memorial Day wreath at the Tomb of the Unknown Soldier in the morning, the president, along with Eleanor and Anna, was driven to Arlington and, largely unnoticed by other visitors, had slowly traversed the winding roads of the cemetery and, on the way back to the White House, had driven up to the Lincoln Memorial.

In the afternoon press conference, after affirming his support for the league in 1919—"I was quite right in supporting it at the time"—he stressed the differences between then and now.

> We hoped that there would never be any more wars. . . . Today we are a little older; we have gone through some pretty tough times together. And perhaps we are not saying that we can devise a method of ending all wars for all time. . . .
>
> And so we have an objective today, and that is to join with the other Nations of the world not in such a way that some other nation would decide whether we were to build a new dam on the Conestoga Creek, but for general world peace in setting up some machinery of talking things over with other Nations, without taking away the independence of the United States in any shape, manner, or form, or destroying—what's the other word?—the *integrity* of the United States in any shape, manner or form; with the effort

of working so closely that if some nation in the world started to run amuck, or some combination of nations, and seeks to grab territory or invade its neighbors, that there would be a unanimity of opinion that the time to stop them was before they got started; that is, all the other nations that weren't in with them.[51]

This vague and somewhat simplistic soliloquy represents, it seems to me, an accurate snapshot of Roosevelt's general hopes for world organization as he waited for the outcome of the largest military operation in American history, which he knew would kill thousands of young men whom he had sent into battle.

11 The Last Campaign
1944

VETERAN CORRESPONDENT CHARLES HURD (1903–68), who had covered the president as early as the 1932 convention and recently begun an encore stint as the *Times'* White House correspondent, wrote in an early June feature that for a time, it seemed "Mr. Roosevelt was losing the facility of making the conferences sprightly, pre-eminent as news developers; that possibly he was bored with them. . . . Now [after his month at Hobcaw] Mr. Roosevelt reflects his new energy in the vigor with which he conducts the conferences."

An examination of the transcripts of six consecutive scheduled press conferences plus a special one between May 26 and June 13, 1944, supports Hurd's contention that these conferences again could be described as "one of the most potent political forces in the history of the White House." In that period, Roosevelt spoke to the American people for the first time since January, gave a reception for House members, and had numerous appointments, although his schedule remained somewhat restricted.[1]

In the final May press conference, Roosevelt, responding to a question he clearly expected, began to unveil the scheme that represents his most lasting positive contribution to American immigration policy.

> Q: Mr. President, there has been considerable agitation recently for this establishment of the—what have been termed free ports for Jewish refugees in this country. What is your reaction to this proposal?
>
> THE PRESIDENT: I like—I like the—I don't like the name, but I like the idea, and we are working on it now. And well, when you said "this country," I'd take those two words out, because it is not, in my judgment, necessary to decide that we have to have a free port right here in the United States. There are lots of other places in the world where refugees conceivably could go to.

The free-ports idea, essentially a scheme of allowing refugees into the United States temporarily, to house and feed them at restricted sites—Ellis Island and surplus army camps were most frequently discussed—had been pushed by a number of interest groups, most prominently the National Committee against

Persecution of the Jews, chaired by Supreme Court Justice Frank Murphy, and had been endorsed by several newspapers, including the *New York Times*.

At the next press conference, though the president continued to talk about the possibility of bringing some refugees to the United States, and mentioned the possibility of using a surplus army camp to house them, he stressed the practical utility of taking care of most refugees in overseas locations, what are now called camps of first asylum. He spoke of meeting with Secretary Morgenthau and John Pehle of the War Refugee Board about the situation; he also met with UNRRA head Lehman. Asked whether refugees brought here would have to return:

THE PRESIDENT: Oh, absolutely.

Q: Wouldn't stay here—not as citizens?

THE PRESIDENT: No, no. Not a bit.

Q: Sir—Mr. President, is that the "free port" idea, which would allow the refugees to come in for this temporary residence, regardless of quotas and visas?

THE PRESIDENT: I think that's it. If you have some starving and perfectly helpless people—after all they are human beings—and we can give them—what?—the assurance of life somewhere else, it seems like it's the humanitarian thing to do.

That morning New York City's Samuel Dickstein (1885–1954), longtime chair of the House Committee on Immigration and Naturalization, introduced a congressional resolution to permit the president to declare "free ports" open to refugees for "religious or racial reasons" for the duration plus six months, which was not the course the president would pursue, at a time of his choosing.[2]

After the long-delayed capture of Rome by Mark Clark's Fifth Army on June 4, the White House announced a fifteen-minute presidential talk on the city's liberation for the next evening at an unusual day and hour, Monday night at 8:30 Washington time. Roosevelt, but not his speechwriters, knew that the D-Day invasion was scheduled for that morning and expected to be able to speak of it. The president, along with Anna and her husband, had spent the weekend at Pa Watson's home in Charlottesville, Virginia, and while there had written a prayer of some five hundred words that he had intended to read at the end of the June 5 talk. A stormy weather forecast caused a postponement of the landings.

The speech aired on schedule and was a confident if subdued account, with a curious, nonidiomatic phrase counting the fall of the first enemy capital as "One up and two to go!" It contained a long tribute to the Italian people and to their contributions as immigrants to the United States and other countries that would have been comfortable in a Columbus Day tribute. He did warn against overconfidence—"It would be a mistake to inflate in our own minds the military importance of the capture of Rome"—and cautioned that "victory still lies some distance ahead." He closed with a tribute to both American and British commanders, naming six generals and two admirals, ending, in place of his prayer with the benediction, "May God bless them and watch over them and over all of our gallant fighting men."

He went up to his bedroom early on the night of June 5; he was awakened at about 3:00 a.m. with the first news of successful landings in Normandy coming to him from the Pentagon as it was announced from Eisenhower's headquarters. Later in the morning, copies of the prayer he had written were sent to Congress, where it was read in each house, and to the wire services, so it could be printed in afternoon papers along with the announcement that it would be read by the president on the air at 10:00 p.m. After a brief introduction, the president read his prayer to the people with no comment. The words were those of a man steeped in the cadences of the King James Version of the Bible.

My fellow Americans:

Almighty God: Our sons, pride of our Nation, this day have set upon a mighty endeavor, a struggle to preserve our Republic, our religion, and our civilization, and to set free a suffering humanity.

Lead them straight and true; give strength to their arms, stoutness to their hearts, steadfastness in their faith. They will need Thy blessings. Their road will be long and hard. For the enemy is strong. He may hurl back our forces. Success may not come with rushing speed, but we shall return again and again; and we know that by Thy grace, and by the righteousness of our cause, our sons will triumph.

They will be sore tried, by night and by day, without rest—until the victory is won. The darkness will be rent by noise and flame. Men's souls will be shaken with the violences of war.

For these men are lately drawn from the ways of peace. They fight not for the lust of conquest. They fight to end conquest. They fight to liberate. They fight to let justice arise, and tolerance and good will among all Thy people. They yearn but for the end of battle, for their return to the haven of home.

Some will never return. Embrace these, Father, and receive them, Thy heroic servants, into Thy kingdom.

And for us at home—fathers, mothers, children, wives, sisters and brothers of brave men overseas—whose thoughts and prayers are ever with them—help us, Almighty God, to rededicate ourselves in renewed faith in Thee in this hour of great sacrifice.

Many people have urged that I call the nation into a single day of special prayer. But because the road is long and the desire is great, I ask that our people devote themselves in a continuance of prayer. As we rise to each new day, and again when each day is spent, let words of prayer be on our lips, invoking Thy help in our efforts.

Give us strength, too—strength in our daily tasks, to redouble the contributions we make in the physical and material support of our armed forces.

And let our hearts be stout, to wait out the long travail, to bear sorrows that may come, to impart our courage unto our sons wheresoever they may be.

And, O Lord, give us Faith. Give us Faith in Thee; Faith in our sons; Faith in each other; Faith in our united crusade. Let not the keenness of our spirit ever be dulled. Let not the impacts of temporary events, of temporal matters of but fleeting moment—let not these deter us in our unconquerable purpose.

With Thy blessing, we shall prevail over the unholy forces of our enemy. Help us to conquer the apostles of greed and racial arrogancies. Lead us to the saving of our country, and with our sister Nations into a world unity that will spell a sure peace, a peace invulnerable to the schemings of unworthy men. And a peace that will let all of men live in freedom, reaping the just rewards of their honest toil. Thy will be done, Almighty God.

Amen.

Roosevelt, in shirtsleeves and looking tired but happy, efficiently conducted a fairly full briefing and answered many questions directly, a relatively rare occurrence in wartime. He was not entirely frank, saying that the planning "goes all the way back to December 1941" when a proper answer would have been "early 1941." He did reveal that the general decision had been made at Tehran, that Stalin had been fully informed about the date and was satisfied, that the precise date, later postponed one day because of weather, had been made by Eisenhower, and that no such second front could have taken place in 1943 because of the lack of trained men and equipment. Only when questions touched future operations was discussion closed down. After Roosevelt said that perhaps "half a dozen different places" could have been chosen for the landings, he was asked:

Q: Mr. President, may there still be a half dozen different places?
THE PRESIDENT: Gosh! What an awful question. You know they are all improper, highly improper.[3]

Much of the following day was spent with Stanislaw Mikolajczyk, described by the White House as the prime minister of Poland, but he was actually the leader of an exile group, often described as the London Poles, as opposed to a government recognized by the USSR, known as the Moscow Poles. As Roosevelt had explained to Stalin, the opinions of Polish American voters, particularly numerous in western New York, Pennsylvania, Michigan, and Illinois, whose leaders overwhelmingly favored the London group, were of concern to him. At a June 7 state dinner, the president made what the White House called a "toast" to Mikolajczyk, noting that he and his guest had had a "frank talk about the future of Poland." "Within his lifetime and mine we have seen the rebirth of Poland. In my boyhood and his, there was no independent Poland."

After pointing out that one historic map showed a Poland that included "most of Russia and a good part of Germany and Czechoslovakia," Roosevelt insisted, "We have got to do the practical thing. . . . And I hope sometime very soon that steps will be taken by which the people of Poland and the very large nation that lies to the East will become not merely good neighbors—that is an essential—but also two Nations, one very, very large and the other a good deal smaller, that will be able to work out a mutual economic system by which there will be complete independence on the part of Poland."

Roosevelt went on to note that "at Tehran," Stalin said that he wanted Poland to be "a completely independent nation." The message was clear. Poland had to accommodate itself to its eastern neighbor, which had already liberated some of Poland and would presumably soon control all of prewar Poland. A few days later, Roosevelt, in a message to Stalin, described the Polish leader as "a very sincere and reasonable man whose sole desire is to do what is best for his country. He is fully cognizant that the whole future of Poland depends on the establishment of good relations with the Soviet Union."[4]

Almost two weeks after Roosevelt's May 26 physical examination, Dr. McIntire convoked an "informal" press conference—that is, no transcript—in Steve Early's office to fulfill the promise of a "full report" about it. What he said was more relevant to the art of public relations than of medicine. He claimed that Roosevelt's health was "excellent in all respects" and better than average for a man of his age. He added that "all the checks are well within normal limits" and "extremely satisfactory"; there was no mention of the president's enlarged heart or blood pressure.[5]

The president's press conferences continued to be jam-packed with news, both on and off the record. The most significant stories from the June 9 conference announcements were of a long-delayed White House visit by the skittish General de Gaulle in the coming weeks and of "some fairly definite action on the problem of the refugees." After noting that their number in Italy continued to rise and that non-Italians were being shipped to camps in North Africa, Sicily, and Cyprus with a capacity of forty thousand, Roosevelt added, "In the meantime, we found that we had a camp which was not being used for training purposes on a big scale: Fort Ontario, New York—this is just across the river from Oswego—and we are going to bring over a thousand, that's all, to go into that camp."

When a veteran correspondent, who understood that immigration was a traditional congressional preserve and tried to get him to comment on a flurry of bills and resolutions that had been introduced on the topic of "free ports," the president's response was, an improbable, "No. I never heard of it," which signaled an end of the discussion.

Later that day, the White House released the text of a cable of presidential instructions to Ambassador Robert Murphy in Algiers:

> I feel that it is important that the United States indicate that it is ready to share the burden of caring for refugees during the war. Accordingly, I have decided that approximately 1,000 refugees should be immediately brought from Italy to this country, to be placed in an Emergency Refugee Shelter to be established at Fort Ontario near Oswego, New York, where under appropriate security restrictions they will remain for the duration of the war. These refugees will be brought into this country outside of the regular immigration procedure just as civilian internees from Latin American countries and prisoners of war have been brought here. The Emergency Refugee Shelter will be well equipped to take good care of these people. It is contemplated that at the end of the war they will be returned to their homelands.

The thousand sent to Fort Ontario has been described, quite properly, as a "token shipment." Roosevelt clearly had multiple motives. First, he wanted to show other nations that the United States was doing something for refugees. He also wanted to have something to talk about during the fall presidential campaign. In addition, and in the long run more important, he was also creating a precedent for bold executive action in an area that had been an almost exclusive congressional preserve. The president's timing, as Congress was busily trying to wind up a number of important legislative measures prior to a late June adjournment to attend national conventions and mend fences back home, meant that it might not attract much attention.

He sent up a message on June 12 notifying Congress of what he had done. After beginning with an overstatement of what he called Congress's "deep concern" about the "plight of persecuted minorities in Europe," the president restated Nazi intentions: "As the hour of the final defeat of the Hitlerite forces draws near, the fury of their insane desire to wipe out the Jewish race in Europe continues undiminished." He reprised the activities of his War Refugee Board that "operating quietly . . . has actually succeeded in saving the lives of innocent people. . . . Above all the efforts of the Board have brought new hope to the oppressed peoples of Europe" by what the president claimed was "the concrete manifestation of this Government's desire to do all possible to aid and rescue the distressed." Roosevelt reiterated his determination "to punish all participants in these acts of savagery" and admitted that "the numbers of those rescued from the jaws of death have been small." He went on to tell Congress what he had done "in an effort to save additional lives," adding new details worked out since his press conference, "and which I am certain will meet with your approval."

The major new detail was that the camp at Fort Ontario would be administered by the War Relocation Authority. This move obviated the need to go to Congress for extra money, as the WRA had released many thousands of its prisoners, mostly Nisei, and had surplus funds and personnel. As things turned out, none of the nearly thousand refugees were sent back. Just before Christmas 1945, President Truman ordered that the immigration status of those who wanted to stay be adjusted and the twenty-three babies born in the camp before it closed recognized as American citizens. Later, the Eisenhower administration ruled that Roosevelt's action had created a "parole authority," which it invoked initially to admit Hungarian refugees in 1956.[6]

On June 12, the president went on the air for the third time in seven days with a Fireside Chat to kick off the Fifth War Loan. Besides urging everyone to buy bonds and stamps, he reported on a "panorama of world war" and spoke of having "firm footholds in France with losses lower than expected." "While I know that the chief interest tonight is centered on the English Channel and on the beaches and farms and the cities of Normandy, we should not lose sight of the fact that our armed forces are engaged on other battlefronts all over the world, and that no one front can be considered alone without its proper relation to all."

He then compared the current situation with June 1942, when "Germany [controlled] practically all of Europe" and was pushing "the Russians back toward the Ural Mountains" and threatening the Suez Canal. "Italy was still an important factor," and Japan was knocking at the gates of Australia and New Zealand and controlled "the western Aleutian Islands."

> American armed forces on land and sea and in the air were definitely on the defensive, and in the building up stage. Our allies were bearing the heat and the brunt of the attack. . . .
>
> But today we are on the offensive all over the world—bringing the attack to our enemies . . .
>
> True, we still have a long way to go to Tokyo. But carrying out our original strategy of eliminating our European enemy first and then turning all our strength to the Pacific, we can force the Japanese to unconditional surrender or to national suicide much more rapidly than has been thought possible.

Returning to the European theater and "our enemy who is first on the list for destruction," Roosevelt depicted a Germany with "her back against the wall—in fact three walls at once."

From the south, "Allied armies" had taken Rome and "broken the German hold on central Italy." From the east, "our gallant Soviet allies" had driven the enemy back from the "lands . . . invaded three years ago."

> Overhead—vast Allied air fleets . . . have been waging a bitter air war [with] two major objectives: to destroy German war industries . . . and to shoot German Luftwaffe out of the air. . . .

And on the west—the hammer blow which struck the coast of France last Tuesday . . . was the culmination of many months of planning and strenuous preparation.

Millions of tons of weapons and supplies, and hundreds of thousands of men assembled in England are being poured into the great battle in Europe . . .

What has been done in the United States since those days of 1940—when France fell—in raising and equipping and transporting our fighting forces, and in producing weapons supplies for war, has been nothing short of a miracle. It was largely due to American teamwork—teamwork among capital and labor and agriculture, between the armed forces and the civilian economy—indeed among all of them. And everyone—every man or woman or child—who bought a war bond helped—and helped mightily.

In the final sentences of his fifteen-minute talk, Roosevelt urged everyone to buy more war bonds. He was clearly successful in doing that. He was also making the best possible campaign speech—without even hinting at an election—by associating himself with the most vital issue, winning the war.[7]

The highlight of the June 13 press conference, which ended a string of six consecutive Friday–Tuesday gatherings actually held, was Roosevelt reading a personal report to him from Eisenhower that "came in yesterday" and was much more vital than the regular communiqué.

The first great obstacle has been surmounted—that is the breaching of the beach defenses that the enemy by lavish employment of enslaved labor had installed in forest-like density along the entire lateral of northwest Europe. . . .

This battle is but a mere beginning to the tremendous struggle that must follow before final victory. . . .

Through the opening thus made, and through others yet to come, the flood of our fighting strength must be poured. Our operations, vast and important as they are, are only part of the larger pattern of a combined assault against the fortress of Germany by the great Russian armies from the East and our forces from the Mediterranean.

The Nazis will be forced to fight throughout the perimeter of their stronghold, daily expending their dwindling resources until overwhelmed by the hopelessness of their position. To this end, we need every man, every weapon, and all the courage of our respective peoples. The Allied soldier will do his duty.

Roosevelt sloughed off with good humor questions about his electoral intentions and when asked about the vice presidential slot suggested that the reporter "go to China," where Henry Wallace had been sent. Asked about the progress of the war, the president replied that what he had said in his talk "last night . . . was still current."

Later that day, despite recommendations from Stimson and Forrestal to the contrary, Roosevelt signed a congressional joint resolution extending by six months the statutory limit for instituting court-martial or other proceedings about responsibility for Pearl Harbor. He noted that his cabinet officers feared that interference with the war effort might result, but he was sure that Congress intended no such thing. This was the second extension he had approved; he would approve another in December, and a final extension was approved by Truman in June 1945. The congressional Pearl Harbor Attack Hearings of 1946, as well as separate investigations by each service, settled nothing. No court-martial proceedings were ever instituted against anyone for the obvious failures of the Hawaiian command. None were even hinted at for the failures in the Philippines.

On June 15, just before leaving for an unannounced week in Hyde Park and after a series of conferences with Secretary Hull and other State Department officials, Roosevelt issued his first detailed statement about postwar international organization. As we know, he had been talking about the United Nations since the 1941 Argentia conference. He neither mentioned the League of Nations nor gave his proposed organization a name, but he was obviously seeking to replace the body created at Versailles in 1919. His statement, fewer than five hundred words, called for creating "a fully representative body with broad responsibilities for promoting and facilitating international cooperation, through such agencies as may be found necessary, to consider and deal with the problems of world relations. It is our further thought that the organization would provide for a council, elected annually by the fully representative body of all Nations, which would include the four major Nations and a suitable number of other Nations. The council would concern itself with peaceful settlement of international disputes."

The president did not identify "the four major Nations," but the State Department announced that invitations would be sent to Britain, the Soviet Union, and China for a meeting, with a date not yet set, to discuss the proposed organization. He made no mention of the two international agencies already functioning, the UNRRA and the Food and Agriculture Organization (FAO).[8]

After the flurry of activities leading up to and after D-Day, the president's stay at Hyde Park was quiet and uneventful. He and Eleanor gave a picnic at Val-Kill for Norwegian crown princess Martha and her children, who were their guests for most of the week. On their return to the White House, Hassett commented that the president was "looking in the pink of condition."

The first order of business was a signing ceremony in the Oval Office for the G.I. Bill of Rights, a measure that had been originally drafted by the Armed Forces Committee on Post-War Educational Opportunities for Service Personnel, which the president had created in October 1942 and whose roots went back to studies made by the Veterans Administration in the aftermath of the bonus marches. A year later, after his committee had reported, the president sent its report to Congress and urged action. The statute the president signed covered more than education: it provided veterans with loan guarantees for the purchase or renovation of homes, farms, and businesses; offered a no-questions-asked fifty-two weeks of unemployment insurance at twenty dollars a week—the so-called 52–20 club—even if the veteran had never held a civilian job, and included funds for building hospitals and for better management of them. But the educational benefits that Roosevelt described as giving "servicemen and women the opportunity of resuming their education or technical training, not only without tuition charge up to $500 per school year, but with the right to receive a monthly living allowance while pursuing their studies" were the most important part of the complex measure. Roosevelt expressed the hope that Congress would soon make members of the merchant marine eligible for similar benefits, but legislation to do that was narrowly defeated.

Many of the leaders of elite universities opposed the G.I. Bill. Robert M. Hutchins, the celebrated president of the University of Chicago, predicted that it would turn American universities into "hobo jungles." Five years later, *Fortune* reported that the postwar veterans had produced the most mature and most disciplined classes of college students in American history, a verdict endorsed by public opinion and historians.[9]

In a brief press conference the next day, Roosevelt expressed disappointment that the Battle of the Philippine Sea, or the Marianas Turkey Shoot (June 19–21), did not result in destruction of the Japanese fleet, commenting that "it is rather difficult to destroy a fleet that runs away." He also released the names of the twelve American delegates to the forthcoming monetary conference at Bretton Woods, New Hampshire. The list included two Republican members of Congress, reinforcing, at a highly partisan time, the bipartisan aspects of his international policies initiated in 1940 with the Stimson and Knox appointments.[10]

At another brief press conference on Tuesday, Roosevelt told the press that the long-bruited White House meeting with de Gaulle would probably take place between July 5 and 9. This flurry of late May and June press conferences—there were nine between May 26 and June 27—was the last of its kind. In the remaining nine-plus months of his presidency there would be only fifteen of the supposedly twice-weekly press conferences. This was due in part to the president's extensive travels, particularly the trips to the Pacific theater and to the Crimea, and in part to his fluctuating health.

On July 29, Roosevelt signed eight appropriation bills, chief among them an additional forty-nine billion dollars for the army; more than a hundred other bills followed him to Hyde Park when he went there for a week that included the July 4 holiday. Accompanying him, in addition to Hassett and staff, were Anna, her three children, and their Labrador retriever.

The most important of the bills signed at Hyde Park were one whose major provisions extended the life of the Office of Price Administration for a year and another strengthening the U.S. Public Health Service (USPHS). In signing the OPA extension, he congratulated Congress for renewing "the general authority vested in the executive agencies . . . to hold the line against inflation." He noted that during the three months of congressional debate over the "Extension Act . . . the clamor of pressure groups was loud in the land [but happily] Congress has stood firm against any departure from the basic principles" that had kept the cost of living level during the past year.

Unlike the OPA, the USPHS had not been a bone of contention. The service itself had existed since 1798; as part of the 1939 reorganization, it had been moved from the Treasury into the new Federal Security Agency. The 1944 act made it a research funding agency with authority to make grants-in-aid to public and private institutions "for investigation in any field related to the public health" and provided twenty million dollars annually for such grants. This largely un-heralded measure made the federal government a major source of funding for medical research. It also established a national tuberculosis program within the USPHS and gave commissions to public health nurses, "just as the nurses of the Army and the Navy are commissioned." "In establishing a national program of war and post-war prevention, [the president concluded], we will be making as sound an investment as any government can make; the dividends are payable in human life and health."

In a message read at the opening of the Bretton Woods Conference, Roosevelt welcomed the delegates from forty-four nations who had responded to his call and observed that "the war has prodded us into the healthy habit of coming together in conference" to discuss and solve problems. He referred to the recent conferences creating the FAO and UNRRA. Those, he noted, had been "essentially emergency matters." Without referring directly to the two immediate objectives at Bretton Woods, the establishment of an international monetary stabilization fund and a world bank, Roosevelt instead spoke of its long-term goal. "Commerce is the life blood of a free society. We must see to it that the arteries which carry that blood stream are not clogged as they have been in the past, by artificial barriers created through senseless economic rivalries. . . . This conference will test our ability to cooperate in peace as we have in war. I know that you will approach your task with a high sense of responsibility to those who have sacrificed so much in their hopes for a better world."

Roosevelt seems never to have been too busy to intervene on behalf of individuals about to be run over by the government juggernaut. The president had demonstrated on a number of occasions that he was particularly interested in the welfare of the female members of the military. Hassett relates in some detail what his boss did about a navy nurse who had gone AWOL (absent without leave) after her superior officer had denied her request for a delayed honeymoon with her sailor husband. Roosevelt refused to sign the navy's dismissal papers and ordered her placed on probation.[11]

Before leaving for the White House, he set out the parameters for the meeting with de Gaulle. Annoyed by the French leader's pretensions, the president ordered that under no circumstances was de Gaulle, who claimed to be president of a Provisional Government of the French Republic, to be recognized as a chief of state. Thus, when the U.S. Army transport bringing him to Washington landed at National Airport, he received only the seventeen-gun salute due a general—we can be sure that de Gaulle counted—his escorts to the White House were to be the president's two military aides and not the secretary of state, and his domicile was at Blair House rather than the White House. But the airport reception was, otherwise, what a chief of state could expect. His hosts had arranged for two honor guards, one of French pilots being trained in the United States, the other of army air force soldiers. He was greeted by the three chiefs of staff, Marshall, King, and Arnold, and the air force band played the "Marseillaise" and "The Star-Spangled Banner." De Gaulle, on his part, had memorized a brief speech in English, a language in which he was never comfortable. After saluting "brave American boys . . . fighting . . . against the common enemy," he said that in organizing for "peace," the "United States and France must continue to cooperate . . . as today they are working together for the common victory."

Roosevelt, despite his annoyance with his guest, recognized the same necessity, as his actions that afternoon and his words the next day would indicate. He accorded de Gaulle the same kind of reception a head of state would receive. The president, seated in an armchair before the fireplace in the Diplomatic Reception Room and flanked by Anna standing on his left with the cabinet members arrayed on his right, greeted his guest with "My, I'm glad to see you" as the tall Frenchman shook his hand. De Gaulle's response was inaudible to the press. While the newsreel cameras rolled, the two men chatted in French.

At his morning press conference, the president said unequivocally that recognition of a French government had not come up and would not come up until a more significant portion of France had been liberated. At the state luncheon the next day, Roosevelt, after some nostalgic remarks about the special affection for France that he shared with many Americans, offered a toast not to the guest but to his nation and its liberation. In further remarks, he insisted that there were "no great problems between the French and the Americans or between General de Gaulle and myself." After some further pleasantries, he made a second toast: "So I propose the health of General de Gaulle, our friend."

Although de Gaulle and his supporters failed to gain recognition, they avowed that progress had been made, which events soon demonstrated. After the French leader had left the capital, Roosevelt announced that the Algiers-based French Committee of National Liberation had been given "de facto authority" in liberated areas of France, with Eisenhower retaining final authority. In August, when Paris fell, French troops were allowed to enter the city first, with a French general accepting the capitulation of the remaining German garrison. Only on October 23, 1944, did the State Department, not the White House, announce formal recognition of de Gaulle's government.[12]

Since the GOP had already chosen a ticket of New York governor Thomas E. Dewey for president and Ohio governor John W. Bricker (1893–1986) as his running mate, the ninety-nine reporters crowding into the July 11 press conference knew that a formal announcement of the president's expected candidacy for a fourth term was quite likely.

After a considerable discussion of matters related to the de Gaulle visit and the expected declaration of war by Mexico, the president announced that the doors were closed and the press couldn't leave. Obviously enjoying himself, he proceeded to read aloud an exchange of letters between Democratic National Committee chairman Robert Hannegan and himself. Hannegan wrote "Dear Mr. President" that since communications from various state party officials had informed him that a clear majority of the delegates were legally bound to vote for him at the convention, "I would respectfully request that you send to the Convention or otherwise convey to the people of the United States an expression that you will again respond to the call of the Party and the people."

The president's long-awaited acceptance began with a positive version of Civil War general William T. Sherman's negative of 1884: "If the Convention should carry this out, and nominate me for the Presidency, I shall accept. If the people elect me, I will serve." The rest of his letter can be considered his first campaign address.

> Every one of our sons serving in this war has officers from whom he takes his orders. Such officers have superior officers. The President is the Commander in Chief and he, too, has his superior officer—the people of the United States.
>
> I would accept and serve, but I would not run, in the usual partisan, political sense. But if the people command me to continue in this office and in this war, I have as little right to withdraw as the soldier has to leave his post in the line.
>
> At the same time, I think I have a right to say to you and to the delegates to the coming Convention something which is personal—purely personal.
>
> For myself, I do not want to run. By next Spring, I shall have been President and Commander in Chief of the Armed Forces for twelve years—three times elected by the people of this country under the American Constitutional system. From the personal point of view, I believe that our economic system is on a sounder, more human basis than it was at the time of my first inauguration.
>
> It is perhaps unnecessary to say that I have thought only of the good of the American people. My principal objective, as you know, has been the

protection of the rights and privileges and fortunes of what has been so well called the average of American citizens.

After many years of public service, therefore, my personal thoughts have turned to the day when I could return to civil life. All that is within me cries out to go back to my home on the Hudson River, to avoid public responsibilities, and to avoid also the publicity which in our democracy follows every step of the Nation's Chief Executive.

Such would be my choice. But we of this generation chance to live in a day and hour when our Nation has been attacked, and when its future existence and the future existence of our chosen method of government are at stake.

To win this war wholeheartedly, unequivocally, and as quickly as we can is our task of the first importance. To win this war in such a way that there be no further world wars in the foreseeable future is our second objective. To provide occupations, and to provide a decent standard of living for our men in the armed forces after the war, and for all Americans, are the final objectives.

Therefore, reluctantly, but as a good soldier, I repeat that I will accept and serve in this office, if I am so ordered by the Commander in Chief of us all—the sovereign people of the United States.

He finished the letter and invited the press "to go out quietly."

Q: (Interposing) Mr. President, there is one more question. What about your talk with Vice President Wallace yesterday? Did that have any—
THE PRESIDENT: (Interposing) No—
Q: (Continuing)—bearing—
THE PRESIDENT: (Continuing)—Talked about China. Now get out! (Much laughter).
Q: (Hurriedly) Thank you.[13]

The reporter's unanswered question was pertinent. Although various figures in the administration and in Democratic politics told somewhat different stories, it seems clear that Wallace had become so unpalatable to most of the party leaders that Roosevelt had already decided he was not to remain as vice president, and he may well have decided to exclude him from the ticket as far back as July 1943 when he publicly admonished him and Jesse Jones. Among other influences, Pa Watson made sure that anti-Wallace figures in the party had easy access to the president.

Roosevelt, who was notoriously reluctant to dismiss anyone in a face-to-face situation, had tasked both Rosenman and Ickes with breaking the news to Wallace, who was returning from almost two months in China, but neither had managed to get the job done. Wallace had met with the president the day before Roosevelt's announcement of his candidacy and emerged from it with the notion that he would have some support from the president, although both he and the president said that they had discussed only China.

According to Sam Rosenman, who was performing some of the tasks that Harry Hopkins would have done had he been fit, the president had convoked a meeting in his study on the evening of his announcement attended by five party insiders—Hannegan; Chicago mayor Edward J. Kelly (1876–1950); the ubiquitous Frank Walker, George E. Allen (1896–1973), treasurer of the Democratic National Committee; Bronx boss Edward J. Flynn; plus son-in-law John Boettiger, because he liked to have "family" present—to pick a vice presidential candidate, although Roosevelt may well have already made his decision. The possible choices included Wallace, Sam Rayburn, Justice William O. Douglas, Jimmy Byrnes, Truman, and John Winant. According to Rosenman, who was not present, "When all the names had been fully canvassed the President said with an air of finality: 'It's Truman.' The conference was over."

Hannegan stayed behind and got a handwritten note from the president dated July 19, the opening day of the convention.

Dear Bob,
You have written me about Harry Truman and Bill Douglas. I should, of course, be very glad to run with either of them and believe that either one of them would bring real strength to the ticket.
Always sincerely,

Franklin Roosevelt

Rosenman writes further that the next day, Hannegan came to ask the president to have Grace Tully type the note on White House stationery. Rosenman dismisses "stories that the original handwritten note named Douglas first, and that Hannegan induced the President a few days later in the railroad yards in Chicago to change the order." But that is exactly what Grace Tully says happened. In her 1949 memoir—published three years before Rosenman's—she wrote that in the Chicago yards, Hannegan emerged from the president's compartment with a typed letter in his hand and told her, "Grace, the President wants you to retype this letter and switch those names so it will read 'Harry Truman or Bill Douglas'!"

I know of no way to resolve the differences between the two versions. By the time the memorialists wrote, Truman was in the White House and anything that called into question how he had received the nomination was one more burden on his embattled presidency. It is certainly possible that Roosevelt had originally provided himself a little extra "wiggle room" and, closer to the event, used it. The notion that Hannegan somehow maneuvered Truman into the vice presidency and thus the White House fails to account for the manipulator in chief.

The text of a second Roosevelt letter dated July 14 is not in dispute. Sent to Indiana senator Samuel D. Jackson, who was slated to be permanent chair of the Democratic convention—with a copy apparently furnished immediately to Wallace or one of his aides—it related that "because I expect to be away from Washington for the next few days," he was "wholly willing to give you my own personal thought about" the vice presidential candidacy. "The easiest way of putting it is this. I have been associated with Henry Wallace [for more than twelve years.] I like him and I respect him and he is my personal friend. For those reasons I would personally vote for his renomination if I were a delegate to the convention." He added that he was not dictating to the convention, which should "give great consideration to the pros and cons of its choice."

Since delegates remembered that four years earlier, Roosevelt had demanded that the convention nominate Wallace before he himself would accept the presidential nomination, and this time he didn't even request that anyone vote for Wallace, Roosevelt's endorsement was, in reality, permission not to vote for Wallace. We must also remember, as some writers have forgotten, that delegates learned first about the letter to Senator Jackson and later about the "Truman and Douglas" letter and understood that the second was the president's latest word.[14]

The "few days" away from the White House mentioned in the letter to Jackson were actually a thirty-five-day trip. Roosevelt's train left the capital on July 13 for Hyde Park, Chicago, and then San Diego; from there naval vessels took him to Honolulu, the Aleutians, and Bremerton, Washington, where his train was waiting to take him back to the White House.

Roosevelt's desire to be in San Diego just in time to speak to the convention by telephone, and then board his ship for Hawaii, meant that what could have been a two-day-plus trip was stretched to four days. It was a meandering journey with nighttime halts for better sleeping. Most of the party was bored, but the president loved it.[15]

The streamlined Democratic convention, cut to three days as a wartime measure, went like clockwork. On the evening of the second day, Roosevelt won renomination with 1,086 votes, while noncandidates Virginia senator Harry Byrd and Jim Farley got 89 votes and 1 protest vote, respectively. A telegram was sent to notify the president, who was listening to the proceedings on his train.

Dr. Bruenn reports that he witnessed a well-rested Roosevelt broadcast his speech from a car of his train facing a small audience, including his son James, two daughters-in-law, Admiral Leahy, Pa Watson, Sam Rosenman, and Elmer Davis. Unlike 1940, this preceded the vice presidential ballot.

Roosevelt told the delegates and the nation that he was speaking from "a naval base . . . in the performance of my duties under the Constitution." According to the *Times'* Turner Catledge, his "words came strong and magic-like through the loud speaker system." The president insisted that a sense of duty compelled him to run "in spite of my desire to retire to the quiet of private life."

He would "not campaign, in the usual sense," because he thought it unfitting "in these days of tragic sorrow" and because, given "global warfare, I shall not be able to find the time. However," he noted, "I shall . . . feel free to report to the people the facts about matters of concern to them and especially to correct any misrepresentations."

Most of the speech orchestrated three of the four main themes of the Democratic campaign: "First, to win the war—to win the war fast, to win it overpoweringly. Second, to form worldwide international organizations, and to arrange to use the armed forces of the sovereign Nations of the world to make another war impossible within the foreseeable future. And third, to build an economy for our returning veterans and for all Americans—which will provide employment and provide decent standards of living."

The fourth theme, the relative inexperience of the moderately known forty-two-year-old New York governor, was left to others; Harold Ickes had set the tone early by announcing that "Dewey has thrown his diaper into the ring." Roosevelt effectively played off this theme by emphasizing his experience and effective leadership of an all-victorious military, something he had not been able to do in the off-year elections in 1942.

Roosevelt ended his speech, as he often did, with a reference to the Almighty, but, unlike his usual practice, he used a quotation from a predecessor.

The greatest wartime President in our history, after a wartime election which he called the "most reliable indication of public purpose in this country," set the goal for the United States, a goal in terms as applicable today as they were in 1865—terms which the human mind cannot improve:

> ". . . with firmness in the right, as God gives us to see the right, let us strive on to finish the work we are in; to bind up the Nation's wounds; to care for him who shall have borne the battle, and for his widow, and his orphan—to do all which may achieve and cherish a just and lasting peace among ourselves, and with all Nations."[16]

Voting on twelve vice presidential nominees took two ballots. On the first, Wallace led with 429.5 votes, Truman was second with 319.5, while fifteen others (five of them, including Justice Douglas, not even nominated) divided the remaining 427 votes. On the second ballot, as more and more votes went to Truman, most of Wallace's first-ballot supporters abandoned him, while others later switched their votes to the victor. The final tally was announced as Truman 1,100, Wallace 66, and 4 votes for Douglas. Wallace quickly pledged his support for Truman.

A threatened southern revolt was largely stifled; only in Texas, where the convention awarded half the state's votes to an anti-Roosevelt faction that provided the majority of the votes against him, was the growing southern discomfort fully visible. Many southern Democratic leaders and almost all the northern ones understood that some retreat from segregationist positions was necessary to retain the support of growing numbers of northern black voters that Roosevelt and his policies had drawn to the party since 1934. The fact that the Republican platform had set a high bar—endorsing a permanent FEPC, a constitutional amendment abolishing poll taxes, and antilynching legislation, and pledging "an immediate Congressional inquiry to ascertain the extent to which mistreatment, segregation and discrimination against Negroes who are in our armed forces are impairing morale and efficiency, and the adoption of corrective legislation"—caused the Democratic platform committee, which included Senator Truman, to take a very tentative step toward a civil rights plank: "We believe that racial and religious minorities have the right to live, develop and vote equally with all citizens and share the rights that are guaranteed by our Constitution. Congress should exert its full constitutional powers to protect those rights."

Devout segregationists on the committee wrote a substitute plank supporting the right of states to segregate their schools and their voting registers without federal interference unless required to do so by a constitutional amendment. Convention rules provided that the formal support of twelve state delegations was required to bring a minority report to the floor, but only eight states did so. A potentially costly floor debate was thus avoided. The entire platform was adopted by voice vote.[17]

After the speech, Roosevelt visited the naval hospital in Balboa Park and by ten o'clock, he and his Hawaii-bound party had been installed in their quarters aboard the heavy cruiser USS *Baltimore,* but, since it was a Friday, sailing was delayed until after midnight. The three-and-a-half-day run to Honolulu was more rest and relaxation for the president. Some fifty miles east of Molokai, the little flotilla was met by eighteen naval aircraft that escorted it into Pearl Harbor. On entering port, Roosevelt saw that all the ships' crews were in white uniforms at man-the-rails stations and the piers packed with military and civilian personnel. Remarking that "it was no secret who was coming," he ordered that his presidential flag be hoisted, and the vessel moored at three in the afternoon.

Waiting on the pier were CincPac Fleet admiral Chester W. Nimitz and other military dignitaries, all in dress uniform, who came aboard to greet the president. About an hour later, MacArthur, who had flown in from Australia earlier that day, came aboard wearing what Rigdon describes as an "old battered leather jacket." At five the president's party was driven across downtown Honolulu through cheering crowds to a Waikiki Beach mansion that the navy was using as a rest home for carrier pilots. A third-floor suite with a private elevator had been prepared for Roosevelt.

After a quiet evening, he had a very full schedule for the next three days, inspecting a number of military installations, including Schofield Barracks,

Hickam Field, a jungle-warfare training camp, and, as was his wartime custom, three different hospitals. At one of the hospitals, he had himself wheeled slowly through the wards in which there were amputees to let them see his useless legs, which, as a public figure, he so diligently strove to keep hidden.

Security concerns by the Secret Service about Roosevelt's drives amid crowds, which included large numbers of persons of Japanese ancestry and birth, were overridden by Roosevelt. Rosenman, who shared these fears, wrote, "Many of the inhabitants were pure Japanese or descended from mixed marriages of Japanese. The President, however, insisted on riding through these crowds—and in an open car. . . . I could not help thinking how dreadful a toll one well-placed bomb would take."

Other members of the president's party as well as the Hawaiian military establishment obviously had other views. "Not the least impressive moment of the whole Hawaii stay [McIntire wrote] was when the President rode through long lines of Japanese-American soldiers. . . . There was some effort to dissuade him out of the fear that there might be a fanatic in the ranks who would leap at the chance to shoot the President at point blank range. 'Nonsense!' he exclaimed. 'I would never forgive myself if I shamed them by an open showing of their President's distrust.'"

Despite these and other strenuous activities, Bruenn writes that "the time from the middle of May to the early part of August was without incident relative to the President's health." McIntire was able to persuade the president to remain seated in his open car when he reviewed the Seventh Division with MacArthur at Schofield Barracks.[18]

In terms of affecting Pacific strategy, the much-discussed presidential conference in Honolulu settled little or nothing. Roosevelt, so willing to shape and reshape strategic decisions in North Africa and Europe, did not resolve the long-standing disagreement between MacArthur and Nimitz. The view from Brisbane was that a steady northward push, bypassing some enemy strongholds but ousting the Japanese from the Philippines, was a necessary prelude to defeating Japan. The view from Honolulu was that invasion of the Philippines was not necessary, that air and sea bombardment might force Japan to surrender. The steady western push through the central Pacific had already secured Saipan (July 8), and Guam, invaded on July 21, would fall on August 8. These islands would provide secure and reinforceable bases for B-29s to bomb Japan, just thirteen hundred miles away. B-29 bombers based deep in China had begun such raids in mid-June; raids from Saipan would begin by the end of November. The reconquest of the Philippines began on October 20 with the landings on Leyte.

Leahy's notes for the conference, more accurately a presidential briefing, show Roosevelt acting as an intermediary between the two commanders, attempting to minimize their profound differences. The president's man concluded that for

"Roosevelt it was an excellent lesson in geography, one of his favorite subjects." The comment of MacArthur's biographer that the meeting was "a conversational game played by the master politician and his most politically minded general" is certainly a part of the truth.[19]

The only reason for the two-week detour that took the president north to Adak, in the Aleutians, then east to Alaska proper and south to Puget Sound was that the gadabout Roosevelt wanted to go. Two days out, Roosevelt was notified of the death of his longtime right-hand woman, Missy LeHand, who had lived with the Roosevelts for more than two decades in Hyde Park, Albany, and the White House until she was permanently incapacitated by a stroke in the summer of 1941. On desolate Adak, the president ate and joked with enlisted men.[20]

Roosevelt wanted to broadcast a report to the people as soon as he returned to the United States, but the botched physical arrangements for it and their consequences are more significant than the speech itself. He originally wanted to speak in Seattle's baseball park, but Secret Service fears about security caused him to agree to speak in the Bremerton Navy Yard just after arrival. Offered a choice between speaking from a stand on the dock or from his ship, he chose the latter as more fitting for the commander in chief mode in which he wanted to campaign. Neither he nor the Secret Service seems to have been aware that the destroyer *Cummings,* which he had boarded in Alaska, would be in drydock and tilted. Dr. Bruenn described the physical consequences and the medical result. "For the first time in many months the braces for his legs were applied and he delivered the speech while standing upright and resting his arms on the speaker's stand which was erected on the fan-tail of the destroyer. He began his address at 5 PM and spoke for 35 min. During the early part of the speech the President for the first time experienced substernal oppression with radiation to both shoulders. The discomfort lasted about 15 min, gradually subsiding."

In a 1990 interview for a nonprofessional audience, Bruenn used simpler language: "He went on with the speech and came below and said 'I had a severe pain.' We stripped him down in the cabin of the ship, took a cardiogram, some blood, and so forth, and fortunately it was a transient episode, a so-called angina, not a myocardial infarction. But that was a very disturbing situation. That was the first time under my observation that he had something like this. He had denied any pain before. But this was proof positive that he had coronary disease, no doubt about it." McIntire's take on the episode was, again, mendacious: "A stiff wind was blowing, and there was quite a slant to the deck, two things that called for considerable bracing on his part, and, as a result he finished up with considerable pain. Purely muscular, as it turned out; and when we got back to Washington . . . he was in better shape than when we left."[21]

The speech itself—a casual account of where Roosevelt had gone, whom he had talked to, and the progress of the war—was not very effective. That

Roosevelt managed to deliver it at all is further evidence of his iron will to overcome physical frailties. Rigdon notes that Roosevelt was exhausted and caused concern to his doctors, but in about an hour "he seemed to be himself again." He reboarded his train, which proceeded on the five-day trip back to the capital without incident.[22]

Back in the White House on the morning of August 17, he had a long meeting with Harry Hopkins and was briefed by General Marshall on the two-day-old invasion of southern France, which quickly liberated the port of Marseille. Before leaving for three days at Hyde Park, Roosevelt discussed plans for the election campaign with Bob Hannegan. Briefly sloughed off were the final battles in what WPB head Donald Nelson called "The War Within a War," the struggle between civilian and military government planners over the timing and management of economic reconversion. Asked about that struggle, he told the press that "I haven't had time" for that. The allocation problems had been acute long before Roosevelt left for the Pacific. In mid-June, Nelson had warned that "the next three months" might be "most critical" in terms of allocation of materials and labor. He soon issued four orders relaxing civilian usage of certain strategic materials, such as aluminum. These orders were strongly opposed by the military, which delayed their application, and public controversy followed. Roosevelt reverted to his indirect way of settling high-level disputes. He met with Nelson and got him to agree to go on a mission to China, while retaining his WPB post. Roosevelt named WPB vice chairman Charles E. Wilson (1886–1972), former and future president of General Electric, as acting chairman, which Nelson endorsed. Five days later, in the midst of a media tempest over reconversion policy, Wilson resigned, making bitter charges against Nelson and his staff. In a temporary stopgap suggested by Nelson, Roosevelt appointed a low-profile technocrat, Julius A. Krug (1907–70), an engineer who had been a manager in the TVA and headed the WPB's power division, as acting chairman. He, in effect, replaced both dollar-a-year men and ran a less aggressive WPB until its dissolution in November 1945. Nelson went to China. On September 30, Nelson's resignation for an unspecified "major" position and Krug's appointment as his replacement were announced. Nelson returned from China to campaign for Roosevelt, who, in a November 2 letter, gave him a face-saving appointment as "personal representative of the president," with cabinet rank, but not cabinet salary. Krug became Truman's secretary of the interior.[23]

The major piece of international business on the president's return to the White House was to speak to the delegations attending the conference being held at the Dumbarton Oaks mansion in D.C. from August 21 to October 7; its decisions about the structure of the nascent United Nations organization would be modified at Yalta and at San Francisco in 1945. Roosevelt spoke to the delegations led by Stettinius, Britain's Alexander Cadogan, and Soviet ambassador to the United States Andrei Gromyko (1909–89).

Roosevelt's message was clear. Ignoring the temporary absence of the Chinese, he put it to them that "we have got to make not merely a peace, but a peace that will last, and a peace in which the larger Nations will work absolutely in unison in preventing war by force. But the four of us have to be friends, conferring all the time—the basis of getting to know each other—'putting their feet on the table.'"

Along with other Americans and much of the rest of the world, Roosevelt expressed his "joy" at the liberation of Paris, calling it a "brilliant presage of total victory." He sent Congress a required report on the progress of Lend-Lease and recommended that the program be extended until the surrender of both Germany and Japan, whose dates he refused to predict.[24]

Roosevelt spent five quiet days at Hyde Park, saying that he was anxious to catch up on his sleep, Hassett noting that "he isn't rested yet from the Pacific trip." While he was there, the White House released his Labor Day message, which, like so many of his statements now, was directed largely toward the postwar world and its problems. "Once the forces of tyranny have been overcome, we shall be faced with difficult problems of transition from war to peace. There will be matters of international arrangements as well as questions of internal economic policy. What we do in both spheres will affect our success in attaining a durable world peace—a peace that will contribute to the progress of mankind, and will give to all who work and produce an opportunity constantly to better their lives."

Back in Washington on Wednesday, he had a number of meetings, mostly about the upcoming conference with Churchill. After considering Scotland or Bermuda as a site, they chose to return to Quebec.

That evening the president left, unannounced, for Hyde Park, where Admiral Leahy, Dr. McIntire, Steve Early, and the two military aides, Admiral Brown and General Watson, joined the Roosevelts for "a pleasant Sunday" before all, including Eleanor, took the overnight train ride timed to arrive in Quebec Monday morning shortly before Churchill and his wife, Clementine (1885–1977), arrived from Halifax. The housing arrangements were similar to Quebec I: both delegations were in the luxurious Château Frontenac, except for the Roosevelts and the Churchills. They, with a few aides and servants, were housed in the Citadel, where meetings with the president took place. Harry Hopkins, who had returned to work on a limited scale after six months of hospitalization before Roosevelt's Pacific voyages, remained in Washington, not yet ready for the rigors of a conference with Churchill.

It can be argued that Quebec II is best understood in the light of Yalta and Potsdam in 1945 rather than anything that had gone before. There were no military decisions to be made at Quebec in 1944. There were political decisions, but they were about Germany, not Japan.

The one big decision that the two leaders made—agreeing to the so-called Morgenthau Plan, which would not only have dismantled most of Germany's industrial plants but also have made the coal mines of the Saar unusable—was soon canceled, with each leader giving several explanations of why they had approved their quickly disavowed decision in the first place. One important factor, which the president did not mention, is that he had no diplomatic adviser present. Hopkins was not there, Hull had been invited but declined, Stettinius had his hands full with Dumbarton Oaks, and no one had emerged to play the Sumner Welles role. Something of Roosevelt's mind-set in the run-up to the conference can be seen in his reaction to a draft of an army manual for the governance of conquered Germany. In late August, he wrote War Secretary Stimson, "It gives me the impression that Germany is to be restored just as much as the Netherlands or Belgium, and the people of Germany brought back as quickly as possible to their pre-war estate. . . . The fact that they are a defeated nation, collectively and individually, must be so impressed upon them that they will hesitate to start any new war. . . . I see no reason to start a WPA, PWA or a CCC for Germany when we go in with our Army of Occupation."

On the last day of the conference, after discussions between the president, the prime minister, and Morgenthau, the two leaders each initialed a brief typed statement dated September 16, 1944.

At a conference between the President and the Prime Minister upon the best measures to prevent renewed rearmament by Germany, it was felt that an essential feature was the future disposition of the Ruhr and the Saar.

The ease with which the metallurgical, chemical and electric industries in Germany can be converted from peace to war has already been impressed upon us by bitter experience. It must also be remembered that the Germans have devastated a large portion of the industries of Russia, and of other neighboring Allies, and it is only in accordance with justice that these injured countries should be entitled to remove the machinery they require in order to repair the losses they have suffered. The industries referred to in the Ruhr and in the Saar would therefore be necessarily put out of action and closed down. It was felt that the two districts should be put under some body under the world organization which would supervise the dismantling of these industries and make sure that they were not started up again by some subterfuge.

This programme for eliminating the war-making industries in the Ruhr and in the Saar is looking forward to converting Germany into a country primarily agricultural and pastoral in its character.

The Prime Minister and the President were in agreement upon this programme.

No public mention of the initialed document or of the Morgenthau Plan was made in Quebec or immediately afterward. Few would agree with Morgenthau's notion, expressed to his staff after his return to Washington, that this was "the high point" of his government career; surely, his presentation of the document on the murder of the Jews would be a sounder choice.

Quebec II, like its predecessor, ended with a Roosevelt-Churchill outdoor press conference on the parapet of the Citadel, presided over by Mackenzie King, at which no questions were allowed. Both leaders spoke about complete agreement and victory to come, without either saying anything particularly memorable. A two-paragraph summary for the press gave the gist of their comments and claimed that they had "discussed all aspects of the war . . . [and] reached decisions on all points" at issue to complete "the war in Europe" and "the destruction of the barbarians of the Pacific."[25]

Roosevelt's party left Quebec by train immediately after the press conference; Franklin, Eleanor, Leahy, and Dr. Bruenn went to Hyde Park, arriving the next morning to enjoy a quiet Sunday, while others continued on to Washington. The next morning, the Churchills arrived by train after breakfast with a sizable party, and by lunchtime Harry Hopkins and the Duke of Windsor arrived together.

While much of the Churchills' two-day stay was devoted to meals and group conversation, the two leaders managed again, without any scientific advisers present, to make an important decision about "tube alloys." The existence of the brief memorandum, which each initialed, was a very closely held secret for many years. "The suggestion that the world should be informed regarding TUBE ALLOYS, with a view to an international agreement regarding its control and use, is not accepted. The matter should continue to be regarded as of the utmost secrecy, but when a 'bomb' is finally available, it might perhaps, after mature consideration, be used against the Japanese, who should be warned that this bombardment will be repeated until they surrender."

Roosevelt, of course, had received extensive scientific advice from his regular advisers and, shortly before Quebec II, had met in Washington with one of the giants of theoretical physics, the Dane Niels Bohr (1885–1962). Felix Frankfurter, who did not allow his position on the Supreme Court to inhibit his penchant for promoting intellectual exchanges, had forwarded to the president a memorandum by Bohr on nuclear policy, which led to Bohr's ninety-minute White House meeting with the president on August 26. This meeting was later described by Bohr's son, who accompanied him to the United States, as warm, while in an earlier meeting Churchill didn't even give the physicist the time of day. Yet like so many other meetings with Roosevelt, its pleasant atmosphere did not translate into the results his visitor envisioned. In both the memorandum and the meeting, Bohr argued on pragmatic grounds that informing Stalin that research toward creating a bomb was going on while not passing on any technical information would be a worthwhile first step toward postwar international control of atomic energy. As the Hyde Park memo shows, Roosevelt ignored this wise and cautious advice, although he might have acted on it once a breakthrough had been made.

The Churchills left for home late on the evening of September 19, which pleased Roosevelt's staff. The nocturnal Churchill had kept the president up until one in the morning on the first day of his visit. Churchill was one of two persons—Eleanor was the other—who regularly caused the president stress. Each could be labeled "dangerous to his health," though neither meant him harm. Visibly tired, the president left word for Hassett that he wanted to sleep right through the morning and might have lunch in bed, but at ten in the morning he asked to have his mail brought up. That evening he left for Washington with Anna, Leahy, and Dr. Bruenn, arriving on the morning of September 21, two days before his speech to the Teamsters. He was feeling tired and worried about his voice, which had been somewhat feeble during the Quebec press conference.

Although Congress adjourned that afternoon until a week after the election, the White House continued to send up messages. The most ambitious was Roosevelt's final attempt to get a TVA-like project approved. In the postelection euphoria of early 1937, bills for "little TVAs" had been introduced, but none had been passed or ever would be. Using the occasion of a recent resolution by the governors of eight Missouri Valley states urging adoption of overall planning for their valley rather that a piecemeal approach, Roosevelt asked for congressional action for the Missouri Valley region and reminded them of his previous requests for the other areas.[26]

In answering a question about Italy, he said that he and Churchill had agreed in Quebec gradually to place "more responsibility on the Italian government" in the management of Italy's domestic affairs. Later, a joint statement that had been drafted by Leahy and Hopkins with help from John Boettiger at Hyde Park during Churchill's visit was released providing more details.

That day, as rumors flew around Washington about the Morgenthau Plan, the Office of War Information's Elmer Davis and Bob Sherwood held a joint press conference in Washington, which the White House correspondents had been advised to attend to learn the administration's version of its policy toward Germany. The OWI men, speaking explicitly for the president, described Roosevelt's attitude as insisting that the Germans not be treated as well as liberated peoples and stipulating a "hard" policy. It was coordinated with a press statement from Eisenhower's headquarters bearing a similar message that shared a page 1 headline in the *Times*. Sherwood, when asked what the first job of the OWI in Germany would be, replied that "the first thing is to convince the Germans that they have really lost the war." The president's spokesmen made no mention of the Morgenthau Plan, and the phrase *Morgenthau Plan* had not yet appeared in print. The following day's papers were full of it, but neither Roosevelt nor his spokesmen used the phrase publicly. Responding to a direct question in the third week of his presidency, Harry Truman said, "I don't know anything about the Morgenthau Plan. I haven't studied it at all, so I can't answer you."[27]

By the time Roosevelt made his first openly political speech, Dewey had been campaigning for weeks. The New York governor did not emphasize policy differences, domestic or foreign, but rather attacked government by "tired old men." Dewey was twenty years younger—and kept insisting that it was time for a change, and did so with prosecutorial vigor. Throughout Roosevelt's presidency, there had been false rumors about his health, and these increased with his illness after Tehran. The incident of the Bremerton speech, and, above all, photographs in which he appeared haggard, seemed to some to provide a basis for fears about his ability to handle the tasks and stress of his office. Dr. Bruenn insists in his memoir that Roosevelt's weight loss—he had dropped from 190 pounds before his post-Tehran illnesses to 168 pounds—was what made him look "somewhat haggard."

The task of the speech to the Teamsters was to reestablish in the minds of his listeners the image of the wise, confident leader who knew what was best for them and the country. No matter what the words said, they had to be delivered in a way that matched the text. The key passage, both his chief writers tell us, was dictated to Grace Tully by the president during Quebec II. The talk's setting was ideal: a hotel ballroom filled with a thousand enthusiastic and eventually boisterous supporters. Roosevelt, eschewing his braces, sat on the banquet dais between the AFL's William Green and industrialist Henry J. Kaiser. The president's tone throughout was largely in the conversational idiom of the familiar Fireside Chats rather than of more formal campaign speeches.

He began casually: "Well, here we are together again—after four years—and what years they have been! You know, I am actually four years older, which is a fact that seems to annoy some people. In fact, in the mathematical field there are millions of Americans who are more than eleven years older than when we started to clean up the mess that was dumped in our laps in 1933."

After noting that "certain people" deprecated and attacked "labor" for "three years and six months" only to "change their tune . . . just before election day," he quoted a plank of the current Republican platform pledging to maintain the Social Security Act and other named New Deal reforms, remarking that Republicans had spent time and money fighting every one of those laws that "they would not even recognize . . . if they met them in broad daylight." "The whole purpose of Republican oratory these days . . . is to persuade the American people that the Democratic Party was responsible for the 1929 crash and the depression and that the Republican Party was responsible for social progress under the New Deal."

He moved on to talk about the foreign policy history of many Republicans, "in Congress and out," who opposed preparedness before 1939 and after war came said that "Lend-lease" would end "free government in the United States" and said "only hysteria entertains the idea that Germany, Italy, or Japan contemplates war on us" and now say, "Don't leave the task of making peace to those old men . . . just turn it over to us." "I think there is one thing that you know: I am too old for that; I cannot talk out of both sides of my mouth at the same time."

Toward the end of his half-hour talk, after further recitations of various Republican exaggerations and distortions, the president read the paragraph he had dictated in Quebec.

These Republican leaders have not been content with attacks on me, or my wife, or on my sons. No, not content with that, they now include my little dog, Fala. Well, of course, I don't resent attacks, and my family doesn't resent attacks, but Fala *does* resent them. You know, Fala is Scotch, and being a Scottie, as soon as he learned that the Republican fiction writers in Congress and out had concocted a story that I had left him behind on the Aleutian Islands, and had sent a destroyer back to find him—at a cost to the taxpayers of two or three, or eight or twenty million dollars—his Scotch soul was furious. He has not been the same dog since. I am accustomed to hearing malicious falsehoods about myself—such as the old worm-eaten chestnut that I have represented myself as indispensable. But I think I have a right to resent, to object to libelous statements about my dog.

Well, I think we all recognize the old technique. The people of this country know the past too well to be deceived into forgetting. Too much is at stake to forget.

Roosevelt's tone then changed as he moved into the speech's final passages, which were about the nation's business: the tasks of setting up the machinery to keep the peace and those of switching the economy from peace to war. He closed on a note of triumph and confidence in a glorious future.

We are even now organizing the logistics of peace, just as Marshall and King and Arnold, MacArthur, Eisenhower and Nimitz are organizing the logistics of this war.

I think that the victory of the American people and their allies in this war will be far more than a victory against Fascism and reaction and the dead hand of despotism of the past. The victory of the American people and their allies in this war will be a victory for democracy. It will constitute such an affirmation of the strength and power and vitality of government by the people as history has never before witnessed.

And so, my friends, we have had affirmation of the vitality of democratic government behind us, that demonstration of its resilience and its capacity for decision and for action—we have that knowledge of our own strength and power—we move forward with God's help to the greatest epoch of free achievement by free men that the world has ever known.[28]

Rosenman called the speech Roosevelt "at his vigorous best" and told Hassett that it was "his greatest campaign address." It became quickly known as "the speech about Fala," but it was much more than that. The famous paragraph did make the country laugh with Roosevelt and at his opponents, assured supporters that the champion campaigner still had that magic touch, and clearly rattled Dewey, who went off-message for a few speeches as he vainly tried to land a blow on his elusive target. But equally or even more important was that the speech helped many to believe, for a time at least, that what most Americans hoped for—not just victory, but peace in their time—was possible. And it was important that the war news continued to be favorable. A month later and just three weeks before the election, when MacArthur waded ashore at Leyte and proclaimed "I have returned," he destroyed an important argument of many Republican campaigners, that Roosevelt had leashed the Southwest Pacific commander. If a temporary setback, like December's Battle of the Bulge, had occurred before the election, the results might have been somewhat different.

The president, clearly satisfied with his reception, went straight to his train and spent three relaxed days at Hyde Park.

Meanwhile, controversy over the Morgenthau Plan moved to the front pages, and after Roosevelt's return to Washington two separate foreign policy statements were handed out at his brief end of September press conference. One was a letter to Leo Crowley, spelling out details of the "hard" economic policy to be followed in Germany; the other was a severe criticism of Argentina, the future sanctuary of Adolf Eichmann, for the "growth of Nazi-Fascist influence" there. Roosevelt had held back on public criticism out of consideration for food-short Britain's dependence on Argentine beef. Argentine officials were reportedly shocked because Roosevelt's statement followed an announcement in Buenos Aires that those charged with war crimes would not be given refuge there.[29]

On October 2, in the first of a series of actions to speed reconversion, the president took power away from the military and transferred it to Krug's WPB. The military had long held the power to issue "certificates of non-necessity," which were needed before a private factory devoted to war production could be reconverted to civilian production, but had never issued one. An administration spokesman told reporters that few certificates would be issued before the end of the war in Europe. The next day, Roosevelt read two signing statements in his press conference about bills that were less than he desired but did move reconversion forward. The first, which gave duties and powers over Reconversion to the Office of War Mobilization, was "quite satisfactory" in its organizational provisions, but "does not deal adequately with the human side of reconversion."

The chief lack was legislation providing uniform standards for state-controlled, federally funded unemployment benefits to war workers. The bill also renamed Byrnes's agency to match its expanded function, so that it became the Office of War Mobilization and Reconversion (OWMR). Roosevelt explained that Byrnes wanted to be relieved but had agreed to stay on to oversee the transition until the Senate, which had to confirm the director of the revised agency, returned from recess, a week after the election.

It is instructive to note the different responses Roosevelt made to questions about China and Poland.

> Q: Mr. President, . . . yesterday a Chinese military spokesman [said] that our aid to China . . . was "pitifully inadequate." Anything you can say about that?

Roosevelt gave a fairly long account of the problems in supplying China: the now closed Burma Road, the rigors of the route from the eastern Caspian Sea through Tibet over which trucks had to carry their own gasoline, and, finally, the flights over the Himalayas, which had initially been limited to two thousand tons a month and had been raised to twenty thousand tons a month. He acknowledged that much of that—he gave no figure—was gasoline for Chennault's planes and for the newly arrived B-29s. After several follow-up questions about details, the same reporter asked:

> Q: Mr. President, what is the reason for the sudden complaints by the Chinese on the aid we have given them?
> THE PRESIDENT: They would like to have more. [And, after a brief response] There is nothing new in it.

But when a reporter tried to get him to comment on the fact that the more than two-month-long Warsaw uprising had been quelled by the Germans while Soviet armies in position to intervene did not do so, Roosevelt cut off discussion: "I don't know enough to talk about it."

Actually, the president knew more than enough. He and Churchill had asked Stalin to help the Warsaw Poles at the start of the revolt, but the Soviet leader refused. Stalin's final message on the subject blamed "a handful of criminals," including his enemies the Polish government in London, who "used the trustfulness of the Warsawites" in a desperate grasp for power and claimed that nearby Soviet armies were unable to help them. Roosevelt, still concerned about Polish American voters, wanted as little discussion as possible of this and other aspects of the Polish question before the election.[30]

If there was little Roosevelt could do to attract those voters for whom the well-being of Poland was important, he could and did make sure that Italian American voters knew about his efforts to improve the lives of Italians. He made a formal public statement detailing current aid to the Italian people, copies of which were distributed to voters in Italian American neighborhoods and featured in the ethnic press.

He also found time to speak to the two hundred delegates, mostly educators and government officials, to the first White House Conference on Rural Education. He opened humbly: "I feel like a fish out of water. I haven't thought of education in this country for three years"—a strange comment for the chief promoter of the G.I. Bill. Before the war, he had spoken about the problems of rural schools, often using personal anecdotes about the underprepared and underpaid teachers he encountered in and around Warm Springs. He used one of the same anecdotes, but supported it with contemporary data, noting that the war, which had led to so many positive effects on the standards of American life, had had some disastrous effects on rural education. "Within one school year after Pearl Harbor, several thousand rural schools had been closed because of lack of teachers. . . . In one agricultural State in the Midwest, nearly a third of the teachers in one-room schools are persons holding only emergency licenses to teach, and nearly 800 schools face this coming school year without a teacher."

Without offering details, the president set out a decidedly conservative agenda for future federal aid to education: some kinds of direct grants to poor schools that "should, of course, never involve Government interference with State and local administration and control." The conference itself, dominated by the National Education Association, was even more conservative. Despite Roosevelt's endorsement, its eight-point program ignored the topic of federal aid.[31]

Roosevelt's second admittedly political speech was more like a Fireside Chat than a campaign speech and in part it was devoted, as he had said would be the case, to correcting Republican misstatements. After the political pyrotechnics of the Fala speech, it was the calm voice that Americans had been hearing for nearly a dozen years. He began casually, saying, "I am speaking to you tonight from the White House." He spoke of the importance of having "a large registration and a large vote this fall." "We are holding a national election despite all the prophecies of some politicians and a few newspapers who have stated, time and again in the past, that it was my horrid and sinister purpose to abolish all elections and to deprive the American people of the right to vote."

Stressing that right, he insisted on the need for all voters, regardless of party, to exercise that "sacred obligation." Two sentences attacked the poll tax but, like the party platform, did not name it: "The right to vote must be open to our citizens irrespective of race, color, or creed—without tax or artificial restriction of any kind. The sooner we get to that basis of political equality, the better it will be for the country as a whole."

Observing that "all of us" who run for office want to win, he had the confidence to mention the possibility of losing. "But, speaking personally, I should be very sorry to be elected President of the United States on a small turnout of voters. And by the same token, if I were to be defeated, I should be much happier to be defeated in a large outpouring of voters. Then there could not be any question of doubt in anybody's mind as to which way the masses of the American people wanted this election to go."

After restressing the importance of a large vote, Roosevelt pointed out that "for many millions of our young men in the armed forces . . . it will be difficult in many cases—and impossible in some cases—to register and vote." Without specifying party, he said that the people knew who was responsible, and therefore "we here at home must not be slackers on registration day or on election day." He made a special appeal for all women to vote, arguing that they "have a double obligation . . . to themselves as citizens and . . . to their fighting husbands, and sons, and brothers and sweethearts."

> [It] is my plain duty to reiterate to you that this war for the preservation of our civilization is not won yet [even though the] Allied Armies under General Eisenhower have waged during the past four months one of the most brilliant campaigns in military history [while in] the Pacific, our naval task forces and our Army forces have advanced to attack the Japanese, more than five thousand miles west of Pearl Harbor. . . .
>
> Nor will all of our goals have been achieved when the shooting stops. We must be able to present to our returning heroes an America which is stronger and more prosperous, and more deeply devoted to the ways of democracy, than ever before.
>
> "The land of opportunity"—that's what our forefathers called this country. By God's grace, it must always be the land of opportunity for the individual citizen—ever broader opportunity.
>
> We have fought our way out of economic crisis—we are fighting our way through the bitterest of all wars—and our fighting men and women—our plain, everyday citizens—have a right to enjoy the fruits of victory.

Only then did the candidate respond to false Republican claims. What is usually referred to as the postwar Red Scare was already alive and well in the speeches of Republican candidates from the top of the ticket on down, and the president felt it necessary to formally reject communist support. "I have never sought, and I do not welcome the support of any person or group committed to Communism, or Fascism, or any other foreign ideology which would undermine the American system of government, or the American system of free competitive enterprise and private property."

This was immediately followed by a longer paragraph affirming the "friendly relationship which this Nation has . . . with the people of the Soviet Union" and that the "American people are glad and proud to be allied with the gallant people of Russia." Not a word here about the man whom he and Winston referred to in their messages as "UJ" (Uncle Joe), but merely the statement that "the kind of economy that suits the Russian people, I take it is their own affair." His closing sentences stressed international amity and postwar prosperity summed up in a closing homily: "We owe it to our posterity, we owe it to our heritage of freedom, we owe it to our God, to devote the rest of our lives and all of our capabilities to the building of a solid and durable structure of world peace."[32]

The president left for Hyde Park right after the speech, spending five full days there, conserving his strength for the campaign rigors ahead. In that short span, Roosevelt deputized his wife to attend two political funerals in New York City in his stead. Al Smith's death at seventy-one was not unexpected, but that of Wendell Willkie of a heart attack at fifty-two was a shock. By 1944 the 1940 Republican standard-bearer had become politically marginalized; his attempt to win a second presidential nomination fizzled after a disastrous showing in the Wisconsin primary. Had Willkie lived longer, Roosevelt might have found a role for him, but the much-rumored notion of their joining to create a new party of liberals was a pipe dream.

Most foreign policy issues were kept out of the campaign; the successful completion of the second session of the Dumbarton Oaks meeting (China, the United States, and Britain) drew praise from both Roosevelt and Dewey. But Roosevelt had to deal with a contentious foreign policy issue as soon as he returned to the White House on October 11. He told a delegation of the Polish American Congress that "Poland must be reconstituted as a great nation" and that he did not know exactly what was happening in Poland or the circumstances of what had happened in the Warsaw uprising. He did not share with them what he and Churchill feared: a unilateral Soviet solution of the Polish question.

Roosevelt broadcast a brief address made to the chiefs of mission from the other American republics—minus Argentina—in the White House's Diplomatic Cloak Room. The president described it as "absolutely nonpolitical"—an impossibility less than a month before election day. In the ten-minute Columbus Day talk, he praised Latin American support for the war, which the "people of the United States will never forget," and urged that those nations join with the United States in pressing "forward to bring into existence [the world organization] to maintain peace and security. There is no time to lose." In addition, he paid tribute to the "millions of Italians [who] have come to the Western Hemisphere seeking freedom and opportunity."

That evening, in a telephoned talk to an Italian American Labor Council dinner in Manhattan, he noted that the "act of the Attorney General—removing the status of enemy aliens from Italian aliens—has been justified by their corresponding effort to help us wage war." He also told the group that at Quebec II, he and Churchill had agreed on increased aid to Italy. Six days later, a delegation from the council presented the president with its Four Freedoms Award in his office.

Dr. McIntire, "asked for an authoritative statement on the President's health, in view of rumors in political circles and elsewhere," responded with comments about Roosevelt's weight loss and his vanity about his "flat tummy" wholly consistent with what Dr. Bruenn revealed in 1970 and later. But one statement was another deliberate lie. "The president's health is perfectly O.K. There are absolutely no organic difficulties at all." Persons who are "perfectly O.K." do not keep a cardiologist in constant attendance, nor are they described as "in heart failure."[33]

Most of the president's answers to press questions were negative or vague. He didn't "know [and had] no idea" when a meeting with Churchill and Stalin would occur. Where will "the formal United Nations' conference be held?" The president didn't "even know when." And asked if he had made his election predictions, he replied, "No, not yet. I have been too busy."

The president was more responsive about the defiance of James Caesar Petrillo (1892–1984), the autocratic but effective leader of the American Federation of Musicians (AFL), whose members were violating the no-strike pledge by refusing to play in recording studios until an agreement about sharing record royalties was reached. Roosevelt had asked the NWLB to intervene, and it ordered the union to cease and desist, but Petrillo refused.

Q: [Petrillo's] union has rejected your request to remove the ban on recording. Do you contemplate any further action, or have you anything further to say?

THE PRESIDENT: I don't know. I am going into that. . . . It is largely a question of the law. People write a story that I am acting as a dictator, in the next moment they say that I should act on this musician trouble, without seeing whether, under the law I can act or not. . . . It is a very interesting question.

Eventually, the strikes were ended by a series of royalty-sharing agreements. Although Petrillo was portrayed, not inaccurately, as an uncouth labor autocrat—he refused to differentiate between "Heifetz . . . and the fiddler in a tavern"—he nevertheless pioneered an effective adjustment to the impact of changing technology for musicians of all kinds.[34]

The next press conference was held in the White House Fish Room rather than in the Oval Office so that elaborate scale models of one of the two artificial harbors, code-named Mulberrys, that were crucial elements in the Normandy landings could be shown to and later examined by reporters. Roosevelt, augmented and sometimes gently corrected or amplified by three of his military aides, told reporters how the Mulberrys functioned. Roosevelt, holding a long pointer and being pushed or pulled in his unmentioned wheelchair when necessary, obviously enjoyed himself.

Questions about the authority that the American delegation to "this world security organization would have" and "what authority Congress would have" clearly annoyed the president, who spoke of such questions being raised by "people . . . who are not friendly to the idea of a United Nations organization" and didn't attempt to answer. Instead, he embarked on a long disquisition in which he argued that "we are after a very great objective in this whole thing. We don't know if it is going to work. It doesn't guarantee peace forever, but we hope at least it will guarantee world peace while any of us today are still alive. That will be something."

In the course of his discussion, the president, who had never visited the League of Nations headquarters in Geneva, seemed to be opposed to a regular meeting site, adding that Washington would be a "horrible place" for the permanent organization, which he thought could be contained in one office building. He speculated that it might be well to have the annual meetings in different places, as the Organization of American States did.

Later that day, Roosevelt spent more than two hours with Francis J. Cardinal Spellman, whom he had named military vicar of the U.S. armed forces shortly after the outbreak of war in 1939, hearing about his recent visit to the troops in the Mediterranean theater. As he emerged from lunch on trays in the Oval Office, Spellman made his contribution to the discussion of the president's health by telling reporters that "he had found the President well and looking the same as he did in July, when he last saw him."[35]

On October 20, Roosevelt naturally made the most of MacArthur's return to the Philippines, announcing the news himself; what the general would describe in the first person, the president made plural.

> This morning American troops landed on the island of Leyte in the Philippines. The invasion forces, under the command of General Douglas MacArthur, are supported by the greatest concentration of naval and air power ever massed in the Pacific Ocean.
>
> We have landed in the Philippines to redeem the pledge we made over two years ago when the last American troops surrendered on Corregidor after five months and twenty-eight days of bitter resistance against overwhelming enemy strength.
>
> We promised to return; we *have* returned.
>
> In my last message to General Wainwright, sent on the fifth of May, 1942, just before he was captured, I told him that the gallant struggle of his comrades had inspired every soldier, sailor, and marine and all the workers in our shipyards and munitions plants. I said that he and his devoted followers had become the living symbol of our war aims and the guarantee of our victory.
>
> That was true in 1942. It is still true in 1944. . . .

We have learned our lesson about Japan. We trusted her, and treated her with the decency due a civilized neighbor. We were foully betrayed. The price of the lesson was high.

Now we are going to teach Japan her lesson.

We have the will and the power to teach her the cost of treachery and deceit, and the cost of stealing from her neighbors. With our steadfast allies, we shall teach this lesson so that Japan will never forget it.

We shall free the enslaved peoples. We shall restore stolen lands and looted wealth to their rightful owners. We shall strangle the Black Dragon of Japanese militarism forever.

Roosevelt also sent separate congratulatory messages to General MacArthur, to Admirals Nimitz and Halsey, and to Philippine president Sergio Osmeña. At his press conference, he added that the losses in the landing were "extremely light" and that there was "general satisfaction" about it "all over the country."

Described as "in a jovial and animated mood," he spoke of the weather forecast as "rain and a fifty-mile gale in New York which is not cheerful." He was scheduled to tour New York City before an evening speech there. He agreed that he would wear his navy cape, "about the best garment I have got. I have been wearing that—it is about the third I have had since 1913." He soon ended the brief conference, telling reporters that he had no appointments as he had to write a speech, adding, "I hope you don't get wet, those of you who are going." Recording the departure in his journal, Hassett noted it was the first time the president has been entirely "'on the record'" outside of Washington since the nation went to war.[36]

Writing the speech he was going to make before the Foreign Policy Association was of course important, but in this instance the tour of New York City seemed more consequential, as it would be judged as a demonstration of Roosevelt's physical fitness, or lack of it. The weather, the cold wet tail of a hurricane, made the test more difficult, but also more useful.

Wartime security rules about details of the president's itinerary were abandoned. A timetable of his schedule, street by street and bridge by bridge, was printed in the papers before the trip, beginning with a 7:00 a.m. arrival at the rail terminal of a Brooklyn army base followed by inspections of the base and the nearby navy yard. Then came a rally for Senator Wagner at Ebbets Field, an inspection of a navy training station for WAVES at Hunter College in the Bronx, and a description of his route in Manhattan from 155th Street and Seventh Avenue downtown through Harlem and Times Square to Washington Square, where he was to be brought to Eleanor Roosevelt's apartment at 1:07 p.m. All of this was done with the president seated, bareheaded, in the back seat of an open car in a driving icy rain; he had a heater under his feet and wore a suit of flannel underwear and a fur robe around most of his body, under his heavy navy cape, which masked everything. The police estimated that three million people jammed the sidewalks to see him, and countless others watched from windows and rooftops.

The president wore his braces as far as the stop at Ebbets Field. There he told the crowd to send Wagner back to the Senate and admitted that it was his first visit to the Dodgers' ballpark but claimed to have rooted for them. In an unannounced stop, the Secret Service had arranged to have dry clothes for the president in an adjacent Coast Guard motor pool, where he was undressed, given a rubdown, and redressed in dry clothes, which were soon soaked again during the rest of the drive.

What effect, if any, Roosevelt's bravura performance had on the election results, no one can say. The president obviously thought that it was important, and it was good for his morale and that of his supporters that he had done well. The whisperings about his health continued, but the members of the middle fifth of the electorate that decides most elections were certainly more likely to continue to support a visibly active and vigorous campaigner.[37]

The broadcast speech at the Foreign Policy Association dinner at the Waldorf Astoria Hotel was directed both to the elite audience, perhaps two-thirds of whom were internationally minded Republicans like War Secretary Stimson, who was present, and to a nationwide radio audience.

The basic strategy of the speech was simple. Roosevelt's foreign policy initiatives had been successful; at every opportunity, most Republicans in Congress had opposed them. The same was true of many pre–Pearl Harbor steps to build up the armed forces and to aid the nations resisting Hitler and the Japanese. Roosevelt merely had to remind listeners that the "majority of Republican members of Congress voted . . . against" the Selective Service law, the repeal of the arms embargo, Lend-Lease, and "four months before Pearl Harbor" against extension of the Selective Service, "which meant voting against keeping our Army together." He then named various isolationists—including Hiram Johnson, Gerald Nye, Hamilton Fish, and Joe Martin—who, with others, would hold key leadership positions if Republicans gained control of Congress. And, he pointed out, "every one of them is now actively campaigning for the national Republican ticket this year." As was his custom, Roosevelt did not mention his opponent or refer to him.

Within that overt strategy was a hidden ploy. Wendell Willkie had died without revealing for whom he would vote, and there was a struggle among his supporters about his political legacy. At Willkie's funeral earlier that month, Minnesota's Republican senator Joseph H. Ball (1905–93), a key Willkie supporter and a strong voice for internationalism, had approached Ben Cohen to say that he would challenge both candidates to make their positions clear on internationalist issues, and since he thought that the most important question was whether a candidate was prepared to support the use of force by the United Nations without recourse to Congress, he would support the candidate who took the stronger approach.

Cohen passed this information on to both Hopkins and Rosenman. Since the president already supported such a provision, this was not a problem.

Ball later made a public declaration that he was "on the fence" in regard to the presidential election and that he would make his decision after he heard Dewey's speech before the *New York Herald Tribune* Forum and Roosevelt's talk to the Foreign Policy Association. It was easy for the president and his speechwriters to make the kind of declaration that Ball asked for; Dewey and his advisers did not choose to do so. Ball subsequently endorsed the president, who made the requested declaration and followed it up with a homey example that unsophisticated listeners could understand:

> So to my simple mind it is clear that, if the world organization is to have any reality at all, our American representative must be endowed in advance by the people themselves, by constitutional means through their representatives in Congress, with authority to act.
>
> If we do not catch the international felon when we have our hands on him, if we let him get away with his loot because the Town Council has not passed an ordinance authorizing his arrest, then we are *not* doing our share to prevent another world war. I think, and I have had some experience, that the people of this nation want their Government to work, they want their Government to act, and not merely talk, whenever and wherever there is a threat to world peace.

His conclusion, with its echoes of the great 1936 acceptance speech, and perhaps the moral peak of the year's campaign, stressed:

> The task ahead of us will not be easy. Indeed it will be as difficult and complex as any task as has ever faced any American administration.
>
> I will not say to you now, or ever, that we of the Democratic Party know all of the answers. I am certain, for myself, that *I* do not know how all the unforeseen difficulties can be met. What I can say to you is this—that I have unlimited faith that the task can be done. And that faith is based on knowledge gained in the arduous, practical, and continuing experience of these past eventful years.
>
> I speak to the present generations of Americans with a reverent participation in its sorrows and in its hopes. No generation has undergone a greater test, or has met the test with a greater heroism and I think greater wisdom, and no generation has had a more exalted mission.
>
> For this generation must act not only for itself, but as a trustee for all those who fell in the last war—a part of their mission unfulfilled.
>
> It must also act for all those who have paid the supreme price in this war— lest their mission, too, be betrayed. And finally it must act for the generations to come—that must be granted a heritage of peace.

I do not exaggerate that mission. We are not fighting for, and we shall not attain a Utopia. Indeed, in our own land, the work to be done is never finished. We have yet to realize the full and equal enjoyment of our freedom. So, in embarking on the building of a world fellowship, we have set ourselves a long and arduous task, which will challenge our patience, our intelligence, our imagination, as well as our faith.

That task, my friends, calls for the judgment of a seasoned and a mature people. This, I think, the American people have become. We shall not again be thwarted in our will to live as a mature Nation, confronting limitless horizons. We shall bear our full responsibility, exercise our full influence, and bring our full help and encouragement to all who aspire to peace and freedom.

We now are, and shall continue to be, strong brothers in the family of mankind—the family of the children of God.

The speech completed, the president and his party were ushered into an elevator to a private railroad siding, where his train was waiting to take him to Hyde Park for two days of rest. Wartime secrecy was restored, so no reporters accompanied him.[38]

Until the election was over, Roosevelt would be, except for what soon came to be called "the China tangle," almost exclusively in a campaign mode. Five formal efforts remained: a speech on the war in Shibe Park, Philadelphia, on October 27; another in Chicago's Soldier Field on postwar domestic problems, the next day; a brief campaign address from the White House, on November 2; what Sherwood calls a "general roundup" in Fenway Park, Boston, on November 4; and the customary Fireside Chat from Hyde Park on election eve, November 6. His public papers also include the texts of seven extemporaneous remarks given from the rear platform of his train or from a touring car.

Roosevelt's vigor and resiliency bucked up the spirits of his staff. Hassett recorded his impressions at Hyde Park the night of the Waldorf speech: "All that I have seen today . . . again convinces me that the election is in the bag. Best of all my own fears and misgivings about the President's health under the terrific load he is carrying are dissipated, vanished like the morning dew. He will bury most of his detractors yet. So I went early to bed."

Back in Washington, the president, in a mood to quibble, opened his press conference by volunteering, "Yes, I haven't even got the sniffles!" He refused to confirm details of his speaking schedule that had been announced by the Democratic National Committee and local party officials. He acknowledged that he had talked to Ambassador Harriman, just back from Moscow, but revealed nothing about their talks, except:

Q: Did you get into the Polish situation, sir?
THE PRESIDENT: No, didn't talk about it at all.

In his 1975 memoir, Harriman writes of a nearly two-hour lunch with the president and Anna and noted that Roosevelt "consistently shows very little interest in Eastern European matters except as they affect sentiment in America." This comports with what the president had said to Stalin at Tehran.

The next afternoon, at 5:20, Steve Early excitedly summoned the half dozen reporters left in the press room and rushed them to the Oval Office, where Roosevelt awaited them with a single sheet of paper written in his own hand, which he said "just came over from Admiral Leahy."

THE PRESIDENT: (Reading) The President received today a report from Admiral Halsey that the Japanese navy in the Philippine area has been defeated, seriously damaged, and routed by the American Navy.

The president's flash was the first word of the Battle of Leyte Gulf, the final sortie of the Imperial Japanese Navy.[39]

The president's campaign train, thirteen cars long and filled with press, Secret Service, technicians, and the president's party, including Early, Hassett, Dr. McIntire, Dr. Bruenn, Grace Tully, Dorothy Brady (a White House stenographer), Sherwood, and Rosenman, left Washington late Thursday night for the speeches in Philadelphia and Chicago on Friday and Saturday evenings, October 27–28. After a two-hour run into Delaware, it laid by for most of the morning on a siding near Wilmington. Resuming, the train paused there briefly, as it had done in 1936 and 1940—Roosevelt liked familiar routines—and he had his braces put on so he could stand, bareheaded in blustery weather, on the rear platform of his train and speak briefly to a noon-hour crowd of perhaps 7,000. He reminded them that he had been there before, but that this election was in wartime, the first such since Lincoln was reelected in 1864. He quoted Lincoln, derided "Republican political oratory," but thought that it was not "disturbing the progress of events here in Wilmington," whose products—meaning the Du Pont explosives factories—"have made quite a lot of noise around the world." He spoke of those workers and "the ship builders—the industrial engineers—the chemists—and the plain citizens of the State of Delaware . . . who have contributed to the victories we have won." He closed by expressing the hope that "every man and woman . . . will step up to the polls on election day." He did not ask them to vote for him, but said that "I won't advise you to vote early and often, because I might go to jail." He urged that "a large vote . . . will speak powerfully for the cause of democracy in the world." The president rarely said, "vote for me," though that was the general idea.

Wearing the braces necessary for these stops was now quite painful. Because of his weight loss and the muscular atrophy exacerbated by lack of exercise—during the war years he swam very little—the braces, made long before he was president, no longer fit. Apparently, no one thought to see to it that they were replaced or modified.

The train proceeded to Philadelphia, where Roosevelt made a four-hour tour in mostly wet and windy forty-degree October weather through the city's streets and those of Camden, across the river in New Jersey, and inspected military installations and a huge shipyard. Police estimated that he was seen by 750,000 persons, and the press reported crowds even in staunchly Republican suburbs.

After a break for a drink, dinner, and dry clothes aboard his train, he returned to the open automobile, which was driven to the center of the baseball park before 50,000 demonstrative spectators. The president sat in full view with a board reaching across the back seat before him, like a kind of desktop with several microphones on it.

The strategy of his speech was similar to that of the talk at the Waldorf, but concentrated on the military rather than the diplomatic record. His speech was in part a celebration of victories, in part a catalog of Republican charges of mal-administration followed by refutations, accompanied by a listing of selected votes of Republican legislators. He began by pointing out that October 27 was Navy Day, so chosen because it was the birthday of Theodore Roosevelt, who would have been proud that "our American fleet today" was larger than all other navies combined. "And when I say all the navies, I am including what was—until three days ago—the Japanese fleet. Since Navy Day a year ago, our armed forces—Army, Navy, and Air forces—have participated in no fewer than twenty-seven different D-Days—twenty-seven landings in force on enemy held soil. . . . And every one of these twenty-seven D-Days has been a triumphant success."

After discussing his constitutional role as commander in chief and pointing out his duties, including appointing the civilian and military heads of the armed forces,

> I feel called upon to offer no apologies for my selection of Henry Stimson, the late Frank Knox, and Jim Forrestal, or of Admiral Leahy, General Marshall, Admiral King, and General Arnold.
>
> . . . The other day, I am told, a prominent Republican orator stated that: 'There are not five civilians in the entire national government who have the confidence and respect of the American people' [and] went on to describe your present Administration as 'the most spectacular collection of incompetent people who ever held public office.'
>
> Well, you know, that is pretty serious, because the only conclusion to be drawn from that is that we are losing this war. If so, that will be news to most of us—And it will certainly be news to the Nazis and the Japs.
>
> Now, I like a thing called the record, and the record will show that from almost the very first minute of this Administration—twelve years ago, nearly—I tried to rebuild the United States Navy. . . .
>
> Take, for example, just the other day, the ships of Admiral Halsey's powerful Third Fleet that helped to give the Japanese Navy the worst licking in its

history. . . . All of the aircraft carriers in that Fleet had been authorized by the present Administration before Pearl Harbor, and half of them were actually under construction. . . .

He gave similar data featuring land and air forces along with examples of Republican votes against military preparedness before Pearl Harbor. Post–Pearl Harbor support by Republicans was ignored.

Roosevelt closed with a litany of hopes for the nation, a series of "May this country":

... never forget that its power . . . has come from . . . its citizens.
... hold in piety . . . those who have battled and died [for it].
... reserve its contempt for . . . selfish interests.
... marshal its righteous wrath against those who would divide it by racial struggles.
... lavish its scorn upon the fainthearted.
... always . . . support . . . those who . . . struggle for a righteous peace.
God bless the United States of America.

Roosevelt returned to his train, which pulled out for Chicago. The next day, in western Ohio, the president had the train slowed to a snail's pace going through the city of Lima so he could wave to the crowd that lined the track for blocks. He repeated the ploy in Gary, Indiana. At Fort Wayne, Indiana, he left the train to speak to the crowd, telling them that he was campaigning to correct Republican misrepresentations. He repeated his earlier statements about wanting a big vote, win or lose, and closed by saying, "I hope to come back once more in the next four years—as President of the United States." If he did, "you will find me just the same and I will wear the same sized hat."

Since he would arrive in Chicago about 6:30 p.m., there was no time to tour the city, so the Democratic machine brought the city to him. Soldier Field's 100,000 seats were filled, and another 150,000 supporters surrounded the stadium and listened thanks to dozens of loudspeakers. Mike Reilly recorded that "Mayor Kelly turned out a crowd that scared the daylights out of all of us," but nothing untoward happened.

The president had not spoken in Chicago since the 1937 "quarantine the aggressor" speech. This time he would twit rather than attack the now vanquished isolationists. This speech, focused on postwar domestic goals, contained another memorable phrase.

After quoting, line by line, the eight generalized rights he had advocated in the State of the Union message back in January, he now added a specific numerical goal: "To assure the full realization of the right to a useful and remunerative employment, an adequate program must, and if I have anything to do about it will, provide America with close to sixty million productive jobs."

Like the 1940 goal of fifty thousand planes, the target of sixty million jobs was scoffed at by many but soon achieved. In each case, Roosevelt chose, on his own responsibility, a round number a little above the experts' guesses; in the case of jobs, the statistics Rosenman had assembled mostly had an upper limit of fifty-seven or fifty-eight million.

"In the America of tomorrow," the president continued, alluding to the "World of Tomorrow" slogan of the New York World's Fair of 1939–40, "we think of many things."

> The demand for . . . well over a million homes a year for at least ten years. . . . New highways, new parkways . . . thousands of new airports . . . new planes . . . small, new cheap automobiles, with low maintenance and operation costs . . . new hospitals and new health clinics . . . a new merchant marine for our expanded world trade.
>
> . . . [O]ur Economic Bill of Rights—like the sacred Bill of Rights of our Constitution itself, must be applied to all our citizens, irrespective of race, color, or creed. . . . Back in 1941, I appointed a Fair Employment Practice[s] Committee to prevent discrimination in war industry and Government employment. The work of that Committee and the results obtained more than justify its creation.
>
> I believe that the Congress should by law make the Committee permanent.

Much of the latter part of the speech was an attempt to placate businessmen; in doing so, Roosevelt iterated conventional economic wisdom. "I believe in free enterprise—and always have. I believe in the profit system—and always have. I believe that private enterprise can give full employment to our people." He also spoke about ending price and wage restraints as soon as possible.

The speech over, the train headed back to Washington. Unlike the 1940 campaign train that remained tense and worried, this was a relaxed and confident group. Sherwood remembered that there was "none of the frantic strain or epidemics of jitters that marked" the 1940 campaign. The wartime president still had environmental problems on his mind. He used the occasion of a brief stop in Clarksburg, West Virginia, to speak to ten thousand people about the conservation of resources. Pointing to the region's denuded hills, he explained why it was both necessary and profitable to replant and restore the trees in what he called a "sermon."

Back in the White House on Monday, Hassett found the "Big Boss brisk as a bee, brimming with health and spirits when we went to the bedroom this morning," despite the exertions of the trip.[40]

Roosevelt opened his press conference the next afternoon saying that he had no news but was just back from a half-hour visit with Secretary Hull at the naval hospital and that Hull looked "awfully well." He made it clear that "*I* wasn't examined." Asked when Hull would leave the hospital, he said he didn't ask the doctor and, showing his annoyance at the attention paid to his own health, added that "unlike some people, who are not doctors, I dislike to give medical information." The real news about that meeting, which Roosevelt had no intention of releasing, was that Hull had told him at the end of September that he was too ill to continue. In his memoirs, Hull comments that Roosevelt "did not seem to want to believe me." On October 2, his seventy-third birthday, he had left the State Department and remained in his apartment for eighteen days before checking into Bethesda, where he would remain for seven months. During Roosevelt's hospital visit, he urged Hull not to resign; Hull told him that despite his strong desire to help execute the plans for peace he had presided over, he simply could not continue. Roosevelt then asked him to defer his resignation until the start of the fourth term, January 20; Hull again refused. Finally, Roosevelt asked him to defer his resignation until after the election, to which Hull agreed. Stettinius, who would succeed him, had been functioning as secretary of state for some time but was not made privy to this arrangement until after the election. Roosevelt did try again to persuade Hull to stay on, without success. Hull's retirement and Stettinius's appointment would be announced only on November 27.

When a reporter asked, "Mr. President, is there anything that you can tell us in the way of background, or general shedding of light, on why it was necessary to call Stilwell home?" the question could not have been a surprise. Three days earlier, the War Department had made a detailed announcement, and the papers had been full of it ever since. Roosevelt gave an unusually full and relatively straightforward account: "General Stilwell has done extremely well. I am very fond of him personally. I think that his record has been excellent."

After characterizing Stilwell's dismissal—a word the president did not use—as "just one of 'them' things," he tried to put the best possible face on it.

> In this particular case, General Stilwell had the—really three commands. One was the Burma command—I am talking about areas—one was with Admiral Mountbatten, and one was chief of staff to General Chiang Kai-shek. And General Chiang Kai-shek and the General had had certain fallings out—oh, quite a while ago—and it finally ended the other day.
>
> The Generalissimo asked if we could send someone to replace General Stilwell with him as his chief of staff. And we did it. You have to remember that General Chiang Kai-shek is head of the Chinese Republic of 450 million people—head of state. He is also the head of the government, and he is commander-in-chief of the army.

It became apparent in the months after his death that Roosevelt's China policy had begun to fall apart just at the time of Stilwell's recall. That policy had been based on one incredibly perceptive insight—that China would become a major power in the postwar world—that no other Western leader shared. Thus, Roosevelt had insisted that China be one of the "four policemen," which resulted in a permanent China seat on the United Nations Security Council. But the corollaries of that insight were not only that a corrupt, brutal, and inefficient regime had to be supported up to a point—Roosevelt never envisaged sending armies to fight on the Asian mainland—but that a slavish continuation of that policy kept the seat in the hands of a repudiated government in exile for decades. From a purely wartime strategic point of view, the failure of Stilwell's doomed mission simplified matters. As an official army history pointed out, "The removal of Stilwell in October 1944 served to relieve the situation somewhat and paved the way for a more impersonal approach to the problem of China's role in the war, but with little consistent political guidance at the top level and with U.S. postwar objectives in the Far East largely idealistic and the methods of attaining them still undefined, the Army's task of preparing China's forces for the challenges that lay ahead were tremendous, and time was fast running out."[41]

Responding to urgings from party chairman Hannegan, Roosevelt made a quarter-hour campaign speech from the White House on November 2 that was also piped in to a rally at Madison Square Garden. After reporting on the excellent progress in the war against Japan, he turned to politics. "We have been told during this political campaign that unless the American people elect the Republican presidential choice, the Congress will not cooperate in the peace. That is a threat to build a party spite fence between us and the peace."

The president questioned the authority of "these men to speak for the Congress" and pointed out that congressional resolutions pledging support for international cooperation for peace had been adopted overwhelmingly. In his closing remarks, he returned to the theme of the Chicago speech and spoke about ensuring postwar economic prosperity, adding that he looked forward to "new highways . . . airplanes and airports; to television, and other miraculous new inventions and discoveries, made during this war, which will be adapted to the peacetime uses of a peace-loving people.

Roosevelt's very brief Friday press conference was chiefly devoted to his laying out the details of his final campaign trip and a statement about the importance of allowing employees time off to vote, which was put out later in the day as a formal statement. That evening the president's train, which had grown to fourteen cars, carrying the largest press complement since the 1940 campaign, left for Boston, where the president would make his last major campaign appearance on Saturday night.

Brief Saturday stops at Bridgeport and Hartford, Connecticut, and Springfield, Massachusetts, to deliver what the president called "a few kind words" produced no surprises. At Bridgeport he let his real animosity toward Dewey and the kind of campaign the Republicans were running show a little by saying, "I can't say all the things I would like to say about my opponent the way I would like to sometimes," because "I try to think I am a Christian," and "someday . . .

[will] go to Heaven," and "don't believe there is anything to be gained in saying dreadful things about other people in any campaign."

At Hartford he left the train for a rally in a downtown dominated by the buildings of insurance companies. He attacked his favorite target, Herbert Hoover, reminding his audience that despite his own election in 1932, the "grass did not grow in the streets" and that "four years ago . . . people . . . were being told that if I got reelected, all of the Hartford insurance companies would go broke."

He drew laughter from the crowd by claiming, as he made a sweeping gesture that took in many of the buildings surrounding him, that "coming in here I expected to see vast, empty buildings not being used and employing no people." After the laughter faded, he continued:

> And, of course, the joke is that the insurance companies, not only in Hartford but other places, are better off than they have ever been before. They are pretty good insurance companies, you know. They subscribe to the war loans. They have been patriotic. They just have only one unfortunate habit which they acquire every four years—in fact, the last four months of every four years. They say, "If this man Roosevelt gets elected president, we will have to get out of business!" So it is good to see them still going—good to see that Hartford is not a city of empty homes.

The president was ending his campaign as it had begun, by getting his audiences to laugh with him at his opponents. A little later, in Springfield, again leaving the train to speak in the center of town to a crowd of from thirty-five to fifty thousand and where, he noted, he had never spoken before, he was brief and his tone serious. Referring to his 1940 pledge of "no foreign wars," Roosevelt deliberately misquoted it, adding the words that Sherwood could not persuade him to use in 1940. "[In 1940] We had the stern resolve . . . that we would not send our boys to fight abroad unless we were attacked. The attack came—treacherous, deadly attack. Our pledge was kept—we fought back when we were attacked—obviously rightly."[42]

The speech in Boston's Fenway Park was set up like the other major outdoor affairs—the president's car driven onto a platform in the middle of the field—but somehow there was an interaction between speaker and audience not present in the earlier events. As the car circled the field, "wave after wave of applause" came from the seventy-five thousand partisans, and when it was in position the crowd took up the chant, "We want Roosevelt!"

The Fala speech opening the campaign was marked by good-natured humor, but the closing Boston speech was often bitter ridicule. Dewey's campaign had gotten under Roosevelt's skin, and as United Press reporter Merriman Smith noted, the president viewed him with "unvarnished contempt." Roosevelt's insistence, in public and private, that the campaign was the dirtiest in his lifetime overstates the case, but he clearly believed it.

He began, amiably enough, by talking about Boston's hero Al Smith, reminding the crowd that he had nominated Al for president twice and that, when he ran for governor of New York at Al's request in 1928, "people were then, even then, saying that my health would not permit me to discharge the duties of public office. Well, you know, I think that it is by now a pretty well established fact that I managed to survive my four years as Governor of New York. And at the end of that time I went elsewhere."

He mentioned that when he had spoken for Smith in Boston, he had focused on racial and religious intolerance, which was and is "a menace to the liberties of America." All the bigots were "gunning for Al Smith," he said. Noting that in New England, "you have been fighting bigotry and injustice for centuries," he repeated his line about everyone but "pure blooded Indians" being immigrants or descendants of immigrants, "even those who came here on the *Mayflower*."

He spoke of "our boys" who were winning the war, and among them were the Murphys and the Kellys, the Smiths and the Joneses, the Cohens, the Carusos, the Kowalskis, the Schultzes, the Olsens, the Swobodas, and—right in with all the rest of them—the Cabots and the Lowells. Unlike Roosevelt, immigrant songwriter Irving Berlin (1888–1989) sang in 1942 of an army composed of men named Jones, Green, and Brown. The president's list ignored names originating in Asia or Latin America. The president assured his listeners that "victory over the Nazis and Japanese is certain and inevitable," but he warned that "tough, hard, bloody fighting lay ahead." Alluding to his still controversial 1940 speech in Boston without mentioning it, he reminded his audience that "we got into this war because the Japanese. . . . Hitler's Germany and Mussolini's Italy declared war on us." He followed with the self-quotation: in the same situation, he would do it "again, again, and again." Sherwood, still sensitive about his role in the 1940 speech, notes that the crowd, many of whom had heard that triad before, "roared its approval."

After a vigorous defense of the New Deal and his conduct of the war, Roosevelt granted: that "this administration has made mistakes, that I freely assert. *Assert*. And I hope my friends of the press will not change that to admit. But, my friends, I think it is a pretty good batting average."

Roosevelt then turned his attention to his opponent. Adhering to his custom, he never spoke Dewey's name, though he referred to him an unprecedented seven separate times in a long passage. He focused on two separate quotations from the Republican's recent swing through Massachusetts. In Boston, "quote, 'the Communists are seizing control of the New Deal, through which they aim to control the Government of the United States.' Unquote." And in Worcester on the same day, he said that after a November victory "quote, 'we can end one-man government in the United States, and we can forever remove the threat of monarchy in the United States.'"

Roosevelt asked, "Now really—which is it—Communism or monarchy?" He added, somewhat muddily, "I do not think that we could have both in this country, even if we wanted either, which we do not." The president went on to confess that

> often in this campaign I have been tempted to speak my mind with sharper vigor and greater indignation.
>
> Everyone knows that I was reluctant to run for president this year.
>
> But now [he explained] I am most anxious to win because never before in my lifetime has a campaign been filled with such misrepresentation, distortion and falsehood. . . .
>
> When any candidate . . . stands up and says . . . the Government of the United States—your Government—could be sold out to the Communists . . . that candidate reveals—I'll be polite—a shocking lack of trust in America . . . in democracy, in the spiritual strength of our people.

Roosevelt then spoke of the darkest days of the Depression when "our people might have turned to alien ideas . . . Communism or Fascism. But . . . the American people demanded in 1933 . . . not less democracy but more democracy, and that's what they got." Then, using words he wanted to be remembered by, "The only thing we have to fear is fear itself."

He ended what was his last stump speech with a vision of the postwar world in which "this country will have the greatest material power of any Nation in the world."

> It will be a shining America. . . .
>
> It will be an America [of] abundant jobs and an expanding economy.
>
> All around us we see an unfinished world . . . of awakened peoples struggling to achieve a higher cultural and material standard of living.
>
> I say we must wage the coming battle for America and for civilization on a scale worthy of [the war effort]. And I say that we must wage it in association with the United Nations.
>
> I say that we must wage a peace to attract the highest hearts, the most competent hands and brains. That, my friends, is the conception that I have of the meaning of total victory.
>
> And that conception is founded on faith—faith in the unlimited destiny— the unconquerable spirit of the United States of America.[43]

The president reboarded his train immediately after the speech, and early the next morning the last two cars were shunted onto the siding below Springwood; after he got up, Eleanor drove her car down to pick him up and bring him home, where he spent a quiet, private Sunday.

The Monday ritual before election day began after lunch with the president being driven into Poughkeepsie where he picked up the county Democratic chairman, who, with Secretary Morgenthau, rode in the president's open car. The sixty-eight-mile tour in what Roosevelt called a "sentimental journey" in "raw autumn weather" was punctuated by a light snowfall. His remarks in a number of places rarely touched national issues; in one he joshed about his chances of winning locally and claimed that someone in New England had told him that if he ran enough times, he might carry Maine and Vermont. As a presidential candidate, he never carried either the county or the village of Hyde Park, although he did carry the electoral district he lived in. His crowds ran from a few hundred to several thousand and were largely composed of schoolchildren, except when he spoke at a Newburgh shipyard, where he told workers that they would have jobs after the war. Back in Poughkeepsie, his old friend Judge Julian Mack, who had placed him in nomination at the 1932 convention, wondered whether he should introduce him "as fellow-Communist or as the man who is backing up MacArthur." Roosevelt, with Eleanor beside him, closed the tour with the hope that tomorrow "it is going to be said . . . that the war has been conducted constitutionally and with the approval of the people."

His broadcast remarks that evening from his study, though part of an hour-long national program paid for by the DNC, were more civic than political. "I do not want," he said, "to talk to you tonight of partisan politics. The political battle is finished." Like other Americans, "We are thinking of our own sons—all of them far from home—and of our neighbors sons and the sons of our friends."

He warned that any future war "would be bound to bring even more devilish and powerful instruments of destruction . . . crashing deep within the United States itself. . . . [W]e must be certain that the peace-loving Nations . . . band together . . . to outlaw and to prevent war."

Tomorrow, you the people of the United States again vote as free men and women, with full freedom of choice—with no secret police watching over your shoulders. . . . But when the ballots are cast your responsibilities do not cease. The public servants you elect cannot fulfill their trust unless you, the people, watch and advise them, raise your voices in protest when you believe your public servants to be wrong, back them up when you believe them to be right.

But not for one single moment can you now or later forget the all important goals for which we are aiming—to win the war and unite our fighting men with their families . . . to see that all have honorable jobs . . . to create a world peace organization which will prevent this disaster—or one like it—from ever coming upon us again.

Roosevelt closed by reading a fairly substantial prayer for those in the armed forces that had been sent to him by Angus Dun (1892–1971), the Episcopal bishop of Washington, which included this passage: "Be Thou their strength when they are set in the midst of so many and great dangers. And grant that, whether by life or by death, they may win for the whole world the fruits of their sacrifice and a just peace."[44]

On election day, a little after noon, the president was driven with Eleanor, Johnny Boettiger, and Fala "in an open phaeton" to the local elementary school, where the children came out, greeted him and sang some songs, and received a presidential greeting. The car then proceeded to the town hall, where officials and a good-sized crowd were waiting to see the Roosevelts. Franklin entered the booth first, but unbeknownst to him a cable that the newsreel photographers had strung over the booth prevented the curtain from closing completely, and shortly a familiar voice was heard to complain, "The damned thing won't work!" The offending cable was noticed and moved, and the president voted; Eleanor followed suit without incident. (The *New York Times* found this mishap unfit to print, but some other papers and diarist Hassett were less inhibited.)

That evening the Roosevelts dined en famille, and by 9:00 p.m. the dining room had been readied for results, with two wire-service printers and extra telephones installed. A shirtsleeved president sat with pads and pencils to record the results, which Grace Tully and other aides passed on to him. A fair-size crowd, including Steve Early, Pa Watson, Henry and Elinor Morgenthau, Sam and Dorothy Rosenman, Bob and Madeline Sherwood, and a number of local friends and relatives, were gathered in the big library, listening to results on the radio. There was little tension among the insiders: a twenty-five-dollar pool set up in the last week of the campaign among Watson, Rosenman, Hopkins, Early, and Sherwood on the number of electoral votes Roosevelt would get produced guesses ranging from 400 to 484, with 266 necessary to elect: Roosevelt rang up 432.

The president and the Secret Service had arranged with the town supervisor that a torchlight parade several thousand strong be admitted to the grounds after 11:00 p.m. It was an old tradition; Roosevelt claimed to remember coming downstairs "in my old-fashioned nightgown" to witness the 1892 parade celebrating Grover Cleveland's reelection, but the tradition of its coming to Springwood ceased with his father's death, to be resumed only in 1928. In a rare public allusion to Roosevelt's disability, John Crider wrote in the *Times* that "the president wheeled out onto the front porch at 11:25," with Eleanor and Anna "leaning on the back of his chair."

After being serenaded by the crowd, which included a drum and bugle corps and the Vassar College chorus, the president first reminisced about local events, then said that the reports he had "are not so bad." Although he couldn't "make any statement at all," he made his victory sound like a sentence: "It looks as if I will have to come back here on a train from Washington for four more years. But it's worth while still, and always will be, to leave Washington on a Friday night and get here Saturday morning, just for two days up here. It will always be worth it. And so I am glad to be here on election day again—I might say again and again and again! But I'll be perfectly happy to come back here for good, as you all know."

He then thanked them for coming, told them about his telephone calls to and from all over, and "the ticker in there" that gave him returns. "It has been good to see you, and I will have to go back and do some more telephoning." The crowd then said good-bye by singing "For He's a Jolly Good Fellow."

Within an hour or so, what had seemed probable was all but certain; Dewey—"graceless," according to Hassett—broadcast a concession at 3:16 a.m. but sent no message to the president, who, nevertheless, wired that "I thank you for your statement which I have heard over the air a few minutes ago." At 4:00 a.m., as Roosevelt headed up to bed, he answered Hassett's good night with: "I still think he is a son of a bitch!"

Wednesday morning the president and many others slept almost to noon. After lunch Roosevelt dictated answers to a few of the flood of congratulatory telegrams and issued a formal statement: "For the first time in eighty years we have held a national election in the midst of a war. What is really important is that after all of the changes and vicissitudes of fourscore years, we have demonstrated to the world that democracy is a living, vital force, that our faith in American institutions is unshaken; that conscience and not force is the source of power in the government of man. In that faith let us unite to win the war and to achieve a lasting peace."

Early briefed the press in Poughkeepsie, as wartime rules now applied again and journalists no longer had direct access to the reelected president. However, the rules were relaxed enough so that they could be told that the president would leave for the capital Thursday night.[45]

The president's train arrived at Union Station at 8:20 a.m. in a downpour, and after he received a number of cabinet officials, led by War Secretary Stimson on the train, he emerged, ordered the top of his touring car taken down, and got in with Vice President Wallace on one side and Vice President-elect Truman on the other, with Johnny Boettiger up front beside the chauffeur. His car led a procession around to the station plaza facing the Capitol, where he made a brief talk, thanking everyone for welcoming him on a rather rainy morning and hoping that "the scribes in the papers" wouldn't hint that "I expect to make Washington my permanent home for the rest of my life." The motorcade then proceeded down Pennsylvania Avenue before crowds of perhaps 250,000 persons, largely pupils dismissed from school and government workers given time off for the occasion. At the White House, a large contingent of staff was waiting to greet him in the Diplomatic Cloak Room, where he accepted congratulations and shook hands as an orchestral contingent of the Marine Band played.

At a brief press conference before lunch, in response to requests, he rummaged around in his desk drawer and found his electoral vote prediction, made at some unspecified time before he left on his last campaign swing. He had guessed that there would be only 335 votes "for me," leaving 196 for Dewey, an overestimation of nearly 100 percent. He denied a number of rumors, answered "I suppose so" when asked if he expected Secretary Hull to be "back in the State Department," and "No" when asked if he had heard from Mr. Dewey yet.

By the time the president reached Washington, almost all the national election results were in hand. The turnout was two million lower than the fifty million Roosevelt had hoped for, but in view of the difficulties—both physical and legal—of getting the soldier vote in and the fact that large numbers of war workers had moved and often faced delays in being able to register in new precincts, the turnout was good. It was clear that most of those unable to vote would have been Roosevelt voters, whose popularity among workers was high and ran consistently 60 percent or better among military voters.

Of those who actually voted, Roosevelt won 53.4 percent, down 0.5 percent from 1940, and the lowest of his presidency. Dewey received 45.9 percent, up 1.2 percent from Willkie's tally, while minor candidates drew 0.7 percent, up 0.3 percent from 1940. Given the total circumstances of the election, it is not meaningful to speak of any change in Roosevelt's overall popularity between 1940 and 1944.

The congressional races were a different matter. In the House, Democrats, who had lost 50 seats in the 1942 election, gained 24 seats in 1944, but their total, 242 seats, as opposed to 190 Republicans and just 2 independents, was the second smallest of Roosevelt's presidency. In the less volatile Senate, the steady decline in Democratic seats from the high of 79 of 96 seats after the 1936 landslide continued as the total fell 2 more seats to a Roosevelt-era low of 56. But it was significant that isolationist support continued to shrivel through the defeat of key isolationist senators such as North Dakota's Nye and, more significantly, the conversion of such key figures as Michigan's Vandenberg. In domestic matters, a shifting coalition of southern Democrats and conservative northern Republicans continued to be able to block or reshape many administration nonmilitary initiatives.[46]

Concerns about Roosevelt's health within his circle were somewhat abated. Bruenn noted that during the brief but intensive campaign, "there was a complete disregard of the rest regimen, and there were prolonged periods of intense activity. . . . It may be noted that during this period of stress he was very animated. He really enjoyed going to the 'hustings,' and despite this his blood pressure levels, if anything, were lower than before. He was eating somewhat better, and, despite prolonged periods of exposure he did not contract any upper respiratory infections. The physical examination remained unchanged."

A relaxed air prevailed at the White House; Congress would remain in recess until November 14. On Armistice Day, the president was driven to Arlington for the annual wreath-laying ceremony, accompanied by Eleanor, Johnny Boettiger, and his two military aides. He felt well enough to leave the car and stand watching while Pa Watson went forward and placed his wreath. That afternoon he met with the secretary of the Senate and the architect of the Capitol to discuss plans for his fourth inauguration. He spent the rest of the weekend in the White House.

Just as Congress was getting back to work, Steve Early called reporters into his office and announced that after meeting with the president, Justice Byrnes, who had in August agreed to stay on only until the Senate reconvened and confirmed his successor, had now bowed to the president's wishes and agreed to stay on and direct the new OWMR until Germany was defeated. As soon as his nomination was read in the Senate, his former colleagues confirmed him by unanimous consent. The president used Byrnes's example to urge others to stay on. A week later, Leo Crowley resigned but agreed to stay on as head of the Foreign Economic Administration (FEA) until Germany was beaten.

At his press conference later that afternoon, Roosevelt answered or deflected a number of questions. Asked what "you could tell us" about the announced resignation of three public members of the War Labor Board, he answered, "Nothing at all. . . . I can't even tell you when there will be any action." The next day, he canceled their resignations, and they complied, setting a pattern that was expected to prevail until V-E Day.

Asked about his plans for the inaugural, he remarked, obviously enjoying himself, that economy-minded senators—he mentioned Virginia's Harry Byrd—had appropriated twenty-five thousand dollars for it but that he could "save an awful lot of money" by cutting out the parade and having a small ceremony, including the swearing in of Vice President Truman, on the South Portico of the White House with a limited, invited audience and do without an inaugural chairman.

Asked whether he had heard from Dewey, he said that he received "a letter yesterday."

Q: What kind of letter was it?
THE PRESIDENT: No, you can't see my personal files.

The next morning, the president met for an hour and a half with the Democratic leaders of the old Congress—Vice President Wallace, Speaker Rayburn, and Majority Leader Barkley—to plan for its final weeks. They agreed that the one piece of must legislation was the renewal of the Second War Powers Act from which many of the president's extraordinary powers stemmed before its expiration on December 31.

Henry J. Kaiser, one of Roosevelt's strong supporters, emerged from a White House meeting delivering a familiar message: war workers who quit their jobs to take others in the now expanding civilian economy imperiled the war effort.[47]

Roosevelt devoted most of his brief Friday-afternoon press conference to a pitch for compulsory service, which he said, in response to a query, need not be military. He wanted "one year of service out of the life of every boy in this country to his own government . . . between the ages of 18 and 23." He cited the nonmilitary service in the CCC.

By Saturday, November 18, Dr. Bruenn noticed a distinct regression in Roosevelt's general health, though his lungs were clear and the heart functions no worse: "His appetite had again become poor and he had lost a little more weight. . . . The President looked tired."

On Sunday evening, Roosevelt, speaking from the White House, opened the sixth war loan drive with a brief broadcast appeal. With his talent for the telling statistic, he pointed out that the war was costing "two hundred and fifty millions a day. That is why every war bond you buy is important." He noted that "we have every reason to be . . . optimistic about the ultimate outcome [but] a rough road lies in front of us." He concluded, "There is an old saying about sticking to the plow until you have reached the end of the furrow. . . . And so in the name of our wounded and sick, in the name of our dead, and in the name of future generations of Americans, I ask you to plow out this furrow to a successful and victorious end." The drive, conducted from November 20 through December 16, raised more than twenty-one billion dollars, just over one and a half times its target.[48]

As part of his postwar planning, Roosevelt sent a public letter to his chief scientific adviser, Vannevar Bush, whose Office of Scientific Research and Development had overseen federal research since 1940. Noting that the scientific work was being carried out "in utmost secrecy," he said that there was no reason the same methods should not be used openly "in the days of peace ahead" to "improve the national health" and to create "new enterprises bringing new jobs and the betterment of the national standard of living."

He asked Bush for recommendations on four major points.

1. What can be done, consistent with military security . . . to make known to the world as soon as possible the contributions which have been made during our war effort to scientific knowledge? . . .

2. With particular reference to the war of science against disease, what can be done now to organize a program for continuing in the future the work that has been done in medicine and related sciences? . . .

3. What can the Government do now and in the future to aid research activities by private and public organizations? The proper roles of public and private research, and their interrelation, should be carefully considered.

4. Can an effective program be proposed for discovering and developing scientific talent in American youth so that the continuing future of scientific research in the country may be assured on a level comparable to what has been done during the war?

Roosevelt followed these questions, about which he asked for the "considered judgment" of Bush and his associates, with a statement of his vision of the possibilities for the future: "New frontiers of the mind are before us, and if they are pioneered with the same vision, boldness, and drive with which we have waged this war we can create a fuller and more fruitful employment and a fuller and more fruitful life."

At his Tuesday-afternoon news conference, the president again stressed the importance of war workers staying at their jobs—many of which would not last long—and not taking jobs in the civilian sector that were more likely to be permanent. In response to a question about the status of Lend-Lease, he unknowingly challenged a phrase about "second stage Lend-lease" that had been used publicly by Secretary Morgenthau in describing his meetings with Keynes. The president insisted that Lend-Lease would continue unchanged until Japan was defeated, while Keynes and Morgenthau assumed, correctly, that Britain's needs and focus would be altered once the war in Europe ended.

Three days later, the president expanded his remarks on Lend-Lease in his seventeenth quarterly report on the program. He repeated his statement that it "should end with the war" but said that economic assistance through the United Nations would be necessary in the postwar years. By the end of the month, the results of the Morgenthau-Keynes negotiations were announced: after Germany was defeated, Lend-Lease would be reduced by 43 percent.[49]

Later in the press conference, a question about the possibility of allowing Japanese Americans to return to the Pacific Coast drew from the president his longest press-conference statement about Japanese Americans.

> THE PRESIDENT: In most of the cases. That doesn't mean all of them. . . . I am now talking about . . . Japanese Americans. I am not talking about the Japanese themselves. A good deal of progress has been made in scattering them around the country, and that is going on almost every day. . . . There are about . . . a hundred thousand Japanese-origin citizens in this country. And it is felt by a great many lawyers that under the Constitution they can't be kept locked up in concentration camps. And a good number of them . . . you had better check with the Secretary of the Interior on this—somewhere around 20 to 25 percent of all those citizens have replaced themselves, and in a great many parts of the country.

The president went on to speak about "scattering" the released Japanese Americans in rural counties—typically, he spoke of the "the Hudson River valley" and "western 'Joe-gia' (Georgia)"—but the vast majority of these twice-relocated people were in midwestern cities, particularly Chicago and Minneapolis. He never mentioned resettlement on the Pacific Coast. He did say that "after all they are American citizens, and we all know that American citizens have certain privileges," and added, "And, of course we are actuated . . . in part by the very wonderful record that the Japanese in that battalion in Italy have been making in the war. It is one of the outstanding battalions we have." When a reporter followed up by asking whether the restrictions on returning to their former homes would be changed, the president ignored him and answered a question on another topic.

What had changed? For one thing, the election was over. By mid-1944, leaders of the War Department and the War Relocation Authority were ready to allow some Japanese Americans to return to their West Coast homes, but the president had insisted that this not be done before the election. His expressed concern about the Constitution was perhaps triggered by his knowledge that lawyers in the Justice Department expected to lose the fourth of the so-called Japanese American cases, a habeas corpus petition from Mitsuye Endo (1920–2006), a Japanese American woman of undisputed loyalty who wanted to return to her home in Sacramento. The Court's decision, announced on December 18, 1944, meant that Japanese American citizens, if certified loyal by the government, could no longer be restrained from returning to the West Coast, although many no longer had homes to return to. Every aspect of Roosevelt's wartime treatment of Japanese Americans is a permanent deserved stain on his reputation.[50]

On Tuesday evening, Roosevelt left to spend Thanksgiving in Hyde Park; encouraged by Dr. Bruenn, he planned for an extended rest at Warm Springs. As they planned the Saturday-night return to the capital, he told Hassett that in addition to Eleanor, his cousins Laura Delano (1885–1972) and Margaret Suckley (1891–1991) would be on the train and that the cousins would go down to Georgia with him on Monday evening. In Washington, on Sunday, he paid yet another visit to Secretary Hull.

In a rare Monday press conference on November 27, the president finally announced Hull's resignation and later released an exchange of letters dated November 21. The president feigned surprise—"hit me between the wind and the water"—at Hull's resigning. During the conference, he refused to say anything about who would be appointed:

Q: How about a successor?
THE PRESIDENT: I just said that there was no more news on that.

Yet most of the details had been leaked and were in that morning's newspapers. Asked if he was going to see Stettinius, Roosevelt said that they would have lunch. It was perhaps at that lunch that Roosevelt made it clear to Stettinius that the president and not the secretary of state would deal with matters concerning Churchill and Stalin and formulate overall policy and that he wanted someone who would work in harmony with him. For that reason, he had rejected Byrnes, who had been favored by many, including Harry Hopkins. When Stettinius remarked, "In other words, Jimmy might question who was boss," Roosevelt responded that this was "exactly the point."

The president may have been concerned by an AP story indicating strong Senate support for Byrnes as Hull's replacement. During his lunch hour, he "summoned" Senators Tom Connally and Walter F. George, the two ranking Democrats on the Senate Foreign Relations Committee, who came and returned to the Hill without saying what they had talked about. Sometime after 2:00 p.m., the president announced his nomination of Edward Stettinius as secretary of state.[51]

At 5:00 p.m., the president's train pulled out for Warm Springs; he would not return until December 19, twenty-two days later. Unlike his condition in April when he went to Baruch's estate, Roosevelt was able to handle the paper workload, but was spared appointments, so a very different contingent went with him. Nine White House staffers, headed by Bill Hassett, set up a fully functioning office: Grace Tully and three others to handle the paperwork, Louise Hackmeister and a technician to run and maintain a switchboard, and Dewey Long and an assistant to take care of transportation. Of the president's regular companions, only Dr. McIntire came, and he returned to Washington after three days. Roosevelt's health care was seen to by Dr. Bruenn and a "chest specialist," Captain Robert E. Duncan, executive officer of the naval hospital, while George Fox was there for massage and physiotherapy. In addition to the usual Secret Service contingent, there was a detachment of Marines for the president's protection. Although Roosevelt's location was supposed to be secret, the "whole town" of Warm Springs turned out in midafternoon to meet his train, and the cooks at the foundation were already preparing the post-Thanksgiving turkey dinner that the president would preside over that evening.

There was no crisis in the president's health at that time, but there were indications of a further deterioration. Dr. Bruenn said of the stay at Warm Springs:

In this relaxed and familiar environment his appetite improved somewhat, but his weight remained unchanged at 165 pounds. A lower right molar tooth . . . was removed under local anesthetic without difficulty. He had very few visitors, and, except for attending to [the daily batch of documents] from Washington, the days were spent in reading, motoring . . . and in conversation with his intimates. [Some days after] his arrival, he entered the pool for the first time. . . . He seemed to enjoy it and thought that some contraction of the hips had developed. Blood pressure determinations taken before and after showed an alarming rise (260/150 mm Hg). Because of this, further swimming was definitely discouraged. . . . His general condition remained essentially unchanged. He continued to have difficulty in eating ("Can't eat"— "cannot taste food"), and as a result he had lost a little more weight. He was urged to eat and its importance was stressed. An electrocardiogram (trac-

ing) showed no change, and there was no evidence of digitalis toxicity. . . .
With the routine of rest and relaxation being more carefully observed, the
blood pressure levels tended to be a little lower. There was no change in the
physical examination.

Since Congress stayed in session until the day the president returned to
Washington, there was plenty of work for him and the staff in Georgia. More
than seventy-five bills were signed and several minor ones vetoed. The most
vital new laws were the renewal of the Second War Powers Act and an increase
of 1 percent in the payroll tax for Social Security beginning on January 1, 1945.
In a signing statement, he said that he approved the bill "reluctantly" because
the original 1935 act had called for a 2 percent tax increase to go into effect in
1941 that had now been postponed by Congress three times. Had Roosevelt
vetoed the bill, no payroll tax increase would have resulted. He warned:

> The Congress should realize that this bill deferring a statutory increase in
> contributions toward existing Social Security merely defers . . . the necessary
> fiscal receipts to pay the benefits. Also it does not seem to me to be wholly
> sound to enact a tax law and then defer the taxes year after year.
>
> The public will understand that as a nation we are committed to Social
> Security and will undoubtedly increase and not decrease its benefits. . . .
> But it will be incumbent upon the next Congress thoroughly to review the
> methods of financing them.

Roosevelt sent Congress a number of messages, including a request for $75.9
million to finance loans for public works to cities and states and his first quarterly report on UNRRA. In the latter, he warned that many of the one hundred
million liberated people in Europe would need significant food assistance to
avert the danger of "famine" and "pestilence" that might otherwise occur. Using
the figures supplied by the new agency, he overestimated the ability of Europeans
to feed themselves, claiming that they could raise 90 percent of their needs.

Public announcements from the White House made it seem that the president
was in residence. Legal niceties were observed. When several appointments to
the State Department were confirmed by the Senate, the commissions were sent
in the daily pouch to Warm Springs; only after the president had signed them
and Hassett phoned Maurice Latta (1869–1948), Rudolph Forster's successor as
White House usher, to say that they had been signed were the new appointees
sworn in. Of course, many in Washington knew or deduced that the president
was not there, and rumors abounded. The most prevalent was that he was
undergoing an operation; the favored locales for this nonevent were the local
naval hospital and Boston.

Roosevelt's other long-distance executive actions included an intervention
in a public dispute between Attorney General Biddle and one of his assistant

attorney generals that had been going on since July; he dismissed the subordinate, whom he had previously warned, calling his subsequent insubordination "inexcusable." A letter to all department heads directed them and their subordinates to refrain from predicting "an early termination of the war," and he averted a railroad strike by appointing a special board.

His public statements included a letter for a special "United States at War" issue of the *Army and Navy Journal* to be published on December 7, which closed with an appeal for an effective peace: "The effective cooperation among the United Nations which has done so much to insure victory must continue after war for building a structure of peace. . . . Everything we do must be dedicated to that objective."

When Roosevelt left Warm Springs on Sunday afternoon, December 17, he spoke briefly from the train's rear platform and reminded the crowd that in 1941, he had said that he would be back "next year" unless there was a war. This time he said that he would be back in the spring, war or no war. The train took him to Camp Lejeune, North Carolina, which he inspected on Monday afternoon and saw a training exercise with war dogs and their handlers while explosions simulated battlefield conditions. The president's train brought him back to the Bureau of Printing and Engraving's underground siding at 7:30 Tuesday morning. Only after he returned to the White House was news of his absence released.[52]

At his press conference that afternoon, Roosevelt, described as "tanned and looking much rested," warned reporters about asking "contentious questions." The redoubtable May Craig countered:

MAY CRAIG: Well, Mr. President, this is a contentious question, but I would like a serious answer.

THE PRESIDENT: You would find it awfully hard to get, May.

MAY CRAIG: There's a good deal of question as to whether you are going right or left politically, and I would like your opinion on which way you are going?

THE PRESIDENT: I am going down the whole line a little left of center. I think that was answered, that question, eleven and a half years ago, and still holds.

MAY CRAIG: But you told us a little while ago that you were going to have Dr. Win-The-War and not Dr. New Deal.

THE PRESIDENT: (Interjecting) That's right.

MAY CRAIG: (Continuing) The question is whether you are going back to be Dr. New Deal after the war—

THE PRESIDENT: (Interposing) No, no. No. Keep right along a little to the left of center, which includes winning the war. That's not much of an answer, is it?

MAY CRAIG: No.

THE PRESIDENT: However, you have broken the ice, May.

A minute later, another reporter drew a more revealing appraisal than the oft-quoted "a little left of center" remark.

Q: Mr. President, if you are going down a little left of center, how does that match with the six appointments you sent up to the Hill on the State Department?

THE PRESIDENT: Very well.

Q: Would you call them a little left of center? . . .

THE PRESIDENT: I call myself a little left of center. I have got a lot of people in the Administration—oh, I know some of them are extreme right and extreme left, and everything else—a lot of people in the Administration, and I cannot vouch for them all. They work out pretty well, on the whole. Just think, this crowd here in this room—my gracious, you will find every opinion between left and extreme right. . . .

Q: (Interposing) Do you find them all for you? . . .

THE PRESIDENT: No. A surprising number are.

The following day, the most talked about event in Washington was the president's two-hour lunch with Henry Wallace. For once the prevalent rumors—that the lame-duck vice president would become secretary of commerce and that the future role of Jesse Jones, the incumbent interior secretary, was unclear—were essentially correct. Wallace's account in his diary reports that Roosevelt, after an opening monologue about a variety of topics, ended Wallace's suspense by saying, "It is all right. You can have Commerce." Neither man made any public statement at the time.

In an important public action, the president signed a bill for aid to state highways, providing $1.5 billion spread over the next three years. As his signing statement pointed out, it included authorization "of an interregional highway system," as he had recommended to Congress in January, which would be essential as "a part of an expanding, prosperous economy that will insure jobs."

Lunch with the incoming vice president the next day was noncontentious. The major decision, according to Truman, was that both men would wear business suits rather than formal attire during the inaugural. The afternoon was largely devoted to two receptions for White House employees, presided over by both Roosevelts, one for those employed in the residence and their children, the other for those employed in the offices as 278 of them crowded into the Oval Office.

Roosevelt's return to Washington from Warm Springs coincided with the most crucial period of the German offensive in the Ardennes, the eight-day successful defense of the Belgian town of Bastogne in what became known as the Battle of the Bulge. He was asked about it at his Friday press conference and said, off the record, that he didn't "know much more about it" than the press did. His comments about the war in the following days should be read with that in mind.

Saturday evening the president and a small party entrained for Hyde Park; only Hassett and Hackmeister of his office staff were aboard, as he planned to do no work there, apart from the incessant signings of documents from the pouch; Grace Tully joined them after Christmas. His Christmas Eve message the next day for the fourth wartime Christmas was particularly somber, concluding:

> On this Christmas Day, we cannot yet say when our victory will come. Our enemies still fight fanatically. . . . But, they themselves know that they and their evil works are doomed. We may hasten their day of doom if we at home continue to do our full share.
>
> And we pray that that day will come soon. We pray that until then, God will protect our gallant men and women in the uniforms of the United Nations—that He will receive into His infinite grace those who make their supreme sacrifice in the cause of righteousness, in the cause of love of Him and His teachings.
>
> We pray that with victory will come a new day of peace on earth in which all the Nations of the earth will join together for all time. That is the spirit of Christmas, the holy day. May that spirit live and grow throughout the world in all the years to come.

Roosevelt had three generations of his family present: Anna's three children, Anna and Elliott and their spouses, Franklin Jr.'s wife, plus Eleanor and the widow of his half brother. Hassett, who joined Henry and Elinor Morgenthau and their daughter, Joan, as the only nonfamily guests at Christmas dinner, recorded: "To me the President seemed tired and weary—not his old self as he led the conversation. I fear for his health despite assurances from the doctors that he is O.K."

On each of the two evenings after Christmas, the first couple hosted parties in the library for the military-police detachment. On the twenty-seventh, he issued the first of the two significant presidential actions to emanate from Hyde Park during the six-day stay: an executive order for yet another seizure of Montgomery Ward facilities. Ward's president, Sewell Avery, in no way fazed by his earlier physical ouster, had become, like John L. Lewis, a serial violator of presidential orders.

The other was a matter close to one of Roosevelt's overriding concerns, the preservation of the natural wonders of the nation. In its closing hours, Congress had enacted a bill abolishing the Jackson Hole National Monument, which Roosevelt had created by executive order the year before. The president, by withholding his signature, had killed the bill—the so-called pocket veto—and, as was his custom, issued a statement explaining the authority (the Antiquities Act of 1906) and giving his reasons: to preserve "for the interests of the people of the United States as a whole" Jackson Hole's "scenery, its scientific interest, its wildlife, and its history." It is significant that, in the midst of global warfare, Roosevelt found the time to continue his massive expansion of the federal trusteeship of the national landscape.[53]

12 The Final Triumph
1945

ON NEW YEAR'S DAY, FRANCE WAS ADMITTED to the United Nations in a ceremony at the State Department. The years of American opposition to de Gaulle's regime were ignored but surely not forgotten. Stettinius read Roosevelt's statement: "France was the first ally of our country in our own war of liberation. For 150 years her traditions of liberty have been an inspiration to freemen everywhere. In this war all the brutalities of four years of Nazi occupation could not quench the flame of her unconquerable spirit or suppress the resistance of her people to the enemy. And now France stands beside us as a strong ally—once more in the first rank of the free and peace-loving nations of the world."

Most of the fruitless discussion at the year's first press conference stemmed from remarks by Barkley and Rayburn. After meeting with the president, they had told reporters that there would be a Big Three meeting "soon"; Roosevelt gave the press a synonym, *anon,* and no further information. Actually, by December 27, the decision for the three to meet at Yalta had been made, with Roosevelt and Churchill meeting at Malta beforehand. As the prime minister's New Year's doggerel to the president put it:

No more let us falter!
From Malta to Yalta!
Let nobody alter!

Asked about his future plans for Vice President Wallace, the president said that he had no news—"today." He volunteered that the traditional budget message "seminar" for financial specialists would again be conducted by budget director Smith, a clear indication that the president had had little to do with its details.

Reporters wondered if two Nazi saboteurs, one an American citizen, who had just been seized shortly after landing on a beach in Maine, would be tried as their predecessors had been in 1943. Roosevelt replied that he assumed so, but couldn't say "definitively." Warned by Stimson that another high-profile trial might jeopardize American POWs in German hands, the president, over Biddle's objections, issued an unpublicized military order on January 12 to try the two saboteurs and let the War Department handle the details. After a nine-day low-profile closed trial on New York's Governors Island in February, the tribunal deliberated for three hours, found both men guilty, and sentenced them to death. While the complex review procedures specified in army regulations were still going on, the war in Europe ended. In April President Truman commuted their sentences to life imprisonment. In 1955 the German was released and deported to West Germany. Five years later, the American was released on parole; he lived until 2002.[1]

For the second time, the annual message was read in Congress by clerks at midday and by the president on the air that night. As had been true since he returned from Tehran in the midst of war, Roosevelt also talked about peace. Confident of "ultimate total victory," he spoke publicly for the first time about the December "setback" delivered by the "ferocious" German counterattack. It was stemmed with "indescribable and unforgettable gallantry . . . two days after Christmas." Noting the speedy resumption of the American push into Germany, he expressed his "complete confidence" in General Eisenhower.

Switching to the home front, the president described a need for twenty thousand additional military nurses and asked that Congress amend the draft law to allow the induction of registered nurses. He also endorsed a request from the two service secretaries for a national service law and immediate enactment of legislation utilizing the services of "the four million men now classified as 4F."

Turning to "foreign policy," the president stressed the need "to stand together with the United Nations" in peace as well as in war. He admitted "concern" over situations in Greece and Poland and spoke of "obligations" to governments in exile and to "our major Allies who came much nearer to the shadows than we did." He emphasized the difficulties of achieving "international peace and well being," a phrase he repeated, without specifics. Conversely, he explicitly referred to the cooperation with France without mentioning the previous difficulties.

Roosevelt then reminded that he had already set forth "an American Economic Bill of Rights" and that the most fundamental of these was the right to a "job." Other rights included "a decent home . . . a good education . . . good medical care . . . social security . . . a reasonable farm income." After again stressing that winning the war must come first, the president closed with an exhortation:

I quote from an editorial in the *Stars and Stripes,* our soldiers' own newspaper in Europe.
    "For the holy love of God let's listen to the dead. Let's learn from the living. Let's join ranks against the foe. The bugles of battle are heard again above the bickering." That is the demand of our fighting men. We cannot fail to heed it.
    This new year of 1945 can be the greatest year of achievement in human history.

Nineteen forty-five can see the final ending of the Nazi-Fascist reign of terror in Europe.

Nineteen forty-five can see the closing in of the forces of retribution about the center of the malignant power of imperialistic Japan.

Most important of all, 1945 can, and must, see the substantial beginning of the organization of world peace—for we all know what such an organization means in terms of security, and human rights, and religious freedom. We Americans of today, together with our Allies, are making history—and I hope it will be better history than ever has been made before.

We pray that we may be worthy of the unlimited opportunities that God has given us.[2]

Early congressional reactions to the president's speech indicated that while the proposal to draft 4Fs had a good chance of success, the proposals both to draft nurses and to institute a national service law would face serious opposition. As administration leaders in Congress began the legislative process, Roosevelt himself kept a low profile, spending an hour visiting Hull in the hospital and agreeing that a brief moratorium on newly Court-approved antitrust actions against insurance companies was appropriate.

The budget message began with a concise statement of national objectives: "We . . . must back our fighting men and women to the limit . . . be ready to throw our whole effort . . . against Japan as fast as the war in Europe permits . . . begin plans to transform an all-out war economy into a full-employment peace economy."

The message noted that the expected early end to the war in Europe had reduced previous estimates for war expenditures so that the prior estimate of spending "about $100 billion" for "July 1, 1945–June 30, 1946" were now reduced to "$83 billion." Placing those then astronomical figures in perspective, during the year Roosevelt became president total federal expenditures were $4.6 billion. In the budget under discussion, that was roughly the amount necessary to cover the interest on the national debt. The president closed the budget message with an exhortation about the future and the need to provide sixty million jobs. "We must attack the employment problem on every front. . . . Our program should include provision for extending social security, including medical care, for better education, public health and nutrition; for the improvement of our homes, cities, and farms; and for the development of our transportation facilities and river valleys. We must plan now so that these programs can become effective when manpower and material are available."[3]

The president continued on a very light public schedule, knowing that he faced an arduous trip. He awarded seven Congressional Medals of Honor to five officers—one of whom had won a battlefield promotion—and two enlisted men in a ceremony witnessed by many relatives as well as General Marshall and

Admiral King. In "a rare wartime evening out," the president attended the annual dinner of the Radio Correspondents Association at the Hotel Statler, which included performances by stars of radio. Master of ceremonies Jack Benny got one of Roosevelt's "biggest laughs" when he reported that his trip east included a stopover in Chicago, where he bought a shirt at "Montgomery, Roosevelt, and Ward's." After the Thursday-night affair, the president was driven to his train and went to Hyde Park for five days. His time there, amid frigid temperatures and snow, was largely restful: he dictated a draft of his inaugural address and worked on a message to Congress calling for national service, which eventually became a letter to a committee chairman.

He returned to the White House on Tuesday of inauguration week. As he told his press conference, he had met with various members of Congress and with General Marshall and Admiral King to talk about national service legislation and would send a letter about it to Congress. Among other questions about national service, he was asked if he still felt that baseball could continue.

> THE PRESIDENT: [If] it's possible to continue it without hurting the employment of people, or the building up of the Army. I still am in favor of baseball, but I don't think that a perfectly healthy young man should play baseball at this time.

Most other questions were brushed aside. He would say nothing about the upcoming Big Three meeting, including who might go with him or any other aspects of foreign affairs, nor would he disclose anything about coming cabinet changes.

The president's letter on what the press called a "work or fight" bill went to the chair of the House Committee on Military Affairs who had been holding hearings on the administration bill, which provided that any draft registrant between the ages of eighteen and forty-five who left a job classified as essential without good reason, or who failed to take an essential job, should be immediately reclassified as "available for induction." It had been opposed in the committee's hearings by both the National Association of Manufacturers and the CIO.

Roosevelt's letter, accompanied by a letter backing the bill signed by Marshall and King, noted that the bill was "not a complete national service law" but insisted "it will go far to insure" that the offensive against the Axis "should not slacken because of any less than total utilization of our manpower on the home front." The House committee immediately adjourned its hearings and sent the measure to the floor; it passed on February 1 by a vote of 246–167. A modified measure passed the Senate, and a conference report was issued March 27. By the time the Senate voted on it, April 6, the war in Europe was so clearly about to end that the Senate killed the measure by rejecting the conference report, 46–29.

Roosevelt began the final press conference of his third term with a brief statement by himself, Churchill, and Mackenzie King extending the life of their various combined boards that had helped to coordinate wartime production and supply until the end of the war with Japan and instructing them "to collaborate increasingly with representatives of other United Nations."

Once the questioning began, the president, in obvious good humor, continued not answering questions about foreign affairs—"Ask the State Department." But when Henry Wallace's future came up again:

Q: What's he going to do for a living after tomorrow?
THE PRESIDENT: I don't think that he'll starve. Now there's a real tip.

Asked for "reflections" about "the last four years, and where do we go from here?" the president said he would tell them "a great secret. . . . I was asked that same question at the last Cabinet meeting," and he "sort of guessed" that he and Mr. Ickes and Miss Perkins had all "come to the same conclusion . . . the first twelve years were the hardest."[4]

The president's inaugural day began, as had each of the other three, with a religious service, but this time it was in the East Room and not conducted by Endicott Peabody, who had died in November. Roosevelt's truncated, paradeless fourth inaugural lasted about a quarter hour, including his six-minute address. Although the back of the White House provided a different venue, there were many familiar elements: as had been the case in the previous three, he was sworn in with his hand on the family Bible by a Republican chief justice, with his eldest son, now a Marine colonel, by his side. After Truman had been sworn in by former vice president Wallace, Roosevelt shed his navy cape, rose, and with James's assistance thrust himself the few feet to the podium, where he took the oath and immediately began his speech. With him on the portico were just a hundred others, including thirteen of his grandchildren. Facing him on the snow-covered lawn were "shivering thousands, stamping in the snow," some five thousand invited guests, and, beyond the south fence of the White House, a good two football fields away, some three thousand others. When the president looked up from his text, he could see the monument to the first president.

After explaining that the inaugural's form was "simple and its words brief," he noted:

We Americans . . . are passing through a . . . supreme test of our courage . . . resolve . . . wisdom . . . our essential democracy. If we meet that test . . . we shall perform a service . . . which men and women and children will honor throughout all time. . . . I know that it is America's purpose that we shall not fail. In the days and years that are to come, we shall work for a just and honorable peace . . .
We can and we will achieve such a peace.

The president then referenced his old schoolmaster Dr. Peabody as saying: "The great fact to remember is the trend of civilization itself is forever upward."

Reaching back even further, Roosevelt spoke of "our Constitution of 1787" as "not a perfect instrument" and "not perfect yet," trusting his audience to see the analogy to the still nascent United Nations. Coming back to "this year of war, 1945," he said, "We have learned lessons at a fearful cost—and we shall profit from them." "We have learned that we cannot live alone . . . that our well-being is dependent on the well-being of other Nations,. . . . that we must live as men, and not as ostriches, nor as dogs in the manger. We have learned to be citizens of the world, members of the human community." He closed with a final short prayer for peace.

The president and his supporting son remained standing at the speaker's stand as his old friend Monsignor John Ryan asked God's blessing on the "re-inaugurated" man who was bearing responsibilities "weightier and more complex than those that burdened any of his predecessors." Roosevelt, smiling broadly, shook Ryan's hand and remained standing while the Marine Band played the national anthem. He then raised his right arm in a wave to the people before him and, as the band played "Hail to the Chief," proceeded slowly back into the White House.

Many observers remarked favorably on the president's performance and appearance; the *New York Times*' Crider, in a think piece, held that Roosevelt "did not look more than four years older" since the third inaugural and "shows no outward sign of illness, and when he has been away from the White House for a few days of rest he looks as well as he did several years ago." Dr. Bruenn noted that he gave the address "without difficulty" and at the evening reception "seemed to be in good spirits."[5]

Sometime on Sunday, January 21, Jesse Jones unexpectedly released an exchange of inauguration-day letters about his as-yet-unannounced but widely rumored replacement in the cabinet by Henry Wallace. The president's letter, which apparently only Grace Tully had seen before it left the White House, informed Jones that he was being replaced despite "your splendid services to the Government and the excellent way in which you have carried out the many difficult tasks during these years [because] Henry Wallace deserves almost any service which he believes he can satisfactorily perform [since during the campaign] he displayed the utmost devotion to our cause [although] not on the ticket himself. [He wants to be secretary of commerce.] It is for this reason only that I am asking you to relinquish this present post for Henry."

Roosevelt thus put himself in the awkward position of holding that service to party was more important than service to country. He went on to say that he hoped Jones would "continue to be part of the government" and pointed out that ambassadorial positions were available. If that interested him, he should speak "to Ed Stettinius."

Why Roosevelt, the shrewd judge of political tactics and public opinion, should leave himself so open to criticism is difficult if not impossible to explain. There is an adage that even great soccer teams are often most vulnerable just after they have scored a goal. Unlike his Court-packing blunder after the 1936 election, replacing Jones with Wallace was part of no larger purpose.

Jones's reply was a well-crafted attack on his old enemy Henry Wallace, whom he described as "a man inexperienced in business and finance." His letter used and expanded upon Roosevelt's remarks. "I have your letter . . . asking that I relinquish my post as Secretary of Commerce, which carries with it the vast . . . Reconstruction Finance Corporation . . . so that you can give it to Henry Wallace as a reward for his support of you in the campaign. You state that Henry thinks he [could succeed] and that you consider him fully suited for the post. With all due respect, Mr. President, while I must accede to your decision, I cannot agree with either of you." While he spoke of desiring further service, he rejected a diplomatic assignment.

That the White House made no immediate effort to support Wallace or counter Jones's attack seems extraordinary. Jones's hostility to Wallace was well known. A week before the inauguration, Wallace noted in his diary, "Of course, there is the possibility that Jesse may try to cause trouble in the Senate."

Even though the president was in the White House for a good thirty-six hours after Jones's letter appeared in the Sunday-morning papers, he did nothing to support a nomination that surely would have faced difficulties even without Jones's assault. That the president and Steve Early were leaving the White House Tuesday evening and turning the press office over to presidential assistant Jonathan Daniels surely contributed to the public relations failure. The Wallace nomination was sent routinely to the Senate, and a presidential statement on the importance of victory gardens was issued, but nothing was done to offset Jones's letter. Early merely announced that the White House had "no knowledge" that Jones planned to release the letters.

In contrast, Roosevelt's enemies in the Senate were quick off the mark. As the nomination papers for Wallace reached the Senate, purge survivor Walter George dropped a bill into the hopper to separate the RFC and its related loan agencies from the authority of the secretary of commerce. Few Democrats wanted to reject the president's right to choose his cabinet members, and George spoke for many when he said that once the lending bodies were removed he would support Wallace's nomination.

Five days after George's bill was enrolled, Eleanor Roosevelt, Rosenman, and Daniels met to attempt some belated damage control. A message, signed by Rosenman and associating Morgenthau with it, was sent to the president at sea, suggesting that he issue an executive order separating the RFC and other fiscal agencies from control of the secretary of commerce. Roosevelt did not reply to it or to a second message from Eleanor, two days later, asking him to issue a statement supporting Wallace.

In a diary entry describing their meeting, Daniels quotes the president's wife saying of the unfortunate letter: "That is just like Franklin, he always hopes to get things settled pleasantly and he won't realize that there are times when you have to do an unpleasant thing directly, and, perhaps, unpleasantly."

Only after the White House informed Congress that the president had signed the George bill "on board an American warship" on February 28 did the Senate agree to vote on Wallace's confirmation. The next day, he was confirmed by a vote of 56–32; five Democrats and twenty-seven Republicans voted against him, while ten Republicans and one independent joined forty-five Democrats in approval.[6]

Meanwhile, the president and his party had left the White House on January 22 to meet Stalin at Yalta. An overnight train run to Newport News, Virginia, began the arduous trip. The departure was secret, but the fact that the president had left for a Big Three meeting somewhere was soon an open secret in Washington. With him on the train were daughter Anna, Admiral Leahy, Dr. McIntire, Edward J. Flynn, his two military aides General Watson and Admiral Brown, Steve Early, and Dr. Bruenn. The inclusion of the Bronx boss in the party was ridiculed in the press and by some insiders, but in fact Roosevelt had asked Flynn, a prominent Catholic layman as well as a politician, to go to Moscow with Harriman from Yalta in the ambassador's airplane to discuss with Soviet leaders the status of religion in the USSR, a topic long of great interest to the president. Key members of the American delegation General Marshall and Admiral King, and their staffs, would fly out to Malta and meet with their British counterparts before the president arrived there. Harry Hopkins, had flown to London the day after the inauguration to confer with Churchill. He and Charles Bohlen, who again would interpret for Roosevelt at Yalta, went to Paris for meetings with Eisenhower and de Gaulle; to Rome, where Hopkins had an audience with Pius XII; and to Naples, where they met with Ed Stettinius and two State Department colleagues, H. Freeman Matthews (1899–1986) and Alger Hiss (1905–96), for two days before they all went to Malta to await the president. Stettinius would be the first secretary of state to attend a summit meeting. Finally, Ambassador Harriman arrived from Moscow. These were just the principals. Altogether some 350 persons composed the American party in Yalta.

In Virginia the president's train pulled into the army's port-of-embarkation area and right alongside the heavy cruiser USS *Quincy* on the morning of January 23. Roosevelt and the others boarded, and the vessel cast off for the ten-day passage to Malta, zigzagging at around twenty knots. It was accompanied by three destroyers and later by a light cruiser as well and had air cover first from planes based in the United States, then from the Azores, and finally from North Africa. On the few occasions when it was necessary to transmit radio messages, they would be given to one of the destroyers, which would speed away for some distance before transmitting, and then return.

Two days into the voyage, Roosevelt received a message from Hopkins in London, indicating that the mercurial Churchill had lost some of his New Year's enthusiasm for Yalta. "[Churchill] says that if we had spent ten years in research we could not have found a worse place in the world than [Yalta] but he feels that he can survive it by bringing in an adequate supply of whiskey. He claims that it is good for typhus and deadly on lice which thrive in those parts."

Secret Service agent Mike Reilly had observed the lice and other deficiencies in his preconference inspection of the site, and a navy medical team had sanitized the war-damaged Livadia Palace where Roosevelt and other Americans would stay and the conference itself take place. The Soviets reinstalled plumbing and made other improvements to make the site more comfortable.

On January 30, Roosevelt's sixty-third birthday was duly celebrated aboard the *Quincy*, even though there had been an early celebration at the White House the night before he departed. Back in Washington and across the nation, the annual Birthday Balls went on as usual, with Eleanor reading her husband's message on the air without revealing where he was. In speaking of the fight against polio, the president used wartime metaphors: "Our national concern for the handicapped and the infirm is one of our national characteristics. Indeed it caused our enemies to laugh at us as soft. 'Decadent' was the word they used. But not any more. They are learning—and learning the hard way—that there are many things that we are tough about. . . . We combat this evil enemy of disease at home just as unremittingly as we fight our evil enemies abroad."

Reporting on the 1944 polio epidemic—"the worst . . . since 1916"—he claimed that "the National Foundation for Infantile Paralysis and its community chapters" had ensured medical help for "everyone . . . stricken by this disease." "But as any fighting man will tell you, we cannot rest on defense alone. [Treatment] does not take the place of prevention and cure. . . . We must give our scientists and research workers the necessary equipment to find this insidious enemy, to corner and destroy him. The task is not an easy one. The mystery shrouding the infantile paralysis virus is not easily penetrated. But we will persist—and we will triumph."

Although there were a few matters Roosevelt had to deal with, the days aboard the *Quincy* were not stressful. In conversations with Leahy and Byrnes, the president set forth his two principal objectives for the Yalta Conference: he wanted "to complete plans for the defeat of Germany" and "to secure Russian cooperation in his efforts to achieve a permanent world peace" through the agency of the United Nations. In addition, as Harriman put it, the president "held fast to his belief that he personally could accomplish more in man-to-man talks with Stalin than Churchill, the State Department or the British Foreign Office."[7]

On February 2, the *Quincy* entered Valletta harbor at about 9:30 a.m. Bohlen, who was there waiting, wrote, "The entry of the President . . . was a memorable spectacle . . . as the oversized cruiser *Quincy* sailed [in slowly]. Roosevelt sat on the deck, his black cape around his shoulders, acknowledging salutes from the British men-of-war and the rolling cheer of the spectators crowding the quays."

Roosevelt put in a busy fifteen hours in Malta, most of them aboard the *Quincy*. Churchill had been there, along with his military leaders, since January 30. Doubtless at his behest, his men were in acrimonious debate with the American chiefs over more Mediterranean sideshows, which the Americans rejected. Churchill, bringing his daughter Sarah, and Foreign Minister Eden, came aboard to confer, as did Hopkins, Marshall, King, Harriman, and Bohlen. The British trio stayed for lunch with the president and Anna, Stettinius, Byrnes, and Leahy, who commented grumpily that the table talk "was, as usual, monopolized by the Prime Minister." In the afternoon, a whole stream of second-rank military and civilian Allied officials came aboard, which is perhaps why the president arranged to take a half-hour drive to show Anna the island.

Churchill and the British Joint Chiefs returned to the ship for a two-hour late-afternoon conference. Churchill, his daughter, who was a serving officer, and Eden stayed for a late dinner. Roosevelt, according to Leahy, spoke of wanting to broker an agreement between the Arabs and the Jews in Palestine; Churchill expressed doubts about its likely success.

Moving more than seven hundred American and British participants the fourteen hundred miles from Malta to Yalta by air was an extraordinary feat. (The Soviets had not yet cleared the extensive German minefields in the Black Sea.) Throughout the night and early morning hours of February 2–3, twenty-five four-motored aircraft took off at ten-minute intervals for the almost seven-hour flight east across the Mediterranean, avoiding Cyprus, still in German hands, then across the Dardanelles over the Black Sea, and then north to the Crimea, landing at Saki, which was ninety miles from the conference site, reached by a three-hour drive up a steep, unpaved mountain road. The president took off with just eleven of his party at 3:30 a.m. in a special plane the air force referred to as the *Sacred Cow*. It was a version of the Douglas DC-4 Skymaster, a four-motored commercial airliner secretly commissioned by the army air force for the president's use. It had an elevator and a private room for the president, extra radio equipment, and all the latest gadgets. Roosevelt hadn't been aware of it, thought it an unnecessary extravagance, and had refused to use it for domestic travel. He used it only for the trip to and from Yalta, although he had arranged for it to fly Hopkins to London. Only the planes of the president and the prime minister were escorted by fighter aircraft. Dr. Bruenn reported that the flight's altitude—six to eight thousand feet—"did not cause the President any discomfort" but that the noise and vibration interfered with his sleep.

After landing at Saki, Roosevelt remained aboard for some twenty minutes until after Churchill's plane had landed and then took the elevator to the ground and was pushed out in his wheelchair to meet Churchill and be greeted by Molotov and other Soviet dignitaries. After a Red Army band played "The Star Spangled Banner," "God Save the King," and "The Internationale," Roosevelt got into a Lend-Lease Jeep, and, with Churchill walking beside him, the two leaders reviewed the Soviet honor guard.

Not all Americans came by air. Four U.S. Navy vessels, two minesweepers, a Liberty ship, and the USS *Catoctin* braved the German mines and were anchored in Sevastopol. The augmented minesweepers' crews supplied an armed guard for the president, and the Liberty carried supplies. The *Catoctin,* a combined operations and communications headquarters ship, had served those purposes during the invasion of southern France in August 1944. Arriving at the Crimean port on January 29, it had been specially fitted to accommodate the president. It functioned as a base for the advance party and provided a secure communications facility for the American officials. Roosevelt and those traveling with him spent their last night in the Crimea aboard it.

After the formalities at the airport, Roosevelt and his party were driven the ninety miles up to Yalta in cars supplied by the Soviet government. In a spectacular and profligate use of military personnel, both sides of the road for the entire route were lined by armed soldiers, many of them women, who saluted as the president passed. The Livadia Palace, outside of Yalta and overlooking the sea, had been built for the last czar. It served as the American billet and was also the site of the political meetings and formal dinners. Churchill and the British were in a palace and three other buildings about twelve miles away, while Stalin, who had not yet arrived, was in a palace halfway between the two; that palace would be the site of most of the military meetings.

Kathleen Harriman—the third Western daughter attending, and acting as hostess for her father, as she did in Moscow—greeted Roosevelt on his arrival. She wrote her sister in America: "Well, I've had my wish and met the president. . . . He's absolutely charming, easy to talk to, with a lovely sense of humor. He's in fine form, very happy with the accommodations and all set for the best."[8]

The Yalta Conference began, the next day, February 4, and ended on February 11, twice as long as the Tehran Conference of November 28–December 1, 1943. Any understanding of what happened there must consider the transformation of the military situation in the fourteen months after Tehran. If Roosevelt had been able to open that morning's *New York Times* as he awakened on the opening day at Yalta, he would have read that the ring around Germany was closing tighter. The Russian winter offensive was nearing the Oder River, forty-four miles from Berlin, which had been subjected to a raid by a thousand American bombers dropping three thousand tons of bombs. In the West, the largely American armies were, at one point, eleven miles inside Germany and approaching the

Rhine and had cleared Belgium of German troops. In Italy stalemate continued amid rumors of German withdrawal. Unconfirmed reports had it that "the Big Three conference has begun somewhere in the Black Sea area near the southern borders of the Soviet Union" and that the "hopeless Germans" had sent peace feelers there. In the Pacific, two American columns were closing in on Manila. Although there was nothing about China in that day's summary, the president would have known that Chiang's armies were in desperate straits and that the American air bases there were in some peril. Later that day, the White House released the text of a message from Roosevelt to Philippine president Osmeña celebrating the capture of Manila.

The following account of the long and complex Yalta Conference makes no attempt to go over it session by session; I discuss the more important issues without regard to chronology. There have been adequate descriptions since the immediate postwar period. Three of the most useful are the participant memoirs of Jimmy Byrnes (1947), Ed Stettinius (1949), and Admiral Leahy (1950); in 1955 the State Department published its documentary volume, *From Malta to Yalta*. In a large historical literature, Diane Shaver Clemens's *Yalta* (1975) is probably still the most important single work. A 2010 book, S. M. Plokhy's *Yalta: The Price of Peace*, the first by a Western historian to utilize large amounts of Soviet archival material, makes no significant alteration to the conclusions reported in Clemens's book thirty-five years before, but it does provide a much-needed look at what military historians call the other side of the hill.

Most of the decisions made at Yalta about Europe were largely prefigured both by what had been agreed upon at Tehran and by what had been obtained by Stalin's armies. The myth of a "sellout at Yalta," created by right-wing politicians and publicists, hinges largely on the fate of Poland and the other states of central and southeastern Europe. As Roosevelt put it to Leahy about what he had accepted for Poland at Yalta, "It's the best I can do for Poland at this time." Molotov had promised free elections in Poland "within a month's time." Elections actually took place on January 19, 1947, twenty-three months later, but they were not free. The first free elections in postwar Poland were held in 1989.

In theory, Roosevelt could have washed his hands of the whole matter and not agreed to anything about Poland, but that would have accomplished nothing for the Poles, made an orderly conclusion of the war in Europe more difficult, and, most important from Roosevelt's point of view, probably would have scuttled his plans for a postwar United Nations including all major powers. And if he had frankly said to the public what he said to Leahy, it would have strengthened the considerable resistance to U.S. membership in the United Nations and called into question the assumption of great-power compatibility that was its major premise.

Roosevelt had the notion, from the outset, that he might overcome some of Stalin's well-founded belief about a basic sympathy between him and Churchill by refusing to meet for even a full day with Churchill in Malta and not meeting with him alone at Yalta until the fifth day. It annoyed Churchill, but produced no perceptible change in Stalin's positions. But Roosevelt could no more resist trying to use his charm than some persons can resist flirting at almost any opportunity.

Stalin did show Roosevelt personal respect. Why not? He was, after all, the source of those machines that Stalin needed. As at Tehran, he deferred to him in many small ways. When Roosevelt sent word that he would like the Soviet leader to call on him just before the first session of the leaders, as Stalin had done on his own initiative at Tehran, he came as requested. Another example was on a substantive issue: whether France should have a zone of occupation and participate in the control commission to manage the occupation of Germany. Initially, only Churchill favored it, with Roosevelt and Stalin opposed. At one session, Roosevelt agreed to let France have a zone on the western side of the divide but not participate in the control commission. At the next interval, some of his aides convinced the president that this simply would not be feasible for administrative reasons. So at the next session when the president reversed himself and supported having France on the control commission too, Stalin threw his hands up above his head and said, "*Sdalyous,*" Russian for "I surrender." It was not a matter of great concern to the Soviets and in no way lessened the size of their zone, or their authority.

Contrary to the popular notion, Stalin made some genuine concessions at Yalta. On the fourth day, in the midst of discussions about the future of Poland—about which he conceded nothing—Stalin yielded on a vital procedural matter about voting in what became the Security Council of the United Nations, a concession that Harriman felt was "the most concrete political achievement of the Yalta Conference." It provided that no single permanent member could prevent discussion of a topic, though it could prevent action.

Not everything was controversial. Most of the military matters were resolved at the separate staff meetings and merely ratified by the leaders. Churchill briefly tried to push an incursion into Yugoslavia from Italy, which was summarily rejected by Roosevelt and Stalin. On February 7, a brief interim communiqué of fewer than two hundred words was issued in all three capitals, stating officially, for the first time, that the three leaders were meeting, that it was "in the Black Sea area," and that they were planning for the final "defeat of the common enemy" and to build, "with their Allies, firm foundations for a lasting peace." It reported "complete agreement for joint military operations in the final phase of the war against Nazi Germany" and said that military staffs were jointly working out plans. Future discussions would treat "the occupation and control of Germany, the political and economic problems of liberated Europe," and proposals for "the earliest possible establishment of a permanent international organization to maintain peace." An end-of-conference communiqué was promised.

The limitation to Nazi Germany did not mean that the war against Japan was ignored. In late January, the American Joint Chiefs had advised the president that "Russia's entry at as early a date as possible . . . is necessary to provide maximum possible assistance to our Pacific operations." As noted earlier, Roosevelt had never wanted to commit troops to fight on the Asian mainland as opposed to setting up and protecting air bases. In fact, Stalin would renew his Tehran pledge to go to war with Japan after Germany was defeated, but he now raised with the president the matter of "the political conditions under which the USSR would enter the war." These had been briefly referred to at Tehran, and since then Harriman had prepared Roosevelt for what Stalin would demand, though the president surely had always known that there would be a price. He told Stalin that he could have the southern half of Sakhalin Island, which Japan had taken from Russia as part of the price of peace in 1905 and now had a population of four hundred thousand Japanese, and the Kurile Islands, which had never been completely Russian and which Japan had controlled since an 1875 agreement with Russia.

Stalin also wanted territorial concessions and guarantees along the northern borders of China. It was one thing to dispose of the property of an enemy and quite another to concede the territory of an ally, but Roosevelt, while saying that he could not speak for China, raised no objection to a series of demands. They included use of the port of Darien on the Kwantung Peninsula or its internationalization, Russian use of the Manchurian railroad, and a guarantee of the status quo of Outer Mongolia, a Soviet-controlled state. Roosevelt commented that anything revealed to the government in Chungking was known to the world within twenty-four hours. Stalin suggested, and Roosevelt agreed, that discussions with China about these matters be delayed until after the German surrender and his subsequent transfer of twenty-five divisions to the Far East.

There was real danger that if the Soviet agreement to enter the war with Japan two or three months after V-E Day became known, the still potent two-million-man Kwantung army in Manchuria might make a preemptive strike at the depleted Soviet forces in Siberia. Conversely, the Joint Chiefs anticipated that the augmented Soviet forces would overwhelm the Japanese forces in North China. These bilateral decisions were later ratified and became part of the final protocol but left out of the communiqué. Stalin also indicated a belief that China would survive and that he favored a reinstitution of the united front that had existed between Chiang and the Chinese Communists, something that Roosevelt's military envoys in Chungking were also working toward.

The conference's closing statement, signed by the three leaders in alphabetical order, was issued simultaneously from their capitals the day after the conference ended. It contained just over two thousand words arranged under nine topical headings. The first three dealt with Germany: its defeat, occupation, and reparations. The first concluded that "Nazi Germany," "attacked from the East, West, North, and South," was "doomed" and resistance "hopeless." It credited the meetings of the three military staffs with achieving greater coordination that would shorten the war. Each of the three powers would occupy a separate zone of Germany, and France would be invited to take over a zone and participate in the control commission. It announced "an inflexible purpose to destroy German militarism and Nazism and to ensure that Germany will never again be able to disturb the peace of the world." It promised to "bring all war criminals to just and swift punishment" and "wipe out the Nazi Party, Nazi laws . . . and take in harmony such other measures . . . as may be necessary to the future peace and safety of the world." A brief paragraph acknowledged the need of Germany to make "reparation in kind" for war damage and announced that a commission working in Moscow would arrange details.

In a section on the United Nations, the leaders called for "the earliest possible establishment . . . of a general international organization to maintain peace and security" and announced a conference to meet in San Francisco on April 25, 1945, to create it, based on "foundations . . . laid at Dumbarton Oaks." China and France were invited to "sponsor" conference invitations jointly with the Big Three, and "the texts of the voting proposals" would be released later, suggesting that Roosevelt's four policemen might become five.

The next three sections dealt with the liberated European nations. After a formal "Declaration on Liberated Europe," briefer sections dealt with Poland and Yugoslavia. In the declaration, the three leaders mutually agreed "to concert during the temporary period of instability in liberated Europe" their policies "in assisting the peoples liberated from the domination of Nazi Germany and of the former Axis satellite states to solve by democratic means their pressing political and economic problems." The three would "establish conditions of internal peace . . . emergency . . . relief . . . form interim governmental authorities broadly representative [to hold] free elections" and "to facilitate where necessary the holding of such elections."

They reaffirmed "our faith in the principles of the Atlantic Charter, our pledge in the declaration by the United Nations, our determination to build in cooperation with other peace-loving Nations world order under law, dedicated to peace, security, freedom, and general well-being of all mankind."

About Poland, the focal point of contention, the language papered over the cracks. It provided that the government created and partially installed by the USSR "should" be broadened by "inclusion of democratic leaders from Poland and from Poles abroad." A committee—Molotov and the two Western ambassadors in Moscow—was charged with overseeing the formation of a new provisional Polish government that would hold "free and unfettered elections as soon as possible." The eastern boundaries of Poland were set at the Curzon line, and it was recognized that Poland was entitled "to receive substantial accessions of territory in the North and West."

A brief statement recommended that Marshal Tito and the prime minister of the Yugoslavian government in exile should agree to form a government, while another praised the functioning of the daily meetings of the three foreign secretaries and provided that they should meet regularly three or four times a year.

A final section, headed "Unity for Peace as for War," is painful reading seven decades later. It claimed that the Crimean meeting had confirmed the leaders' "common determination" to continue in the peace "the unity of purpose and action" achieved in war. "We believe that this is a sacred obligation. . . . Victory in this war and the establishment of the proposed international organization will provide the greatest opportunity in all history to create in the years to come the essential conditions of such a peace."

The White House followed up its release of the joint statement on Yalta by releasing a long prepared message to Congress, urging "immediate action" to approve the agreements reached at the Bretton Woods meeting the previous July to establish the International Monetary Fund and create what became the World Bank. The two projects were described as necessary if there was to be "a peaceful and prosperous world," as they would together provide "a cornerstone" for global prosperity. Despite Roosevelt's call for urgency, Congress did not complete action on the proposals until the end of July. Although the fund soon had more than $8 billion in assets, it was slow and cautious in its operations. Its first loan—$250 million to France—was not made until May 1947, and after four years of operation it had loaned a total of only $634 million.[9]

Roosevelt had informed his partners on the tenth that he would be leaving Yalta at three on the afternoon of the eleventh, which caused some concern, but everything got done promptly on the last day. The president's party was driven in several cars down to Sevastopol, where the USS *Catoctin* was moored. He was delighted to see the "Valley of Death" where the "Light Brigade" had come to grief some ninety years previously. Leahy described the president as tired but happy as they had a late steak dinner aboard. He had every reason to be both. Roosevelt had worked very hard and achieved agreement on the two points he was most concerned about—securing firm commitments for Soviet intervention in the Pacific war and its participation in the United Nations—and had paid for it largely with other people's property. That evening Pa Watson suffered a heart attack; there seemed no alternative to taking him along with the rest of the president's party. The next morning, just after seven, the party was driven to the airfield. Harriman, Stettinius, and Flynn left for Moscow in the ambassador's plane; Byrnes had left for Washington the day before, concerned about the status of the "work or fight" legislation. The others, after a ceremonial Soviet farewell, reboarded the *Sacred Cow* and flew to Egypt for what Roosevelt had described to Churchill as a meeting with "with three kings": Egypt's Farouk, Ethiopia's Haile Selassie, and Saudi Arabia's Ibn Saud. As on the prior flight, the altitude—not higher than nine thousand feet—did not give the president problems.

Since the image of an ill or even dying president at Yalta has become firmly embedded in the historical tradition, it is important to understand that the only direct evidence we have about Roosevelt's health at Yalta is based on medical data rather than visual reactions to external appearances from lay and professional witnesses. Here is everything Dr. Bruenn reported in 1975 about Roosevelt's health while he was at Yalta.

> The President slept well that [first] night, and the conferences began the next morning, Sunday, February 4. He worked very hard, both before and during the conferences. There was a constant stream of visitors from the time he awakened in the morning until lunch, and on occasion he had no time to take his afternoon rest. For the first three or four nights he developed a paroxysmal cough that was moderately productive but would awaken him at night after which he would go back to sleep. He denied dyspnea, orthopnea or cardiac pain. The lungs were clear. The heart and blood pressure were unchanged and there were no electrocardiographic changes. The nose was obstructed and this was treated with nose drops before he retired at night. The cough disappeared with the use of terpin hydrate and codeine. He continued to eat well and had no gastric discomfort.
>
> [After describing the formal procedures of the conference, Bruenn continued his report on the president.] On February 8, after an especially arduous day and an emotionally disturbing conference (he was worried and upset about the trend of discussions that day at the Conference, namely Poland) he was obviously greatly fatigued. His color was very poor (gray), but examination showed that his lungs were clear and the heart sounds were of good quality—regular in rhythm and rate (84/min). The blood pressure however, for the first time showed pulsus alternans. A change in his routine was enforced. His hours of activity were rigidly controlled so that he could obtain adequate rest. No visitors were allowed until noon, and at least an hour of rest was enforced in the afternoon before the [4:00 p.m.] Conference.
>
> Within two days he appeared to be much better. His appetite was excellent and he appeared to enjoy Russian food and cooking. There was no cough and the pulsus alternans had disappeared. The weather throughout this period, February 2 to 12, was pleasant; the average temperature was 40F.

It is possible to adduce a kind of repeating pattern in the final thirteen months of Roosevelt's life. Aware that he has a big test ahead of him—a conference, a long trip, or an election campaign—he rests to renew his declining physical strength. He then works hard at the task and is energized by both the task and its successes, real and imagined, and achieves his results. When the crisis is safely over, he seems to regress until his powers are restored.

The following is an extract from the last known interview with Dr. Bruenn in 1990.

> *What was the President's health just prior to going to Yalta, because when he got back he certainly looked terrible.*
>
> There was no great change. There were a few times when I really got worried about him. He had an attack of gallbladder colic down at Baruch's place. And I'm no surgeon but with a few simple things, the thing subsided and that was that. When we got back we took an x-ray and he did have stones in his gallbladder.
>
> But there were one or two other situations. He had seen a movie about *Wilson* and the League of Nations in which Wilson really got pummeled. The President said, "By God, that's not going to happen to me!" And his blood pressure was [gesturing] about that high that night. Then it came down the next morning.
>
> Another time out at Yalta, they were having a set-to, particularly about Poland. That night, after the meeting, he had something we call *pulsus alternans* which means that every alternate beat was less strong than the previous one. That's a very bad sign. But that too subsided after twelve hours.
>
> *What's that a precursor of?*
>
> It's a combination of heart and blood pressure. We certainly put the clamps on him by cutting down his activities for the next 24 hours and that too subsided. And on the way back he was fine.[10]

The *Sacred Cow* landed in mid-afternoon at an airfield in the Suez Canal Zone near Ismailia, Egypt, operated by the U.S. Army. The president and his party were taken to the canal company's landing, where boats from the USS *Quincy* took them to its anchorage in Great Bitter Lake. Roosevelt would spend three days aboard the moored cruiser while middle-eastern monarchs were brought to him.

The three kings brought exotic keepsakes for the president and his family (perfumes; native costumes, male and female; a gold cigarette case; and bejeweled scimitars), while the president gave both trinkets (autographed copies of his inaugural addresses and medallions) and big-ticket items: Egypt's Farouk got a Douglas C-47, Ethiopia's Haile Selassie received four command and reconnaissance cars, and Saudi Arabia's Ibn Saud, who was lame, got the president's own wheelchair (the Secret Service always carried a spare) and a C-47 with a crew to fly it until replacements could be trained or imported.

Late on the morning of the thirteenth, the wastrel King Farouk (1920–65) of Egypt came to lunch with the president. Admiral Leahy, while stating that he didn't hear everything that was said, reports that the president and the king, who spoke "perfect English," exchanged small talk. The American minister to Egypt, S. Pinkney Tuck (1891–1967), who discreetly removed himself, reported to Grew in Washington that he had "briefed" the president to urge Farouk, a constitutional monarch, to stop intervening in Egypt's politics, the kind of advice that had caused the president to despair of American diplomats. In fact, the week he returned to Washington, Roosevelt wrote to an economic adviser in the Cairo legation that he had suggested to the king that "many of the large landed estates in Egypt be broken up and made available for ownership to the fellaheen who worked them."

Haile Selassie (1892–1975), who claimed descent from Solomon and Sheba, was a small, dignified person who had won the sympathy of much of the Western world by his futile appeal for help against Mussolini's armies before the League of Nations. He came at five and stayed for tea. He talked with Roosevelt in French during their tea in the president's cabin; after tea the emperor spoke to him in Amharic through an Ethiopian interpreter for more than an hour, chiefly about the disposition of Italy's colonies, access to the sea for Ethiopia, and the development of its railroads.

The brief encounter with Ibn Saud (1880–1953) the next day was both spectacular and significant, as it seemed to cement what had already become a promising and entangling American relationship. Those aboard the *Quincy* knew that the king was arriving aboard a destroyer, the USS *Murphy*, which had been sent to Jidda, some eight hundred miles away, to fetch him. But they were amazed at what they saw, as stated by the usually prosaic Rigdon: "High on the destroyer's super-structure deck sat a huge man, an Arabian King, on a large gilded chair, with gorgeous oriental rugs all about, and dozens of retainers, guards, members of the royal family in their native dress, their long robes beautifully ornamented in brocaded work of many colors. King Ibn Saud and members of the royal family wore red and white checked headscarves, with gold ropes entwined around them [while on the stern] were live sheep . . . nibbling at food [with] an animal slaughter scaffold rigged to the flagstaff."

Since Saudi protocol insisted that the king not be exposed to the presence of foreign women, Anna had been dispatched to Cairo for a day of shopping and sightseeing. The king was accompanied by the American minister Marine lieutenant colonel William A. Eddy, a fluent Arabist who translated for each and provided an account to the State Department. In their hour-and-a-half "very friendly" conversation before lunch:

> The King spoke of being the "twin" brother of the President, in years, in responsibility as Chief of State, and in physical disability. The President said, "but you are fortunate to still have the use of your legs to take you wherever you wish to go." The King replied, "It is you, Mr. President, who are fortunate.

My legs grow feebler every year, with your more reliable wheel-chair you are assured that you will arrive." The President then said, "I have two of these chairs which are also twins. Would you accept one as a personal gift from me? The King said. "Gratefully. I shall use it daily and always recall affectionately the giver, my great and good friend."

After lunch the king spoke with Roosevelt about the oil properties in his country and said that he liked the American oilmen and wanted to continue doing business with them. Roosevelt then gently trashed the English, telling the king, "We like the English, but we also know the English and the way they insist on doing good themselves. You and I want freedom and prosperity for our people and their neighbors after the war and by whose hand freedom and prosperity arrive concerns us but little. The English also work and sacrifice to bring freedom and prosperity to the world, but on the condition that it be brought by them and marked 'Made in Britain.'"

Bohlen, sitting in for the ailing Hopkins, reported the king's intransigent position against the immigration of even ten thousand additional Jewish victims of Hitler, asking why the Arabs had to atone for Hitler's sins and insisting that his opposition was not to Jews but to Europeans who were technically and culturally on a higher level and with whom the Arabs had difficulty in competing. "Arabs would choose to die rather than yield their land to the Jews," he said. Roosevelt thus became the first in what has become an unbroken chain of American presidents to encounter difficulty in trying to mediate between Arabs and Jews.[11]

After the king reboarded the *Murphy* for his return, the *Quincy* reentered the Suez Canal and stood north to Alexandria for a refueling stop, arriving on the morning of February 15. It had been learned that Churchill, who had planned to return to London after Yalta, had, after Roosevelt told him he was visiting the three kings and, concerned about American influence on what the old imperialist considered British turf, decided to meet with the same three leaders and would first meet Roosevelt in Alexandria. There it was learned that de Gaulle, whom Roosevelt had invited to meet with him in Algiers, had sent word to the Paris embassy that he would not come. Leahy reports that the president shrugged it off, but Bohlen writes that Roosevelt was furious and had dictated "a terse and insulting statement" to Steve Early.

Hopkins, learning of it and too ill to leave his bed, had sent word via Early that such a statement would anger the French people as well as de Gaulle. He was told by the press secretary that the president's "Dutch" was up, and he was insisting that the statement be released. Hopkins then told Bohlen "to go and see what you can do with the President." Reluctantly, Bohlen went and found Roosevelt working on his stamp collection. Bohlen repeated Hopkins's argument, which the president again rejected, saying, "No, no, what you don't seem to realize is that the United States has been insulted through its President and this requires an appropriate answer." Bohlen continued the conversation, finally saying. "We can all admit that de Gaulle is being one of the biggest sons of bitches who ever straddled a pot." This remark, he reports, "tickled" Roosevelt, whose "tired eyes suddenly twinkled." He flashed "his famous smile . . . threw back his head . . . laughed and said, 'Oh, go ahead, you and Harry try your hand at a draft.'" Their draft, which expressed only polite regret, was sent.

As the *Quincy* reached Alexandria, Stettinius, who had flown into Egypt from Moscow the previous day, took a launch out to meet it and had a half-hour talk with Roosevelt. The president told him that his conversation with Ibn Saud had convinced him that "if nature took its course there would be bloodshed between the Arabs and the Jews" and that some formula had to be found to prevent it. Without waiting for lunch, Stettinius left to begin his return to Washington. After the ship docked, Churchill came aboard and had a private half-hour talk with the president during which they discussed the Pacific war and atomic research and then lunched along with Anna, two of his sons, John Winant from London, Hopkins, and Leahy. The cruiser left the harbor at four, turned west, and arrived in Algiers on February 18.[12]

During the brief stop in Algiers, the American ambassadors from Paris and Rome called on the president, as did a number of military commanders, but Eisenhower was too busy. There were several changes of personnel in the president's party. Roosevelt had summoned Sam Rosenman from London to work on the speech to Congress about Yalta, work that the ailing Hopkins was unable to do. Rosenman met with Hopkins and Bohlen for two hours, getting briefed on what happened at Yalta, and Bohlen provided him with conference documents and dictated a six-page memo about Roosevelt's talks with Stalin. The three wire-service pool reporters, who had been kept away from Yalta and Great Bitter Lake, were in Algiers waiting for the *Quincy*, which they boarded. Hopkins went to Marrakech to rest for a few days and took Bohlen with him. They both then flew to Washington, with Hopkins continuing on to the Mayo Clinic. Steve Early, after briefing the reporters on what had happened on the trip, left for Paris, where he undertook a study of press relations at Eisenhower's headquarters, returning to Washington only on March 22. After taking on fuel, the *Quincy* steamed out of Algiers on February 18, headed back to Newport News.

On February 20, Major General Edwin M. Watson, almost two years younger than the president, died. He had suffered what Dr. Bruenn diagnosed as "acute congestive heart failure" on the drive down to Sevastopol and once aboard the *Quincy* had been confined to his cabin, where an eventually fatal "cerebral hemorrhage and right hemiplegia" occurred. All observers agreed that Roosevelt was deeply affected by Watson's death. Pa, then a colonel, was originally assigned as FDR's military aide in June 1933 at the suggestion of Admiral Cary Grayson, who also recommended Dr. McIntire. He not only had experience as one of Woodrow Wilson's military aides in postwar Europe and as a military attaché in the Low Countries but had a distinguished combat record in 1918. In addition to his invaluable service as aide and appointments secretary, he became the president's close friend and entertained him in his home more than any other nonrelative. Many have commented on the effect of Pa's death on Roosevelt. Dr. Bruenn, the inside outsider, comments sensibly, "Outwardly the President took the death of General Watson calmly, but it was obvious that he was deeply moved." He went on to describe Roosevelt's health as the voyage came to an end. "The President's general health remained good. His nose bothered him from time to time because of some nasal stuffiness, but he had no cough. Physical examination and electrocardiogram were unchanged. Blood pressure during these past few days had been quite variable."

The president held what the White House called press conferences for the three pool reporters in his cabin on February 19 and 23, but they were not press conferences in the normal use of the word. The president spoke about important matters in off-the-record words that they could not report then or later. The reporters regarded only the second hour-long session as a "real" press conference, as only it contained some "real news" that they could eventually print—"his plans to go before Congress right away with a report on Yalta, that there had been no secret agreements reached at the meeting." But reading the transcripts, taken down by Rigdon and edited by the president, gives us a glimpse into what Roosevelt was thinking as he prepared his address to Congress and the public. Perhaps most interesting for twenty-first-century readers are his musings about colonialism and what we call the third world.

> Q: De Gaulle has announced that French Indo-China is to be soon liberated. By whom, Mr. President?
>
> THE PRESIDENT: This is very much off the record. For two whole years I have been terribly worried about Indo-China. I talked to Chiang Kai-shek in Cairo, Stalin in Teheran. They both agreed with me. The French have been in there some hundred years. The Indo-Chinese are not like the Chinese.
>
> The first thing I asked Chiang was "Do you want Indo-China."
>
> He said, "It's no help to us. We don't want it. They are not Chinese. They would not assimilate into the Chinese people."
>
> I said "What are you going to advocate? It will take a long time to educate them for self-government."
>
> He said they should not go back to the French. They have been there over a hundred years and have done nothing about educating them. For every dollar they have put in they have taken out ten. The situation

there is a good deal like the Philippines were in 1898. The French have done nothing about it.

With the Indo-Chinese there is a feeling that they ought to be independent but are not ready for it. I suggested at the time, to Chiang, that Indo-China be set up under a trusteeship—have a Frenchman, one or two Indo-Chinese, and a Chinese and a Russian because they are on the Coast, and maybe a Filipino and an American—to educate them for self-government. It took us fifty years in the Philippines.

Stalin liked the idea. China liked the idea. The British didn't like it. It might bust up their empire, because if the Indo-Chinese were to work together and eventually get their independence, the Burmese might do the same thing to the King of England. The French have talked about how they expect to re-capture Indo-China, but they haven't got any shipping to do it with. It would only get the British mad. Chiang would go along. Stalin would go along. As for the British, it would only make the British mad. Better to keep quiet just now.

Q: Is that Churchill's idea on all that territory out there, he wants them all back just like they were?

THE PRESIDENT: Yes, he is mid-Victorian on all things like that.

After a long presidential statement, his reading of Queen Wilhelmina's gradualist notions about independence for what is now Indonesia, a question brought Roosevelt back to Churchill.

Q: This idea of Churchill's seems inconsistent with the policy of self-determination?

THE PRESIDENT: Yes, that is true.

Q: He seems to undercut the Atlantic Charter. He made a statement the other day that it was not a rule, just a guide.

THE PRESIDENT: The Atlantic Charter is a beautiful idea. When it was drawn up, the situation was that England was about to lose the war. They needed hope, and it gave it to them. We have improved the military situation since then at every chance, so that really you might say we have a much better chance of winning the war now than ever before. . . .

Q: Do you remember the speech the Prime Minister made about the fact that he was not made the Prime Minister in Great Britain to see the empire fall apart?

THE PRESIDENT: Dear old Winston will never learn on that point. We [He?] had made his specialty on that point. This is, of course off the record.[13]

The *Quincy* sailed into Chesapeake Bay in the late afternoon of February 27 and moored to the army dock at Newport News at 6:30 p.m. The president and his party immediately boarded his train for the return to Washington, arriving well before dawn. Mrs. Roosevelt, with General Watson's widow, met the train in the Fourteenth Street yard, where General Watson's body was taken off and sent to Arlington; the train then took the president and his party to the underground siding near the White House at 6:00 a.m. Roosevelt, as was his custom, remained aboard sleeping and arrived at the White House a little before 9:00; Hassett and Daniels accompanied him up to the family quarters, where he had his usual scrambled eggs and bacon. Hassett recorded that he was "in the pink of condition—hasn't looked better in a year. . . . His color good and spirits high."

Later that day at the interment ceremony at Arlington Cemetery, as rain and sleet fell, the president remained in his limousine, but Eleanor, Anna, and her husband, Lt. Col. John Boettiger, stood by the car in the bitter weather during the ceremony, as did General Marshall, Admiral Leahy, and a number of military and civilian dignitaries. A small group of Pa's White House colleagues stood with Mrs. Watson underneath the canopy that sheltered the grave. The next morning, Eleanor, but not the president, attended the funeral mass in St. Matthew's Cathedral, for which Hassett had made the arrangements.

During the day, the White House released the texts of the invitation letters sent to the American delegates to the San Francisco United Nations Conference, confirming that of the six delegates who would serve with the secretary of state, four were members of Congress, three were Republicans, and one was a woman.[14]

On March 1, the president went up to the Capitol at midday to deliver his report to Congress and the American people on the Yalta Conference. Although it was not one of Roosevelt's better performances, it was effective and well received—but it contained a major blunder. At Yalta it had been agreed that the Soviets would get two extra votes in what became the Assembly of the United Nations. It had been omitted from the brief summary that had been publicly released in mid-February, and, Rosenman tells us, the president "decided to keep [it] secret." Rosenman says that he had "never been able to understand" why Roosevelt did it, but does not say that he tried to talk him out of it. It is difficult to understand, since, even if it weren't leaked—and it was—the matter was bound to come out when the Republican delegates to the San Francisco meeting were briefed. What it points up is that Roosevelt was deprived of a foreign policy adviser after Hopkins left at Algiers, taking Bohlen with him. Bohlen, in his memoir, does not mention the voting issue, but says, "On reflection the thought came to me that the President might have wanted me to continue working with his special counsel, Samuel I. Rosenman, who had boarded the *Quincy* at Alexandria, on his report to Congress. I had helped Rosenman with the speech for a few days."

As previously noted, Rosenman boarded not at Alexandria on February 15 but in Algiers three days later, so Bohlen can have worked with him for only a few hours, for which Rosenman thanks him in his memoir.

The speech began, famously, with Roosevelt's first and only direct public reference during his presidency, outside of Warm Springs, to his disability. "I hope that you will pardon me for the unusual posture of sitting down during the presentation of what I want to say, but I know that you will realize that it makes it a lot easier for me not to have to carry about ten pounds of steel around on the bottom of my legs, and also because I have just completed a fourteen-thousand-mile trip."

Roosevelt spoke for roughly an hour about what had been accomplished at Yalta and the importance of those actions for America and the world. And right at the beginning, he put the responsibility on those before him. After saying that it was "good to be home" from "a long journey" and "a fruitful one," he admonished: "Speaking in all frankness, the question of whether it is entirely fruitful or not lies to a great extent in your hands. For unless you here in the halls of the American Congress—with the support of the American people— concur in the general conclusions reached at Yalta, and give them your active support, the meeting will not have produced lasting results." In a long speech filled with obvious ad-libs, the president expanded on what had been revealed in the mid-February joint statement. In defending his much-criticized "unconditional surrender" policy, he explained that it meant "the temporary control of Germany by" Britain, Russia, France, and the United States, each in charge of a separate zone and coordinated from Berlin. "It also means the end of Nazism . . . the termination of all militaristic influence in the . . . life of Germany . . . [and punishment for] Nazi war criminals . . . that is speedy and just—and severe."

The president mentioned his visits with the three kings, ad-libbing the only detail: "For instance, on the problem of Arabia, I learned more about that whole problem—the Moslem problem, the Jewish problem—by talking with Ibn Saud for five minutes, than I could have learned in the exchange of two or three dozen letters."

Closing, the president put before both his audiences what seemed to be the essential choice.

Twenty-five years ago, American fighting men looked to the statesmen of the world to finish the work of peace for which they fought and suffered. We failed them then. We cannot fail them again, and expect the world to survive.

The Crimea Conference was a successful effort by the three leading Nations to find a common ground for peace. It ought to spell the end of the system of unilateral action, the exclusive alliances, the spheres of influence, the balances of power, and all the other expedients that have been tried for centuries—and have always failed.

We propose to substitute for all these, a universal organization which all peace-loving Nations will finally have a chance to join.

I am confident that the Congress and the American people will accept the results of this Conference as the beginnings of a permanent structure of peace upon which we can begin to build, under God, that better world in which our children and grand-children—yours and mine, the children and grand-children of the whole world—must live, and can live.

And that, my friends, is the principal message I can give you. But I feel it very deeply, as I know that all of you are feeling it today, and are going to feel it in the future.[15]

In the White House, Bill Hassett took over Pa Watson's duties as appointment secretary, pending a new appointee, while Jonathan Daniels continued to act as press secretary and to second the president at his press conferences. At his regular Friday press conference the next day, Roosevelt faced the full press corps for the first time in forty-two days. The president had no news and parried most questions. He said that he didn't think that the labor of POWs should count as reparations in kind but did observe that "if I were Russian and I wanted to do something in the Crimea . . . I don't think that it would be a bad idea to get some German soldiers—ex soldiers—down there to clean up that mess."

Asked about the status of Jesse Jones—Wallace had been confirmed as commerce secretary the preceding day—Roosevelt answered that he was "ex-Secretary of Commerce." In response to a question about Jones's status as RFC head, he explained that Jones had held that post after he entered the cabinet by virtue of being commerce secretary. What he did not say—and some reporters clearly knew—was that Jones had clung to power even after he had been fired. Although Roosevelt had immediately named his deputy as acting secretary, Jones had sent letters to the White House—and presumably elsewhere—signed as secretary of commerce as late as February 28. Roosevelt quickly appointed Fred Vinson as federal loan administrator to run the RFC and other lending agencies, an appointment both Wallace and Jones praised publicly. This was soon followed by the appointment of War Labor Board head W. H. Davis to Vinson's post as director of economic stabilization and the promotion of NWLB vice chairman Dr. George W. Taylor (1901–71), an academic who became one of the nation's leading arbitrators, as Davis's successor. As both jobs were within the EOP, no Senate confirmation was necessary. Roosevelt continued to push, without significant success, for meaningful "work or fight" legislation. Congress, anxious not to annoy many constituents, was clearly stalling, hoping that the impending collapse of Germany would obviate the need for action. One radio commentator quipped that "work or fight" had become "work or loaf." Roosevelt and his successor saw the manpower control legislation as a step toward universal military training.

On Saturday night, the president left for a Hyde Park weekend, which he extended so that he returned Thursday morning. His time there was quiet with a good deal of chilly rain. While there he made plans to return for the weekend of March 24–26 and then leave on Tuesday, March 27, for two weeks in Warm Springs. He planned to leave Washington by train on April 20 to open the San Francisco Conference on April 25. Daniels announced a relaxation of security regulations so that once the president was back in the White House, the press could report that he had been away and what he had done. Reporters could travel with him, but advance or contemporary notice of presidential travel or absence still could not be printed.

Hassett describes the president as "in a gay mood" when he, Daniels, and Anna went up to see him at breakfast time on March 9 and noted often in the days that followed that the president's appointments were numerous and he was usually running late. The second post-Yalta Friday press conference was even more cursory than the first. Roosevelt did indicate dissatisfaction with the manpower bill being discussed by the Senate. He refused to answer a question about when the war with Germany might end, calling it a "crystal ball question," and brushed off several queries as "speculation." Asked if he would open the San Francisco Conference or go out later, the president answered, "Sometime during the conference; that's all I can tell you now." Finally:

> Q: Can you tell us, sir, whether there is any significance in the fact that
>   Admiral Nimitz, Admiral Halsey, General [Albert] Wedemeyer, General
>   [Patrick] Hurley are all here at this time?
> THE PRESIDENT: I suppose it's good flying weather.
> Q: Thank you, Mr. President.

More news followed the conference than was produced during it. Roosevelt spoke to a group of visiting French journalists, as American reporters listened, about his regard for de Gaulle and that he had bicycled in France as a boy, visited it during the Great War, and hoped to visit it again soon. A dispatch from Paris said that the French papers made a great deal of the president's friendly statement.

On Monday the War Department announced that, in response to a directive from the president in the fall, it had appointed the leading members of what became the all-civilian United States Strategic Bombing Survey to study the effects of the bombing of Germany. It was to begin its fieldwork as soon as possible after the end of hostilities in Europe.

When Clark Griffith, owner of the once potent Washington Senators baseball team, emerged from the Oval Office after presenting the president his customary annual pass, he told reporters that the president continued to favor the continuance of Major League Baseball. This produced a question about it in the Tuesday press conference, which the president answered with "Why not?"

He went on, for the third time, to sanction the continuance of the game despite the war.

The press conference, with Mackenzie King a silent visitor, had begun with the president reading an exceedingly bland declaration of mutual amity between the United States and Canada about good relations and mutual purposes, which was of little interest south of the forty-ninth parallel but important to most of those to its north. Roosevelt pointed to the bilateral relationship as a model for international cooperation. The president understood that the Canadian's high visibility in Washington was important to folks back home, so when asked about a rumor, probably planted by his guest, that he was being considered as chairman of the San Francisco Conference, Roosevelt didn't deny it. When the prime minister returned to Ottawa, he told reporters that Roosevelt was "looking well" and that both of them were "optimistic" about the looming San Francisco Conference. That was the general view in Washington, where some observers continued to be amazed about how little was heard from once powerful isolationist sources. There was little doubt that the Senate would approve Roosevelt's plan to join the yet-unnamed international organization.

Most of the newsmen's questions in the press conference, which followed a closed meeting, with a photo opportunity, for the American delegation to San Francisco, were about details of the conference, which the president did not satisfactorily answer, and many of which he could not answer. But when asked about when he would go, he pretended that he had no idea.[16]

At this time, "during the two weeks after his return from Yalta," Dr. Bruenn reported that his patient

> again began to ignore his rest regimen. In addition to a heavy schedule during the day he began to work much too late in the evenings. His appetite had become poor, and, although he had not been weighed, it appeared that he had lost more weight. He complained of not being able to taste his food. There was no nausea. Because of this anorexia, digitalis was withheld for several days, although no digitalis toxicity was discernable in the electrocardiogram. There was no cough or cardiac symptoms. Heart size was unchanged. The sounds were clear and of good quality. The rhythm was regular, and the apical systolic murmur had not changed. Blood pressure values were somewhat lower. Despite the withdrawal of digitalis, he was still troubled by his loss of appetite. Otherwise he insisted that he felt well. Digitalis therapy was renewed.

The president made several appointments dealing with impending post-European war problems, including sending Bernard Baruch to London to discuss such matters with Churchill and others, naming former commissioner of immigration and naturalization Earl G. Harrison (1890–1955) to replace Myron C. Taylor on the Intergovernmental Committee on Refugees and, after a meeting with Rabbi Stephen J. Wise, reaffirming his support for what the Democratic platform in 1944 had called "the opening of Palestine to unrestricted immigration and colonization, and such a policy as to result in the establishment there of a free and democratic commonwealth." This called into question the statement in his report on Yalta about learning from his encounter with Ibn Saud, an apparent contradiction he never resolved.

In his brief Friday press conference, much of the time was taken up by an opening presidential monologue about the need to increase restrictions on the consumption of some foods in the United States so that supplies could be shipped to liberated peoples in Europe. The president pointed to the Netherlands where famine and near-famine conditions existed in what had been a particularly bitter winter. He said, after searching for the right word, that it was a matter of "*decency*" and that "we have got to tighten our belts" until both "the German war and the Japanese war" were won.

Two events marked the Roosevelts' fortieth wedding anniversary. A family luncheon threesome with just Anna, and a small formal dinner in the State Dining Room with Princess Juliana of the Netherlands and members of her party, the widow of the president's onetime law partner, Mrs. Kermit Roosevelt, Justice and Mrs. Robert Jackson, Judge Marvin Jones, the war food administrator, Mr. and Mrs. Nelson Rockefeller, and Hassett were among the fewer than twenty guests who honored the presidential couple.

The Tuesday press conference was, again, largely perfunctory. Roosevelt spoke of a letter he sent to Byrnes instructing him ("I wish") to have an existing advisory board investigate the feasibility of guaranteed annual wage plans in collective bargaining agreements. He also urged a divided Congress to pass the "Work or Fight Bill," without favoring either the House version, which called for "limited national service" and subjected workers who refused to take war jobs with fines and jail, or the Senate version, which provided penalties only for employers. Later, he made a brief radio address, which was also filmed for newsreels, appealing for donations to the American Red Cross as an integral part of the war effort.

Roosevelt insisted that the Earl of Athlone, governor-general of Canada, and his wife, Princess Alice, be given all the honors of a head of state during a three-day visit, during which he and Eleanor greeted them, gave a dinner in their honor, and saw them off at Union Station.

The president, with much paperwork to take care of before his departure for Hyde Park and a planned sojourn at Warm Springs, briefed Baruch prior to his leaving for London, met with Pat Hurley (who was going back to Chungking), and lunched with the manpower maven Anna Rosenberg. He announced that Jonathan Daniels would be the new press secretary and that Steve Early, recently returned from Europe, would take charge, temporarily, of appointments. By early June, he hoped to appoint a replacement, after which "Steve will be free to enter private employment." Once aboard his train to Hyde Park, Hassett reports, Roosevelt, "weary after his long day," went straight to bed.[17]

A few hours before his departure, Roosevelt had suffered a small but stinging defeat from the Senate, which refused to confirm his nomination of Aubrey Williams to head the Rural Electrification Administration (REA). When Williams had left the government as his NYA was being phased out in late 1943, the president had said publicly that he wanted him back in government soon. In January 1944, he offered Williams the executive directorship of the War Refugee Board, which did not require Senate confirmation, but Williams turned it down. On January 22, 1945, Roosevelt sent Williams's nomination to head the Rural Electrification Administration to the Senate, which was embroiled with Henry Wallace's nomination as commerce secretary. On March 2, the Senate Agriculture Committee voted twelve to eight against the nomination: the negative votes came from five of the seven southern Democrats plus seven of the eight Republicans. Criticism included the unfounded charge that Williams was a Communist and the statement that he denied the divinity of Christ—once planning to become a Presbyterian minister, he was now a Unitarian. What was perhaps crucial to the ensuing rejection by the full Senate was Williams's refusal to downplay his advanced views on race relations. While he could not deny his role in the creation of the FEPC, he made it clear that he favored further intervention by the federal government to protect the rights of Negroes. The final vote was fifty-two to thirty-two. Only eight of twenty-six southern Democrats voted for him. The president made no public statement, but Mrs. Roosevelt spoke at what was styled as a "victory dinner" in Williams's honor held in the capital five days after his rejection.[18]

On Palm Sunday morning, both Roosevelts began four quiet days at Hyde Park, yet the White House continued to issue a flow of information and previously prepared statements, suggesting that the president was working there. He gave friendly advice on how "to extend the life and service" of motor vehicles and sent two formal messages to Congress on new legislation, one urging an expansion of his ability to negotiate mutual tariff reductions, the other asking that it approve active participation in the nascent Food and Agriculture Organization of the United Nations. And, in a fourth attempt to get some kind of work or fight bill out of Congress, he sent a letter to the Senate Military Affairs Committee, arguing that lack of manpower control was jeopardizing the rapid winning of the war and urging acceptance of a compromise bill.

At about this time, Dr. Bruenn's concerns about his patient peaked: "By the end of March he began to look bad. His color was poor, and he appeared to be very tired, although he continued to sleep well. Heart and lungs were unchanged. A period of total rest was urged. Accordingly, on March 29 the President left Washington for Warm Springs, Georgia."[19]

Actually, the trip began on the evening before in Hyde Park when both Roosevelts, several staff members, Margaret Suckley, and Laura Delano took the president's train to Washington. The president arrived at the White House at eight, went upstairs and had breakfast, and worked in his office with Archibald MacLeish and Jonathan Daniels on a statement about the arrangement at Yalta that had led to the granting of three votes to the Soviet Union in what became the UN General Assembly that had been publicly revealed in that morning's *New York Herald Tribune*. The president then had lunch with Anna, her son Curtis, Suckley, and Delano.

After lunch, Daniels writes:

> He was in his upstairs oval study working with Grace Tully when MacLeish and I appeared with the statement. . . . Tully, obviously protective, was tending papers he was tediously signing. . . . He looked bone tired, haggard, almost torpid. Apologetically we presented the paper. His eyes became alert above the words. With seeming precision he made a slight change in the first paragraph and pushed the paper back to me. We departed in haste. Then—when we reached the elevator in the hall we discovered that the change he had made in the first paragraph turned into confusion the rest of the statement. We had to go back into the room of that gaunt man. MacLeish wrote me of that moment later: "I remember particularly the pain in the decision to go back and ask the President to reconsider. You had a great deal more courage than I. If the decision had depended on me, I would have let it go as it was—which would have been very bad indeed." The truth is that it took whatever joint courage we had. We did go back and without any rebuke to either of us, the President corrected the paper. That was the last time I ever saw him.

Tully's memoir affirms the president's extreme fatigue.

Roosevelt was driven to the nearby underground siding and boarded his train, which left at 4:00 p.m. His party included, in addition to Suckley and Delano, two other friends, Leighton McCarthy and Basil O'Connor; staffers Bill Hassett, Grace Tully, Dorothy Brady, Toi Bachelder, Alice Winegar, and Louise Hackmeister; Dr. Bruenn; physiotherapist Lieutenant Commander George Fox; his valet, Arthur Prettyman; Secret Service personnel; the three wire-service reporters; some Filipino kitchen staff; and, of course, Fala. The reporters were along under the revised wartime restraints that nothing be published until the president returned to the White House. Anna was prevented from going to Hyde Park by the illness of her younger son, who was eventually hospitalized.

After lunch the next day, the train pulled into the Warm Springs station, where wartime rules were ignored and the usual crowd was waiting. The president was driven to the Little White House in warm, pleasant weather and remained there for the rest of the day.

The next morning's papers were full of the leaked news about the extra seats for the Soviets, and the responsible stories noted the MacLeish-Daniels White House statement that the president had okayed just before he left:

Soviet representatives at the Yalta Conference indicated their desire to raise at the San Francisco Conference of the United Nations the question of representation for the Ukrainian Soviet Republic and the White Russian Soviet Republic in the assembly of the proposed United Nations organization. The American and British representatives at the Yalta Conference were requested by the Soviet representatives to support this proposal when submitted to the United Nations at San Francisco. They agreed to do so, but the American representatives stated that if the United Nations organization agreed to let the Soviet republics have three votes, the United States would ask for three votes also.

[After noting that Britain and the USSR agreed to this, the statement concluded:] These conversations at Yalta related to the submission to the San Francisco conference where the ultimate decision will be made.

That the preparation of this statement had not been done earlier further demonstrates the deficiency in the management of foreign policy matters after Yalta. That day the White House also announced that Lieutenant General Lucius D. Clay (1898–1978), who had been serving as Byrnes's deputy, would soon leave for Germany, where he would be Eisenhower's deputy for civil affairs. This set a precedent, followed by Truman, so that the postwar occupation of Germany and Japan would be under military auspices.[20]

The president's days at Warm Springs were largely uneventful. He had gotten very little work done on the train, but Hassett reports that on Saturday morning—the first full day in Georgia—he signed "an enormous amount of mail" from that day's pouch plus papers brought from Hyde Park so that everything was "cleared up" for that evening's return pouch. (It went to Fort Benning and was flown to the capital.) Hassett returned to the president's cottage at five to get his signature on a letter accepting Byrnes's resignation and was "shocked at his appearance—worn, weary, exhausted. He seemed all right when I saw him in the morning."

When Hassett commented that Byrnes's retirement was a loss to him and to the government, Roosevelt agreed and added, "It's too bad some people are prima-donnaish." Of course, this was not reflected in the letter, which was full of praise. The next day, Easter Sunday, the president was undecided about going to church when signing the morning mail, but he showed up at eleven and stayed through what the Secret Service thought a long service. The next day, Hassett found Roosevelt "in good spirits" when he signed papers in the morning but "weary and tired" when Hassett brought a phone message from Stettinius just after lunch. He approved the action that Stettinius would announce from Washington the next day, saying that the United States would not request extra seats in the assembly of the new world body. The next two days were quiet, with the president taking afternoon drives. Preparations were made for the arrival of the only official visitor to Warm Springs, President Sergio Osmeña of the Philippines, on April 5. Hassett was sent in the president's limousine to Fort Benning to bring Osmeña and a small retinue back to Warm Springs; only Osmeña was taken to Roosevelt's cabin for lunch. Hassett was told to bring the three reporters at two.

The president opened with a long and newsy monologue, noting that he and Osmeña, who was present, "have been having a nice talk." He reminded the newsmen that their stories would have to be held until he got back to Washington, in "another week or ten days," which was news they couldn't print until it wasn't news anymore. He then recounted some of what Osmeña, who had just returned from the Philippines, had told him about the destruction there and the resistance of Filipino and American guerrillas. He said that American policy about Filipino independence was "absolutely unchanged" and that the United States had the responsibility for relief and a good deal of reconstruction of war-damaged infrastructure.

He then laid out, more fully than in any other public statement, his notions about postwar security policy in the western Pacific. It was "obvious," he said, that the United States would be "more or less responsible for security in all the Pacific waters" and must prevent Japan, as Germany would be prevented, from "setting up a military force," and it was necessary "to throw them out of their mandated ports." "We were talking about what base or bases, not for us nationally, but for us in the world, to prevent anything from being built up by the Japanese, and at the same time give us a chance to operate in those waters. . . . [A]nd undoubtedly we accept a mandate to keep security in that part of the world. The Filipinos and ourselves would in propinquity maintain adequate naval and air bases to take care of that section of the Pacific."

The president then accepted—and answered—many more questions than he had for quite some time, including one directed to and answered by Osmeña about his personal plans. The most interesting response was Roosevelt's imaginative recollection of a conversation with Stalin concerning what a reporter called "the three-to-one vote," which ended the conference.

THE PRESIDENT: As a matter of fact this plea for votes was handled in a very quiet way. Stalin said to me—and this is the essence of it—"You know there are two parts of Russia that have been completely devastated. Every building is gone, every farm house, and there are millions of people living in there [sic] territories—and it is very important from the point of view of humanity—and we thought, as a gesture, they ought to be given something as a result of this coming victory. They have had very little civilization. One is the Ukraine, and the other is White Russia. We all felt—not any of us coming from there in the government—we think it would be grand to give them a vote in the Assembly."

He asked me what I thought.

I said to Stalin, "Are you going to make that request of the Assembly?"

He said, "I think we should."

I said, "I think it would be alright—I don't know how the Assembly will vote."

He said, "Would you favor it?"

I said, "Yes, largely on sentimental grounds. If I were on the delegation—which I am not—I would probably vote 'yes.'"

That has not come out in any paper.

He said, "That would be the Soviet Union, plus White Russia, plus the Ukraine."

Then I said, "By the way, if the conference in San Francisco should give you three votes in the Assembly—if you get three votes—I do not know what would happen if I don't put in a plea for three votes and insist on it."

It is not really of any great importance. It is an investigative body only. I told Stettinius to forget it. I am not awfully keen for three votes in the Assembly. It is the little fellow who needs the vote in the Assembly. This business about the number of votes in the Assembly does not make a great deal of difference.

Q: They don't decide anything, do they?

THE PRESIDENT: No. [Apparently after a significant pause] By the way, this is all off the record.[21]

The last week at Warm Springs began quietly and with some confidence. Dr. Bruenn reported:

The weather there was ideal, and within a week there was an obvious improvement in his appearance and sense of well-being. He had begun to eat with appetite, rested beautifully, and was in excellent spirits. He began to go out every afternoon for short motor trips, which he clearly enjoyed. He had given up the eggnogs in favor of a gruel between meals. The physical examination was unchanged except for the blood pressure, the level of which had become extremely wide, ranging from 177/88 to 249/130 mm. Hg. There was no apparent cause and effect. By April 10 improvement had continued. His color was much better, and his appetite was very good; he asked for double helpings of food. Although he had not been weighed, it was apparent that he had begun to gain a little weight. He had been resting very well and began to increase his activities. He was in excellent spirits and began to plan a weekend, involving a barbeque and attendance at a minstrel show.

We know something about the last three of those motor trips.

For the first, the only witness account is that of Elizabeth Shoumatoff. She relates that a long series of telephone conversations between her friend and patron, Lucy Mercer Rutherfurd, and the president had resulted in her being allowed to paint her second portrait of Roosevelt during a stay of several days at Warm Springs while Lucy would spend time with the president. On April 9, she drove Lucy and the photographer who assisted her from the Rutherfurd home in Aiken, South Carolina, toward a planned meeting with the president in Macon, Georgia. They arrived late, and Roosevelt was not there. Continuing on their 186-mile journey, they reached Manchester, five miles from Warm Springs, and saw the president's limousine surrounded by townspeople, with Roosevelt in the backseat, drinking a bottle of Coca-Cola. The two women joined Roosevelt in the backseat, and his companions, Margaret Suckley and Fala, moved up front with his Secret Service driver, while Shoumatoff's photographer drove her car to the Warm Springs hotel. The two women were accommodated in the guest cottage adjacent to the Little White House, and both dined with the president on each of the three nights of their visit.

For the second drive, Mike Reilly is the only witness. He says that it was on April 11; Shoumatoff's account of the departure says April 10. Reilly writes that Roosevelt was accompanied by his two cousins; Shoumatoff that the passengers were Suckley, Lucy, and Fala. Roosevelt's loyal bodyguard never mentioned the name of the woman who wasn't supposed to be there. Reilly wrote:

> The day was perfect for driving. . . . Near La Grange, Georgia, we came upon a bridge which bore a sign: "Load limit, 4,000 pounds." I honked the horn of the Detail car and the president's auto stopped.
>
> "I'm sorry Mr. President . . . but your auto has a lot of steel armoring in it and weighs 7,500 pounds. This bridge can take only about half that."
>
> "Okay Mike, we'll turn around."
>
> Miss Suckley seemed disappointed. She turned to the President and said, "Oh, Franklin, don't you think if we go real fast we could get across?" The Boss did a sort of double take at her and burst into a roar of laughter. Almost choking, he said, "Margaret, I don't think Mike would approve of your suggestion." I wouldn't, of course, but now I'm awfully glad she made it, because I'm pretty sure that was the last time the Boss laughed on earth. That is, laughed the way he so loved to—a hearty yell, his head thrown back and his eyes closed tightly.

We have no direct testimony about the third drive on April 11. Roosevelt, Lucy, and Fala were the only passengers. They drove out to a favorite local overlook, Dowdell's Knob, and watched the sunset.

On Tuesday the photographer took photos of Roosevelt for the artist's later use, and she made some preliminary sketches while the president worked at the card table that served as his desk. He accepted an invitation to attend a Thursday-afternoon barbecue being held by the mayor of Warm Springs. The president specified that he did not care for barbecued pork and asked that he be served Brunswick stew, preceded by an old-fashioned.

On Wednesday Roosevelt made detailed plans for his appearance at the San Francisco Conference, which he had been talking about for some time. He would leave Warm Springs on April 18, just a week away; host a White House dinner for the regent of Iraq the next evening; and leave on his train for San Francisco on the twentieth, arriving at the army embarkation reservation in Oakland at noon on the twenty-fifth. He would then be driven over to San Francisco and address the conference, return to Oakland, and leave for Los Angeles at 6:00 p.m. (After dinner that evening, he would tell Henry Morgenthau that "at three o'clock in the afternoon I will appear on the stage in my wheelchair and I will make the speech.") That he was willing to be seen in his wheelchair is a clear sign that he had no further electoral ambitions. Eleanor and Romelle Schneider Roosevelt, his son James's second wife, would accompany him to San Francisco. He would then go on to Los Angeles, where his daughter-in-law would leave the train, and perhaps he would go on to San Diego to visit his son John's family. His return trip would begin at 6:00 p.m. on April 26 and end on May 1 at Hyde Park, where he would rest for a few days. Although he had evinced growing concern over Soviet actions in Poland and elsewhere, Roosevelt sent a conciliatory cable to Stalin about a minor dispute over a meeting between American and German military in Switzerland.

> Personal from the President for Marshall Stalin
>
> Thank you for your frank explanation of the Soviet point of view of the Bern incident which now appears to have faded into the past without having accomplished any useful purpose.
>
> There must not, in any event, be mutual distrust and minor misunderstandings of this character should not arise in the future. I feel sure that when our armies make contact in Germany and join in a fully coordinated offensive the Nazi Armies will disintegrate.

Later that afternoon, using a draft sent down by Robert Sherwood, he dictated to Dorothy Brady the final version of his Jefferson Day speech, which he planned to broadcast on Saturday evening. Hassett, who read it that evening, thought it "a good speech."

At twelve o'clock Wednesday, Shoumatoff came for the first of what she told a New York press conference were a planned four sittings. The president continued to work. At dinner that night, they were joined by Henry Morgenthau, who recorded in his "diary" how terrible the president looked but noted his healthy appetite. He was there to get Roosevelt's approval for a book he wanted to write and publish on postwar policy toward Germany and came away with what he thought was approval: "The President said, 'Henry, I am with you 100 per cent.'" After Morgenthau left, the conversation continued until Dr. Bruenn arrived to tell the president that it was his bedtime.[22]

On Thursday, April 12, Bruenn reports, "I saw the President shortly after 9:20 AM, a few minutes after he had awakened. He had slept well but complained of a slight headache and some stiffness of the neck. He ascribed this to a soreness of the muscles, and relief was experienced after a slight massage."

Bruenn left the president's bedroom, used the phone to make his daily report to Dr. McIntire, and left the cottage. Roosevelt had breakfast and read the papers in bed and at about eleven had his valet, Chief Steward Arthur Prettyman, put him in and out of his bath and help him dress. A little before noon, he came to the living room, where his cousins and Lucy were waiting for him. As the pouch was late, neither Hassett nor Grace Tully went to the president's cottage that morning, though he did work out details of his trip to San Francisco with Dewey Long, who managed domestic travel.

Sometime after noon, Hassett came with the pouch, a "heavy batch," and the president, "with the usual wisecracks," began to sign the mail. Soon Shoumatoff came in, set up her easel, and annoyed Hassett, who wrote that she "interrupted the paper work constantly." When the president signed what was his final bill—a measure extending the life of the Commodity Credit Corporation and increasing its borrowing power—he remarked to Laura Delano, as he often did, "Here's where I make a law." When Hassett left the cottage, a little before one, he was "fully resolved to ask Bruenn to put an end to this unnecessary hounding of a sick man" by the artist.

Shoumatoff, for her part, reports that as soon as "the Filipino butler" (actually Chief Steward Irineo Esperancilla) began setting the table for lunch, Roosevelt said to her, "We have fifteen minutes more to work," which she believed were his last words. (Laura Delano told Dr. Bruenn that she thought the president said, "I have a terrific headache.")

Shoumatoff was apparently the only one to notice the president collapse about 1:15 p.m. She says that Lucy and Margaret were in conversation on the couch and that she called to them that something had happened; one of them called, "Get a doctor!" Disentangling herself from her painting equipment, she ran to the porch and shouted to a Secret Service agent to get a doctor. By the time she came back inside, Prettyman and Esperancilla were carrying the unconscious president into his bedroom. The Secret Service drove Dr. Bruenn, who had been swimming, to the cottage at about 1:30 and moments later delivered physiotherapist George Fox, who brought Bruenn's bag and assisted him.

Dr. Bruenn's report follows:

1:30 PM to 2:30: When I saw him 15 min later, he was cold, pale, and sweating profusely. He was totally unconscious with fairly frequent generalized tetanic contractions of mild degree. Pupils of the eyes were at first equal, but in a few minutes the right pupil became widely dilated. The lungs were clear, bur he was breathing stertorously but regularly. Heart sounds were excellent, heart rate was 96/min. Systolic blood pressure was well over 300 mm Hg; diastolic pressure was 190 mm Hg. He had voided involuntarily.

Warmth in the form of hot water bottles and blankets was applied, and papavarine, 1 grain, was administered intravenously. Amylnitrite was also given to relieve the apparent intense vasoconstriction. Reflexes were unobtainable in the legs; right elbow was +++. It was apparent that the president had suffered a massive cerebral hemorrhage. I immediately called Washington on the private telephone line and contacted Dr. McIntire and informed him of the catastrophe. He told me that he would call Dr. Paullin in Atlanta immediately.

2:45 PM. Color was much improved. Breathing was a little irregular and stertorous. Blood pressure had fallen to 240/120 mm Hg. Heart sounds were good—rate 90/min.

3:15 PM. Blood pressure was 210/110 mm Hg; heart rate, 96/min; right pupil, still widely dilated, but the left pupil, from moderate constriction, had become moderately dilated. Occasional spasm of rigidity with marked slowing of respiration was noted. During latter phases, he had become mildly cyanotic.

3:30 PM: Pupils were approximately equal. Breathing had become irregular but of some amplitude.

3:31 PM: Breathing suddenly stopped but was replaced by occasional gasps. Heart sounds were not audible. Artificial respiration was begun and caffeine sodium benzoate given muscularly. At this moment Dr. Paullin arrived from Atlanta. Adrenalin was administered into the heart muscle.

3:35 PM: I pronounced him dead.[23]

*   *   *

The death of a serving president marks a change of course in the life of the nation; that new course will not be plotted here. Even before the president died, someone (Grace Tully?) had told Lucy that his family was coming, and she told Shoumatoff that they must leave immediately. As the women packed in haste, Secret Service men brought the photographer and Shoumatoff's car to the Little White House, and Shoumatoff drove the three of them away for a return to Aiken. The announcement of the president's death was delayed until Eleanor Roosevelt, in Washington, could be notified. Then Hassett summoned the three wire-service reporters to his cottage (which had four telephones), announced that the president had died at 3:35, and then had Bruenn give them an account of the president's final hours. Almost simultaneously, Steve Early was alerting the Washington press and radio. Later, Hassett used the name of Shoumatoff's photographer to identify the artist painting the president. He ignored this falsification in his published diary, which properly identified her, but continued to suppress Lucy's presence. Eleanor Roosevelt, Steve Early, and Dr. McIntire flew down that night in a navy plane, leaving Washington at 7:45 and arriving at Warm Springs about 11:00. Hassett and Bruenn had been delegated by Mrs. Roosevelt to get a suitable coffin. Dr. Paullin recommended an Atlanta undertaker, who managed to get a large solid bronze coffin to Warm Springs that night. In Washington General Marshall set in motion the plans for military ceremonies honoring the commander in chief.

In the wee hours, what Hassett described as "the admirals, generals, and colonels from Southern Army and Navy Commands" made plans for the funeral. An honor guard of some two thousand drawn from all military services, with the band from Fort Benning, would see the coffin to what was now the funeral train, where it would rest on a catafalque, fully visible from the outside, with a rotating guard of four sentinels drawn from the various branches of the service. The train left Warm Springs at 10:00 a.m. Friday, and, as had been the case with Lincoln's funeral train in the same month eighty years before, crowds stood waiting in stations and along the right-of-way to see the president's body pass.

In Washington the next morning, the coffin was placed on a black, flag-draped caisson drawn by six white horses, which led a long, slow military procession, including elements of WAACs, WAVES, SPARS, and women Marines, which took more than an hour to escort the body to the White House. The body did not lie in state.

The brief funeral service, conducted by Bishop Dun in the East Room, began at 4:00, attended by dignitaries, domestic and foreign, headed by President Truman and Anthony Eden. Of Roosevelt's four serving sons, only Brigadier General Elliott Roosevelt was able to join his mother and sister at the service. At 4:25 a limousine left the White House, taking the coffin back to the train, which left for Hyde Park at 11:00 p.m. There, on Sunday morning in an austere military ceremony lasting just seventeen minutes, Franklin Delano Roosevelt was buried in the garden of his home at the precise location he had prescribed in an instruction written and signed in 1937. The document further provided that a plain rectangular marble headstone should contain only his name and the name of his wife and their dates of birth and death.[24]

* * *

It seems appropriate to include the text of Roosevelt's last speech, the radio address to the Jefferson Day Dinners that he planned to deliver on April 14, 1945. In some ways, this forward-looking talk is as germane to a post-9/11 audience as it was to the postwar generation at which it was aimed.

Americans are gathered together this evening in communities all over the country to pay tribute to the living memory of Thomas Jefferson—one of the greatest of all democrats: and I want to make it clear that I am spelling that word "democrats" with a small "d."

I wish I had the power, just for this evening, to be present at all of these gatherings.

In this historic year, more than ever before, we do well to consider the character of Thomas Jefferson as an American citizen of the world. As Minister to France, as our first Secretary of State and as our third President, Jefferson was instrumental in the establishment of the United States as a vital factor in international affairs.

It was he who first sent our Navy into far distant waters to defend our rights. And the promulgation of the Monroe Doctrine was the logical development of Jefferson's far-seeing foreign policy.

Today, this nation which Jefferson helped so greatly to build, is playing a tremendous part in the battle for the rights of man all over the world.

Today we are part of the vast allied force—a force composed of flesh and blood and steel and spirit—which is today destroying the makers of war, the breeders of hate, in Europe and in Asia. In Jefferson's time our Navy consisted of only a handful of frigates—but that tiny Navy taught nations across the Atlantic that piracy in the Mediterranean—acts of aggression against peaceful commerce, and the enslavement of their crews, was one of those things which, among neighbors, simply was not done. Today, we have learned in the agony of war that great power involves great responsibility. Today, we can no more escape the consequences of German and Japanese aggression than could we avoid the consequences of attacks by the Barbary corsairs a century and a half before.

We as Americans, do not choose to deny our responsibility. Nor do we intend to abandon our determination that, within the lives of our children and our children's children, there will not be a Third World War.

We seek peace—enduring peace. More than an end to war, we want an end to the beginnings of all wars—yes, an end to this brutal, inhuman and thoroughly impractical method of settling the differences between governments.

The once powerful, malignant Nazi state is crumbling, the Japanese warlords are receiving, in their own homeland, the retribution for which they asked when they attacked Pearl Harbor.

But the mere conquest of our enemies is not enough. We must go on to do all in our power to conquer the doubts and the fears, the ignorance and the greed, which made this horror possible.

Thomas Jefferson, himself a distinguished scientist, once spoke of "the brotherly spirit of science, which unites into one family all of its votaries of whatever grade, and however widely dispersed throughout the different quarters of the globe."

Today science has brought the different quarters so close together that it is impossible to isolate them one from another. Today we are faced with the pre-eminent fact that, if civilization is to survive, we must cultivate the science of human relationships, the ability of all peoples, of all kinds, to live together and work together, in the same world, at peace. Let me assure you that my hand is the steadier for the work that is to be done, that I move more firmly into the task, knowing that you—millions and millions of you—are joined with me in the resolve to make this work endure.

The work, my friends, is peace, more than an end to this war—an end to the beginnings of all wars, yes, an end, forever, to this impractical, unrealistic settlement of the differences between governments, by the mass killing of peoples.

Today as we move against the terrible scourge of war—as we go forward toward the greatest contribution any generation of human beings can make in this world—the contribution of lasting peace, I ask you to keep up your faith. I measure the sound solid achievement that can be made at this time by the straight-edge of your own confidence and your resolve. And to you, and to all Americans who dedicate themselves with us in the making of an abiding peace, I say: The only limit of our realization of tomorrow will be our doubts of today. Let us move forward with strong and active faith.[25]

*　　*　　*

As a stunned nation mourned Roosevelt, tributes from abroad poured in for the man who had made himself the undisputed world leader. In London an obviously moved and uncharacteristically brief Churchill told the House of Commons, "The House will have heard, with the deepest sorrow, the grievous news that has come to us from across the Atlantic, which conveys to us the loss of the famous president of the United States, whose friendship for the cause of freedom and for the weak and poor has won him immortal fame. It is not fitting that we should continue our work this day."

Most positive assessments of Roosevelt's more than twelve years in the White House stress, properly, the crises of the Great Depression and of World War II. Perhaps equally notable, he transformed the magnetic field of American politics. He changed the Democratic Party from an agrarian-oriented party dominated by southerners and with strong conservative elements into a party dependent on big-city voters, ethnic minorities, and African Americans. His breaking of the southern stranglehold on the party began even before he became president, when the 1932 Democratic National Convention effectively abolished the two-thirds rule. In the long run, after Roosevelt was gone, this pushed most white southerners into the Republican Party and gradually cleansed that party's traditional liberal element, making the national parties largely ideological.

Evaluations of what Roosevelt called the New Deal have, far too often, focused on the fabled hundred days, but the first serious attempt to confront the greatest problem of those years, mass unemployment, began with the Civil Works Administration, created by executive order when Congress was not sitting on the two hundred and fiftieth day. After—long after—it was clear that its positive stimulus had not been nearly enough, Roosevelt pushed the Emergency Relief Appropriation Act of April 1935 through Congress. He then created the Works Projects Administration. It provided a continuing stimulus effective enough to trim the unemployment rate to less than half of the putative 25 percent prevailing when the New Deal began. This accomplishment, before the effects of defense and war spending set in, is only part of the achievements of the first seven years of the Roosevelt era.

Despite being a man who cast a huge shadow, Roosevelt managed to surround himself with a large cast of highly skilled public servants and acolytes; in addition, the example of a chief executive who did exciting things made government service attractive to many of the best and the brightest. Without these constantly refreshed cadres, New Deal reform would have been less effective than it was. During the war years, Roosevelt, limited by the existing army and navy rosters, showed an amazing skill in assembling an effective group of top military leaders who ran the entire war.

Also vital in both peace and war was Roosevelt's ability to gain and maintain public confidence throughout his entire presidency. While he catered to public prejudices, he successfully managed, time and again, to lead public opinion in the direction in which he wished it to go. His accomplishment is demonstrated not only by his electoral success and persistent high ratings in the various polls but also in the way he weaned substantial segments of the public away from their support of isolationism.

Perhaps Roosevelt's least appreciated major peacetime achievements were intellectual ones. His real postgraduate education began at age forty-seven with private tutorials in Albany, culminating late in his second term in his gradual conversion to a kind of Keynesianism. He had demonstrated an almost instinctive ability for administration during his navy years, but that was inside-the-box stuff. Also instinctive was his penchant for taking the long view, as the callow *Whither Bound?* of 1926 demonstrates. By the time he put the finishing touches on the Reorganization Act plans in 1939, he had the foresight and the guile to create a "sleeper" Office of Emergency Management that he could activate should the war that he expected come to pass.

Although he became an effective world leader, his early attempts to achieve international influence were ineffective outside the Western Hemisphere, and his successes within it were largely ignored and often reversed by subsequent administrations. His more enduring efforts, beginning with the Atlantic Charter, were dependent on victory. He made desperate bets on Britain and the Soviet Union being able to hold out. Few have even tried to calculate what the effects on Roosevelt's reputation would have been if even one of those bets had been lost.

Roosevelt's contributions to that victory by his management of the war economy are often vitiated by negative comments about "the mess in Washington." A distinguished contemporary historian has concluded that at the end of 1943, "After years of indifference, muddle, and make do, the United States was at last prepared to fight its kind of war."[26] To thus describe Roosevelt's activities between 1939 and late 1943—between the outbreak of war through the Tehran Conference—is more like a political campaign ad than historical scholarship. Roosevelt's marshaling of the nation's productive facilities, raising and supplying a vast armed force as well as shipping vital aid to his European allies, was no mean feat. That it was accompanied by shameless profiteering, wasteful extravagance, and a great deal of confusion by both civilian and military authorities is true, regrettable, but, in the final analysis, largely irrelevant.

Beyond the victory that American men and machines helped achieve, Roosevelt in his final days was most concerned about ensuring a durable peace by establishing a viable international organization. The United Nations came into existence because Roosevelt insisted on it. None of the other major leaders placed great value on its creation or survival. It is an important part of his legacy. So is atomic energy, which he enabled, but did not live to see.

Professional critics of a conservative bent today tend to criticize Roosevelt for trying to do too much in regard to such matters as taxation and economic regulation, while many of those on the Left complain that he did not do enough to curb discrimination and end poverty. Time, a string of failed presidencies, and what Paul Krugman calls a "Great Recession" have caused there to be more interest in Roosevelt's presidency in the early twenty-first century than during most of the later twentieth. As I write, in the fall of 2015, two pressing issues, health care and unemployment, that were on Roosevelt's postwar to-do list are still pressing issues.

With victory assured, the issue that most concerned Roosevelt in April 1945 and sometime before was world peace and what became the United Nations. He and his contemporaries would have been amazed if it had been revealed to them that repeated "small wars" would occur in various parts of the world involving, in one way or another, both the United States and the Soviet Union, despite the establishment and growth of the United Nations. They would have been less surprised by the development, first, of American-Soviet summits and, after the Cold War, the meetings of heads of state or chief ministers of the larger powers in varying combinations. Roosevelt hoped, as we have seen, not for perpetual peace but for no great war during the lifetime of anyone then alive. Surviving babies born the day Roosevelt died are already past normal retirement age, so in that sense the awkward postwar settlement that he largely helped organize now seems not as unstable as it did to his surviving contemporaries.

Franklin Delano Roosevelt, born in the last years of the Victorian era, successfully led the United States into the modern world and pulled a large number of his countrymen with him. Like all leaders, he was limited, to a degree, by what he had to work with—in his case a Congress in which the least progressive segments of the population were overrepresented by a Constitution designed to limit sudden change. Where his fifth cousin had yearned to be president "and Congress too," he devised ways to govern without Congress. Although a civil libertarian on most issues, most of the time his actions toward the guilty Nazi saboteurs and the innocent Japanese Americans have provided elements of the still growing national security state, as did his giving largely free rein to the unprincipled J. Edgar Hoover and the dedicated William J. Donovan.

Like most great leaders, it is easier to describe his flaws than his virtues. Perhaps the greatest of the latter was his determination: determination to overcome his crippling disability, his political opponents, and his nation's enemies. Almost equally important was his vision: of a nation in which all could prosper, of an environment that was preserved and improved, of a world at peace. And to those virtues, apparent to millions of his fellow citizens, we can now add the continuing ability to inspire others to pursue his most important goals.

Notes

Chapter 1. Reform, Neutrality, and War

1. "Annual Message to Congress, Jan. 4, 1939," in *Public Papers and Addresses of Franklin D. Roosevelt,* edited by Samuel I. Rosenman, hereafter cited as *PPA;* Turner Catledge, "Aims of President," *NYT,* January 5, 1939, 1.

2. Samuel I. Rosenman, *Working with Roosevelt,* 181–84, 257.

3. *PPA,* "The Annual Budget Message, Jan. 5, 1939"; Felix Belair Jr., "Debt Is Near Limit," *NYT,* January 6, 1939, 1; Turner Catledge, "WPA Cost Amazes," *NYT,* January 6, 1939, 1.

4. "New Deal Spending Is Held Wasteful," *NYT,* January 6, 1939, 13; "Survey Indicates Roosevelt Gains," *NYT,* January 8, 1939, 35.

5. *PPA,* "A Message on the Needs of the Works Progress Administration, Jan. 5, 1939," and appended note, and "The President Urges the Congress to Pass Additional Appropriations for National Defense, Jan. 12, 1939."

6. *PPA,* "The President Recommends Additional [WPA] Appropriations . . ., February 7, 1939" and "The President Again Urges Additional [WPA] . . . Appropriations, Mar. 14, 1939," and appended note.

7. "Frankfurter Wins; Murphy Vote, 78–7," *NYT,* January 18, 1939, 6; "Hopkins Confirmed; Glass Leads Foes in Acrid Attacks," *NYT,* January 24, 1939, 1; Associated Press (AP), "12 Named by Roosevelt Met Senate Rejection," *NYT,* August 6, 1939, 27. In addition to the two judges, the Senate rejected ten of the 3,338 postmasters nominated during the 1939 session. "Roberts Rejected, by Senate, 72–9, in Sweeping Blot," *NYT,* February 7, 1939, 1. *PPA,* "A Letter on the Constitutional Role of the Senate in Confirming Presidential Appointments—and on Its Occasional Misuse by the Senate, Feb. 7, 1939." For a convenient summary of the history of "senatorial courtesy," see Congressional Research Service Report, "Evolution of the Senate's Role in the Nomination and Confirmation Process: A Brief History," by Betsy Palmer, updated July 2, 2008, Order Code RL31948, available online.

8. *PPA,* "Address at Jackson Day Dinner, Washington, D.C., Jan. 7, 1939"; "Roosevelt Asks Democrats to Unite Behind New Deal; Urges Others to Join G.O.P.," *NYT,* January 8, 1939, 1. Monroe served 1817–25, Jackson 1829–37.

9. Kent Roberts Greenfield, "Franklin D. Roosevelt: Commander-in-Chief," in *American Strategy in World War II: A Reconsideration,* 49–84, has a list and description of twenty-two "Decisions of F.D.R. against the advice, or over the protests of his military advisors." See also Eric Larrabee, *Commander in Chief: Franklin D. Roosevelt, His Lieutenants & Their War.* Article II, Section 2: "The President shall be Commander in Chief of the Army and Navy of the United States, and of the Militia of the several States, when called into the actual Service of the United States."

10. *PPA,* "The President Urges Congress to Pass Additional Appropriations for National Defense, Jan. 12, 1939" (the online version of *PPA,* in a rare error, misdates this message as January 2, 1939); Felix Belair Jr., "$552,000,000 for Defense Is Asked by Roosevelt; Mostly for New Planes," *NYT,* January 13, 1939, 1; John W. Hutson, "Arnold, Henry Harley ('Hap')," in *Franklin D. Roosevelt: His Life and Times; An Encyclopedic View,* edited by Otis L. Graham Jr. and Meghan R. Wander. For details of air force developments, see Wesley F. Craven and James L. Cate, eds., *The Army Air Forces in World War II.*

11. *PPA,* "Further Appropriations Are Requested for National Defense, Apr. 29, 1939." Only after World War II would there be a separate air force.

12. Jean Monnet, *Memoirs,* 122; John M. Haight, *American Aid to France, 1938–1940.*

13. Frank Freidel, *Franklin D. Roosevelt: A Rendezvous with Destiny,* 309–13; Wayne S. Cole, *Roosevelt and the Isolationists, 1932–1945,* 297–302; "Bomber Pilot Killed in Coast Plane Crash," *NYT,* January 24, 1939, 5; "French Observer in Coast Crash," *NYT,* January 27, 1939, 5; "Spurs Air Works," *NYT,* January 28, 1939, 11; "President Helped French Air Mission Despite Protests," *NYT,* February 17, 1939, 1; Arthur Krock, "Behind the Scenes in French Plane Affair," *NYT,* February 21, 1939, 14.

14. *PPA,* "A Message Transmitting to the Congress a Report of the Social Security Board, Jan. 16, 1939," and appended note, and "Presidential Statement on Signing Some Amendments to the Social Security Act, Aug. 11, 1939."

15. Larry DeWitt on the "1939 Amendments" in "Historical Background and Development of Social Security."

16. *PPA,* "A Request for Consideration of the Recommendations of the Interdepartmental Committee to Coordinate Health Activities with Respect to the National Health Program, Jan. 23, 1939," and appended note; "Roosevelt Urges Broad Health Plan as Need of Nation," *NYT,* January 24, 1939, 1; "National Health Program Reported by Committee," *NYT,* January 24, 1939, 12, is the official summary.

17. Ronald L. Numbers, *Almost Persuaded: American Physicians and Compulsory Health Insurance, 1912–1920;* I. S. Falk, "The Committee on the Costs of Medical Care: 25 Years of Progress"; Daniel S. Hirschfield, *The Lost Reform: The Campaign for Compulsory Health Insurance in the United States from 1932 to 1943,* is fundamental.

18. "National Health Program Offered by Wagner in Social Security Bill," *NYT,* March 1, 1939, 1; J. Joseph Huthmacher, *Senator Robert F. Wagner and the Rise of Urban Liberalism,* 263–66 (Fishbein quote on 265). For Fishbein, see Lester S. King's *American National Biography (ANB)* sketch.

19. FDR, *The Complete Presidential Press Conferences of Franklin D. Roosevelt,* #608 (December 22, 1939), 14:375–82, hereafter cited as *Press Conf.*

20. "New Appeal Made in Paralysis Drive," *NYT,* January 6, 1939, 8; *PPA,* "A Letter by the President on the Raising of Funds on His Birthday, Jan. 18, 1939" and "Radio Address on the Occasion of the President's Birthday Ball, Jan. 30, 1939"; "President Thanks Paralysis Donors," *NYT,* January 31, 1939, 10.

21. "Justice Brandeis Retires from the Supreme Court," *NYT,* February 14, 1939, 1; "President, Recovered, Set for Caribbean Tour," *NYT,* February 15, 1939, 1; "Senate Confirms Douglas," *NYT,* April 5, 1939, 1. The bill, the so-called Court Proctor statute,

created a post, to be filled by a nominee of the chief justice, to oversee and regulate the finances of all federal courts (53 Stat. 1293).

22. *PPA*, "President's Statement on Attaining the Objectives of the Court Fight of 1937, Aug. 7, 1939"; Felix Belair Jr., "Roosevelt Claims Victory on Courts," *NYT*, August 8, 1937, 1.

23. *PPA*, "Statement on Removal of Federal Trade Commissioner Humphrey, Oct. 7, 1933"; *Humphrey's Executor v. United States*, 295 U.S. 302 (1935). William E. Leuchtenburg's essay "The Case of the Contentious Commissioner" (1967), revised in his 1995 volume *The Supreme Court Reborn: The Constitutional Revolution in the Age of Roosevelt*, 52–81, brought the case into the literature. In a three-paragraph essay in a reference book he added the conclusion, without additional documentation: "More angered by [the Humphrey decision] because of its implication that he had willfully violated the Constitution than by the more important ruling in *Schechter Poultry Corp. v. U.S.* handed down the same day, Roosevelt was determined to seek ways to curb the court, a course that led to his ill-fated *court-packing* plan of 1937." "*Humphrey's Executor v. United States*," in *The Oxford Guide to Supreme Court Decisions*, edited by Kermit J. Hall, 131–32. Cf. the "Contentious Commissioner" essay cited above, at 79. Leuchtenburg nowhere cites FDR directly. There is one relevant quotation, hiding in plain sight in the note to the *PPA* document cited above: "The Supreme Court later held that it was not within my power as president to remove Commissioner Humphrey except after charges" (*Humphrey's Executor v. United States*, 295 U.S. 602). Such procedure was not followed by me. It seems advisable at this time not to discuss the reasons for my action. The president's signed introduction to the 1933 volume is dated November 1, 1937.

24. The exempted agencies were Army Corps of Engineers, Board of Governors of the Federal Reserve System, Board of Tax Appeals, Civil Service Commission, Coast Guard, U.S. Employees' Compensation Commission, Federal Communications Commission, Federal Deposit Insurance Corporation, Federal Power Commission, Federal Trade Commission, General Accounting Office, Interstate Commerce Commission, Maritime Commission, Mississippi River Commission, National Labor Relations Board, National Defense Mediation Board, Railroad Retirement Board, National Railway Readjustment Board, Securities and Exchange Commission, Tariff Commission, and Veterans Administration.

25. "Reorganizing Bill Is Passed by House by Vote of 246–153," *NYT*, March 9, 1939, 1; "Senate Votes Bill on Reorganization with Curb Dropped," *NYT*, March 23, 1939, 1; Felix Belair Jr., "Roosevelt Signs Reorganization Bill," *NYT*, April 4, 1939, 1.

26. Louis Brownlow, *A Passion for Anonymity*, 417–18.

27. "Budget Director Sworn," *NYT*, April 16, 1939, 30, matches the story from Freidel, *Rendezvous with Destiny*, 278–79. A variant version is in Barbara Blumberg's *ANB* sketch of Smith. Brownlow, *A Passion for Anonymity*, 414–29.

28. Robert E. Sherwood, *Roosevelt and Hopkins: An Intimate History*, 72–73; James MacGregor Burns, *Roosevelt: The Soldier of Freedom*, 348–49. Smith's untimely death at fifty just as he became head of the World Bank is largely responsible for his relatively unknown status. There is no biography, and, apart from Sherwood, none of the first generation of chroniclers of the Roosevelt era interviewed him.

29. *PPA*, "The President Presents Plan No. 1 to Carry Out the Provisions of the Reorganization Act, Apr. 25, 1939," and appended note.

30. Brownlow, *A Passion for Anonymity*, 419–20. Ickes's published diary does not mention this lunch, but the entry for April 29, 1939, complains about his losses from Plan No. 1, including the Office of Education. Harold L. Ickes, *The Secret Diary of Harold L. Ickes*, 2:623.

31. *PPA*, "The President Presents Plan No. 2 to Carry Out the Provisions of the Reorganization Act, May 9, 1939," and appended note; "Roosevelt Plan II Changes or Dooms Scores of Agencies," *NYT*, May 10, 1939, 1.

32. *Press Conf #536* (April 4, 1939), 13:248; *PPA*, "The Reorganization of the Executive Office of the President, Executive Order (EO) 8248, Sept. 8, 1939." The appended note is a long first-person account of the experience of the presidential assistants up to mid-1941.

33. "President Promotes Col. Watson from Military 1 Aide to Secretary," *NYT*, March 7, 1939, 2; "Watson Now a General," *NYT*, April 4, 1939, 11.

34. "Roosevelt Names three New Aides," *NYT*, July 13, 1939, 3; Felix Belair Jr., "Roosevelt Staff Grows with Tasks," *NYT*, July 23, 1939, E6; "J. H. Rowe to Be Biddle Aide," *NYT*, November 17, 1941. Rowe's later career included a two-year stint as a naval lieutenant in the Pacific theater and service on the staff of the International War Crimes Tribunal in Nuremburg, after which he entered a successful Washington law practice with Corcoran. He served on many public boards and commissions and managed two unsuccessful campaigns for the presidency: Lyndon Johnson's in 1960 and Hubert Humphrey's in 1968. A witty and thoughtful man, Rowe, who had a successful postwar legal partnership with Corcoran, once remarked that although he and many of his New Deal colleagues made a lot of money, "quite frankly a lot of us are bored to death." His oral history interview on the Truman Library website is illuminating about his experience working in the White House and about the Budget Bureau for which he worked after the war. Seth S. King. "James Rowe, New Deal Aid and an Assistant to Roosevelt," *NYT*, June 19, 1984, B10.

35. "Roosevelt Ex-Aide Dies," *NYT*, January 17, 1951; Brownlow, *A Passion for Anonymity*, 421.

36. Marriner S. Eccles, *Beckoning Frontiers: Public and Personal Recollections*, 333. The council was created by the Full Employment Act of 1946.

37. Much of my account of Currie comes from Roger J. Sandilands, *The Life and Political Economy of Lauchlin Currie*, esp. 96–140, quote on 98; Albert Lepawsky, "The Planning Apparatus: A Vignette of the New Deal."

38. *PPA*, "The Reorganization of the Executive Office of the President, EO 8248, Sept. 8, 1939." For an early academic account, see A. J. Wann, *The President as Chief Administrator: A Study of Franklin D. Roosevelt* and "Franklin D. Roosevelt's Administrative Contributions to the Presidency."

39. *PPA*, "The Reorganization of the Executive Office of the President, EO 8248, Sept. 8, 1939."

40. Raymond Arsenault, *The Sound of Freedom: Marian Anderson, the Lincoln Memorial and the Concert That Awakened America*, 97–188, is a superior account and analysis. See also Ickes, *Secret Diary*, 2:612–13. The interior secretary had been

working with local black organizations and Walter White and the NAACP. "Throng Honors Marian Anderson in Concert at Lincoln Memorial," *NYT,* April 10, 1939, 15. The paper ran a full page of pictures the following Sunday: "Concert for 75,000," *NYT,* April 16, 1939, RP7. There is no known verifiable comment about the concert by the president. One alleged quotation exists in two versions. In 1983 Nancy J. Weiss quoted an item from the *Chicago Defender* in 1943 with some skepticism: "Tell Oscar he has my permission to have Marian sing from the top of the Washington Monument if he wants it" (Weiss, *Farewell to the Party of Lincoln,* 260). Ten years later, Scott A. Sandage quoted Roosevelt without reservation, saying, "She can sing from the top of the Washington Monument as far as I am concerned," based on his 1989 interview with an otherwise unidentified "Ann Chapman," presumably a relative of Oscar L. Chapman (1896–1978), who was Ickes's assistant secretary. Sandage, "A Marble House Divided: The Lincoln Memorial, the Civil Rights Movement, and the Politics of Memory, 1939–1963," 135.

41. *PPA,* "Informal, Extemporaneous Remarks at Tuskegee Institute, Tuskegee Alabama, Mar. 30, 1939," "Informal, Extemporaneous Remarks at Alabama Polytechnic Institution, Auburn, Alabama, Mar. 30, 1939," and "Statement on the New Agricultural Building at Tuskegee Institute, Dec. 14, 1939"; Felix Belair Jr., "Roosevelt Urges Self-Reliant South," *NYT,* March 31, 1939, 1. The hospital was the site of the now infamous New Deal Tuskegee syphilis experiment in which a control group of black patients, thinking that they were being treated, were given placebos for many years while the disease ravaged their bodies. There is no reason to believe that Roosevelt knew anything about it. See James H. Jones, *Bad Blood: The Tuskegee Syphilis Experiment.*

42. "Paralysis Center Set Up for Negroes," *NYT,* May 22, 1939, 15; David Oshinsky, *Polio: An American Story,* gives a different dollar amount for the Tuskegee grant, citing two presidential documents in which no figures appear. See also Naomi Rogers, "Race and the Politics of Polio: Warm Springs, Tuskegee, and the March of Dimes." For black health professionals, see Darlene Clark Hine, "Black Professionals and Race Consciousness: Origins of the Civil Rights Movement, 1890–1950."

43. *Press Conf* #534–37 (March 31–April 8, 1939), 13:235–62; Felix Belair Jr., "Roosevelt Happy in Georgia," *NYT,* April 9, 1939, E9; "President Voices Fear of Early War," *NYT,* April 10, 1939, 1; *PPA,* "Extemporaneous Warning of Approaching War, Warm Springs, Georgia, Apr. 9, 1939." Both the *Times* and the *Washington Post* quote the president as saying "don't" rather than the "do not" of the official text in *PPA.*

44. "President Returns to Anxious Capital" and "President Envies Egg Rollers," *NYT,* April 11, 1939, 1, 20.

45. *Press Conf* #538 (April 11, 1939), 13:265–68; Felix Belair Jr., "President's Views," *NYT,* April 12, 1939, 1.

46. *PPA,* "Address at Governing Board of the Pan American Union, Apr. 14, 1939"; Bertram D. Hulen, "America's Way Urged," *NYT,* April 15, 1939, 1; *PPA,* "Address on the One Hundred and Fiftieth Anniversary of the Formal Announcement of the Election of the First President of the United States, Apr. 14, 1939"; Felix Belair Jr., "Roosevelt Extols Washington of 1789," *NYT,* April 15, 1939, 9.

47. *PPA,* "A Message to Chancellor Adolf Hitler and Premier Benito Mussolini, Apr. 14, 1939"; *Press Conf* #539 (April 15, 1939), 13:270–78; AP, "Reporters Suddenly Called

to White House Hear President Disclose His Peace Appeal," *NYT,* April 16, 1939, 40; "President Appeals," *NYT,* April 16, 1939, 1.

48. "Berlin Sees Rejection; Incredible Says Rome," *NYT,* April 16, 1939, 1; "London and Paris Quickly Approve the President's Message to Dictators," *NYT,* April 16, 1939, 40; "President's Plea for Peace Stirs Washington and the Latin American Capitals," *NYT,* April 16, 1939, 41; Robert E. Burke, ed., *Diary Letters of Hiram Johnson, 1917–1945,* April 29, 1939, 7:171–98, is a good summary of the last months of prewar diplomacy.

49. For Bloom, see the *ANB* sketch. In his autobiography, Bloom says that Tammany boss Murphy selected him to run for a Manhattan House seat in a 1923 special election because he was "an amiable and solvent Jew" (Harold B. Hinton, "Embargo Injected in Neutrality Bill by Sudden Move," *NYT,* June 30, 1939, 1).

50. Harold D. Hinton, "Senate Committee Votes for Delay on Neutrality," *NYT,* July 12, 1939, 1; *PPA,* "The President Strongly Urges Revision of Our Neutrality Laws, July 14, 1939" and "White House Release on the Conference on Neutrality Held at the White House, July 18, 1939"; "No Neutrality Revision This Session," *NYT,* July 19, 1939, 1. The other Democrats in opposition on the committee vote were Clark of Missouri, Gillette, Reynolds of North Carolina, and Van Nuys.

51. *Press Conf* #564 (July 21, 1939), 14:35–36. Borah's friendly biographer quotes him as saying that he did "not believe that there is going to be any war in Europe between now and the first of January or for some time thereafter" and revealed that Borah's source had been the private weekly newsletter published by British journalist Claude Cockburn that British historian A. J. P. Taylor describes as "an instrument of Communist penetration." Marian C. McKenna, *Borah,* 362–64; Taylor, *English History, 1914–1945,* 397n1.

52. Turner Catledge, "Blow to President," *NYT,* August 2, 1939, 1; "Housing Bill Killed, 191–170," *NYT,* August 4, 1939, 1; "Congress to Adjourn Today," *NYT,* August 5, 1; "Clash Marks End: Scene in House as 76th Congress Adjourns," *NYT,* August 6, 1939, 1. For a very different view of the 1939 session, see James T. Patterson, *Congressional Conservatism and the New Deal: The Growth of the Congressional Coalition in Congress, 1933–1939,* 288–324. Only part of our differences can be explained by his view that the Social Security changes were "mild" (311).

53. *Press Conf* #568 (August 1, 1939) 14:63–66. The statement on 63 that "147" Democrats joined the Republicans is a typo for "47." Felix Belair Jr., "President Retorts," *NYT,* August 2, 1939, 1; *PPA,* "The President Signs and Discusses the Hatch Act, Aug. 2, 1940"; Felix Belair Jr., "Backs Politics Ban," *NYT,* August 3, 1939, 1. Cf. David F. Porter, "The Hatch Act of 1939," in *Encyclopedia of the Great Depression,* edited by Robert S. McElvaine, 426–27.

54. *Press Conf* #569 (August 4, 1939), 14:75–80; Felix Belair Jr., "President Quotes Latin on Congress," *NYT,* August 5, 1939, 1.

55. *PPA,* "President's Statement on Attaining the Objectives of the Court Fight of 1937" and "The President Directs Department Surveys to Reduce Government Costs, Aug. 7, 1939"; Felix Belair Jr., "Roosevelt Claims Victory on Courts Despite Congress," *NYT,* August 8, 1939, 1.

56. *Press Conf* #570 (August 8, 1939), 14:91–93; *PPA,* "Some Political Advice to the Convention of Young Democratic Clubs of America, Aug. 8, 1939"; Felix Belair Jr.,

"Roosevelt Depicts His Congress Foes in Gamblers' Role," *NYT,* August 9, 1939, 1; "Roosevelt Plans New 'Must' Bills," *NYT,* August 10, 1939, 2.

57. *PPA,* "Presidential Statement on Signing Some Amendments to the Social Security Act, Aug. 11, 1939"; *Press Conf* #571 (August 11, 1939), 14:108–10; Felix Belair Jr., "President Ready to Call Congress If War Threatens," *NYT,* August 12, 1939, 1.

58. *PPA,* "The President Opens the Golden Gate Exposition in San Francisco from Key West, Florida, Feb. 18, 1939" and "The President Opens the New York World's Fair, Apr. 30, 1939." This was the first televised presidential speech. There were perhaps two hundred sets in existence; it could be seen within fifty miles of New York City. "Ceremony Is Carried by Television . . .," *NYT,* May 1, 1939.

59. Press coverage was extensive. From June 9 to June 12, the *New York Times* devoted, successively, five, six, nine, and four front-page stories to the royal visit, with numerous smaller stories and sidebars on inside pages.

60. Felix Belair Jr., "Informal Atmosphere Is Stressed for Royal Visit with President," *NYT,* June 11, 1939, 1; "King Tries Hot Dog and Asks for More," *NYT,* June 12, 1939, 1. Queen Elizabeth's letter from Franklin Delano Roosevelt Library (FDRL) website (access "Royal Visit, 1939").

61. *Press Conf* #552 (June 9, 1939), 13:410; "Transcript of King George VI's Handwritten Notes for a Memorandum on His Conversations with President Roosevelt on June 10 and 11, 1939," FDRL website (access "Royal Visit, 1939").

62. Felix Belair Jr., "President Ready to Call Congress If War Threatens," *NYT,* August 12, 1939, 1; "Mayor, President Talk on WPA Today," *NYT,* August 12, 1939, 5; Roosevelt Sails on 10-Day Sea Trip," *NYT,* August 13, 1939, 1; "Roosevelt Views Squalus Salvaging," *NYT,* August 14, 1939, 4. The *Squalus* sank after a catastrophic valve failure during a test dive in 240 feet of water; one officer, twenty-three seamen, and two civilian electricians perished. A dramatic rescue using a diving bell brought the thirty-three survivors to the surface.

63. James A. Hagerty, "Young Democrats Cheer Call to Draft Roosevelt," *NYT,* August 13, 1939, 1; *Press Conf* #572 (August 14, 1939), 14:115–19; Felix Belair Jr., "President Silent on Kelly's Speech" and "Roosevelt to Move Thanksgiving; Retailers for It, Plymouth Is Not," *NYT,* August 15, 1939, 7, 1; *PPA,* "A Thanksgiving Day Proclamation, Oct. 31, 1939."

64. "Roosevelt Visits Halifax, Sails On," "Roosevelt Beset by Fog at Sydney," "Roosevelt Sails on in Fog Ridden Seas," "Aide of Roosevelt Lands Humber Salmon," "Roosevelt at Bonne Bay," "Roosevelt Speeds Return as Fog Bars Mail," and "Roosevelt Puts in at Halifax Harbor," *NYT,* August 16–22, 1939.

65. Felix Belair Jr., "President Speeds to Act on Crisis," *NYT,* August 24, 1939, 1; *PPA,* "The President Again Seeks the Way of Peace in the New Crisis over Poland. Messages to Adolf Hitler of Germany; King Victor Emmanuel of Italy; and President Mozicki of Poland, Aug. 24, 1939" (the listing is achronological) and "A Further Attempt for Peace in the Polish Crisis: A Second Letter to Chancellor Hitler," August 25, 1939; Felix Belair Jr., "President Moves," *NYT,* August 25, 1939, 1; *Press Conf* #573 (August 25, 1939), 14:120–23; Felix Belair Jr., "President Hopeful," *NYT,* August 26, 1939, 1; Robert Dallek, *Franklin D. Roosevelt and American Foreign Policy, 1932–1945,* 196 (hereafter cited as DALLEK).

66. *Press Conf* #575 (September 1, 1939), 14:131.

Chapter 2. Beginning an Undeclared War

1. *Press Conf* #575 (September 1, 1939), 14:130–34; Felix Belair Jr., "Roosevelt Pledge" and "War Industries Buoy the Markets Here," *NYT,* September 2, 1939, 1.

2. Woodrow Wilson, "Message on Neutrality, Aug. 19, 1914," http://www.presidency.ucsb.edu.

3. *PPA,* "Fireside Chat, Washington, D.C., Sept. 3, 1939."

4. William L. Neumann, "Franklin D. Roosevelt and Japan, 1913–1933."

5. U.S. Department of State, *Peace and War: United States Foreign Policy, 1931–1941,* 473–74; Cordell Hull, "*Japan* on the Eve," in *The Memoirs of Cordell Hull,* 1:627–40; *Press Conf* #567 (July 28, 1939), 14:61; Bertram H. Hulen, "U.S. Denounces Japanese Trade Treaty," *NYT,* July 27, 1939, 1.

6. For extreme examples of actions against chimerical threats to the safety of the New World ordered by Roosevelt, see the luminous monograph by Max Paul Friedman, *Nazis and Good Neighbors: The United States Campaign against the Germans of Latin America in World War II.* Since I composed this paragraph, an entire unbalanced volume, Ira Katznelson's *Fear Itself: The New Deal and the Origins of Our Time,* that posits fear as the lietmotif of Roosevelt's political career. Hope and faith, as even a casual reading of Roosevelt's words will show, were predominant.

7. Stetson Conn and Byron Fairchild, *The Framework of Hemisphere Defense,* 11.

8. For Marshall, the best source is Forrest C. Pogue's four-volume biography, *George C. Marshall;* more accessible is Thomas Parrish, *Roosevelt and Marshall.* "Marshall Named as Chief of Staff," *NYT,* April 28, 1939, 4.

9. Ray S. Cline, *Washington Command Post: The Operations Division,* 45. The EO 8193-B was classified "Confidential," and not even its title was printed in *PPA* in the listing of second-term EOs at 595 of the 1937 volume. See also William Emerson, "Franklin Roosevelt as Commander-in-Chief in World War II"; and Greenfield, *American Strategy,* 49ff.

10. *PPA,* "A Proclamation of Neutrality of the United States Pursuant to General International Law, Proclamation No. 2348, Sept. 5, 1939" and "The Export of Arms and Munitions to Belligerent Powers Is Prohibited under the Neutrality Act of 1937, Proclamation No. 2349, Sept. 5, 1939."

11. *Press Conf* #576 (September 5, 1939), 14:135–45; Felix Belair Jr., "President Puts Our Ships in Open," *NYT,* September 6, 1939, 6. The *Athenia* was carrying 1,103 passengers, including 316 Americans from Liverpool to Canada; 118 passengers drowned, 18 of them Americans.

12. *PPA,* "The Federal Bureau of Investigation Is Placed in Charge of Espionage Investigation, Sept. 6, 1939"; *Press Conf* #514 (January 4, 1939), 13:40. There is a growing literature demystifying the work of Hoover's FBI. A good place to start is Athan G. Theoharis, *J. Edgar Hoover, Sex, and Crime: An Historical Antidote.* For naval intelligence, see Jeffery M. Dorwart, *Conflict of Duty: The U.S. Navy's Intelligence Dilemma, 1919–1945.*

13. *Press Conf* #577 (September 8, 1939), 14:146–57; *PPA,* "Proclaiming a Limited National Emergency, Proclamation No. 2352"; "EO 8246, Sept. 8, 1939." The other EOs, not in *PPA,* are 8244, 8245, and 8247. Felix Belair Jr., "100,000 More Men," *NYT,* September 9, 1939.

14. *PPA,* "The Reorganization of the Executive Office of the President, EO 8248, Sept. 8, 1939," and appended note; Felix Belair Jr., "Roosevelt Unifies White House Task," *NYT,* September 10, 1939, 1. On wartime information, see Allan M. Winkler, *The Politics of Propaganda: The Office of War Information, 1842–1945.* See also Richard W. Steele, *Propaganda in an Open Society: The Roosevelt Administration and the Media, 1933–1941.*

15. White House statement, *NYT,* September 10, 1939, 50. For an inside perception of the "mess," see Jonathan Daniels, *White House Witness, 1942–1945.* He was one of the "anonymous six" and briefly FDR's last press secretary.

16. *PPA,* "The Marketing Limitations on Sugar Are Suspended for the Emergency, Proclamation No. 2361, Sept. 11, 1939," and appended note, and "A Statement on Terminating the Suspension of the Marketing Quota Provisions on the Sugar Act of 1937," revoked by "Proclamation No. 2378, Dec. 26, 1939."

17. Felix Belair Jr., "Roosevelt Unifies White House Task," *NYT,* September 10, 1939, 1; Freidel, *Rendezvous with Destiny,* 325.

18. *PPA,* "The Congress Is Called into Extraordinary Session, Proclamation No. 2365, September 13, 1939; Felix Belair Jr. "Congress Called to Meet Sept. 21 on Embargo Issue," *NYT,* September 13, 1939, 1.

19. Turner Catledge, "On Eve of Congress," *NYT,* September 21, 1939, 1; W. Cole, *Roosevelt and the Isolationists,* 310–30; transcript, "Copy of the President with Democratic and Republican Leaders Preceding the Opening of a Special Session of the Congress, Executive Offices of the White House, Sept. 20, 1939, 3:05 P.M.," OF 1569, FDRL, as cited in W. Cole, *Roosevelt and the Isolationists,* 610n33. FDR's rant to Morgenthau is from the diary entry of June 30, 1939. See the comments in Freidel, *Rendezvous with Destiny,* 315; AP, "Tighten Capital Rules to Protect the President," *NYT,* September 21, 1939, 16.

20. *PPA,* "The President Urges the Extraordinary Session to Repeal the Embargo Provisions of the Neutrality Law, Sept. 21, 1939," and appended note; Turner Catledge, "A Solemn Message," *NYT,* September 22, 1939, 1. The closing phrase is from Psalm 56:13.

21. "Editorials Back Presidents Plea," "A Solemn Message," "Knox Acclaims the Message," and "Roosevelt Nears 1936 Popularity," *NYT,* January 22, 1939, 19, 1, 19; "Change Favored in Neutrality Act," *NYT,* September 24, 1939, 30; "3D Term Sentiment Increased by War," *NYT,* October 1, 1939, 26.

22. DALLEK, 205–6; Harold B. Hinton, "Americas Set Up Sea Safety Zone," *NYT,* October 3, 1939, 8, which also has the text of the Declaration, and "American Nations Stress Unanimity," *NYT,* October 4, 1939, 7; *Press Conf* #587 (October 10, 1939), 14:226; Samuel E. Morison, *The Two-Ocean War: A Short History of the United States Navy in World War Two,* 26–27. This is a distillation, with revisions, of his fifteen-volume *History of United States Naval Operations in World War II.*

23. "American Fronts," *NYT,* September 24, 1939, 70. A good summary of congressional action in the special session can be found in the appended note to the president's speech cited above. *PPA,* "Proclamation of Neutrality"; "Proclamation of Combat Areas . . ., Nov. 4, 1939." The combat areas proclamation had to be amended a number of times before December 7, 1941, as the war spread. Ironically, the Far East was not declared a war zone before December 7, 1941.

24. *PPA,* "Radio Address to the New York 'Herald Tribune' Forum, Oct. 26, 1939."

25. W. Cole, *Roosevelt and the Isolationists*, 310–30, quote on 310.

26. Charles A. Lindbergh, *The Wartime Journals of Charles A. Lindbergh*, 257–58; Freidel, *Rendezvous with Destiny*, 307–8, 323; Frank L. Kluckhohn, "Lindbergh Urges We Shun War," *NYT*, September 16, 1939, 1.

27. The Einstein letter, with a brilliant short commentary, is in Donald Fleming, "Albert Einstein: Letter to Franklin D. Roosevelt, 1939." For a detailed account, see Martin J. Sherwin, *A World Destroyed: The Atomic Bomb and the Grand Alliance;* and "Alexander Sachs, Economist, Dead," *NYT*, June 24, 1973, 47. Szilard, Fermi, Briggs, and Leahy are in *ANB*.

28. *PPA*, "Exchange of Messages with President Kalinin of Russia, Oct. 11, 1939, and Oct. 16, 1939"; *Press Conf* #588 (December 1, 1939), 14:229–30; *PPA*, "Statement on the Conflict between Russia and Finland" and "The President Appeals to Russia and Finland to Desist from Bombing of Civilians, Dec. 1, 1939"; "The President Suggests to Manufacturers Not to Sell Airplanes to Belligerents Who Bomb Civilians, Dec. 2, 1939"; "A Greeting to Finland on the Twenty-Second Anniversary of Its Independence, Dec. 6, 1939." For general information about the larger war, I rely on Gerhard L. Weinberg's authoritative *A World at Arms: A Global History of World War II*, which will not be cited again unless quoted directly.

29. Warren F. Kimball, ed., *Roosevelt and Churchill: The Complete Correspondence*, 1:28–34; Warren F. Kimball, *Forged in War: Roosevelt, Churchill, and the Second World War.*

30. Michael R. Beschloss, *Kennedy and Roosevelt: The Uneasy Alliance*, 200. The September 11, 1939, note began correspondence ending on April 11, 1945: 1,949 items, 788 from Roosevelt, 1,161 from Churchill. Warren Kimball's collection cited in note 29 above a monument of scholarship. His eighteen-page introduction is a useful guide to a fateful relationship.

31. Felix Belair Jr., "Roosevelt Rests at Warm Springs," *NYT*, November 23, 1939, 3; *PPA*, "Informal, Extemporaneous Remarks at Thanksgiving Dinner, Warm Springs, Georgia, Nov. 23, 1939"; Felix Belair Jr., "Roosevelt Hopes for Spring Peace," *NYT*, November 24, 1939, 18.

32. *Press Conf* #601 (November 28, 1939), 13:325–28; Felix Belair Jr., "Roosevelt Acts in Budget Dispute: Summons Director," *NYT*, November 27, 1939, 1; "Roosevelt Whittles Estimates for Budget," *NYT*, November 28, 1939, 1; "Roosevelt Decides to Have Two Budgets," *NYT*, November 29, 1939, 1.

33. *PPA*, "A Letter to the Pope, Dec. 23, 1939"; "Church and Public Hail Peace Moves," *NYT*, December 27, 1939, 1; "Vatican Tie Scored by Three Church Groups," *NYT*, January 5, 1940, 8.

34. *PPA*, "A Radio Christmas Greeting to the Nation, Dec. 23, 1939." The Beatitudes are Matthew 5:3–11 and Luke 6:20–22; the 1938 Christmas text was Isaiah 2:4. *PPA*, "Address on Lighting the Community Christmas Tree, Dec. 24, 1939"; "President Exalts Neighbor Spirit in Christmas Rite," *NYT*, December 25, 1939, 1.

35. "Edison Appointed Naval Secretary by the President," *NYT*, December 31, 1939, 1; "Charles Edison, 78, Ex-Governor of Jersey, and U.S. Aide, Dies, Aug. 1, 1969," *NYT*, August 1, 1969, 33. Sketches of Swanson and Edison are in Paolo E. Coletta, ed., *American Secretaries of the Navy.*

36. *PPA,* "Annual Message to the Congress, Jan. 3, 1940"; Turner Catledge, "For Unity in Action" and "Borah Eschews Opening Fearing Roosevelt's Voice," *NYT,* January 4, 1940, 1, 14.

37. *PPA,* "The Annual Budget Message, Jan. 3, 1940"; Turner Catledge, "Roosevelt Fixes the Outlay in '41 Budget at $8,424,000,000," *NYT,* January 5, 1940, 1.

38. "Democrats Invite Republican Chiefs to Jackson Dinner," *NYT,* December 31, 1939, 1; *PPA,* "Address at Jackson Day Dinner, Jan. 8, 1940"; Turner Catledge, "Roosevelt Says Party Must Hold Independent Vote" and "Third-Term Talkers Get No Executive Rebuke Now," *NYT,* January 9, 1940, 1, 14.

39. *PPA,* "[Letter on Aid to Finland], Jan. 16, 1940," and appended note; DALLEK, 208–10. The statute doubled the lending authority of the Export-Import Bank to $200 million and allowed loans of up to $20 million per nation. Congress laid down certain guidelines but did not have to approve individual loans.

40. *PPA,* "A Recommendation for the Construction of Small Hospitals, Jan. 30, 1940," and appended note; "President Urges 50 New Hospitals," *NYT,* January 31, 1940, 22; "Fishbein Praises Hospital Program," *NYT,* December 31, 1939, 19; Charles W. Hurd, "Josephine Roche Returns to Guide a Health Program," *NYT,* February 11, 1940, 61. The word *Negro* had been used fourteen times previously in his *Public Papers:* three in connection with celebrations of the Emancipation Proclamation; three in dedicating segregated facilities; two in greetings to the NAACP; two in talks at white colleges; and one each in a statement on the Virgin Islands, a press conference, remarks to NYA directors, and a private letter on a literary matter.

41. *PPA,* "Radio Address before the White House Conference on Children, Washington, D.C., Jan. 19, 1940"; "Roosevelt Backs Child Aid Program," *NYT,* January 20, 1940, 13; Kathleen McLaughlin, "Child Group Forms Ten-Year Program," *NYT,* January 19, 1940, 24. For the significance of the conference, see Kriste Lindenmeyer, *"A Right to Childhood": The U.S. Children's Bureau and Child Welfare, 1912–1946,* 203–47. For the limited federal programs for transients, see Helen S. Hawkins, *A New Deal for the Newcomer: The Federal Transient Service.* John Steinbeck's *The Grapes of Wrath* (1939) won the Pulitzer Prize that year. It and the John Ford film version (1940) along with the images of Dorothea Lange and other FSA photographers have embedded deeply in the national consciousness the false notion of the Depression as primarily a rural phenomenon.

42. *PPA,* "Radio Address on the Occasion of the President's Seventh Birthday Ball, Jan. 30, 1940"; "Nation Observes President's Day," *NYT,* January 31, 1940, 1.

43. For a useful account of the CP's switch after the Nazi-Soviet pact, see Fraser M. Ottanelli, *The Communist Party of the United States,* 197–212.

44. *PPA,* "Address to the Delegates of the American Youth Congress, Washington, D.C., Feb. 10, 1940"; "Alliance Derides Roosevelt in New Song," *NYT,* January 14, 1940, 19; Frank S. Adams, "Youth Told Stand," Delbert Clark, "CIO Chief's Offer," and Frank S. Adams, "Youth Congress Moves on Turbulent Course," *NYT,* February 11, 1940, 1, 1, 80. Joseph P. Lash's chapter "FDR Administers a Spanking" in his *Eleanor and Franklin: The Story of Their Relationship, Based on Eleanor Roosevelt's Private Papers,* 612–33, is a detailed account. For the ongoing concern of both Roosevelts about youth, see Richard A. Reiman, *The New Deal and American Youth: Ideas and Ideals in a Depression Decade.*

45. "John L. Lewis' Speech Criticizing Policies of President Roosevelt before Youth Congress," *NYT*, February 11, 1940, 45.

46. Eleanor Roosevelt, "Why I Still Believe in the Youth Conference"; *Press Conf* #649A (June 5, 1940), 15:452–540.

47. *Press Conf* #621 (February 5, 1940), 15:127–29; Felix Belair Jr., "Roosevelt Cites Gains in New Deal," *NYT*, February 6, 1940, 1.

48. *Press Conf* #623–27 (February 13, 15, 19, 27, March 2, 1940), 15:152–79; "President Decides on Vacation at Sea in Air of Mystery," *NYT*, February 14, 1940, 1; Felix Belair Jr., "Roosevelt Sails on Mystery Cruise," *NYT*, February 16, 1940, 1; "President Warns Congress on Delay in Canal Defense," *NYT*, March 3, 1941, 1.

49. Felix Belair Jr., "Roosevelt Marks 7 New Deal Years, Silent on 3d Term," *NYT*, March 5, 1940, 1; Arthur Krock, "New Deal Anniversary Raises Two Questions," *NYT*, March 4, 1940, 8.

50. *PPA*, "The President Presents Plan No. III to Carry Out the Provisions of the Reorganization Act, Apr. 2, 1940."

51. DALLEK, 216–18; *Press Conf* #622 (February 9, 1940), 15:139; *PPA*, "Statement on the Return of Welles, Mar. 20, 1940"; "Welles Trip Gets Approval in U.S.," *NYT*, March 10, 1940, 27.

Chapter 3. Breaking Precedents in War and Politics

1. Bertram D. Hulen, "Roosevelt Defers U.S. Action on War after Night Talks," *NYT*, April 10, 1940, 1; *PPA*, "The War Spreads: And the Definition of the Combat Area Is Extended. Proclamation No. 2394, Apr. 10, 1940" and "Funds in the United States of Victims of Aggression Are Protected, EO 8389, Apr. 10, 1940," and appended note. Governments in exile could obtain licenses to use the money. Felix Belair Jr., "New Curbs in U.S.," *NYT*, April 11, 1940, 1; *PPA*, "Statement by the President on the Nazi Invasion of Denmark and Norway, Apr. 13, 1940." A Proclamation of Neutrality "in the War between Germany and Norway" was not issued until April 25, 1940. *PPA*, "Proclamation No. 2399." See Felix Belair Jr., "War Zone Widened," *NYT*, April 26, 1940, 1.

2. U.S. Department of State, *Foreign Relations of the United States, 1940*, 2:343–76 (hereafter cited as *FRUS*); "Iceland Assumes Sovereign Power," *NYT*, April 11, 1940, 6; James MacDonald, "Iceland Occupied by British Force," *NYT*, May 10, 1940, 1; Frederick T. Birchall, "Greenland Raises Hemisphere Issue," *NYT*, April 11, 1940, 1; "Roosevelt Studies Greenland Status," *NYT*, April 13, 1940, 4; "Consul to Greenland to Be Rushed by U.S.," *NYT*, May 2, 1940, 13. For Roosevelt's specific concerns, see *Press Conf* #634–636 (April 9, 12, 18, 1940), 15:240–61; and "U.S. to Establish Ties with Iceland," *NYT*, April 17, 1940, 1. Denmark, unlike Norway, did not resist. It became a Nazi "protectorate"; its parliament continued to sit, and its king retained certain powers and remained in his Copenhagen palace. The Norwegian monarch escaped and set up a government in exile in London, joining similar Czech and Polish bodies.

3. *PPA*, "The President Presents Plan No. IV . . ., Apr. 11, 1940"; Felix Belair Jr., "Roosevelt Urges CAA Merger Plan," *NYT*, April 12, 1940, 14; *PPA*, "Statement on Signing the Bill Continuing the Reciprocal Trade Agreements Program, Apr. 12, 1940"

and "Presidential Statement [on CAA Reorganization], Apr. 30, 1940," and appended note; "President Hails Hull Plan Gains," *NYT*, April 13, 1940, 9.

4. *PPA*, "Radio Address . . . Pan American Governing Board, Apr. 15, 1940" and "Radio Address to the Young Democratic Clubs of America, Apr. 20, 1940."

5. Felix Belair Jr., "Roosevelt in South," "President Confers on Fiscal Affairs," "President Starts Return to Capital," and "President Returns from Vacation in South," *NYT*, April 20, 23, 24, 25, 28, 29, 1940, 1, 9, 5, 6; *Press Conf* #637 (April 21, 1940), 15:293–96. Roosevelt's officer aides were always large men, and at least one of them was almost always present on trips to lift and otherwise physically assist the crippled president when he was on public view.

6. *Press Conf* #640 (May 3, 1940), 15:317; #641 (May 6, 1940), 15:319–20; Felix Belair Jr., "Our Defense Steps Satisfy President," *NYT*, May 4, 1940, 1.

7. FDR to John Cudahy, in *F.D.R.: His Personal Letters*, edited by Elliott Roosevelt (hereafter cited as *FDR Letters*), May 8, 1940, 1024; EO 8405, May 10, 1940; "U.S. Freezes Credit," *NYT*, May 10, 1940, 1; *Press Conf* #642 (May 10, 1940), 15:326–29; Felix Belair Jr., "America Angered, Says Roosevelt," *NYT*, May 11, 1940, 1; "Holland's Queen Protests Invasion," *NYT*, May 10, 1940, 1.

8. *PPA*, "Radio Address Pan American Scientific Congress, Washington, D.C., May 10, 1940."

9. "Roosevelt to Ask for Increase in Funds for Defense Uses," *NYT*, May 14, 1940, 1; *Press Conf* #643 (May 14, 1940), 15:335; "Roosevelt Calls for Preparedness," *NYT*, May 15, 1940, 1; Frank L. Kluckhohn, "President to Ask Billion to Equip an Army of 750,000," *NYT*, May 16, 1940, 1.

10. Conn and Fairchild, *Framework of Hemisphere Defense*, 41–42.

11. *PPA*, "Message to the Congress Asking Additional Appropriations for National Defense, May 16, 1940"; "Roosevelt Asks Billion Fund, 50,000 Planes," *NYT*, May 17, 1940, 1; Greenfield, *American Strategy*, 53. See also Emerson, "Roosevelt as Commander-in-Chief," 185–87.

12. "Congressional Comment Favors Roosevelt Plea Overwhelmingly," *NYT*, May 17, 1940, 12.

13. "Hoover and Dewey Back Defense Plan," *NYT*, May 17, 1940, 15; "Landon Supports New Defense Plan," *NYT*, May 18, 1940, 9; Turner Catledge, "Vandenberg Urges 'Insulated America,'" *NYT*, May 17, 1940, 15; "Gannett Says Speech Indicates a Failure," *NYT*, May 17, 1940, 10.

14. "Public Approves Defense Program," *NYT*, May 26, 1940, 3.

15. *Press Conf* #644 (May 17, 1940), 15:338–49; Felix Belair Jr., "Roosevelt Is Busy," *NYT*, May 18, 1940, 1.

16. *PPA*, "The President Presents Plan No. V of the Reorganization Act, May 22, 1940"; Felix Belair Jr., "President Offers Alien Control Plan," *NYT*, May 23, 1940.

17. 54 Stat. 670; *PPA*, "Statement by the President on Signing the Alien Registration Act, June 29, 1940," and appended note; Francis Biddle, *In Brief Authority*, 106–22.

18. "29 Reds Indicted in Overthrow Plot," *NYT*, July 17, 1941, 7; "18 Guilty of Plot to Disrupt Army," *NYT*, December 2, 1941, 1; "18 Are Sentenced in Sedition Trial," *NYT*, December 9, 1941, 64.

19. Churchill to Roosevelt, May 15, 1940, in Kimball, *Roosevelt and Churchill*, 1:37–38.

20. Roosevelt to Churchill, May 16, 1940, in ibid., 38–39.

21. Churchill to Roosevelt, May 16 and 20, 1940, in ibid., 39–49. The sudden death of Philip Kerr, Lord Lothian (1882–1940), in December was regretted on both sides of the Atlantic.

22. Frank L. Kluckhohn, "President to Form a Defense Board of All Segments," *NYT*, May 26, 1940, 1.

23. *PPA*, "Fireside Chat on National Defense, May 26, 1940"; "President Assures Nation of Safety," *NYT*, May 27, 1940, 1. For an assessment of the fifth-column threat, see Louis de Jong, *The German Fifth Column in the Second World War*.

24. "War Sentiment Seen Rising in U.S.," *NYT*, May 29, 1940, 10; Hadley Cantril, "Impact of the War on the Nation's Viewpoint," *NYT*, June 2, 1940, 67. For the White Committee, see Walter Johnson, *The Battle against Isolation;* and "White Organizes Aid to the Allies," *NYT*, May 20, 1941, 11.

25. "Roosevelt Speaks Tonight on World Crisis," *NYT*, June 10, 1940, 1; *PPA*, "Address, University of Virginia, June 10, 1940"; Felix Belair Jr., "Our Help Is Pledged," *NYT*, June 11, 1940, 1.

26. Churchill to Roosevelt, June 11, 1940 (emphasis in the original), Roosevelt to Churchill, August 15, 1940, in Kimball, *Roosevelt and Churchill*, 1:43–59. Roosevelt's quoted words are from a formal set of hypotheses the president sent to the army planners, from a section headed "The Planners Overruled" in the official U.S. Army history, Maurice Matloff and Edwin N. Snell, *The War Department . . . 1941–42*, 13–21.

27. "Congress Members Applaud the Speech," "Editorials Praise Roosevelt's Speech," and "Dewey Assails Tone of Roosevelt's Talk," *NYT*, June 11, 1940, 7; "Willkie Predicts Six-Ballot Choice," *NYT*, July 11, 1940, 10; "Vandenberg Urges Wide Aid to Allies," *NYT*, June 10, 1940, 7; "Taft's Defense Program," *NYT*, June 11, 1940, 12.

28. *PPA*, "A Request for Appropriations to Relieve Civilian Distress in War-Torn Areas, June 11, 1940"; *Press Conf* #651 (June 11, 1940), 15:557; Felix Belair Jr., "Roosevelt Praises Stop Hitler Ad," *NYT*, June 12, 1940. The ad appeared in eighty-five newspapers. See *NYT*, June 10, 1940, 36. The "Bob" was Roosevelt's habitual informality. Sherwood tells us that, at the time, they had not yet met. Sherwood, *Roosevelt and Hopkins*, 165–68.

29. Turner Catledge, "We Take 'Action Short of War' to Aid Allies," *NYT*, June 9, 1940, E3; "Defense Tax Bill Adopted by House," *NYT*, June 12, 1940, 1; *Press Conf* #643 (May 14, 1940), 15:336; #651 (June 11, 1940), 15:557; "Congress to Stay in Capital in Fear of New War Crisis," *NYT*, June 14, 1940, 1. A 1942 definition of "command economy": "an economic system in which activity is controlled by a central authority and the means of production are publicly owned."

30. Two of the earliest are the muckraking Bruce Catton, *The War Lords of Washington;* and the pseudoscholarly Eliot Janeway, *The Struggle for Survival*.

31. "6 Civilians Named for Coordination of War Resources," *NYT*, August 10, 1939, 1; *PPA*, "A Letter of Thanks [to] the War Resources Board of 1939, Nov. 24, 1939."

32. Frank L. Kluckhohn, "New Dealers See Another Victory," *NYT*, September 28, 1939, 10; "Asked United Rule of War Materials," *NYT*, May 28, 1940, 10, 1. That Early gave the story to Kluckhohn, not to the *Times'* White House correspondent, was no accident: he wanted to point at the older story. Kluckhohn, a respected reporter, made

sure the inspirer's identity was made plain and did not in these stories refer merely to informed sources.

33. *Press Conf* #647 (May 28, 1940), 15:385–94; Felix Belair Jr., "President Sets Up Defense Council to Hasten Arming," *NYT*, May 29, 1940, 1.

34. *PPA*, "The Office of Price Administration and Civilian Supply Is Established, EO 8734, April 11, 1941." The notes and introductions to this and the other three volumes covering the third and fourth terms were written by Rosenman and never seen by the president.

35. Brownlow, *A Passion for Anonymity*, 428–31. Brownlow is in error on one detail: the OEM was brought to life by an administrative order, not an executive order. Freidel, *Rendezvous with Destiny*, 341.

36. *Press Conf* #647A (May 30, 1940), "Conference on National Defense," 15:395–424. This, as noted, is not a press conference—no reporters are present—but a transcript of the initial meeting of the National Defense Advisory Committee. I imagine it is here because of a filing error. The meeting, which took place at the White House, was followed, after a seventy-minute lunch break, by a regular press conference. The notes for both were taken by Roosevelt's shorthand reporter, Henry Kannee, and somehow filed together. When Da Capo Press published the transcripts from FDRL files in 1972, they were printed as found and given a special number, 647A.

37. *Press Conf* #652 (June 14, 1940), 15:564–65. The NDRC was established on June 27, 1940: see *PPA*, "Administrative Order, Jan. 7, 1941." *PPA*, "The Office of Scientific Research Is Established, EO 8807, June 28, 1941," and appended note; Nathan Reingold, "Vannevar Bush's New Deal for Research," pt. 2. During his years as a professor and administrator at MIT, Bush had been an important figure in the development of analog computers. See James Hershberg, *James B. Conant: Harvard to Hiroshima and the Making of the Nuclear Age*. A good brief summary of the achievements of the Bush-Conant organization is George H. Daniels, "Office of Scientific Research and Development," in *Government Agencies*, edited by Donald R. Whitnah, 426–32.

38. *Press Conf* #648 (May 30, 1940), 15:425–38; "Roosevelt Sifts Tools Export Curb," *NYT*, June 14, 1940, 13; "Billions More Aim of Arms Program," *NYT*, June 29, 1940, 1; *Press Conf* #656 (June 28, 1940), 15:601; "The Day in Washington," *NYT*, August 27, 1940, 15.

39. "Knox and Stimson Approved in Survey," *NYT*, July 5, 1940, 28; "Stimson Confirmed by Vote of 56–28," *NYT*, July 10, 1940, 1; "Knox Confirmed by Vote of 66–16," *NYT*, July 11, 1940, 1. Twelve of twenty-two Republicans voted against Stimson; three of the twelve, Vandenberg, Taft, and Danaher of Connecticut, voted for Knox. Louis Johnson was replaced by Stimson's choice, another Republican, Robert P. Patterson (1891–1952), a federal appellate judge originally appointed by Hoover and promoted by Roosevelt in 1939. "Johnson Resigns as Stimson Aide; Patterson Appointed," *NYT*, July 26, 1940, 1. Roosevelt had discussed with Knox appointing him as navy secretary and William J. Donovan as war secretary (*FDR Letters*, December 29, 1939, 975–77).

40. Felix Belair Jr., "Capital Surprised," *NYT*, June 21, 1940, 1. Henry L. Stimson and McGeorge Bundy, *On Active Service in Peace and War*, is an apologia; the quote from his diary is on 353. Richard N. Current, *Secretary Stimson*, is an important brief book-length critique.

41. *Press Conf* #665 (June 18, 1940), 15:181–82; Felix Belair Jr., "Roosevelt Proposes Training for Youth in Vast Training Program," *NYT,* June 19, 1940, 1.

42. For party platforms, see http://presidency.ucsb.edu/ws/. See also Anne O'Hare McCormick, "War Plank Called Shaky Compromise," *NYT,* June 27, 1940, 7.

43. The best contemporary account I have seen is Charles W. Hurd, "Choice Was Made in Day of 15 Hours," *NYT,* June 28, 1940, 3.

44. Charles W. Hurd, "Delegates at Final Session Complete Ticket and Greet Party Leader," *NYT,* June 29, 1940, 2; James A. Hagerty, "Willkie Approves Platform, Opposes Big Campaign Gifts," *NYT,* June 29, 1940, 1; *Press Conf* #656 (June 28, 1940), 15:601; "Roosevelt Willing to Talk to Willkie" and "Billions More Aim of Arms Program," *NYT,* June 29, 1940, 1; Willkie's 1934 comment from Freidel, *Rendezvous with Destiny,* 342.

45. Freidel gives his view, that essentially it was the war that caused him to run, in *Rendezvous with Destiny,* 327–28. For Hopkins's view of both his and Roosevelt's candidacies, see Sherwood, *Roosevelt and Hopkins,* 91–99, 172n92, 938–39. See also George McJimsey, *Harry Hopkins: Ally of the Poor and Defender of Democracy,* 119ff.

46. Sherwood, *Roosevelt and Hopkins,* 172; Freidel, *Rendezvous with Destiny,* 327; Felix Belair Jr., "Will Roosevelt Run?," *NYT,* June 30, 1940, 59.

47. "Tax Bill Is Signed; 2,200,000 Drawn In," *NYT,* June 26, 1940, 9; *PPA,* "A Recommendation for the Enactment of a Steeply Graduated Excess Profits Tax, July 1, 1940," and appended note.

48. *PPA,* "The President Asks for Additional Appropriations for National Defense, July 10, 1940," and appended note; "$4,848,171,957 More Is Asked by Roosevelt for Defense, Not to Send Men to Europe" and "Training Endorsed," *NYT,* July 11, 1940, 1.

49. "War Issues, Led by Aircraft, Strengthen on Plan to Remove Tax Obstacles to Defense Production," *NYT,* July 12, 1940, 23.

50. Rosenman, *Working with Roosevelt,* 104–21; Freidel, *Rendezvous with Destiny,* 343–46; Hull, *Memoirs of Hull,* 1:858–62; David Robertson, *Sly and Able: A Political Biography of James F. Byrnes,* 28–29, 92–93, 290–94.

51. *Press Conf* #660 (July 12, 1940), 16:31–38.

52. For party platforms, see http://presidency.ucsb.edu/ws/. Rosenman, *Working with Roosevelt,* 211–12; Turner Catledge, "Platform Trouble," *NYT,* July 16, 1940, 1.

53. Turner Catledge, "Platform Trouble," *NYT,* July 16, 1940, 1; James A. Hagerty, "'Stay Out' Plank," *NYT,* July 18, 1940, 1.

54. Charles W. Hurd, "Opponents of Third Term Ponder on How to Put Issue to Convention," *NYT,* July 15, 1940, 1; Anne O'Hare McCormick, "Democrats Glum Facing Inevitable," *NYT,* July 16, 1940, 6. The only previous use of the word *Negro* had been the 1868 Democratic platform, which denounced the Freedmen's Bureau and "Negro supremacy."

55. *Press Conf* #661 (July 16, 1940), 16:148.

56. *PPA,* "The President States He Does Not Seek to Be a Candidate for a Third Term, July 16, 1940."

57. Hull, *Memoirs,* 1:858–59.

58. Freidel, *Rendezvous with Destiny,* 344; "Roosevelt Renominated on First Ballot," *NYT,* July 17, 1940.

59. Kathleen McLaughlin, "No Campaigning, First Lady States," *NYT,* July 19, 1940, 1. This contains the text of ER's speech.

60. Rosenman, *Working with Roosevelt,* 215–18, prints both the initial and the final versions and names "Pa and Mrs. Watson, Steve Early, Ross McIntire, Dan Callaghan, Missy, Grace, and several others" as present.

61. Henry N. Dorris, "Delegates Balked at Wallace Choice," "For Vice President," "Stadium Crowded for Balloting," and "Sharp Floor Fight," *NYT,* July 19, 1940, 3, 1; Rosenman, *Working with Roosevelt,* 219.

62. *PPA,* "The President Accepts the Nomination for a Third Term, July 19, 1940"; Sidney M. Shallett, "But Silence Came as Leader Spoke," "Roosevelt, Accepting, Feels He Must Serve," and "President Speaks as If in Presence," *NYT,* July 19, 1940, 2, 1.

Chapter 4. Winning an Election, Addressing the World

1. "President Sleeps Far into Forenoon," *NYT,* July 20, 1940, 1; "President Prolongs Cruise on Potomac," *NYT,* July 21, 1940, 2; *PPA,* "A Recommendation for Legislation to Assist the Other American Republics to Finance the Marketing of Their Surplus Products, July 22, 1940," and attached note, and "The President Recommends Adoption of Habana Agreement . . ., Sept. 13, 1940," and attached note; Hull, *Memoirs,* 1:791–92, 813–30. Hull's overheated chapter is titled "Assault on the Hemisphere."

2. *Press Conf* #662 (July 23, 1940), 16:50–60; "Burke Bolts Party over Third Term," *NYT,* July 19, 1940, 1; "Third Term Revolt Voiced in Chicago," *NYT,* July 22, 1940, 1; "Douglas and Hanes Join Willkie Ranks," *NYT,* July 23, 1940, 1; Charles W. Hurd, "Roosevelt Ironic on Former Backers Who Go to Willkie," *NYT,* July 24, 1940, 1.

3. James A. Hagerty, "Farley Explains," *NYT,* July 20, 1940, 1; "2 Reverse Stand against 3d Term" and "Ban on Third Term Opposed in Survey," *NYT,* July 24, 1940, 15.

4. Charles W. Hurd, "France Discussed in Hyde Park Talks," *NYT,* July 22, 1940, 11; "104 War Refugees Get New Mass Visa," *NYT,* July 24, 1940, 1; *Press Conf* #663 (July 26, 1940), 16:70; "Refugee Aid Funds Asked by President; $125,000 Sought for Expenses of Federal Children's Bureau," *NYT,* August 2, 1940, 17; Frank L. Kluckhohn, "Roosevelt Moves to Help Red Cross and Refugees," *NYT,* July 28, 1940, 1. For the French-based rescue operation, see the memoir by one of FDR's agents: Varian Fry, *Surrender on Demand*; and essays in Jarrell C. Jackman and Carla M. Borden, eds., *The Muses Flee Hitler: Cultural Transfer and Adaptation, 1930–1945.* Among those rescued were Marc Chagall, Marcel Duchamp, Lion Feuchtwanger, Wanda Landowska, Jacques Lipchitz, Heinrich Mann, Anna Mahler Werfel, and Franz Werfel. For the Children's Bureau's efforts, see Lindenmeyer, *"Right to Childhood,"* 210–14. For a memoir by one of the British children, see Anthony Bailey, *America, Lost & Found.* The United States Committee for the Care of European Children was founded in the summer of 1940 by Clarence E. Pickett (1884–1965), leader of the American Friends Service Committee. See Allan W. Austin, *Quaker Brotherhood: Interracial Activism and the American Friends Service Committee, 1917–1950.*

5. John Morton Blum, *Roosevelt and Morgenthau,* 329–31. Purvis is a little-known but important figure in the history of the British American collaboration in World War II. Robert Skidelsky, *John Maynard Keynes,* 3:96, 113, 115.

6. John H. Crider, "Ban Affects Japan," *NYT*, July 26, 1940, 1; *Press Conf* #663 (July 26, 1940), 16:62–63.

7. "President Goes on Cruise," *NYT*, July 28, 1940, 25; *Press Conf* #664 (July 29, 1940), 16:71–77; Charles W. Hurd, "President Views Our New Defenses," *NYT*, July 30, 1940, 1.

8. *PPA*, "The President Asks Authority to Call Out the National Guard, July 29, 1940," and appended note; Frank N. Kluckhohn, "Roosevelt Asks a Year's Training of National Guard" and "President's National Guard Plan," *NYT*, July 30, 1940, 1, 11.

9. *Press Conf* #666 (August 2, 1940), 16:84–89; Charles Hurd, "Need of Men Vital," *NYT*, August 3, 1940, 1; "Marshall Urges Speeding of Draft," *NYT*, August 6, 1940.

10. "Democrats Elect Flynn to Succeed Farley," *NYT*, August 2, 1940, 1; "Farley Withdraws from Cabinet," *NYT*, August 9, 1940, 1, letters appended; "Roosevelt Names Walker to Succeed Farley," *NYT*, September 1, 1940, 1.

11. "Wickard Is Named to Wallace's Post," *NYT*, August 20, 1940, 13, letters appended; Dean Albertson, *Roosevelt's Farmer: Claude R. Wickard in the New Deal*.

12. Charles Hurd, "Hopkins: Right-Hand Man," 6, 22; Bertram D. Hulen, "Hopkins Resigns from Cabinet," *NYT*, August 25, 1940, 34, letters appended.

13. UP, "Jones Silent on Offer," *NYT*, August 25, 1940, 34; "Would Let Jones Keep Loan Post," *NYT*, August 7, 1940, 34; "Jesse Jones to Take Oath," *NYT*, September 19, 1940, 32; "Text of Roosevelt Speech at Washington Airport," *NYT*, September 29, 1940, 22. The ad-lib is *not* in the version in *PPA*, "An Airport Like This Is Important to the National Defense.' Address at New Washington National Airport," September 28, 1940.

14. *Press Conf* #667 (August 6, 1940), 16:98. Kimball, *Forged in War*, 56, says Churchill "repeatedly begged" for the destroyers.

15. *Press Conf* #669 and #670 (August 10, 12, 1940), 16:110–22; Charles Hurd, "Defense Program Hitting Its Stride, President Asserts," *NYT*, August 11, 1940, 1; "President Visits Newport and New London," *NYT*, August 12, 1940, 1.

16. *Press Conf* #671 (August 16, 1940), 16:123–29; "U.S. Is Negotiating for British Bases, Plan for Canada," *NYT*, August 17, 1940, 1; Charles Hurd, "Roosevelt to See Mackenzie King," August 17, 1940, 9.

17. Frank L. Kluckhohn, "Leases Proposed," *NYT*, August 16, 1940, 1.

18. Kenneth Campbell, "Army Is Inspected by the President," *NYT*, August 18, 1940, 3.

19. *PPA*, "White House Statement on Establishment of Joint Board on Defense of Canada and the United States, Aug. 18, 1940," and appended note; *Press Conf* #672 (August 17, 1940), 16:130–33; Charles Hurd, "U.S.-Canada Ties Welded by President and Premier," *NYT*, August 18, 1940, 1; "Joint-Board to Act," *NYT*, August 19, 1940, 1; "President Hurries U.S.-Canada Plan," *NYT*, August 20, 1940, 1; "Roosevelt Puts Canada Pact First," *NYT*, August 21, 1940, 1; "President Works on Canada Accord," *NYT*, August 22, 1940, 1; "Two Capitals Act," *NYT*, August 23, 1940, 1; William R. Conklin, "Board to Stress Canadian Coast," *NYT*, August 28, 1940, 7. For the Joint Board, see Stanley W. Dziuban, *Military Relations between the United States and Canada, 1939–1945*. It was most useful in coordinating logistic support for Alaska after Pearl Harbor.

20. "Elwood Visitors Nearly Swamp It," *NYT*, August 18, 1940, 35; Anne O'Hare McCormick, "Man of the Middle West."

21. James A. Hagerty, "Willkie for Draft Training" and "Text of the Address of Wendell Willkie," *NYT*, August 18, 1940, 1, 33. Willkie's text is also at http://presidency.ucsb.edu/ws/ in the category "Convention Speeches." "'No Real Choice' Left, Says Norman Thomas," *NYT*, August 18, 1940, 31. The first was Kennedy-Nixon in 1960; the first with an incumbent president, Carter-Ford in 1976; and the first with an elected incumbent, Carter-Reagan in 1980.

22. *Press Conf* #673 (August 20, 1940), 16:137; Turner Catledge, "Ickes Belittles Willkie Address as Demagoguery" and "Text of Secretary Ickes' Address . . .," *NYT*, August 20, 1940, 1, 14; Ickes, *Secret Diary*, 3:300–308.

23. *PPA*, "President's Statement on Signing Two More Statutes, Aug. 23, 1940"; "Roosevelt Signs Trust Measure," *NYT*, August 24, 1940, 17; "U.S. Voters Favor Calling of Guard," *NYT*, August 16, 1940, 6.

24. *PPA*, "The President Begins to Call Out the National Guard, EO 8530, Aug. 31, 1940"; Henry R. Dorris, "House Approves Final Guard Bill," *NYT*, August 23, 1940, 1; "Roosevelt Signs Bill to Call Guard," *NYT*, August 29, 1940, 1.

25. I have combined remarks made in *Press Conf* #675 (August 27, 1940), 16:156–57, with those written in *PPA* (appended note on National Defense, 1940 volume, 206).

26. Charles Hurd, "Roosevelt Aide Hits Willkie's Use of Defense Report," *NYT*, September 2, 1940, 1; *PPA*, "Address at Chickamauga Dam, Sept. 2, 1940," and appended note, and " . . . Address at Dedication of Great Smoky Mountains National Park, Sept. 2, 1940"; Charles Hurd, "Roosevelt Calls on Nation to Unite for Total Defense; Won't Sacrifice Social Gains," *NYT*, September 3, 1940, 1. The huge complex erected at Oak Ridge, Tennessee, in which TVA electricity was essential in creating the first atomic devices. See Charles W. Johnson and Charles O. Jackson, *City behind a Fence: Oak Ridge, Tennessee, 1942–1946*.

27. Charles Hurd, "Roosevelt Hails Gain of New Bases," *NYT*, September 4, 1940, 1; *Press Conf* #667 (September 3, 1940), 16:173–91; *PPA*, "The President Informs the Congress of [Destroyer-Bases Deal], Sept. 3, 1940"; James A. Hagerty, "Willkie for Pact, but Hits Secrecy," *NYT*, September 4, 1940, 1. The version of the press conference printed in his *Public Papers* calls it "a good trade." *PPA*, "Press Conference. . . . Sep. 3, 1940." In his memoir, Alsop names the leaker as John Foster but says nothing about alerting Cohen but mentions giving it to the "Century Group" (*"I've Seen the Best of It,"* 145–46).

28. Conn and Fairchild, *Framework of Hemisphere Defense*, 39–61; William Lasser, *Benjamin V. Cohen: Architect of the New Deal*, 216–31; Kimball, *Roosevelt and Churchill*, 1:56–69; J. R. M. Butler, *History of the Second World War*, 244–45; Ickes, *Secret Diary*, 3:233; W. Johnson, *The Battle against Isolation*, 114–17; "No Legal Bar Seen to Transfer of Destroyers," *NYT*, August 11, 1940, 58–59; Robert H. Jackson, *That Man: An Insider's Portrait of Franklin D. Roosevelt*, 103; Hull, *Memoirs*, 1:831–43; *FDR Letters*, 4:1056–57. The short-lived use of "Pan-American" was intended to disguise the fact that these were, essentially, military facilities. The signers were Charles C. Burlingham (1859–1959), a leading member of the New York Bar who had opposed FDR's Court-packing plan, Thomas D. Thacher (1881–1950), Hoover's solicitor general; George

Rublee; and Dean Acheson. All were members of the Century Group. Cohen was not publicly associated with the letter.

29. "Comment by Press on British Accord" and "Congress Ranks Split on Accord," *NYT,* September 4, 1940, 13, 16; Charles Hurd, "Democrats Hail Action on Bases," *NYT,* September 5, 1940, 1; "Ship Deal Backed in Gallup Survey," *NYT,* September 6, 1940, 12; James A. Hagerty, "Willkie Condemns Destroyer Trade," *NYT,* September 7, 1940, 8.

30. "The President Greets a New Cabinet Member," *NYT,* September 12, 1940, 16; *PPA,* "Address at Teamsters Union Convention, Washington, D.C., Sept. 11, 1940"; Louis Stark, "Roosevelt Backs Draft of Industry; Hails Labor Gains," *NYT,* September 12, 1940, 1.

31. Charles Hurd, "President Asks Fitness Training," *NYT,* September 13, 1940, 10; *Press Conf* #680 (September 13, 1940), 16:206–15; *PPA,* "A Statement of General Principles Governing the Letting of Defense Contracts, Sept. 13, 1940"; "Basic Policies Set on Defense Work," *NYT,* September 14, 1940, 9.

32. "Final Roll Calls on Draft Bill," *NYT,* September 15, 1940, 31; Frank L. Kluckhohn, "Final Vote 58 to 31," *NYT,* August 29, 1940, 1; Harold B. Hinton, "House Votes 185–155 for Delaying Draft to Test Recruitment," *NYT,* September 6, 1940, 1; "House Bars Change in 21–45 Age Limits of Draft Measure," *NYT,* September 7, 1940, 1; "House Votes Conscription; 60-Day Delay," *NYT,* September 8, 1940, 1; Harold B. Hinton, "Draft Bill Ready for Passage Today," *NYT,* September 13, 1940, 10; "Upset in Senate Sends Draft Bill Back for Revision," *NYT,* September 14, 1940, 1; "Draft Fund Asked," *NYT,* September 15, 1940, 1; "Health Committee Set Up for Defense," *NYT,* September 20, 1940, 13.

33. "How the Draft Will Affect the Nation's Manpower and Industrial Resources" and "Text of the Selective Service Measure," *NYT,* September 15, 1940, 30–31; *PPA,* "Registration Day Is Proclaimed, Proclamation No. 2425, Sept. 16, 1940"; Charles Hurd, "400,000 by Jan. 1," *NYT,* September 17, 1940, 1; *PPA,* "A Letter to All Governors Asking Their Cooperation in Carrying Out the Selective Service Act, Sept. 21, 1940"; Charles Hurd, "Roosevelt Asks the 48 Governors to Help the Draft," *NYT,* September 24, 1940, 1; "Roosevelt Signs Excess Profits Tax," *NYT,* October 10, 1940, 39.

34. "Hershey Is Named to High Draft Post," *NYT,* September 30, 1940, 9; "Draft Directorate Offered Dykstra," *NYT,* October 10, 1940, 14; "Confirms Dykstra as Head of Draft," *NYT,* October 16, 1940, 10; George Q. Flynn, *Louis B. Hershey;* Wolfgang Saxon, "General Became a Symbol," *NYT,* May 21, 1977, 1.

35. Allan M. Winkler, *"To Everything There Is a Season": Pete Seeger and the Power of Song,* 29; "First Lady Assails Guild on Draft," *NYT,* September 15, 1940, 28; "First Lady Expands Her Views on Draft," *NYT,* September 17, 1940, 23.

36. "Roosevelt Leads in Honoring Bankhead for Long Career," *NYT,* September 16, 1940, 10; "Rayburn Elected in House Tradition," *NYT,* September 17, 1940, 19; Anthony Champagne, *Congressman Sam Rayburn;* "President Mourns at Bankhead Bier," *NYT,* September 18, 1940, 16; "House Democrats Name McCormack as Their Leader," *NYT,* September 26, 1940, 1.

37. *Press Conf* #681 (September 20, 1940), 16:216–18; *PPA,* "Address at the University of Pennsylvania, Sept. 20, 1940"; "President Voices Faith in the Many Rather than the 'Elite,'" *NYT,* September 21, 1940, 1.

38. "Roosevelts Honor Head of Family, 86," *NYT*, September 22, 1940, 41; Charles Hurd, "Roosevelt Names Advisers on Draft," *NYT*, September 22, 1940, 41; "Channing Tobias of NAACP Dead," *NYT*, November 6, 1961, 37; Charles Hurd, "Petition President to Spur British Aid," *NYT*, September 28, 1940, 2.

39. Robert L. Zangrando, *The NAACP Crusade against Lynching, 1909–1950*, 155; N. Weiss, *Farewell to the Party of Lincoln*, 246–48; Charles Hurd, "Independents Join to Back Roosevelt," *NYT*, September 25, 1940, 1; "Mayor Says Labor Backs Roosevelt . . . First Lady Also Addresses the Convention," *NYT*, September 17, 1940, 23.

40. N. Weiss, *Farewell to the Party of Lincoln*, 274–76; John Prados, *The White House Tapes: Eavesdropping on the President*, 30–38. See Prados's *White House Tapes*, which contains DVDs of some tapes including that of the September 27, 1940, conference. The quality of the FDR era recordings is poor. An earlier work, William Doyle, *Inside the Oval Office: The White House Tapes from FDR to Clinton*, provides a wider sampling of the FDR recordings. Both books report Stimson in the conference; he was not present.

41. N. Weiss, *Farewell to the Party of Lincoln*, 277–80; "Draft Directorate Offered Dykstra," *NYT*, October 10, 1940, 24; *Press Conf* #692 (October 25, 1940), 16:286–87; "Emmons Promoted as Army Air Head; Colonel B. O. Davis Is First Negro to Be Brig. General," *NYT*, October 26, 1940, 4.

42. Frank L. Kluckhohn, "Roosevelt Moves," *NYT*, September 27, 1940, 1; DALLEK, 240–41; *Press Conf* #683 (September 27, 1940), 16:227–32; Charles Hurd, "Hull Sees No Shift," *NYT*, September 28, 1940, 1.

43. *PPA*, "Procedure for Taking over Plants, Sept. 26, 1940"; "President Defines Plant Draft Steps," *NYT*, September 29, 1940; "Roosevelt Holds 2 Parties Eternal," *NYT*, September 28, 1940, 6.

44. "President on Cruise," *NYT*, September 29, 1940, 24; *Press Conf* #684 (September 30, 1940), 16:233–38; Charles Hurd, "President Views Expansion of Defense," *NYT*, October 1, 1940, 1.

45. "Willkie Treated for Hoarse Throat," *NYT*, September 15, 1940, 3; James A. Hagerty, "Willkie Improved, Will Speak Today," *NYT*, September 16, 1940, 1; Robert E. Burke, "The Election of 1940," in *History of American Presidential Elections*, edited by Arthur M. Schlesinger Jr., 291–46.

46. James A. Hagerty, "Willkie Says That Roosevelt 'Promoted' the Munich Pact," *NYT*, September 15, 1940, 1; "Willkie Predicts Dictatorship If Roosevelt Wins," *NYT*, September 17, 1940, 1; "Willkie Acclaims Senator Johnson as True Liberal," *NYT*, September 19, 1940, 1; "Willkie Charges New Deal Policies Helped Bring War," September 22, 1940, 1.

47. *Press Conf* #685 (October 1, 1940), 16:240; "Roosevelt Scores Willkie Attacker," *NYT*, October 2, 1940, 15; Rosenman, *Working with Roosevelt*, 127–55; John Mason Brown, *The Worlds of Robert E. Sherwood: Mirror to His Times, 1896–1939* and *The Ordeal of a Playwright*; Sherwood, *Roosevelt and Hopkins*, 49–50.

48. Robert J. C. Butow, "The FDR Tapes: Secret Recordings Made in the Oval Office of the President in the Autumn of 1940."

49. *PPA*, "Address at Dedication of Three New Schools, Hyde Park, N.Y., Oct. 5, 1940"; Charles Hurd, "Roosevelt Calls Our Free Schools a Bar to Tyranny," *NYT*, October 6, 1940, 1.

50. Charles Hurd, "Roosevelt Visits Watervliet Today," *NYT*, October 7, 1940, 5; "President Views Cannon Assembly," *NYT*, October 8, 1940, 11; *Press Conf* #687 (October 7, 1940), 16:257–58.

51. "President Starts on 2-State Tour," *NYT*, October 11, 1940, 1; Charles Hurd, "We Can Avoid War If We Speed Arms, President Asserts," *NYT*, October 12, 1940, 1; "Reply to Axis," *NYT*, October 13, 1940, 1; *PPA*, "Address on Hemisphere Defense, Dayton, Ohio, Oct. 12, 1940."

52. *PPA*, "Radio Address for the 1940 Mobilization on Human Needs, Oct. 13, 1940"; "Roosevelt Urges Private Gifts to Aid National Morale," *NYT*, October 14, 1940, 1; *PPA*, "A Message to the Registrants under the Selective Service Law from the President, Oct. 16, 1940" and "Radio Address on Registration Day, Oct. 16, 1940"; Charles Hurd, "President Speaks," *NYT*, October 17, 1940, 1.

53. "Roosevelt Plans Two Political Talks," *NYT*, October 16, 1940, 1; *Press Conf* #689 (October 15, 1940), 16:272; "Roosevelt to Make Political Tour, with 5 Major Speeches," *NYT*, October 18, 1940, 1; *Press Conf* #690 (October 18, 1940), 16:275–80; "Rivals Falsifying, Roosevelt Asserts," *NYT*, October 19, 1940, 1.

54. Charles Hurd, "Roosevelt Is Host to Earl of Athlone in Hyde Park Home," *NYT*, October 20, 1940, 1; "Earl of Athlone in Hyde Park Talks," *NYT*, October 21, 1940, 1; *PPA*, "A Greeting on the Anniversary Celebration of the New York World's Fair, Oct. 16, 1940"; "President Praises Negroes at Fair," *NYT*, October 21, 1940, 20.

55. *Press Conf* #691 (October 22, 1940), 16:281–85; Charles Hurd, "Roosevelt Again Voices Confidence on Campaign Trend," *NYT*, October 23, 1940, 1; "Roosevelt Attacks 'Falsifications' in Opening Campaign in Philadelphia" and "Mr. Roosevelt in Rebuttal," October 24, 1940, 1, 24; *PPA*, "Rear Platform Remarks on Liberty at Wilmington, Delaware, Oct. 23, 1940" and "Address at Philadelphia, Pennsylvania, Oct. 23, 1940."

56. *PPA*, "Radio Address to the New York 'Herald Tribune' Forum, Oct. 24, 1940"; "Nation Undaunted, Roosevelt Asserts," *NYT*, October 25, 1940, 1.

57. Louis Stark, "Lewis Declares for Willkie," *NYT*, October 26, 1940, 1, Lewis's prepared text at 12; "Lewis Repudiated, Backed by Labor; Hull Hits Address," *NYT*, October 27, 1940, 1; "Lewis Stand Laid to Demands Defied," *NYT*, October 31, 1940, 1.

58. "Crowds in Jersey Block Cavalcade," "Roosevelt Is Seen by 2,000,000 in City," and "Farley Rides to Garden in the President's Car," *NYT*, October 29, 1940, 13, 14, 17; *PPA*, "Campaign Address at Madison Square Garden, Oct. 28, 1940"; Frank S. Adams, "Roosevelt Says Opposition Hindered Defense," *NYT*, October 29, 1940, 1.

59. "Early Admits 'Giving the Knee' to Policeman Who Tried to Bar Him from President's Train," *NYT*, October 30, 1940, 16; "'Kneed' Policeman Gives Interview with the Sanction of Valentine," *NYT*, October 31, 1941, 25; Byron Darnton, "Joe Louis Tours City for Willkie," *NYT*, November 1, 1940, 20; N. Weiss, *Farewell to the Party of Lincoln*, 280–82; Linda Lotridge Levin, *The Making of FDR: The Story of Stephen T. Early, America's First Modern Press Secretary*, 224–25; *Press Conf* #698 (November 29, 1940), 16:330. The index to the 1940 press conferences lists, under "Early, Steve": "Jokes about recent publicity about Early."

60. *PPA*, "Radio Address on the Occasion [Drawing Draft Numbers], Washington, D.C., Oct. 29, 1940"; "First Draft Number Is 158," "Kennedy Urges Re-election of Roo-

sevelt," and "Roosevelt Starts Trip to Boston," *NYT*, October 30, 1940, 1, 16, Kennedy's speech on 8.

61. "President Assails Appeals to 'Fear,'" *NYT*, October 31, 1941, 14.

62. Sherwood, *Roosevelt and Hopkins*, 191; Rosenman, *Working with Roosevelt*, 241–42. Sherwood's full version of the final quotation is: "Of course we'll fight if attacked. If somebody attacks us, then it isn't a foreign war is it? Or do they want me to guarantee that our troops will not be sent into battle only in the event of another Civil War?"

63. *PPA*, "Campaign Address at Boston, Massachusetts, Oct. 30, 1940." The *New York Times* gave roughly equal space to Roosevelt's speech and one by Willkie in Baltimore. Charles Hurd, "President Moves. But Our Youth Won't Go into Any Foreign War, He Says at Boston," and James A. Haggerty, "Willkie Cites Past. Says President's Failure on 1932 Pledges Means War If He Is Elected," *NYT*, October 31, 1940, 1. Note that the playwright gives himself the best line. Rosenman mentions only the president and himself in his account published four years after Sherwood's. Rosenman, *Working with Roosevelt*, 242–43. Surely, some of the others said something.

64. "Willkie's Boston Speech Urging a Responsible Government," *NYT*, October 12, 1940, 9; Ellsworth Barnard, *Wendell Willkie, Fighter for Freedom*, 258; Steve Neal, *Dark Horse: A Biography of Wendell Willkie*, 158; "Verbatim Testimony of Wendell Willkie in Answer to Questions Put to Him by Senators," *NYT*, February 12, 1941, 4–6.

65. Rosenman, *Working with Roosevelt*, 242.

66. *PPA*, "Address at the Dedication of the National Institute of Health, Bethesda, Maryland, Oct. 31, 1940," and appended note; "President Assures Medical Freedom," *NYT*, November 1, 1940, 1.

67. *Press Conf* #693 (November 1, 1940), 16:292–97; *PPA*, "Campaign Address in Brooklyn, Nov. 1, 1940"; Russell B. Porter, "Roosevelt Charges 'Unholy Alliance' of Radicals-Reactionaries," *NYT*, November 2, 1940, 1; U.S. Department of Commerce. *Historical Statistics of the United States: Colonial Times to 1957*, Series D 696–707, 95 (hereafter cited as *HIST STATS*).

68. *PPA*, "Extemporaneous Remarks at Rochester, N.Y., . . . at Buffalo, N.Y., Nov. 2, 1940"; "President Assails 'War Whispering'" and Charles Hurd, "Third Term Last," *NYT*, November 3, 1940, 41, 1; Rosenman, *Working with Roosevelt*, 248. Dorothy Thompson (1893–1961), who once shared the op-ed page of the *Herald Tribune* with Walter Lippmann, is now largely forgotten. Her second husband, Sinclair Lewis, once quipped, only half in jest, that he hoped for her to be elected president so he could write "My Day."

69. Charles Hurd, "Goes to Hyde Park," *NYT*, November 4, 1940, 1; *PPA*, "Final Radio Speech of the 1940 Presidential Campaign, Hyde Park, N.Y., Nov. 4, 1940"; "Hyde Park Appeal," *NYT*, November 5, 1940, 1; Sherwood, *Roosevelt and Hopkins*, 197.

70. Charles Hurd, "Roosevelt Looks to Difficult Days" and "Willkie Retires, Refusing to Give Up; He Declines Any Statement before Today," *NYT*, November 6, 1940, 1; Charles Hurd, "Willkie Telegram," *NYT*, November 7, 1940, 1; James C. Hagerty, "'Loyal Opposition' to New Deal Urged in Willkie Speech," *NYT*, November 12, 1940, 1, Willkie's speech on 12.

71. The most convenient compilation of election data is the county-by-county re-sults, 1932–44, in Edgar E. Robinson, *They Voted for Roosevelt,* 41–182. *Press Conf* #694 (November 8, 1940), 16:298–307; "Surveys of the Election," "Result in Balance in Gallup Survey," "55.2% of Popular Vote Given to Roosevelt in Survey That Ended on Oct. 31," *NYT,* November 4, 1940, 1, 11. For efforts of Gallup and others to rationalize their "success," see "Gallup Cites Surveys' Success," *NYT,* November 7, 1940, 15; "Re-publican Center Shifts Westward," *NYT,* November 9, 1940, 8; "Majority Believed That President Would Win," *NYT,* November 13, 1940, 16; "Dr. Gallup Defends Accuracy of Poll" and "Value of Public Opinion Polls Reweighed," November 17, 1940, 28, 76.

72. David M. Kennedy, *Freedom from Fear: The American People in Depression and War,* 453–64; David Reynolds, *From Munich to Pearl Harbor: Roosevelt's America and the Origins of the Second World War,* 101.

73. Charles Hurd, "Washington Hails Roosevelt Return," *NYT,* November 8, 1941, 1; "President Allots Planes to Britain on a Basis of 50–50," November 9, 1941, 1; *Press Conf* #694 (November 8, 1940), 16:298–307.

74. *PPA,* "An Increase in Funds for the FHA, Nov. 8, 1940," and appended note; Lee E. Cooper, "Higher Loan Fund to Aid FHA Work," *NYT,* November 24, 1940, RE1; *PPA,* "Address on Armistice Day, Arlington National Cemetery, Nov. 11, 1940," "A Greeting to the American Federation of Labor, Nov. 13, 1940," and "The Neutrality of the United States in the War between Italy and Greece, Proclamation No. 2444, Nov. 15, 1940."

75. *PPA,* "The President Thanks the Many Senders of Congratulations on His Re-election, Nov. 13, 1940"; "The President Calls for Unity in U.S.," *NYT,* November 14, 1940, 17; "Roosevelt Fishing on York River," *NYT,* November 18, 1940, 2; Wayne S. Cole, *America First: The Battle against Intervention.*

76. "Envoy Flies Here," *NYT,* November 23, 1940, 1; Frank L. Kluckhohn, "Lothian to Discuss Britain's Credits with Roosevelt," and Turner Catledge, "Hope High, Lothian Tells Roosevelt," November 25, 1940, 1; *Press Conf* #697 (November 26, 1940), 16:324, DALLEK, 242–43. Many accounts have Lothian saying "Well, boys, Britain's broke; it's your money we want." The curious source for this seems to be John W. Wheeler-Bennett, *King George VI: His Life and Reign,* 521, which gives no source. It is all but impossible to believe that those words, if spoken, were not reported at a well-covered press conference with New York City reporters.

77. "Defense Taxes Levy Is Next Capital Task," *NYT,* November 26, 1940, 17; *Press Conf* #697 (November 26, 1940), 16:320–29; Frank L. Kluckhohn, "President Carves Spending for All Except Defenses," *NYT,* November 27, 1940, 1; *Press Conf* #698 (No-vember 29, 1940), 16:332.

78. *PPA,* "Presidential Statement on Financial Aid to China, Nov. 30, 1940," and appended note; "Roosevelt Holds War Relief Conference," *NYT,* November 29, 1940, 1; "Knudsen Sees President," *NYT,* December 11, 1940, 47; Frank L. Kluckhohn, "Presi-dent Leaves Capital for Miami," *NYT,* December 3, 1940, 14.

79. *Press Conf* #699 (December 3, 1940), 16:337–39; "President Sails with Naval Pomp on Silent Cruise," *NYT,* December 4, 1940, 1; Milton Bracker, "Windsor Confers with Roosevelt on Island Bases," *NYT,* December 14, 1940; *Press Conf* #700 and #701 (December 13–14, 1940), 16:340–49; Frank L. Kluckhohn, "President Implies Agency Bill Veto," *NYT,* December 15, 1949, 1; Sherwood, *Roosevelt and Hopkins,* 224.

80. The *New York Times* first used the term in a business-page story apparently quoting from the trade magazine *Iron Age*. "Speeding-Up Seen in Steel Industry," *NYT*, December 25, 1940, 35. A reporter used it in a press conference question on December 31. *Press Conf* #705, 16:393. Roosevelt used it repeatedly from January 1941.

81. Frank L. Kluckhohn, "Roosevelt Hints at Crisis in Saying 'If World Survives,'" *NYT*, December 16, 1940, 1; "More War Buying Hinges on U.S. Aid," *NYT*, December 18, 1940, 10; *Press Conf* #702 (December 17, 1940), 16:350–65; Frank L. Kluckhohn, "Roosevelt Would Lend Arms to Britain," *NYT*, December 18, 1940, 1.

82. *Press Conf* #703, 703A (December 20, 1940), 16:366–83; Frank L. Kluckhohn, "President Names a Four-Man Board for Defense Drive," *NYT*, December 21, 1940, 1; *PPA*, "The Office of Production Management Is Set Up, EO 8629 and Administrative Order, Jan. 7, 1941."

83. *PPA*, "The President's Christmas Greeting to the Nation, Dec. 24, 1940"; "Nation Will See Gayest Christmas since the Slump" and Frank L. Kluckhohn, "President Says Christmas Signifies Bettering World in 'Voluntary Way,'" *NYT*, December 25, 1940, 1.

84. Rosenman, *Working with Roosevelt*, 256–65; Sherwood, *Roosevelt and Hopkins*, 226–28; Lawrence W. Levine and Cornelia R. Levine, *The People and the President: America's Conversation with FDR*, 308–15; Frank L. Kluckhohn, "Roosevelt to Specify Aid to Britain," *NYT*, December 27, 1940, 1; Harold B. Hinton, "President Works All Day on Chat," and "President's Radio Audience Alone Is Estimated 80,000,000," *NYT*, December 29, 1940, 1, 12; *PPA*, "Fireside Chat on National Security, Dec. 29, 1940"; Turner Catledge, "Roosevelt Calls for Greater Aid to Britain," *NYT*, December 30, 1940, 1.

Chapter 5. Sailing toward War

1. *Press Conf* #706 (January 3, 1941), 17:1–9; Frank L. Kluckhohn, "Roosevelt Starts Rush Plan to Build 200 Merchant Ships," and Turner Catledge, "President Sending Hopkins to Britain," *NYT*, January 4, 1941, 1.

2. Raymond Daniell, "U.S. Aid Is Decisive, Churchill Asserts," *NYT*, January 10, 1941, 1; Sherwood, *Roosevelt and Hopkins*, 230–33; Henry H. Adams, *Harry Hopkins: A Biography*, 189–230.

3. *PPA*, "Annual Message . . ., Jan. 6, 1941," plus appended note; Frank L. Kluckhohn, "Roosevelt Asks All-Out Aid for Democracies," *NYT*, January 7, 1941, 1; Rosenman, *Working with Roosevelt*, 263.

4. Laurie Norton Moffatt, "Norman Rockwell," *ANB*. See also Susan E. Meyers, *Norman Rockwell's World War II: Impressions from the Homefront*; and Stuart Murray and James McCabe, *Norman Rockwell's Four Freedoms: Images That Inspired a Nation*.

5. "Congress Reaction Largely Favorable," *NYT*, January 7, 1941, 1.

6. *PPA*, "Annual Budget Message, Jan. 3, 1941"; Turner Catledge, "1942 Defense Budget $17,485,528,049," and "Plans Offered to Control Budget," January 1, 1941, 1.

7. *Press Conf* #708 (January 8, 1941), 17:52–53; *PPA*, "The Office of Production Management Is Set Up . . ., EO 8629 and Administrative Order, Jan. 7, 1941," and appended note; Frank L. Kluckhohn, "Full Power Given Knudsen, Hillman in Defense Output," *NYT*, January 8, 1941, 1. For Minton, see David N. Anderson, "From New Deal Liberal to Supreme Court Conservative."

8. *Press Conf* #709 (January 11, 1941), 17:56–57; Turner Catledge, "Congress Gets Bill Today to Give Roosevelt Power for 'All Out' Anti-Axis Aid," *NYT*, January 10, 1940, 1; "President Calls for Swift Action," "Bill Interpreted by Two Leaders," "Opposition Starts," and "Hoover and Dewey Criticize Bill," *NYT*, January 11, 1941, 1; UP, "Landon Condemns Bill," *NYT*, January 11, 1941, 4.

9. "Willkie Endorses 'All-Out' Aid Bill," *NYT*, January 13, 1941, 1 (his statement is on 4); "Congress Reaction on Willkie Varies," *NYT*, January 13, 1941, 4; Turner Catledge, "Roosevelt Has a Talk with Willkie," *NYT*, January 20, 1941, 1; Neal, *Dark Horse*, 181–230; *FDR Letters*, January 19, 1941, 2:1109. The verse is from Longfellow, "The Building of the Ship" (1850). Willkie's biographer tells us that Churchill's staff could not identify the lines for him and that Willkie told him that it was Longfellow. Neal, *Dark Horse*, 196. See also Winston S. Churchill, *The Grand Alliance*, 25.

10. *Press Conf* #710 (January 14, 1941), 17:76; Frank L. Kluckhohn, "'Rotten,' 'Dastardly,' Roosevelt Says of War Charge by Wheeler," *NYT*, January 15, 1941, 1. The bracketed remark may be assumed to have been approved by Roosevelt as it appears in the 1940 volume of *PPA*, the last volume to appear in his lifetime. That volume actually went up to the third inaugural.

11. Warren E. Kimball, *The Most Unsordid Act: Lend Lease, 1939–1941*, 119–230, contains a blow-by-blow account of the bills. For extreme hawks, see Mark L. Chadwin, *The Hawks of World War II*. The *New York Times* ran a front-page story on each day of the hearings: the quotations of testimony may be found in those stories. *Press Conf* #738 (April 25, 1941), 17:293.

12. "Roosevelt Trend at Record High," *NYT*, March 15, 1941, 5. See also Kimball, *Most Unsordid Act*, 191–92.

13. Turner Catledge, "President Signs, Starts War Aid," Frank L. Kluckhohn, "President Meets Congress Leaders," and "Roosevelt Signs Aid Measure," *NYT*, March 12, 1941, 1, 4; *PPA*, "The President Requests an Appropriation of $7,000,000,000, Mar. 12, 1941," and appended note.

14. "Roosevelt Leaves Today for Fishing Cruise," *NYT*, March 19, 1941, 1; Frank L. Kluckhohn, "Roosevelt Sails on Fishing Cruise" and "President Off in Search of Rest," *NYT*, March 23, 1941, 27, E7.

15. "[Hopkins] Returns" and "[Hopkins] Confers with President," *NYT*, February 17, 1941, 1, 5; "Harriman Leaves as Special Envoy," *NYT*, March 11, 1941, 12; Sherwood, *Roosevelt and Hopkins*, 230–63.

16. Turner Catledge, "Roosevelt and Hopkins Shape Allied Aid Set Up," *NYT*, March 30, 1941, 17; "Hopkins Set Up as Head of Lend-Lease Program," *NYT*, April 15, 1941, 9; FDR to Hopkins, March 27, 1941, Box 214, Hopkins Papers, FDRL, as cited in Adams, *Harry Hopkins: A Biography*, 418, 6; *Press Conf* #735 (April 15, 1941), 17:57–58; Frank L. Kluckhohn, "Roosevelt Holds Ships' Protection Required by Law," *NYT*, April 16, 1941, 1; *PPA*, "The Division of Defense Aid Reports Is Established, EO 8751, May 2, 1941," and attached note; *Press Conf* #741 (May 16, 1941), 17:320; "President Answers Question of Hopkins," *NYT*, May 17, 1941, 5; "President Appoints Coy as Assistant on Defense," *NYT*, April 25, 1941; W. H. Lawrence, "Roosevelt Names New 7-Man Board to Fix Priorities," *NYT*, August 29, 1941, 1; *Press Conf* #775 (October 14, 1941), 17:227; *PPA*, "The Office of Lend Lease Administrator Is Established, EO 8926, Oct. 28, 1941,"

and attached note; Sherwood, *Roosevelt and Hopkins*, 376; Edward R. Stettinius, *Lend-Lease, Weapon for Victory*; "Roosevelt Signs New Leasing Bill . . . Delegates Blanket Powers to Stettinius," *NYT*, October 29, 1941.

17. See, for example, Ickes, *Secret Diary*, 3:479; Stimson and Bundy, *On Active Service*, 334, citing diary, March 3, 1941; *Press Conf* #735 (April 15, 1941), 17:251–52.

18. David Anderson, "Envoy Is Selected," *NYT*, July 21, 1941, 1; "Minister to Aid Winant," *NYT*, January 21, 1941, 9; "President Silent on Naming Envoy," *NYT*, January 22, 1941, 5; Frank L. Kluckhohn, "Winant Is Named as London Envoy," *NYT*, February 7, 1941, 1; *Press Conf* #716 (February 7, 1941), 17:110–12; Louis Stark, "A New Kind of Envoy to a New Kind of Britain," *NYT*, February 16, 1941, SM6; Frank L. Kluckhohn, "Breaks Precedent," *NYT*, January 25, 1941, 1; *Press Conf* #719 (February 18, 1941), 17:128–31; John G. Winant, *A Letter from Grosvenor Square*, 10–29; Bernard Bellush, *He Walked Alone: A Biography of John G. Winant*.

19. Winant, *Letter from Grosvenor Square*, 21–22, 70–86. Telegram and Attlee quotation from Bellush, *He Walked Alone*, 176, 169.

20. AP, "Roosevelt Aide in Conference," *NYT*, January 2, 1941, 12; Frank L. Kluckhohn, "Roosevelt Sending Aide to Chungking," *NYT*, January 24, 1941, 4; *Press Conf* #725 (March 11, 1941), 17:184; AP, "American Will Direct Burma Road Operations," *NYT*, March 12, 1941, 8.

21. *PPA*, "Presidential Statement on Financial Aid to China, Nov. 30, 1940," and attached note, which contains a long review, written in the first person, of American relations with China—and to a lesser extent with Japan—since 1933; Frank L. Kluckhohn, "U.S. Lending China $100 Million More, Countering Japan," *NYT*, December 1, 1940, 1; *Press Conf* #725 (March 11, 1941), 17:183–84; *PPA*, " . . . Address at Annual Dinner, Mar. 15, 1941"; for the declaration about China, see the extended note to *PPA*, "EO 8751, May 2, 1941"; Braxton Eisel, *The Flying Tigers: Chennault's American Volunteer Group in China*; Sandilands, *Life and Political Economy*, 112–14.

22. Richard M. Leighton and Robert W. Coakey, *Global Logistics and Strategy, 1940–1943*, 44, 61. See also Greenfield, *American Strategy*, 75.

23. Maurice Matloff and Edwin M. Snell, *Strategic Planning for Coalition Warfare, 1941–42*, 32–63, quote on 33.

24. *Press Conf* #712 (January 21, 1941), 17:86–87; Frank L. Kluckhohn, "No Plan to Convoy, President States," *NYT*, January 22, 1941, 1.

25. *PPA*, " . . . United States Will Establish Bases in Greenland, Apr. 10, 1941," and appended note; Frank L. Kluckhohn, "Agreement Signed," *NYT*, April 12, 1941, 1; Conn and Fairchild, *Framework of Hemisphere Defense*, chap. 5; *PPA*, "Message to the Congress Asking Power to Requisition Idle Foreign Ships, Apr. 10, 1941"; Charles Hurd, "U.S. Moves to Seize Idle Foreign Ships," *NYT*, April 11, 1941, 1; *Press Conf* #734 (April 11, 1941), 17:242–47; Frank L. Kluckhohn, "Move for Ship Aid," *NYT*, April 12, 1941, 1.

26. *PPA*, "Radio Address on Defense Savings Bonds . . .," April 30, 1941," and appended note; John MacCormack, "Roosevelt Buys First Savings Bond for Defense Fund," *NYT*, May 1, 1941, 1.

27. *Press Conf* #734 (April 11, 1941), 17:241–43; *PPA*, "The Office of Price Administration and Civilian Supply Is Established, EO 8734, Apr. 11, 1941," and appended

note; W. H. Lawrence, "President Creates Price-Fixing Set-Up," *NYT,* April 12, 1941, 1; "Henderson Points to Price Weapons," *NYT,* April 13, 1941, 32. In this original creation, the agency was called the Office of Price Administration and Civilian Supply (OPACS).

28. *PPA,* "The President Requests That Bituminous Coal Mining Be Resumed, Apr. 21, 1941," and appended note; Louis Stark, "Roosevelt Urges Immediate Opening of Soft Coal Mines," *NYT,* April 22, 1941, 1; "Soft Coal Strike Is Ended," *NYT,* April 29, 1941, 1.

29. *Press Conf* #738 (April 25, 1941), 17:285–89; Frank L. Kluckhohn, "Greenland Alarm," *NYT,* April 25, 1941, 1.

30. Conn and Fairchild, *Framework of Hemisphere Defense,* 107–8. Defense Plan #1, never promulgated, authorized U.S. Navy convoys.

31. Conn and Fairchild, *Framework of Hemisphere Defense,* 112–13, citing the series entitled Fuehrer Conferences on Matters Dealing with the German Navy, reproduced in translation by the Office of Naval Information in 1947, 1:62–76, entry of May 22, 1941.

32. *PPA,* "The President Recommends the Levying of $3,500,000,000 in Taxes, May 1, 1941," and appended note; Frank L. Kluckhohn, "Advises Doughton," *NYT,* May 2, 1941, 1.

33. Conn and Fairchild, *Framework of Hemisphere Defense,* 110–29; *PPA,* "The President Orders Construction of a Fleet of Heavy Bombers . . ., May 5, 1941," and appended note; "Two Stimson Aides Advanced in Rank," *NYT,* April 1, 1941, 16. For Roosevelt and airpower, see Kent Roberts Greenfield's essay "Air Power and Strategy," in his *American Strategy,* 85–121. Portuguese dictator Antonio Salazar told the British that if Hitler invaded Portugal, their intervention would be welcomed, but not an American one. One reason given was that public opinion had been alarmed by Roosevelt's May 27 speech. Conn and Fairchild, *Framework of Hemisphere Defense,* 122.

34. *PPA,* "President Requests Funds for the NYA to Train Workers for Defense, May 14, 1941," "The Office of Civilian Defense Is Established, EO 8757, May 20, 1941," and "The Congress Is Asked for an Oil Pipeline to Supply Middle Atlantic Refineries, May 20, 1941," and appended notes; "La Guardia Has 3 Posts in Addition to Mayor's Job," *NYT,* May 21, 1941, 1; "Mayor Tells City He Will Run Again If Voters Call Him," *NYT,* May 22, 1941, 1.

35. "Roosevelt Has Quiet Day," *NYT,* May 4, 1941; *PPA,* "Remarks at Staunton, Virginia . . ., May 4, 1941"; Frank L. Kluckhohn, "U.S. 'Ever Ready to Fight Again' for Democracy, Roosevelt Says," *NYT,* May 5, 1941, 1.

36. Sherwood, *Roosevelt and Hopkins,* 294–96; cf. Rosenman, *Working with Roosevelt,* 278–83; Patrick Abbazia, *Mr. Roosevelt's Navy: The Private War of the U.S. Atlantic Fleet, 1939–1942,* 183–90.

37. *PPA,* "A Radio Address Announcing . . . an Unlimited National Emergency, May 27, 1941" and "Proclamation No. 2487, May 27, 1941"; Frank L. Kluckhohn, "A Call to Nation," "Speech Echoes in a Hushed City as Radios Go in Homes, on Streets," "Canada Parliament Listens to Roosevelt," "British Ban Sleep to Hear President," and "Says Speech Didn't Mean Convoys in Old Sense," *NYT,* May 28, 1941, 1, 21, 20. Levine and Levine, *People and the President,* 340–48, quote on 348. Sometimes listed as a Fireside

Chat, it could not have had the personal communication feeling that Roosevelt could imbue. See "Cameras Dominate Scene of Address," *NYT,* May 28, 1941, 21.

38. Sherwood, *Roosevelt and Hopkins,* 298; Levine and Levine, *People and the President,* 347; Dr. George Gallup, "Convoy Sentiment Seen Rising after Roosevelt Emergency Talk," *NYT,* June 15, 1941, 33; July 4, 24; September 1, 11, 1941, 26; October 9, 27, 1941; and September 16, 1942.

39. *Press Conf* #745 (May 28, 1941), 17:370; Turner Catledge, "Roosevelt Does Not Plan Convoys or Change in the Neutrality Laws," *NYT,* May 29, 1941, 1; Sherwood, *Roosevelt and Hopkins,* 298–99.

40. Abbazia, *Mr. Roosevelt's Navy,* 191–96; Ickes, *Secret Diary,* 3:539–40; "Wheeler Accepts Depth Bomb Story," *NYT,* June 10, 1941, 19.

41. *PPA,* "Harold L. Ickes Is Named Petroleum Coordinator . . .," May 28, 1941," and appended note; Conn and Fairchild, *Framework of Hemisphere Defense,* 121–29; *PPA,* "A Statement by the President Taking Possession of the Plant of the North American Aviation Company . . ., EO 8773, June 9, 1941," and appended note; Louis Stark, "U.S. Plans to Take over N.A. Aviation in California unless Strike Ends Soon," *NYT,* June 7, 1941, 1; "Roosevelt Explains Seizure; Jackson Cites Insurrection" and Foster Hailey, "Bayonets on Coast," *NYT,* June 10, 1941, 1; "Troops Arrival Brings Quick Shift," *NYT,* June 10, 1941, 14; *Press Conf* #748 (June 10, 1941), 17:392–97; Frank L. Kluckhohn, "President Returns Plane Plant Rule," *NYT,* July 3, 1941, 1.

42. "U.S. Ship Sunk in Atlantic," *NYT,* June 10, 1941, 1; *Press Conf* #748 (June 10, 1941), 17:392; #749 (June 17, 1941), 17:400–401, 403; Frank L. Kluckhohn, "Roosevelt Urges Delayed Judgment on Sinking of Ship," *NYT,* June 11, 1941, 1; "Fifth Column Curb; Nazi Consulates Are Ordered Shut," *NYT,* June 17, 1941, 1, includes the text of the order; *Press Conf* #749 (June 17, 1941), 17:402; *PPA,* "Message to the Congress on the Sinking of the *Robin Moor,* June 20, 1941," and appended note; Frank L. Kluckhohn, "'Piracy' Is Assailed," and Turner Catledge, "Congress Endorses Protest Message," *NYT,* June 21, 1941, 1.

43. Sherwood, *Roosevelt and Hopkins,* 299; *Press Conf* #765 (August 29, 1941), 18:125; Conn and Fairchild, *Framework of Hemisphere Defense,* 127.

44. Kimball, *Forged in War,* 87–92; Conn and Fairchild, *Framework of Hemisphere Defense,* 129.

45. Sherwood, *Roosevelt and Hopkins,* 304–5; "Churchill on Radio Today," *NYT,* June 22, 1941, 7; "Churchill Audience Vast" and Robert P. Post, "Churchill Promises to Aid All Who Are Hitler's Foes," and "Prime Minister Churchill's Broadcast on the War," *NYT,* June 23, 1941, 8, 1, 8.

46. Turner Catledge, "U.S. Hits Communism, but May Aid Russia," *NYT,* June 24, 1941, 1; *Press Conf* #750 (June 24, 1941), 17:408–11; Frank L. Kluckhohn, "Red Credits Freed," *NYT,* June 25, 1941, 1; Bertrand Hulen, "Pacific Port Free," *NYT,* June 26, 1941, 1; *PPA,* "The President Freezes the Assets of Certain European Countries, EO 8785, June 14, 1941."

47. "U.S. Hits Communism, but May Aid Russia," *NYT,* June 24, 1941, 1; "Taft Warns . . . on Aiding Russia," *NYT,* June 26, 1941, 7; "Hoover Condemns Aid to Soviet," *NYT,* June 30, 1941, 1.

48. George Gallup, "Victory for Russia Favored," *NYT,* July 13, 1941, 2; "Survey Finds 76% Back Roosevelt," *NYT,* June 27, 1941, 1.

49. For Hopkins's trip, see Sherwood, *Roosevelt and Hopkins,* 317–19, 323–48; George C. Herring, *Aid to Russia, 1941–46.*

50. *Press Conf* #753 (July 1, 1941), 18:2, 9; Frank L. Kluckhohn, "President Hopes We Can Avoid War," *NYT,* July 2, 1941, 1.

51. Conn and Fairchild, *Framework of Hemisphere Defense,* 133. For details of occupation, see Abbazia, *Mr. Roosevelt's Navy,* 197–212. *PPA,* "The President Informs Congress of the Landing of American Troops in Iceland, Trinidad, and British Guiana . . ., July 7, 1941," and appended note; Frank L. Kluckhohn, "U.S. Occupies Iceland," *NYT,* July 7, 1941, 1; *Press Conf* #753 (July 8, 1941), 18:17–18; Turner Catledge, "Hemisphere No Bar," *NYT,* July 9, 1941, 1. For a somewhat overheated treatment, see Neil Smith, *American Empire: Roosevelt's Geographer and the Prelude to Globalization.*

52. Sherwood, *Roosevelt and Hopkins,* 308–22; Winant, *Letter from Grosvenor Square,* 206–9.

53. Frank L. Kluckhohn, "Meeting of Churchill and Roosevelt on President's Cruise Is Reported," *NYT,* August 6, 1941, 1. The best firsthand American accounts are Sumner Welles, *Where Are We Heading?,* 2–18, and *The Time for Decision,* 174–77; and Sherwood, *Roosevelt and Hopkins,* 349–65.

54. DALLEK, 282; Theodore Wilson, *The First Summit: Roosevelt and Churchill at Placentia Bay, 1941;* Conn and Fairchild, *Framework of Hemisphere Defense,* 133–34; Churchill as quoted in Freidel, *Rendezvous with Destiny,* 386. Fala, more properly Murray the Outlaw of Fala Hill, a gift from his cousin Margaret Suckley (1891–1991) in 1940, was the last of Roosevelt's several Scotties.

55. Churchill, *The Grand Alliance,* 434; *PPA,* "The Atlantic Charter, Official Statement, Aug. 14, 1941," and appended note; UP, "Official Statement," *NYT,* August 15, 1941, 1. The UP dispatch places the names of Roosevelt and Churchill at the foot of the document, but they do not appear in the version in *PPA.* Frank L. Kluckhohn, "Roosevelt, Churchill Draft 8 Peace Aims, Pledging Destruction of Nazi Tyranny," *NYT,* August 15, 1941, 1; Turner Catledge, "Another Aid Bill Is Seen in Capital," *NYT,* August 15, 1941, 1; "Views of U.S. Press on Parlays at Sea," *NYT,* August 15, 1941, 6; Robert P. Post, "London Expects More from Talks," *NYT,* August 15, 1941, 1; *PPA,* "Joint Declaration of the United Nations, Jan. 1, 1942." The opening words of the declaration of the conference illustrate this nicely: "The President of the United States of America and the Prime Minister, Mr. Churchill, representing His Majesty's Government in the United Kingdom. . . ."

56. *PPA,* "Joint Roosevelt-Churchill Message Asking for Moscow Conference, Aug. 15, 1941"; Frank L. Kluckhohn, "U.S., Britain and Soviet to Confer in Moscow," *NYT,* August 16, 1941, 1.

57. *Press Conf* #761 (August 16, 1941), 18:76–84; John H. Crider, "President Debarks," *NYT,* August 17, 1941, 1; Levin, *Making of FDR,* 244–45. For Hassett, see Jonathan Daniels's introduction to *Off the Record with F.D.R., 1942–1945,* by William D. Hassett, hereafter cited as HASSETT.

58. John H. Crider, "Roosevelt Back in Capital; Sees Hull on Far East," *NYT,* August 18, 1941, 1; Hull, *Memoirs,* 2:974–76; Frank L. Kluckhohn, "U.S. Planes to Be Flown to British in Near East; Ferry System to Run by Way of West Africa," *NYT,* August 19, 1941, 1; "Ferry to Near East Delights the British," *NYT,* August 20, 1941, 3; Conn

and Fairchild, *Framework of Hemisphere Defense*, 248S; Frank K. Kluckhohn, "Tacit Approval by U.S. Indicated in Hull's Comment on Iran Move," *NYT*, August 26, 1941, 3; "American Tanker Is at Vladivostok," *NYT*, September 5, 1941, 1.

59. For example, David M. Kennedy writes: "The president also faced a nasty fight in the Congress over the extension of the Selective Service Act. Particularly nettlesome was a clause extending draftees' tour of duty for eighteen additional months beyond the twelve months specified in the original legislation of 1940. The recruits called up under that act a year earlier, chafing under the unfamiliar military discipline, confused about their part in a war the president was insistent they would never have to fight, were scrawling 'OHIO' on the walls of their encampments. Had the fledgling troops in fact melted away—either by statutory release from duty, or by mass desertion, as the ubiquitously chalked code for 'Over the Hill in October' threatened—the army would have had to start all over again, inflicting catastrophic delays on the Victory Program's timetable. Congress on August 12 approved the extension of service (while upholding the prohibition of deployment outside the Western Hemisphere) by a margin of a single vote in the House. The threatened desertions did not occur, and the army continued to grow, but the perilously thin margin in the House vote provided a sobering reminder of the nation's continuing reluctance to move to a full war footing" (*Freedom from Fear*, 496–97).

60. Senate Joint Resolution 95, July 28, 1941; George Gallup, "50% of U.S. Voters for Longer Draft," *NYT*, August 6, 1941, 9; "Senate to Speed Draft Extension," *NYT*, August 4, 1941, 7; Turner Catledge, "Senate Defeats Taft Draft Plan, Faces New Curb," *NYT*, August 6, 1941, 1; "Two-Year Limit on Draft Beaten in Senate, 50–21," *NYT*, August 7, 1941, 1; "2½ Years Service, 2D-Year Pay Rise, Voted by Senate," *NYT*, August 8, 1941; Frederick R. Barkley, "Debate on Draft Opened in House, Result in Doubt," *NYT*, August 9, 1941, 1; AP, "Draft Bill Foes Push House Fight," *NYT*, August 10, 1941, 1; Frederick R. Barkley, "Vote Is 203 to 202," *NYT*, August 13, 1941, 1; AP, "House Vote on Draft Bill," *NYT*, August 13, 1941, 10; "Fight on Draft Ends in Senate, Due to Act Today," *NYT*, August 14, 1941, 1; *Press Conf* #755 (July 15, 1941), 18:36–37; UP, "Service Bill Support Rallied," *NYT*, August 11, 1941, 1; "Roosevelt Signs Draft Extension," *NYT*, August 19, 1941, 19; "President Extends Army Service to 18 Months of Amended Law," *NYT*, August 23, 1941, 6; *Press Conf* #771 (September 30, 1941), 18:186–87. The vote breakdown was 182 Democrats and 21 Republicans for; 65 Democrats, 133 Republicans, and 4 others against. "House Vote on Draft Bill," *NYT*, August 13, 1941, 10.

61. *Press Conf* #762 (August 19, 1941), 18:87–89, 91–93; AP, "President in High Spirits"; Frank L. Kluckhohn, "Roosevelt Is Grim"; "President Quotes Lincoln and Draws Parallel"; and Turner Catledge, "Roosevelt Calls for Arms Survey of Allied Needs through 1941," *NYT*, August 20, 1941, 2, 1, 2, 1.

62. *PPA*, "The President Reports . . . on His Meeting with Churchill, Aug. 21, 1941"; Frank L. Kluckhohn, "Religion Secure, Roosevelt Says," *NYT*, August 22, 1941, 1.

63. *Press Conf* #763 (August 22, 1941), 18:98–110; AP, "President Calls Byrd Inaccurate" and Turner Catledge, "Byrd Reiterates Plane Lag Data," *NYT*, April 24, 1941, 1, 5; Charles Hurd, "500 of Our Tanks Sent to British," *NYT*, August 29, 1941, 1.

64. Frank L. Kluckhohn, "U.S. Takes over Kearney Shipyard, Open Tomorrow," *NYT*, August 24, 1941, 1, the order is on 16; "Roosevelt Acts on Oil Shortage," *NYT*, August 25,

1941, 1. (The headline is misleading; it was tankers that were in short supply.) John H. Crider, "26 Axis Tankers in South America to Move U.S. Oil," *NYT,* August 30, 1941, 1.

65. *Press Conf* #764 (August 26, 1941), 18:111–13; Frank L. Kluckhohn, "U.S. Army Mission Will Assist China," *NYT,* August 27, 1941, 1; Sandilands, *Life and Political Economy,* 114–15.

66. *PPA,* "The President [Introduces] Harriman to Stalin, Oct. 8, 1941," and attached note; *Press Conf* #765 (August 29, 1941), 18:125–26; "W. A. Harriman Will Head U.S. Mission to Moscow," *NYT,* August 30, 1941, 1; John H. Crider, "President Names Moscow Mission," *NYT,* September 4, 1941, 1. Sherwood, *Roosevelt and Hopkins,* 384–402, traces the beginnings of Chinese and Russian aid.

67. *Press Conf* #762 (August 19, 1941), 18:93; #764 (August 26, 1941), 18:122–23; "To Check on Defense," *NYT,* August 20, 1941, 13; W. H. Lawrence, "Weighs Forming Priorities Board," *NYT,* August 29, 1941, 13; *PPA,* "The Supply Priorities and Allocations Control Board Is Created, EO 8875, Aug. 28, 1941," and appended note; *Press Conf* #765 (August 29, 1941), 18:130; W. H. Lawrence, "Roosevelt Names New 7-Man Board to Fix Priorities" and "Order Creating Board and Outline of Duties," *NYT,* August 29, 1941, 1, 8. For an insider's view, see Donald M. Nelson, *Arsenal of Democracy: The Story of American War Production,* chap. 8.

68. *Press Conf* #765 (August 29, 1941), 18:129; "Hints at Important Statement," *NYT,* August 30, 1941, 4; "Roosevelt Gives Labor Day Theme," *NYT,* August 31, 1941, 18; *PPA,* "Informal Extended Remarks to Roosevelt Home Club, Hyde Park, NY, Aug. 30, 1941"; Frank L. Kluckhohn, "Roosevelt Sees Peril to U.S. Growing," *NYT,* September 1, 1941, 1; *PPA,* " . . . Labor Day Radio Address. Sep. 1, 1941"; Frank L. Kluckhohn, "Roosevelt Calls for 'More Energy' to Defeat Hitler's 'Insane Violence,'" and "President Starts Back," September 2, 1941, 1, 10. The underlined words are omitted from the version printed in *PPA* without ellipsis. The president did not then know that the culprit was Assistant Press Secretary William D. Hassett (1880–1965), who became increasingly important in Roosevelt's entourage.

69. Sherwood, *Roosevelt and Hopkins,* 370; "Roosevelt Speech Hailed in Capital," *NYT,* September 2, 1941, 11.

70. Conn and Fairchild, *Framework of Hemisphere Defense,* 149.

Chapter 6. The Last Days of Peace

1. *Press Conf* #762 (August 19, 1941), 18:94–97; #764 (August 26, 41), 18:113–17; #765 (August 29), 124, 127–29; #766 (September 2, 1941), 18:133–35; "War Department Will House Only 20,000," *NYT,* September 3, 1941, 16; Steve Vogel, *The Pentagon,* 67–103, quotes on 101–2; for Somervell, see John K. Ohl, *Supplying the Troops: General Somervell and American Logistics in WWII.*

2. *Press Conf* #766 (September 2, 1941), 18:132–39; Frank L. Kluckhohn, "President to Ask New Arms Fund; More Night Work," and W. H. Lawrence, "Nation Warned to Tighten Belt," *NYT,* September 3, 1941, 1, 16.

3. *PPA,* "The President Establishes the Office of Defense Health and Welfare Services, EO 8890, Sept. 3, 1941"; "President Sets Up New Health Body," *NYT,* September 4, 1941, 14.

4. *PPA*, "The President Recommends the Levying of [$3.5 Billion] in Taxes, May 1, 1941," and appended note; Henry N. Dorris, "Roosevelt Backs Defense Tax Bill," *NYT*, September 3, 1941, 15; "Roosevelt Signs Record Tax Bill; Estate Levies Up," *NYT*, September 20, 1941, 1.

5. Abbazia, *Mr. Roosevelt's Navy*, 223–31. Abbazia was able to consult the logs of both the *Greer* and the U-652.

6. "Submarine Attacks U.S. Destroyer Greer; Latter, Undamaged, Fires Depth Charges," *NYT*, September 5, 1941, 1.

7. *Press Conf* #767 (September 5, 1941), 18:140–54; Frank L. Kluckhohn, "Fleet to 'Eliminate' Attacking Submarine," *NYT*, September 6, 1941, 1.

8. AP, "British Airman Helped Repel Attack," *NYT*, September 6, 1941, 1.

9. "Mother of President Dies at Her Home in Hyde Park" and Frank L. Kluckhohn, "President Postpones His Address on World Crisis to Thursday Night," September 8, 1941, 1; Eleanor Roosevelt, *This I Remember*, 227; Kathleen McLaughlin, "President Shuts Self from World," *NYT*, September 9, 1941; "Sara D. Roosevelt Has Simple Burial," *NYT*, September 10, 1941, 1, 24. "Mother's Estate Left to President," *NYT*, September 11, 1941, 46, contains the text of the will.

10. Frank L. Kluckhohn, "President Starts Return to Capital," *NYT*, September 10, 1941, 14; "Picks Rail Board, Averts Strike," *NYT*, September 11, 1941, 1; Rosenman, *Working with Roosevelt*, 290–93; Frank L. Kluckhohn, "President Likely to Announce Navy Will Protect U.S. Shipments on Seas," *NYT*, September 11, 1941, 1; "Congress Leaders See President for Advance View of His Speech," *NYT*, September 12, 1941, 3.

11. *PPA*, "Fireside Chat, Sep. 11, 1941"; Frank L. Kluckhohn, "President Orders Navy to Shoot First If Axis Enter Our Defense Zones," *NYT*, September 12, 1941, 1; Levine and Levine, *People and the President*, 374–79. For an excellent and detailed account of the overheated government reaction to the Nazi influence on Latin America, see Friedman, *Nazis and Good Neighbors*.

12. "Willkie Applauds," AP, "Capital Comment Is Split," and "Press Comments on Roosevelt's Talk," *NYT*, September 12, 1941, 1, 4, 3.

13. "Lindbergh Sees a 'Plot' for War," *NYT*, September 12, 1941, 2. See also W. Cole, *Roosevelt and the Isolationists*, 465–66.

14. "American Opinion," *NYT*, October 1, 1941, C20; George Gallup, "'Keep-Out-of-War' Party Opposed by Most Voters," *NYT*, September 21, 1941, 39; "Majority Favors 'Shoot on Sight,'" *NYT*, September 26, 1941, 9; "Republicans Back U.S. Foreign Policy," *NYT*, September 28, 1941, 45; "Plan to Change Neutrality Act Favored by Voters," *NYT*, October 1, 1941, 8.

15. Frank L. Kluckhohn, "U.S. Owned Ship Sunk in Iceland Defense Zone," *NYT*, September 23, 1941, 1; *Press Conf* #770 (September 23, 1941), 18:174–78; Frank L. Kluckhohn, "President Plans to Arm Our Merchant Ships," *NYT*, September 24, 1941, 1.

16. *PPA*, "The President Asks Congress to Revise the Neutrality Act, Oct. 9, 1941," and appended note; Turner Catledge, "Roosevelt Asks Authority to Arm Ships," *NYT*, October 10, 1941, 1.

17. Abbazia, *Mr. Roosevelt's Navy*, 262–74; Turner Catledge, "U.S. Destroyer Hit by Torpedo off Iceland," and James B. Reston, "House Debate Fiery," *NYT*, October 18, 1941, 1; *Press Conf* #776 (October 17, 1941), 18:229–35; #777 (October 21, 1941),

18:243; #778 (October 24, 1941), 18:257; Frank L. Kluckhohn, "Kearny in Limits, Says President," *NYT*, October 18, 1941, 3; "Kearny Casualties," *NYT*, October 20, 1941, 1. Immediately after the September 11 Fireside Chat, the press characterized it as the "Shoot-on-Sight" speech, even though Roosevelt did not use the term publicly until his Navy Day speech on October 27, 1941.

18. *PPA*, "Navy and Total Defense Day Address, Oct. 27, 1941"; Frank L. Kluckhohn, "'Shooting' on, Roosevelt Says; Bares Nazi Plot on Americas," *NYT*, October 28, 1941, 1. Rosenman, *Working with Roosevelt*, 294–303, treats the Nazi documents as if they were authentic, but Friedman, *Nazis and Good Neighbors*, 58–59, shows that forged documents by British intelligence were foisted on Roosevelt who was ready to believe them.

19. "Roosevelt 'Trick' Charged by Taft," *NYT*, October 29, 1941, 1.

20. *Press Conf* #781 (November 3, 1941), 18:278–79.

21. Sherwood, *Roosevelt and Hopkins*, 383. See also Burns, *Soldier of Freedom*, 148–49; and Freidel, *Rendezvous with Destiny*, 394–95.

22. "Vote on War Asked by America First," *NYT*, October 22, 1941, 4; James B. Reston, "Sinking Quickens Congress Action," *NYT*, November 1, 1941, 2; W. Cole, *Roosevelt and the Isolationists*, 448–55.

23. Joe Klein, *Woody Guthrie: A Life*, 217–18.

24. James B. Reston, "Senate Votes to Put Arms on Ships and Permit Sailings to War Ports," *NYT*, November 8, 1941, 1; AP, "House to Debate Ship Bans 2 Days," *NYT*, November 9, 1941, 26; "Ship Ban Battle Shaped in House," *NYT*, November 10, 1941; "Predict Passage of Ship Bans Bill," *NYT*, November 11, 1941, 6; James B. Reston, "House Passage of Neutrality Act Imperiled," *NYT*, November 13, 1941, 1; *PPA*, "The President Renews Request for Amendment of the Neutrality Act, Nov. 13, 1941," and appended note with the legislators' letter; James B. Reston, "House Votes 242–194 to Amend Neutrality Laws after Pledge by Roosevelt to Quell Strikes," *NYT*, November 14, 1941, 1; "Secretary Hull's Letter," *NYT*, November 14, 1941, 4. Six Republicans joined 1 independent and 43 Democrats in voting for repeal, while 15 Democrats and 1 Progressive joined 21 Republicans in voting against repeal. Opponents included 9 senators who had never previously opposed the president on a major defense matter—5 Democrats and 4 Republicans.

25. George Gallup, "Neutrality Shift Finds More Favor," *NYT*, November 5, 1941, 5. Twenty-two Republicans joined 1 American Laborite and 189 Democrats in voting for repeal, while 53 Democrats, 3 Progressives, and 1 Farmer Laborite joined 137 Republicans in voting against it.

26. George Gallup, "Law Forbidding Defense Strikes Widely Favored," *NYT*, November 2, 1941, 34; "60% Are Opposed to Coal Walkout," *NYT*, November 20, 1941, 33.

27. *HIST STATS*, D46–47, 73; Joel Seidman, *American Labor from Defense to Reconversion*, 41–52; *PPA*, "The National Defense Mediation Board Is Established, EO 8716, Mar. 19, 1941," and appended note; Louis Stark, "Dykstra Heads Agency to Avert Strikes in Defense Industries," *NYT*, March 29, 1941, 1; "Davis Appointed Mediation Chief," *NYT*, June 22, 1941, 28.

28. "Defense Unit Asks Miners to Go Back," *NYT*, September 16, 1941, 30; "Dykstra Resigns as Mediation Head," *NYT*, June 20, 1941, 10; "Davis Appointed Mediation

Chief," *NYT,* June 21, 1941, 28; Louis Stark, "Strike Impends in Captive Mines," *NYT,* October 22, 1941, 13; "Roosevelt Asks Lewis Bar [Strike] in Captive Mines," *NYT,* October 25, 1941, 1; "Deadline Passes President Defied on Plea to Lewis," *NYT,* October 26, 1941, 1. (The OEM statement is printed in Stark's October 25 story and Lewis's first letter in his October 26 story.) *PPA,* "The President Asks John L. Lewis to Avert the Strike in the Captive Coal Mines, Oct. 26–27, 1941," and appended note; Louis Stark, "Roosevelt Is Firm" and "The President's and Lewis' Letters," *NYT,* October 28, 1941, 1, 18; *PPA,* " . . . Navy and Total Defense Day Address, Oct. 27, 1941"; Frank L. Kluckhohn, "'Shooting' on, Roosevelt Says," *NYT,* October 28, 1941, 1; Seidman, *American Labor,* 64–66. William H. Davis, a New York patent attorney, served as deputy administrator of the NRA: on its dissolution, he returned to New York and achieved a reputation as a labor mediator. He returned to Washington in 1941 to head the NDMB and continued to serve in increasingly more responsible positions into the Truman administration.

29. "Lewis Flayed by Congressmen" and UP, "President May Ask Legislation," *NYT,* October 28, 1941, 19, 18; *Press Conf* #779 (October 28, 1941), 18:260–69; Louis Stark, "Curb on Strikes Planned by President and Congress" and "Anti-Sabotage Bill Aimed in Congress at Mine Tie-Up," *NYT,* October 29, 1941, 1; Louis Stark, "Lewis in Parlays," *NYT,* October 30, 1941, 1. For Lewis, see Melvin Dubofsky and Warren Van Tine, *John L. Lewis: A Biography,* and the shorter Robert H. Ziegler, *John L. Lewis: Labor Leader.*

30. Louis Stark, "Deadline by Lewis," *NYT,* October 31, 1941, 1; "Coal Talks Open; Both Sides Firm," *NYT,* November 4, 1941, 17; "Mediation Board Takes Coal Case," *NYT,* November 5, 1941, 25; "Four Mediators Fight Union Shop," *NYT,* November 7, 1941, 14; "Setback to Lewis," *NYT,* November 11, 1941, 1; "Boycott Is in View," *NYT,* November 12, 1941, 1. The absurdity of having two members of the UMW sitting on a quasi-judicial body judging a dispute to which the UMW was a party seems not to have been apparent to most contemporary observers.

31. Louis Stark, "Coal Truce Sought," *NYT,* November 13, 1941, 1; "Test on Coal Today," *NYT,* November 14, 1941, 1; *PPA,* "The President Renews Request for Amendment of the Neutrality, Nov. 13, 1941."

32. *PPA,* "The President Directs Management and Labor to Resume Collective Bargaining Covering, Nov. 14, 1941," and appended note, includes text of Roosevelt's letters to Lewis, November 18 and 22; Louis Stark, "President Is Stern," *NYT,* November 15, 1941, 1.

33. W. H. Lawrence, "53,000 Told to Quit," *NYT,* November 16, 1941, 1; "Refuse Union Shop," *NYT,* November 17, 1941, 1; "President Defied," "Report of the Two Sides to Roosevelt," "Text of John L. Lewis's Speech on the Failure of Coal Strike Conference," and A. H. Raskin, "C.I.O. Vote Backs Lewis on Strike," November 18, 1941, 1, 17, 15, 1; "C.I.O. Backs Foreign Policy in Rout of Lewis Forces," *NYT,* November 19, 1941, 1.

34. *Press Conf* #784 (November 18, 1941), 18:311–12; W. H. Lawrence, "Roosevelt Disputes Lewis but Takes No Action on Coal Strike," *NYT,* November 19, 1941, 1; "President Would Arbitrate or Postpone Closed Shop; Lewis Balks" and "Texts of Roosevelt's Plea and Replies," November 20, 1941, 1, 34.

35. W. H. Lawrence, "Lewis Calls Off Coal Strike," "Letters Ending Coal Strike," and "Sketches of the Coal Conferees," *NYT,* November 23, 1941, 1, 41, 44.

36. Milton Bracker, "Miners Endorse Arbitration Plan and Resume Jobs," *NYT,* November 24, 1941, 1; "Coal Parley On: 'Little Steel' Out," *NYT,* November 27, 1941, 16; "Steel Leaders See All Accepting Pact," *NYT,* November 29, 1941, 9; "Only One Company Spurns Steel Talk," *NYT,* November 30, 1941, 54; "Arbitration Board on Coal Recesses," December 3, 1941, 17; "Crucible Steel Co. to Agree on Mines," *NYT,* December 5, 1941, 16; "Captive Mine Decision Expected by Tomorrow," *NYT,* December 7, 1941, 33; "Lewis Wins Captive Mine Fight; Arbitrators Grant Union Shop," *NYT,* December 8, 1941, 1.

37. For the "fish pond" image, see Robert J. C. Butow, *Tojo and the Coming of War,* 245. Hiroyuki Agawa, *The Reluctant Admiral: Yamamoto and the Imperial Navy,* is a useful biography of Yamamoto.

38. George F. Kennan, *American Diplomacy, 1900–1950,* 46.

39. Churchill's remark first cited in Francis L. Loewenheim, Harold D. Langley, and Manfred Jonas, *Roosevelt and Churchill, Their Secret Wartime Correspondence,* 95. For Roosevelt in the 1920s, see William L. Neumann, "Franklin D. Roosevelt and Japan, 1913–1933," and his own "Must We Fight Japan?" and "Our Foreign Policy: A Democratic View." His original title for the first was "The Japs: A Habit of Mind." For a summary of the "yellow peril" literature of war between Japan and the West, see Roger Daniels, *The Politics of Prejudice: The Anti-Japanese Movement in California and the Struggle for Japanese Exclusion,* 65–78. The most nuanced account of trans-Pacific relationships is still Akira Iriye, *Across the Pacific: An Inner History of American–East Asian Relations.* For the border war, see Alvin D. Coox, *Nomonhan: Japan against Russia, 1939.* For a brief account, see Butow, *Tojo and the Coming of War,* 125–28. Hitler did not have much faith in his Japanese ally before December 7, 1941. As noted he speculated that if he declared war on the United States, Japan might not join in. The Pearl Harbor attack was a surprise to him too.

40. *Press Conf* #717 (February 11, 1941), 17:120–21; Bertram D. Hulen, "Roosevelt, Nomura Emphasize Anxiety for Peace in Orient," *NYT,* February 15, 1941, 1. For the State Department's account of the White House meeting, see *FRUS, The Far East* (1941), 4:387–89.

41. Bertram D. Hulen, "U.S. Policy Stated," July 25, 1941, 1; "Text of Welles's Statement on Japan," *NYT,* July 25, 1941, 5; *PPA,* " . . . Extemporaneous Remarks to Volunteer Participation Committee of the Office of Civilian Defense, July 24, 1941." For a detailed, document-by-document account of U.S.-Japan negotiations, see *FRUS, The Far East* (1941), 4:1–729.

42. *PPA,* "The President Freezes Japanese and Chinese Assets in the United States, White House Statement and EO 8832, July 26, 1941" and "Military Order Placing Land and Sea Forces of Philippines under United States Commands, July 26, 1941"; John H. Crider, "Roosevelt Puts Filipino Forces in U.S. Army as Japan Freezes American, British Funds" and "M'Arthur Made Chief in Far East," *NYT,* July 27, 1941, 1, 17; Matloff and Snell, *Strategic Planning,* 67; Louis Morton, "War Plan Orange: Evolution of a Strategy"; Mark S. Watson, *Chief of Staff: Prewar Plans and Preparations,* 434–38.

43. Butow, *Tojo and the Coming of War,* 236–61, quote on 255, poem on 291. See also his *John Doe Associates* for exhaustive analyses of the negotiations and some of

the bizarre influences thereon. For a contrary view, see Paul W. Schroeder, *The Axis Alliance and Japanese-American Relations, 1941*.

44. *Press Conf* #783 (November 14, 1941), 18:298–305; Frank L. Kluckhohn, "President Indicates Situation in Far East Might Lead to War," *NYT*, November 15, 1941, 1. The president had previously announced that he was giving consideration to withdrawing the Marines from China. *Press Conf* #782 (November 7, 1941), 18:289–90, as recommended on September 1 by the consul-general in Shanghai and the navy and marine commanders in China.

45. *FRUS, Japan: 1931–1941* 2:362, 375; Hull, *Memoirs*, 2:1074; Kimball, *Roosevelt and Churchill*, 1:276; Frank L. Kluckhohn, "Kurusu and Roosevelt Talk . . .," *NYT*, November 18, 1941, 1; Bertram D. Hulen, "Talks Are Bogged," *NYT*, November 28, 1941, 1.

46. *FRUS, Japan: 1931–1941*, 2:376–77; "The Day in Washington," *NYT*, November 18, 1941, 10; "Roosevelts Dine with Two Guests," *NYT*, November 21, 1941, 13; Frank L. Kluckhohn, "Hull Relays Data," *NYT*, November 30, 1941, 1; "Roosevelt Is Grim," *NYT*, December 1, 1941, 1.

47. *Press Conf* #788 (December 2, 1941), 18:333–336; #789 (December 5, 1941), 18:339.

48. *FRUS, Japan: 1931–1941*, 2:378.

49. *PPA*, "The President Sends a Personal Message to Emperor Hirohito, Dec. 6, 1941"; Hull, *Memoirs*, 2:1093–94; Freidel, *Rendezvous with Destiny*, 402. For a precise timetable and mechanics of the disrupted delivery in Tokyo, see Butow, *Tojo and the Coming of War*, 387–401.

50. U.S. Congress, Joint Committee on the Investigation of the Pearl Harbor Attack, *Pearl Harbor Attack*, pt. 10, 4659–63. For a brief description of the prewar navy security protocol, see George M. Elsey, *An Unplanned Life*, 16–17.

Chapter 7. A War Presidency, Pearl Harbor to Midway

1. Lieutenant Schulz's testimony as cited in chap. 6, n. 50. Hopkins's note is in Sherwood, *Roosevelt and Hopkins*, 430–34. Hopkins's times are not precise. He says that after Stark's call (2:28), the president called Early at home, who called the three wire services. Their subsequent bulletins were timed at 2:22. Levin, *Making of FDR*, 251–53.

2. Hull, *Memoirs*, 2:1097. When Marshall read the Magic intercept in the morning, he sent a further warning telegram to General Short that was delivered as bombs were falling. If Marshall had been alerted Saturday night, the message might have been delivered earlier. It is hard to believe that it would have significantly affected the result, but the administration would have looked a little less inept if he had done so. Stimson's diary entry for the November 25 meeting has Roosevelt saying: "The Japanese are notorious for making an attack without warning."

3. Winant, *Letter from Grosvenor Square*, 278; Churchill, *Second World War*, 3:608; Kimball, *Forged in War*, 122–23.

4. Proclamation 2525, December 7, 1941. This and the proclamations listed in note 10 were in compliance with Section 21 of Title 50, U.S. Code; "Japanese Seizure Ordered by Biddle," *NYT*, December 8, 1941, 6; Roger Daniels, "The Internment of Japanese Nationals in the United States during World War II," 66–75.

5. For Fish, see Burns, *Soldier of Freedom,* 164. The other attendees were Speaker Rayburn and Senators Barkley, McNary, Connally, Austin, and Bloom. Charles Eaton (R-NJ) attended in place of Fish.

6. Alexander Kendrick, *Prime Time: The Life of Edward R. Murrow,* 240.

7. Hopkins note, FDRL, as cited in Rosenman, *Working with Roosevelt,* 307.

8. *PPA,* "Address to the Congress," December 8, 1941. For other comments on the text, see Rosenman, *Working with Roosevelt,* 307–8.

9. Frank L. Kluckhohn, "Unity in Congress," *NYT,* December 9, 1941, 1. The vote was 82–0 in the Senate and 388–1 in the House.

10. Proclamations 2526 and 2527, December 8, 1941, for Germans and Italians; "Axis Aliens Held with Japanese," *NYT,* December 10, 1941, 30.

11. John Joel Culley, "Enemy Alien Control in the United States during World War II." I have benefited from reading Culley's large unpublished manuscript on the Justice Department in World War II.

12. Rosenman, *Working with Roosevelt,* 307–10.

13. *Press Conf* #790 (December 9, 1941), 18:343–57; "Washington News on Fighting Scant" and "Censorship Rules Set by President," *NYT,* December 10, 1941, 4, 5.

14. Rosenman, *Working with Roosevelt,* 310–11.

15. *PPA,* "Fireside Chat, Dec. 9, 1941"; Frank L. Kluckhohn, "Roosevelt Sees a Long, World-Wide War," *NYT,* December 10, 1941. *PPA,* "A Message to the Congress Outlining the History of Relations between the United States and Japan, Dec. 15, 1941" is the Rosenman-Sherwood rewrite of Welles's paper. "U.S. 'White Paper,'" *NYT,* December 16, 1941. 1.

16. Matloff and Snell, *Strategic Planning,* 83–84; Louis Morton, *The Fall of the Philippines,* 1145–48. American planners could not know that the Japanese plan had been for a second attack after the planes had refueled and rearmed on their carriers, but when the cautious battleship admiral in charge learned that the two American carriers in the Pacific had not been in harbor at the time of attack, he scrubbed the second attack and headed back to Japan. Roland H. Spector, *Eagle against the Sun: The American War against Japan,* 128.

17. *PPA,* "Message to the Congress Asking That a State of War Be Recognized between Germany and Italy and the United States, Dec. 11, 1941," and appended note; Frank L. Kluckhohn, "U.S. Now at War with Germany and Italy," *NYT,* December 12, 1941, 1.

18. *Press Conf* #791 (December 12, 1941), 18:362; "Secretary Knox Visits Honolulu," *NYT,* December 12, 1941, 1; Frank L. Kluckhohn, "President Holds Naval Conference," *NYT,* December 14, 1941, 1.

19. Knox Press Conference Transcript, December 15, 1941, Knox Collection, Office of Naval History, Washington Navy Yard; Charles Hurd, "Knox Reports One Battleship Sunk at Hawaii, Five Other Craft Lost, but Main Fleet Is at Sea" and "Knox Statement on Hawaii," *NYT,* December 16, 1941, 1. A detailed "Damage Report for Ships after Pearl Harbor Attack," Enclosure (21C) to Commander in Chief, Pacific Fleet Report of Japanese Raid on Pearl Harbor, February 15, 1942, http://www.history.navy.mil/docs/wwii/pearl/CinCPac-D.htm. For an effective sample of the Hawaiian rumors, see S. Morison, *Two-Ocean War,* 67–68. For Japanese in Hawaii, see Stetson Conn,

Rose C. Engleman, and Byron Fairchild, *Guarding the United States and Its Outposts*, 206–14.

20. "Board of Inquiry Set Up on Hawaii," *NYT*, December 17, 1941; *PPA*, "The President Appoints a Commission to Investigate the Pearl Harbor Attack, Executive Order No. 8983, Dec. 18, 1941."

21. Charles Hurd, "Hawaii Naval, Army, Air Commanders Ousted," *NYT*, December 18, 1941, 1. For Nimitz, see E. B. Potter, *Fleet Admiral Chester W. Nimitz*. The third officer relieved was the departmental army air force commander, Major General Frederick L. Martin, who was replaced by Brigadier General Clarence L. Tinker. Harry N. Scheiber and Jane L. Scheiber, *Bayonets in Paradise: Martial Law in Hawaii, 1941–1946* is a transforming work.

22. "Admiral King Heads Navy, Rules All Sea and Air Fleets Special," *NYT*, December 21, 1941, 1; Charles Hurd, "King in Top Post in Navy Shake-Up," *NYT*, March 10, 1942, 1; S. Morison, *Two-Ocean War*, 34–35, 102–3, 579–80. See also Thomas B. Buell, *Master of Sea Power: A Biography of Fleet Admiral Ernest J. King*. For a short list, headed by Stimson and Churchill, of those who "hated" King, see S. Morison, *Two-Ocean War*, 35.

23. *Press Conf* #792 (December 16, 1941), 18:370–72; *PPA*, "[Establishment of] the Office of Censorship, EO 8985, Dec. 19, 1941"; Frank L. Kluckhohn, "President Appoints Byron Price to Direct Wartime Censorship," *NYT*, December 17, 1941, 1; Arthur Krock, "Freedom of the Press Restricted for the War," *NYT*, December 21, 1941, E3; "Censorship Code Issued for Press," *NYT*, January 15, 1942, 12. See Theodore F. Koop, *Weapon of Silence*.

24. *PPA*, "White House Statement Announcing the Arrival of Prime Minister Churchill and the Beginning of Conferences, Dec. 22, 1941"; *Press Conf* #794 (December 23, 1941), 18:382–92; Frank L. Kluckhohn, "2 Leaders Confer," *NYT*, December 23, 1941, 1; "Churchill Talks," *NYT*, December 24, 1941, 1; *PPA*, " . . . Christmas Eve Message to the Nation, Dec. 24, 1941"; "Roosevelt, Churchill Voice Faith to War-Weary World" and "Yule Messages of Roosevelt and Churchill," *NYT*, December 25, 1941, 1, 13; Frank L. Kluckhohn, "Congress Thrilled," *NYT*, December 27, 1941, 1; Jon Meacham, *Franklin and Winston*, 141–65. For example, in April 1942, when Burmese nationalists were negotiating with the Japanese, Roosevelt sounded like an old-style imperialist, telling Churchill that he "never liked Burma and the Burmese! . . . You people must have had a terrible time with them for the last fifty years" (DALLEK, 327).

25. For the Arcadia military talks, see Matloff and Snell, *Strategic Planning*, especially 97–113, 124–26, 164–73. For the British debacle, see Christopher Bayly and Tim Harper, *Forgotten Armies: The Fall of British Asia, 1941–1945*. See *PPA*, "White House Statement on Combined [Boards], Jan. 26, 1942."

26. *Press Conf* #859 (November 10, 1942), 20:223–24.

27. *PPA*, "A Pledge to the Philippines, Dec. 29, 1941"; P. J. Phillips, "Churchill Sees Two Tasks before Final Blow at Enemy," *NYT*, December 31, 1941, 1, speech on 6; *PPA*, "Joint Declaration of the United Nations . . ., Jan. 1, 1941"; Frank L. Kluckhohn, "War Pact Is Signed," *NYT*, January 3, 1942, 1; AP, "Signing of Declaration Spread over Two Days" and "Term 'United Nations' Selected by Roosevelt," *NYT*, January 3, 1942, 4.

Soong (1894–1971), Chiang's brother-in-law, managed the funding of the Flying Tigers and later Lend-Lease for China in Washington.

28. *Press Conf* #795 (December 30, 1941), 18:393–403; Frank L. Kluckhohn, "50 Billion a Year Is Set by President as Our War Outlay," *NYT*, December 31, 1941, 1; *PPA*, "The Annual Budget Message, Jan. 5, 1942" and "Address to the Congress on the State of the Union, Jan. 6, 1942"; Frank L. Kluckhohn, "President Says We Will Carry War to the Foe," Frederick R. Barkley, "President Stern in War Address," and "'Fighting Address' Hailed in Congress," *NYT*, January 7, 1942, 1, 4; UP, "Taft and Vandenberg Approve," *NYT*, January 7, 1942, 4; George Gallup, "Roosevelt Gains in Public Esteem," *NYT*, January 28, 1942, 17; "Germany Is Held Main Threat to U.S.," *NYT*, December 23, 1941, 4; *PPA*, "The President Establishes the National War Labor Board, EO 9017, Jan. 12, 1942" and "The War Production Board Is Established, EO 9024, Jan. 16, 1942," and appended notes.

29. *PPA*, "Statement by the President on Signing the Emergency Price Control Act, Jan. 30, 1942"; Frank L. Kluckhohn, "Price Bill Signed; 110 P.C. Parity Hit," *NYT*, January 31, 1942, 1; John Kenneth Galbraith, *A Life in Our Times*, 108.

30. Robert P. Post, "Churchill Wins 464–1 Vote . . . ," *NYT*, Jan. 30, 1942, 1; Freidel, *Rendezvous with Destiny*, 417 (quote); *PPA*, "The President Establishes the National War Labor Board, EO 9017, Jan. 12, 1942," "The War Production Board Is Established, EO 9024, Jan. 16, 1942," and "Statement by the President on Signing the Emergency Price Control Act, Jan. 30, 1942"; *Press Conf* #802 (January 30, 1942), 19:102–12; *PPA*, "The President Approves the Continuation of Professional Baseball, Jan. 16, 1942," and appended note; *Press Conf* #810 (March 10, 1941), 19:185–86; "Roosevelt Backs Wartime Sports," *NYT*, March 11, 1943, 21; George Gallup, "Pro Sports for Duration of War Favored in Poll," *NYT*, April 15, 1942, 29; Gerald Bazer, "Baseball during World War II: The Reaction and Encouragement of Franklin Delano Roosevelt and Others."

31. Report of Roberts Commission, January 23, 1942, is contained in U.S. Congress, Joint Committee on the Investigation of the Pearl Harbor Attack, *Pearl Harbor Attack*, pt. 39. An analysis of the Roberts Report and of some of the testimony before it may be found in Commission on Wartime Relocation and Internment of Civilians, *Personal Justice Denied*, 57–58. Stimson Diary, January 20, 1942; James B. Reston, "Raid Signs Ignored," *NYT*, January 25, 1942, 1; Report of Roberts Commission, 31–32.

32. *PPA*, "Radio Address on the President's Birthday, Jan. 30, 1942"; James B. Reston, "Nations Hail President at 60," "A Prayer from MacArthur," "President Hailed at Tea in London," and "Latin Americans Acclaim President," *NYT*, January 31, 1942, 1, 9; verse from Morton, *Fall of the Philippines*, 368.

33. Frank L. Kluckhohn, "President and Churchill Pray in George Washington's Pew," *NYT*, January 2, 1942, 1; HASSETT, 91, 105.

34. Elsey, *An Unplanned Life*, 18–66. Elsey, a doctoral candidate in history at Harvard, came to the White House Map Room on April 28, 1942, as a junior watch officer. He became a senior adviser to President Truman. The cited pages are a chapter entitled "The Map Room." See also his oral history online at the Truman Presidential Library.

35. *Press Conf* #836 (July 21, 1942), 20:14–18; Frank L. Kluckhohn, "Leahy Will Do Detail Work to Help President Plan War," *NYT*, July 22, 1942, 1; William D. Leahy, *I Was There*, 172. For an example of how he operated as more than a conduit between Roosevelt and the JCS, see Matloff and Snell, *Strategic Planning*, 282–83.

36. HASSETT, January 6, 1942, 1; Frank L. Kluckhohn, "Report Due Soon on Pearl Harbor," *NYT,* January 24, 1942, 4. The "unprecedentedly brief" conference was *Press Conf* #800 (January 23, 1942), 19:87–89.

37. Levin, *Making of FDR,* 218ff.

38. *PPA,* "[Letter to] Robert E. Hannegan, July 11, 1944"; HASSETT, May 10, 1942, 45.

39. S. Morison, *Two-Ocean War,* 108–21.

40. The first informed account of the process that set up the incarceration of the West Coast Japanese Americans was Stetson Conn, "The Decision to Relocate the Japanese from the Pacific Coast." See Roger Daniels, *Concentration Camps, USA: Japanese Americans and World War II.*

41. Biddle, "Memorandum to the President," February 17, 1942, FDRL. It is printed in full in vol. 2 of Roger Daniels, ed., *American Concentration Camps: A Documentary History of the Relocation and Incarceration of Japanese Americans, 1941–1945.* See also Biddle to Stimson, February 12, 1942, Record Group (RG) 107, National Archives (NA); and Biddle, *In Brief Authority,* 212–26. Telephone conversation between John J. McCloy and Karl R. Bendetsen, February 11, 1942, RG 107, NA. The army regularly recorded telephone conversations, which is a great boon to historians. Stimson, however, refused to allow his conversations with the president to be recorded. McCloy's "we talked" is not accurate. Only Stimson spoke to the president.

42. Benjamin V. Cohen, Oscar Cox, and Joseph L. Rauh, "The Japanese Situation on the West Coast," in folder "Dealer and Dreamers: Japanese Exclusion Order, 1942," Joseph P. Lash Papers, FDRL. For Cohen's role, see Lasser, *Benjamin V. Cohen,* 261–65. "EO 9066, Authorizing the Secretary of War to Prescribe Military Areas, Feb. 19, 1942," in U.S. House of Representatives, Tolan Committee, *House Report 2124.* It does not appear in *PPA,* perhaps because the *Federal Register* for 1942 was not compiled, but it is in the electronic edition. "Army Gets Power to Move Citizens or Aliens Inland: President's Order Is Designed Primarily to Allow Round-up of West Coast Japanese," *NYT,* February 21, 1942, 1, EO 9066 text on 6.

43. Filed under "Recommendations" in Assistant Secretary of War, RG 107, NA. There are various drafts, some with handwritten corrections dated February 12, 1942, in the Hiram W. Johnson Mss., Bancroft Library, University of California, Berkeley.

44. *PPA,* "The Establishment of the War Relocation Authority, EO 9102, Mar. 18, 1942"; "'Work Corps' Set Up for Coast Aliens," *NYT,* March 19, 1942; Eisenhower to Wickard, April 1, 1942, "Correspondence of the Secretary of Agriculture, Foreign Relations, 2–1, Aliens-Refugees, RG 16, NA. For the most detailed examination of Roosevelt's motives, see Greg Robinson, *By Order of the President: FDR and the Internment of Japanese Americans,* argues otherwise, laying great stress on Roosevelt's long-felt resentments of Japan's behavior. His chapter "FDR's Decision to Intern" (73–124) concludes: "The sin that pervades the President's decision to approve evacuation was not one of malice but of indifference."

45. Roger Daniels, *Prisoners without Trial: Japanese Americans in World War II,* 53–54.

46. *Press Conf* #853 (October 29, 1942), 20:156–57.

47. Olson to FDR, April 25, 1942, and FDR to Olson, May 18, 1942, FDRL; Austin, *From Concentration Camp to Campus.* Among those advocating for Nisei students

were Elmer Davis, Harry Hopkins, Milton Eisenhower, and Archibald MacLeish. In addition, the support of Assistant War Secretary McCloy, the War Department's point man on the Japanese Americans, was particularly important.

48. Rosenman, *Working with Roosevelt*, 329–33; "President to Speak to Nation Tonight" and "Map . . .," *NYT*, February 23, 1942, 1, 12; *PPA*, "Fireside Chat on Progress of the War, Feb. 23, 1942"; W. H. Lawrence, "President Speaks," *NYT*, February 24, 1942, 1; Levine and Levine, *People and the President*, 413–19.

49. Lawrence E. Davies, "Refinery Fired On: Big Craft Hurls Dozen Shells at an Oil Field near Santa Barbara," *NYT*, February 24, 1942, 1; U.S. Army, *Submarine Operations, December 1941–April 1942*; Conn, Engelman, an Fairchild, *Guarding the United States*, 87–88.

50. Morton, *Fall of the Philippines*, 77–97.

51. Ibid., 334–60, 385–88; S. Morison, *Two-Ocean War*, 98; *Press Conf* #812 (March 17, 1942), 19:208–10; Charles Hurd, "MacArthur in Australia as Allied Commander," *NYT*, March 18, 1942, 1; W. L. White, *They Were Expendable*. John Ford's film version was released in 1945. Louis Morton wrote: "The fate of the Philippine garrison had been decided [by events] at Pearl Harbor" (*Fall of the Philippines*, 583).

52. Morton, *Fall of the Philippines*, 562–84; *PPA*, "Message to Lieutenant General Jonathan Wainwright, May 5, 1942"; Jonathan M. Wainwright, *General Wainwright's Story*. There are many harrowing accounts; for a general view, see Gavan Daws, *Prisoners of the Japanese: POWs of World War II in the Pacific*.

53. MacArthur's medal was awarded April 1, 1942, Wainwright's September 19, 1945. For details, see the website of the Congressional Medal of Honor Society.

54. Rosenman, *Working with Roosevelt*, 327–28; *PPA*, "The President Submits a Plan to Guarantee Uninterrupted Production, Dec. 23, 1941"; Frances Perkins, *The Roosevelt I Knew*, 369–70; *PPA*, "The President Creates the National War Labor Board, EO 9017, Jan. 12, 1942," and appended note; W. H. Lawrence, "War Labor Board Created," *NYT*, January 13, 1942, 1; "Labor Is Warned of Treason Action," *NYT*, July 22, 1942, 1; Seidman, *American Labor*.

55. *PPA*, "The War Production Board Is Established, EO No. 9024, Jan. 16, 1942"; W. H. Lawrence, "Nelson Receives Over-All Powers; Knudsen, Army Job," *NYT*, January 17, 1942, 1; Nelson, *Arsenal of Democracy*.

56. *PPA*, "EO 8757, May 20, 1941"; "First Lady Named to Defense Post," *NYT*, September 14, 1941, 20; Anna Rosenberg Hoffman, "Oral History," FDRL, as cited in Doris Kearns Goodwin, *No Ordinary Time: Franklin and Eleanor Roosevelt; The Home Front in World War II*, 281; Frank L. Kluckhohn, "Dean Landis Made Executive of OCD as La Guardia Aide," *NYT*, January 10, 1942, 1; "House Reversal Keeps OCD Set-up: Senate Votes $100,000,000 Fund," *NYT*, January 20, 1942, 1; W. H. Lawrence, "La Guardia Resigns as Defense Head; Landis Gets Post," *NYT*, February 11, 1942, 1; Thomas Kessner, *Fiorello H. La Guardia and the Making of Modern New York*, 505; AP, "Melvyn Douglas Is Made Director of Information," *NYT*, February 3, 1942, 22; "Melvyn Douglas Works at His OCD Desk," *NYT*, February 6, 1942, 21; "Douglas Replies to Criticism," *NYT*, February 11, 1942, 15; AP, "Mayris Cheney in OCD Post," *NYT*, February 5, 1942, 2; UP, "Appointment of Dancer Causes a Stir," and AP, "Eleanor Glide" picture with caption, *NYT*, February 5, 1942, 21; C. P. Trussell, "House Fights Looms on 'Frills'

for OCD," *NYT,* February 9, 1942, 1; *Press Conf* #804 (February 10, 1942), 19:125; AP, "Jesse Owens on OCD Staff," *NYT,* February 7, 1942, 30. For Cheney's other relations with the Roosevelts, see Jonathan Daniels, *White House Witness,* 7; "Mrs. Roosevelt Quits OCD to Free Agency of Attack" and "Mrs. Roosevelt Berates Critics, Defends Course as OCD Official," *NYT,* February 21, 1942, 1, 21. For the postwar history of civil defense, see Allan M. Winkler, "A Forty-Year History of Civil Defense"; and Robert E. Miller, "The War That Never Came: Civilian Defense, Mobilization, and Morale during World War II."

57. *PPA,* "The War Manpower Commission Is Created, EO 9139, Apr. 18, 1942," and attached note; Frank L. Kluckhohn, "M'Nutt Made Head of a New Board to Rule Manpower," *NYT,* April 19, 1942, 1; "Paul McNutt Dies," *NYT,* March 25, 1955, 23; James H. Madison, *The Indiana Way: A State History;* Eric Pace, "Anna Rosenberg Hoffman Dead," *NYT,* May 10, 1983, D25.

58. *PPA,* "The President Outlines a Seven-Point Economic Stabilization Program, Apr. 27, 1941"; Frank L. Kluckhohn, "$25,000 Income Limit, Ceilings on Prices, Stable Wages, Taxes, Asked by President," *NYT,* April 28, 1942, 1; *PPA,* "Fireside Chat, Apr. 28, 1942"; Frank L. Kluckhohn, "Roosevelt Sees Axis Cracking," *NYT,* April 29, 1942, 1.

59. *Press Conf* #820 (April 21, 1942), 19:291–92; "President Puts Raiders of Tokyo at 'Shangri-La,'" *NYT,* April 22, 1942, 6.

60. W. H. Lawrence, "Doolittle, Leader of Raid on Japan, Says Navy Yard, Plane Plant, Were Hit," *NYT,* May 20, 1942, 1. For the fullest account of the raid, see Carroll V. Glines, *Doolittle's Tokyo Raiders;* H. H. Arnold to Rosenman, April 29, 1949, extract in *PPA,* appended note to "Press Conference . . . Apr. 21, 1942"; Spector, *Eagle against the Sun,* 154–55; S. Morison, *Two-Ocean War,* 139–40; Greenfield, "Franklin D. Roosevelt," 83.

61. George Gallup, "Roosevelt's Conduct of War Approved by 8 Out of 10 Voters," *NYT,* May 13, 1942, 10.

62. *PPA,* "Establishment of the Women's Army Auxiliary Corps, EO 9163, May 15, 1942," and attached note; Mattie E. Treadwell, *The Women's Army Corps,* 22; Nona Baldwin, "Bill for Women's Auxiliary Corps Passed by the House," *NYT,* March 18, 1942, 1; "Bill to Put Women in Army Is Passed" and "Mrs. Hobby Slated to Become Head of the WAAC," *NYT,* May 15, 1942, 21, 23; "Mrs. Hobby Named Director of WAAC," *NYT,* May 16, 1943, 15; "Mrs. Hobby Sworn in as WAAC Director," *NYT,* May 17, 1942, 32; "Urges Navy Women Be Auxiliary Unit," *NYT,* May 28, 1942, 14; EO 9274, November 19, 1942; "President Hails Waacs on First Birthday; Trust in Them 'Magnificently Justified,'" *NYT,* May 16, 1943, 39; "WAACs Now in Army; Name Now WACs," *NYT,* July 3, 1943, 16; "Mrs. Hobby a Colonel; Marshall Approves a Wac Goal of 600,000," *NYT,* July 6, 1943, 16; James Baron, "Oveta Culp Hobby, Founder of the WACs and First Secretary of Health, Dies at 90," *NYT,* August 19, 1995, B13.

63. For American women in wartime, see Susan M. Hartmann, *The Home Front and Beyond: American Women in the 1940s.* For evolving feminist scholarship, see Karen Anderson, *Wartime Women: Sex Roles, Family Relations, and the Status of Women during World War II;* and Leisa D. Meyer, *Creating G.I. Jane: Sexuality and Power in the Women's Army Corps during World War II.*

64. S. Morison, *Two-Ocean War*, 140–63; Spector, *Eagle against the Sun*, 158–76.

65. Conn and Fairchild, *Framework of Hemisphere Defense*, 423–24.

Chapter 8. Taking the Offensive

1. *PPA*, "Statement on Roosevelt-Molotov Conversations, June 11, 1942," and appended note; Sherwood, *Roosevelt and Hopkins*, contains accounts of the meetings written by the American interpreter, Samuel H. Cross of Harvard, and by Hopkins, and the text of Roosevelt's June 6 cable to Churchill, 557–79, quotes on 561, 577, and 579. Molotov's adieu is in Susan Butler, *My Dear Mr. Stalin*, 70. W. H. Lawrence, "U.S., Soviet Agree. Russian Here Secretly . . .," *NYT*, June 12, 1942, 1.

2. HASSETT, June 17–20, 1942, 60–69; *PPA*, "Joint Statement of President Roosevelt and Prime Minister Churchill on Their Conferences, June 27, 1942," and appended note; Martin Gilbert, *Churchill: A Life*, 722; Frank L. Kluckhohn, "Premier's 2nd Visit," *NYT*, June 19, 1943, 1; "World Plans Made: Pacific—China Strategy, Russian, and 'Second Front' Discussed," *NYT*, June 20, 1942, 1; "Churchill Said to Oppose Call for an Invasion," *NYT*, June 21, 1942, 1.

3. For this counterfactual proposition, see Chester Wilmot, *The Struggle for Europe*.

4. HASSETT, June 21, 1942, 69–70; Gilbert, *Churchill: A Life*, 723; Meacham, *Franklin and Winston*, 185; Winston S. Churchill, *The Hinge of Fate*, 383; Kimball, *Forged in War*, 149–53; Map Room messages between Roosevelt and Stalin, July 5 and 7, 1942, FDRL, as printed in S. Butler, *My Dear Mr. Stalin*, 75–76. General John Burgoyne (1722–1792) surrendered a British army at Saratoga, New York, in 1777, a turning point in the American Revolution.

5. *PPA*, "White House Statement Announcing War Production Figures, June 25, 1942" and "Joint Statement of President Roosevelt and Prime Minister Churchill on Their Conferences, June 27, 1942"; W. H. Lawrence, "Allies Strategy Heartens Leaders," *NYT*, June 28, 1942, 1.

6. Gilbert, *Churchill: A Life*, 723–24.

7. "Memorandum for Hon. Harry L. Hopkins, General Marshall, Admiral King, July 16, 1942," in Sherwood, *Roosevelt and Hopkins*, 603–5.

8. Matloff and Snell, *Strategic Planning*, 217–94. This differs from the analysis by Greenfield in *American Strategy*, 56–60, who could not factor in the Roosevelt-Churchill conferences at Hyde Park.

9. For an amusing but somewhat inaccurate account of early efforts to deal with the rubber crisis, see Galbraith, *Life in Our Times*, 152–55; "Tire Rationing Comes as Blow to Auto Owners and Truckmen," *NYT*, December 28, 1941, 1; *PPA*, "The President Appeals to the State Governors to Conserve Rubber by Reducing Speed Limits, Mar. 14, 1942" and "Radio Appeal on the Scrap Rubber Campaign, June 12, 1942," and appended notes.

10. "Farm Rubber Bill Opposed by Nelson," *NYT*, July 7, 1942, 11; C. P. Trussell, "Farm Rubber Bill Is Voted by Senate," *NYT*, July 23, 1942, 1; "Farm Rubber Bill Is Passed by House," *NYT*, July 5, 1942, 1; "Farm Rubber Bill Is Viewed as Doomed," *NYT*, August 2, 1942, 1; *PPA*, "The President Vetoes a Bill to Promote the Production of Synthetic Rubber from Grain, Aug. 6, 1942" and "The President Asks Bernard M.

Baruch to Make a Survey and Report on Rubber, Aug. 6, 1942," and appended note; W. H. Lawrence, "Roosevelt Vetoes Farm Bill, Names Own Board," *NYT,* August 7, 1942, 1.

11. W. H. Lawrence, "Nation-Wide Gasoline Curb Pledged Soon by Roosevelt after Baruch Asks" and "Digest of Report by Baruch Committee," *NYT,* September 11, 1942, 1, 15; "Henderson Asks Reduced Auto Use All over Country," *NYT,* September 13, 1942, 1.

12. "Jeffers Appointed Ruler over Rubber," *NYT,* September 16, 1942, 1; "Rubber Administrator," *NYT,* September 17, 1942, 24; *PPA,* "The President Provides for Coordination and Control of Rubber Program, EO 9246, Sept. 17, 1942," and appended note; "Roosevelt Vests Power in Jeffers," *NYT,* September 19, 1942, 7; Charles E. Egan, "Gasoline Rationing Ordered Widened to Entire Country," *NYT,* September 26, 1942, 1; "Gasoline Rationing in Entire Country in Effect, Nov. 22," *NYT,* September 27, 1942, 1; "35-Mile Speed in Force," *NYT,* October 1, 14; Nelson, *Arsenal of Democracy,* 290–306; *PPA,* "[Letter to Rubber Director and Price Administrator], Nov. 26, 1942"; "Full 'Gas' Rationing Dec. 1 Ordered by the President," *NYT,* November 27, 1942, 1.

13. *PPA,* "The President Establishes the Office of War Information, EO 9128, June 13, 1942," and appended note, and "Military Order Establishing the Office of Strategic Services, June 13, 1942," and appended note; "President Forms Top News Agency; Elmer Davis Chief," *NYT,* June 14, 1942, 1.

14. *PPA,* "The Reorganization of the Executive Office of the President, EO 8248, Sept. 8, 1939," and appended note; Frank L. Kluckhohn, "President Puts Defense Secrecy up to Press, Radio, and Congress," *NYT,* February 22, 1941, 1; *PPA,* "White House Statement Announcing the President's Appointment of William J. Donovan as Coordinator of Information, July 11, 1941," and appended note; "Lowell Mellett, Ex-U.S. Aide, Dies," *NYT,* April 7, 1960, 35; *PPA,* "The President Establishes the Office of Facts and Figures, Oct. 21, 1941," and appended note. For Donovan, see Thomas F. Troy, *Donovan and the CIA: A History of the Establishment of the Central Intelligence Agency.* Sherwood, *Roosevelt and Hopkins,* notes his own work with Donovan in 943n273. Winkler, *Politics of Propaganda,* is the best account of the OWI. For an account of prewar information policy, see Steele, *Propaganda in an Open Society.*

15. *PPA,* "[OWI], June 13, 1941"; "President Forms Top News Agency; Elmer Davis Chief," *NYT,* June 14, 1942, 1; "Davis Is Sworn in as News Director," *NYT,* June 18, 1942, 19; "Davis Long Writer and Commentator," *NYT,* June 14, 1943, 31; E. B. White. "Talk of the Town," *New Yorker,* March 14, 1942, 14; *Press Conf* #833 (June 16, 1942), 19:395; Roger Burlingame, *Don't Let Them Scare You: The Life and Times of Elmer Davis.* The well-known internal dispute is treated thoroughly in Winkler's *Politics of Propaganda,* and will not be further addressed.

16. *PPA,* "White House Statement Announcing the Appointment of William J. Donovan as Coordinator of Information, July 11, 1941," and appended note, and "Military Order Establishing the Office of Strategic Services, June 13, 1942," and appended note; "Military Order," *NYT,* June 14, 1942, 31; *Press Conf* #851 (October 13, 1942), 20:143–44; #859 (November 10, 1942), 20:134.

17. *Press Conf* #831 (June 9, 1942), 19:380–81; Edmund F. Wehrle, *Catoctin Mountain Park,* chap. 6. A number of detailed maps are included as is a list of FDR's guests at

each visit and its duration. Rosenman, *Working with Roosevelt*, 348; Churchill, *The Hinge of Fate*, 797; HASSETT, August 28–30, 1942, 109–16. Apparently, some Washington newspaperwomen were the first to use "Shangri-La" to refer to the Catoctin site, which FDR thought was "lovely." *Press Conf* #831 (June 9, 1942), 19:381.

18. Will Lissner, "FBI Seizes 8 Saboteurs Landed by U-Boats Here and in Florida to Blow Up War Plants," *NYT*, July 28, 1942, 1; "War on Our Own Shores," *NYT*, July 29, 1942, C14; Biddle, *In Brief Authority*, 325–43, memo on 328, quote on 329; *PPA*, "The President . . . Establishes a Military Commission . . ., July 2, 1942," and appended note; *Ex parte Milligan*, 71 U.S. 2 (1866); *Ex parte Quirin*, 317 U.S. 1 (1942); Lewis Wood, "Spy Court Session Viewed by Press," *NYT*, July 12, 1942, 1; *Press Conf* #839 (August 4, 1942), 20:34–37; Lewis Wood, "Decision Is Near on Saboteur Raid," *NYT*, August 8, 1942, 1; "Clemency for Two," *NYT*, August 9, 1942, 1; HASSETT, June 28, July 2, 9, 12, August 1, 2, 3, 1942, 74–75, 83, 86, 90, 97, 98. Louis Fisher, *Nazi Saboteurs on Trial: A Military Tribunal and American Law*, quote on 96, is heavily drawn upon. The *New York Times* ran a page 1 story by Lewis Wood on most days of the trial. A brief look at twenty-first-century evaluations is provided in Michael R. Belknap, "A Putrid Pedigree: The Bush Administration's Military Tribunals in Historical Perspective." Art. I, Sec. 9: " . . . No Bill of Attainder or ex post facto Law shall be passed."

19. John Miller Jr., *Guadalcanal: The First Offensive*; S. Morison, *Two-Ocean War*, 167–77; Charles Hurd, "Sea Battle in Dark," *NYT*, October 13, 1942, 1; *Press Conf* #844 (August 28, 1942), 20:74–75; *PPA*, "The President Addresses a Letter to Each Federal Department and Agency, Aug. 21, 1943"; Lewis Woods, "Roosevelt Orders Agencies to Cease Fights in Public," *NYT*, August 22, 1941, 1; Franklin D. Roosevelt to JCS, October 24, 1942, as cited in J. Miller, *Guadalcanal: The First Offensive*, 172n3. See also Greenfield, *American Strategy*, 73. Richard Tregaskis, *Guadalcanal Diary*, is a vivid account.

20. *PPA*, "A Statement on Labor Day, Sept. 5, 1942," "A Message to Congress Asking for Quick Action to Stabilize the Economy, Sept. 7, 1941," and appended note, and " . . . Fireside Chat on the Cost of Living and the Progress of the War, Sept. 7, 1942"; Bertram D. Hulen, "President Praises Labor, Warning of War Sacrifices," *NYT*, September 6, 1942, 1; W. H. Lawrence, "The Ultimatum," "The President Speaks," and Frederick R. Barkley, "Roosevelt Stirs Congress by Threat to Act on Prices," *NYT*, September 8, 1942, 1; George Gallup, "Farmers Ready to Accept Price Control . . .," *NYT*, September 25, 1942, 13; Levine and Levine, *People and the President*, 451–58. Presumably, Roosevelt would have relied on the Second War Powers Act, P.L. 507, 77th Cong., 2d sess., approved March 27, 1942. For some of its uses, see Margo J. Anderson and William Seltzer, "Federal Statistical Confidentiality and Business Data: Twentieth Century Challenges and Continuing Issues." The full citation for John Robert Powers (1912–42), and all other Medal of Honor citations, by war and in alphabetical order, are at http://www.history.army.mil/moh.html.

21. *PPA*, "Letter to the Chairman of the Banking and Currency Committees . . .," September 17, 1941, and appended note; "President Strikes at Any Parity Rise," *NYT*, September 18, 1942, 1; *Press Conf* #848 (October 1, 1942), 20:127–29; C. P. Trussel, "Price Bill Delays Hit by President," *NYT*, October 2, 1942, 1; "Sept. 15 Rates Set," *NYT*, October 3, 1942, 1; Thomas G. Manning, *The Office of Price Administration: A World War II Agency of Control*; Galbraith, *Life in Our Times*, 124–44.

22. *PPA*, "The Office of Economic Stabilization Is Established, EO 9250, Oct. 3, 1942," and appended note, and "Letters to Leon Henderson," October 3, 1942; C. P. Trussel, "Roosevelt Freezes Wages, Rents, Farm Prices; Names Justice Byrnes Director" and Godfrey N. Nelson, "Order Qualifies Policy on Salaries," *NYT*, October 4, 1942, 1, 19. Byrnes (1879–1972) was the last person appointed to the Court who had no formal judicial education save for "reading law" in a lawyer's office during 1903. A U.S. senator since 1931, he was confirmed the day he was nominated. He resigned the day of his appointment as economic stabilizer. See Robertson, *Sly and Able*.

23. AP, "9 Billion Tax Bill Voted in Congress," and UP, "Features of New Tax Bill," *NYT*, October 21, 1942, 1, 10; "Roosevelt Signs Record Tax Bill," *NYT*, October 22, 1942, 1.

24. AP, "President's [Itinerary]," *NYT*, October 3, 1942, 6; *Press Conf* #848 (October 1, 1942), 20:103–28; W. H. Lawrence, "Nation-Wide Roosevelt Trip to War Plants Is Revealed"; Bertram Hulen, "President Seems Untired and Calm Despite Grueling Two-Week Trip," "Banned from Trip, Reporters Protest," "Roosevelt Story Cuts Paper," "Press and Radio Praised for Silence on President," and "Charges Politics in Roosevelt Trip," *NYT*, October 2, 1941, 1, 15, 14.

25. *PPA*, "The President Announces the Plan to Try Nazi War Criminals," October 7, 1942"; Bertram D. Hulen, "Roosevelt Says U.S. Will Join in Investigation of Atrocities," and Raymond Daniell, "British Announce Plan," *NYT*, October 8, 1942, 1, 11; *PPA*, "The President Denounces the Nazi Murder of French Hostages, Oct. 25, 1941" and "Statement Warning against Axis Crimes in Occupied Countries, Aug. 21, 1942"; *Press Conf* #842 (August 21, 1942), 20:52–57; Kimball, *Forged in War*, 277. But Kimball ignores the October 1942 announcement, and his text treatment first discusses war crimes in connection with the 1944 Quebec Conference, though an endnote (379n73) mentions information given Roosevelt by Rabbi Stephen Wise in December 1942. Few historians mention FDR's October 1942 announcement. Burns, *Soldier of Freedom*, 395, says, "Late in 1942 [the president] announced the plan of the United Nations to establish a commission to investigate war crimes." But of course there was no United Nations plan, or even an FDR plan at that time. There was a firm intention that bore fruit. A well-received book, Arieh J. Kochavi, *Prelude to Nuremberg: Allied War Crimes Policy and the Question of Punishment*, 4, 88, 90, 91, 126, 237, insists in at least six places that Roosevelt favored "summary execution" for war criminals, without ever citing his public papers that I have quoted.

26. *PPA*, " . . . Statement on Columbus Day, Oct. 12, 1942" and "The President Reports on the Home Front, Fireside Chat, Oct. 12, 1942"; W. H. Lawrence, "President for Drafting Youths at 18 Years; Says Our Offensives Will Aid Russia, China," *NYT*, October 13, 1932, 1.

27. *PPA*, "Signing the Bill Reducing the Draft Age, Nov. 13, 1942," and appended note; Frederick R. Barkley, "House by 345 to 16 Lowers Draft Age to Take Boys of 18," *NYT*, October 18, 1942, 1; C. P. Trussell, "Year of Training of 18, 19-Year-Olds Is Voted by Senate," *NYT*, October 25, 1942; "Year of Training Is Voted by Senate," *NYT*, October 25, 1941, 1; "Youth Draft Bill Is Adopted by Senate, Sent to White House," *NYT*, November 13, 1942, 1; "President Signs 18–19 Draft Bill," *NYT*, November 14, 1942, 16. The Census Bureau would later note that between October 1940 and October 1942, 1.9 million women entered the labor force as 2.3 million men left it. "Census Shows Changes in Nation Due to War," *NYT*, December 4, 1942, E8.

28. *PPA*, " . . . Letter to John J. Bennett . . ., Oct. 23, 1942" and " . . . The Hope That All Will Vote . . ., Oct. 20, 1942"; "Roosevelt Votes at Hyde Park Hall," *NYT,* November 4, 1942, 5; "Midterm Verdict," *NYT,* November 11, 142, E1.

29. *Press Conf* #857 (November 6, 1942), 20:196–200; W. H. Lawrence, "President Elated by British Victory," *NYT,* November 7, 1942, 1; George F. Howe, *Northwest Africa: Seizing the Initiative in the West,* 14. McNarney (1903–72), Marshall's deputy, was filling in for his absent chief.

30. *PPA,* "The President Broadcasts to the French People, Nov. 7, 1942," and appended note; "The President Sends a Message of Assurance to Marshal Petain, Nov. 8, 1942," and appended note; "The President Assures Portugal, Nov. 8, 1942," and appended note; "White House Statement on [Laval], Nov. 9, 1941"; and "A Message to the Governor General of Algeria, Nov. 14, 1942"; Robert D. Murphy, *Diplomat among Warriors,* 66–161, quotes on 69 and 101; Sherwood, *Roosevelt and Hopkins,* 641–57. See, for example, the excerpt from a Marshall oral history interview and Pogue's comment on it in Pogue, *George C. Marshall,* 2:336.

31. Howe, *Northwest Africa,* 89–272; R. Murphy, *Diplomat among Warriors,* 131; Sherwood, *Roosevelt and Hopkins,* 648–55, quote on 649.

32. Hull, *Memoirs,* 2:948–66, 1128–37; *PPA,* "Statement on the Temporary Political Arrangements in North and West Africa, Nov. 19, 1942"; *Press Conf* #861 (November 17, 1942), 20:247; Sherwood, *Roosevelt and Hopkins,* 634, 651; S. Butler, *My Dear Mr. Stalin,* November 14, 1942, 94; W. H. Lawrence, "President Says Darlan Deal Is 'a Temporary Expedient,'" *NYT,* November 18, 1942, 1; "Willkie Assails 'Expediency,'" *NYT,* December 6, 1942, 57. Roosevelt, naturally sympathetic, later had the son sent to Warm Springs. Freidel, *Rendezvous with Destiny,* 456.

33. Sherwood, *Roosevelt and Hopkins,* 648; *PPA,* address to the *New York Herald Tribune* Forum, November 17, 1942; "Roosevelt Says Tide of War Is Turning," *NYT,* November 18, 1942, 1. For the naval battle of Guadalcanal, see S. Morison, *Two-Ocean War,* 196–208. Eisenhower's memoir does not mention this instruction from his commander in chief, although he cites his own message to which it was a response. Dwight D. Eisenhower, *Crusade in Europe,* 109–10.

34. HASSETT, November 26–30, 1942, 141–46; December 18–23, 1942, 146–49.

35. Charles E. Egan, "Foreign Needs Sharpen Anxieties over Food," *NYT,* November 29, 1942, E6; "Lehman, Hoover Confer on Relief," *NYT,* December 4, 1942, 17; "Lehman Sworn in as Relief Director," *NYT,* December 5, 1942, 17; *Press Conf* #863 (November 24, 1942), 20:264–65; Allan Nevins, *Herbert H. Lehman and His Era,* 221–38.

36. *PPA,* "Establishment of the Petroleum Administration for War, EO 9276, Dec. 2, 1943"; W. H. Lawrence, "President Widens Control by Ickes over Oil Industry," *NYT,* December 3, 1942, 1; *PPA,* "Delegation of Authority over the Food Program, EO 9280, Dec. 5, 1942," and appended note; "Food Men Repeat Shortage Warning" and John MacCormack, "Wickard Named Food Administrator," *NYT,* December 7, 1942, F7, 1; "Will Work with Lehman," *NYT,* December 7, 1942, 18; Irvin M. May, *Marvin Jones: The Public Life of an Agrarian Advocate,* 208–27.

37. "Navy Reveals Damage Done at Pearl Harbor" and "Navy Statement on the Pearl Harbor Attack," *NYT,* December 6, 1942, 1, 69; "Roosevelt Hails Unity for Victory," *NYT,* December 7, 1941, 8.

38. *PPA,* "The President Announces Discontinuation of W.P.A., Dec. 4, 1941," and appended note; "WPA Is Abolished, Roosevelt Points to War Work Rise," *NYT,* December 5, 1942, 1.

Chapter 9. Advancing on All Fronts

1. *PPA,* "State of the Union, Jan. 7, 1943"; W. H. Lawrence, "Roosevelt Sees Allies on the Road to Victory; Urges a Post-war America Free from Want," *NYT,* January 8, 1943, 1; Sherwood, *Roosevelt and Hopkins,* 667–68; Rosenman, *Working with Roosevelt,* 366–68. I do not think that the distinction between bombing "Japanese people" and Axis facilities was merely rhetorical. Cf. John Dower, *Japan in War & Peace,* 257–306.

2. *PPA,* "Annual Budget Message, Jan. 6, 1943," and appended note; *Press Conf* #874 (January 9, 1943), 21:28–85; W. H. Lawrence, "President Asks 109 Billions in War Budget; New Taxes" and "One Year of War Costs More than 1789 to 1933," *NYT,* January 13, 1941, 1, 15.

3. "The Day in Washington," *NYT,* January 12, 1943, 10; *NYT,* January 14, 1943, 11; Lewis Wood, "Rutledge Joins Supreme Court; Civil Liberties Cases Are Reopened," *NYT,* February 16, 1943, 1; "Justice Wiley Rutledge Dies of Brain Hemorrhage at 55," *NYT,* September 11, 1949, 9; W. H. Lawrence, "A Cool Man on a Hot Spot," 7, 23.

4. Sherwood, *Roosevelt and Hopkins,* 667–74; *Press Conf* #879 (February 12, 1943), 32:141.

5. *Press Conf* #875 (January 24, 1943), 21:86–96. This is printed in *PPA* with an appended note. S. Butler, *My Dear Mr. Stalin,* 101–4.

6. Maurice Matloff, *Strategic Planning for Coalition Warfare, 1943–44,* 18–42, quote on 21.

7. *Press Conf* #875 (January 24, 1943), 21:86–96; *PPA,* "Official Communiqué Casablanca Conference, Jan. 26, 1943"; Drew Middleton, "Roosevelt, Churchill Map 1943 War Strategy in Ten-Day Conference Held in Casablanca," "London Press Sees Parlay as Augury," and "Historic Meeting Informal in Tone," *NYT,* January 27, 1943, 1, 2, 3. These and a number of other embargoed stories appeared in the *New York Times* and other papers with a "Jan. 24 (Delayed)" dateline. Michael F. Reilly, *Reilly of the White House,* 159. For de Gaulle's jaundiced view, see *The Complete War Memoirs of Charles de Gaulle,* 396–99. At the joint press conference, Roosevelt spoke 3,114 words, Churchill 832.

8. Walter Logan, UP, "Roosevelt Pays Surprise Visit to U.S. Troops in Morocco," *NYT,* January 27, 1943, 1; Meacham, *Franklin and Winston,* 209–12; S. Butler, *My Dear Mr. Stalin,* 112–13; Sherwood, *Roosevelt and Hopkins,* 694–95; Ross T. McIntire, *White House Physician,* 156. Most of the comments about McIntyre's concerns for the president's health during the Casablanca trip come from Hopkins's contemporary notes. The subtext of Dr. McIntire's memoir is the robust health of the president until shortly before his death.

9. *PPA,* "Joint Statement on the Meeting of President Roosevelt and President Vargas, Jan. 29, 1943"; UP, "Roosevelt Stops Off in Brazil after a Short Visit to Liberia," and "Left Morocco by Plane," *NYT,* January 29, 1943, 1; Bertram Hulen, "Roosevelt, Vargas, Affirm Aim to Make Atlantic Safe for All," and AP, "Roosevelt-Vargas Conference Held

on U.S. Destroyer in Natal Harbor," *NYT,* January 30, 1943, 1; Bertram D. Hulen, "Visits West Indies," *NYT,* January 31, 1943, 1; Sidney M. Shallett, "Roosevelt Is Back in the White House," *NYT,* February 1, 1943, 1; "President Asserts We Fight Two Wars," *NYT,* January 31, 1943, 6. Brazil had declared war on Germany and Italy in August 1942. Its major active contribution was a 25,000 man infantry division sent to Italy; 1,889 of its soldiers and sailors were killed, and three warships, thirty-one merchant vessels, and twenty-two fighter aircraft were lost.

10. *Press Conf* #876 (February 2, 1943), 21:97–123, long quote on 116; "President Tells War Plans Secretly to Congress Group," *NYT,* February 2, 1943, 1; W. H. Lawrence, "President Implies 1943 Invasion Plan"; Bertram D. Hulen, "President Depicts His Trip with Zest"; Harold Callender, "Roosevelt's View of Africa Hopeful"; "Press and Radio Praised"; "Roosevelt on Trip, Kept in Touch with U.S."; and "Guard Tricks in Morocco Recounted by President," *NYT,* February 3, 1943, 1, 4, 5; *Press Conf* #879 (February 12, 1943), 21:137–41.

11. *PPA,* "Address to the White House Correspondents' Association, Feb. 12, 1943"; W. H. Lawrence, "President Pledges Many Invasions in Europe, Ousting Foe from China and Attack on Japan," *NYT,* February 13, 1943, 1.

12. *PPA,* "President Sends a Message of Congratulation to Marshal Stalin, Feb. 4, 1943" and "Message to Marshall Stalin . . ., Feb. 22, 1943"; Matloff, *Strategic Planning,* 26–27; S. Butler, *My Dear Mr. Stalin,* 116–18; Kimball, *Forged in War,* 211.

13. S. Butler, *My Dear Mr. Stalin,* 122–27; Kimball, *Forged in War,* 211–12. The initial *New York Times* story was a tiny paragraph, "Nazis Accuse Russians," April 16, 1943, 4; eleven stories later, it had migrated to the front page: Ralph Parker, "Soviet Breaks Ties with Poland," *NYT,* April 27, 1943, 1. Janusz K. Zawodny, *Death in the Forest: The Story of the Katyn Forest Massacre.* Forty-two years after the mass murders, the Russian government admitted what it had done. Celestine Bohlen, "Russian Files Show Stalin Ordered Massacre of 20,000 Poles in 1940," *NYT,* October 15, 1992, A1. General Wladyslaw Sikorski (1881–1943) was prime minister of the London exiles.

14. *PPA,* "The President Urges the Congress Not to Repeal the $25,000 Salary Limitation, Feb. 6, 1943"; C. P. Trussell, "Roosevelt Urges Salary Rider Ban," *NYT,* February 7, 1943, 36; *PPA,* "A Letter to [Robert Doughton] on Salary Limitation, Feb. 15, 1943"; *Press Conf* #880 (February 16, 1943), 21:149; John H. Crider, "Roosevelt Backs $25,000 and $50,000 as Income Limits," *NYT,* February 18, 1943, 1; *PPA,* "The President Criticizes the Rider Method of Legislation . . ., Apr. 11, 1943"; John MacCormack, "$25,000 Pay Limit Repealed Minus Roosevelt Signature; He Assails Congress," *NYT,* April 12, 1943, 1.

15. *PPA,* "White House Statement and EO 9328, Apr. 8, 1943," and appended note; W. H. Lawrence, "Roosevelt Order Freezes Wages and Prices and Bars Shifting of Jobs for Higher Pay," and "Order Is Acclaimed," *NYT,* April 9, 1943, 1, 1. The Consumer Price Index, All Items, rose from 59.4 in 1939 to 74.0 in 1943; in 1945 it was 76.9 and 95.5 in 1947. *HIST STATS,* Series E 113, p. 125.

16. Ickes, *Secret Diary,* after 1937 is filled with items about Dies and his committee; for the meeting with FDR, see 3:579–81 (December 1, 1940). Kenneth O'Reilly, ed., *The FBI File on the House Committee on Un-American Activities; ANB; PPA,* "The Interdepartmental Committee to Consider Cases of Subversive Activities by Federal

Employees Is Established, EO 9300, Feb. 5, 1943," and appended note; "Names Committee on Subversion," *NYT*, February 7, 1943, 20.

17. *PPA*, "Establishment of a Minimum Wartime Work Week of Forty-Eight Hours, EO 9301, Feb. 9, 1943"; "President Orders 48-Hour Week in War Effort," *NYT*, February 10, 1943, 1. The Dies Committee was the common usage until Dies left Congress in 1945, when it became known as HUAC until its eventual demise in 1975.

18. Sherwood, *Roosevelt and Hopkins*, 644, 660–61; HASSETT, November 27, 1942, 143–44; June 21–22, 1943, 181–82; November 3, 1943, 288; Jonathan Daniels, *White House Witness*, 167; "Chiang Plans a Nation-Wide Tour," *NYT*, February 13, 1943, 4; W. H. Lawrence, "Mme. Chiang Guest of the President," *NYT*, February 18, 1943, 1; "Mme. Chiang Asks Defeat of Japan and House Cheers," Nancy MacLennan, "China's First Lady Charms Congress," and "Text of the Two Addresses before Congress by Mme. Chiang Kai-shek," *NYT*, February 19, 1943, 1, 2, 4; *Press Conf* #881 (February 19, 1943), 21:157–74; W. H. Lawrence, "President Tells Mme. Chiang More Arms Will Be Rushed," and Nancy MacLennan, "Mme. Chiang Poises as If for Flight," *NYT*, February 20, 1943, 1, 3.

19. Charles Hurd, "Guadalcanal Is Ours," *NYT*, February 10, 1943, 1; J. Miller, *Guadalcanal: The First Offensive*, 349. Samuel Morison says, "The number of sailors lost on each side . . . the aviators lost . . . have never been computed" (*Two-Ocean War*, 214). "Gen. Vandegrift Gets Honor Medal for Victories Won on Guadalcanal," *NYT*, February 5, 1943. 1.

20. Howe, *Northwest Africa*, 438ff, quotes on 480, 476, 675; Charles Hurd, "Stimson Reports 'a Sharp Reverse,'" *NYT*, February 19, 1943, 1; A. J. Liebling, *World War II Writings*, 320; Sherwood, *Roosevelt and Hopkins*, 689; "Eisenhower Gets Full Generalship," *NYT*, February 12, 1943, 3. Comparable figures for British troops were 35,940: 6,475, 21,630, 7,835.

21. *PPA*, "Informal Extemporaneous Remarks at Reception for New Senators and Representatives, Mar. 10, 1943"; "President Greets 117 New Members," *NYT*, March 11, 1943, 19.

22. *Press Conf* #880 (February 16, 1943), 21:152–55; "Offices Bill Total Is [$2.6 Billion]," *NYT*, February 10, 1943, 11; *PPA*, "Message to the Congress Transmitting National Resources Planning Board Report, Mar. 10, 1943," and appended note; "Roosevelt Offers Plan to Congress for Birth-to-Grave Social Security"; W. H. Lawrence, "Postwar Program"; Louis Stark, "Federalized Welfare Is Asked . . ."; AP, "Planning Board's Ideas Told in 450,000 Words"; "Resources Board's Findings and Recommendations to Congress on Expanded Social Security System"; and "Plan Is Compared with Beveridge's," *NYT*, March 11, 1943, 1, 12, 13; Louis Stark, "Congress at Odds on Security Plan" and "Security Program Lauded at Parley," *NYT*, March 12, 1943, 1, 14; Henry M. Dorris, "Lend-Lease Wins 407–6 in House; Senate Group Unanimous for It," *NYT*, March 11, 1943, 1; *Press Conf* #883 (March 12, 1945), 21:191–92. J. M. Burns, in his only reference to the National Resources Planning Board, says "planning, to Roosevelt, was a sharply limited exercise. It was segmental; he was interested in plans for specific regions, watersheds, industries, not—despite his critics—in 'economic planning' or in some grand reshaping of the nation" (*Soldier of Freedom*, 353). This is a serious misreading.

23. *Press Conf* #888 (March 30, 1943), 21:239–55; Harold Callender, "President Expects Talks with Russia," and W. H. Lawrence, "President Tells Farm Labor Plan," *NYT*, March 31, 1943, 1; *Press Conf* #883 (March 12, 1943), 21:201; W. H. Lawrence, "Briton in Capital"; "Text on Farm Labor"; and Bertram D. Hulen, "38 Nations Called to Parley on Food," *NYT*, March 31, 1943, 1, 13, 7; Frederick R. Barkley, "Congressmen See President on Food," and P. J. Philip, "President's Views Endorsed by Eden," *NYT*, April 1, 1943, 15, 9. See also *Press Conf* #912 (July 30, 1943), 22:143–45.

24. HASSETT, April 1–6, 1943, 163–68, *PPA*, "The President Vetoes a Parity Computing Bill, Apr. 2, 1943"; John H. Crider, "Bankhead Farm Bill Vetoed; President Warns Congress of 'Inflationary Tornado,'" *NYT*, April 3, 1943, 1, text on 8, Rosenman, *Working with Roosevelt*, 378–79; "Now He Is the President's Official Adviser," *NYT*, October 2, 1943, 8. Henrietta Nesbitt (1874–1963), installed as executive housekeeper by the new mistress of the White House in 1933, pleased almost no one but Eleanor, so she remained. After his mother's death, the president brought Mary Campbell, his mother's cook, to Washington to preside over the family kitchen on the second floor. See Nesbitt's *White House Diary*.

25. *PPA*, "Address at Monterrey, Mexico, Apr. 20, 1943," and appended note, "Extemporaneous Remarks to Naval Air Cadets at Corpus Christi, Texas, April 21, 1943," and "Statement on the Execution of the Tokyo Raiders by the Japanese, Apr. 21, 1943," and appended note; *Press Conf* #891 (April 19,1943), 21:275–84; #892 (April 29, 1943), 21:285–92; W. H. Lawrence, "Roosevelt, on Tour, Meets Mexican President," and "President Stirred by Visits to Camps," plus seven delayed dispatches, and Camille M. Clanfarra, "Monterrey Crowd Greets 2 Leaders," *NYT*, April 21, 1943, 1, 10, 11; Bertram D. Hulen, "President Aghast," *NYT*, April 22, 1942, 1; AP, "President Stirred by Trip to Camps and War Plants," and W. H. Lawrence, "Ends Camps Tours," *NYT*, April 30, 1943, 7. The date of the first sinking of a Mexican oil tanker bringing oil to the American East Coast, killing thirteen crewmen, which resulted in a Mexican declaration of war against the Axis the next month. Camacho, who became president in 1940, cooperated with the United States from the beginning of his presidency. One Mexican air force squadron participated in liberating the Philippines, flying P-47s. Five of its fifty-one pilots were killed in action.

26. *Press Conf* #892 (April 29, 1943), 21:285–92; *PPA*, "White House Statement and EO 9340 on Seizure of Coal Mines, May 1, 1943," and appended note, and "Fireside Chat on the Federal Seizure of the Coal Mines, May 2, 1942," and appended note; Louis Stark, "Roosevelt Seizes All Struck Coal Mines," and AP, "Texts of Pronouncements on Coal," *NYT*, May 2, 1943, 1, 37; Joseph Shaplen, "Lewis Announces 15-Day Truce in Coal Strike Just before Roosevelt Rebukes Mine Union; New Contract to Be Negotiated in Interim," and "Speech Hits Lewis," *NYT*, May 3, 1943, 1; Sherwood, *Roosevelt and Hopkins*, 727–28.

27. Louis Stark, "Guarantee of Six-Day Week Seen as Mine Peace Step," *NYT*, May 3, 1943, 1. The existing contract called for overtime after seven hours in any day, or thirty-five hours in any week.

28. *PPA*, "Messages on the Victory in Tunisia, May 9, 1943," "Letter to the United Nations Conference on Food and Agriculture, May 18, 1943," and appended note, and "Address to the Delegates of [UN Food Conference], June 8, 1943"; Howe, *Northwest*

Africa, 665–68; Russell B. Porter, "Roosevelt Urges Food Parlay Waive Tariffs for Health," *NYT*, May 19, 1943, 1; "President Hails Food Conference as Sign of Unity," *NYT*, June 8, 1943, 1; I. May, *Marvin Jones*, 200–203.

29. Matloff, *Strategic Planning*, 125–45; Leahy, *I Was There*, 156–58; Sherwood, *Roosevelt and Hopkins*, 727–29. For a description of British preparations, see Churchill, *The Hinge of Fate*, 782–89; Burns, *Soldier of Freedom*, 368; Kimball, *Forged in War*, 214–18; *Press Conf* #895 (May 11, 1943), 21:311; W. H. Lawrence, "Churchill Arrives for Talk with Roosevelt," *NYT*, May 12, 1943, 1; HASSETT, May 27–June 2, 1943, 170–74; S. Butler, *My Dear Mr. Stalin*, 135–39.

30. W. H. Lawrence, "Blows in Europe and Far East Promised," *NYT*, May 15, 1943, 1; "Churchill Pledges Japan's Ruin, but Reaffirms Nazis Come First," *NYT*, May 20, 1943, 1; "Churchill's Text," *NYT*, May 20, 1943, 4; *Press Conf* #899 (May 25, 1943), 21:336–54; W. H. Lawrence, "Briton Predicts Equal Blows Will Fall in Europe and Asia," and Bertram D. Hulen, "Churchill Is Calm under Question Barrage," *NYT*, May 26, 1943, 1, 6; W. H. Lawrence, "U.S.-British Staffs in Full Accord," *NYT*, May 28, 1943, 1.

31. *PPA*, "The President Establishes the Office of War Mobilization, EO 9347, May 27, 1943," and attached note; "President's Texts on the OWM," W. H. Lawrence, "Byrnes Heads New 6-Man Board to Direct All War Mobilization," and "Vinson Was Expert on Taxes in House," *NYT*, May 29, 1943, 3, 1, 3; "Byrnes Speech to Be on Air," *NYT*, May 30, 1943, 20; Robertson, *Sly and Able*, 326–27. This was to prevent appeals from the OES, whose director was a subordinate of the OWM's director.

32. AP, "Byrnes Declares War Is Entering Many-Front Stage," and "Text of Byrnes Address," *NYT*, June 1, 1943, 1, 15; James F. Byrnes, *All in One Lifetime*, 220–21. Cf. Robertson, *Sly and Able*, 327–31.

33. *PPA*, "The President Establishes the [FEPC], EO 8802, June 25, 1941," and appended note; "President Orders an Even Break for Minorities in Defense Jobs," *NYT*, June 26, 1941, 1; Andrew E. Kersten, *Race, Jobs, and the War: The FEPC in the Midwest, 1941–46*; Robertson, *Sly and Able*, 335–36; A. Philip Randolph, "Why and How the March Was Postponed," reprinted in Andrew E. Kersten, *A. Philip Randolph: A Life in the Vanguard*, 141–46; Walter White, *A Man Called White: The Autobiography of Walter White*, 189–93; Studs Terkel, Rauh interview in *"The Good War,"* 337–42; Goodwin, *No Ordinary Time*, 249–53.

34. Kersten, *A. Philip Randolph*, 142; "Roosevelt Reviews Job Gains for Negro," *NYT*, April 6, 1942, 8; "Fair Employment," *NYT*, April 14, 1942, 20; "Negroes to Fight Employment Bias," *NYT*, June 11, 1942, 21; "Asks Discrimination End," *NYT*, August 28, 1941, 12; "President Orders Race Bars Lifted," *NYT*, September 7, 1942; "Roosevelt Reviews Job Gains for Negro," *NYT*, April 6, 1942, 8; "Fair Employment," *NYT*, April 24, 1942, 20; Kersten, *Race, Jobs, and the War*, 38–41; "Protest to President: 22 Groups Fight Transfer of Fair Employment Committee," *NYT*, August 17, 1942, 8; "Defends Transfer of Fair Hiring Body," *NYT*, August 18, 1942, 40.

35. "M'Nutt Calls Off Hearing on Hiring," *NYT*, January 12, 1943, 14; "Calls Conference on Discrimination," *NYT*, February 4, 1943, 3; *Press Conf* #897 (May 18, 1943), 21:234; "Msgr. Haas Takes Labor Post," *NYT*, May 20, 1943, 23. Haas, a protégé of Msgr. John A. Ryan, became bishop of Grand Rapids and an important clerical figure in the civil rights movement. *PPA*, "A New [FEPC] Is Established, EO 9346, May 27, 1943,"

and attached note; "New Board Set Up to End Hiring Bias," *NYT,* May 27, 1943, 6; *PPA,* "Campaign Address . . . Chicago . . . , Oct. 28, 1944"; Kersten, *Race, Jobs and the War,* 40–46, 5–6.

36. *PPA,* "State of the Union, Jan. 6, 1942"; Roger Daniels and Harry H. L. Kitano, *American Racism: Exploration of the Nature of Prejudice,* 73–79. For a national view, see *NYT* West Coast correspondent Lawrence E. Davies's stories on June 11, 12, 13 (2), 20, 1943. "CIO Asks President Act in 'Zoot' Cases," *NYT,* June 20, 1943; *PPA,* "The President Orders the Detroit Race Rioters to Disperse," Proclamation No. 2588, June 21, 1943; HASSETT, June 21, 1943, 181–82; "23 Dead in Detroit Rioting: Federal Troops Enter City on the Orders of Roosevelt," *NYT,* June 22, 1943, 1; "Army Patrols End Detroit Rioting," *NYT,* June 23, 1943, 1; Turner Catledge, "To Seek Remedies for Racial Tension," *NYT,* September 28, 1943, 17; *Press Conf* #933 (February 5, 1944), 23:23–35; "Negroes Meet President," *NYT,* February 6, 1944, 35. See also Freidel, *Rendezvous with Destiny,* 520–21. Dominic J. Capeci Jr., *The Harlem Riot of 1943,* is broader than its title indicates; for the spectrum of advice given Roosevelt, see 148–56. Allen D. Grimshaw, ed., *Racial Violence in the United States,* is a broad collection of documents. Zoot suits—coat knee length, shoulders overly padded, trousers so severely pegged at the ankles that a shoehorn was needed to get them on—were, like so much of youth culture, pioneered by blacks. Invented in 1939, popular in Harlem by 1940, their appeal was increased when cloth-saving edicts by the WPB made them illegal, along with such frills as cuffs on trousers. The Los Angeles Mexican American variant included a heavily pomaded ducktail hairstyle. Zoot suits were relatively expensive, and only a tiny fraction of L.A. youths wore them. See Meyer Berger, "Zoot Suit . . . ," *NYT,* June 11, 1943, 21. Finally, Cheryl L. Greenberg's broad study *Troubling the Waters: Black-Jewish Relations in the American Century* illuminates a crucial aspect of American race relations.

37. *PPA,* "The President Vetoes the Smith-Connally Bill, June 25, 1943," and appended note; W. H. Lawrence, "Congress Rebels," and "CIO Blames Absentees," *NYT,* June 26, 1943, 1, 2; *PPA,* "Veto of a Bill on the Commodity Credit Corporation, July 2, 1943," and appended note; Samuel B. Bledsoe, "Subsidies Upheld as House Sustains Veto by President," *NYT,* July 3, 1942, 1; *PPA,* "Statement on Signing a [Joint Resolution], July 16, 1943," and appended note; "Qualifies Signing of CCC Extension," *NYT,* July 17, 1943. This figure, although counterintuitive, is accurate. In 1937, the most turbulent year for labor, the official figure was 43/100 of 1 percent, the highest then recorded. *HIST STATS,* Series D 764–768 at 99.

38. *PPA,* "Extemporaneous Remarks at State Dinner in Honor of General Giraud, July 9, 1943," "Pope Pius XII Is Given Assurances on the Allied Invasion of Italian Soil, July 10, 1943," and "Joint Message of President Roosevelt and Prime Minister Churchill to the Italian People, July 9, 1943"; Sherwood, *Roosevelt and Hopkins,* 741.

39. *PPA,* "The Economic Defense Board Is Established, EO 8839, July 30, 1941," "The President Defines the Relations between the Department of State and the Board of Economic Warfare, May 20, 1943," and "EO 9361 Establishing the Office of Economic Warfare, July 15, 1943," and appended note; *Press Conf* #906 (June 29, 1943), 21:412–14; #908 (July 13, 1943), 22:10; #910 (July 23, 1943), 22:39–40; "President Tells BEW Hull Ranks It," *NYT,* May 22, 1942, 6; C. P. Trussel, "War Agency Row Left Smoldering,"

NYT, July 11, 1943, E7; *PPA,* "Letter to Wallace and Jones, EO 9361, July 16, 1943"; John H. Crider, "Roosevelt Strips Wallace, Jones of Power over War Purchases," *NYT,* July 16, 1942, 1; "Byrnes Is Shaping Economic Policy for Foreign Field" and "F.D.R. Cracks Down," *NYT,* July 18, 1943, 1; HASSETT, July 16, 1943, 190–91.

40. Rosenman, *Working with Roosevelt,* 383–84; Sherwood, *Roosevelt and Hopkins,* 741–44; Harold Callender, "Italy Seen Making First Peace Step," *NYT,* July 26, 1943, 1; *PPA,* "Fireside Chat, July 28, 1943." For a brief summary of the Italian situation, see Weinberg, *World at Arms,* 483–88. See Marian Clawson, *New Deal Planning: The National Resources Planning Board,* for the fullest account of the board.

41. *Press Conf* #912 (July 30, 1943), 22:41–51; *PPA,* "The President Warns Neutral Nations against Providing Asylum for War Criminals," July 30, 1943; Harold Callender, "Roosevelt Bars Only a Fascist Deal," *NYT,* July 31, 1943, 1; *Press Conf* #911 (July 27, 1943), 22:36; "Eisenhower Offers Italy Peace Terms" and "Gen. Eisenhower's Appeal," *NYT,* July 30, 1943, 1, 3; "OWI Broadcast Excerpts," *NYT,* July 28, 1943, 8.

Chapter 10. Waiting for D-Day

1. *Press Conf* #913 (August 10, 1943), 22:52–56; Martin Gilbert, *Churchill and America,* 180–81; Will Lissner, "Churchill Is Back in Quebec," and "Churchill Visit Disclosed," *NYT,* August 16, 1943, 1, 6; W. Averell Harriman and Elie Abel, *Special Envoy to Churchill and Stalin, 1941–1946,* 222; Leahy, *I Was There,* 174; S. Butler, *My Dear Mr. Stalin,* 150–51; John Crider, "Talks to Be Anglo-American Roosevelt Asserts in Capital," *NYT,* August 11, 1943, 1. Some scholars make much of the fact that Roosevelt lied to Churchill about his efforts to have a meeting with Stalin without the Briton. They were often less than frank with each other.

2. Matloff, *Strategic Planning,* 211–43, Stimson quote on 214, summary of Brooke's position on 220; Leahy, *I Was There,* 174–79; Elsey, *An Unplanned Life,* 37–40; Rosenman, *Working with Roosevelt,* 185. The American planners apparently did not then know that this issue had been settled at Hyde Park.

3. *PPA,* "Joint Statement of President Roosevelt and Prime Minister Churchill, Aug. 24, 1943." Negotiations with Stalin can be followed in messages August 18–November 8. S. Butler, *My Dear Mr. Stalin,* 151–82; Harold Callender, "A Quebec Decision," and "The Roosevelt Statement," *NYT,* August 27, 1943, 1, 3.

4. *Press Conf* #914 (August 24, 1943), 22:57–75; John H. Crider, "Conference Ends," *NYT,* August 25, 1943, 1.

5. *PPA,* "Address at Ottawa, Canada, Aug. 25, 1943"; "30,000 Cheer Roosevelt on History Making Ottawa Visit" and "Roosevelt Warns Hitler to Surrender," *NYT,* August 26, 1943, 3, 1; P. J. Philip, "Churchill to Join Roosevelt Again," *NYT,* August 28, 1943, 6.

6. Arthur Krock, "Welles Has Quit, Washington Hears," *NYT,* August 25, 1943, 1; Lewis Wood, "Capital Convinced Welles Resigned," *NYT,* August 26, 1943, 1; John D. Morris, "Roosevelt Holds 'Post-Quebec' Talks," *NYT,* August 31, 1943, 1; *Press Conf* #915 (August 31, 1943), 22:77–84; John H. Crider, "President Brands Columnist a Liar," *NYT,* September 1, 1943, 1; "Hull Denies Hostility to Soviets: Calls Writer's Story 'Monstrous,'" *NYT,* August 31, 1943, 1; Irwin F. Gellman, *Secret Affairs: Franklin D. Roosevelt, Cordell Hull, and Sumner Welles,* 302–31. For examples of the range of views, see "Diplomatic

Differences" and Arthur Krock, "Welles' Passing Ends a Long Disagreement," *NYT,* August 29, 1943, E2, E3; and Anne O'Hare McCormick, "The Changes in the State Department," *NYT,* September 27, 1943, 18. Hull says that his differences with Welles were due to his insubordination and that Roosevelt agreed with him. Hull, *Memoirs,* 2:1227–31, 56. See the detailed account in Benjamin Welles, *Sumner Welles: FDR's Global Strategist,* 1–3, 541–54, 375–80.

7. Freidel, *Rendezvous with Destiny,* 474–75; E. Roosevelt, *This I Remember,* 63; HASSETT, September 24, 1943, 208. Freidel, who consulted with ER, says that FDR told her about his dismissal of Bullitt after her return from the South Pacific on September 24 and that Bullitt had come to ask for Welles's old job.

8. Elsey, *An Unplanned Life,* 42–43.

9. "Stettinius Named for Welles Post: Crowley Shifted," *NYT,* September 26, 1943, 1; *Press Conf* #918 (September 28, 1943), 22:105. There had been a similar exchange in #917 (September 7, 1943), 22:92. For Crowley's job, see *PPA,* "The Foreign Economic Administration Is Established, EO 9389, Sept. 25, 1943," and appended note.

10. *PPA,* "Letter to Aubrey Williams, Sept. 7, 1943"; *Press Conf* #916 (September 7, 1943), 22:85–86; "NYA Head Resigns, President Accepts," *NYT,* September 8, 1943, 25; *PPA,* "Fireside Chat, Sept. 8, 1943, and appended note; "President Opens Third War Loan Drive" and John H. Crider, "President Hails Victory but Warns of Real Foes," *NYT,* September 9, 1943, 1.

11. "Praises Army Plan for Japanese Unit," *NYT,* February 5, 1943, 6; U.S. Selective Service System, *Special Groups,* 2:142–54; *PPA,* "A Message to the Senate on the Segregation Program of the War Relocation Authority, Sept. 14, 1943"; "Evacuees Divided, President Declares," *NYT,* September 15, 1943, 14; Roger Daniels, *Asian America: Chinese and Japanese in the United States since 1850,* 250–59. The classic account of the Hawaiian element of the 442nd is Thomas D. Murphy, *Ambassadors in Arms: The Story of Hawaii's 100th Battalion.*

12. *PPA,* "A Message to the Senate on the Segregation Program of the War Relocation Authority, Sept. 14, 1943"; "Curbs on Evacuees Will Stay in Force," *NYT,* July 18, 1943, 20; "Evacuees Divided, President Declares," *NYT,* September 15, 1943, 14; Executive Order 9423, "Transfer of the War Relocation Authority to the Department of the Interior," February 16, 1944, in *Federal Register* (February 18, 1944), 9:1903. For the loyalty program, see Eric L. Muller, *American Inquisition: The Hunt for Japanese American Disloyalty in World War II.* There is no full history of the Tule Lake Camp, but see Barbara Takei, "Legalizing Detention: Segregated Japanese Americans and the Justice Department's Renunciation Program." This comment and much that has been written about Japanese American soldiers ignore those who served in various secret military intelligence units from early 1942. See James C. McNaughton, *Nisei Linguists: Japanese Americans in the Military Intelligence Service in World War II.*

13. *PPA,* "Message to the Congress on the Progress of the War, Sept. 17, 1943," and appended note; Bertram D. Hulen, "Dates Set for New Invasions, President Says," *NYT,* September 18, 1943, 1.

14. Gilbert, *Churchill and America,* 282–86; Alexander Cadogan, *The Diaries of Sir Alexander Cadogan, O.M., 1938–1945,* 559; Hastings Lionel Ismay, *Memoirs,* 310; HASSETT, September 10–13, 1943, 197–202.

15. *Press Conf* #918 (September 28, 1943), 22:103–4; *PPA,* "Joint Roosevelt-Churchill Message [to] Italian People . . ., Sept. 10, 1943"; Matloff, *Strategic Planning,* 245–47; Albert N. Garland and Howard McGaw Smyth, *Sicily and the Surrender of Italy;* Martin Blumenson, *Salerno to Cassino.*

16. *Press Conf* #917 (September 14, 1943), 22:95–96; *PPA,* "Message to Congress, Oct. 6, 1943," and appended note, and "Statement of the President, June 29, 1944," and appended note; *Press Conf* #998 (April 5, 1945), 25:113–16; Rosenman, *Working with Roosevelt,* 389–93; "President Names Rosenman as Aide," *NYT,* September 15, 1943, 20. In the event, independence was granted on the original Tydings-McDuffie date, July 4, 1946.

17. *PPA,* "The President Transmits [Extraterritoriality Treaty], Feb. 1, 1943"; "Senate for China Treaty," *NYT,* February 2, 1943, 11; *PPA,* "The President Urges the Congress to Repeal the Chinese Exclusion Laws, Oct. 11, 1943" and "The President Approves the Bill to Repeal the Chinese Exclusion Laws, Dec. 17, 1943"; "President Urges Congress Repeal the Chinese Exclusion as War Aid," *NYT,* October 12, 1943, 1; "House Paves Way to Lift Chinese Ban," *NYT,* October 20, 1943, 9; "Senate Sends Bill to Admit Chinese to the President for His Signature," *NYT,* November 27, 1943, 5; "Sends Congress Thanks," *NYT,* December 4, 1943, 1; Fred W. Riggs, *Pressures on Congress: A Study of the Repeal of Chinese Exclusion;* R. Daniels, *Asian America,* 193–98, and *Guarding the Golden Door: American Immigration Policy and Immigrants since 1882,* 81–174.

18. *Press Conf* #934 (October 29, 1943), 22:189–90; #935 (November 5, 1943), 22:195–98; Bertram D. Hulen, "Harriman Named Envoy to Russia after Admiral Standly Resigns," *NYT,* October 2, 1943, 1; S. Butler, *My Dear Mr. Stalin,* 168–70; Hull, *Memoirs,* 2:1274–1318; *PPA,* "Statement Regarding Atrocities, Nov. 1, 1943"; W. H. Lawrence, "Accord in Moscow," and "Texts of Three-Power Conference Documents," *NYT,* November 2, 1943, 1, 14; "Hull, Returning in Triumph, Finds President at Airport," *NYT,* November 11, 1943, 1; C. P. Trussell, "Senate Votes 85–5 to Cooperate in Peace," *NYT,* November 6, 1943, 1.

19. S. Butler, *My Dear Mr. Stalin,* 172–85; Rosenman, *Working with Roosevelt,* 405. Art. 1, Sec. 7: "If any Bill shall not be returned by the President within ten Days (Sundays excepted) after it shall have been presented to him, the Same shall be a Law, in like Manner as if he had signed it, unless the Congress by their *Adjournment* prevent its Return, in which Case it shall not be a Law." Note that Roosevelt left out the Sunday provision so that there was actually an eleven or twelve day window. He, Rosenman, Hopkins, Sherwood and many historians speak of "ten days."

20. *PPA,* "Agreement Establishing [UNRRA], Nov. 9, 1943," and appended note; Russell B. Porter, "44 Nations Sign Relief Pact," *NYT,* November 10, 1943, 1; "War Relief Body Headed by Lehman," *NYT,* November 12, 1943, 1; "Cost of UNRRA Cut to $2,000,000,000," *NYT,* November 24, 1943, 11; "UNRRA Completes Relief Machinery," *NYT,* November 30, 1943, 10.

21. Leahy, *I Was There,* 195–202; William M. Rigdon, *White House Sailor,* 64–65; Sherwood, *Roosevelt and Hopkins,* 770–79, long quote on 770. Eisenhower, *Crusade in Europe,* 197, gives a terser version; neither cites a source. Harriman and Abel, *Special Envoy,* 256–61; *Press Conf* #924 (October 29, 1943), 22:181–82; *PPA,* "Joint Communiqué

on the Cairo Conference, Dec. 1, 1943"; C. L. Sulzberger, "Crushing of Japan Mapped at Cairo Parlay," *NYT,* December 2, 1943, 1.

22. *Press Conf* #888 (March 11, 1943), 21:349–50; Freidel, *Rendezvous with Destiny,* 478–94; Harriman and Abel, *Special Envoy,* 262–83; Leahy, *I Was There,* 202–13; Baron Moran, *Churchill, Taken from the Diaries of Lord Moran: The Struggle for Survival, 1940–1965; FDR Letters,* November 8, 1943, 1468; Reilly, *Reilly of the White House,* 168–88, quote on 178–79, de Gaulle on 157–58; Charles E. Bohlen, *Witness to History, 1929–1969,* 134–54, quotes on 136–37.

23. Matloff, *Strategic Planning,* 356–68; *FRUS, Cairo and Teheran,* 469 (long Stalin quote); Bohlen, *Witness to History,* 146–47; Zawodny, *Death in the Forest.*

24. *PPA,* "The Anglo-American Russian Declaration at Teheran, Dec. 1, 1943," and attached note; James B. Reston, "Roosevelt, Stalin, Churchill Agree on Plans for War on Germany," *NYT,* December 4, 1943, 1. It seems to me that this and the two similar remarks to serving forces on this trip cited below are a good informal summary of what Roosevelt thought he was accomplishing. Cf. Rosenman, *Working with Roosevelt,* 409–10, and the Christmas Eve broadcast shortly after Roosevelt returned. *PPA,* "Remarks at Camp Amirabad, Iran, Dec. 2, 1943," "Remarks to Military Policemen Cairo . . . , Dec. 6, 1943," and "Communiqué on Meeting with the President of Turkey, Dec. 7, 1943," and appended note; Sherwood, *Roosevelt and Hopkins,* 776–99, quote on 799; Bohlen, *Witness to History,* 150; Leahy, *I Was There,* 206.

25. Sherwood, *Roosevelt and Hopkins,* 803; Eisenhower, *Crusade in Europe,* 207–9; S. Butler, *My Dear Mr. Stalin,* 193; "Eisenhower Named Commander for Invasion," *NYT,* December 25, 1943, 1.

26. *PPA,* "Remarks at Malta, Dec. 8, 1943," and appended note; "Roosevelt Acclaims Malta for Heroism," *NYT,* December 11, 1943, 1; *PPA,* "Statement of the President on the Death of Marvin McIntyre, Dec. 13, 1943"; "Marvin M'Intyre Is Dead in Capital," *NYT,* December 14, 1943, 27; *PPA,* "Remarks on Leaving the USS *Iowa,* Dec. 16, 1943"; Leahy, *I Was There,* 214–16. His phrase aboard the *Iowa* is somewhat more ambitious than Chamberlain's "peace in our time" and decidedly less so than Hitler's "thousand year Reich."

27. *Press Conf* #927 (December 17, 1943), 22:212–29; "Roosevelt Welcomed Home, Hails Success of Parlays" and James B. Reston, "Churchill Gains in Pneumonia Fight," *NYT,* December 18, 1943, 1, 7.

28. *PPA,* "Presidential Statement and EO on the Seizure and Operation of the Railroads, EO 9412, Dec. 27, 1943," and appended note; Louis Stark, "Rail Wage Issue Reaching a Climax," *NYT,* December 19, 1943, E7. Stark's page 1 stories on December 20, 21, 23, 24, 28, and 30 are a good account. "Statement by White House," *NYT,* December 28, 1943, 8; HASSETT, December 23–24, 1943, 222–26; "President Enjoys a Stay-at-Home Day," *NYT,* December 26, 1943, 5. An AP wire photo titled "A Grandfather and His Grandchildren at Hyde Park for Christmas," December 25, 1943, 9.

29. *PPA,* "Fireside Chat, Dec. 24, 1943"; "Simplicity Marks Broadcast Scene," *NYT,* December 25, 1943, 9; "Eisenhower Named Commander for Invasion: 3,000 Planes Smash French Coast; Berlin Hit; Roosevelt Promises Nation a Durable Peace," *NYT,* December 25, 1943, 1.

30. HASSETT, December 25–27, 1943, 224–26; *PPA*, "Presidential Statement and EO 9412, Dec. 27, 1943," and appended note; *Press Conf* #927 (December 17, 1943), 22:223–24; #928 (December 21, 1943), 22:230–35; #929 (December 28, 1943), 22:239–45; #930 (January 18, 1944), 23:1–5; Louis Stark, "Roosevelt Moves to Take over Railroads," *NYT,* December 24, 1943, 1; Sidney Shalett, "Army Held Ready to Man Railroads," *NYT,* December 29, 1943, 10; Louis Stark, "3 Rail Unions End Holdout on Raises; Others Given Terms," *NYT,* January 15, 1944, 1; John H. Crider, "Rail Wage Dispute Is Ended and Lines Go Back to Owners," *NYT,* January 19, 1944, 1.

31. HASSETT, December 26–27, 1943, 225–26; "70,000 in 4 States Begin Steel Halt; Spread Indicated," *NYT,* December 26, 1943, 1; John H. Crider, "Roosevelt Calls on All Steel Men to Avert a Tieup," *NYT,* December 27, 1943, 1; "Industry Members Hit NWLB Reversal," December 28, 1943, 10; AP, "Steel Strike Ends with Rush to Work," *NYT,* December 29, 1943, 1.

32. *Press Conf* #929 (December 28, 1943), 22:238–54; John H. Crider, "Roosevelt Drops 'New Deal' for 'Win-the-War' Slogan," *NYT,* December 24, 1943, 1; "U.S. at War: Death of a Cause" and John H. Crider, "Roosevelt Uses Allegory to Explain 'Win the War,'" *NYT,* December 29, 1943, 1; Rosenman, *Working with Roosevelt,* 414–16. Cf. the account in Burns, *Soldier of Freedom,* 422–24.

33. *PPA,* "The President's Statement on New Year's Day, Jan. 1, 1944"; "Roosevelt Urges War Cooperation Go on into Peace," *NYT,* January 2, 1944, 1; *PPA,* "Roosevelts Deed Their Hyde Park Home to Government as National Historic Site, Jan. 4, 1944," 19; "Congress Leaders Advise President," *NYT,* January 11, 1944, 17; Rosenman, *Working with Roosevelt,* 417–27. To fit a thirty-minute time slot, the chat was some seven hundred words shorter than the message that is not in *PPA* but is in the *Congressional Record* for January 11, 1944. There was a new introduction to the radio version.

34. *PPA,* "State of the Union Message, Jan. 11, 1944," and appended note; "Congress Leaders Advise President" and John H. Crider, "President Asks Civilian Draft to Bar Strikes, Realistic Taxes, Subsidies, New Bill of Rights," *NYT,* January 11, 1944, 17, 1; Burns, *Soldier of Freedom,* 424; Rosenman, *Working with Roosevelt,* 417–27. Levine and Levine, *People and the President,* 515–24, is a balanced analysis.

35. "Labor Fights Compulsion: 'Quack Medicine,' Murray" and C. P. Trussell, "Congress Is Balky," *NYT,* January 12, 1944, 1; "Congress Leaders Advise President," *NYT,* January 11, 1944, 17; Louis Stark, "Labor Chiefs Warn against Draft Law," *NYT,* January 13, 1945, 1; "Bridges-CIO Union Endorses Labor Draft . . .," *NYT,* January 15, 1944, 7; Seidman, *American Labor,* 163–64; Nelson Lichtenstein, *Labor's War at Home,* 183–84; Rosenman, *Working with Roosevelt,* 420–25. Lichtenstein's treatment is confused; he has Roosevelt capitulating to Stimson's demands in early 1943 but says, correctly, that the president's support for national service legislation late in the year was a surprise. His note 15 on 186 cites the Rosenman passage cited above, which correctly dates FDR's change after his return from Tehran.

36. John H. Crider, "Roosevelt Offers 34,000-Mile Roads for Post-war Jobs," *NYT,* January 13, 1944, 1; "Roosevelt Urges City Peace Works," *NYT,* January 20, 1944, 10; U.S. House of Representatives, *A Message from the President Transmitting a Report of the National Interregional Highway Committee;* Richard Weingroff, "President Roosevelt and Excess Condemnation." For a fine overview, see Mark H. Rose, *Interstate: Express*

Highway Politics, 1941–1956. Weingroff, an official of the Department of Transportation, has been a most helpful guide.

37. *PPA,* "The Annual Budget Message, Jan 10, 1944"; John H. Crider, "A Victory Budget," *NYT,* January 14, 1944, 1.

38. *PPA,* "The War Refugee Board Is Established, EO 9417, Jan. 22, 1944," and appended note. Written by the Treasury's general counsel Randolph E. Paul (1890–1956), it was originally titled "Report to the Secretary on the Acquiescence of This Government in the Murder of the Jews." Morgenthau retitled it "Report to the President." "Roosevelt Board Is Negotiating to Save Refugees from Nazis," *NYT,* January 30, 1944, 1; John Morton Blum, *From the Morgenthau Diaries: Years of War, 1941–1945,* 221–23. Verne Newton, ed., *FDR and the Holocaust,* contains essays presenting widely varying opinions. Richard Breitman and Allan J. Lichtman, *FDR and the Jews,* surveys the president's meetings with Jewish leaders about the fate of the Jews of Europe.

39. *PPA,* "Annual Appeal for the National Foundation for Infantile Paralysis, Radio Broadcast, Jan. 29, 1944"; "Roosevelt Calls on People to Give 'Victory Dollars'"; "Celebration of Birthday Eve," *NYT,* January 30, 1944, 1, 33.

40. *PPA,* "Message to Congress on Soldier Vote Legislation, Jan. 25, 1944," and appended note, and "[Signing Statement] on Allowing Soldier Vote Bill to Become Law, Mar. 31, 1944"; HASSETT, January 25, 1944, 232; C. P. Trussell, "Soldier Vote Shifted by Senate to Let States Rule," *NYT,* December 1, 1943; "President Calls Vote Bill Fraud," *NYT,* January 27, 1944; "Vote Bill Allowed to Become Law," *NYT,* April 1, 1944; Rosenman, *Working with Roosevelt,* 427–28; Richard Polenberg, *War and Society,* 195–97.

41. *PPA,* "The President Vetoes a Bill, Feb. 18, 1955," and appended note; *Press Conf* #937 (February 18, 1944), 23:57–58; "House, 248 to 118, Bans Price Subsidy," *NYT,* February 18, 1944, 1; C. P. Trussell, "President Upheld by House Veto of Subsidies Ban," *NYT,* February 19, 1944, 1; Rosenman, *Working with Roosevelt,* 428.

42. *PPA,* "The President Vetoes a Revenue Bill, Feb. 22, 1944," and appended note; *Press Conf* #938 (February 23, 1944), 23:63–68; Rosenman, *Working with Roosevelt,* 429; John H. Crider, "President Vetoes Tax Bill, Calls It Relief for the Greedy," and C. P. Trussell, "Congress Wrathy over the Tax Veto," *NYT,* February 23, 1944, 1, 14; HASSETT, February 22–29, 1944, 235–38; AP, "Barkley's Address in Senate Assailing President's Tax Bill," and C. P. Trussell, "Congress Rebels," *NYT,* February 24, 1944, 12, 1; *PPA,* "A Telegram to Senator Alben Barkley, Feb. 23, 1944"; C. P. Trussell, "Moves for Unity," and "Barkley to the President," *NYT,* February 25, 1944, 1, 12; C. P. Trussell, "Taxes Voted Law by 72–14 in Senate," *NYT,* February 26, 1944, 1.

43. *Press Conf* #939–44 (March 3, 10, 14, 17, 24, 1944), 23:69–118; "Roosevelt Starts His 12th Year with Prayers in White House," *NYT,* March 5, 1944, 1; HASSETT, March 4, 24–27, 1944, 238–41; "President Goes to Office" and John H. Crider, "President Warns Germans on Jews," *NYT,* March 25, 1944, 12, 1; *Press Conf* #945 (March 28, 1944), 23:119–26; John H. Crider, "Roosevelt Was Ill of Bronchitis, but Says That He Is Feeling Fine," *NYT,* March 29, 1944, 1.

44. Anna Eleanor Roosevelt (1906–75) married: Curtis B. Dahl, 1926, divorced 1934; Clarence John Boettiger, 1935, divorced 1949; James A. Halsted, 1956. HASSETT, March 24–27, 1944, 239–41; Bernard Asbell, *Mother and Daughter: The Letters of Eleanor and*

Anna Roosevelt, 171–81; John R. Boettiger, *A Love in Shadow,* 251–61; Grace G. Tully, *FDR, My Boss,* 274.

45. Norimitsu Onishi, "Howard Bruenn, 90, Roosevelt's Doctor in Last Year of Life," *NYT,* August 2, 1995, D20; Howard G. Bruenn, "Clinical Notes on the Illness and Death of President Franklin D. Roosevelt," 571–80; Harold M. Schmeck Jr., "Roosevelt's Doctor Says Last Illness Did Not Prevent President from Performing Duties," *NYT,* April 12, 1970, 73; Jan Kenneth Herman, "The President's Cardiologist"; Robert H. Ferrell, *The Dying President: Franklin D. Roosevelt, 1944–45,* 27–46; Barron H. Lerner, "Crafting Medical History: Revisiting the 'Definitive' Account of Franklin D. Roosevelt's Terminal Illness"; Lawrence K. Altman, M.D., "When Alzheimer's Waited Outside the Oval Office," *NYT,* February 21, 2011, Science section.

46. John H. Crider, "President's Health 'Satisfactory'; Unique Report Made by McIntire," *NYT,* April 5, 1944, 1; McIntire, *White House Physician,* 235–44. For a contemporary assessment of McIntire's memoir, see Cabell Phillips, "President's Doctor," *NYT,* November 24, 1946, 181. For an analysis of public comments in the decade after Roosevelt's death, see Herman E. Bateman, "Observations on President Roosevelt's Health during World War II."

47. Burns, *Soldier of Freedom,* 448–50, 668–69, and passim. Burns did not reveal that he had collaborated with Anna and her husband Dr. James A. Halsted in persuading Bruenn to write and publish his "Clinical Notes" or that he interviewed Bruenn. He thanks the Halsteds in his acknowledgments (615–16) but does not thank Bruenn. For details of the Halsted-Bruenn-Burns collaboration, see the Lerner essay cited in note 45 above.

48. Bruenn, "Clinical Notes," 580–83. In Bruenn's article, the date is misprinted as March 27. Subsequent March dates in his narrative are similarly in error: March 28 should be March 29, and so forth. Robert H. Ferrell, who interviewed him, says that the date is correct in Bruenn's typescript (*Dying President,* 160n17). *Press Conf* #946 (April 7, 1944), 23:127–36; "President Is Better; Goes to His Office," *NYT,* April 8, 1944, 1; AP, "'I Have a Terrific Headache,'" *NYT,* April 13, 1945, 1; Herman, "Cardiologist," 9.

49. Bruenn, "Clinical Notes," 583–84; *Press Conf* #947 (April 28, 1944), 23:138. The quoted words are a reconstruction as stenographic notes of the conference had not yet begun. *Press Conf* #948 (May 6, 1944), 23:142–51; A. Merriman Smith, *Thank You, Mr. President,* 133–44. Other visitors included Australian prime minister Curtin and President-elect Picado of Costa Rica flown in and out for lunches; his son Franklin, now a lieutenant commander, spent one night; General Mark Clark, the American commander in Italy, reported to him as part of a brief Stateside consultation; and Lucy Mercer Rutherfurd came with her daughter-in-law. It may have been their first meeting since Roosevelt became crippled. UP, "Roosevelt Rested at Quiet Manor," *NYT,* May 8, 1944, 36; McIntire, *White House Physician,* 185; Rigdon, *White House Sailor,* 96–107; Margaret Coit, *Mr. Baruch,* 641; Bernard Baruch, *The Public Years,* 335–37; "Roosevelt Goes South for 2 Weeks to Rest and Recuperate," *NYT,* April 11, 1944, 1; Sidney Shalett, "Knox Dies in Home of Heart Attacks," *NYT,* April 29, 1944, 1.

50. HASSETT, May 8–11, 1944, 242–43; *Press Conf* #949 (May 9, 1944), 23:152–64; AP, "President Returns from Month's Rest on Baruch Estate," *NYT,* May 8, 1944, 1; Warren Moscow, "Roosevelt Drive Started Here," *NYT,* May 9, 1944, 1; "Avery Arrested

by Army," caption "Action on the Chicago Front," *NYT*, April 28, 1944, 1. Avery was evicted twice. On April 26, he left the building voluntarily. Somehow he was allowed back in the next day and, in the presence of Attorney General Biddle, conducted a one-man sit down strike and was carried out. The firm continued in operation.

51. *Press Conf* #951 (May 26, 1944), 23:176–89; #953 (May 30, 1944), 23:190–205, long quote on 192–93; "President Undergoes Physical Examination," *NYT*, May 31, 1944, 9; Turner Catledge, "President Hints of Stay in Office," *NYT*, May 27, 1944, 1; "President Explains Timing of Big Events," *NYT*, May 31, 1944, 1; John H. Crider, "Monetary Parlay May Be Set Today," *NYT*, May 26, 1944, 1; "Monetary Parlay Called for July 1," *NYT*, May 27, 1944, 1; "Paying Homage to American War Heroes . . ." and AP, "Roosevelts Visit Tomb," *NYT*, May 31, 1944, 21, 1.

Chapter 11. The Last Campaign

1. Charles Hurd, "Roosevelt Press Sessions Back in Lively, Newsy Role," *NYT*, June 4, 1944, E10; *Press Conf* #951–957 (May 26–June 13, 1944), 23:176–265.

2. *Press Conf* #952 (May 30, 1944), 23:203; #953 (June 2, 1944), 23:212–16; "'Free Ports' for Refugees," *NYT*, May 4, 1944, 18; "Murphy Group Backs 'Free Port' Proposal," *NYT*, May 29, 1944, 10; "Roosevelt Backs Refugee 'Ports," *NYT*, May 31, 1944, 4; "May Use Army Camp as Refugee Haven," *NYT*, June 3, 1944, 15.

3. "Rome Captured Intact by Fifth Army" and "President to Talk on Rome Tonight," *NYT*, June 5, 1944, 1; *PPA*, "Fireside Chat on the Fall of Rome, June 5, 1944"; *Press Conf* #954 (June 6, 1944), 23:218–32; *PPA*, "The President's D-Day Prayer, June 6, 1944"; Charles Hurd, "Roosevelt Speaks," *NYT*, June 6, 1944, 1; "President Kept Vigil on the News," "Roosevelt Pleased by Invasion Gains," and Lawrence Resner, "Country in Prayer," *NYT*, June 7, 1944, 7, 1; Rosenman, *Working with Roosevelt*, 433–35.

4. *PPA*, "The President Offers a Toast . . ., June 7, 1944"; AP, "Roosevelt Is Host to Poland's Premier," *NYT*, June, 7, 1944, 4; S. Butler, *My Dear Mr. Stalin*, June 17, 1944, 237; DALLEK, 453–55.

5. Charles Hurd, "President's Health 'Excellent,' Admiral McIntire Reports," *NYT*, June 9, 1944, 7; Bruenn, "Clinical Notes," 584.

6. *Press Conf* #955 (June 9, 1944), 23:233–49; *PPA*, "Cablegram to Ambassador Robert Murphy in Algiers, June 9, 1944" and "Message to the Congress on Refugee Policy, June 12, 1944," and attached note; Charles Hurd, "Roosevelt Agrees," "1,000 Refugees Will Enter, to Be Housed at Fort Ontario," and "Ports of Refuge," *NYT*, June 10, 1944, 1, 14; "President Predicts Murder Orgy by Nazis . . .," *NYT*, June 13, 1944, 1; Edward B. Marks Jr., *Token Refuge: The Story of America's War Refugee Shelter;* Sharon R. Lowenstein, *Token Refuge: The Story of the Jewish Refugee Shelter at Oswego, 1944–1946;* R. Daniels, *Guarding the Golden Door*, 86–87, 127.

7. *PPA*, " . . . Fireside Chat Opening Fifth War Loan Drive, June 12, 1944," and attached note; Charles Hurd, "President Says Invasion Speeds Pacific War," *NYT*, June 13, 1944, 1. The first quotation is an ad-lib from Hurd's story.

8. *Press Conf* #957 (June 13, 1944), 23:250–65; "Sweden to Slash Ball-Bearing Aid," *NYT*, June 14, 1944, 7; Charles Hurd, "A Mere Beginning'[Says Eisenhower]," *NYT*,

June 14, 1944, 1 (I use the version of Eisenhower's message printed in Hurd's story as the stenographic text in *PPA* contains verbal errors); "Fourth Term Questions Meet Presidential Banter," *NYT*, June 14, 1944, 34; *PPA*, "Statement Approving Joint Resolution, June 15, 1944," and attached note, and "Statement of the President on the Postwar Security Organization Program, June 15, 1944"; "Signs Bill to Try Pearl Harbor Men," *NYT*, June 15, 1944, 10; Charles Hurd, "President Outlines U.S. World Security Union," *NYT*, June 16, 1944, 1; Harriman and Abel, *Special Envoy*, 314. For Crowley and FEA, see Stuart L. Weiss, *The President's Man: Leo T. Crowley and Franklin D. Roosevelt in Peace and War*, chap. 11.

9. HASSETT, June 15–24, 1944, 252–55; *PPA*, "Message to Congress on Education of War Veterans, Oct. 27, 1943" and "The President Signs the G.I. Bill of Rights, June 22, 1944," and appended note; "G.I. Rights Bill Goes to the White House," *NYT*, June 14, 1944, 19; "Roosevelt Signs G.I. Bill of Rights"; AP, "Roosevelt on Rights Bill," *NYT*, June 23, 1944, 1, 32; Roger Daniels, *Guarding the Golden Door*, 288; Davis R. B. Ross, *Preparing for Ulysses: Politics and Veterans during WW II*. For Hutchins and postwar impact, see Harold G. Vatter, *The U.S. Economy in World War II*, 613.

10. *Press Conf* #958 (June 23, 1944), 23:266–72; "Congress Quits till Aug. 1," "Japanese Fleet's Flight Disappoints Roosevelt" and John H. Crider, "Roosevelt Names Money Delegates," *NYT*, June 24, 1944, 1, 5, 7; S. Morison, *Two-Ocean War*, 330–45.

11. *Press Conf* #959–960 (June 27, 1944), 23:273–311; HASSETT, June 26–July 5, 1944, 255–59; *PPA*, "Statement on Signing the Stabilization Extension Act, July 1, 1944," and appended note, and "Statement on Signing the Public Health Service Act, July 1, 1944," and appended note; "De Gaulle's Visit Set Early in July," *NYT*, June 28, 1944, 7; "Big Fund Bills Signed," *NYT*, June 30, 1944, 21; "Roosevelt Signs but Criticizes Changes in OPA Extension Bill," *NYT*, July 1, 1944, 1; Russell Porter, "Roosevelt Appeal for Unity Starts Monetary Policy," and AP, "Message of the President," July 2, 1944, 1, 14; "Signs Broadening of Health Service," *NYT*, July 4, 1944, 17.

12. HASSETT, July 6–8, 1944, 259–60; *Press Conf* #960 (July 7, 1944), 24:1–11; *PPA*, "The President Offers a Toast for General Charles De Gaulle, July 7, 1944"; Harold Callender, "De Gaulle Arrives, Meets Roosevelt," *NYT*, July 7, 1944, 1; Edwin L. James, "De Gaulle Does Better and Washington Also," *NYT*, July 9, 1944, E3; Harold Callender, "De Gaulle Believes Frank Talks with Roosevelt Aid Understanding," *NYT*, July 11, 1944, 17; "Roosevelt Gives Algiers a Top Role," *NYT*, July 12, 1944, 1; Harold Callender, "De Gaulle Scores a Double Triumph," *NYT*, October 24, 1944, 4; Freidel, *Rendezvous with Destiny*, 527–28.

13. *Press Conf* #961 (July 11, 1944), 24:12–25; *PPA*, "The President Announces He Will Accept a Nomination for a Fourth Term, July 11, 1944"; Charles Hurd, "Roosevelt Agrees to Run for a Fourth Term," *NYT*, July 12, 1944, 1. General Sherman had said, "I will not accept if nominated and will not serve if elected."

14. *PPA*, "A Letter on the Vice-Presidential Nomination, July 14, 1944" and "Letter to Robert E. Hannegan, July 19, 1944"; Rosenman, *Working with Roosevelt*, 438–54; Tully, *FDR, My Boss*, 276; George E. Allen, *Presidents Who Have Known Me*, 118–36; C. P. Trussell, "Wallace Friends Plan How to Use Roosevelt Letter," *NYT*, July 15, 1944, 1. For Pa Watson, see Appendix B of the George E. Allen oral history interview online

at the Truman Library. Cf. Freidel, *Rendezvous with Destiny*, 533–38, especially the paragraph beginning "These hasty words" on 534.

15. HASSETT, July 13, 1944, 263; Rigdon, *White House Sailor*, 108–13, 283–85. Hassett has Eleanor boarding in D.C., but Rigdon's itinerary says Hyde Park. A. Smith, *Thank You, Mr. President*, 145–47.

16. *PPA*, "Address to the Democratic National Convention in Chicago, July 20, 1944"; Turner Catledge, "Democrats Press 'War Chief' Issue; Second Place Open," *NYT*, July 20, 1944, 1; "Roosevelt Nominated for Fourth Term," *NYT*, July 21, 1944, 1. Quotation from Lincoln's second inaugural, March 4, 1865. Interestingly, Roosevelt omitted the first eight words of the peroration: "With malice toward none, with charity for all."

17. "Truman Nominated for Vice Presidency," *NYT*, July 22, 1944, 1. For a contemporary account of platform disputes, see two *NYT* accounts by Charles E. Egan, "Drafters Troubled by Racial Plank," July 20, 1944, 1; and "Arms Use to Keep Peace Is Pledged," July 21, 1944, 1. A good brief summary of the convention and election is Leon Friedman, "Election of 1944," in *History of American Presidential Elections*, edited by Schlesinger, 3009–96. For a longer account, see Michael J. Anderson, "The Presidential Election of 1944." Campaign planks are at http://www.presidency.ucsb. edu. Bruenn, "Clinical Notes," 584.

18. Rigdon, *White House Sailor*, 113–23; Leahy, *I Was There*, 249–52; McIntire, *White House Physician*, 198–200. It is not clear whether this came before or after he had come across wounded Nisei veterans from Italy. Rigdon, *White House Sailor*, has a similar comment and explicitly names Reilly as expressing his concerns that the Secret Service executive does not mention in his memoir. Rosenman, *Working with Roosevelt*, 458; Bruenn, "Clinical Notes," 584; *Press Conf* #962 (July 29, 1944), 24:26–37.

19. Leahy, *I Was There*, 243, 250–53; Matloff, *Strategic Planning*, 482; James, *MacArthur*, 2:526–33, quote on 532.

20. *PPA*, "Statement on the Death of LeHand, July 31, 1944," and appended note, and "Extemporaneous Remarks . . ., Adak, Alaska," August 3, 1944; Rigdon, *White House Sailor*, 123–29; Leahy, *I Was There*, 252–54; McIntire, *White House Physician*, 201–2; Bruenn, "Clinical Notes," 586; "Miss Le Hand Dies; Aide to Roosevelt" and "Tribute by President," *NYT*, August 1, 1944, 15.

21. Reilly, *Reilly of the White House*, 192–94; Leahy, *I Was There*, 254; Bruenn, "Clinical Notes," 586; Herman, "The President's Cardiologist," 8–9; McIntire, *White House Physician*, 202. Bruenn forget that Roosevelt had gone to the fantail to take a bow and respond to the plaudits of the crowd for some fifteen minutes before the speech started.

22. *PPA*, "Radio Address at Bremerton, Wash., Aug. 12, 1944," and appended note; UP, "President on Air," *NYT*, August 13, 1944, 1; *Press Conf* #963 (August 15, 1944), 24:38–53.

23. *Press Conf* #964 (August 18, 1944), 24:54–66; HASSETT, August 17–23, 1944, 264–67; Charles Hurd, "Roosevelt Urges Training of Youth" and "President, Truman Map the Campaign," *NYT*, August 19, 1944, 1, 6; "Roosevelt Confers with Hannegan," *NYT*, August 20, 1944, 28; Nelson, *Arsenal of Democracy*, 391–416; *Press Conf* #964 (August 18, 1944), 24:66; "War Needs Acute, WPB Head States," *NYT*, June 20, 1944, 25; Charles E. Egan, "Army, Navy Fight Nelson Civil Plan," *NYT*, July 9, 1944, 1; "Hurley and Nelson Are Going to China," *NYT*, August 19, 1944, 1; Charles E. Egan, "Wilson

Quits WPB; Says Nelson Aides Impaired His Work"; AP, "Texts of Wilson-Roosevelt Letters," *NYT*, August 25, 1944, 1, 28; Charles E. Egan, "WPB Gets a New Chairman in Spectacular Shake-Up," *NYT*, August 27, 1944, E10; Frederick R. Barkley, "Krug Ready to Fire All WPB Feudists," *NYT*, August 29, 1944, 1; *Press Conf* #965 (August 25, 1944), 24:67–88; #966 (August 29, 1944), 24:87–88; John H. Crider, "Nelson Quits WPB for 'Major' Task; Krug Succeeds Him," *NYT*, October 1, 1944; "Nelson Is Named to Cabinet Rank as 'Personal Agent' of President," *NYT*, November 21, 1944, 1; "Nelson . . . Lauded by Truman," *NYT*, May 13, 1945, 3.

24. *PPA*, "Remarks [to] Delegates to the Dumbarton Oaks Conference, Aug. 23, 1944," and attached note. Because the USSR was not yet at war with Japan, the conference was divided. The United States and Britain met with the USSR until September 29 and then with China until October 7. James B. Reston, "President Tells Delegates 'Four of Us' Can Keep Peace," *NYT*, August 24, 1944, 1; *PPA*, "The President Hails the Liberation of Paris, Aug. 24, 1944"; John H. Crider, "Keep Lend-Lease, President Asks," *NYT*, August 26, 1944, 8.

25. HASSETT, September 1–5, 1944, 268–70; *PPA*, "The President's Labor Day Statement, Sept. 2, 1944"; *Press Conf* #967 (September 9, 1944), 24:97–104; #968 (September 16, 1944), 24:105–20; John H. Crider, "Roosevelt-Churchill Talks to Be in Quebec's Citadel," *NYT*, September 11, 1944, 1; "Roosevelt and Churchill Pledge . . . to Crush 'Barbarians of the East,'" *NYT*, September 17, 1944, 1; Roosevelt to Stimson, August 26, 1944, as quoted in Freidel, *Rendezvous with Destiny*, 550; Matloff, *Strategic Planning*, 508–31; Leahy, *I Was There*, 257–63; McIntire, *White House Physician*, 202–4; Bruenn, "Clinical Notes," 587; E. Roosevelt, *This I Remember*, 331–36; Levine and Levine, *People and the President*, 390–92; Blum, *Roosevelt and Morgenthau*, 584–607; Blum, *Morgenthau Diaries: Years of War*, 373. This poorly written document—apparently dictated by Churchill to a British secretary—first saw the light of day in E. Roosevelt, *This I Remember*, 333.

26. HASSETT, September 16–20, 1944, 271–72; Leahy, *I Was There*, 263–66, 269. Max Freedman, ed., *Roosevelt and Frankfurter: Their Correspondence, 1928–1945*, 723–36, includes the text of the Bohr memo; see Sherwin, *World Destroyed*, 6–7, 90–114. Freidel, *Rendezvous with Destiny*, 553–55; "Roosevelt at Work on Campaign Talk," *NYT*, September 21, 1944, 34; *PPA*, "Message on the Missouri River Development Plan, Sept. 21, 1944," and appended note; "Roosevelt Urges a Missouri 'TVA,'" *NYT*, September 22, 1944, 1; William E. Leuchtenburg, "Little TVAs," in *The FDR Years: On Roosevelt and His Legacy*, 159–95.

27. *Press Conf* #969 (September 22, 1944), 24:121–30; *PPA*, "Joint Statement of the President and Prime Minister on Conditions in Italy," September 26, 1944; Truman Public Papers, "The President's News Conference (May 2, 1945)"; C. P. Trussell, "Roosevelt Shuns Pearl Harbor Row," "Italian Program Mapped at Quebec," and John H. Crider and Raymond Daniell, "U.S. to Be Hard with Germans; Eisenhower Orders Strict Rule," *NYT*, September 23, 1944, 8, 7, 1; "Text of Eisenhower Statement on Reich," *NYT*, September 23, 1944, 1, 3; AP, "Morgenthau Plan on Germany Splits Cabinet Committee," *NYT*, September 24, 1944, 1; AP, "Morgenthau Plan Shelved," *NYT*, September 28, 1944, 12; Leahy, *I Was There*, 264. Cf. Sherwood, *Roosevelt and Hopkins*, 818–19, 832.

28. *PPA*, "[Teamsters Speech], Washington, D.C., Sept. 23, 1944"; Bertram D. Hulen, "Roosevelt Asserts 'Old Guard' Poses Now as 'New Deal,'" *NYT*, September 24, 1944, 1.

29. "There had been no reduction in his vigor and feeling of well being. But . . . the President had lost some flesh from his face. His features had become sharpened and he looked somewhat haggard in place of his normal robust appearance" (Bruenn, "Clinical Notes," 586–87). Rosenman, *Working with Roosevelt*, 471–79, quote on 478; HASSETT, September 24–26, 1944, 272–73; AP, "Morgenthau Plan on Germany Splits Cabinet Committee," *NYT*, September 24, 1944, 1; *Press Conf* #970 (September 29, 1944), 24:131–38; *PPA*, "[Letter to Leo Crowley], Sept. 29, 1944" and "Statement of the President on Argentina, Sept. 29, 1944"; John H. Crider, "President Assails Trend in Argentina," and Arnaldo Cortesi, "Roosevelt's Tone Stuns Argentina," *NYT*, September 30, 1944, 1, 8.

30. C. P. Trussell, "President Shifts Changeover Power," *NYT*, October 3, 1944, 1; *Press Conf* #971 (October 3, 1944), 24:138–53; *PPA*, "The President Issues a Statement on Reconversion, Oct. 3, 1944," and appended note, and "The President's Statement on Signing the Surplus Property Act, Oct. 3, 1944," and appended note; C. P. Trussell, "Reconversion Bill Criticized, Signed," and Sydney Gruson, "Warsaw Gives Up after 63-Day Fight," *NYT*, October 4, 1944, 1; S. Butler, *My Dear Mr. Stalin*, 252–54. This should not be confused with the Warsaw Ghetto uprising of 1943. Polish Jews and Christians resisted the Nazis separately, with few exceptions.

31. *PPA*, "Statement on Relief Aid to Italy, Oct. 4, 1944"; "Needs of Italians under Survey," *NYT*, October 5, 1944, 6; *PPA*, "Remarks to the Conference on Rural Education, Oct. 4, 1944"; Benjamin Fine, "President Urges Rural School Aid," *NYT*, October 5, 1944, 14; "Charter Proposed for Rural Schools," *NYT*, October 6, 1944, 25; "Education in Review," *NYT*, October 8, 1944, 77.

32. *PPA*, "Radio Address from the White House, Oct. 5, 1944"; C. P. Trussell, "President Spurns Aid of Communists," *NYT*, October 6, 1944, 1. There was little danger of Roosevelt getting fascist support, but in 1944, following the transformation of the Communist Party USA into the Communist Political Association by CP leader Earl R. Browder (1891–1973), most Communist voters surely voted for Roosevelt. In 1940 Browder had been a presidential candidate and received forty-six thousand of almost fifty million votes cast. "Text of Dewey's Address Assailing New Deal as Linked to Communism," *NYT*, October 8, 1944, 36. Cf. Freidel, *Rendezvous with Destiny*, 562; and Rosenman, *Working with Roosevelt*, 479–80.

33. HASSETT, October 5–11, 1944, 273–77; *PPA*, "Statement on the Death of Al Smith, Oct. 4, 1944" and "Statement on the Death of Wendell Willkie, Oct. 8, 1944." Cf. Rosenman, *Working with Roosevelt*, 463–70; *PPA*, "Statement on the Completion of the Dumbarton Oaks Conversations, Oct. 9, 1944"; "Dewey Lauds Dumbarton Plan as 'Fine Beginning' for Peace," *NYT*, October 10, 1944, 13; C. P. Trussell, "Roosevelt Backs Restored Poland," *NYT*, October 12, 1944, 1, contains White House statement text; *PPA*, "Columbus Day Address, Oct. 12, 1942"; C. P. Trussell, "Roosevelt Urges Quick Peace Plan," *NYT*, October 13, 1944; *PPA*, "The President's Address on Accepting the Four Freedoms Award, Oct. 12, 1944"; "Four Freedoms Award Given to President," *NYT*, October 19, 1944, 25; "President Renews Pledge to Aid Italy" and North American

Newspaper Alliance, "President Is Well, His Physician Says," *NYT,* October 13, 1944, 1, 20.

34. *Press Conf* #972 (October 13, 1944), 24:154–66; *PPA,* "Letter to the Chairman of the War Production Board [on] Farm Machinery, Oct. 13, 1944"; "Roosevelt Urges Farm Machine Rise," "President to Search Laws for a Way to Answer Petrillo," and C. P. Trussell, "President Thinks of Other Speeches after Oct. 21 Talk," *NYT,* October 14, 1944, 26, 1.

35. *Press Conf* #973 (October 17, 1944), 24:167–85; "Roosevelt Traces Invasion Pier Move"; C. P. Trussell, "Roosevelt to Make Philadelphia Talk"; AP, "Health Pretty Good, Roosevelt Declares"; and Lansing Warren, "President Assails Sniping at Security by Dissensionists," *NYT,* October 18, 1944, 4, 1; "Spellman and Roosevelt Talk," *NYT,* October 19, 1944, 21. For Spellman and Roosevelt, see Gerald P. Fogarty, S.J., *The Vatican and the American Hierarchy from 1870 to 1965.*

36. *PPA,* "Statement and Messages Hailing Landing of American Troops in the Philippines, Oct. 20, 1944"; *Press Conf* #974 (October 20, 1944), 24:186–91; "M'Arthur Invades Central Philippines" and "Text of Roosevelt's Statements," *NYT,* October 20, 1944, 1, 11; C. P. Trussell, "Rain Fails to Dim Roosevelt's Mood," *NYT,* October 21, 1944, 1; HASSETT, October 20, 1944, 278.

37. HASSETT, October 21, 1944, 278–82; "10,000 Police Ready to Guard Itinerary of President Here," *NYT,* October 20, 1944, 1; C. P. Trussell, "President Defies Rain, Wind to Let New York See Him," and Alexander Feinberg, "Vast Throngs See Roosevelt on Tour," *NYT,* October 22, 1944, 1, 35; Reilly, *Reilly of the White House,* 197–99; A. Smith, *Thank You, Mr. President,* 156.

38. *PPA,* "Radio Address at Dinner of Foreign Policy Association, New York, N.Y., Oct. 21, 1944"; HASSETT, October 21, 1944, 278–82; UP, "Ball Will Choose Candidate Soon," *NYT,* October 18, 1944, 17; Leo Egan, "Roosevelt Wants World Peace Force Free to Act Quickly," *NYT,* October 22, 1944, 1; Sherwood, *Roosevelt and Hopkins,* 825–27; Rosenman, *Working with Roosevelt,* 480–90.

39. Sherwood, *Roosevelt and Hopkins,* 824; HASSETT, October 21–23, 1944, 280–83; "Ball to Support Roosevelt," *NYT,* October 23, 1944, 1; *Press Conf* #975 (October 24, 1944), 24:192–99; "President Hopeful on Moscow Talks," *NYT,* October 25, 1944, 1; Harriman and Abel, *Special Envoy,* 366; *Press Conf* #976 (October 25, 1944), 24:200–201; Lewis Wood, "President Elated," *NYT,* October 26, 1944, 1; C. Vann Woodward, *The Battle for Leyte Gulf;* Herbert Feis, *The China Tangle: The American Effort in China from Pearl Harbor to the Marshall Mission.*

40. HASSETT, October 26–30, 1944, 383–87; *PPA,* ". . . Campaign Remarks at Wilmington, DL, Oct. 27, 1944" and "Campaign Address, Shibe Park, Philadelphia, Oct. 27, 1944"; "Roosevelt Derides Republican Talks," Walter W. Ruch, "800,000 Cheer President in Philadelphia and Camden," and C. P. Trussell, "Victories Prove Our Preparedness, President Asserts," *NYT,* October 28, 1944, 8, 1; *PPA,* "Campaign Remarks at Ft. Wayne, IN," "Campaign Address at Soldier Field, Chicago, Oct. 28, 1944," "President Recalls Campaign Warning," and C. P. Trussell, "President Offers Post-war Program for Aiding Business," *NYT,* October 29, 1944, 35, 1; Reilly, *Reilly of the White House,* 199; *PPA,* "Extemporaneous Remarks at Clarksburg, WV, Oct. 29, 1944"; C. P. Trussell, "Roosevelt Gives 'Sermon' on Need of Reforestation," *NYT,* October 29, 1944, 1.

41. *Press Conf* #977 (October 31, 1944), 24:202–12; "Roosevelt Visits Hull," *NYT,* November 1, 1944, 17; Hull, *Memoirs,* 2:1714–20. In his next press conference when asked if there were "any indications" that Hull "planned to resign," the president flatly and falsely denied it. "No, of course not." *Press Conf* #978 (November 3, 1944), 24:216. Bertram D. Hulen, "Stilwell Moved from Orient at Request Laid to Chiang," *NYT,* October 29, 1944; "Stillwell-Chiang Differences Personal," *NYT,* November 1, 1944; Brooks Atkinson, "Long Schism Seen," *NYT,* October 31, 1944, 1; Matloff, *Strategic Planning,* 530.

42. *PPA,* "Radio Address, Nov. 2, 1944"; C. P. Trussell, "Roosevelt Adds Campaign Speech to Be Broadcast Tomorrow Night," *NYT,* November 1, 1944, 1; "Party 'Spite Fence' May Imperil Peace, President Asserts," *NYT,* November 3, 1944, 1; *Press Conf* #978 (November 3, 1944), 24:213–16; *PPA,* "The President Urges Employers to Allow Workers Time Off [to Vote], Nov. 3, 1944"; HASSETT, November 2–4, 1944, 288–91; C. P. Trussell, "President Travels to New England for Strong Drive," *NYT,* November 4, 1944, 1; *PPA,* "[Extemporaneous Campaign Addresses in] Bridgeport, CT . . . Hartford, CT . . . and Springfield, MA, Nov. 4, 1944"; "Roosevelt Strikes Foes in Two States," *NYT,* November 5, 1944, 39.

43. HASSETT, November 4, 1944, 290–91; *PPA,* "Campaign Address at Fenway Park, Boston, MA, Nov. 4, 1944"; C. P. Trussell, "Falsehood Marks Republican Pleas, Roosevelt Asserts," *NYT,* November 5, 1944, 1; Sherwood, *Roosevelt and Hopkins,* 828–31; Rosenman, *Working with Roosevelt,* 499–506; A. Smith, *Thank You, Mr. President,* 145. Unlike Roosevelt, immigrant songwriter Irving Berlin (1888–1989) sang in 1942 of an army composed of men named Jones, Green, and Brown. The president's list ignored names originating in Asia or Latin America.

44. HASSETT, November 6–7, 1944, 291–94; *PPA,* "Extemporaneous Remarks at Kingston, NY, . . . Poughkeepsie, NY, Nov. 6, 1944" and "Radio Address at Hyde Park, NY, Nov. 6, 1944"; John H. Crider, "President Rests in Hyde Park Home before Tour Today"; "President Calls upon All to Vote," *NYT,* November 6, 7, 1944, 1.

45. HASSETT, November 7–9, 1944, 292–95; *PPA,* "Extemporaneous Remarks . . . Election Night, Hyde Park, NY, Nov. 7, 1944"; John H. Crider, "Torchlight Parade Honors President," and "President Says That Election Shows 'Reviving Democracy,'" *NYT,* November 8, 9, 1944, 3, 1; C. P. Trussell, "Roosevelt Guess on Majority Low," *NYT,* November 11, 1944, 8. Some authorities, including E. Robinson, *They Voted for Roosevelt,* table 1, 47, use figures of 24,780,943 (51.7 percent), the number of votes cast for Roosevelt on the Democratic line, which ignores the 825,640 votes for Roosevelt on the American Labor and Liberal lines in New York. A close reading of Robinson's text in two separate places, 46 and 199, will give a careful reader the information necessary to calculate the number and percentage of those who voted for Roosevelt in 1944, but Robinson never provides them.

46. *PPA,* "Extemporaneous Remarks at Union Station, Washington, D.C., Nov. 10, 1944"; *Press Conf* #979 (November 10, 1944), 24:217–21; John H. Crider, "200,000 Welcome Roosevelt in Rain to Capital 'Home,'" *NYT,* November 11, 1944, 1.

47. Bruenn, "Clinical Notes," 587; HASSETT, November 11, 14–15, 1944, 296–98; Bertram D. Hulen, "President Visits Unknown's Tomb," *NYT,* November 12, 1944, 32; C. P. Trussell, "President Gets Byrnes to Stay in War Post until Reich Falls," *NYT,*

November 15, 1944, 1; "Senate Confirms Byrnes Quickly," *NYT*, November 17, 1944, 1; John H. Crider, "Crowley Resigns, Then Stays at FEA," *NYT*, November 23, 1941, 22; *Press Conf* #980 (November 14, 1944), 24:223–35; "President Presses for River Projects," "Roosevelt Asks Simple Inaugural," and "Dewey Writes President," *NYT*, November 15, 1944, 19, 18, 29; "President Meets Congress Leaders" and "War Effort Periled by Workers, Who Quit Vital Jobs, Kaiser Says," *NYT*, November 16, 1944, 1; Louis Stark, "President Halts WLB Resignations," *NYT*, November 17, 1944, 1.

48. HASSETT, November 17, 1944, 298; *Press Conf* #981 (November 17, 1944), 24:236–41; C. P. Trussell, "President Presses Compulsory Plan of Youth Training," *NYT*, November 18, 1944, 1; Bruenn, "Clinical Notes," 587; *PPA*, "The President Opens Sixth War Loan Drive, Nov. 19, 1944," and appended note; "War Is Costing $250,000,000 a Day, President Reveals," *NYT*, November 20, 1944, 1.

49. *PPA*, "The President Requests Plan for Future Scientific Research and Development, Nov. 20, 1944," and appended note; "Roosevelt Urges Peace Science Plan," *NYT*, November 21, 1944, 4; Reingold, "Vannevar Bush's New Deal"; Bertram D. Hulen, "$33,000,000 for Research Yearly Asked as a Policy; Dr. Bush Proposes That a Foundation with Federal Funds Aid Colleges and Develop Trained Personnel," *NYT*, July 19, 1945, 1; Waldemar Kaempffert, "Science in Review," *NYT*, July 23, 1945, 71; *Press Conf* #981 (November 21, 1943), 24:243–53; C. P. Trussell, "President Assails War-Job Quitting," *NYT*, November 22, 1944, 15; John H. Crider, "Leasing to Go on, President Asserts," *NYT*, November 22, 1944, 13; "Peace Should End Lend-Lease Plan, Roosevelt Says," *NYT*, November 23, 1944, 1, Roosevelt's letter on 10; John H. Crider, "Lease Aid to Britain Will Be Cut 43%," December 1, 1944, 1. In July 1945, Bush presented a report to President Truman calling for establishing a National Science Foundation with funding of thirty-three million dollars. Five years later a bill establishing the NSF was enacted with an initial annual budget of fifteen million dollars. Funding remained at roughly that level until well after the Sputnik crisis of 1957.

50. *Press Conf* #982 (November 21, 1944), 24:247–48; Lawrence E. Davies, "Return of Japanese to the West Coast Poses New Problem," *NYT*, November 19, 1944, E6; *Ex parte Endo,* 323 U.S. 283 (December 18, 1944). *Endo* was actually decided unanimously by the justices on October 26, but Chief Justice Stone delayed the announcement, apparently to accommodate the president. It is likely that the White House was informed of its nature in advance; the Western Defense Command in San Francisco was able to announce that it was lifting the ban on Sunday, December 17, hours before the Court's "decision Monday" announcement. The Court's heads-up to the White House, if it took place, was unethical and violated the separation-of-powers dictum, but was not illegal; as Roosevelt liked to say, "There's no law against it." Lawrence E. Davies, "Ban on Japanese Lifted on the Coast," *NYT*, December 18, 1944, 1; Lewis Wood, "Supreme Court Upholds Return of Loyal Japanese to West Coast," *NYT*, December 19, 1944, 1. For the first of many devastating analyses of the Japanese American cases, see Eugene V. Rostow, "The Japanese American Cases: A Disaster"; and a more accessible version, "Our Worst Wartime Mistake." See also Roger Daniels, *Guarding the Golden Door*.

51. HASSETT, November 24–26, 1944, 299–302; *Press Conf* #983 (November 27, 1944), 24:254–58; *PPA*, "Exchange of Letters on the Resignation of Cordell Hull, Nov.

21, 1944"; Bertram D. Hulen, "Hull Leaving Post," and AP, "Byrnes Backing on Hill Seen," *NYT,* November 27, 1944, 1; C. P. Trussell, "President Accepts Hull's Resignation, Names Stettinius," *NYT,* November 28, 1944, 1; Walter Johnson, "Edward R. Stettinius, Jr.," 215.

52. HASSETT, November 27–December 19, 1944, 299–306; Bruenn, "Clinical Notes," 587–88; *PPA,* "Letter to Department Heads . . ., Dec. 1, 1944"; "Asks $75.9 Million for Public Works," *NYT,* November 29, 1944, 10; C. P. Trussell, "Roosevelt Ousts Littell in Dispute," *NYT,* December 1, 1944, 1; "President Pleads to Put Peace First," *NYT,* December 3, 1944, 1; "War Powers Bill Is Approved," *NYT,* December 5, 1944, 38; "Says Europe's Need for Relief Is Great," *NYT,* December 6, 1944, 5; "Roosevelt Averts Railroad Strike," *NYT,* December 15, 1944, 15; "Roosevelt Signs Tax Freeze Bill, but Says It Handicaps Security," *NYT,* December 17, 1944, 1; AP, "Roosevelt Ends Warm Springs Trip," and "Congress Expires with Few on Hand," *NYT,* December 20, 1944, 15, 1. The AP story about the trip, which was submitted to Roosevelt for "editing," named and identified the two navy doctors as investigating the treatment of polio patients to enable them to improve the treatment of postpolio care at Bethesda. "Roosevelt Ends Warm Springs Trip," *NYT,* December 20, 1944, 13.

53. HASSETT, December 23–30, 1944, 306–8; *Press Conf* #984 (December 19, 1944), 24:259–71. Elisabeth May Adams Craig (1889–1975) was a correspondent for a string of Maine newspapers. See Jane L. Twomey, "May Craig: Journalist and Liberal Feminist"; and *Press Conf* #985 (December 22, 1944), 24:272–81. *PPA,* "Christmas Eve Address, Dec. 24, 1944," "The President's . . . Seizure of Montgomery Ward, Dec. 27, 1944," and "The President Vetoes a Bill Abolishing the Jackson Hole National Monument, Dec. 29, 1944"; C. P. Trussell, "Atlantic Charter, Unsigned but Intact, Roosevelt Says," *NYT,* December 20, 1944, 1; "Wallace Confers with Roosevelt" and "President Allows $1,500,000,000 for Federal Aid to Highways," *NYT,* December 21, 1944, 24, 11; "President, Truman Meet," *NYT,* December 22, 1944, 30; "Roosevelts Begin Yule Celebration," C. P. Trussell, "Roosevelt Urges Homefolks to Back Soldiers at Front," and Sidney Shalett, "Stimson Remains Calm over Battle," *NYT,* December 23, 1944, 10, 1, 5; "President Broadcasts Demand Christmas Be Freed of Wars," *NYT,* December 25, 1944, 1; Louis Stark, "President Orders Army to Take over Ward's in Chicago," *NYT,* December 28, 1944, 1; C. P. Trussell, "President Vetoes Jackson Hole Bill," *NYT,* December 30, 1944, 1; John Morton Blum, ed., *The Price of Vision: The Diary of Henry A. Wallace, 1942–1946,* 407; Hugh M. Cole, *The Ardennes: Battle of the Bulge.*

Chapter 12. The Final Triumph

1. *Press Conf* #988 (January 2, 1945), 25:1–10; "Roosevelt Is Working on His Annual Message," *NYT,* December 31, 1944, 19; "France Admitted to United Nations," *NYT,* January 2, 1945; John H. Crider, "Roosevelt Admits Differences but Hints at Big 3 Talk 'Anon'" and "Army to Try Spies, Roosevelt Hints," January 3, 1945, 1; Fisher, *Nazi Saboteurs,* 138–44.

2. *PPA,* "Annual Message, Jan. 6, 1945" and "Radio Address State of the Union Message, Jan. 6, 1945"; John H. Crider, "Roosevelt Demands a National Service Act, Draft of Nurses and 4Fs, Postwar Training," *NYT,* January 7, 1945, 1; Rosenman, *Working*

with Roosevelt, 510–16; Sherwood, *Roosevelt and Hopkins*, 845–46; Levine and Levine, *People and the President*, 542–45.

3. *PPA*, "Annual Budget Message, Jan. 3, 1945"; *Press Conf* #988 (January 9, 1945), 25:23–27; Robert F. Whitney, "Congress Leaders Map Bills to Push Roosevelt Plans," and AP, "President Visits Hull, Finds Him Much Better," *NYT*, January 8, 1945, 1, 10; "Roosevelt Backs Plea of Insurance," *NYT*, January 9, 1945, 21; John H. Crider, "70 Billion for War," *NYT*, January 10, 1945, 1; *HIST STATS*, Series Y 354, 718.

4. HASSETT, January 10–20, 1945, 309–13; *Press Conf* #989 (January 16, 1945), 25:28–35; *PPA*, "The President [Recommends] National Service Legislation, Jan. 17, 1945," and appended note; *Press Conf* #990 (January 19, 1945), 25:37–56; "Top Award Given to 7 by President," *NYT*, January 11, 1945, 25; AP, "Roosevelt Attends Fete of Radio Folk," *NYT*, January 12, 1945, 10; C. P. Trussell, "Roosevelt Renews Demand Congress Pass Total Draft," and "Wartime Baseball Is Put on an 'If' Basis," *NYT*, January 17, 1945, 1, 24; C. P. Trussell, "Roosevelt Urges Work or Fight Bill to Back Offensives," *NYT*, January 18, 1945, 1; John H. Crider, "Wartime Severity to Open 4th Term without Fanfare," *NYT*, January 20, 1945, 1.

5. *PPA*, "Fourth Inaugural Address, Jan. 20, 1945"; HASSETT, January 20, 1945, 312–13; Bruenn, "Clinical Notes," 588; "Services Start President's Day," John H. Crider, "Roosevelt Sworn in for Fourth Term" and "A Grim Roosevelt Begins a New Term," and Bertram D. Hulen, "Shivering Thousands Stamp in the Snow at Inauguration," *NYT*, January 21, 1945, 21, 1, 69, 1; UP, "Housekeeper Vetoes Roosevelt on Menu," *NYT*, January 20, 1945, 1; Bess Furman, "Luncheon Marked by Informality," *NYT*, January 21, 1945, 27; Rosenman, *Working with Roosevelt*, 516–17; Sherwood, *Roosevelt and Hopkins*, 646–47.

6. "Wallace Will Get All Jones' Posts as Party Rewards," AP, "The President's and Jones's Letters," and "Floor Fight Seen in Jones' Ouster," *NYT*, January 22, 1945, 1, 30; James B. Reston, "Senators Start Fight on Wallace to Succeed Jones," "Roosevelt Extols Victory Gardeners," and "The Day in Washington," *NYT*, January 23, 1946, 11, 14; "Way Is Cleared for Wallace Vote" and Lewis Wood, "Senate Confirms Wallace as Secretary by 56 to 32," *NYT*, March 2, 1945, 19, 1; Jonathan Daniels, *White House Witness*, 257–60; Leahy, *I Was There*, 293–94.

7. HASSETT, January 22, 1945, 313–14; Rigdon, *White House Sailor*, 136–51; Sherwood, *Roosevelt and Hopkins*, 847–49; Thomas M. Campbell and George C. Herring, eds., *The Diaries of Edward R. Stettinius, Jr., 1943–1946*, 222–59; Leahy, *I Was There*, 291–323; Harriman, *Special Envoy*, 388–91; Bohlen, *Witness to History*, 167–73; Edward J. Flynn, *You're the Boss*, 200–222; *FRUS, Malta to Yalta*, 39–40; Reilly, *Reilly of the White House*, 200–206; *PPA*, "Appeal for National Foundation for Infantile Paralysis, Jan. 30, 1945"; "President Hails 'Stream of Dimes,'" *NYT*, January 31, 1945, 23.

8. Reilly, *Reilly of the White House*, 212; Bohlen, *Witness to History*, 171–72; Leahy, *I Was There*, 291–96; Harriman, *Special Envoy*, 388–417. This first presidential aircraft got heavy use by President Truman, and it was in his time that the name was emblazoned on its fuselage.

9. *PPA*, "Message to President Osmeña, Feb. 4, 1945"; *FRUS, From Malta to Yalta*, 396; *PPA*, "Joint Statement, Yalta, Feb. 11, 1945"; "War News Summarized," *NYT*, February 4, 1945, 1; "Roosevelt Hails Entry into Manila," *NYT*, February 5, 1945, 1; Bertram D.

Hulen, "Big Three Set Final Steps to Crush Germany," and AP, "Text of White House Announcement on Big Three Parlay in Black Sea Area," *NYT*, February 8, 1945, 1, 4; *PPA*, "Joint Statement on Crimea Conference—Yalta, Feb. 11, 1945"; Lansing Warren, "Big 3 Doom Nazism and Reich Militarism," *NYT*, February 13, 1945, 1; *PPA*, "The President Urges Immediate Adoption of the Bretton Woods Agreements, Feb. 12, 1945," and appended note; "Roosevelt Presses World Money Plan," *NYT*, February 13, 1945, 1; Leahy, *I Was There*, 298–323; James F. Byrnes, *Speaking Frankly*, 21–45; Edward R. Stettinius Jr., *Roosevelt and the Russians*; Diane Shaver Clemens, *Yalta*; S. M. Plokhy, *Yalta: The Price of Peace*, 36–52.

10. Leahy, *I Was There*, 324–25; Harriman, *Special Envoy*, 417; Bruenn, "Clinical Notes," 588–89; Rigdon, *White House Sailor*, 152–54; Robertson, *Sly and Able*, 382–85; Herman, "The President's Cardiologist," 12–13. Roosevelt saw the film *Wilson* (1944) at the second Quebec Conference. An expensive Technicolor production, it won an Academy Award for Best Direction but lost money. Its producer, Darryl F. Zanuck, was known for producing films focusing on contemporary topics, including *The Grapes of Wrath* (1940) and *Gentlemen's Agreement* (1947), which examined contemporary American anti-Semitism. In *Wilson* the president was the tragic hero and Senator Henry Cabot Lodge the villain; Navy Secretary Josephus Daniels was depicted, but not his assistant secretary.

11. Bruenn, "Clinical Notes," 589; *PPA*, "The President Urges Immediate Adoption of the Bretton Woods Agreement, Feb. 12, 1945," and appended note; Rigdon, *White House Sailor*, 154–73; Leahy, *I Was There*, 325–27; Bohlen, *Witness to History*, 202–5; *FRUS, Diplomatic Papers, The Near East and Africa* (1945), 1–10; Thomas W. Lippman, *Arabian Knight: Colonel Bill Eddy USMC and the Rise of American Power in the Middle East*, 133–43; William A. Eddy, *F.D.R. Meets Ibn Saud*.

12. Leahy, *I Was There*, 327–38; Bohlen, *Witness to History*, 204–5; Stettinius, *Roosevelt and the Russians*, 289.

13. Rosenman, *Working with Roosevelt*, 521; cf. A. Smith, *Thank You, Mr. President*, 170–71, 172–73. Bruenn, "Clinical Notes," 599; *Press Conf* #991 (January 19, 1945), 25:47–56; #992 (January 23, 1945), 25:57–73, quote on 70–73; "Gen. Watson Dead; Roosevelt's Aide," *NYT*, February 28, 1945, 21.

14. HASSETT, February 28, 1945, 317–18; Jonathan Daniels, *White House Witness*, 263–66. (Daniels's "diary" is confused by an entry for "Thursday Feb. 29" that must be Thursday, March 1.) "Arlington Burial for Gen. Watson" and "Roosevelt's Trip Made by Sea, Air," *NYT*, March 1, 1945, 21, 12; *PPA*, "The President Invites Delegates to the United Nations Conference, Washington, D.C., Feb. 28, 1945"; "Formal Parlay Bid Sent by President," *NYT*, March 2, 1945, 13. Democrats Tom Connally, Sol Bloom, and Barnard College dean Virginia Guildersleeve (1877–1965) and Republicans Arthur Vandenberg, New Jersey representative Charles A. Eaton (1868–1953), and Harold Stassen.

15. *PPA*, " . . . Address to the Congress Reporting on the Yalta Conference, Mar. 1, 1945"; John H. Crider, "Roosevelt Puts World Peace Up to Senate," *NYT*, March 2, 1945, 1; Rosenman, *Working with Roosevelt*, 530–37, quote on 537; Bohlen, *Witness to History*, 295–96.

16. HASSETT, March 2–13, 1945, 319–23; *Press Conf* #993 (March 2, 1945), 25:74–84; #994 (March 9, 1945), 25:85–89; #995 (March 13, 1945), 25:90–99; John H. Crider,

"Roosevelt Thinks It Good Idea to Let Nazis Repair Soviet," *NYT*, March 3, 1945, 1; C. P. Trussell, "Vinson Is Named to Head the RFC," *NYT*, March 6, 1945, 1; Joseph H. Loftus, "W. H. Davis Named to Succeed Vinson," *NYT*, March 7, 1945, 1; "Roosevelt Is Back from Hyde Park," *NYT*, March 9, 1945, 17; C. P. Trussell, "Roosevelt Keeps Manpower Stand"; "Roosevelt Avows Amity for French," *NYT*, March 10, 1945, 13, 5; Harold Callender, "Roosevelt Amity Big News in Paris," *NYT*, March 11, 1945, 6; "U.S. Peace Group to See Roosevelt, May Hear Oaks Data Talk Today" and "Civilians to Survey Bombing in Europe," *NYT*, May 13, 1945, 10, 4; "President Greets Parlay Delegates" and "Roosevelt Wants Baseball to Go On," *NYT*, May 14, 1945, 1, 14; "Roosevelt Optimistic, Mackenzie King Reports," *NYT*, March 16, 1945, 10.

17. Bruenn, "Clinical Notes," 590; *Press Conf* #996 (March 16, 1945), 25:100–106; #997 (March 20, 1945), 25:108–12; HASSETT, March 17, 24, 1945, 323–26; *PPA*, "[Letter to Justice Byrnes on] Guaranteed Annual Wage Plans, Mar. 20, 1945" and "Radio Address Opening the Red Cross Fund Drive, Mar. 20, 1945"; "E. G. Harrison Appointed," *NYT*, March 16, 1945, 17; "Baruch Will Go on London Mission; Expected to Discuss Reparations," "President Again Asks Palestine's Freedom," and Bertram D. Hulen, "Roosevelt Asks Belt Tightening," *NYT*, March 17, 1945, 1, 13, 1; "Roosevelts 40 Years Wed," *NYT*, March 18, 1945, 32; C. P. Trussell, "Get the Manpower, President Demands," and "Roosevelt Urges Gift to Red Cross," *NYT*, March 21, 1945, 1, 21; "Roosevelts Greet Athlone, Princess," *NYT*, March 23, 1945, 4; "Earl of Athlone Departs" and AP, "President Transfers Daniels to Press Job," March 25, 1945, 26, 40.

18. "Aubrey Williams Named Head of REA," *NYT*, January 23, 1945, 11; Lansing Warren, "Senate Group, 12–8, Opposes Williams," *NYT*, March 3, 1945, 1; "Williams Defiant on Idea He Step Down," *NYT*, March 4, 1945, 32; William S. White, "Senate, by 52 to 36, Rejects Williams as Director of REA," *NYT*, March 24, 1945, 1; Arthur Krock, "A 'Liberal' View of Appointive Power," *NYT*, March 30, 1945, 16.

19. HASSETT, March 25–28, 1945, 326; *PPA*, "The President Urges the Congress to Strengthen the Trade Agreements Act, Mar. 26, 1945," and appended note, and "Transmitting Report on United Nations Interim Commission on Food and Agriculture, Mar. 26, 1945," and appended note; Bruenn, "Clinical Notes," 590; UP, "Roosevelt Warns Public on Car Care," *NYT*, March 26, 1945, 12; Lansing Warren, "President Seeks Powers to Slash Rates 50%"; AP, "President Urges World Food Pact" and "President Sets Aid in Cancer Control," *NYT*, March 27, 1945, 1, 26, 15; C. P. Trussell, "President Urges Senate to Adopt Manpower Truce," *NYT*, March 29, 1945, 1.

20. HASSETT, March 29–30, 1945, 329–33; Jonathan Daniels, *White House Witness*, 277–78; Tully, *FDR, My Boss*, 355–59; Bertram D. Hulen, "United States, Russia to Seek 3 Votes in Security Assembly," and "Gen. Clay to Aid Reich Occupation," *NYT*, March 30, 1945, 1. The *Times* story also said that "President Roosevelt and Secretary of State Stettinius conferred today after returning here from brief vacations." There is no reference to any such contact in Stettinius's voluminous published diaries. Cf. Campbell and Herring, *Diaries of Stettinius*. Perhaps they talked on the phone.

21. HASSETT, March 31–April 5, 1945, 329–31; Tully, *FDR, My Boss*, 358–59; Reilly, *Reilly of the White House*, 225–57; *Press Conf* #998 (April 5, 1945), 25:113–21; Lansing Warren, "Byrnes Will Quit Mobilization Post; Vinson Appointed," and "Letters of

Byrnes and Roosevelt," *NYT,* April 3, 1945, 1, 14; James B. Reston, "U.S. Will Not Seek 3 Assembly Votes; Insists on Parlay," *NYT,* April 4, 1945, 1.

22. Bruenn, "Clinical Notes," 590; Elizabeth Shoumatoff, *FDR's Unfinished Portrait,* 71–114; Reilly, *Reilly of the White House,* 228; Freidel, *Rendezvous with Destiny,* 604; Sherwood, *Roosevelt and Hopkins,* 878–80; HASSETT, April 10–11, 1945, 332–33; "Roosevelt Jovial before Collapse," *NYT,* April 16, 1945, 10; Blum, *Roosevelt and Morgenthau,* 626–31; Henry Morgenthau III, "The Last Night at Warm Springs," *NYT,* April 12, 1945, A2. Shoumatoff (1888–1980) came to the United States in 1917 with her husband, a trade representative of the short-lived Kerensky government; after the Bolsheviks took power, they remained. After her husband's death, she turned her painting hobby into a source of livelihood. Shoumatoff is best known for her portraits of Roosevelt and Lyndon Johnson.

23. HASSETT, April 12, 1945, 333–37; Bruenn, "Clinical Notes," 590; Shoumatoff, *FDR's Unfinished Portrait,* 114–19; Reilly, *Reilly of the White House,* 229–34; Tully, *FDR, My Boss,* 360–63; Jim Bishop, *FDR's Last Year,* 573–74; S. Butler, *My Dear Mr. Stalin,* 321; AP, "Last Words: 'I Have Terrific Headache,'" *NYT,* April 13, 1945, 1.

24. HASSETT, April 12–15, 1945, 337–47; A. Smith, *Thank You, Mr. President,* 182–84; "Mrs. Roosevelt Flies to Georgia," *NYT,* April 13, 1945, 4; Frank Kluckhohn, "Nation Pays Final Tribute to Roosevelt as World Mourns," and William S. White, "500,000 in Capital View Final March," *NYT,* April 15, 1945, 1; Frank Kluckhohn, "Grave Is in Garden," *NYT,* April 16, 1945, 1.

25. "Text of Jefferson Day Address," *NYT,* April 14, 1945, 7.

26. D. Kennedy, *Freedom from Fear,* 668.

Works Consulted

Abbazia, Patrick. *Mr. Roosevelt's Navy: The Private War of the U.S. Atlantic Fleet, 1939–1942.* Annapolis, Md.: Naval Institute Press, 1975.

Adams, Henry H. *Harry Hopkins: A Biography.* New York: Putnam, 1977.

Agawa, Hiroyuki. *The Reluctant Admiral: Yamamoto and the Imperial Navy.* Translated by John Bester. New York: Kodansha International, 1979.

Albertson, Dean. *Roosevelt's Farmer: Claude R. Wickard in the New Deal.* New York: Columbia University Press, 1955.

Allen, Frederick Lewis. *Since Yesterday: The Nineteen-Thirties in America.* New York: Harper, 1939.

Allen, George E. *Presidents Who Have Known Me.* New York: Simon and Schuster, 1950.

Allen, William C. *History of the United States Capitol.* Washington, D.C.: Government Printing Office, 2001.

Alsop, Joseph W., with Adam Platt. *"I've Seen the Best of It."* New York: W. W. Norton, 1992.

American Defense League. *Gardner or Daniels?* New York: American Defense Society, [1915?].

American Legion. *Proceedings of the Sixteenth National Convention of the American Legion, Miami, Florida, October 22–25, 1934.* Washington, D.C.: Government Printing Office, 1935.

American National Biography. http://www.anb.org.

Anderson, David N. "From New Deal Liberal to Supreme Court Conservative." *Washington University Law Quarterly* (1975): 361–94.

Anderson, Karen. *Wartime Women: Sex Roles, Family Relations, and the Status of Women during World War II.* Westport, Conn.: Greenwood Press, 1981.

Anderson, Margo. *The American Census: A Social History.* New Haven, Conn.: Yale University Press, 1988.

Anderson, Margo J., and William Seltzer. "Federal Statistical Confidentiality and Business Data: Twentieth Century Challenges and Continuing Issues." *Journal of Privacy and Confidentiality* (2009). http://repository.cmu.edu/jpc/vol1/iss1/2.

Anderson, Michael J. "The Presidential Election of 1944." Ph.D. diss., University of Cincinnati, 1990.

Anderson, Paul Y. "Armed Rebellion on the Right." *Nation,* August 7, 1937, 146–47.

Anderson, William. *The Wild Man from Sugar Creek: The Political Career of Eugene Talmadge.* Baton Rouge: Louisiana State University Press, 1975.

Annunziata, Frank. "Governor of New York." In *Franklin D. Roosevelt: His Life and Times; An Encyclopedic View,* edited by Otis L. Graham Jr. and Meghan R. Wander, 159–61. Boston: G. K. Hall, 1983.

Arnold, Henry Harley. *Global Mission*. New York: Harper, 1949.

Arsenault, Raymond. *The Sound of Freedom: Marian Anderson, the Lincoln Memorial, and the Concert That Awakened America*. New York: Bloomsbury Press, 2009.

Asbell, Bernard. *Mother and Daughter: The Letters of Eleanor and Anna Roosevelt*. New York: Coward, McCann, and Geoghegan, 1982.

Ashburn, Frank D. *Peabody of Groton: A Portrait*. New York: Coward, McCann, 1944.

Ashley, Clifford W. *Whaleships of New Bedford*. Boston: Houghton Mifflin, 1929.

Auerbach, Jerold S. *Labor and Liberty: The La Follette Committee and the New Deal*. Indianapolis: Bobbs-Merrill, 1966.

———. "New Deal, Old Deal, or Raw Deal: Some Thoughts on New Left Historiography." *Journal of Southern History* 35 (1969): 18–30.

Austin, Allan W. *From Concentration Camp to Campus: Japanese American Students and World War II*. Urbana: University of Illinois Press, 2004.

———. *Quaker Brotherhood: Interracial Activism and the American Friends Service Committee, 1917–1950*. Urbana: University of Illinois Press, 2012.

Baer, George W. *The Coming of the Italian-Ethiopian War*. Cambridge, Mass.: Harvard University Press, 1967.

Bagby, Wesley M. *The Road to Normalcy: The Presidential Campaign and Election of 1920*. Baltimore: Johns Hopkins University Press, 1962.

Bailey, Anthony. *America, Lost & Found*. New York: Random House, 1980.

Barnard, Ellsworth. *Wendell Willkie, Fighter for Freedom*. Marquette: Northern Michigan University Press, 1966.

Barnouw, Eric. *The Golden Web: A History of Broadcasting in the United States, 1933 to 1953*. New York: Oxford University Press, 1968.

Baruch, Bernard. *The Public Years*. New York: Holt, 1960.

Bateman, Herman E. "Observations on President Roosevelt's Health during World War II." *Mississippi Valley Historical Review* 56 (1956): 82–102.

Bayly, Christopher, and Tim Harper. *Forgotten Armies: The Fall of British Asia, 1941–1945*. Cambridge, Mass.: Harvard University Press, 2005.

Bazer, Gerald. "Baseball during World War II: The Reaction and Encouragement of Franklin Delano Roosevelt and Others." *Nine: A Journal of Baseball History and Culture* 10 (Fall 2001): 114–29.

Beard, Charles A. *American Foreign Policy in the Making, 1932–1940: A Study in Responsibilities*. New Haven, Conn.: Yale University Press, 1946.

———. *President Roosevelt and the Coming of War, 1941: A Study in Appearances and Realities*. New Haven, Conn.: Yale University Press, 1948.

Beasley, Maurine H. *Eleanor Roosevelt and the Media: A Public Quest for Self-fulfillment*. Urbana: University of Illinois Press, 1987.

———, ed. *The White House Press Conferences of Eleanor Roosevelt*. New York: Garland, 1983.

Belair, Felix. "F. D. Roosevelt: Assistant Secretary." *New York Times Magazine*, March 17, 1940, 8, 18.

Belknap, Michal K. "A Putrid Pedigree: The Bush Administration's Military Tribunals in Historical Perspective." *California Western Law Review* 38 (2002): 433, 471–79.

———. "The Supreme Court Goes to War: The Meaning and Implications of the Nazi Saboteurs Case." *Military Law Review* 89 (1980): 59.

Bellush, Bernard. *The Failure of the NRA.* New York: W. W. Norton, 1975.

———. *Franklin D. Roosevelt as Governor of New York.* New York: Columbia University Press, 1955.

———. *He Walked Alone: A Biography of John G. Winant.* The Hague: Mouton, 1968.

Berg, A. Scott. *Lindbergh.* New York: Putnam, 1998.

Berle, Adolf A. *Navigating the Rapids, 1918–1971: From the Papers of Adolf A. Berle.* Edited by Beatrice Bishop Berle and Travis Beal Jacobs. New York: Harcourt Brace Jovanovich, 1973.

Bernstein, Barton J. "The New Deal: The Conservative Achievements of Liberal Reform." In *Towards a New Past: Dissenting Essays in American History,* edited by Barton J. Bernstein, 263–88. New York: Pantheon, 1968.

Bernstein, Irving. *A Caring Society: The New Deal, the Worker and the Great Depression.* Boston: Houghton Mifflin, 1985.

———. *The New Deal Collective Bargaining Policy.* Berkeley: University of California Press, 1950.

———. *Turbulent Years: A History of the American Worker, 1933–1941.* Boston: Houghton Mifflin, 1969.

Beschloss, Michael R. *Kennedy and Roosevelt: The Uneasy Alliance.* New York: W. W. Norton, 1980.

Biddle, Francis. *In Brief Authority.* New York: Doubleday, 1962.

Biles, Roger. *Big City Boss in Depression and War: Mayor Edward J. Kelly of Chicago.* DeKalb: Northern Illinois University Press, 1984.

———. *Crusading Liberal: Paul H. Douglas of Illinois.* DeKalb: Northern Illinois University Press, 2002.

Biographical Directory of the United States Congress, 1774–Present. http://bioguide.congress.gov.

Birmingham, Stephen. *Our Crowd: The Great Jewish Families of New York.* New York: Harper & Row, 1967.

Bishop, Jim. *FDR's Last Year.* New York: William Morrow, 1974.

Blackorby, Edwin C. *Prairie Rebel: The Public Life of William Lemke.* Lincoln: University of Nebraska Press, 1963.

Blum, John Morton. *From the Morgenthau Diaries: Years of Crisis, 1928–1938.* Boston: Houghton Mifflin, 1959.

———. *From the Morgenthau Diaries: Years of War, 1941–1945.* Boston: Houghton Mifflin, 1967.

———, ed. *The Price of Vision: The Diary of Henry A. Wallace, 1942–1946.* Boston: Houghton Mifflin, 1973.

———. *Roosevelt and Morgenthau.* Boston: Houghton Mifflin, 1970.

Blumenson, Martin. *Salerno to Cassino.* Washington, D.C.: Office of the Chief of Military History, U.S. Army, 1969.

Boettiger, John R. *A Love in Shadow.* New York: W. W. Norton, 1978.

Bohlen, Charles E. *Witness to History, 1929–1969.* New York: W. W. Norton, 1973.

Borg, Dorothy. "Notes on Roosevelt's Quarantine Speech." *Political Science Quarterly* 72 (1957): 405–33.

Bower, Kevin P. "Relief, Reform, and Youth: The National Youth Administration in Ohio, 1935–1943." Ph.D. diss., University of Cincinnati, 2003.

Boyer, Paul S., ed. *The Oxford Companion to United States History.* New York: Oxford University Press, 2001.

Braeman, John, Robert H. Bremner, and Everett Walters, eds. *Change and Continuity in Twentieth Century America.* Columbus: Ohio State University Press, 1964.

Brandeis, Louis D. *Other People's Money and How the Bankers Use It.* New York: Stokes, 1914.

Brandes, Stuart D. *American Welfare Capitalism, 1880–1940.* Chicago: University of Chicago Press, 1976.

Brandt, Irving. *Adventures in Conservation with Franklin D. Roosevelt.* Flagstaff, Ariz.: Northland, 1988.

Breitman, Richard, and Allan J. Lichtman. *FDR and the Jews.* Cambridge, Mass.: Harvard University Press, 2013.

Breitman, Richard, Barbara McDonald Stewart, and Severin Hochberg, eds. *Advocate for the Doomed: James G. McDonald.* Bloomington: Indiana University Press, 2007.

———. *Refugees and Rescue: The Diaries and Papers of James G. McDonald, 1935–1945.* Bloomington: Indiana University Press, 2009.

Bremer, William W. *Depression Winters: New York Social Workers and the New Deal.* Philadelphia: Temple University Press, 1984.

Brinkley, Alan. *The End of Reform: New Deal Liberalism in Recession and War.* New York: Alfred A. Knopf, 1995.

———. "The National Resources Planning Board and the Reconstruction of Planning." In *The American Planning Tradition: Culture and Policy,* edited by Robert Fishman, 173–92. Baltimore: Johns Hopkins University Press, 2000.

———. *Voices of Protest: Huey Long, Father Coughlin, and the Great Depression.* New York: Alfred A. Knopf, 1982.

Brock, William R. *Welfare, Democracy and the New Deal.* Cambridge: Cambridge University Press, 1988.

Broesamle, John J. *William Gibbs McAdoo: A Passion for Change, 1863–1917.* Port Washington, N.Y.: Kennikat, 1973.

Browder, Robert Paul, and Thomas G. Smith. *Independent: A Biography of Lewis W. Douglas.* New York: Alfred A. Knopf, 1986.

Brown, D. Clayton. *Electricity for Rural America: The Fight for REA.* Westport, Conn.: Greenwood Press, 1980.

Brown, John Mason. *The Ordeal of a Playwright.* New York: Harper, 1970.

———. *The Worlds of Robert E. Sherwood: Mirror to His Times, 1896–1939.* New York: Harper, 1965.

Brownlow, Louis. *Administrative Management in the Government of the United States.* Washington, D.C.: Government Printing Office, 1937. [United States, President's Committee on Administrative Management.]

———. *A Passion for Anonymity.* Chicago: University of Chicago Press, 1958.

Bruenn, Howard G. "Clinical Notes on the Illness and Death of President Franklin D. Roosevelt." *Annals of Internal Medicine* 72 (1970): 571–92.

Bruère, Henry. *America's Unemployment Problem.* Philadelphia: n.p., 1915.

Buell, Thomas B. *Master of Sea Power: A Biography of Fleet Admiral Ernest J. King.* Boston: Little, Brown, 1980.

Buenker, John D. *Urban Liberalism and Progressive Reform.* New York: Scribner's, 1973.

Buhite, Russell D., and David Levy, eds. *FDR's Fireside Chats.* Norman: University of Oklahoma Press, 1992.

Bunche, Ralph J. *The Political Status of the Negro in the Age of FDR.* Chicago: University of Chicago Press, 1973.

Buni, Andrew. *Robert L. Vann and the "Pittsburgh Courier": Politics and Black Journalism.* Pittsburgh: University of Pittsburgh Press, 1974.

Burke, Robert E., ed. *Diary Letters of Hiram Johnson, 1917–1945.* 7 vols. New York: Garland, 1983.

———. *Olson's New Deal for California.* Berkeley: University of California Press, 1953.

Burlingame, Roger. *Don't Let Them Scare You: The Life and Times of Elmer Davis.* Westport, Conn.: Greenwood Press, 1961.

Burns, James MacGregor. *Roosevelt: The Lion and the Fox.* New York: Harcourt, Brace, 1956.

———. *Roosevelt: The Soldier of Freedom.* New York: Harcourt Brace Jovanovich, 1970.

Burns, James MacGregor, and Susan Dunn. *The Three Roosevelts: Patrician Leaders Who Transformed America.* Boston: Atlantic Monthly Press, 2001.

Butler, J. R. M. *History of the Second World War.* United Kingdom Military Series, Grand Strategy. Vol. 2, *September 1939–June 1941.* London: Her Majesty's Stationery Office, 1957.

Butler, Susan. *My Dear Mr. Stalin.* New Haven, Conn.: Yale University Press, 2005.

Butow, Robert J. C. "The FDR Tapes: Secret Recordings Made in the Oval Office of the President in the Autumn of 1940." *American Heritage* (February–March 1982): 23–24.

———. *The John Doe Associates: Backdoor Diplomacy for Peace.* Stanford, Calif.: Stanford University Press, 1974.

———. "A Notable Passage to China: Myth and Memory in FDR's Family History." *Prologue* 31 (Fall 1999): 159–77.

———. *Tojo and the Coming of War.* Stanford, Calif.: Stanford University Press, 1961.

Byrnes, James F. *All in One Lifetime.* New York: Harper, 1958.

———. *Speaking Frankly.* New York: Harper, 1947.

Cadogan, Alexander. *The Diaries of Sir Alexander Cadogan, O.M., 1938–1945.* New York: Putnam, 1972.

Calef, Wesley C. *Private Grazing and Public Lands: Studies of the Local Management of the Taylor Grazing Act.* Chicago: University of Chicago Press, 1960.

Campbell, Thomas M., and George C. Herring, eds. *The Diaries of Edward R. Stettinius, Jr., 1943–1946.* New York: New Viewpoints, 1975.

Cannadine, David. *Mellon: An American Life.* New York: Alfred A. Knopf, 2006.

Capeci, Dominic J., Jr. *The Harlem Riot of 1943.* Philadelphia: Temple University Press, 1977.

———. *Race Relations in Wartime Detroit: The Sojourner Truth Housing Controversy of 1942.* Philadelphia: Temple University Press, 1984.

Caro, Robert A. *The Power Broker: Robert Moses and the Fall of New York.* New York: Alfred A. Knopf, 1974.

Caroli, Betty Boyd. *The Roosevelt Women: A Portrait in Five Generations.* New York: Basic Books, 1998.

Carosso, Vincent P., with the assistance of Rose C. Carosso. *The Morgans: Private Investment Bankers, 1854–1913.* Cambridge, Mass.: Harvard University Press, 1987.

Carter, Dan T. *Scottsboro: A Tragedy of the American South.* New York: Oxford University Press, 1969.

Catton, Bruce. *The War Lords of Washington.* New York: Harcourt, Brace, 1948.

Cebula, James E. *James M. Cox: Journalist and Politician.* New York: Garland, 1985.

Chadwin, Mark L. *The Hawks of World War II.* Chapel Hill: University of North Carolina Press, 1968.

Champagne, Anthony. *Congressman Sam Rayburn.* New Brunswick, N.J.: Rutgers University Press, 1984.

Chang, Hsin-pao. *Commissioner Lin and the Opium War.* Cambridge, Mass.: Harvard University Press, 1964.

Churchill, Winston S. *The Grand Alliance.* Boston: Houghton Mifflin, 1950.

———. *The Hinge of Fate.* Boston: Houghton Mifflin, 1950.

———. *The World Crisis, 1916–1918.* New York: Scribner's, 1927.

Clawson, Marian. *New Deal Planning: The National Resources Planning Board.* Baltimore: Johns Hopkins University Press, 1981.

Clemens, Diane Shaver. *Yalta.* New York: Oxford University Press, 1975.

Cline, Ray S. *Washington Command Post: The Operations Division.* 1951. Reprint, Washington, D.C.: Center for Military History, 2003.

Coady, Joseph W. "Franklin D. Roosevelt's Early Washington Years (1913–1920)." Ph.D. diss., St. John's University, 1968.

Coben, Stanley. *A. Mitchell Palmer: Politician.* New York: Columbia University Press, 1963.

Cohen, Adam. *Nothing to Fear: FDR's Inner Circle and the Hundred Days That Created Modern America.* New York: Penguin, 2009.

Cohodas, Nadine. *Strom Thurmond and the Politics of Southern Change.* New York: Simon and Schuster, 1993.

Coit, Margaret. *Mr. Baruch.* Boston: Houghton Mifflin, 1957.

Cole, Hugh M. *The Ardennes: Battle of the Bulge.* Washington, D.C.: Government Printing Office, 1965.

Cole, Olen, Jr. *The African-American Experience in the Civilian Conservation Corps.* Gainesville: University Press of Florida, 1999.

Cole, Wayne S. *America First: The Battle against Intervention.* Madison: University of Wisconsin Press, 1953.

———. *Roosevelt and the Isolationists, 1932–1945.* Lincoln: University of Nebraska Press, 1983.

Coletta, Paolo E., ed. *American Secretaries of the Navy.* Annapolis, Md.: Naval Institute Press, 1980.

Commission on Wartime Relocation and Internment of Civilians. *Personal Justice Denied.* Washington, D.C.: Government Printing Office, 1982.

Conkin, Paul. *Tomorrow a New World: The New Deal Community Program.* Ithaca, N.Y.: Cornell University Press, 1958.

Conn, Stetson. "The Decision to Relocate the Japanese from the Pacific Coast." In *Command Decisions,* edited by Kent Roberts Greenfield, 125–49. New York: Harcourt, 1959.

Conn, Stetson, Rose C. Engleman, and Byron Fairchild. *Guarding the United States and Its Outposts.* Washington, D.C.: Office of the Chief of Military History, Department of the Army, 1964.

Conn, Stetson, and Byron Fairchild. *The Framework of Hemisphere Defense.* Washington, D.C.: Government Reprints Press, 1989.

Cook, Blanche Wiesen. *Eleanor Roosevelt.* Vol. 1, *1884–1933.* Vol. 2, *1933–1938.* New York: Viking, 1992, 1999.

Coox, Alvin D. *Nomonhan: Japan against Russia, 1939.* 2 vols. Stanford, Calif.: Stanford University Press, 1985.

Cordery, Stacy A. *Alice: Alice Roosevelt Longworth, from White House Princess to Washington Power Broker.* New York: Viking, 2007.

Cox, James M. *Journey through My Years.* New York: Simon and Schuster, 1946.

Craven, Wesley F., and James L. Cate, eds. *The Army Air Forces in World War II.* 7 vols. Washington, D.C.: Government Printing Office, 1948–58.

Creel, George. *Rebel at Large: Recollections of Fifty Crowded Years.* New York: G. P. Putnam's Sons, 1947.

Cronon, E. David, ed. *The Cabinet Diaries of Josephus Daniels, 1913–1921.* Lincoln: University of Nebraska Press, 1963.

———. *Josephus Daniels in Mexico.* Madison: University of Wisconsin Press, 1960.

Crosby, Alfred W. *America's Forgotten Pandemic: The Influenza of 1918.* New York: Cambridge University Press, 1989.

Cross, Robert F. *Sailor in the White House: The Seafaring Life of FDR.* Annapolis, Md.: Naval Institute Press, 1999.

Culley, John Joel. "Enemy Alien Control in the United States during World War II." In *Alien Justice: Wartime Internment in Australia and North America,* edited by Kay Saunders and Roger Daniels, 138–51. St. Lucia: University of Queensland, 2000.

Current, Richard N. *Secretary Stimson.* New Brunswick, N.J.: Rutgers University Press, 1954.

Curtis, James C. *Mind's Eye, Mind's Truth: FSA Photography Reconsidered.* Philadelphia: Temple University Press, 1989.

Cutlip, Scott M. *Fund Raising in the United States: Its Role in American Philanthropy.* 1965. Reprint, New Brunswick, N.J.: Transaction, 1990.

Dallek, Robert. *Democrat and Diplomat: The Life of William E. Dodd.* New York: Oxford University Press, 1968.

———. *Franklin D. Roosevelt and American Foreign Policy, 1932–1945.* New York: Oxford University Press, 1979.

Dangerfield, George. *Chancellor Robert R. Livingston of New York, 1746–1813.* New York: Harcourt, Brace, 1960.

Daniels, Jonathan. *The Time between the Wars: Armistice to Pearl Harbor.* New York: Doubleday, 1966.

——. *Washington Quadrille: The Dance beside the Documents.* New York: Doubleday, 1968.

——. *White House Witness, 1942–1945.* New York: Doubleday, 1975.

Daniels, Josephus. *Editor in Politics.* Chapel Hill: University of North Carolina Press, 1941.

——. *Shirt-Sleeve Diplomat.* Chapel Hill: University of North Carolina Press, 1947.

——. *The Wilson Era: Years of Peace, 1910–1917.* Chapel Hill: University of North Carolina Press, 1944.

——. *The Wilson Era: Years of War and After, 1917–1923.* Chapel Hill: University of North Carolina Press, 1946.

Daniels, Roger, ed. *American Concentration Camps: A Documentary History of the Relocation and Incarceration of Japanese Americans, 1941–1945.* 9 vols. New York: Garland, 1989.

——. "American Refugee Policy in Historical Perspective." In *The Muses Flee Hitler: Cultural Transfer and Adaptation, 1930–1945,* edited by Jarrell C. Jackman and Carla M. Borden, 61–77. Washington, D.C.: Smithsonian Institution Press, 1983.

——. *Asian America: Chinese and Japanese in the United States since 1850.* Seattle: University of Washington Press, 1988.

——. *The Bonus March: An Episode of the Great Depression.* Westport, Conn.: Greenwood Press, 1971.

——. *Concentration Camps, USA: Japanese Americans and World War II.* New York: Holt, Rinehart, and Winston, 1972.

——. *The Decision to Relocate the Japanese Americans.* Philadelphia: Lippincott, 1975.

——. *Guarding the Golden Door: American Immigration Policy and Immigrants since 1882.* New York: Hill and Wang, 2004.

——. "The Internment of Japanese Nationals in the United States during World War II." *Halcyon* (1995): 66–75.

——. *The Japanese American Cases: The Rule of War in Time of War.* Lawrence: University Press of Kansas, 2013.

——. *The Politics of Prejudice: The Anti-Japanese Movement in California and the Struggle for Japanese Exclusion.* Berkeley: University of California Press, 1962.

——. *Prisoners without Trial: Japanese Americans in World War II.* New York: Hill and Wang, 1993.

Daniels, Roger, and Harry H. L. Kitano. *American Racism: Exploration of the Nature of Prejudice.* Englewood Cliffs, N.J.: Prentice Hall, 1970.

Davis, Kenneth S. *FDR: The Beckoning of Destiny.* New York: Putnam, 1972.

——. *FDR: The New York Years, 1928–1933.* New York: Random House, 1985.

——. *The Hero: Charles A. Lindbergh and the American Dream.* New York: Doubleday, 1959.

Davis, Polly. *Alben Barkley: Senate Majority Leader and Vice President.* New York: Garland, 1979.

Dawes, Charles G. *Journal as Ambassador to Great Britain.* New York: Macmillan, 1939.

Dawley, Alan. *Changing the World: American Progressives in War and Revolution.* Princeton, N.J.: Princeton University Press, 2003.

Daws, Gavan. *Prisoners of the Japanese: POWs of World War II in the Pacific.* New York: Morrow, 1994.

de Gaulle, Charles. *The Complete War Memoirs of Charles de Gaulle.* New York: Simon and Schuster, 1964.

Delano, Amasa. *Narrative of Voyages and Travels in the Northern and Southern Hemispheres, Comprising Three Voyages Round the World.* Boston: E. G. House, 1817.

Delano, Daniel W., Jr. *Franklin Roosevelt and the Delano Influence.* Pittsburgh: James S. Nudi, 1946.

Dewey, George. *Autobiography of George Dewey, Admiral of the Navy.* New York: Scribner's, 1913.

DeWitt, Larry. "Historical Background and Development of Social Security." http://www.ssa.gov/history/briefhistory3.html.

Dierenfield, Bruce J. *Keeper of the Rules: Howard W. Smith of Virginia.* Charlottesville: University Press of Virginia, 1987.

Divine, Robert A. *Roosevelt and World War II.* Baltimore: Johns Hopkins University Press, 1969.

Dorsett, Lyle W. *Franklin D. Roosevelt and the City Bosses.* Port Washington, N.Y.: Kennikat, 1977.

Dorwart, Jeffery M. *Conflict of Duty: The U.S. Navy's Intelligence Dilemma, 1919–1945.* Annapolis, Md.: Naval Institute Press, 1983.

Douglas, Paul H. *The Coming of a New Party.* New York: McGraw-Hill, 1931.

———. *In the Fullness of Time: The Memoirs of Paul H. Douglas.* New York: Harcourt Brace Jovanovich, 1972.

Dower, John. *Japan in War & Peace.* New York: New Press, 1993.

Downey, Kirstin. *The Woman behind the New Deal.* New York: Doubleday, 2009.

Downs, Jacques M. *The Golden Ghetto: The American Commercial Community at Canton and the Shaping of American China Policy, 1784–1844.* Bethlehem, Pa.: Lehigh University Press, 1997.

Doyle, William. *Inside the Oval Office: The White House Tapes from FDR to Clinton.* New York: Kodansha International, 1999.

Droze, Wilmon H. *Trees, Prairies, and People: A History of Tree Planting in the Plains States.* Denton: Texas Woman's University, 1997.

Dubofsky, Melvin, and Warren Van Tine. *John L. Lewis: A Biography.* New York: Quadrangle, 1977.

Dunne, Gerald T. *Grenville Clark: Public Citizen.* New York: Farrar, Straus, and Giroux, 1986.

Dykeman, Wilma. *Seeds of Southern Change: The Life of Will Alexander.* Chicago: University of Chicago Press, 1962.

Dziuban, Stanley W. *Military Relations between the United States and Canada, 1939–1945.* Washington, D.C.: Government Printing Office, 1959.

Eccles, Marriner S. *Beckoning Frontiers: Public and Personal Recollections.* Edited by Sidney Hymon. New York: Alfred A. Knopf, 1951.

Eddy, William A. *F.D.R. Meets Ibn Saud.* New York: American Friends of the Middle East, 1954.

Egerton, John. *Speak Now against the Day: The Generation before the Civil Rights Movement in the South.* New York: Alfred A. Knopf, 1994.

Eichengreen, Barry. *Hall of Mirrors: The Great Depression, the Great Recession, and the Uses—and Misuses—of History.* New York: Oxford University Press, 2015.

Eisel, Braxton. *The Flying Tigers: Chennault's American Volunteer Group in China.* Washington, D.C.: Air Force History and Museums Program, 2009.

Eisenhower, Dwight D. *Crusade in Europe.* New York: Doubleday, 1948.

Eliot, Thomas Hopkinson. *Recollections of the New Deal: When the People Mattered.* Boston: Northeastern University Press, 1992.

Elsey, George M. *An Unplanned Life.* Columbia: University of Missouri Press, 2005.

Emerson, William. "Franklin Roosevelt as Commander-in-Chief in World War II." *Military Affairs* 22 (Winter 1958–59): 181–207.

"F. D. Roosevelt: The World's Best Known Stamp Collector." *Stamp & Coin Collector* 3 (January 1966).

Falk, I. S. "The Committee on the Costs of Medical Care: 25 Years of Progress." *American Journal of Public Health* 48 (1958): 979–82.

Farley, James A. *Behind the Ballots: The Personal History of a Politician.* New York: Harcourt, Brace, 1938.

———. *Jim Farley's Story: The Roosevelt Years.* New York: Whittlesey House, 1948.

Feingold, Henry L. *The Politics of Rescue: The Roosevelt Administration and the Holocaust, 1938–1945.* New Brunswick, N.J.: Rutgers University Press, 1970.

Feis, Herbert. *The China Tangle: The American Effort in China from Pearl Harbor to the Marshall Mission.* Princeton, N.J.: Princeton University Press, 1953.

———. *1933: Characters in Crisis.* Boston: Little, Brown, 1966.

Ferrell, Robert H. *The Dying President: Franklin D. Roosevelt, 1944–45.* Columbia: University of Missouri Press, 1998.

Fielding, Raymond. *The American Newsreel, 1911–1967.* Norman: University of Oklahoma Press, 1972.

Finan, Christopher M. *Alfred E. Smith: The Happy Warrior.* New York: Hill and Wang, 2002.

Fine, Sidney. *Frank Murphy: The Detroit Years.* Ann Arbor: University of Michigan Press, 1975.

———. *Frank Murphy: The New Deal Years.* Ann Arbor: University of Michigan Press, 1979.

Fisher, Louis. *Nazi Saboteurs on Trial: A Military Tribunal and American Law.* Lawrence: University Press of Kansas, 2003.

Fleming, Donald. "Albert Einstein: Letter to Franklin D. Roosevelt, 1939." In *An American Primer,* edited by Daniel J. Boorstin, 857–62. Chicago: University of Chicago Press, 1966.

Flynn, Edward J. *You're the Boss.* 1947. Reprint, New York: Collier Books, 1962.

Flynn, George Q. *Louis B. Hershey.* Chapel Hill: University of North Carolina Press, 1985.

Flynn, John T. *Country Squire in the White House.* New York: Doubleday, Doran, 1940.

Flynt, Wayne. *Duncan Upshaw Fletcher, Dixie's Reluctant Progressive.* Tallahassee: Florida State University Press, 1971.

Fogarty, Gerald P., S.J. *The Vatican and the American Hierarchy from 1870 to 1965.* Stuttgart: Hiersmann, 1982.

Frankfurter, Felix. *Felix Frankfurter Reminisces: Recorded in Talks with Dr. Harlan B. Phillips.* New York: Reynal, 1990.

Freedman, Max, ed. *Roosevelt and Frankfurter: Their Correspondence, 1928–1945.* Boston: Little, Brown, 1967.

Freidel, Frank. "The Dutchness of the Roosevelts." In *A Bilateral Bicentennial: A History of Dutch American Relations, 1782–1982,* edited by J. W. Schulte Nordholt and Robert P. Swierenga, 157–67. New York: Octagon Books, 1982.

———. *Franklin D. Roosevelt: The Apprenticeship.* Boston: Little, Brown, 1952.

———. *Franklin D. Roosevelt: Launching the New Deal.* Boston: Little, Brown, 1973.

———. *Franklin D. Roosevelt: The Ordeal.* Boston: Little, Brown, 1954.

———. *Franklin D. Roosevelt: A Rendezvous with Destiny.* Boston: Little, Brown, 1990.

———. *Franklin D. Roosevelt: The Triumph.* Boston: Little, Brown, 1956.

———. "Franklin D. Roosevelt in the Northwest: Informal Glimpses." *Pacific Northwest Quarterly* 76 (1985): 122–31.

———. "Herbert Hoover and Franklin Roosevelt: Reminiscent Reflections." In *Understanding Herbert Hoover: Ten Perspectives,* edited by Lee Nash, 125–40. Stanford, Calif.: Hoover Institution, 1987.

Friedman, Max Paul. *Nazis and Good Neighbors: The United States Campaign against the Germans of Latin America in World War II.* Cambridge: Cambridge University Press, 2003.

Friend, Theodore. *Between Two Empires: Philippine Ordeal and Development from the Great Depression through the Pacific War, 1929–1946.* New Haven, Conn.: Yale University Press, 1965.

Fritz, Sherilyn C. "Twentieth-Century Salinity and Water-Level Fluctuations in Devils Lake, North Dakota: Test of a Diatom-Based Transfer Function." *Limnology and Oceanography* 35 (1990): 1771–81.

Fry, Varian. *Surrender on Demand.* New York: Random House, 1945.

Galbraith, John Kenneth. *The Great Crash.* London: Hamish Hamilton, 1955.

———. "How Keynes Came to America." In *A Contemporary Guide to Economics, Peace, and Laughter,* by John Kenneth Galbraith, 43–59. Boston: Houghton Mifflin, 1971.

———. *A Life in Our Times.* Boston: Houghton Mifflin, 1981.

———. *Name Dropping: From F.D.R. On.* Boston: Houghton Mifflin, 1999.

Gallagher, Hugh G. *FDR's Splendid Deception.* New York: Dodd, Mead, 1985.

Garland, Albert N., and Howard McGaw Smyth. *Sicily and the Surrender of Italy.* Washington, D.C.: Office of the Chief of Military History, U.S. Army, 1965.

Garrison, Lloyd K. "The National Labor Boards." *Annals* 184 (1936): 138–46.

Gaydowski, J. D. "Eight Letters to the Editor: The Genesis of the Townsend Plan." *Southern California Quarterly* 52 (1970): 365–82.

Gellman, Irwin F. *Good Neighbor Diplomacy: United States Policies in Latin America, 1933–1945.* Baltimore: Johns Hopkins University Press, 1979.

———. *Secret Affairs: Franklin D. Roosevelt, Cordell Hull, and Sumner Welles.* Baltimore: Johns Hopkins University Press, 1995.

Gilbert, Martin. *Churchill: A Life.* New York: Henry Holt, 1991.

———. *Churchill and America.* New York: Free Press, 2005.

Glennon, Robert J. *The Iconoclast as Reformer.* Ithaca, N.Y.: Cornell University Press, 1985.

Glines, Carroll V. *Doolittle's Tokyo Raiders.* Princeton, N.J.: Van Nostrand, 1964.

Goldberg, Richard Thayer. *The Making of Franklin D. Roosevelt: Triumph over Disability.* Cambridge, Mass.: Abt Books, 1981.

González, Gilbert G. *Labor and Community: Mexican Citrus Worker Villages in a Southern California County, 1900–1950.* Urbana: University of Illinois Press, 1994.

Goodwin, Doris Kearns. *The Fitzgeralds and the Kennedys.* New York: Simon and Schuster, 1987.

———. *No Ordinary Time: Franklin and Eleanor Roosevelt; The Home Front in World War II.* New York: Simon and Schuster, 1994.

Gosnell, Harold F. *Boss Platt and His New York Machine: A Study of the Political Leadership of Thomas C. Platt, Theodore Roosevelt, and Others.* Chicago: University of Chicago Press, 1924.

———. *Champion Campaigner: Franklin D. Roosevelt.* New York: Macmillan, 1952.

Graebner, Norman A., ed. *An Uncertain Tradition: American Secretaries of State in the Twentieth Century.* New York: McGraw-Hill, 1961.

Graham, Otis L. *An Encore for Reform: Old Progressives and the New Deal.* New York: Oxford University Press, 1967.

Graham, Otis L., Jr., and Meghan R. Wander, eds. *Franklin D. Roosevelt: His Life and Times; An Encyclopedic View.* Boston: G. K. Hall, 1983.

Gravlee, G. Jack. "Stephen T. Early: The 'Advance Man.'" *Speech Monographs* 30 (1963): 441–49.

Green, Marguerite. *The National Civic Federation and the American Labor Movement.* Westport, Conn.: Greenwood Press, 1956.

Greenberg, Cheryl L. *Troubling the Waters: Black-Jewish Relations in the American Century.* Princeton, N.J.: Princeton University Press, 2006.

Greenfield, Kent Roberts. *American Strategy in World War II: A Reconsideration.* Baltimore: Johns Hopkins University Press, 1963, especially "Franklin D. Roosevelt: Commander-in-Chief," 49–84, 126–31.

Greer, Thomas H. *What Roosevelt Thought: The Social and Political Ideas of Franklin D. Roosevelt.* East Lansing: Michigan State University Press, 1958.

Gregory, Cleburne F. "Franklin D. Roosevelt Will Swim to Health." *Atlanta Journal Sunday Magazine,* October 26, 1924.

Grimshaw, Allen D., ed. *Racial Violence in the United States.* Chicago: Aldine, 1956.

Griswold, Erwin W. "Government in Ignorance of the Law: A Plea for Better Publication of Executive Legislation." *Harvard Law Review* 48 (1934).

Gruening, Ernest. *Many Battles: The Autobiography of Ernest Gruening.* New York: Liveright, 1973.

Gunther, John. *Roosevelt in Retrospect: A Profile in History.* New York: Harper, 1950.

Haight, John M. *American Aid to France, 1938–1940.* New York: Atheneum, 1970.

Hall, Kermit L., ed. *The Oxford Guide to Supreme Court Decisions*. New York: Oxford University Press, 1999.

Halsey, William F., and J. Bryan III. *Admiral Halsey's Story*. New York: Whittlesey House, 1947.

Hamilton, Nigel. *The Mantle of Command: FDR at War, 1941–1942*. Boston: Houghton Mifflin Harcourt, 2014.

Hand, Samuel B. *Counsel and Advise: A Political Biography of Samuel I. Rosenman*. New York: Garland, 1979.

Handlin, Oscar. *Al Smith and His America*. Boston: Little, Brown, 1958.

Harbaugh, William H. *The Life and Times of Theodore Roosevelt*. New York: Oxford University Press, 1975.

———. "Roosevelt, Theodore." In *American National Biography*. New York: Oxford University Press, 2000.

Hargrove, Erwin C. "The Task of Leadership: The Board Chairman." In *TVA: Fifty Years of Grass Roots Democracy*, edited by Erwin C. Hargrove and Paul K. Conkin. Urbana: University of Illinois Press, 1984

Harriman, W. Averell, and Elie Abel. *Special Envoy to Churchill and Stalin, 1941–1946*. New York: Random House, 1975.

Harrington, Jerry. "Senator Guy Gillette Foils the Execution Committee." *Palimpsest* 62 (1981): 170–80.

Harris, Joseph E. *African-American Reactions to War in Ethiopia, 1936–1941*. Baton Rouge: Louisiana State University Press, 1994.

Harriss, C. Lowell. *History and Policies of the Home Owners' Loan Corporation*. New York: National Bureau of Economic Research, 1951.

Harrod, Frederick S. *Manning the New Navy: Development of a Modern Naval Enlisted Force, 1899–1940*. Westport, Conn.: Greenwood Press, 1978.

Hartmann, Susan M. *The Home Front and Beyond: American Women in the 1940s*. Boston: Twayne, 1982.

Harvard Alumni Bulletin 47 (April 28, 1945).

Hassett, William D. *Off the Record with FDR, 1942–1945*. New Brunswick, N.J.: Rutgers University Press, 1958.

Hawkins, Helen S. *A New Deal for the Newcomer: The Federal Transient Service*. New York: Garland, 1991.

Hawley, Ellis W. *The New Deal and the Problem of Monopoly*. Princeton, N.J.: Princeton University Press, 1966.

Healy, David. *Gunboat Diplomacy in the Wilson Era: The U.S. Navy in Haiti, 1915–1916*. Madison: University of Wisconsin Press, 1976.

Heinemann, Ronald L. *Depression and New Deal in Virginia*. Charlottesville: University Press of Virginia, 1986.

Herman, Jan Kenneth. "The President's Cardiologist." *Navy Medicine* 81 (March–April 1990): 6–13.

Herring, E. Pendleton. "Second Session of the Seventy-Third Congress, January 3rd, 1934, to June 18th, 1934." *American Political Science Review* 28 (1934): 852–66.

Herring, George C. *Aid to Russia, 1941–46*. New York: Columbia University Press, 1973.

Hershberg, James. *James B. Conant: Harvard to Hiroshima and the Making of the Nuclear Age.* New York: Alfred A. Knopf, 1993.

Hess, Stephen. "The Roosevelt Dynasty." In *America's Political Dynasties,* by Stephen Hess, 167–217. 2nd ed. New Brunswick, N.J.: Transaction, 1997.

Higham, John. *Strangers in the Land: Patterns of American Nativism, 1860–1924.* New Brunswick, N.J.: Rutgers University Press, 1955.

Hine, Darlene Clark. "Black Professionals and Race Consciousness: Origins of the Civil Rights Movement, 1890–1950." *Journal of American History* 89 (2003): 1279–95.

Hirschfield, Daniel S. *The Lost Reform: The Campaign for Compulsory Health Insurance in the United States from 1932 to 1943.* Cambridge, Mass.: Harvard University Press, 1970.

Hofstadter, Richard. *The American Political Tradition and the Men Who Made It.* New York: Alfred A. Knopf, 1948.

Hofstadter, Richard, William Miller, and Daniel Aaron. *The United States: The History of a Republic.* Englewood Cliffs, N.J.: Prentice Hall, 1957.

Holley, Donald. "Trouble in Paradise: Dyess Colony and Arkansas Politics." *Arkansas Historical Quarterly* 32 (Autumn 1973): 203–16.

———. *Uncle Sam's Farmers: The New Deal Communities in the Lower Mississippi Valley.* Urbana: University of Illinois Press, 1975.

Holtzman, Abraham. *The Townsend Movement: A Study of Old Age Pressure Politics.* New York: Bookman Associates, 1963.

Hoover, Herbert C. *The Memoirs of Herbert Hoover: The Great Depression, 1929–1941.* New York: Macmillan, 1952.

———. *Public Papers of the Presidents of the United States.* 4 vols. Washington, D.C.: Government Printing Office, 1974.

Hoover, Irwin H. *Forty-Two Years in the White House.* Boston: Houghton Mifflin, 1934.

Hopkins, Harry L. *Spending to Save: The Complete Story of Relief.* New York: W. W. Norton, 1936.

Hopkins, June. *Harry Hopkins: Sudden Hero, Brash Reformer.* New York: St. Martin's, 1999.

Howard, Donald S. *The WPA and Federal Relief Policy.* New York: Russell Sage Foundation, 1943.

Howe, George F. *Northwest Africa: Seizing the Initiative in the West.* Washington, D.C.: Office of the Chief of Military History, Department of the Army, 1957.

Howe, Louis McHenry. "The President's Mailbag." *American Magazine,* June 1934, 34.

———. "The Winner." *Saturday Evening Post,* February 25, 1935.

Howlett, Charles F., ed. *History of the American Peace Movement, 1890–2000: The Emergence of a New Scholarly Tradition.* Lewiston, N.Y.: Edwin Mellen Press, 2005.

Hull, Cordell. *The Memoirs of Cordell Hull.* New York: Macmillan, 1948.

Hurd, Charles W. "Hopkins: Right-Hand Man." *New York Times Magazine,* April 11, 1940, 6, 22.

———. *When the New Deal Was Young and Gay.* New York: Hawthorn Books, 1965.

Huthmacher, J. Joseph. *Senator Robert F. Wagner and the Rise of Urban Liberalism.* Cambridge, Mass.: Harvard University Press, 1968.

Hyman, Sidney. *Marriner S. Eccles: Private Entrepreneur and Public Servant.* Stanford, Calif.: Stanford University, School of Business Administration, 1976.

Ickes, Harold L. *The Autobiography of a Curmudgeon.* New York: Reynal and Hitchcock, 1943.

———. *The Secret Diary of Harold L. Ickes.* 3 vols. New York: Simon and Schuster, 1954.

Iriye, Akira. *Across the Pacific: An Inner History of American–East Asian Relations.* New York: Harcourt, Brace & World, 1961.

Ismay, Hastings Lionel. *Memoirs.* New York: Viking, 1960.

Jackman, Jarrell C., and Carla M. Borden, eds. *The Muses Flee Hitler: Cultural Transfer and Adaptation, 1930–1945.* Washington, D.C.: Smithsonian Institution Press, 1983.

Jackson, Carlton. *Presidential Vetoes, 1792–1945.* Athens: University of Georgia Press, 1967.

Jackson, Kenneth T. "Race, Ethnicity, and Real Estate Appraisal: The Home Owners Loan Corporation and the Federal Housing Administration." *Journal of Urban History* 6 (1980): 419–62.

Jackson, Robert H. *That Man: An Insider's Portrait of Franklin D. Roosevelt.* New York: Oxford University Press, 2003.

James, D. Clayton. *The Years of MacArthur.* Vols. 1–2. Boston: Houghton Mifflin, 1970, 1975.

Janeway, Eliot. *The Struggle for Survival.* New Haven, Conn.: Yale University Press, 1951.

Jeffries, John. "A 'Third New Deal'? Liberal Policy and the American State, 1937–1945." *Journal of Policy History* 8 (1996): 387–409.

———. *Wartime America: The World War II Home Front.* Chicago: Ivan R. Dee, 1998.

Jensen, Joan M. *The Price of Vigilance.* Chicago: Rand McNally, 1968.

Johnson, Charles W., and Charles O. Jackson. *City behind a Fence: Oak Ridge, Tennessee, 1942–1946.* Knoxville: University of Tennessee Press, 1981.

Johnson, Hugh S. *The Blue Eagle from Egg to Earth.* New York: Doubleday, 1935.

Johnson, Walter. *The Battle against Isolation.* Chicago: University of Chicago Press, 1944.

———. "Edward R. Stettinius, Jr." In *An Uncertain Tradition: American Secretaries of State in the Twentieth Century,* edited by Norman A. Graebner, 2110–23. New York: McGraw-Hill, 1961.

———, ed. *Selected Letters of William Allen White.* New York: Holt, 1947.

Jones, Benjamin. "Hawai'i's Kibei under Martial Law." *Western Legal History* 22, nos. 1–2 (2009).

Jones, James H. *Bad Blood: The Tuskegee Syphilis Experiment.* New York: Free Press, 1981.

Jones, Jesse H., with Edward Angly. *Fifty Billion Dollars: My Thirteen Years with the RFC.* New York: Macmillan, 1951.

Jong, Louis de. *The German Fifth Column in the Second World War.* Chicago: University of Chicago Press, 1956.

Kaiser, David. *No End Save Victory: How FDR Led the Nation Into War.* New York: Basic Books, 2014.

Kantowicz, Edward R. "Cardinal Mundelein of Chicago and the Shaping of Twentieth-Century American Catholicism." *Journal of American History* 68 (1981).

———. *Corporation Sole: Cardinal Mundelein and Chicago Catholicism.* Notre Dame: University of Notre Dame Press, 1983.

Katznelson, Ira. *Fear Itself: The New Deal and the Origins of Our Time*. New York: Liverright, 2013.

Kauffman, Reginald W. *Jesse Isidor Straus: A Biographical Portrait*. New York: n.p., 1973.

Kaye, Harvey J. *The Fight for the Four Freedoms*. New York: Simon and Schuster, 2014.

Kearney, James R. *Anna Eleanor Roosevelt: The Evolution of a Reformer*. Boston: Houghton Mifflin, 1968.

Kelly, Lawrence C. *The Assault on Assimilation: John Collier and the Origins of Indian Policy Reform*. Albuquerque: University of New Mexico Press, 1983.

Kendrick, Alexander. *Prime Time: The Life of Edward R. Murrow*. Boston: Little, Brown, 1969.

Kennan, George F. *American Diplomacy, 1900–1950*. Chicago: University of Chicago Press, 1951.

Kennedy, David M. *Freedom from Fear: The American People in Depression and War*. New York: Oxford University Press, 1999.

Kennedy, Susan E. *The Banking Crisis of 1933*. Lexington: University Press of Kentucky, 1973.

Kersten, Andrew E. *A. Philip Randolph: A Life in the Vanguard*. Lanham, Md.: Rowman & Littlefield, 2007.

——. *Clarence Darrow: American Iconoclast*. New York: Hill and Wang, 2011.

——. *Race, Jobs, and the War: The FEPC in the Midwest, 1941–46*. Urbana: University of Illinois Press, 2000.

Kessner, Thomas. *Fiorello H. La Guardia and the Making of Modern New York*. New York: McGraw-Hill, 1989.

Keynes, John Maynard. *The Economic Consequences of the Peace*. New York: Harcourt, Brace, and Howe, 1920.

——. *Essays in Persuasion*. New York: Harcourt, Brace, 1932.

Kilpatrick, Carroll, ed. *Roosevelt and Daniels: A Friendship in Politics*. Chapel Hill: University of North Carolina Press, 1952.

Kimball, Warren F., ed. *Forged in War: Roosevelt, Churchill, and the Second World War*. New York: Morrow, 1997.

——. *The Juggler: Franklin Roosevelt as Wartime Statesman*. Princeton, N.J.: Princeton University Press, 1991.

——. *The Most Unsordid Act: Lend Lease, 1939–1941*. Baltimore: Johns Hopkins University Press, 1969.

——. *Roosevelt and Churchill: The Complete Correspondence*. 3 vols. Princeton, N.J.: Princeton University Press, 1984. The 1987 paperback edition, with errata, is definitive.

Kirkendall, Richard S. "Agricultural Adjustment Act." In *Franklin D. Roosevelt: His Life and Times; An Encyclopedic View,* edited by Otis L. Graham Jr. and Meghan R. Wander. Boston: G. K. Hall, 1983.

——. "Agriculture." In *Franklin D. Roosevelt: His Life and Times; An Encyclopedic View,* edited by Otis L. Graham Jr. and Meghan R. Wander. Boston: G. K. Hall, 1983.

Klaw, Spencer. "Labor's Non-Partisan League: An Experiment in Labor Politics." Master's thesis, Harvard University, 1941.

Kleeman, Rita Halle. *Gracious Lady: The Life of Sara Delano Roosevelt*. New York: D. Appleton–Century, 1935.

Klehr, Harvey, and John Haynes. "The Comintern's Open Secrets." *American Spectator* 25 (December 1992): 34–41.

Klein, Joe. *Woody Guthrie: A Life*. New York: Dell, 1980.

Kochavi, Arieh J. *Prelude to Nuremberg: Allied War Crimes Policy and the Question of Punishment*. Chapel Hill: University of North Carolina Press, 1998.

Koop, Theodore F. *Weapon of Silence*. Chicago: University of Chicago Press, 1946.

Kruger, Thomas. *And Promises to Keep: The Southern Conference of Human Welfare, 1938–1948*. Nashville: Vanderbilt University Press, 1967.

Kutler, Stanley I. *The American Inquisition: Justice and Injustice in the Cold War*. New York: Hill and Wang, 1982.

Kyvig, David E. *Explicit and Authentic Acts: Amending the U.S. Constitution, 1776–1995*. Lawrence: University Press of Kansas, 1996.

———. *Repealing National Prohibition*. Chicago: University of Chicago Press, 1979.

Lane, Anne Wintermute, and Louise Herrick Wall, eds. *The Letters of Franklin K. Lane, Personal and Political*. Boston: Houghton Mifflin, 1922.

Larrabee, Eric. *Commander in Chief: Franklin D. Roosevelt, His Lieutenants & Their War*. New York: Harper & Row, 1987.

Lash, Joseph P. *Eleanor and Franklin: The Story of Their Relationship, Based on Eleanor Roosevelt's Private Papers*. New York: W. W. Norton, 1971.

———. *Love, Eleanor: Eleanor Roosevelt and Her Friends*. New York: Doubleday, 1982.

Lasser, William. *Benjamin V. Cohen: Architect of the New Deal*. New Haven, Conn.: Yale University Press, 2002.

Lawrence, W. H. "A Cool Man on a Hot Spot." *New York Times Magazine*, January 17, 1943, 7, 23.

Leab, Daniel J. "United We Eat: The Creation and Organization of Unemployed Councils in 1930." *Labor History* 8 (1967): 300–315.

Leahy, William D. *I Was There*. New York: Whittlesey House, 1950.

Leff, Mark H. *The Limits of Symbolic Reform: The New Deal and Taxation, 1933–1939*. New York: Cambridge University Press, 1994.

Leighton, Richard M., and Robert W. Coakey. *Global Logistics and Strategy, 1940–1943*. 1955. Reprint, Washington, D.C.: Government Printing Office, 1995.

Lekachman, Robert. *The Age of Keynes*. New York: Random House, 1966.

Leotta, Louis. "Abraham Epstein and the Movement for Old Age Security." *Labor History* 16 (Summer 1975): 359–77.

Lepawsky, Albert. "The Planning Apparatus: A Vignette of the New Deal." *American Institute of Planners Journal* 42 (January 1976): 25.

Lerner, Barron H. "Crafting Medical History: Revisiting the 'Definitive' Account of Franklin D. Roosevelt's Terminal Illness." *Bulletin of the History of Medicine* 81, no. 2 (2007): 386–406.

Leuchtenburg, William E. "Charles Evans Hughes: The Center Holds." *North Carolina Law Review* 83 (June 2005): 1187–1204.

———. *The FDR Years: On Roosevelt and His Legacy*. New York: Columbia University Press, 1995.

———. *Flood Control Politics: The Connecticut River Valley Problem, 1927–1950.* Cambridge, Mass.: Harvard University Press, 1953.

———. *Franklin D. Roosevelt and the New Deal.* New York: Harper, 1963.

———. *In the Shadow of FDR: From Harry Truman to Barack Obama.* Ithaca, N.Y.: Cornell University Press, 2009.

———. "The New Deal and the Analogue of War." In *Change and Continuity in Twentieth Century America,* edited by John Braeman, Robert H. Bremner, and Everett Walters, 81–144. Columbus: Ohio State University Press, 1964.

———. *The Supreme Court Reborn: The Constitutional Revolution in the Age of Roosevelt.* New York: Oxford University Press, 1995.

———. *The White House Looks South: Franklin D. Roosevelt, Harry S. Truman, Lyndon B. Johnson.* Baton Rouge: Louisiana State University Press, 2005.

Levin, Linda Lotridge. *The Making of FDR: The Story of Stephen T. Early, America's First Modern Press Secretary.* Amherst, N.Y.: Prometheus, 2008.

Levine, Lawrence W., and Cornelia R. Levine. *The People and the President: America's Conversation with FDR.* Boston: Beacon Press, 2002.

Lichtenstein, Nelson. *Labor's War at Home.* New York: Cambridge University Press, 1982.

Liebling, A. J. *World War II Writings.* New York: Library of America, 2008.

Lilienthal, David E. *The Journals of David E. Lilienthal: The TVA Years, 1939–1945.* New York: Harper & Row, 1964.

———. *TVA: Democracy on the March.* New York: Harper, 1944.

Lindbergh, Charles A. *The Wartime Journals of Charles A. Lindbergh.* New York: Harcourt, Brace, Jovanovich, 1970.

Lindenmeyer, Kriste. *The Greatest Generation Grows Up: American Childhood in the 1930s.* Chicago: Ivan R. Dee, 2005.

———. *"A Right to Childhood": The U.S. Children's Bureau and Child Welfare, 1912–1946.* Urbana: University of Illinois Press, 1997.

Lindley, Ernest K. *Franklin D. Roosevelt: A Career in Progressive Democracy.* New York: Blue Ribbon Books, 1931.

Link, Arthur S. *Wilson: The Struggle for Neutrality, 1914–1915.* Princeton, N.J.: Princeton University Press, 1960.

Link, Arthur S., et al., eds. *The Papers of Woodrow Wilson.* 69 vols. Princeton, N.J.: Princeton University Press, 1966–94.

Lippman, Thomas W. *Arabian Knight: Colonel Bill Eddy USMC and the Rise of American Power in the Middle East.* Vista, Calif.: Selwa Press, 2008.

Lippmann, Walter. "First Roosevelt Policies." March 11, 1933. Reprinted in *Interpretations, 1933–1935,* edited by Allan Nevins, 27. New York: Macmillan, 1936.

———. "Governor Roosevelt's Candidacy." January 8, 1932. Reprinted in *Interpretations, 1931–1932,* edited by Allan Nevins, 261–62. New York: Macmillan, 1932.

Livermore, Seward W. *Politics Is Adjourned: Woodrow Wilson and the War Congress, 1916–1918.* Middletown, Conn.: Wesleyan University Press, 1966.

Loewenheim, Francis L., Harold D. Langley, and Manfred Jonas. *Roosevelt and Churchill, Their Secret Wartime Correspondence.* New York: Saturday Review Press, 1975.

Looker, Earle. *This Man Roosevelt.* New York: Brewer, Warren & Putnam, 1932.

Lord, Russell. *The Wallaces of Iowa*. Boston: Houghton Mifflin, 1947.

Lorentz, Pare. *FDR's Moviemaker: Memoirs and Scripts*. Reno: University of Nevada Press, 1992.

Lowenstein, Sharon R. *Token Refuge: The Story of the Jewish Refugee Shelter at Oswego, 1944–1946*. Bloomington: Indiana University Press, 1986.

Lowitt, Richard. *George W. Norris: The Persistence of a Progressive, 1913–1933*. Urbana: University of Illinois Press, 1971.

———. *George W. Norris: The Triumph of a Progressive, 1933–1944*. Urbana: University of Illinois Press, 1978.

Lowitt, Richard, and Maurine Beasley, eds. *One Third of a Nation: Lorena Hickok Reports on the Great Depression*. Urbana: University of Illinois Press, 1981.

Lubell, Samuel. *The Future of American Politics*. New York: Harper, 1952.

Madison, James H. *The Indiana Way: A State History*. Bloomington: Indiana University Press, 1986.

Malcolm, James, ed. *The New York Red Book*. Albany: J. B. Lyon, 1930.

Manning, Thomas G. *The Office of Price Administration: A World War II Agency of Control*. New York: Holy, 1960.

Marks, Edward B., Jr. *Token Refuge: The Story of America's War Refugee Shelter*. Washington, D.C.: Government Printing Office, 1946.

Marolda, Edward J., ed. *FDR and the U.S. Navy*. New York: St. Martin's, 1998.

Marquis, Albert N., ed. *Who's Who in America, 1934–35*. Chicago: A. N. Marquis, 1934.

Martin, George. *Madam Secretary: Frances Perkins*. Boston: Houghton Mifflin, 1976.

Masters, Charles J. *Governor Henry Horner, Chicago Politics and the Great Depression*. Carbondale: Southern Illinois University Press, 2007.

Matloff, Maurice. *Strategic Planning for Coalition Warfare, 1943–44*. 1959. Reprint, Washington, D.C.: Government Printing Office, 1990.

Matloff, Maurice, and Edwin M. Snell. *Strategic Planning for Coalition Warfare, 1941–42*. 1953. Reprint, Washington, D.C.: Government Printing Office, 1999.

———. *The War Department . . . 1941–42*. Washington, D.C.: Government Printing Office, 1953.

May, Dean L. *From the New Deal to the New Economics*. New York: Garland, 1981.

May, Irvin M. *Marvin Jones: The Public Life of an Agrarian Advocate*. College Station: Texas A&M University Press, 1980.

McCormick, Anne O'Hare. "Man of the Middle West." *New York Times Magazine*, August 18, 1940, 3–15.

McCoy, Donald R. "The Good Neighbor League and the Presidential Campaign of 1936." *Western Political Quarterly* 13 (1960): 1011–21.

———. *Landon of Kansas*. Lincoln: University of Nebraska Press, 1966.

McElvaine, Robert S., ed. *Encyclopedia of the Great Depression*. New York: Thompson/Gale, 2004.

McFarland, Keith. *Harry H. Woodring: A Political Biography of FDR's Controversial Secretary of War*. Lawrence: University Press of Kansas, 1975.

McGraw, Thomas K. *Morgan vs. Lilienthal: The Feud within the TVA*. Chicago: University of Chicago Press, 1970.

McIntire, Ross T. *White House Physician*. New York: G. P. Putnam, 1946.

McJimsey, George. *Harry Hopkins: Ally of the Poor and Defender of Democracy.* Cambridge, Mass.: Harvard University Press, 1987.

McKenna, Marian. *Borah.* Ann Arbor: University of Michigan Press, 1961.

———. *Franklin Roosevelt and the Great Constitutional War: The Court-Packing Crisis of 1937.* New York: Fordham University Press, 2002.

McNaughton, James C. *Nisei Linguists: Japanese Americans in the Military Intelligence Service in World War II.* Washington, D.C.: Department of the Army, 2007.

Meacham, Jon. *Franklin and Winston.* New York: Random House, 2003.

Medoff, Rafael. *Blowing the Whistle on Genocide: Josiah E. Dubois, Jr. and the Struggle for a U.S. Response to the Holocaust.* West Lafayette, Ind.: Purdue University Press, 2009.

Meriam, Lewis. *Relief and Social Security.* Washington, D.C.: Brookings Institution, 1946.

Meyer, Leisa D. *Creating G.I. Jane: Sexuality and Power in the Women's Army Corps during World War II.* New York: Columbia University Press, 1996.

Meyers, Susan E. *Norman Rockwell's World War II: Impressions from the Homefront.* San Antonio: USAA Foundation, 1991.

Miller, John, Jr. *Guadalcanal: The First Offensive.* Washington, D.C.: Center for Military History, 1949.

Miller, Robert E. "The War That Never Came: Civilian Defense, Mobilization, and Morale during World War II." Ph.D. diss., University of Cincinnati, 1991.

Millis, Walter. *Arms and Men: A Study in Military History.* New York: Putnam, 1956.

———. *The Road to War: America, 1914–1917.* Boston: Houghton Mifflin, 1935.

Mitchell, Broadus. *The Campaign of the Century: Upton Sinclair's Race for Governor of California and the Birth of Media Politics.* New York: Random House, 1992.

———. *Depression Decade: From New Era through New Deal.* New York: Holt, Rinehart, and Winston, 1961.

Mitgang, Herbert. *The Man Who Rode the Tiger: The Life and Times of Judge Samuel Seabury.* Philadelphia: Lippincott, 1963.

Moe, Richard E. *Roosevelt's Second Act: The Election of 1940 and the Politics of War.* New York: Oxford University Press, 2013.

Moeller, Beverley B. *Phil Swing and Boulder Dam.* Berkeley: University of California Press, 1971.

Moley, Raymond. *After Seven Years.* New York: Harper, 1939.

Monnet, Jean. *Memoirs.* New York: Doubleday, 1978.

Moran, Baron. *Churchill, Taken from the Diaries of Lord Moran: The Struggle for Survival, 1940–1965.* Boston: Houghton Mifflin, 1966.

Morgan, Arthur E. *The Making of the TVA.* Buffalo, N.Y.: Prometheus Books, 1974.

Morgan, Chester M. *Redneck Liberal: Theodore Bilbo and the New Deal.* Baton Rouge: Louisiana State University Press, 1985.

Morgan, H. Wayne. *William McKinley and His America.* Syracuse, N.Y.: Syracuse University Press, 1963.

Morison, Elting E., ed. *The Letters of Theodore Roosevelt.* Vols. 2–3, 6. Cambridge, Mass.: Harvard University Press, 1951–52.

Morison, Samuel E. *History of United States Naval Operations in World War II.* 15 vols. Boston: Little, Brown, 1947–62.

———. *The Two-Ocean War: A Short History of the United States Navy in World War Two.* Boston: Little, Brown, 1963.

Morris, Edmund. *The Rise of Theodore Roosevelt.* New York: Coward, McCann, Geoghegan, 1979.

Morrison, Joseph L. *Josephus Daniels: The Small-d Democrat.* Chapel Hill: University of North Carolina Press, 1966.

———. *Josephus Daniels Says . . . : An Editor's Political Odyssey from Bryan to Wilson and F.D.R., 1894–1913.* Chapel Hill: University of North Carolina Press, 1962.

Morton, Louis. *The Fall of the Philippines.* Washington, D.C.: Center for Military History, 1953.

———. "War Plan Orange: Evolution of a Strategy." *World Politics* 11 (1959): 221–50.

Moscow, Warren. *Politics in the Empire State.* New York: Alfred A. Knopf, 1948.

Mowry, George E. *Theodore Roosevelt and the Progressive Movement.* Madison: University of Wisconsin Press, 1946.

Muller, Eric L. *American Inquisition: The Hunt for Japanese American Disloyalty in World War II.* Chapel Hill: University of North Carolina Press, 2007.

Murphy, Lawrence R. *Perverts by Official Order: The Campaign against Homosexuals by the United States Navy.* New York: Haworth Press, 1988.

Murphy, Robert D. *Diplomat among Warriors.* New York: Doubleday, 1964.

Murphy, Thomas D. *Ambassadors in Arms: The Story of Hawaii's 100th Battalion.* Honolulu: University of Hawaii Press, 1946.

Murray, Robert K. *The 103rd Ballot: Democrats and the Disaster in Madison Square Garden.* New York: Harper & Row, 1976.

———. *Red Scare: A Study in National Hysteria, 1919–1920.* Minneapolis: University of Minnesota Press, 1955.

Murray, Stuart, and James McCabe. *Norman Rockwell's Four Freedoms: Images That Inspired a Nation.* Stockbridge, Mass.: Norman Rockwell Museum, 1993.

Myers, Howard B. "Corrington Calhoun Gill, 1898–1945." *Journal of the American Statistical Association* 41 (September 1948).

Myers, William S., and Walter H. Newton. *The Hoover Administration: A Documented Narrative.* New York: Scribner's, 1936.

Myrdal, Gunnar. *An American Dilemma: The Negro Problem and Modern Democracy.* New York: Harper, 1944.

National Emergency Council. *Report on the Economic Conditions of the South.* Washington, D.C.: Government Printing Office, 1938.

Neal, Steve. *Dark Horse: A Biography of Wendell Willkie.* New York: Doubleday, 1984.

Nelson, Donald M. *Arsenal of Democracy: The Story of American War Production.* New York: Harcourt, Brace, 1946.

Nesbitt, Henrietta. *White House Diary.* Garden City, N.Y.: Doubleday, 1948.

Neumann, William L. "Franklin D. Roosevelt and Japan, 1913–1933." *Pacific Historical Review* 22 (1953): 143–53.

Nevins, Allan. *Herbert H. Lehman and His Era.* New York: Scribner's, 1963.

Newman, Roger K. *Hugo Black: A Biography.* New York: Pantheon, 1994.

Newton, Verne, ed. *FDR and the Holocaust.* New York: St. Martin's, 1996.

New York State. *Old Age Security: Report of the New York State Commission.* Albany: J. B. Lyon, 1930.

New York [State] Governor's Commission on Unemployment. *Less Unemployment through Stabilization of Operations.* Albany: J. B. Lyon, 1930.

———. *Problems: Preventing Unemployment; Preliminary Report. . . .* Albany: J. B. Lyon, 1930.

Nixon, Edgar B., ed. *Franklin D. Roosevelt and Conservation, 1911–1945.* 2 vols. Hyde Park, N.Y.: FDR Library, 1957.

———. *Franklin D. Roosevelt and Foreign Affairs.* 17 vols. Cambridge, Mass.: Harvard University Press, 1969–79.

North, Douglas. *Growth and Welfare in the American Past.* Englewood Cliffs, N.J.: Prentice Hall, 1966.

Numbers, Ronald L. *Almost Persuaded: American Physicians and Compulsory Health Insurance, 1912–1920.* Baltimore: Johns Hopkins University Press, 1978.

O'Brien, David M. *Storm Center: The Supreme Court in American Politics.* New York: W. W. Norton, 1986.

Official Report of the Proceedings of the Democratic National Convention . . . 1920. Indianapolis: Bookwalter-Ball, 1920.

Ohl, John Kennedy. *Hugh S. Johnson and the New Deal.* DeKalb: Northern Illinois University Press, 1985.

———. *Supplying the Troops: General Somervell and American Logistics in WWII.* DeKalb: Northern Illinois University Press, 1994.

Okihiro, Gary Y. *Cane Fires: The Anti-Japanese Movement in Hawaii, 1865–1945.* Philadelphia: Temple University Press, 1991.

Olson, James S. *Saving Capitalism: The Reconstruction Finance Corporation and the New Deal, 1933–1940.* Princeton, N.J.: Princeton University Press, 1988.

O'Reilly, Kenneth, ed. *The FBI File on the House Committee on Un-American Activities.* Microfilm. Wilmington, Del.: Scholarly Resources, 1986.

Osborn, Chase S. *The Iron Hunter.* Edited by Robert M. Warner. 1919. Reprint, Detroit: Wayne State University Press, 2002.

Oshinsky, David. *Polio: An American Story.* New York: Oxford University Press, 2005.

Ottanelli, Fraser M. *The Communist Party of the United States.* New Brunswick, N.J.: Rutgers University Press, 1991.

Parrish, Michael E. *Securities Regulation and the New Deal.* New Haven, Conn.: Yale University Press, 1970.

Parrish, Thomas. *Roosevelt and Marshall.* New York: William Morrow, 1989.

Patterson, James T. *Congressional Conservatism and the New Deal: The Growth of the Congressional Coalition in Congress, 1933–1939.* Lexington: University Press of Kentucky, 1967.

———. *Mr. Republican: A Biography of Robert A. Taft.* Boston: Houghton Mifflin, 1972.

Pecora, Ferdinand. *Wall Street under Oath: The Story of Our Modern Money Changers.* New York: Simon and Schuster, 1939.

Peek, George N., with Samuel Crowther. *Why Quit Our Own*. New York: D. Van Nostrand, 1936.

Perkins, Frances. *The Roosevelt I Knew*. New York: Viking, 1946.

Perry, Elisabeth Israels. *Belle Moskowitz: Feminine Politics and the Exercise of Power in the Age of Alfred E. Smith*. New York: Oxford University Press, 1987.

Persico, Joseph E. *Franklin and Lucy*. New York: Random House, 2008.

Pivar, David J. *Purity and Hygiene: Women, Prostitution, and the "American Plan," 1900–1930*. Westport, Conn.: Greenwood Press, 2002.

Piven, Frances Fox, and Richard Cloward. *Regulating the Poor: The Functions of Public Welfare*. New York: Pantheon, 1971.

Plokhy, S. M. *Yalta: The Price of Peace*. Cambridge, Mass.: Harvard University Press, 2010.

Pogue, Forrest C. *George C. Marshall*. 4 vols. New York: Viking, 1963–87.

Polenberg, Richard. "Franklin Roosevelt and the Purge of John O'Connor: The Impact of Urban Change on Political Parties." *New York History* 49 (1968): 306–26.

———. *Reorganizing Roosevelt's Government*. Cambridge, Mass.: Harvard University Press, 1966.

———. *War and Society*. New York: Lippincott, 1973.

Potter, E. B. *Fleet Admiral Chester W. Nimitz*. New York: St. Martin's, 1993.

Potter, E. B., and Chester W. Nimitz. *Triumph in the Pacific: The Navy's Struggle against Japan*. Englewood Cliffs, N.J.: Prentice Hall, 1963.

Prados, John. *The White House Tapes: Eavesdropping on the President*. New York: New Press, 2003.

Pritchett, C. Herman. *The Roosevelt Court: A Study in Judicial Politics and Values, 1937–1947*. New York: Macmillan, 1948.

———. *The Tennessee Valley Authority: A Study in Public Administration*. Chapel Hill: University of North Carolina Press, 1943.

Proskauer, Joseph M. *A Segment of My Times*. New York: Farrar, Straus, 1956.

Quirk, Robert E. *An Affair of Honor: Woodrow Wilson and the Occupation of Vera Cruz*. Lexington: University Press of Kentucky, 1962.

Radford, Gail. *Modern Housing for America: Policy Struggles in the New Deal Era*. Chicago: University of Chicago Press, 1996.

Radomski, Alexander L. *Work Relief in New York State, 1931–1935*. New York: Kings Crown, 1947.

Randolph, A. Philip. "Why and How the March Was Postponed." *Black Worker* 7, no. 8 (1941): 1–2.

Rauchway, Eric. *Murdering McKinley: The Making of Theodore Roosevelt's America*. New York: Hill and Wang, 2003.

Rawick, George P. "The New Deal and Youth: The Civilian Conservation Corps, the National Youth Administration, and the American Youth Congress." Ph.D. diss., University of Wisconsin, 1957.

Reilly, Michael F. *Reilly of the White House*. New York: Simon and Schuster, 1947.

Reiman, Richard A. *The New Deal and American Youth: Ideas and Ideals in a Depression Decade*. Athens: University of Georgia Press, 1992.

———. "The New Deal for Youth: A Cincinnati Connection." *Queen City Heritage* 44 (1986): 36–48.

Reingold, Nathan. "Vannevar Bush's New Deal for Research." *Historical Studies in the Physical and Biological Sciences* 17, no. 2 (1987).

Reynolds, David. *From Munich to Pearl Harbor: Roosevelt's America and the Origins of the Second World War.* Chicago: Ivan R. Dee, 2001.

Rice, Diana. "Mrs. Roosevelt Takes on Another Task." *New York Times Magazine,* December 2, 1928.

Rigdon, William M. *White House Sailor.* New York: Doubleday, 1974.

Riggs, Fred W. *Pressures on Congress: A Study of the Repeal of Chinese Exclusion.* New York: King's Crown, 1950.

Riis, Jacob A. *Theodore Roosevelt: The Citizen.* Washington, D.C.: Johnson, Wynne, 1904.

Ritchie, Donald. *James M. Landis, Dean of the Regulators.* Cambridge, Mass.: Harvard University Press, 1980.

Robertson, David. *Sly and Able: A Political Biography of James F. Byrnes.* New York: W. W. Norton, 1994.

Robinson, Edgar E. *The Presidential Vote, 1896–1932.* Stanford, Calif.: Stanford University Press, 1934.

———. *They Voted for Roosevelt.* Stanford, Calif.: Stanford University Press, 1947.

Robinson, Greg. *By Order of the President: FDR and the Internment of Japanese Americans.* Cambridge, Mass.: Harvard University Press, 2001.

Rogers, Naomi. *Dirt and Disease: Polio before FDR.* New Brunswick, N.J.: Rutgers University Press, 1992.

———. "Race and the Politics of Polio: Warm Springs, Tuskegee, and the March of Dimes." *American Journal of Public Health* 97 (2007): 784–95.

Roll, David L. *The Hopkins Touch: Harry Hopkins and the Forging of the Alliance to Defeat Hitler.* New York: Oxford University Press, 2013.

Rollins, Alfred B., Jr. *Roosevelt and Howe.* New York: Alfred A. Knopf, 1962.

Romasco, Albert U. *The Poverty of Abundance: Hoover, the Nation, the Depression.* New York: Oxford University Press, 1965.

Roose, Kenneth D. "The Depression of 1937–38." *Journal of Political Economy* 56 (1948): 239–48.

Roosevelt, Eleanor. *On My Own.* New York: Harper, 1958.

———. *This I Remember.* New York: Harper, 1949.

———. *This Is My Story.* New York: Harper, 1937.

———. "Why I Still Believe in the Youth Conference." *Liberty* 17 (April 1940): 30–32.

———. "Women Must Learn to Play the Game as Men Do." *Red Book,* April 1928, 78–79, 141–42.

Roosevelt, Elliott, ed. *F.D.R.: His Personal Letters.* 3 vols. New York: Duell, Sloan, and Pearce, 1950.

———. "The Most Unforgettable Character I've Met." *Reader's Digest,* February 1953, 26–30.

Roosevelt, Franklin D. *The Complete Presidential Press Conferences of Franklin D. Roosevelt.* 25 vols. New York: Da Capo Press, 1972.

———. "Must We Fight Japan?" *Asia* 23 (1923): 475–78, 526, 528.

———. "The New Deal: An Interpretation." *Liberty,* December 10, 1932, 7–8.

———. "Our Foreign Policy: A Democratic View." *Foreign Affairs* 6 (1928): 573–86.

———. *Public Papers of Franklin D. Roosevelt, Forty-Eighth Governor of New York.* 4 vols. Albany: J. B. Lyon, 1929–33.

———. "The Real Meaning of the Power Problem." *Forum* 82 (1929): 327–32.

———. *Whither Bound?* Boston: Houghton Mifflin, 1926.

Roosevelt, James, with Bill Libby. *My Parents: A Differing View.* Chicago: Playboy Press, 1976.

Roosevelt, James, and Sidney Shalett. *Affectionately, F.D.R.: A Son's Story of a Lonely Man.* New York: Harcourt, Brace, 1959.

Roosevelt, Sara Delano. *My Boy Franklin, as Told by Mrs. James Roosevelt to Isabel Leighton and Gabrielle Forbush.* New York: R. Long & R. R. Smith, 1933.

Roosevelt, Theodore. *An Autobiography.* 1913. Reprint, New York: Scribner's, 1923.

———. *Letters from Theodore Roosevelt to Anna Roosevelt Cowles, 1870–1918.* New York: Scribner's, 1924.

Roper, Daniel C., with the collaboration of Frank H. Lovette. *Fifty Years of Public Life.* Durham, N.C.: Duke University Press, 1941.

Rose, Mark H. *Interstate: Express Highway Politics, 1941–1956.* Lawrence: University Press of Kansas, 1969.

Rosenbaum, Herbert D., and Elizabeth Bartelme, eds. *Franklin D. Roosevelt: The Man, the Myth, the Era, 1882–1945.* Westport, Conn.: Greenwood Press, 1987.

Rosenberg, Charles. "Martin Arrowsmith: The Scientist as Hero." *American Quarterly* 15 (1963): 447–58.

Rosenman, Samuel I., ed. *Public Papers and Addresses of Franklin D. Roosevelt.* 13 vols. New York: Random House, 1938–50.

———. *Working with Roosevelt.* New York: Harper, 1952.

Ross, Davis R. B. *Preparing for Ulysses: Politics and Veterans during WW II.* New York: Columbia University Press, 1969.

Rossiter, Clinton. *The American Presidency.* New York: Harcourt, Brace, 1960.

Rostow, Eugene V. "The Japanese American Cases: A Disaster." *Yale Law Journal* 54 (July 1945): 498–533.

———. "Our Worst Wartime Mistake." *Harper's Magazine,* September 1945, 193–201.

Rovere, Richard H. *The Goldwater Caper.* New York: Harcourt, Brace & World, 1965.

Salmond, John A. *The Civilian Conservation Corps, 1933–1942: A New Deal Case Study.* Durham, N.C.: Duke University Press, 1967.

———. *A Southern Rebel: The Life and Times of Aubrey Willis Williams, 1890–1965.* Chapel Hill: University of North Carolina Press, 1985.

Saloutos, Theodore. *The American Farmer and the New Deal.* Ames: Iowa State University Press, 1982.

Sandage, Scott A. "A Marble House Divided: The Lincoln Memorial, the Civil Rights Movement, and the Politics of Memory, 1939–1963." *Journal of American History* 80 (1993): 135–67.

Sandilands, Roger J. *The Life and Political Economy of Lauchlin Currie.* Durham, N.C.: Duke University Press, 1990.

Saunders, Kay, and Roger Daniels, eds. *Alien Justice: Wartime Internment in Australia and North America*. St. Lucia: University of Queensland, 2000.

Sautter, Udo. *Three Cheers for the Unemployed: Government and Unemployment before the New Deal*. New York: Cambridge University Press, 1991.

Scheiber, Harry N., and Jane L. Scheiber. *Bayonets in Paradise: Martial Law in Hawaii, 1941–1946*. Honolulu: University of Hawai'i Press, 2016.

Schlabach, Theron F. *Edwin E. Witte: Cautious Reformer*. Madison: State Historical Society of Wisconsin, 1969.

Schlesinger, Arthur M., Jr. *The Coming of the New Deal*. Boston: Houghton Mifflin, 1958.

———. *The Crisis of the Old Order, 1919–1933*. Boston: Houghton Mifflin, 1957.

———, ed. *History of American Presidential Elections*. New York: Chelsea House, 1985.

———. *The Politics of Upheaval*. Boston: Houghton Mifflin, 1960.

Schlesinger, Robert. *White House Ghosts: Presidents and Their Speechwriters*. New York: Simon and Schuster, 2008.

Schmidt, Hans. *The United States Occupation of Haiti, 1915–1934*. New Brunswick, N.J.: Rutgers University Press, 1971.

Schroeder, Paul W. *The Axis Alliance and Japanese-American Relations, 1941*. Ithaca, N.Y.: Cornell University Press, 1958.

Schwartz, Bonnie Fox. *The Civil Works Administration, 1933–1934: The Business of Emergency Employment in the New Deal*. Princeton, N.J.: Princeton University Press, 1984.

Schwarz, Jordan A. "Al Smith in the 1930s." *New York History* 45 (1964): 316–30.

———. "John Nance Garner and the Sales Tax Rebellion of 1932." *Journal of Southern History* 30 (1964): 162–80.

Scobie, Ingrid Winther. *Center Stage: Helen Gahagan Douglas, a Life*. New York: Oxford University Press, 1992.

Scott, William R. *The Sons of Sheba's Race: African-Americans and the Italo-Ethiopian War, 1935–1941*. Bloomington: Indiana University Press, 1993.

Seeber, Frances M. "I Want You to Write to Me: The Papers of Anna Eleanor Roosevelt." *Prologue* 19 (1987): 95–105.

Seidman, Joel. *American Labor from Defense to Reconversion*. Chicago: University of Chicago Press, 1953.

Seligman, Lester G., and Elmer G. Cornwell, eds. *New Deal Mosaic: Roosevelt Confers with His National Emergency Council*. Eugene: University of Oregon Books, 1965.

Sherwin, Martin J. *A World Destroyed: The Atomic Bomb and the Grand Alliance*. New York: Alfred A. Knopf, 1975.

Sherwood, Robert E. *Roosevelt and Hopkins: An Intimate History*. New York: Harper, 1948.

Shlaes, Amity. *The Forgotten Man: A New History of the Great Depression*. New York: Harper, 2007.

Shoumatoff, Elizabeth. *FDR's Unfinished Portrait*. Pittsburgh: University of Pittsburgh Press, 1990.

Shover, John L. *Cornbelt Rebellion: The Farmer's Holiday Association*. Urbana: University of Illinois Press, 1965.

Sills, David L. *The Volunteers, Means and Ends in a National Organization: A Report.* Glencoe, Ill.: Free Press, 1957.

Silva, Ruth C. *Rum, Religion, and Votes: 1928 Reconsidered.* University Park: Pennsylvania State University Press, 1962.

Sims, William S. *The Victory at Sea.* Garden City, N.Y.: Doubleday, 1920.

Sitkoff, Harvard. *A New Deal for Blacks.* New York: Oxford University Press, 1978.

Skidelsky, Robert. *John Maynard Keynes.* Vol. 1, *Hopes Betrayed, 1883–1920.* Vol. 2, *The Economist as Saviour, 1920–1937.* Vol. 3, *Fighting for Britain, 1937–1946.* London: Macmillan, 1983–2001.

Smiley, Gene. *Rethinking the Great Depression.* Chicago: Ivan R. Dee, 2002.

Smith, A. Merriman. *Thank You, Mr. President.* New York: Harper, 1946.

Smith, Elaine M. "Mary McLeod Bethune and the National Youth Administration." In *Clio Was a Woman: Studies in the History of American Women,* edited by Mabel E. Deutrich and Virginia C. Purdy, 149–77. Washington, D.C.: Howard University Press, 1980.

Smith, Ira Robert Taylor. *"Dear Mr. President . . .": Fifty Years in the White House Mail Room.* New York: J. Messner, 1949.

Smith, Neil. *American Empire: Roosevelt's Geographer and the Prelude to Globalization.* Berkeley: University of California Press, 2003.

Smith, Richard Norton. *Thomas E. Dewey and His Times.* New York: Simon and Schuster, 1982.

Snyder, Robert L. *Pare Lorentz and the Documentary Film.* Norman: University of Oklahoma Press, 1968.

Sosna, Morton. *In Search of the Silent South: Southern Liberals and the Race Issue.* New York: Columbia University Press, 1977.

Speakman, Joseph R. *At Work in Penn's Woods: The Civilian Conservation Corps in Pennsylvania.* University Park: Pennsylvania State University Press, 2006.

Spector, Ronald H. *Eagle against the Sun: The American War against Japan.* New York: Free Press, 1954.

———. "Josephus Daniels, Franklin Roosevelt, and the Reinvention of the Naval Enlisted Man." In *FDR and the U.S. Navy,* edited by Edward J. Marolda, 19–33. New York: St. Martin's, 1998.

Spencer, Thomas T. "Democratic Auxiliary and Non-party Groups in the Election of 1936." Ph.D. diss., University of Notre Dame, 1976.

———. "The Good Neighbor League Colored Committee and the 1936 Democratic Presidential Campaign." *Journal of Negro History* 63 (1978): 307–16.

Starling, Edmund W. *Starling of the White House.* New York: Simon and Schuster, 1946.

Steele, Richard W. *Propaganda in an Open Society: The Roosevelt Administration and the Media, 1933–1941.* Westport, Conn.: Greenwood Press, 1985.

Stein, Herbert. *Presidential Economics: The Making of Economic Policy from Roosevelt to Clinton.* Washington, D.C.: American Enterprise Institute for Public Policy Research, 1994.

Sterner, Richard. *The Negro's Share: A Study of Income, Consumption, Housing, and Public Assistance.* New York: Harper, 1943.

Sternsher, Bernard. *Rexford Tugwell and the New Deal.* New Brunswick, N.J.: Rutgers University Press, 1964.

Stettinius, Edward R. *Lend-Lease, Weapon for Victory*. New York: Macmillan, 1944.

———. *Roosevelt and the Russians*. New York: Doubleday, 1949.

Stewart, Barbara McDonald. *United States Government Policy on Refugees from Nazism, 1933–1940*. New York: Garland, 1982.

Stiles, Lela. *The Man behind Roosevelt: The Story of Louis McHenry Howe*. Cleveland, Ohio: World, 1954.

Stimson, Henry L., and McGeorge Bundy. *On Active Service in Peace and War*. New York: Harper, 1948.

Straus, Nathan. *Two-Thirds of a Nation: A Housing Program*. New York: Alfred A. Knopf, 1952.

Swain, Martha H. *Ellen S. Woodward: New Deal Advocate for Women*. Jackson: University Press of Mississippi, 1995.

———. *Pat Harrison: The New Deal Years*. Jackson: University Press of Mississippi, 1978.

Takei, Barbara. "Legalizing Detention: Segregated Japanese Americans and the Justice Department's Renunciation Program." *Journal of the Shaw Historical Library* 19 (2005): 75–105.

Talbert, Roy. *FDR's Utopian: Arthur Morgan of the TVA*. Jackson: University Press of Mississippi, 1987.

Taylor, A. J. P. *English History, 1914–1945*. Oxford: Oxford University Press, 1965.

Taylor, Graham D. *The New Deal and American Indian Tribalism: The Administration of the Indian Reorganization Act*. Baltimore: Johns Hopkins University Press, 1978.

Taylor, Paul S., and Norman Leon Gold. "San Francisco and the General Strike." *Survey Graphic* 23 (September 1934): 405–11.

Taylor, Quintard. *The Forging of a Black Community: Seattle's Central District, from 1870 through the Civil Rights Era*. Seattle: University of Washington Press, 1994.

Terkel, Studs. *"The Good War."* New York: Pantheon, 1984.

Theoharis, Athan G. *J. Edgar Hoover, Sex, and Crime: An Historical Antidote*. Chicago: Ivan R. Dee, 1995.

Tillett, Paul. *The Army Flies the Mails*. Tuscaloosa: University of Alabama Press, 1955.

Tobin, James. *The Man He Became: How FDR Defied Polio to Win the Presidency*. New York: Simon and Schuster, 2013.

Treadwell, Mattie E. *The Women's Army Corps*. Washington, D.C.: Government Printing Office, 1954.

Tregaskis, Richard. *Guadalcanal Diary*. New York: Random House, 1943.

Troy, Thomas F. *Donovan and the CIA: A History of the Establishment of the Central Intelligence Agency*. Langley, Va.: Central Intelligence Agency, 1981.

Truman, Harry S. *Memoirs*. 2 vols. New York: Doubleday, 1955–56.

Tugwell, Rexford G. *The Brains Trust*. New York: Viking, 1968.

———. *The Democratic Roosevelt*. New York: Doubleday, 1957.

———. *In Search of Roosevelt*. Cambridge, Mass.: Harvard University Press, 1972.

———. "The Two Great Roosevelts." *Western Political Quarterly* 5 (March 1952): 84–93.

Tully, Grace G. *FDR, My Boss*. New York: Scribner's, 1949.

Twomey, Jane L. "May Craig: Journalist and Liberal Feminist." *Journalism History* 27, no. 3 (2001): 129–38.

U.S. Army. *Submarine Operations, December 1941–April 1942*. Japanese Monograph no. 102. Washington, D.C.: Government Printing Office, n.d.

"U.S. at War: Death of a Cause." *Time*, January 3, 1944.

U.S. Congress. Joint Committee on the Investigation of the Pearl Harbor Attack. *Pearl Harbor Attack*. Washington, D.C.: Government Printing Office, 1946.

U.S. Department of Commerce. *Historical Statistics of the United States: Colonial Times to 1957*. Washington, D.C.: Government Printing Office, 1960.

U.S. Department of State. *Foreign Relations of the United States, 1933–1945*. Washington, D.C.: Government Printing Office, 1933–45.

———. *Peace and War: United States Foreign Policy, 1931–1941*. Washington, D.C.: Government Printing Office, 1943.

U.S. House of Representatives. *A Message from the President of the United States Transmitting a Report of the National Interregional Highway Committee*. House Document no. 379. Washington, D.C.: Government Printing Office, 1944.

———. Tolan Committee. 77th Cong. *House Report 2124*. Washington, D.C.: Government Printing Office, 1942.

U.S. Selective Service System. *Special Groups*. Special Monograph 10. Washington, D.C.: Government Printing Office, 1955.

U.S. Senate. *Presidential Vetoes, 1789–1988*. S. Pub. 102-12. Washington, D.C.: Government Printing Office, 1992.

Vadney, Thomas E. *The Wayward Liberal: A Political Biography of Donald Richberg*. Lexington: University Press of Kentucky, 1970.

Vatter, Harold G. *The U.S. Economy in World War II*. New York: Columbia University Press, 1985.

Veritas Foundation. *Keynes at Harvard: Economic Deception as a Political Credo*. New York: Veritas Foundation, 1962.

Villard, Oswald Garrison. "The Plight of the Negro Voter." *Crisis* (November 1934).

Vogel, Steve. *The Pentagon*. New York: Random House, 2007.

Voorhis, Jerry. *Confessions of a Congressman*. New York: Doubleday, 1947.

Wainwright, Jonathan M. *General Wainwright's Story*. New York: Doubleday, 1946.

Walker, Frank C. *FDR's Quiet Confidant: The Autobiography of Frank C. Walker*. Edited by Robert H. Ferrell. Niwot: University Press of Colorado, 1997.

Walker, Turnley. *Roosevelt and the Fight against Polio*. London: Rider, 1954.

———. *Roosevelt and the Warm Springs Story*. London: A. A. Wyn, 1954.

Wann, A. J. "Franklin D. Roosevelt's Administrative Contributions to the Presidency." In *Franklin D. Roosevelt: The Man, the Myth, the Era, 1882–1945*, edited by Herbert D. Rosenbaum and Elizabeth Bartelme, 239–53. Westport, Conn.: Greenwood Press, 1987.

———. *The President as Chief Administrator: A Study of Franklin D. Roosevelt*. Washington, D.C.: Public Affairs Press, 1968.

Ward, Geoffrey C. *Before the Trumpet: Young Franklin Roosevelt, 1882–1905*. New York: Harper & Row, 1985.

———. *A First Class Temperament: The Emergence of Franklin Roosevelt*. New York: Harper & Row, 1989.

Ware, Gilbert. *William Hastie: Grace under Pressure*. New York: Oxford University Press, 1984.

Ware, Susan. *Beyond Suffrage: Women in the New Deal.* Cambridge, Mass.: Harvard University Press, 1981.

———. *Partner and I: Molly Dewson, Feminism, and New Deal Politics.* New Haven, Conn.: Yale University Press, 1987.

Warn, A. W. "Senator F. D. Roosevelt, Chief Insurgent at Albany." *New York Times Sunday Magazine,* January 22, 1911, 11; January 31, 1911, 3.

Warner, Hoyt Landon. *The Life of Mr. Justice Clarke: A Testament to the Power of Liberal Dissent in America.* Cleveland, Ohio: Western Reserve University Press, 1959.

Watson, Mark S. *Chief of Staff: Prewar Plans and Preparations.* 1950. Reprint, Washington, D.C.: Center of Military History, 1991.

Wehrle, Edmund F. *Catoctin Mountain Park.* Washington, D.C.: Government Printing Office, 2000.

Weil, Arthur T. "Exploding the Myth of a 'Jewish Hierarchy.'" *American Hebrew* (1934).

Weinberg, Gerhard L. *A World at Arms: A Global History of World War II.* 2nd ed. New York: Cambridge University Press, 2005.

Weingroff, Richard. "President Roosevelt and Excess Condemnation." http://www.fhwa.dot.gov/infrastructure/excess.cfm.

Weiss, Nancy J. *Charles Francis Murphy, 1858–1924: Respectability and Responsibility in Tammany Politics.* Northampton, Mass.: Smith College, 1968.

———. *Farewell to the Party of Lincoln.* Princeton, N.J.: Princeton University Press, 1983.

Weiss, Stuart L. *The President's Man: Leo T. Crowley and Franklin D. Roosevelt in Peace and War.* Carbondale: Southern Illinois University Press, 1996.

Welles, Benjamin. *Sumner Welles: FDR's Global Strategist.* New York: St. Martin's, 1997.

Welles, Sumner. *The Time for Decision.* New York: Harper, 1944.

———. *Where Are We Heading?* New York: Harper, 1946.

Westbrook, Lawrence. "The Program of Rural Rehabilitation of the FERA." *Journal of Farm Economics* 17 (1935): 89–100.

———. "Rehabilitation of Stranded Families." *Annals* 176 (1934): 74–79.

Whalen, Richard J. *The Founding Father: The Story of Joseph P. Kennedy.* New York: New American Library, 1964.

Wheeler, Burton K., with Paul F. Healy. *Yankee from the West.* New York: Doubleday, 1962.

Wheeler-Bennett, John W. *King George VI: His Life and Reign.* New York: St. Martin's Press, 1958.

White, W. L. *They Were Expendable.* New York: Harcourt, Brace, 1942.

White, Walter. *A Man Called White: The Autobiography of Walter White.* New York: Viking, 1948.

White, William Smith. *Majesty & Mischief: A Mixed Tribute to F.D.R.* New York: McGraw-Hill, 1961.

Whitnah, Donald R., ed. *Government Agencies.* Westport, Conn.: Greenwood Press, 1983.

Williams, T. Harry. *Huey Long.* New York: Alfred A. Knopf, 1969.

Wilmot, Chester. *The Struggle for Europe.* New York: Harper, 1952.

Wilson, Theodore. *The First Summit: Roosevelt and Churchill at Placentia Bay, 1941.* 1969. Reprint, Lawrence: University Press of Kansas, 1991.

Wilson, William H. "The Two New Deals: A Valid Concept?" *Historian* 28 (1966).

Wiltz, John E. *In Search of Peace: The Senate Munitions Inquiry, 1934–1936.* Baton Rouge: Louisiana State University Press, 1963.

Winant, John G. *A Letter from Grosvenor Square.* Boston: Houghton Mifflin, 1947.

Winfield, Betty H. *FDR and the News Media.* New York: Columbia University Press, 1990.

Winkler, Allan M. "A Forty-Year History of Civil Defense." *Bulletin of the Atomic Scientists* 40, no. 6 (1984).

———. *Franklin D. Roosevelt and the Making of Modern America.* New York: Longman, 2005.

———. *The Politics of Propaganda: The Office of War Information, 1842–1945.* New Haven, Conn.: Yale University Press, 1978.

———. *"To Everything There Is a Season": Pete Seeger and the Power of Song.* New York: Oxford University Press, 2009.

Wirth, Conrad L. *Parks, Politics, and the People.* Norman: University of Oklahoma Press, 1940.

Wladaver-Morgan, Susan. "Young Women and the New Deal: Camps and Resident Centers, 1933–1943." Ph.D. diss., Indiana University, 1982.

Wolfskill, George. *The Revolt of the Conservatives.* Boston: Houghton Mifflin, 1962.

Woodward, C. Vann. *The Battle for Leyte Gulf.* New York: Macmillan, 1947.

———. *Origins of the New South, 1877–1913.* Baton Rouge: Louisiana State University Press, 1951.

Woolf, S. J. "The Roosevelt Who Is a Firm Democrat: Governor Smith's Nominator Explains Why He Is Not of the Republican Faith—a Long Fight Won with Honor." *New York Times Sunday Magazine,* August 5, 1928, 66.

———. "A Woman Speaks Her Mind: Mrs. Franklin D. Roosevelt Points Out That in Spite of Equal Suffrage the Men Still Run the Parties." *New York Times Sunday Magazine,* April 10, 1928, 2.

Zangrando, Robert L. *The NAACP Crusade against Lynching, 1909–1950.* Philadelphia: Temple University Press, 1980.

Zawodny, Janusz K. *Death in the Forest: The Story of the Katyn Forest Massacre.* South Bend, Ind.: University of Notre Dame Press, 1962.

Ziegler, Robert H. *John L. Lewis: Labor Leader.* Boston: Twayne, 1988.

Zimand, Gertrude F. "Will the Codes Abolish Child Labor?" *Survey* 69 (August 1933).

Zinn, Howard, ed. *New Deal Thought.* Indianapolis: Bobbs-Merrill, 1966.

Zucker, Bat-Ami. "Frances Perkins and the German-Jewish Refugees." *American Jewish History* (2001): 35–59.

Index

Argentina, 426, 430

Arizona, 86

Arkansas, 87, 254

Arlington Cemetery, 191

Armed Forces Committee on Post-War Educational Opportunities for Service Personnel, 295, 407

Army Corps of Engineers, 27

Army and Navy Journal (journal), 456

Army and Navy Munitions Board, 71

Arnold, Henry Harley "Hap," 6–7, 179, 236, 266, 268, 296, 425, 438

Asia, 24, 58, 73, 147, 215–16, 218, 224, 232, 258, 275, 367, 375, 444, 500

Asia Minor, 273

Athenia (passenger liner), 36, 45

Athlone, Earl of, 126, 489

Atlantic Charter, 181, 241, 256, 339, 346, 353, 475, 483, 502

atomic bomb, 44; Tube Alloys, code name of, 272

Attlee, Clement, 75, 163

Austin, Alan W., 255

Austin, Warren, 38–39, 55

Austin, William R., 25

Australasia, 147

Australia, 217, 220, 234, 239–40, 250, 256, 258–60, 285, 368, 405

Austria, 147, 364

Avery, Sewell L., 261, 395, 458, 565–66n50

Ávila Camacho, Manuel, 324, 556n25

Axis powers, 147–48, 220, 232, 256, 274, 294, 296, 305, 309, 320, 328, 344–45

Azores, 168–69, 173

Bachelder, Toi, 491

Badoglio, Pietro, 343, 346

Bahamas, 104

Bainbridge Island (Washington), 254

Baldwin, Roger, 362

Ball, Joseph H., 434, 435

"Ballad of September 16" (Seeger), 116

Bankhead, William, 81–83, 85–86, 116, 354

Barbour, William, 110

Barkley, Alben, 24–25, 55, 72–73, 82–84, 155, 276, 323, 340, 386, 450, 461

Barton, Bruce Fairchild, 131

Baruch, Bernard M., 71, 102, 277, 331, 381, 392–93, 454, 488–89

Baruch Committee, 277–78

Batt, William H., 186

Battle of Bataan, 250

Battle of Britain, 95

Battle of Kasserine Pass, 320

Battle of Leyte Gulf, 437

Battle of Midway, 268–69, 285

Battle of Stalingrad, 301

Battle of the Atlantic, 110, 165

Battle of the Bulge, 120, 426, 458

Battle of the Coral Sea, 268

Battle of the Java Sea, 258

Battle of the Philippine Sea, 408

Battle of the River Plate, 45

Baylor University Hospital, 9

Beardall, John, 179, 246

Beard, Charles A., 158, 225

Beaverbrook, First Baron (William Maxwell Aitken), 187, 237–38

Belair, Felix, 79

Belgian Congo, 44

Belgium, 59, 66, 125, 147, 240, 421

Bell, Daniel, 14, 36, 46

Benny, Jack, 464

Berlin (Germany), 39, 485

Berlin, Irving, 444, 572n43

Berlin-Rome-Tokyo Axis, 34, 120, 215, 242

Bermuda, 29, 35, 104, 106–7, 109, 420

Bethlehem Steel, 209

Bethune, Mary McLeod, 126

Beveridge Report, 307

Bevin, Ernest, 75, 161, 188

Biddle, Francis, 251, 281–84, 315–16, 365, 375, 455–56, 461, 565–66n50

Biggers, John D., 187

Bismarck (battleship), 170–71

Black, Hugo, 283

Bloom, Sol, 24, 271, 510n49, 576n14

Casablanca Conference, 308–13, 320, 353, 359, 370, 396

Catledge, Turner, 414

Catoctin Mountain Park (Shangri-La), 281, 343, 370

Catton, Bruce, 518n30

Central America, 241

Central Statistical Bureau, 15

Century Group, 106, 523n27, 523–24n28

Chagall, Marc, 521n4

Chamberlain, Neville, 21, 44–45, 59, 562n26

Chemidlin, Paul, 7

Cheney, Mayris, 262–63

Chennault, Claire L., 164, 186, 427

Chiang Kai-shek, 19, 34, 163–64, 215, 247, 299, 365, 367, 373, 375, 441, 472, 482–83

Chiang Kai-shek, Madame, 317–19, 363, 367; China Lobby, cementing of, 316

Chicago (Illinois), 439, 452

Chicago Tribune (newspaper), 110, 181

Chicago World's Fair. *See* World's Columbian Exposition

Children's Bureau, 92

China, 19, 24, 34, 93, 142, 163, 176, 181, 203, 214–15, 222, 239, 241, 256, 310, 316, 318–19, 352, 362–63, 375, 407, 412–13, 417, 419, 430, 441, 472, 474–75, 541n44, 569n24; aid to, 164, 186, 216, 427, 543–44n27; and Burma Road, 164, 186, 220, 427; "four policemen," as one of, 364, 367–69, 442

Chou En-lai, 19

A Christmas Carol (Dickens), 47

Churchill, Clementine, 360, 374, 420

Churchill, Sarah, 470

Churchill, Winston, 59, 66, 68–69, 75, 93, 97–98, 100, 105, 107–9, 133, 141, 149, 150, 156–57, 161–62, 184–85, 187, 218–19, 228, 232, 242, 244, 246–47, 250, 263, 271, 274, 281, 293–94, 296–97, 299–301, 305, 309–12, 328–30, 341, 347, 351–54, 359, 362, 364, 367, 369–74, 393, 395–96, 420, 422, 427,

429–31, 453, 465, 468, 480–81, 483, 488, 501, 530n9, 543n24; America radio network, live coverage of on, 175; Anglo-American alliance, call for, 238, 349–50; Congress, address to, 238, 330; Germany-first doctrine, favoring of, 215; Hopkins, meeting with, 177–78; as leader, 179–80; FDR, relationship between, 45, 63–64, 239, 423, 559n1; FDR, meetings with, 179–82, 237–41; and second front, 272–73; secret messages of, 63, 65; sleep habits of, 360, 423; at White House, 360; at Yalta, 461, 469–71, 473

Civil Aviation Board, 58

Congress of Industrial Organizations (CIO), 129, 209, 211, 464

Citizens Committee to Repeal Chinese Exclusion and Place Immigration on a Quota Basis, 362

Civilian Conservation Corps (CCC), 12, 15, 28

Civil Service Commission (CSC), 19, 264, 315

Civil Works Administration (CWA), 502

Clark, Bennett, 39, 175

Clarke, Gilmore D., 191–92

Clark, Mark W., 297–98, 362, 400, 565n49

Clarksburg (West Virginia), 440

Clay, Lucius D., 492

Clemens, Diane Shaver, 472

Cleveland, Grover, 83, 388, 447

"Clinical Notes on the Illness and Death of President Franklin D. Roosevelt" (Bruenn), 389, 565n47

Cockburn, Claude, 510n51

Cohen, Benjamin V., 18, 106–7, 162–63, 252, 434–35, 523n27, 523–24n28

Coit, Margaret, 392

Cold War, 272, 349–50, 503

Cole, Wayne, 43

Collier's (magazine), 78

Fox, George, 454, 491, 497

France, 7, 24, 31, 33, 35, 41, 43, 59, 61, 63–66, 68–69, 73, 92–93, 134, 147, 161, 205, 216–17, 240, 272, 289, 298, 300, 312–13, 350–52, 406, 410, 473, 485; admission to UN, 461; invasion of, 309, 349; loans to, 476; occupation of, 475; Vichy France, 265, 297, 299, 347

Franco, Francisco, 1, 21, 92, 298

Frankfurter, Felix, 4, 18, 149–50, 262, 422

Freedmen's Bureau, 520n54

Freidel, Frank, 9, 84, 560n7

French Committee of National Liberation, 351, 410

French Indochina (Vietnam), 117, 216, 482

French West Indies, 73

From Malta to Yalta (State Department), 472

Fulbright, J. William, 364

Gable, Clark, 146

Galbraith, John Kenneth, 245, 291

Gannett, Frank, 10, 62

Garner, John Nance, 4, 78, 84, 333

Garry, Thomas F., 84

Gellman, Irwin, 354

General Motors (GM), 4

The General Theory of Employment, Interest, and Money (Keynes), 19

Geneva Convention (1926), 259

Gentleman's Agreement (film), 576n10

George II, 28

George III, 28

George VI, 28; "hot dog" picnic of, 29

George, Walter F., 454, 467–68

German saboteurs, 281–83, 285, 461; condemning of, 63; sentences, commuting of, 462; verdict against, 284

Germany, 31, 33, 35, 45, 57, 59, 73, 92, 105, 129, 134, 164, 174–76, 178, 180, 185, 197, 202–3, 215–16, 219, 231, 233, 236, 239, 242, 244, 275, 289, 295, 305–6, 309–11, 341, 344, 352, 368, 372, 374–75, 403,

405–6, 420, 421, 423, 425–26, 444, 450, 462, 469, 471–72, 486–87, 496, 553–54n9; Ardennes, German offensive in, 457–58; Operation Paukenschlag (Drumbeat), 250; occupation of, 473–75, 485, 492–93; second front against, 271

Geyl, Pieter, 134

G.I. Bill, 428

G.I. Bill of Rights, 268, 295, 407; opposition to, 408

Gibraltar, 168

Gilbert Islands, 250

Giraud, Henri, 299, 300, 310–11, 328, 341, 351, 353

Girdler, Tom, 137

Glass, Carter, 5

Good Neighbor policy, 42, 183, 360

Goodwin, Doris Kearns, 334

Grace, Eugene R., 209, 211

Graf Spee (battleship), 45

Grafton, Samuel, 347

Grant, Ulysses S., 310

The Grapes of Wrath (film), 515n41, 576n10

The Grapes of Wrath (Steinbeck), 52, 515n41

Grayson, Cary, 481, 482

Great American Bund, 281

Great Britain, 21, 24, 28–29, 31, 33, 35, 41, 43, 45, 59, 61, 65, 68–69, 95, 99, 100–101, 105, 111, 117, 125, 131, 147, 149–50, 156, 159, 161–64, 171, 177, 181, 211, 216–17, 236–37, 240, 256, 268, 271, 287, 297, 312, 330, 364, 375, 407, 426, 430, 452, 483, 485, 492, 502, 569n24; aid to, 141–45, 148, 158, 165–66; bombing of, 229; destroyers for, 97–98, 106–10, 157; and Japan, 215; mass visa, granting of toward, 92; war materials to, 198, 205; war orders of, 93

Great Depression, 79, 187, 501, 515n41

Great Recession, 503

Great Smoky Mountains National Park, 102

Great War. *See* World War I

Greece, 141, 158, 163, 165, 343, 462; Italian invasion of, 129, 135, 138

Green, Floyd F., 124

Greenland, 57–58, 60, 165–66, 168, 170, 177, 198, 265

Green, William, 129, 380–81, 424

Grew, Joseph, 222

Griffith, Clark, 487

Gromyko, Andrei, 419

Guadalcanal, 285, 287, 301, 319

Guam, 230, 233, 242

Guildersleeve, Virginia, 576n14

Gullion, Allen W., 251

Guthrie, Woody, 203

Haas, Francis J., 337

Hackmeister, Louise, 454, 458, 491

Hagerty, Jim, 140

Hague, Frank, 48

Haiti, 241

Haldeman, H. R., 15

Hale, Nathan, 281

Halifax (Nova Scotia), 98

Halifax, Lady, 162

Halifax, Lord, 150, 162, 178

Halleck, Charlie, 377

Halsey, William Jr., 433, 437–38, 487

Halsted, James A., 564n44, 565n47

Hamburg (Germany), 111

Hamilton, Alexander, 117

Handy, Thomas T., 301

Hanes, John W., 91

Hannegan, Robert E., 394, 411, 413, 419, 442

Harding, Warren G., 363

Harriman, Kathleen, 471

Harriman, W. Averell, 75, 159, 161–62, 179, 186–87, 277, 349–50, 364, 369–70, 383, 436–37, 468–70, 473–74, 476

Harrison, Earl G., 488

Hartford (Connecticut), 442–43

Hassett, William D., 58, 186, 209, 249, 272, 285, 301–2, 316, 323, 342, 388–89,

394, 407–9, 420, 423, 426, 436–37, 440, 447–48, 453–55, 458, 486–87, 489, 491–93, 496–99, 536n68

Hastie, William H., 120

Hatch Act, 26

Hatch, Carl, 26, 110

Hawaii, 64, 214, 227, 229–30, 232–33, 235–36, 245, 254, 257, 269, 303, 358, 417

Henderson, Leon, 72, 166–67, 187, 245, 291, 308

Hershey, Lewis B., 115, 173

Hillman, Sidney, 72, 129, 145, 153, 155, 173, 187, 205, 261, 334

Hill, T. Arnold, 118

Hines, Frank T., 123

Hirohito, Emperor, 222–23

Hiss, Alger, 468

Hitler, Adolf, 7, 18, 21, 23, 31–32, 38, 43–44, 56, 67, 70, 75, 100, 121, 128, 147, 156, 168–72, 175–76, 181, 186, 189, 196, 198–200, 205, 210, 215, 228, 231, 233, 242, 247, 266, 289, 300, 313, 317, 329, 341, 345, 371, 383, 404, 434–44, 480, 532n33, 540n39, 562n26; *Festung Europa* (Fortress Europe), 239; North African invasion, reaction to, 299; Operation Barbarossa, 174; Poland, attack on, 188

HMS *Prince of Wales* (battleship), 170, 234

HMS *Repulse* (warship), 234

HMS *Royal Oak* (battleship), 45

Hobby, Oveta Culp, 267

Holland, 125. *See also* Netherlands

Holmes, Oliver Wendell, 18

Home Owners' Loan Corporation (HOLC), 96

Homestead Act, 56

Hong Kong (China), 230

Hoover, Herbert, 12, 18, 38, 61, 156, 176, 303, 363, 443, 519n39

Hoover, J. Edgar, 36, 252, 285, 354–55, 504

Madison, James, 84

Madrid (Spain), 21

Magna Carta, 353

Magruder, John, 186

Maine, 446, 461

Major League Baseball, 464, 487

Malaya, 217, 222, 224, 244, 250

Malta meetings, 461, 468, 470, 473

Manchuria, 40, 215, 319, 368, 474

Manhattan Project, 44

Manila (Philippines), 257, 472

Mann, Heinrich, 521n4

Manzanar (California), 254

Mapes, Carl E., 38

Marcantonio, Vito, 61

March on Washington Movement
    (MOWM), 333–35

Marianas Turkey Shoot, 408

Maritime Commission, 178

Marseille (France), 92

Marshall, George C., 35–36, 68, 72, 94,
    108, 164, 174, 179, 184, 186, 191, 204,
    224, 227–28, 234–36, 239, 257, 259–61,
    267–68, 271, 273, 275, 295–96, 309,
    320, 329, 350, 356, 367, 369, 373, 419,
    425, 438, 463–64, 468, 470, 484, 499,
    541n2

Marshall Islands, 250

Martha, Princess, 111

Martin, Frederick L., 543n21

Martin, Joe, 38, 61, 121, 131, 134, 197, 434

Martinique, 166, 170

Maryland, 86, 168

Matloff, Maurice, 309

Matthews, H. Freeman, 468

McCarran, Pat, 58, 113, 197

McCarthy, Leighton, 491

McCloy, John J., 251, 545n41, 523–24n28

McCormack, John W., 116, 155, 203–4,
    209, 244

McCormick, Anne O'Hare, 77, 83, 100

McCrea, John L., 308

McIntire, Ross, 31, 55, 97, 123, 143, 179,
    308, 311, 366, 372, 378, 389, 392, 394,
    403, 417, 420, 431, 437, 454, 468, 482,

497–98, 499, 521n60, 553n8; disinfor-
    mation, campaign of, 390–91, 418

McIntyre, Marvin, 18, 58, 282–83, 374,
    388

McNarney, Joseph T., 296

McNary, Charles, 24–25, 38, 50, 77, 131,
    197

McNutt, Paul V., 13, 51, 78, 85, 102, 192,
    264, 315, 335–37

McReynolds, William H., 18–19, 72–73

Meany, George, 30, 315

Mellett, Lowell, 278, 280

Mellon, Andrew, 265

Merriam, Charles, 16

Messersmith, George, 324

Mexico, 324, 411

Micronesia, 220

Michigan, 402

Middle East, 23, 240, 265, 274, 302, 383

Midway Island, 230, 233, 266

Mikolajczyk, Stanislaw, 402–3

Military Affairs Committee, 358

Miller, Earl, 124

Minneapolis (Minnesota), 452

Minton, Sherman, 153

Miquelon, 299

Missouri, 86

Mitchell, Broadus, 362

Molotov, Vyacheslav M., 236–37, 271–72,
    364–65, 370, 472, 475

Monnet, Jean, 7, 29

Monroe Doctrine, 57, 77, 91, 99, 500

Monroe, James, 5

Montana, 254–55

Montgomery (Ala.) *Advertiser* (newspa-
    per), 197

Montgomery Ward, 458

Morgan, J. P., 207

Morgan, Keith, 11

Morgenthau, Elinor, 263, 323, 447, 458

Morgenthau, Henry, 14, 39, 62, 70, 92–93,
    141–42, 144, 155, 157, 159, 169, 249, 292,
    323, 385, 400, 446–47, 452, 458, 467,
    496–97; Jewish people, slaughter of,
    382–83; Morgenthau Plan, 423–24, 426

Morgenthau, Joan, 458
Morison, Samuel Eliot, 236, 258, 285
Morocco, 275, 296–99
Morrill Act, 295
Morris, James W., 283
Morse, Wayne L., 195, 261
Morton, Louis, 258
Moscow (Russia), 174
Moscow declaration, 364–65, 369
Moton, Robert Russa, 20
Mountbatten, Louis, 351, 369, 441
Munich Agreement, 21
Munitions Assignments Board, 331
Murphy, Charles F., 510n49
Murphy, Frank, 4, 14, 283, 400, 510n49
Murphy, Robert D., 297–99, 404
Murray, Philip, 209, 212, 338, 340,
    376–77, 380–81
Murrow, Edward R., 229, 232
Mussolini, Benito, 21, 23, 56, 63–64, 68,
    121, 128, 232–34, 247, 299, 341, 345, 347,
    360, 444, 479; resignation of, 343–44
Myer, Dillon S., 254
Myrdal, Gunnar, 51

Napoleon, 105
Natal (Brazil), 311
National Association for the Advance-
    ment of Colored People (NAACP),
    333, 515n40
National Association of Manufacturers
    (NAM), 380, 464
National Bureau of Standards, 44
National Capitol Park and Planning
    Commission, 191
National Committee against Persecu-
    tion of the Jews, 399–400
National Committee to Uphold Consti-
    tutional Government, 10
National Council of Defense, 245
National Defense Advisory Commit-
    tee (NDAC), 71–72, 75, 80, 130, 145,
    166–67, 519n36
National Defense Mediation Board
    (NDMB), 167, 173, 206–9, 211–12

National Defense Research Committee
    (NDRC), 74
National Education Association, 428
National Emergency Council (NEC),
    12, 18
National Foundation for Infantile
    Paralysis, 469
National Institute of Health, 135
National Maritime Union, 381
National Recovery Act, 67
National Recovery Administration
    (NRA), 43, 162
National Resources Planning Board, 15,
    321, 322, 344, 555n22
National Science Foundation (NSF),
    573n49
National War Labor Board (NWLB),
    260–61, 323, 325, 376–77, 395, 431
National Youth Administration (NYA),
    15, 357
Naval Expansion Act, 105
Nazi Saboteurs on Trial (Fisher), 284
Nazism, 175, 180, 185, 200, 313, 315, 406,
    475, 485, 500
Neal, Steve, 134
Negro Newspaper Publishers Associa-
    tion, 339
Nelson, Donald M., 75, 153, 187, 261,
    276–78, 331–32, 419
Nesbitt, Henrietta, 323, 556n24
Netherlands, 59, 216, 222, 421. See also
    Holland
Neutrality Acts, 36, 39, 43, 51, 129, 142,
    172, 175, 195, 200, 208–9, 218; amend-
    ing of, 42, 198–99, 201, 203–4; and
    American neutrality, 40, 46
New England, 444
Nevada, 5
New Deal, 1, 9, 12, 19, 28, 47–49, 54–55,
    65, 66, 71, 75–76, 79, 83, 88, 100–101,
    121, 123, 140, 150, 157, 162, 181, 205, 215,
    249, 263, 278, 315, 337, 363, 377, 424,
    444, 456; American Left, alienation
    of from, 53; evaluations of, 501–2
New England, 166, 446

Osmeña, Sergio, 433, 472, 493
Outer Mongolia, 474
Owens, Jesse, 262

Pacific fleet, 235
Pacific Northwest, 52
Palau, 220
Palestine, 470, 489
Panama, 42, 55
Panama Canal, 6, 37
Pan American Airways, 60, 107, 183
Pan-American conference (1939), 41–42
Pan American Union, 22, 58
Panay (gunboat), 34, 215
Paris (France): fall of, 70, 411; liberation of, 420
Patterson, Robert P., 118, 121, 334, 519n39
Patton, George S., 373
Paullin, Dr., 498–99
Paul, Randolph E., 564n38
Pavlov, V. N., 370
Peabody, Endicott, 55, 465–66
Pearl Harbor, 134, 164, 205, 214, 216, 222–24, 227–28, 233–35, 244, 256, 265, 275, 285, 301, 303, 342, 358, 407, 416, 439, 500, 522n19, 540n39; Roberts Commission Report on, 245
Pearl Harbor Attack Hearings, 407
Pearson, Drew, 354–56
Pehle, John W., 383, 400
Pennsylvania, 402
Pentagon, 191–92
Pepper, Claude, 322
Percival, Arthur, 250
Perkins, Frances, 167, 213, 260, 465
Permanent Joint Board on Defense with Canada, 169
Pershing, John J., 35, 97
Pescadores, 368
Pétain, Marshal Philippe, 92, 217, 247, 298–99
Petrillo, James C., 431
Philippine Independence Act, 119
Philippine Islands, 94, 101, 214, 217, 222, 224, 230, 232–34, 240, 242, 246, 250,

256, 258–59, 264, 407, 417, 432, 483, 493
Picado, Teodoro, 565n49
Pickett, Clarence E., 521n4
Pink Star (ship), 198
Pittman, Key, 23, 25, 39
Pius XII, 47, 468
Plokhy, S. M., 472
PM (newspaper), 335
Pogue, Forrest, 297
Poland, 18, 21, 31, 33, 51, 92, 147, 266, 369, 371, 403, 427, 430, 462, 472, 475–77, 496; blitzkrieg campaign against, 44; German invasion of, 32, 188; London Poles, 402; Moscow Poles, 402; Polish officers, murders of, 313, 554n13
Polish American Congress, 430
Porter, Paul A., 291
Portugal, 298, 532n33
Potsdam Conference, 420
Powers, John James, 288
President Roosevelt and the Coming of War (Beard), 225
President's Liaison Committee, 159
Prettyman, Arthur, 491, 497
Prettyman, E. Barrett Jr., 108
Price, Byron, 236, 279, 293
Progressive Era, 9
Proposed Direct Route Highways (MacDonald), 381
Public Debt Act, 314
Public Health Service, 51
Public Papers (Roosevelt), 62, 101, 515n40
Public Works Administration (PWA), 18, 215
Puerto Rico, 37, 247
Purcell, Frank, 209
Purvis, Arthur B., 93, 141

Quebec Conference, 349–54, 359, 551n25
Quebec II, 422–25, 430; and Morgenthau Plan, 420–21
Quezon, Manuel, 257–58, 362

Roosevelt, Franklin Delano (FDR) (*continued*): authority, overstepping of, 181; "Big Inch" pipeline, 169; and Birthday Balls, 10–11, 245, 311, 383, 469; black march on Washington, reaction to, 333–35; campaign mode of, 436; Casablanca Conference, dominance of at, 310; China policy of, 316, 319, 362–63, 367, 369, 441; and "China tangle," 436; Churchill, differences between, 330–31; Churchill, meetings with, 179–82, 237–41; Churchill, relationship between, 45, 63–64, 239, 423, 559n1; coal mining disputes, 325–27; on collective bargaining, 210; conflict, avoidance of, 468; cross-Channel invasion (Operation Overlord), support of, 329; death of, 498; Defense Savings Bonds and Stamps, support of, 166; defense spending plan of, 61–62, 66, 111; de Gaulle, anger toward, 480–81; de Gaulle, dislike of, 299–300; and Democratic convention (1940), 81–90; determination of, 504; as dictator, charges of, 110–11, 129; disability of, direct reference to, 485; draft bill, 94, 96–98, 101, 111; draft extension, support of, 184; draftee inductions, 125; dual budget notions of, 46–47; Economic Bill of Rights, 440; education, federal aid to, 428; election strategy of, as flawless, 140; emergency powers of, 37; and farm bloc, 244–45; female members of military, interest in, 409–10; final motor trips of, 494–95; first televised presidential speech, 511n58; flying, attitude toward, 308; foreign policy, defense of, 88–89; fourth term of, 378, 411; funeral of, 499; and George VI, 28–29; and German plot, 369–70; German saboteurs, 281–85; Germany-first doctrine, favoring of, 215, 275, 285; government agencies, reorganizing of, 260–61, 263–64; Great Britain, aid to, 97–98, 106–10, 156–57; health care, federal role of, 135, 192; hundred days of, 501–2; informality of, 518n28; "jawboning," process of, 167; international law, 40–41; interstate highway system, 381–82; and isolationists, 66, 197–98, 294, 364; Japan, concern over, 216–25; Japanese Americans, mass incarceration of, 228, 250–55, 358–59, 452–53, 504, 545n44; and Jewish refugees, 382–83, 399–400; and Keynesianism, 3, 245, 502; labor disputes, and federal troops, 173; leadership of, 114, 179–80; legacy of, 79, 501–4; Lend-Lease, support of, 156, 159–60, 163; mine workers strike, 205–14; Montgomery Ward case, 394–95; mourning of, 501; national service proposal of, 380–81; NDAC, unveiling of, 71–74; NDRC, formation of, 74; natural rubber, supplies of, 275–78; neutrality, proclamations of, 36; Neutrality Act, revision to, call for, 199, 203–4; neutrality zone, call for, 42; Nisei students, university attendance of, 255; officer aides of, 517n5; Operation Torch (North Africa), 296–97; opposition to, 197; Pacific theater, command of, 285, 287, 362, 417; Pearl Harbor attack, reaction to, 227–28; Pentagon, construction of, 191–92; personal income tax, expansion of, 79; and Philippines, 256–59; polio epidemic, comments on, 469; political campaigning, refraining from, 121–22, 124; Polish American voters, 402; and Polish question, 430; political statements, duplicitous nature of, 134–35; postwar world, concern over, 328, 345, 353, 368–69, 375, 381–82, 396, 407, 420, 493; presidential travel, secrecy of, 248; public opinion toward, 197–98, 204–5; race riots, lack of response to, 338–39; railroad strikes, 195, 374–75; reduced schedule of, 394–95; reelection campaign, theme of, 66; reelection of, 447–49 (1944); refugees, issue of, 92, 404–5; renomination of, 91; *Reuben James*, sinking of, reaction to, 201–3; *Robin Moor* sinking, response to, 174; and Roosevelt's Recession, 79, 114; salary cap, 313–14; second Bill of Rights, 379–80; and second front, 272; secret inspection trips of, 292–93; secret retreat of, 281; security, increase in, 246; security concerns over, 417; shoot on sight orders, 201; Sledgehammer, cross-Channel invasion, 273–74; southern revolt against, 415–16; Stalin, meeting with, 368, 371–72; state highways, aid to, 457; steel disputes, 376–77; tax bills, 192–93, 291–92; Thanksgiving holiday, 30–31; third term of, 23, 30, 69, 78–79, 83–84, 92, 137; "three kings," meeting with, 477–80; United Nations, support of, 241–42, 256, 265, 271, 307, 310, 328, 341, 344, 407, 445, 456, 503; unlimited national emergency, declaration of, 171, 173; vision of, 504; wage and price controls, 315; war bonds, support of, 166, 357, 405–6; war crimes, investigating of, 293–94, 551n25; and war criminals, 293–94; war loan drives, 451; wartime agencies, creation of, 278–80; White House Map Room, 35, 246–47, 272; Willkie, challenge to, 100; and women in military, 268; world leadership, bid for, 151–52; and WPA, 304; at Yalta, 461, 468–74, 476–78, 481

Roosevelt, Franklin Delano—AND CONGRESS: annual message to, 1, 462–63; appointments of, 4–5; budget message to, 3–4, 152, 153, 169, 307–8, 382, 463; defeats in, 26; defense budget, 80; differences with, 27; draft bill, passage of, 112–16; draft extension, 183–84; experimental military aircraft, access to, 6–7; farm prices, 383–85; formal messages to, 184; health care proposals of, 8–9; health insurance, failure to recommend to, 9–10; increased military spending, 25; Lend-Lease, 158–59; messages to, 60, 176, 287–89; military nurses, induction of, 462; national defense message, redefining of, 1, 5–7; National Resources Planning Board report to, 321–22; national service bill, 464; neutrality bill, 24–25; New Deal, achievements of, 1–2; New Deal, expansion of, 1; New Deal liberalism, defense of, 1; personal income tax, expansion of, 79; Philippine independence, 362; public works, finance loans for, 455; and PWA, 10; reorganization plan, 12–16, 18–19; selective service training, 80; seven-point stabilization message to, 264–66; Social Security amendments, 8, 25; soldier vote bill, 383–84; statements to, 24; tax bills, 383, 385; veto messages, 323, 340–41, 385–87; Work or Fight Bill, 489–90; and WPA, 2, 4

Roosevelt, Franklin Delano—HEALTH OF, 249, 394, 417, 419, 433–34, 441, 449, 454–55, 458, 482, 494, 496, 553n8; abdominal pain, 393; blood pressure, 391; fatigue of, 451, 490–91; gallstones, 372–73; heart disease, 389, 391–92, 403, 418; illnesses, concealment of, 388; illnesses, playing down of, 378, 390, 403; iron anemia deficiency, 389; last moments of, 497–98; vigor of, 436; weight loss, 387, 424, 431, 437, 451, 488; at Yalta, 477–78

Roosevelt, Franklin Delano—SPEECHES, 60–61; annual messages of, 1, 48–49, 150–51; anti-Hitler speech, 170–71; "Arsenal of Democracy" speech, 146–48, 170; Boston Garden speech, as controversial, 133–34; Boston speech, 443–45; broadcast speeches of, 58–59, 125, 312, 341, 434, 438, 446, 451; Camden speech, 438–39; campaign addresses of, 411–12, 415, 442–44; Chicago speech, 439–40, 442;

Roosevelt, Franklin Delano—SPEECHES (*continued*): Christmas Eve messages, 458; Christmas greetings of, 47, 146; Columbus Day talk, 430; Date of Infamy speech, 133, 229–33; D-Day prayer, 395, 401–2; Democratic (1940) convention, 87–90; Dumbarton Oaks speech, 419–20; election-eve address, 138–39; extemporaneous remarks, 436; Fala speech, 425–26, 428, 443; "Fellow Citizens" speech, 53; Fenway Park speech, 443–45; Fireside Chats, 2–3, 33–34, 36, 65, 146–48, 153, 194–97, 231, 287–91, 294–95, 326–27, 343–44, 357, 374–75, 376, 378, 405–6, 424, 436; five speeches, 126–28; Foreign Policy Association speech, 434–36; foreign policy statements, 426, 434; formal statements, 39, 448; Four Freedoms, 151–52, 170, 181, 306–7, 353; Hartford speech, 443; informal remarks, 97, 320; "I see an America" speech, 137–38; Jackson Day Dinner speeches, 5, 27, 50; Jefferson Day speech (final speech of), 496, 499–501; Labor Day address, 188–89, 420; last-Saturday-before election speech, 135–36; Lend-Lease, implications of, 163–64; Madison Square Garden speech, 129–31; map speech, 255–56; Mexican speech, 324; national speeches, 39–40, 101–4, 123, 301; Navy Day address, 200–201, 207; off the record remarks, 42, 105, 144–45, 202, 236, 300, 458, 482; Ottawa speech, 353; peace messages, 31–32; press conferences, 21–23, 25, 32–37, 39, 46, 50, 54, 59, 62, 65, 69–70, 76, 78, 82–83, 91–94, 97, 99, 104, 111–12, 117, 120, 122–23, 126, 132, 135, 139, 142–45, 149, 153, 155, 157, 159, 165, 167–68, 172, 181–85, 193–94, 198–202, 208, 218–19, 221, 232, 237, 240–41, 249, 280, 284, 287, 293, 296, 302, 309–11, 317–19, 324, 339, 345–46, 352, 356, 369–70, 374, 377–78, 385, 387–88, 391, 393–97, 399–403, 406, 408, 410–12, 422, 426, 431–33, 436, 440–42, 448–53, 456–58, 461, 464–65, 482–83, 486–89, 493–94; public statements, 21, 456, 493; radio addresses, 42, 47, 51–52, 129, 166, 171, 188, 365, 434, 489; on rear-platform trains, 22, 127, 136, 436–37, 456; Republican misstatements speech, 428–30; second Bill of Rights speech, 378–80; shoot-on-sight speech, 198, 537–38n17; State of the Union addresses, 216, 242, 244, 305–7; Sunday evening talks, 66–69; Teamsters Union speeches, 111–12, 424; Thanksgiving messages, 220; third inaugural address, 464–66; train speeches, 124–25, 143, 414–15; troops, speeches to, 373–74; "unholy alliance" speech, 135–37; unlimited-emergency speech, 171; USS *Cummings* speech, 418–19; Valley Forge, speech, 258; Waldorf speech, 434, 436, 438; White House Conference on Rural Education speech, 428; Woodrow Wilson birthplace speech, 170

Roosevelt, Franklin Delano—WRITING: administrative orders, 72; cables of, 219–20, 496; cross-Channel invasion (Operation Overlord) instructions of, 273–75; "Dear Bob" letter, 314; "Dear Dave" letter, 109; "Dear Jim" letter, 95; executive orders (EO), 12, 19, 36, 37, 57, 59, 112, 134, 155, 160, 169, 185–87, 192, 206, 217, 244–45, 250, 252, 254, 267, 277–80, 290, 303, 313–15, 325, 333–37, 342–43, 358, 383, 458–59, 502; letters, 45, 47, 64, 95–96, 109, 156, 169, 186, 203–4, 207–9, 213, 245, 287, 291, 303, 314, 342, 413–14, 421, 451–52, 464, 466, 468; memos, 422; military orders, 281, 283, 461; "My Dear Mr. Stalin" letter, 186; policy announcements, 36; presidential proclamations, 38, 42, 57, 228, 281–83; press releases, 180; press statements, 209–10; press summaries, 221; public statements of, 57, 336, 428,

ROGER DANIELS is the Charles Phelps Taft Professor Emeritus of History at the University of Cincinnati. His many books include *Prisoners without Trial: Japanese Americans in World War II.*